# Lecture Notes of the Institute for Computer Sciences, Social Informatics and Telecommunications Engineering 686

The LNICST series publishes ICST's conferences, symposia and workshops.

LNICST reports state-of-the-art results in areas related to the scope of the Institute.

The type of material published includes

- Proceedings (published in time for the respective event)
- Other edited monographs (such as project reports or invited volumes)

LNICST topics span the following areas:

- General Computer Science
- E-Economy
- E-Medicine
- Knowledge Management
- Multimedia
- Operations, Management and Policy
- Social Informatics
- Systems

Kim-Kwang Raymond Choo ·
Alexander Perez-Pons · Himanshu Upadhyay ·
Rongxing Lu · Kam Pui Chow
Editors

# Digital Forensics and Cyber Crime

16th EAI International Conference, ICDF2C 2025
Miami, FL, USA, November 17–19, 2025
Proceedings, Part II

*Editors*
Kim-Kwang Raymond Choo
University of Texas at San Antonio
San Antonio, TX, USA

Alexander Perez-Pons
Florida International University
Miami, FL, USA

Himanshu Upadhyay
Florida International University
Miami, FL, USA

Rongxing Lu
Queen's University
Kingston, ON, Canada

Kam Pui Chow
University of Hong Kong
Hong Kong, China

ISSN 1867-8211 ISSN 1867-822X (electronic)
Lecture Notes of the Institute for Computer Sciences, Social Informatics and Telecommunications Engineering
ISBN 978-3-032-22544-3 ISBN 978-3-032-22545-0 (eBook)
https://doi.org/10.1007/978-3-032-22545-0



This Springer imprint is published by the registered company Springer Nature Switzerland AG
The registered company address is: Gewerbestrasse 11, 6330 Cham, Switzerland

# Preface

It is with great pleasure that we present the proceedings of the 16th EAI International Conference on Digital Forensics & Cyber Crime (ICDF2C 2025). The conference was held in Miami, Florida, USA between 17 and 19 November 2025. The focus of this year's conference was on next-generation cyber analytics, security, and forensics including the application and deployment of contemporary technologies (e.g., Generative AI and large language models) in various security and forensic settings.

A total of 163 manuscripts were received, and all submissions went through an extensive single-blind review process by the Technical Program Committee (TPC) members with relevant subject matter expertise. Each manuscript was reviewed by three or more TPC members and eventually only 67 submissions were accepted.

We extend our heartfelt gratitude to the authors for their invaluable contributions, the TPC members and reviewers for their dedication in ensuring a rigorous selection process, and the keynote speakers for sharing their expertise. We are also deeply appreciative of the conference organizers, sponsors, and volunteers whose efforts made this event possible.

We hope the proceedings will serve as a valuable resource for researchers, practitioners, and policymakers, fostering innovation and collaboration to advance the state of the art in secure communications.

Thank you for joining us at ICDF2C 2025, and we look forward to seeing you next year at ICDF2C 2026 in Reykjavik, Iceland.

August 2025

Kim-Kwang Raymond Choo
Alexander Perez-Pons
Himanshu Upadhyay
Rongxing Lu
Kam Pui Chow

# Organization

## Steering Committee

| | |
|---|---|
| Sanjay Goel | University at Albany-SUNY, USA |
| Pavel Gladyshev | University College Dublin, Ireland |

## Organizing Committee

### General Chairs

| | |
|---|---|
| Kim-Kwang Raymond Choo | University of Texas at San Antonio, USA |
| Alexander Perez-Pons | Florida International University, USA |

### TPC Chairs

| | |
|---|---|
| Himanshu Upadhyay | Florida International University, USA |
| Rongxing Lu | Queen's University, Canada |
| Kam Pui Chow | University of Hong Kong, China |

### Publicity and Social Media Chairs

| | |
|---|---|
| Nhien An Le Khac | University College Dublin, Ireland |
| Raymond Chan | Singapore Institute of Technology, Singapore |
| Gaurav Gupta | Ministry of Electronics and Information Technology, India |
| Yizhi Ren | Hangzhou Dianzi University, China |
| Sakshi Singh | Florida International University, USA |

### Workshops Chair

| | |
|---|---|
| Pranav Gangwani | Florida International University, USA |

### Publications Chair

| | |
|---|---|
| Jayesh Soni | Florida International University, USA |

**Sponsorship and Exhibits Chair**

| | |
|---|---|
| Himanshu Upadhyay | Florida International University, USA |

**Web Chair**

| | |
|---|---|
| Lakshika Vaishnav | University at Albany-SUNY, USA |

## Technical Program Committee

| | |
|---|---|
| Cheng Guo | Dalian University of Technology, China |
| Duohe Ma | Chinese Academy of Sciences, China |
| Himanshu Upadhyay | Florida International University, USA |
| Hudan Studiawan | Institut Teknologi Sepuluh Nopember, Indonesia |
| Jingyu Hua | Nanjing University, China |
| Jun Shao | Zhejiang Gongsang University, China |
| Kam Pui Chow | University of Hong Kong, China |
| Kim-Kwang Raymond Choo | University of Texas at San Antonio, USA |
| Laiping Zhao | Tianjin University, China |
| Lakshika Vaishnav | University at Albany-SUNY, USA |
| Md Arafatur Rahman | University of Wolverhampton, UK |
| Niken Dwi Wahyu Cahyani | Telkom University, Indonesia |
| Nurul Hidayah Binti Ab Rahman | Universiti Tun Hussein Onn Malaysia, Malaysia |
| Raymond Chan | Singapore Institute of Technology, Singapore |
| Rongxing Lu | Queen's University, Canada |
| Sakshi Singh | University at Albany-SUNY, USA |
| Shancang Li | Cardiff University, UK |
| Weihan Goh | Singapore Institute of Technology, Singapore |
| Yuksel Celik | University at Albany-SUNY, USA |
| Zhiyuan Tan | Edinburgh Napier University, UK |

# Contents

**Cyber Threat Intelligence and Malware Analysis: Focus on Malware Detection, Honeynets, Phishing, Traffic Analysis, and Intrusion Defense**

An Encrypted Traffic Classification Method Based on Mamba and Wavelet Transform Convolution ........ 3
*Guanxin Chen, Yipeng Liu, and Lancan Yu*

MFETD: Multimodal Feature Fusion for Encrypted Traffic Detection Based on Transformer ........ 20
*Zhiqiang Wang, Shufang Pang, Ying Liu, Shaowei Yuan, and Lei Ju*

Online Learning for Android Malware Detection Under Concept-Drift ........ 36
*Elif Sahin, Bilge Karabacak, Hayretdin Bahsi, and AbdElRahman ElSaid*

Evaluating the Impact of Honeynets on Malicious Activity in Home Network Environments ........ 54
*Eric Edge, James H. Jr Jones, and Kathryn Laskey*

Revealing the Intents: Malware Protocol Semantic Inference Using Large Language Models ........ 68
*Yuyao Huang, Hui Shu, and Fei Kang*

PhishIntentionLLM: Uncovering Phishing Website Intentions Through Multi-agent Retrieval-Augmented Generation ........ 88
*Wenhao Li, Selvakumar Manickam, Yung-Wey Chong, and Shankar Karuppayah*

APT-Agent: A Training-Free, Unsupervised, LLM-Based Multi-agent Framework for Interpretable Advanced Persistent Threat Detection ........ 107
*Wenzhuo Cui, Yibing Hu, Zheng Liu, Jingjing Feng, Shuyi Zhang, and Yu Wen*

**Digital Evidence Management, Blockchain, and Privacy: Addressing Blockchain Forensics, Data Provenance, and Privacy-Preserving Computation**

Blockchain-Based vs. SQL Database Systems for Digital Twin Evidence Management: A Comparative Forensic Analysis ........ 129
*Boyd Franken, Hong-Hanh Nguyen-Le, and Nhien-An Le-Khac*

FAIR-MPC: Secure and Auditable SMPC for Anonymous Financial Collaboration ... 144
*Tao Bai, Yuanqing Feng, Zhi Lu, and Songfeng Lu*

Privacy-Preserving $k$-Bitruss Community Query over Encrypted Bipartite Graphs ... 160
*Xiaoxian Liu, Chen Chen, Xueqiao Liu, and Xiaoyang Wang*

Towards Regulated and Accountable Privacy-Preserving Retrieval for Digital Forensics: A Cryptographic Design Framework ... 176
*Jie Song, Zhen Xu, Yan Zhang, and Hong Miao*

Automatic Recovery of Cryptowallets from Mnemonic Seed Phrases ... 197
*Abhishek Bhattarai, Carlos Imery, and Kemal Akkaya*

AnchorMark: Real-World Anchor-Based Watermarking for Digital Content Authentication and Manipulation Detection ... 213
*Xinyun Liu, Ronghua Xu, and Yu Chen*

**Critical Infrastructure and Cyber-Physical Security: Cyber Resilience in Physical and Industrial Systems, Including IoT, Satellites, and SCADA**

Resilient Satellite Cybersecurity: Integrating NIST and AI Governance ... 233
*Kimberly A. Cornell and Li Huang*

An Enhanced Federated Machine Learning Approach for Decentralized Water Contamination Detection ... 248
*Raja Kumar, Jayesh Soni, and Himanshu Upadhyay*

DepFieldGen: Research on Dependent Field Generation for Secure ICS Protocols ... 264
*Zhanwei Song, Dongliang Fang, Yaowen Zheng, Shichao Lv, Xin Chen, Shuaizong Si, Zhi Li, and Limin Sun*

A ROSI-Based Framework with Zero Trust Architecture: Interdependent Risks and Cybersecurity Investment ... 280
*Li Huang and Kimberly A. Cornell*

Accelerating Criminal Investigations with TRACY ... 295
*Pradeep Rangappa, Petr Motlicek, Dairazalia Sanchez-Cortes, Alejandra Sanchez Lara, Michaela Antonopoulou, Ioannis Fourfouris, Nikos Avgerinos, and Manolis Tsangaris*

## Legal, Policy, and AI Governance in Digital Forensics: Studies Bridging AI Governance, Digital Law, Compliance, and Socio-technical Policy

Retrospective Analysis of Legal Documents Using Hybrid AI - A Preliminary Empirical Study of Historical Search Warrant Processing ....... 313
*Md. Ashiqur Rahman, Gokila Dorai, Thomas E. Kadri, Dane R. Thorley, John B. Meixner Jr., Miguel de Figueiredo, and Gagan Agrawal*

Where the Money Is: Shadow AI Risks to Family Offices and the Wealth Management Sector ........ 333
*Brian H. Nussbaum and Kimberly A. Cornell*

Chances and Challenges of the Model Context Protocol in Digital Forensics and Incident Response ........ 345
*Jan-Niclas Hilgert, Carlo Jakobs, Michael Külper, Martin Lambertz, Axel Mahr, and Elmar Padilla*

SCOPE - Activity Recognition Using Temporally Dominant Topic Identification In Forensic Chat Analysis ........ 363
*Rajon Bardhan, Gokila Dorai, Gagan Agrawal, and Khan Mohammad Al-Farabi*

Automating Cloud Security and Forensics Through a Secure-by-Design GenAI Framework ........ 384
*Dalal Alharthi and Ivan Roberto Kawaminami Garcia*

Understanding Online Grooming Through LLMs: Stage Detection and Linguistic Patterns ........ 403
*Sarah A. J. Hamer, Yi Ting Chua, and Weiping Pei*

## Emerging Research, Tools, and Experimental Frameworks: Novel Methods, Datasets, and Future Directions in Digital Forensics and Cybersecurity

Graph Neural Networks for Video Device Identification ........ 433
*Raghu Sesha Iyengar and Vaibhav Kumar*

WebHunter: An LLM-Agent with Exploit Planning and Tool Collaboration for Automated SQL Injection ........ 451
*Wenkai Ren, Die Hu, He Kong, Yuepeng, Liangxiong Li, and Bingzhen Wu*

AFLTrans: Research on Intelligent Generative Fuzz Testing Method Based on Transformer ........ 464
*Guoyan Cao, Mengjiao Geng, and Xiaobing Xiong*

HLSEn: High-Level Semantic Awareness Pseudo-code Encoding for Binary Code Similarity Detection ..... 491
*Yanlin Li, Lu Zhang, Song Wang, Taiyan Wang, Lu Yu, Qiangpu Chen, Yuwei Li, and Zulie Pan*

SolDataVul-LLaMA Dataset: A LLM-Driven Construction Method and Detection Research of Smart Contract Vulnerability Dataset in Data Trading Scenarios ..... 505
*Wenjie Li, Leixiao Li, Dongjiang Liu, Jinze Du, Hao Lin, and Zhexu Liu*

The Sample Classification Method Accelerates the Efficiency of Robustness Verification ..... 524
*Xuejian Li, Jian Xing, and Hantao Xia*

MuLImg-SCV: Multi-label Vulnerability Classification of Smart Contracts Based on RGB Image ..... 540
*Linlin Zhang, Nianlu Liu, Ke Li, Wenbo Fang, and Kai Zhao*

On the Security of the RDHEI by Binary Symmetric Channel and Polar Code ..... 556
*Xuebin Wang, Hongjie He, Fan Chen, and Yaolin Yang*

**Posters and Demos**

Enhancing Trust in VideoKYC: Deepfake Detection and Source Attribution ..... 579
*Srivallabh Mangrulkar, Aryan Karande, Abhijeet Zilpelwar, and Raghu Sesha Iyengar*

**Author Index** ..... 583

# Cyber Threat Intelligence and Malware Analysis: Focus on Malware Detection, Honeynets, Phishing, Traffic Analysis, and Intrusion Defense

# An Encrypted Traffic Classification Method Based on Mamba and Wavelet Transform Convolution

Guanxin Chen, Yipeng Liu(✉), and Lancan Yu

Xinjiang University, Urumqi, Xinjiang 830000, China
liuyipeng@xju.edu.cn

**Abstract.** The classification of encrypted network traffic is a critical research domain with far-reaching implications for enhancing network security, optimizing quality of service, and streamlining network management. As encryption techniques grow increasingly sophisticated, machine learning and deep learning have emerged as dominant approaches for traffic classification. However, existing methods face two key challenges. First, transformer-based architectures, while powerful, suffer from computational inefficiency due to their quadratic complexity. Second, training models tailored to specific traffic scenarios often demands extensive data labeling, which is both time-consuming and resource-intensive. To overcome these limitations, we propose TrafficConMamba, a novel and efficient method that integrates the unidirectional Mamba architecture with wavelet transform convolution. By replacing the Transformer with Mamba, TrafficConMamba significantly enhances computational efficiency while preserving the ability to model long-range dependencies. Additionally, by leveraging convolutional layers for local feature extraction, the model effectively captures both fine-grained and global traffic patterns. To further reduce reliance on labeled data, we employ a two-stage training strategy: large-scale pretraining on unlabeled data followed by fine-tuning on a small, labeled subset for specific classification tasks. Extensive evaluations across six public datasets and three major classification tasks demonstrate that TrafficConMamba surpasses state-of-the-art encrypted traffic classifiers. It achieves near-perfect classification accuracy, exceeding 99% in some cases, while maintaining the fastest inference speed and the lowest memory footprint. Moreover, TrafficConMamba demonstrates excellent small-sample learning capabilities, achieving good classification performance even with limited labeled data.

**Keywords:** Network encrypted traffic · Pre-training · Deep learning · Mamba

## 1 Introduction

As information technology has advanced rapidly, public awareness of network security has grown. This has led to the widespread adoption of encrypted com-


K.-K. R. Choo et al. (Eds.): ICDF2C 2025, LNICST 686, pp. 3–19, 2026.
https://doi.org/10.1007/978-3-032-22545-0_1

munication protocols and tools. A Firefox [1] survey indicates that the proportion of users utilising SSL/TLS security protocols has risen from 39% in 2016 to an expected 81% by 2024. While encryption technology safeguards user privacy and data security, it also presents significant challenges for network management, particularly with regard to maintaining security and ensuring quality of service (QoS) [2,3]. Traffic classification has emerged as a critical solution, enabling network service providers and equipment manufacturers to effectively manage and optimise network performance. Moreover, it plays a fundamental role in intrusion detection systems, helping to identify threats and reinforce system security [4]. However, the growing adoption of encrypted communication and anonymization techniques has substantially increased the complexity of network traffic analysis, demanding more sophisticated classification methods.

Traditional port-based identification and deep packet inspection (DPI) techniques are ineffective for classifying encrypted network traffic. Port-based methods rely on the static mapping between ports and protocols; however, their efficacy has diminished due to the widespread adoption of port forwarding and dynamic port negotiation [5]. Similarly, DPI analyzes entire IP packets to identify protocol signatures and application-layer data, yet it fails to classify encrypted traffic, as encrypted payloads cannot be parsed [6]. Given the increasing complexity of transport encryption, researchers have explored machine learning (ML) techniques that classify traffic based on statistical features. However, these methods rely on manually engineered features, which often fail to accurately represent the true distribution of network traffic due to the lack of raw packet data. By comparison deep learning techniques extract hierarchical features directly from byte-level data, improving classification performance. Nonetheless, when individual packets are excessively long, the overwhelming presence of bytes from a single packet can obscure critical information from others, leading to suboptimal feature representations. This limitation, combined with the lack of explicit representation design in conventional deep learning-based models, often results in unstable classification performance. Furthermore, deep learning methods typically require vast amounts of labeled training data, and the manual annotation of network traffic is both labor-intensive and costly, posing significant challenges to real-world deployment and model updates.

In recent years, pretraining methods leveraging large-scale unlabeled data have demonstrated remarkable success in computer vision (CV) [7,8] and natural language processing (NLP) [9]. Compared to traditional supervised learning, self-supervised pretraining offers two key advantages: (1) more efficient feature representations, which reduce the reliance on extensive labeled datasets for downstream tasks, and (2) improved model initialization, accelerating convergence and enhancing classification performance. Inspired by this progress, researchers have introduced several Transformer-based pretrained models for traffic classification [10–12]. These models first learn a general traffic representation from vast amounts of unlabeled data before undergoing fine-tuning on a limited set of labeled traffic samples for specific classification tasks. However, most state-of-the-art approaches are built on the Transformer architecture, which leverages a computationally expensive self-attention mechanism with quadratic complexity to model sequence correlations. This design imposes substantial computational and memory overheads, making it impractical for processing long-sequence data efficiently [13,14]. Consequently, these models struggle to meet the real-time constraints of online traffic classification and remain unsuitable for deployment in resource-limited network environments. Moreover, existing methods fail to effectively preserve critical raw traffic information. By discarding essential keyword bytes while retaining unnecessary biases, they generate suboptimal representations that degrade classification accuracy. In complex traffic scenarios, such unreliable representations can compromise model performance and, in extreme cases, lead to complete classification failure.

To overcome these obstacles, we propose TrafficConMamba, a model for traffic classification that integrates unidirectional Mamba with wavelet transform convolution. TrafficConMamba learns latent representations from large-scale unlabeled traffic data, enabling more effective classification. Specifically, we first construct a multilevel traffic representation matrix inspired by the YaTC approach [33], which encodes raw packet bytes into a structured format that captures traffic characteristics at multiple granularities (Fig. 1). This matrix serves as input to our novel traffic converter, which integrates a unidirectional Mamba module with a wavelet transform convolution module, allowing for efficient and robust traffic analysis. Finally, we adopt a two-stage training strategy based on the masked autoencoder (MAE) paradigm. During pretraining, we randomly mask portions of the multilevel traffic representation matrix, and a self-encoder—comprising the TrafficConMamba encoder and decoder—reconstructs the original matrix. The model is able to extract meaningful potential representations from unlabeled traffic data during this pre-training phase. In the fine-tuning phase, we transfer the pretrained encoder's parameters to TrafficConMamba and refine it using a small amount of labeled data for downstream traffic classification tasks. The main contributions of this paper are as follows:

1. We propose TrafficConMamba, a model integrating unidirectional Mamba and wavelet transform convolution. TrafficConMamba advances beyond conventional traffic analysis by innovating in three key areas—traffic representation, classifier architecture, and training methodology. Compared with Transformer-based models, TrafficConMamba achieves superior classification accuracy and computational efficiency.
2. By adopting the MAE-based self-supervised learning paradigm, TrafficConMamba first learns generic latent representations from extensive unlabeled traffic data, then fine-tunes on limited labeled data, enabling adaptability across diverse traffic classification tasks.
3. We assess TrafficConMamba on six real traffic datasets, conducting extensive experiments, including ablation studies, efficiency analysis, and low-data learning evaluations. Experimental results demonstrate that TrafficConMamba significantly outperforms state-of-the-art methods, offering new insights for future research in encrypted traffic classification.

## 2 Related Work

### 2.1 ML-Based Method

With the advent of the big data era, encrypted network traffic has become an important security protection mechanism to maintain the security of network communications. However, while encryption protects user privacy and maintains the security of network communications, it also hides the characteristics of the data, making it more difficult to classify network traffic [15]. The port and protocol-based approach to classifying network traffic is a relatively simple method, but the accuracy of this method has declined as newer applications use common port numbers to mask their traffic or do not use standard registered port numbers. In response to the inability of traditional traffic classification methods to cope with dynamic port negotiation and encrypted loads, the researchers proposed an ML-based approach. Feature selection and optimisation play a vital role in ML-based methods, so researchers have proposed many features based on statistical patterns of traffic and selected appropriate ML classifiers such as Support Vector Machines, Random Forests, etc. to classify them. For example, Alshammari et al. [16] used a machine learning approach to identify encrypted traffic tunnels with high accuracy. Feghhi et al. [17] proposed a method to measure VPN traffic using only uplink packet timing information. Moore et al. [18] designed about 250 flow features based on a priori knowledge. Most of the subsequent ML-based traffic classification methods (e.g. [19] [20] [21]) perform feature extraction based on these 250 features. These traffic features include, but are not limited to, the variance of the packet byte count, the median of the total number of bytes in an IP packet, etc. Zhongsheng et al. [22] applied a support vector machine (SVM) to classify network traffic using packet lengths and TCP flags, and transformed the real-world problem into a high-dimensional feature space using the kernel function.

The Cumulative Packet Size (CUMUL) feature was first introduced in [23] for generating Tor website fingerprints and has since been widely adopted in subsequent research. NetScope et al. [24] leveraged traffic behavior metrics—such as redirection rates and packet exchange patterns—to infer user activities on Android and iOS devices. Dubin et al. [25] proposed a novel feature, Bit-Per-Peak, which quantifies the total number of bits within a peak traffic burst. Shen et al. [26] refined website fingerprinting techniques by integrating CUMUL with packet positioning in the uplink-dominant phase, enhancing fingerprint granularity. Meanwhile, ETC-PS [27] introduced a method for modeling encrypted communication paths by constructing traffic sequences between clients and servers. This approach extracts path signature features from session packet length sequences, providing a structured representation of encrypted traffic flows.

### 2.2 DL-Based Method

While machine learning algorithms have demonstrated high accuracy in classifying encrypted network traffic, they rely heavily on feature engineering and suffer from substantial computational overhead and prolonged processing times. In contrast, deep learning approaches eliminate the need for manual feature selection by directly processing raw traffic data and autonomously extracting relevant features. These methods can be categorized into three levels based on input granularity: sessions, flows, and packets. Due to their ability to learn hierarchical representations, deep learning models have gained widespread adoption in encrypted traffic classification. Among these models, Convolutional Neural Networks (CNNs) have attracted significant research attention, particularly given their success in image classification and object detection. CNNs, known for their effectiveness in automatic feature extraction, have been adapted for network traffic classification. For instance, Deep Packet [28] utilizes a one-dimensional CNN architecture to analyze encrypted traffic, while Wang et al. [29] pioneered the transformation of one-dimensional encrypted traffic data into two-dimensional image representations, enabling CNN-based malware traffic classification. However, many deep learning-based approaches rely on packet bytes within network flows to represent raw traffic. This can lead to information imbalance, where the byte content of long packets dominates and obscures critical details from other packets. Furthermore, these models typically require extensive labeled training datasets, yet collecting and manually labeling sufficient real-world traffic samples remains a significant challenge. To mitigate this dependency, we adopt a two-stage learning strategy: first, pretraining on large-scale unlabeled data to learn robust traffic representations, followed by fine-tuning with a small amount of labeled data for precise traffic classification.

### 2.3 Pre-training Methods

The pretraining paradigm has proven to be a powerful approach for reducing dependence on large-scale labeled datasets by harnessing self-supervised learning. By learning unbiased data representations from vast amounts of unlabeled traffic, pre-training enhances the performance of downstream classification tasks. This approach first trains a model on unlabeled data to capture latent representations, then fine-tunes the learned parameters for specific classification objectives. In natural language processing (NLP), BERT [9] has been widely adopted for pre-training using masked token prediction and next-sentence prediction tasks. Inspired by this, some studies [31] have treated traffic packet bytes as words and introduced BERT-based pre-training to improve classification performance. However, unlike textual data, network traffic lacks well-defined high-level semantic structures, making it more suitable for modeling as a computer vision (CV) problem rather than an NLP task. In CV-based pre-training, traditional methods rely on data augmentation techniques—such as cropping and scaling—to generate positive and negative sample pairs for contrastive learning. However, applying such transformations to traffic-derived images distorts the original byte-level information, limiting the effectiveness of contrastive learning in this context. Masked autoencoders (MAEs) [7] offer an alternative, enabling reconstruction-based pre-training by masking input patches while preserving the integrity of unmasked packet bytes. This property makes MAEs particularly well-suited for structured multi-level traffic representations, where different packet content levels are aligned at fixed positions. Building on this, Zhao et al. [31] introduced the YaTC method, which employs the MAE framework to pre-train on large-scale unlabeled traffic data and fine-tune with limited labeled samples for classification. Similarly, Wang et al. [32] proposed NetMamba, replacing the Transformer architecture with an optimized unidirectional Mamba framework to enhance classification efficiency while maintaining low memory overhead.

# 3 Methodology

## 3.1 Traffic Data Preprocessing

Data preprocessing provides consistent-sized raw inputs for classification models and is a critical step in deep learning network traffic classification. Network encrypted traffic data is typically in PCAP or PCAPNG format and must be preprocessed into grayscale images before it can be used as model inputs. As shown in Fig. 1, data preprocessing converts raw PCAP-format network traffic data into TrafficConMamba input images, which involves four steps:

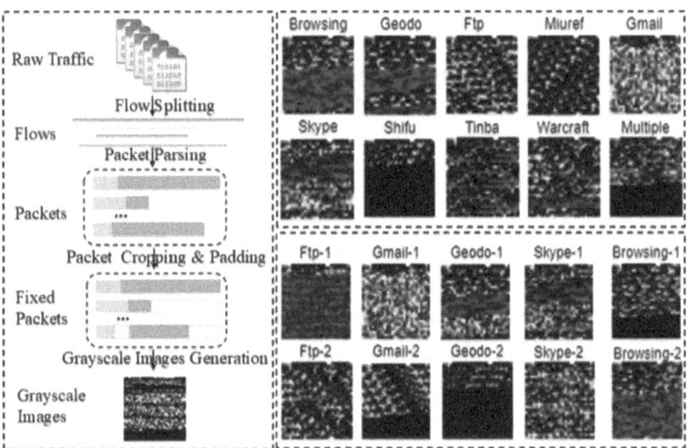


**Fig. 1.** The work process of the Traffic Data Preprocessing

1) Flows Splitting: Network traffic is divided according to specific protocols, and the same traffic data contains key information about host interactions, which is useful for describing and classifying application behavior.
2) Packet Parsing: Process traffic data packets, exclude non-IP protocol packets, retain key information and payloads, and anonymize to eliminate bias.
3) Network packet trimming, padding, and concatenation: To address the issue of variable packet sizes, a uniform size is used, and the first M packets are taken. Assuming that the packet header is $N_h$ bytes and the payload is $N_p$ bytes, the packets are trimmed or padded and then concatenated into a matrix.

4) Grayscale image generation: Set up a matrix containing five data packets, 40 rows and 40 columns, with header and payload rows allocated as needed. If there are insufficient rows, fill them in to form a fixed-size grayscale image.

### 3.2 TrafficConMamba Architecture

The greyscale image $\mathbf{x} \in \mathbf{R}^{\mathrm{H}\times\mathrm{W}}$, used for model matching, is initially partitioned into non-overlapping 2D blocks of size $S \times S$ , resulting in a total of $N = WN/P^2$ patches, represented as $x_s \in \mathcal{R}^{N\times S^2}$. Each patch is then projected into a D-dimensional vector space through a linear layer, forming the patch embeddings. To preserve critical positional information, positional embeddings are incorporated into patch embeddings before they are input to the flow encoder.

$$\mathbf{X}_0 = \left[\mathbf{s}_1\mathbf{E}\ \mathbf{s}_2\mathbf{E} \cdots \mathbf{s}_{N_s}\mathbf{E}\ \mathbf{x}_{\text{cls}}\right] + \mathbf{E}_{\text{enc}}^{\text{pos}} \tag{1}$$

where $E \in \mathcal{R}^{L_S\times D_{enc}}$ denotes the learnable mapping matrix. We set D = 192, S = 2, and $N = 20 \times 20$, ensuring that all elements within a patch correspond to raw bytes of the same type. Each packet matrix is structured with one row of header patches and three rows of payload patches. Drawing inspiration from ViT and NetMamba [32], we incorporate class labels to represent the entire sequence of matrices, denoted as $X_{cls}$.

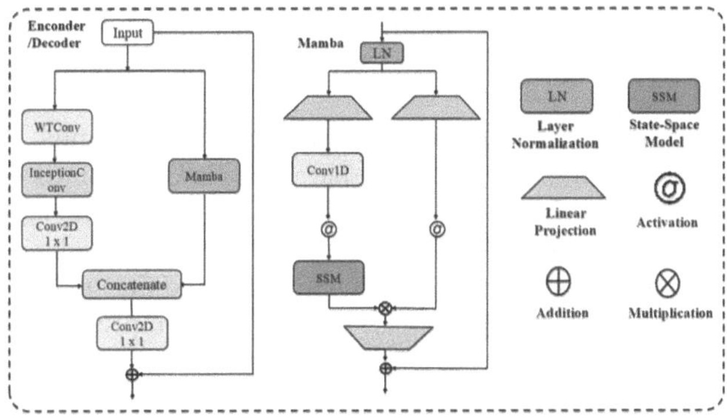


**Fig. 2.** TrafficConMamba Encoder (Decoder)

In recent years, several Mamba variants have been developed to address domain-specific data formats and task requirements. Vision Mamba [13] utilizes bidirectional Mamba blocks to improve spatially-aware understanding in visual tasks, whereas Graph-Mamba [33] integrates a graph-dependent selection mechanism specifically designed for graph learning. We posit that a unidirectional Mamba design, when integrated with wavelet transform, is particularly well-suited for representation learning in visual network traffic. Consequently,

**Algorithm 1. TrafficConMamba Block Forward Pass**

**Require:** $\mathbf{X}_{t-1} : (\mathrm{B}, \mathrm{C}, \mathrm{W}, \mathrm{H})$
**Ensure:** $\mathbf{X}_t : (\mathrm{B}, \mathrm{L}, \mathrm{D})$
1: $\mathbf{X}'_{t-1} : (\mathrm{B}, \mathrm{L}, \mathrm{D}) \leftarrow \mathbf{patchEmbed}(\mathbf{X}_{t-1})$
2: $\mathbf{X}'_{t-1} : (\mathrm{B}, \mathrm{L}, \mathrm{D}) \leftarrow \mathbf{Norm}(\mathbf{X}'_{t-1})$
3: $\mathbf{X}''_{t-1} : (\mathrm{B}, \mathrm{C}, \mathrm{W}, \mathrm{H}) \leftarrow \mathbf{WTConv}(\mathbf{X}_{t-1})$
4: $\mathbf{X}''_{t-1} : (\mathrm{B}, \mathrm{C}, \mathrm{W}, \mathrm{H}) \leftarrow \mathbf{InceptionConv}(\mathbf{X}''_{t-1})$
5: $\mathbf{X}''_{t-1} : (\mathrm{B}, \mathrm{C}, \mathrm{W}, \mathrm{H}) \leftarrow \mathbf{Conv}(\mathbf{X}''_{t-1})$
6: $\mathbf{X}''_{t-1} : (\mathrm{B}, \mathrm{L}, \mathrm{D}) \leftarrow \mathbf{patchEmbed}(\mathbf{X}''_{t-1})$
7: $\mathbf{x} : (\mathrm{B}, \mathrm{L}, \mathrm{E}) \leftarrow \mathbf{Linear}^{\mathbf{x}}(\mathbf{X}'_{t-1})$
8: $\mathbf{z} : (\mathrm{B}, \mathrm{L}, \mathrm{E}) \leftarrow \mathbf{Linear}^{\mathbf{z}}(\mathbf{X}'_{t-1})$
9: $\mathbf{x}' : (\mathrm{B}, \mathrm{L}, \mathrm{E}) \leftarrow \mathsf{SILU}(\mathsf{Convld}(\mathbf{x}))$
10: $\mathbf{B} : (\mathrm{B}, \mathrm{L}, \mathbb{N}) \leftarrow \mathbf{Linear}^{\mathbf{B}}(\mathbf{x}')$
11: $\mathbf{C} : (\mathrm{B}, \mathrm{L}, \mathbb{N}) \leftarrow \mathbf{Linear}^{\mathbf{C}}(\mathbf{x}')$
12: $\boldsymbol{\Delta} : (\mathrm{B}, \mathrm{L}, \mathrm{E}) \leftarrow \log(1 + \exp(\mathbf{Linear}^{\boldsymbol{\Delta}}(\mathbf{x}') + \mathbf{Parameter}^{\boldsymbol{\Delta}}))$
13: $\bar{\boldsymbol{A}} : (\mathrm{B}, \mathrm{L}, \mathrm{E}, \mathbb{N}) \leftarrow \boldsymbol{\Delta} \bigotimes \mathbf{Parameter}^{\bar{\boldsymbol{A}}}$
14: $\overline{\mathbf{B}} : (\mathrm{B}, \mathrm{L}, \mathrm{E}, \mathbb{N}) \leftarrow \boldsymbol{\Delta} \bigotimes \mathbf{B}$
15: $\mathbf{y} : (\mathrm{B}, \mathrm{L}, \mathrm{E}) \leftarrow \mathsf{SSM}(\bar{\boldsymbol{A}}, \overline{\mathbf{B}}, \mathbf{C})(\mathbf{x}')$
16: $\mathbf{y}' : (\mathrm{B}, \mathrm{L}, \mathrm{E}) \leftarrow \mathbf{y} \bigcirc \mathsf{SILU}(\mathbf{z})$
17: $\mathbf{X}_t : (\mathrm{B}, \mathrm{L}, \mathrm{D}) \leftarrow \mathbf{Linear}^{\mathbf{X}}(\mathbf{y}') + \mathbf{X}_{t-1}$
18: $\mathbf{X}_t : (\mathrm{B}, \mathrm{L}, \mathrm{D}) \leftarrow \mathbf{X}''_{t-1} + \mathbf{X}_t$
19: **return** $\mathbf{X}_t$

we have implemented the TrafficConMamba encoder and decoder using unidirectional Mamba blocks combined with wavelet transform convolution, as depicted in Fig. 2.

Algorithm 1 outlines the operation of the TrafficConMamba block forward propagation. For a given input $X_{t-1}$, the batch size is B, the number of channels is C, the length is W, and the width is H. First, we subject the input $X_{t-1}$ to a wavelet convolution operation, followed by a multi-scale convolution to capture the local information of the traffic. Meanwhile, for the linear flow information, we first normalise it after embedding the input, and then project it linearly onto x and z, both of dimension E. We then perform a 1D convolution on the input x to obtain $x'$. Based on $x'$, we compute the step size $\Delta$ associated with the input, as well as the projection parameters B and C of dimension N. We then discretize A and B with $\Delta$. We then use hardware-aware SSM to compute y. Next, y is z-gated and the residuals are added to $X_{t-1}$ to obtain the output token sequence $X_t$ for the tth Mamba block. Finally, we splice the information $X''_t$ captured by the wavelet transform convolution and the multiscale convolution with $X_t$ to obtain the final token sequence $X_t$.

### 3.3 Training Algorithm for TrafficConMamba

As depicted in Fig. 3, during pre-training, TrafficConMamba employs the matrix markers $X_0 \in R^{L \times Denc}$ produced by the embedding layer. A subset of the matrix will be selected at random, while the rest of the elements will be masked. For a given masking ratio $r \in (0, 1)$, the visible token sequence length is calculated as $L_{vis} = \lceil (1 - r)L \rceil$. The visible tokens are subsequently sampled according to the following procedure:

$$\mathbf{X}_0^{\text{vis}} = \text{Shuffle}(\mathbf{X}_0)[1 : \mathcal{L}_{\text{vis}}, :] \in \mathbb{R}^{\mathcal{L}_{\text{vis}} \times D_{\text{enc}}} \tag{2}$$

where the shuffle operation represents a randomised arrangement of the token sequence. It is important to note that the subsequent category token must remain unmasked throughout the process, as it plays a crucial role in aggregating the information of the entire sequence. The main aim of random masking is to eliminate redundancy. The method is a challenging task that rejects direct solutions by inferring them from neighbouring steps alone. In addition, reducing the input length reduces computational and storage costs, allowing for more efficient model training.

The TrafficConMamba encoder captures stepwise dependencies from the visible tokens, while the decoder reconstructs the masked steps by utilizing both the encoder's output tokens and the learnable mask tokens. Each mask token is a common, learnable vector that indicates missing steps in the sequence. To provide spatial context for the mask tokens, new positional embeddings are also included. TrafficConMamba's pre-training process can be formally described as

$$\mathbf{X}_{\text{enc}}^{\text{out}} = \mathbf{MLP}\left(\mathbf{Encoder}(\mathbf{X}_0^{\text{vis}})\right) \in \mathbb{R}^{\mathcal{L}_{\text{vis}} \times D_{\text{dec}}}, \tag{3}$$

$$\mathbf{X}_{\text{dec}}^{\text{in}} = \mathbf{Unshuffle}\left(\mathbf{Concat}(\mathbf{X}_{\text{enc}}^{\text{out}}, \mathbf{X}_{\text{mask}})\right) + \mathbf{E}_{\text{dec}}^{\text{pos}}, \tag{4}$$

$$\mathbf{X}_{\text{dec}}^{\text{out}} = \mathbf{Decoder}(\mathbf{X}_{\text{dec}}^{\text{in}}). \tag{5}$$

Here, The original order is restored by the unshuffle operation, and $\mathbf{E}_{\text{dec}}^{\text{pos}} \in \mathbb{R}^{\text{L} \times \text{D}_{\text{dec}}}$ represents the positional embeddings tailored for the TrafficConMamba decoder. The Mean Squared Error loss for the self-supervised reconstruction task is computed as follows, where $y_{real}$ denotes the true masked tokens and $y_{rec}$ represents the predicted tokens:

$$\mathbf{y}_{\text{real}} = \mathbf{Shuffle}(\mathbf{X}_0)[\mathcal{L}_{\text{vis}} + 1 : \mathcal{L}, :], \tag{6}$$

$$\mathbf{y}_{\text{rec}} = \mathbf{Shuffle}(\mathbf{X}_{\text{dec}}^{\text{out}})[\mathcal{L}_{\text{vis}} + 1 : \mathcal{L}, :], \tag{7}$$

$$\mathcal{L}_{\text{rec}} = \mathbf{MSE}(\mathbf{y}_{\text{real}}, \mathbf{y}_{\text{rec}}). \tag{8}$$

The pre-trained model is used to initialize the encoder parameters, including the embedding module and TrafficConMamba blocks, for downstream tasks. The decoder is replaced by an MLP head to classify the marked traffic data. The process follows a supervised learning approach, as described below, since all step tokens remain visible during fine-tuning:

$$\mathbf{X} = \mathbf{Encoder}(\mathbf{X}_0) \in \mathbb{R}^{\mathcal{L} \times D_{\text{enc}}}, \tag{9}$$

$$\mathbf{f} = \mathbf{X}[\mathcal{L}, :] \in \mathbb{R}^{D_{\text{enc}}}, \tag{10}$$

$$\hat{\mathbf{y}} = \mathbf{MLP}\left(\mathbf{Norm}(\mathbf{f})\right). \tag{11}$$

f represents the final class token, while $\hat{\mathbf{y}} \in \mathbb{R}^{\text{C}}$ denotes the predicted probability distribution across C traffic classes. The classification process is fine-tuned by minimizing the cross-entropy loss between the predicted distribution $\hat{\mathbf{y}}$ and the ground truth label y:

$$\mathcal{L}_{\text{cls}} = \text{CrossEntropy}(\hat{\mathbf{y}}, \mathbf{y}) \tag{12}$$

# 4 Experiments

## 4.1 Experiment Data and Experiment Settings

To evaluate the performance of TrafficConMamba, we conducted experiments on 6 publicly available traffic datasets with three main classification tasks.

1) Cryptographic Application Classification: Classify application traffic under different cryptographic protocols. Among them, CrossPlatform (Android) and CrossPlatform (iOS) contain 254 and 253 applications, respectively. Meanwhile, we use Tor traffic data from 8 communication categories in ISCXTor2016 and VPN traffic data from 7 communication categories in ISCXVPN2016.
2) Attack Traffic Categorization: Identify potential attack traffic such as denial of service (DoS) attacks and brute force attacks. We constructed six categories of data using CICIoT2022.
3) Malicious traffic categorization: distinguishing between malicious and benign traffic. We use all 20 data categories from the USTC-TFC2016 dataset.

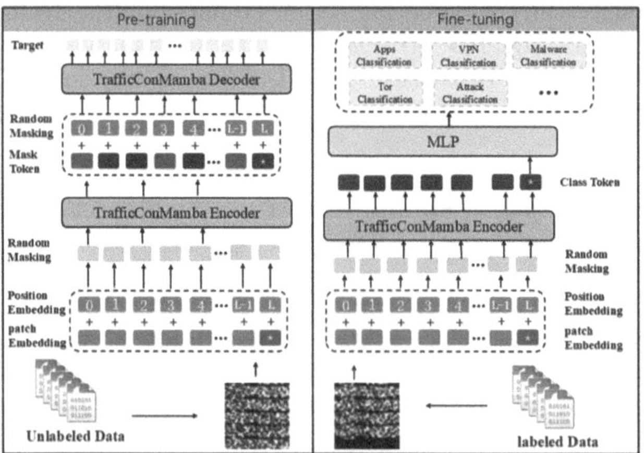


**Fig. 3.** Overview of TrafficConMamba Framework

All experiments described in this study were conducted using PyTorch on an Ubuntu system equipped with a 2080Ti GPU and 24 GB of memory. During the pre-training phase, the model was trained with a batch size of 128 for 150,000 steps. The initial learning rate was set to 0.001 using the AdamW optimizer. At the same time, we used a random masking step with a masking ratio of r = 0.9. In the fine-tuning phase, we set the batch size to 64 and the learning rate to 0.0002. Final evaluations were performed on the test set using the best-performing checkpoint.

To measure the classification performance of our method, we calculated the number of true positives (Tp), true negatives (Tn), false positives (Fp) and false negatives (Fn). Based on the above definitions, recall, precision and F1 can be obtained:

$$\text{Accuracy} = \frac{TP + TN}{TP + TN + FP + FN}, \tag{13}$$

$$\text{Precision} = \frac{TP}{TP + FP}, \tag{14}$$

$$\text{Recall} = \frac{TP}{TP + FN}, \tag{15}$$

$$\text{F1 Score} = \frac{2 \cdot \text{Precision} \cdot \text{Recall}}{\text{Precision} + \text{Recall}}. \tag{16}$$

### 4.2 Experimental Results and Analysis

In this paper, we evaluate the performance of TrafficConMamba on the task of classifying network encrypted traffic in three different network environments, namely encrypted application classification, attack traffic classification, and malware traffic classification, using six publicly available datasets. As shown in Tables 1 and 2, TrafficConMamba shows superior performance over the six datasets compared to ET-BERT, YaTC, and NetMamba. Overall, the average accuracy of TrafficConMamba ranges from 98.71% to 99.99%, with F1 Score values ranging from 98.61% to 99.99%.

**Table 1.** Compare results on Cross-Platform (Android), Cross-Platform (iOS) and ISCXTor2016 datasets

| Models | CrossPlatform(Android) | | | | CrossPlatform(iOS) | | | | ISCXTor2016 | | | |
|---|---|---|---|---|---|---|---|---|---|---|---|---|
| | AC | PR | RC | F1 | AC | PR | RC | F1 | AC | PR | RC | F1 |
| FlowPrint | 87.39% | 89.41% | 87.39% | 87.00% | 87.12% | 86.87% | 87.12% | 86.03% | 13.16% | 1.73% | 13.16% | 3.06% |
| AppScanner | 16.26% | 16.46% | 14.56% | 14.13% | 17.18% | 14.01% | 14.40% | 12.83% | 40.34% | 28.50% | 21.49% | 21.13% |
| FS-Net | 1.47% | 0.23% | 1.47% | 0.34% | 2.93% | 0.14% | 2.93% | 0.25% | 70.20% | 70.10% | 70.20% | 69.99% |
| ET-BERT | 93.86% | 94.51% | 93.86% | 94.01% | 91.05% | 88.09% | 91.05% | 88.50% | 99.80% | 99.81% | 99.80% | 99.80% |
| YaTC | 90.42% | 90.81% | 90.42% | 90.42% | 93.10% | 93.07% | 93.10% | 92.95% | 99.59% | 99.59% | 99.59% | 99.59% |
| NetMamba | 98.35% | 98.42% | 98.35% | 98.36% | 98.81% | 98.85% | 98.81% | 98.81% | 99.79% | 99.80% | 99.79% | 99.79% |
| TrafficConMamba | 98.71% | 98.61% | 98.71% | 98.61% | 98.17% | 98.21% | 98.17% | 98.17% | 99.93% | 99.93% | 99.93% | 99.93% |

As presented in Table 1, TrafficConMamba has some performance improvement on the CrossPlatform (Android) dataset compared to the other benchmark models. Specifically, our model achieves a 4.85% increase in accuracy and a 4.6% improvement in the F1 score compared to ET-BERT, which primarily learns traffic representations from packet payloads while overlooking the critical information embedded in packet headers. In contrast, TrafficConMamba analyzes traffic information more comprehensively by making effective use of header and payload characteristics. On the CrossPlatform (iOS) dataset, TrafficConMamba outperforms all baseline methods, while it far outperforms YaTC in all performance aspects. This performance gain extends beyond architectural differences, as TrafficConMamba constructs a more robust traffic representation than YaTC. Key enhancements, such as IP masking and spanning cuts, contribute to this improvement by refining feature extraction and reducing noise. Furthermore, on the ISCXTor2016 dataset, TrafficConMamba achieves state-of-the-art results, attaining an accuracy of 99.93% and the highest recorded F1 score, demonstrating its effectiveness in encrypted traffic classification.

From the results of CICIoT2022 and USTC-TFC2016 in Table 2, it can be seen that all the models show good performance in both attack traffic classification and malicious traffic classification tasks. Among them, TrafficConMamba slightly outperforms the other models in both accuracy and F1 scores, especially in the accuracy metric, achieving the best performance of 99.93%. This result further validates the effectiveness and advantages of our model.

**Table 2.** Comparative Results for ISCXVPN2016, USTC-TFC2016 and CICIoT2022 Data Sets

| Models | CICIoT2022 | | | | USTC-TFC2016 | | | | ISCXVPN2016 | | | |
|---|---|---|---|---|---|---|---|---|---|---|---|---|
| | AC | PR | RC | F1 | AC | PR | RC | F1 | AC | PR | RC | F1 |
| FlowPrint | 58.20% | 41.64% | 58.20% | 46.43% | 79.92% | 77.45% | 79.92% | 77.55% | 96.66% | 97.33% | 96.66% | 96.81% |
| AppScanner | 75.56% | 80.93% | 72.44% | 69.38% | 69.98% | 85.91% | 60.62% | 66.33% | 76.43% | 80.47% | 70.45% | 72.56% |
| FS-Net | 57.47% | 38.01% | 57.47% | 42.16% | 43.81% | 20.11% | 43.81% | 26.72% | 70.23% | 74.87% | 70.23% | 66.60% |
| ET-BERT | 99.37% | 99.38% | 99.37% | 99.37% | 99.10% | 99.11% | 99.11% | 99.11% | 95.66% | 95.66% | 95.66% | 95.65% |
| YaTC | 99.59% | 99.59% | 99.59% | 99.59% | 99.47% | 99.49% | 99.47% | 99.34% | 98.19% | 98.20% | 98.19% | 98.19% |
| NetMamba | 99.79% | 99.80% | 99.79% | 99.79% | 99.15% | 99.26% | 99.15% | 99.17% | 98.99% | 98.99% | 98.99% | 98.99% |
| TrafficConMamba | 99.93% | 99.93% | 99.93% | 99.93% | 99.91% | 99.91% | 99.91% | 99.91% | 98.92% | 98.92% | 98.92% | 98.92% |

### 4.3 Evaluation of Reasoning Efficiency

The inference speed of a model is crucial for its deployment in real-world scenarios. To assess the inference efficiency of TrafficConMamba, we conducted a comparative analysis with models like YaTC, NetMamba, and FS-Net. As depicted in Fig. 4(a), TrafficConMamba consistently delivers the highest inference speed across various batch sizes. This performance edge is especially pronounced when contrasted with models such as ET-BERT and FS-YaTC, which are hindered by a large number of parameters and less efficient architectures. Even when compared to models with a similar parameter count, TrafficConMamba outperforms YaTC and its optimized versions, showcasing superior computational efficiency. This advantage is largely attributed to Mamba's reduced computational complexity compared to Transformer-based architectures. Consequently, TrafficConMamba provides enhanced scalability, positioning it as a more efficient alternative to Transformer-based models like YaTC and ET-BERT for the classification of encrypted traffic.

As shown in Fig. 4(b), TrafficConMamba demonstrates lower GPU memory consumption for large batch sizes compared to most baseline models, with the exception of FS-Net and YaTC. FS-Net benefits from the memory efficiency of recurrent neural networks (RNNs), which scale linearly with sequence length, thereby reducing overall memory usage. However, this advantage comes at the cost of significantly slower inference speed and weaker classification performance. TrafficConMamba enhances memory efficiency primarily through optimized GPU operator adaptation. Compared to other baselines, the core module of TrafficConMamba improves memory efficiency mainly by adjusting the GPU operators. Overall, TrafficConMamba maintains the highest inference speed with relatively low memory consumption compared to other baselines.

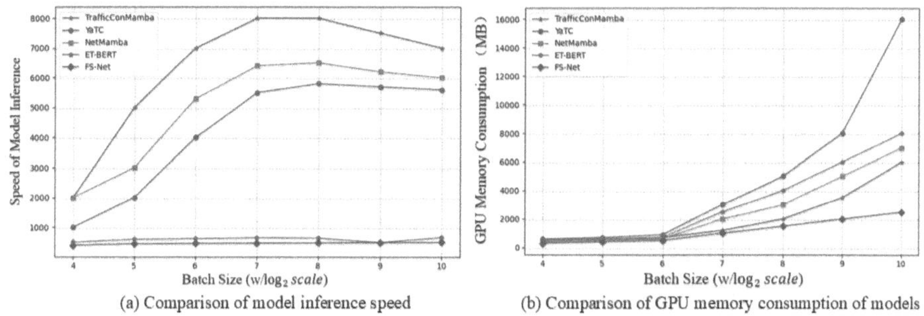


(a) Comparison of model inference speed

(b) Comparison of GPU memory consumption of models

**Fig. 4.** The Inference Speed and GPU Memory Comparison

## 4.4 Ablation Study

To verify the rationality of TrafficConMamba's design, we conducted ablation experiments to evaluate the performance of each module on six public datasets. The corresponding results are shown in Tables 3 and 4.

The experiment first replaced the unidirectional Mamba module in TrafficConMamba with a bidirectional Mamba module. Test data showed that, except for ISCXVPN2016, the accuracy rates of other datasets all decreased slightly. This indicates that the unidirectional Mamba module is more suitable for processing network traffic data, as packets are transmitted in sequence, and earlier packets have limited influence on the information in subsequent packets. Additionally, using bidirectional or omnidirectional Mamba modules introduces additional scanning operations, leading to increased computational load and memory

**Table 3.** Ablation Study of TrafficConMamba on CrossPlatform(Android), CrossPlatform(iOS) and CICIoT2022 Data Sets

| Method | CrossPlatform(Android) | | CrossPlatform(iOS) | | CICIot2022 | |
|---|---|---|---|---|---|---|
| | AC | F1 | AC | F1 | AC | F1 |
| w/Bidirectional Mamba | 98.52% | 98.51% | 97.93% | 97.93% | 99.85% | 99.85% |
| w/WTConv | 97.50% | 97.43% | 97.61% | 98.10% | 98.83% | 98.76% |
| w/InceptionConv | 98.31% | 98.23% | 97.23% | 96.98% | 98.51% | 98.32% |
| w/o Position Embedding | 98.45% | 98.41% | 97.46% | 97.26% | 99.59% | 99.59% |
| w/o Pre-training | 98.07% | 98.10% | 97.79% | 97.61% | 99.49% | 99.49% |
| TrafficConMamba | 98.71% | 98.61% | 98.17% | 98.17% | 99.93% | 99.93% |

**Table 4.** Ablation Study of TrafficConMamba on ISCXVPN2016, USTC-TFC2016 and ISCXTor2016 Data Sets

| Method | USTC-TFC2016 | | ISCXTor2016 | | ISCXVPN2016 | |
|---|---|---|---|---|---|---|
| | AC | F1 | AC | F1 | AC | F1 |
| w/Bidirectional Mamba | 98.52% | 98.51% | 97.93% | 97.93% | 99.85% | 99.85% |
| w/WTConv | 98.53% | 98.31% | 98.51% | 98.73% | 98.36% | 98.31% |
| w/InceptionConv | 98.21% | 98.13% | 98.42% | 98.46% | 98.34% | 98.51% |
| w/o Position Embedding | 98.45% | 98.41% | 97.46% | 97.26% | 99.59% | 99.59% |
| w/o Pre-training | 99.59% | 99.59% | 97.98% | 97.97% | 99.84% | 99.84% |
| TrafficConMamba | 99.91% | 99.91% | 99.93% | 99.93% | 98.92% | 99.91% |

consumption, which ultimately impacts runtime efficiency. Therefore, the unidirectional Mamba module is the optimal choice.

To validate the effectiveness of wavelet convolution, this chapter replaces the wavelet convolution block with a standard convolution block while keeping the rest of the structure unchanged. As shown in Tables 3 and 4, when the wavelet convolution is replaced with a standard convolution, the classification performance of all datasets deteriorates significantly, demonstrating that wavelet convolution is more effective at extracting local features. Although sequence models like Mamba inherently retain positional information, removing explicit positional encoding still results in a decrease in accuracy of 0.03% to 1.35% across all datasets except ISCXTor2016. This indicates that incorporating positional information helps the model better understand traffic features. The purpose of pre-training is to learn general traffic features from massive unlabeled data. Compared to models without pre-training, the pre-trained TrafficConMamba achieved an accuracy improvement of 0.06% to 1.02%, validating the effectiveness of the MAE-based pre-training method.

### 4.5 Few-Shot Analysis

To assess the robustness of TrafficConMamba in low-data scenarios, we evaluated its performance across four datasets using varying proportions of labeled data: 10%, 40%, 50%, and 100%. The results, presented in Fig. 5, demonstrate that pre-training-based methods—TrafficConMamba, YaTC, ET-BERT, and NetMamba—consistently outperform purely supervised approaches, particularly in low-data regimes. While some supervised models achieve competitive results in specific cases, none maintain consistent performance across all datasets. The pre-training approach enables deep learning models to learn high-quality traffic features using large amounts of unlabeled traffic data, dramatically reducing the reliance on labeled data. Notably, TrafficConMamba surpasses ET-BERT and YaTC across all labeled data sizes, highlighting its superior robustness and adaptability in sample-limited settings.

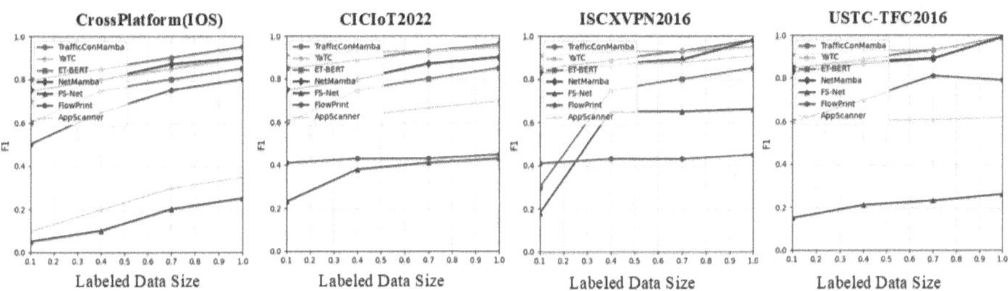


**Fig. 5.** Comparison of performance in a Few-Shot of settings

## 5 Conclusion

In this paper, we present an efficient model for classifying network encrypted traffic: TrafficConMamba.To improve the inference efficiency of the model while maintaining performance, TrafficConMamba combines the local feature extraction capability of convolutional layers with Mamba's ability to capture long-range dependencies.TrafficConMamba has demonstrated excellent performance and efficient inference speed on three network encrypted traffic classification tasks, showing excellent performance and efficient inference speed, demonstrating its effectiveness in classifying network encrypted traffic in different network environments. At the same time, TrafficConMamba outperforms state-of-the-art methods even with small amounts of labeled data.

## References

1. L. Encrypt, Percentage of web pages loaded by firefox using HTTPS (2024). https://letsencrypt.org/stats/
2. Nguyen, T.T.T., Armitage, G.: A survey of techniques for internet traffic classification using machine learning. IEEE Commun. Surv. Tutor. **10**(4), 56–76 (2008)
3. Khatouni, A.S., Zincir-Heywood, N.: Integrating machine learning with off-the-shelf traffic flow features for http/https traffic classification. In: 2019 IEEE Symposium on Computers and Communications (ISCC), pp. 1–7. IEEE (2019)
4. Yao, H., Gao, P., Zhang, P., et al.: Hybrid intrusion detection system for edge-based IIoT relying on machine-learning-aided detection. IEEE Netw. **33**(5), 75–81 (2019)
5. Xu, Y., Cao, J., Song, K., et al.: FastTraffic: a lightweight method for encrypted traffic fast classification. Comput. Netw. **235**, 109965 (2023)
6. Shekhawat, A.S., Di Troia, F., Stamp, M.: Feature analysis of encrypted malicious traffic. Expert Syst. Appl. **125**, 130–141 (2019)
7. He, K., Chen, X., Xie, S., et al.: Masked autoencoders are scalable vision learners. In: Proceedings of the IEEE/CVF Conference on Computer Vision and Pattern Recognition, pp. 16000–16009 (2022)
8. Caron, M., Touvron, H., Misra, I., et al.: Emerging properties in self-supervised vision transformers. In: Proceedings of the IEEE/CVF International Conference on Computer Vision, pp. 9650–9660 (2021)
9. Kenton, J.D.M.W.C., Toutanova, L.K.: Bert: pre-training of deep bidirectional transformers for language understanding. In: Proceedings of NAACL-HLT **1**, 2 (2019)
10. Dias, K.L., Pongelupe, M.A., Caminhas, W.M., de Errico, L.: An innovative approach for real-time network traffic classification. Comput. Netw. **158**, 143–157 (2019). https://doi.org/10.1016/j.comnet.2019.04.004
11. Aceto, G., Ciuonzo, D., Montieri, A., Antonio, P.: Toward effective mobile encrypted traffic classification through deep learning. Neurocomputing **409**, 306–315 (2020). https://doi.org/10.1016/j.neucom.2020.05.036
12. Al-Haija, Q.A., Zein-Sabatto, S.: An efficient deep-learning-based detection and classification system for cyber-attacks in IoT communication networks. Electronics **9**(12), 21–52 (2020). https://doi.org/10.3390/electron-ics9122152
13. Zhu, L., et al.: Vision mamba: efficient visual representation learning with bidirectional state space model. arXiv preprint arXiv:2401.09417 (2024)
14. Qu, J., Ma, X., Li, J.: Trafficgpt: breaking the token barrier for efficient long traffic analysis and generation. arXiv preprint arXiv:2403.05822 (2024)
15. Zheng, J., Zeng, Z., Feng, T.: GCN-eta: high-efficiency encrypted malicious traffic detection. Secur. Commun. Netw., 1–11 (2022)
16. Alshammari, R., Zincir-Heywood, A.N.: Can encrypted traffic be identified without port numbers, IP addresses and payload inspection? Comput. Netw. **55**(6), 1326–1350 (2011)
17. Feghhi, S., Leith, D.J.: A web traffic analysis attack using only timing information. IEEE Trans. Inf. Forensics Secur. **11**(8), 1747–1759 (2016)
18. Moore, A., Zuev, D., Crogan, M.: Discriminators for use in flow-based classification (2013)
19. Liu, C., Cao, Z., Xiong, G., et al.: MAMPF: encrypted traffic classification based on multi-attribute markov probability fingerprints. In: 2018 IEEE/ACM 26th International Symposium on Quality of Service (IWQoS), pp. 1–10. IEEE (2018)

20. Okada, Y., Ata, S., Nakamura, N., et al.: Comparisons of machine learning algorithms for application identification of encrypted traffic. In: 2011 10th International Conference on Machine Learning and Applications and Workshops vol. 2, pp. 358-361. IEEE (2011)
21. Sun, G.L., Xue, Y., Dong, Y., et al.: An novel hybrid method for effectively classifying encrypted traffic. In: 2010 IEEE Global Telecommunications Conference GLOBECOM 2010, pp. 1–5. IEEE (2010)
22. Zhongsheng, W., Jianguo, W., Sen, Y., et al.: Retracted: traffic identification and traffic analysis based on support vector machine. Concurr. Comput. Pract. Exper. **32**(2), e5292 (2020)
23. Panchenko, A., Lanze, F., Pennekamp, J., et al.: Website fingerprinting at internet scale. In: NDSS (2016)
24. Saltaformaggio, B., Choi, H., Johnson, K., et al.: Eavesdropping on fine-grained user activities within smartphone apps over encrypted network traffic. In: 10th USENIX Workshop on Offensive Technologies (WOOT 16) (2016)
25. Dubin, R., Dvir, A., Pele, O., et al.: I know what you saw last minute–encrypted http adaptive video streaming title classification. IEEE Trans. Inf. Forensics Secur. **12**(12), 3039–3049 (2017)
26. Shen, M., Liu, Y., Zhu, L., et al.: Fine-grained webpage fingerprinting using only packet length information of encrypted traffic. IEEE Trans. Inf. Forensics Secur. **16**, 2046–2059 (2020)
27. Xu, S.J., Geng, G.G., Jin, X.B., et al.: Seeing traffic paths: encrypted traffic classification with path signature features. IEEE Trans. Inf. Forensics Secur. **17**, 2166–2181 (2022)
28. Lotfollahi, M., Jafari Siavoshani, M., Shirali Hossein Zade, R., et al.: Deep packet: a novel approach for encrypted traffic classification using deep learning. Soft Comput. **24**(3), 1999–2012 (2020)
29. Wang, W., Zhu, M., Wang, J., et al.: End-to-end encrypted traffic classification with one-dimensional convolution neural networks. In: 2017 IEEE International Conference on Intelligence and Security Informatics (ISI), pp. 43–48. IEEE (2017)
30. He, H., Yang, Z., Chen, X.: PERT: payload encoding representation from transformer for encrypted traffic classification. In: 2020 ITU Kaleidoscope: Industry-Driven Digital Transformation, pp. 1–8 (2020)
31. Zhao, R., Zhan, M., Deng, X., et al.: Yet another traffic classifier: a masked autoencoder based traffic transformer with multi-level flow representation. In: Proceedings of the AAAI Conference on Artificial Intelligence vol. 37, no. 4, pp. 5420–5427 (2023)
32. Wang, T., Xie, X., Wang, W., et al.: NetMamba: efficient network traffic classification via pre-training unidirectional mamba. arXiv preprint arXiv:2405.11449 (2024)
33. Wang, C., Tsepa, O., Ma, J., Wang, B.: Graph-mamba: towards long-range graph sequence modeling with selective state spaces. arXiv preprint arXiv:2402.00789 (2024)

# MFETD: Multimodal Feature Fusion for Encrypted Traffic Detection Based on Transformer

Zhiqiang Wang[1,2](✉), Shufang Pang[1], Ying Liu[1], Shaowei Yuan[1], and Lei Ju[1]

[1] Department of Cyberspace Security, Beijing Electronic Science and Technology Institute, Beijing 102627, China

[2] State Information Center Postdoctoral Research Station, Beijing 100045, China

wangzq@besti.edu.cn

**Abstract.** Malicious network traffic poses a significant threat to Internet security. Although state-of-the-art deep learning (DL)-based detection techniques typically identify malicious traffic by learning traffic-related features, their performance is currently limited by the representational capacity of existing feature extraction methods. This paper proposes a Transformer-based Multimodal Feature Fusion Framework for Encrypted Traffic Detection (MFETD) to address the challenge of effectively representing encrypted traffic data. MFETD is a multimodal architecture that integrates raw byte sequences and extracted statistical features to comprehensively characterize encrypted traffic flows. Specifically, the proposed method extracts image-modal features and tabular-modal features from raw encrypted network traffic, enabling the fusion of low-level raw data characteristics with high-level, domain-specific features. This approach preserves both the intrinsic information and the critical discriminative attributes of the traffic. A Transformer model is employed for classification, achieving superior performance and offering a novel perspective for encrypted traffic detection. Experimental results demonstrate that MFETD achieves a classification accuracy of 99.99%, representing an average improvement of 2.23% over state-of-the-art unimodal machine learning and deep learning approaches. Furthermore, MFETD maintains high classification accuracy even under imbalanced data conditions.

**Keywords:** Multimodal Feature · Feature Fusion · Malicious Encrypted Traffic · Transformer

## 1 Introduction

With the rapid development of the global internet, network traffic has surged, and user demands for privacy have increased. Encryption technologies like Secure

Z. Wang, S. Pang, Y. Liu and S. Yuan—These authors contributed equally to this work.


K.-K. R. Choo et al. (Eds.): ICDF2C 2025, LNICST 686, pp. 20–35, 2026.
https://doi.org/10.1007/978-3-032-22545-0_2

Sockets Layer (SSL) and its successor, Transport Layer Security (TLS), are widely adopted to protect user privacy and data security [1]. However, the rise of malicious encrypted traffic poses a significant cybersecurity threat [2]. Encrypted traffic classification, which identifies the applications or services responsible for generating network traffic, plays a critical role in addressing network issues, enhancing security, and supporting applications such as Quality of Service (QoS) provisioning, intrusion detection, and malware detection [3].

In recent years, machine learning (ML) [5–9] has been applied more and more to network traffic classification. ML methods do not require access to packet port numbers or payload content. Instead, they rely on domain expertise to manually extract and select features that characterize the behavior of specific protocols or applications, thereby enabling the development of effective solutions. For instance, behavior-based network traffic classification analyzes traffic patterns by observing the number of distinct ports accessed by packets or the transport layer protocols in use [4].ML exhibits certain limitations when dealing with increasingly large and complex network traffic. Additionally, the manual feature selection process consumes significant human resources. Deep learning (DL) is currently regarded as one of the most effective techniques for encrypted traffic classification based on automatic feature extraction. Compared to traditional ML, DL possesses superior learning capabilities, enabling it to directly learn complex nonlinear relationships between input data and output without the need to break down the problem into subproblems of feature selection and classification. Due to these advantages, deep learning has gradually become the mainstream technology in the field of encrypted traffic classification.

The main challenge in encrypted traffic classification lies in how to represent the features of encrypted traffic data more effectively. Structurally, network traffic packets consist of components such as the IP, TCP, TLS, and payload. The TLS contains encryption and decryption information. Researchers aim to extract and integrate information from various parts of the TLS traffic as comprehensively as possible to achieve a more accurate classification. Currently, numerous studies have explored this field. On the one hand, machine learning-based methods typically rely on metadata or statistical information from encrypted traffic packets, such as port numbers, packet payload content, byte counts, and data flow durations, to perform encrypted traffic classification [5]. However, machine learning methods often rely on manually designed traffic features, which frequently overlook many packet details and lack fine-grained operations, thereby affecting classification accuracy. Furthermore, end-to-end classification methods generally focus on single-modal features, concentrating on specific types such as payloads, time series, spatial features, or behavioral features [15,16], and often neglect the effective value of critical features. Although past research has aimed to integrate information from different parts and some methods have attempted to make effective use of these features, they frequently overlook the importance of the overall correlation within network traffic [6].

To improve the classification accuracy of encrypted traffic and make full use of all valuable information from the raw traffic while maintaining the integrity of the information and focusing on the most valuable aspects, this paper proposes the Multimodal Feature Fusion for Encrypted Traffic Detection based on Transformer framework. MFETD is a multimodal framework designed to comprehensively describe encrypted data flows by fusing raw data bytes and extracted statistical features. MFETD employs a Transformer for classification, achieving excellent accuracy and offering a new approach to solving the problem of encrypted traffic classification.

The contributions of this paper are summarized as follows:

- **Multimodal Complementary Feature Mechanism for Encrypted Traffic:** This study introduces a multimodal complementary mechanism for feature representation in encrypted traffic, constructing a joint representation through both image and tabular modalities to preserve the integrity of raw data. During the preprocessing phase, raw byte sequences are first transformed into grayscale images, effectively retaining all exploitable information from the original traffic, including the holistic correlations across traffic sessions. Concurrently, salient statistical features are extracted from the traffic and structured as multi-row vectors, capturing critical metadata such as payload content and TLS message types. These vectors serve as an additional modality input, enriching the feature space with domain-specific statistical characteristics.
- **Multimodal Fusion Strategy with Hierarchical Self-Attention Mechanism:** This work pioneers the application of a multimodal multi-head self-attention mechanism in encrypted traffic classification, combining image and tabular modalities within the MFETD framework. The Transformer architecture is employed to simultaneously capture features from both the grayscale image and tabular modes. Leveraging the self-attention mechanism, the model can focus on different aspects of the input data, enabling it to learn both global contextual patterns and local discriminative features. This design retains the advantages of end-to-end learning from raw traffic data while enhancing attention to domain-relevant features, thus achieving comprehensive and fine-grained traffic analysis.
- **Hierarchical Multimodal Fusion and Efficient Modeling:** MFETD employs a hierarchical multimodal fusion strategy for encrypted traffic modeling. Grayscale images are partitioned into multiple patches, which are then converted into one-dimensional vectors through patch embedding. These vectors, along with class and positional embeddings, are fed into the model as input. By capturing both local and global dependencies within the image modality, the model enhances its classification accuracy. Extensive experimental results confirm the effectiveness of the proposed approach, achieving a classification accuracy of 99.99%, with an average improvement of 2.23% over state-of-the-art machine learning and deep learning methods.

# 2 Multimodal Encrypted Malicious Traffic Detection

## 2.1 Multimodal Data Preprocessing

In this section, we will describe the steps of multimodal data preprocessing, focusing on two modalities: Image modes and tabular modes. After data preprocessing, the raw traffic features are represented using both modalities. As shown in Fig. 1

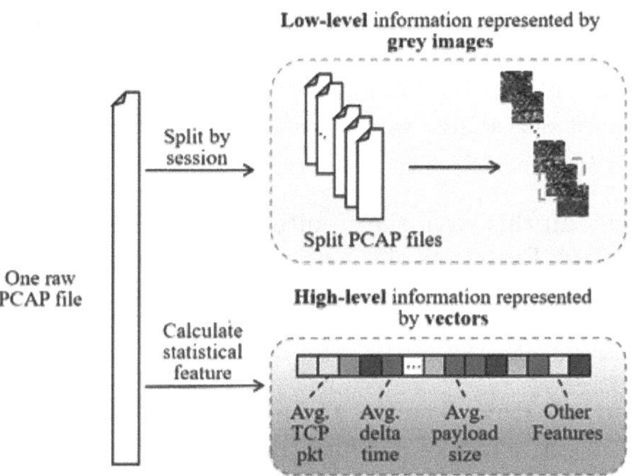


**Fig. 1.** Data Preprocess Procedure. This figure illustrates the preprocessing workflow for network traffic data. The raw traffic data is transformed into two modalities: an image modality, and a tabular modality, derived by extracting features. This workflow provides multimodal inputs for subsequent classification tasks.

### Conversion of Raw Traffic Data Into Image Modes

*Traffic Data Segmentation.* When performing traffic classification, it is essential to segment continuous traffic into discrete units based on a specific granularity to simplify the processing and facilitate the extraction of useful features by the classification model. Wang Wei et al.[?] found that the optimal representation method involves segmenting continuous raw traffic data in packets by session to include all protocol layers' data. In this step, we segment traffic by session into discrete traffic units, which encompass all protocol data from the application layer to the link layer. This approach ensures that each traffic unit fully reflects the entire communication process within a session, including both requests and responses. Currently, most researchers employ session-based traffic segmentation methods.

*Traffic Data Cleaning.* In this step, the traffic data is first anonymized and cleaned. If all traffic originates from the same network, the MAC and IP addresses may no longer serve as effective distinguishing information. Therefore, it is necessary to anonymize and clean invalid features. At the data link layer and the IP layer, MAC addresses and IP addresses are randomly assigned, respectively.

*Data Pruning.* Since many vision transformers do not support processing images of variable sizes, we trim all files to a uniform length to ensure compatibility with various vision transformers. The initial portion of a stream or session typically contains connection and content data, which best reflect the intrinsic characteristics of the stream or session. If the file size exceeds 784 bytes, it is trimmed to 784 bytes. If the file size is less than 784 bytes, $0 \times 00$ padding is added at the end to extend it to 784 bytes.

*Image Generation.* In this step, the resulting files of uniform size are converted into grayscale images. Each byte of the original file represents a pixel, with $0 \times 00$ corresponding to black and 0xff corresponding to white. This method maximizes the retention of information from the original data.

**Transformation of Raw Traffic Data Into Tabular Modes.** Through meticulous feature extraction of network traffic data, we capture and quantify a range of metrics that reflect the characteristics of network communications and potential anomalous behaviors. Within a given observation window, we calculate the average number of packets in which various TCP flags (SYN, URG, FIN, ACK, PSH, RST) are activated. The frequency of these flags can reveal patterns related to connection establishment, urgent data transmission, connection termination, acknowledgment, push operations, and reset requests. Additionally, we compute the average number of DNS, TCP, UDP, and ICMP packets. The activity levels of these protocols help identify normal network service calls and potential anomalous communications.

In the temporal dimension, we record the duration of packets within the observation window, along with the mean, minimum, maximum, and standard deviation of the inter-arrival times. These metrics reflect the dynamic characteristics of network traffic and its potential burstiness. Analyzing packet length and payload, including their mean, minimum, maximum, and standard deviation, provides insights into data transmission efficiency and potential data hiding attempts. Furthermore, we examine the frequency of small payload packets, which may indicate the presence of covert channels. The average DNS/TCP ratio assists in identifying whether DNS queries are using the TCP protocol in a normal manner.

These features collectively form a comprehensive framework for network traffic feature analysis, enabling more in-depth and granular examination of the characteristics and behavior patterns of each session. This allows for more precise detection and identification of complex patterns within network communications. By doing so, we can construct a more extensive and enriched feature space, capturing the characteristics of network activity from multiple perspectives. This cross-modal analysis approach can enhance the accuracy of traffic classification and anomaly detection.

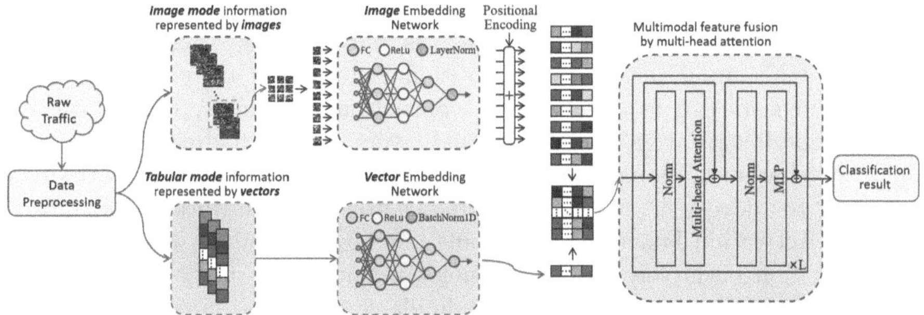


**Fig. 2.** Overview of the MFETD approach. The image modality is transformed into a feature sequence via an image embedding network and positional encoding, while the tabular modality is processed through a vector embedding network. Subsequently, both modalities are fused using an additive fusion strategy (MM-ADD) and input into an enhanced Transformer structure for classification. Finally, a feature enhancement module optimizes the fusion results.

## 2.2 Methodology

In this section, we provide a detailed overview of the multimodal approach based on Vision Transformers, which employs various feature modalities to represent malicious traffic and achieve precise classification. MFETD as shown in Fig. 2.

**Image Segmentation for Constructing Patch Sequences.** Since Transformer models can only process one-dimensional vector sequences, while grayscale images are represented as two-dimensional matrices, it is necessary to first transform the input grayscale image into a sequence of small patches. Specifically, the grayscale image is partitioned along the horizontal and vertical axes with a stride $P \times P$, resulting in $\left(\frac{H}{P}\right) \times \left(\frac{W}{P}\right) = HW/P^2$ patches. This sequence of patches is denoted as $\left\{x_1, x_2, \cdots, x_{HW/P^2}\right\}$,where each small image patch $x_i$ $(1 \leq i \leq HW/P^2)$ has a size of $P \times P$, $x_i \in \mathbb{R}^{P \times P}$.

**Constructing an Embedding Sequence to Represent Image Patches.** To begin, each image patch $x_i \in \mathbb{R}^{P \times P}$ is flattened by concatenating its rows sequentially, resulting in a one-dimensional vector $x_i \in \mathbb{R}^{P^2}$ of length $P^2$. Each one-dimensional vector $x_i$ is then passed through an Image Embedding Network, where it undergoes forward propagation to produce a one-dimensional embedding $e_i \in \mathbb{R}^D$. This embedding vector is generated through a sequence comprising a linear layer, a ReLU activation layer, a LayerNorm normalization layer, and an additional LayerNorm regularization layer. Consequently, the original sequence of patches $\{x_1, x_2, \cdots, x_{HW/P^2}\}$ $(x_i \in \mathbb{R}^{P \times P})$ is ultimately mapped to an embedding sequence $\{e_1, e_2, \cdots, e_{HW/P^2}\}$ $(e_i \in \mathbb{R}^D)$.

**Enhanced Image Embedding Network.** To better accommodate the data characteristics within network traffic images, the proposed Image Embedding Network builds upon the traditional Vision Transformer embedding network with enhanced design features. Unlike conventional methods, which typically rely solely on linear layers or convolutional layers, the method presented in this paper introduces additional ReLU activation layers and LayerNorm normalization layers to address the noise characteristics present in network traffic images.

ReLU Activation Function: By zeroing out negative values, the ReLU activation function effectively suppresses noise within small image patches (such as background features of traffic and redundant, non-discriminative characteristics), while preserving positive regions with stronger features for subsequent training.

LayerNorm Normalization Layer: This layer standardizes each embedding vector, reducing the discrepancies in feature distributions and mitigating the issue of Internal Covariate Shift. This improves the stability of model training. Furthermore, it enhances the comparability between embeddings, making it easier for the model to identify feature patterns within the sequence, thus preventing the model from converging to local optima and improving overall performance.

**Positional Embedding to Preserve Image Spatial Structure.** During the embedding process, the positional information of the original image may be lost, although this information is essential for accurate image classification. As shown in Fig. 3, grayscale images corresponding to "Dowgin" traffic typically exhibit black regions concentrated in the center, while those associated with "Fakeinst" traffic have black regions concentrated in the lower part. This difference in spatial distribution implies that if positional information is disregarded in the embedding sequence, the model may struggle to capture crucial features relevant to classification.

To address this, we introduce learnable positional embeddings $\{p_1, p_2, \cdots, p_{HW/P^2}\}(p_i \in \mathbb{R}^D)$, which are added to the embedding sequence, resulting in the final output of the image embedding network $\{p_1 + e_1, p_2 + e_2, \cdots, p_{HW/P^2} + e_{HW/P^2}\}$. Through supervised learning on large-scale traffic data, the learnable positional embeddings automatically capture the spatial position of each embedding within the original input image, thereby enabling the model to extract spatially relevant information. With effective mapping techniques, the generated image representations can fully capture the underlying structure of the original data, enhancing the model's ability to identify spatial patterns critical for accurate classification.

**Mapping High-Dimensional Information Vectors to the Embedding Space.** High-dimensional information vectors, which represent the features of

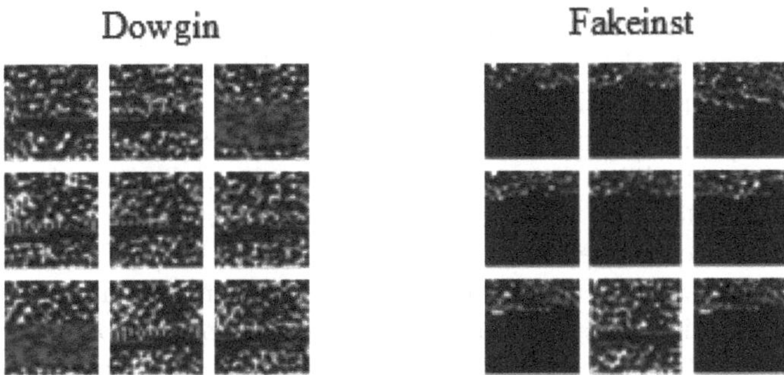


**Fig. 3.** Traffic grayscale image distribution Diagram. This figure illustrates the spatial distribution characteristics of grayscale images corresponding to two types of traffic:"Dowgin" and "Fakeinst". The "Dowgin" traffic samples exhibit central clustering in their image structure, while the "Fakeinst" traffic samples primarily show a concentration of dark regions in the lower half of the image.

raw traffic data, need to be transformed into an embedding sequence for subsequent processing. Initially, the input vector is mapped to an intermediate dimension to reduce computational complexity. Then, each one-dimensional vector $v_i \in \mathbb{R}$ is fed through a specific Vector Embedding Network, where forward propagation transforms it into a one-dimensional embedding $e_i \in \mathbb{R}^D$. Ultimately, the vector sequence $\{v_1, v_2, \cdots, v_i\}$ $(v_i \in \mathbb{R})$ is transformed into an embedding sequence $\{v_1, v_2, \cdots, v_i\}$ $(v_i \in \mathbb{R})$ is converted into an embedding sequence $\{e_1, e_2, \cdots, e_i\}$ $(e_i \in \mathbb{R}^D)$. The Vector Embedding Network consists of a linear layer, a ReLU activation layer, fully connected layers, and a BatchNorm1D layer. Through two fully connected layers with linear transformations and ReLU non-linear activation, the network effectively extracts and combines complex feature relationships. The BatchNorm1D layer further enhances training stability, accelerates convergence, reduces overfitting risk, and improves overall performance.In the modular learning framework, the Image Embedding Network and Vector Embedding Network process different modalities of data separately, and ultimately output distinct modality-specific feature vectors as inputs for the third step of MFETD, ensuring complementary information extraction across different modalities.

**Additive Fusion (MM-ADD) Strategy.** In the multimodal fusion section, this paper proposes an Additive Fusion (MM-ADD) strategy, where image features and CSV features are directly added together to achieve simple yet efficient feature fusion. Let the batch size be $B$, the sequence length be $L$, and the feature dimension be $D$. The fusion process for image features and CSV features can be represented as:

$$\mathbf{X}_{fused} = \mathbf{X}_{img} + \mathbf{X}_{csv} \cdot \mathbf{1}_L^T$$

where $\mathbf{1}_L$ is a vector of ones with length $L$, and the operation $\mathbf{1}_L^T$ broadcasts the table features to the same dimension as the image features, preserving the spatial structure information of the image.

In the patch embedding stage, the image is divided into $4 \times 4$ patches and mapped to the embedding dimension, completing the preliminary fusion between the tabular modality and the image modality. The fused features are then further processed through the hierarchical structure of the Swin Transformer, which includes a window-based self-attention mechanism and hierarchical downsampling strategy. This process gradually reduces the resolution of the feature map while increasing the number of channels, thereby generating multi-scale feature representations and enhancing the model's expressive capacity.

**Feature Enhancement and Recalibration Module.** After each feature fusion layer, we introduce a feature enhancement mechanism that recalibrates the fused features using learnable scaling and offset parameters,

$$E_{\text{img}}^{\text{final}} = \gamma_{\text{img}} \odot E_{\text{img}}^{\text{out}} + \beta_{\text{img}}$$

$$E_{\text{tab}}^{\text{final}} = \gamma_{\text{tab}} \odot E_{\text{tab}}^{\text{out}} + \beta_{\text{tab}}$$

where $\gamma$ and $\beta$ are learnable parameters, and $\odot$ represents element-wise multiplication. In the multi-layer fusion architecture, the output of the $l$-th layer serves as the input to the $(l+1)$-th layer. This progressive fusion approach allows the model to gradually integrate information from both modalities from shallow to deep layers, forming a hierarchical feature representation. It dynamically adjusts the importance of different feature channels, further improving the fusion effectiveness.

# 3 Experimental Results and Analysis

## 3.1 Dataset

To evaluate the effectiveness of MFETD in classifying malicious encrypted traffic, we utilized two public datasets: ISCXVPN2016 and CICAndMal2017. The ISCXVPN2016 contains 12 precisely labeled categories of raw traffic data, including six categories of traditionally encrypted traffic and six categories of protocol-encapsulated traffic. The specific details of datasets are shown in Fig. 4. The malicious traffic data in the CICAndMal2017 comes from 42 malware families.

## 3.2 Evaluation Metrics

MFETD is evaluated using the following four metrics: accuracy, precision, recall, and F1-score.

$$\text{Accuracy} = \frac{TP + TN}{TP + TN + FP + FN} \tag{1}$$

**Algorithm 1.** Training MFETD

**Require:** Sample sets
$S_{x,v}, i \in \{1, 2, \cdots, N\}, z \in \{1, 2, 3\}$;
$S^i_{x,v}, i \in \{1, 2, \cdots, N\}, z \in \{1, 2, 3\}$;
$S_x = \{x_1, x_2, \cdots, x_{HW/P^2}\}$ Where $x_i \in \mathbb{R}^{P^2}$, $x_{HW/P^2}$ represent Image modal feature vector;
$S_v = \{v_1, v_2, \cdots, v_i\}$ $(v_i \in \mathbb{R}^D)$ Where $v_1$ represent Tabular/structured modal feature vectors;
The number of samples is $N$.
**Ensure:** A trained instantiated MFETD network. Net.
**Require:** Image Embedding Network, Vector Embedding Network, Multimodal feature fusion Network
1: Net1 ← ImgEmbNET
2: Net2 ← VecEmbNET
3: Net3 ← FusionNet
4: **for** $i$ in $\{1, 2, \cdots, N\}$ **do**
5: **while** $S^i_x$ **do**
6: Train(Net1, $S_x$) //pretraining stage
7: **while** $S^i_x$ **do**
8: Train(Net2, $S^i_v$) //pretraining stage
9: **end while**
10: **end while**
11: Net ← Combine(Net1, 2, Fusion Network)
12: **end for**
13: Train(Net, $S^i_{x,v}$) // fine-tuning stage

$$\text{Precision} = \frac{TP}{TP + FP} \tag{2}$$

$$\text{Recall} = \frac{TP}{TP + FN} \tag{3}$$

$$F_1 = 2 \times \frac{\text{Precision} \times \text{Recall}}{\text{Precision} + \text{Recall}} \tag{4}$$

TN is number of instances where the actual class is negative, and the prediction is also negative. TP is the number of instances where the actual class is positive, and the prediction is also positive. FN the number of instances where the actual class is positive, but the prediction is negative. FP is the number of instances where the actual class is negative, but the prediction is positive.

### 3.3 Baseline

To verify the effectiveness of the proposed method, we selected four representative baseline models for comparative experiments based on the differences in feature extraction paradigms. Specifically, these models include:

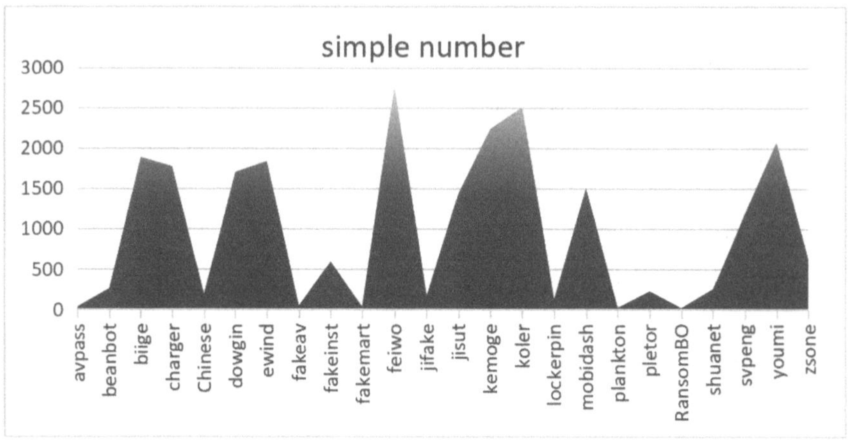


**Fig. 4.** Distribution of Sample Sizes Across Malware Families. This figure illustrates the distribution of sample sizes for various malware families in the dataset. The x-axis lists the names of 42 malware families, while the y-axis indicates the number of samples per family, ranging from 0 to over 3000. There is significant variation in sample sizes across these malware families.

1. **FS-Net**: A deep reconstruction model built upon Bidirectional Gated Recurrent Units (Bi-GRU), which implements encrypted traffic classification through a traffic feature reconstruction mechanism.
2. **Long Short-Term Memory (LSTM)**: A classic temporal modeling architecture that establishes long-range temporal dependencies through gating mechanisms. It has significant advantages in encrypted traffic time-series feature extraction and is widely applied in traffic classification tasks.
3. **Convolutional Neural Network (CNN)**: A spatial feature extractor based on multi-layer convolution operations. It captures the byte-level spatial correlations of encrypted traffic through local perception mechanisms, making it one of the mainstream methods for encrypted traffic representation learning.

The aforementioned baseline models cover the main technological approaches for detecting encrypted malicious traffic from three dimensions: temporal modeling, spatial feature extraction, and traditional feature engineering. According to bibliometric analysis, these methods represent the most effective encrypted malicious traffic detection algorithms currently available. Therefore, comparing our method with these models provides a better reflection of its effectiveness and superiority.

### 3.4 Experimental Results and Analysis

*Comparison Experiments.* In the comparative experiment section, we compare MFETD with the baseline models to verify whether MFETD outperforms existing state-of-the-art methods in detecting malicious encrypted traffic. Figure 5 shows the performance comparison between MFETD and other methods in the encrypted malicious traffic detection task.

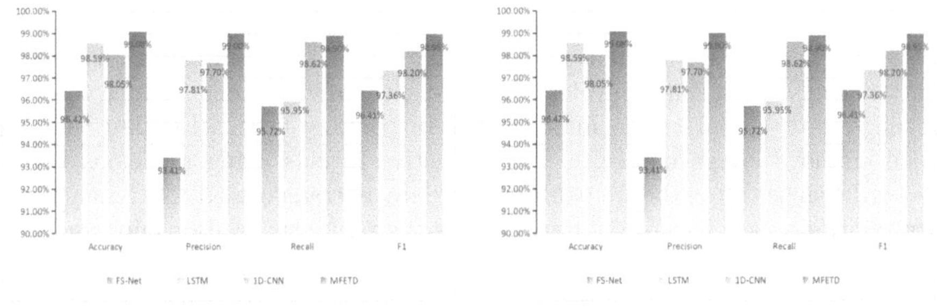


(a) CICAndMal2017 Dateset (b) ISCXVPN2016 Dataset

**Fig. 5.** The result of Comparison Experiments. This figure illustrates the performance comparison of MFETD with existing deep learning models on the CICAndMal2017 and ISCXVPN2016 datasets. The results demonstrate that MFETD outperforms these models in accuracy, precision, recall, and F1 score, achieving an F1 score of 99.68% on the CICAndMal2017 dataset.

Compared to other methods, MFETD achieved the best performance on the CICAndMal2017 dataset and is capable of effectively identifying 42 malicious traffic families. In comparison to other DL models, MFETD outperforms single-modality DL models in terms of Accuracy, Precision, and F1-score. As shown in Fig. 5 , MFETD's F1-score reached 99.68%, indicating that even in the case of imbalanced malicious traffic dataset samples, MFETD can still perform efficient and accurate detection.

Validation on two different datasets reveals that using multimodal features significantly enhances the model's detection performance. MFETD not only uses image features, which are the same as those used by other DL models, but also incorporates additional tabular modality features. These tabular modalities contain crucial raw traffic features and provide detailed traffic information. This feature fusion approach enables the model to perform better when handling complex network traffic. By comprehensively extracting traffic information, MFETD improves detection performance without the need for complex network structures. This indicates that the performance of the MFETD method far surpasses that of current state-of-the-art DL methods.

*Ablation Experiment.* This paper investigates the performance impact of various modalities on the MFETD framework by exploring different variants of MFETD to validate the effectiveness of the modality fusion approach. The variants include MFETD-T (which uses only tabular modes) and MFETD-I (which uses only image modality). By comparatively analyzing the performance of these different variants, we comprehensively evaluate each modality's contribution to enhancing the framework's detection performance, further demonstrating the superiority of the multi-modal fusion strategy. The experimental results are shown in Table 1.

Both tabular modes and image modes contain classification information that effectively distinguishes network traffic and can identify encrypted malicious traffic. However, the performance when using only tabular modes is significantly inferior to that when using image modes. This is primarily because tabular modes tend to focus on specific key features and over-rely on them, which leads to the neglect of global traffic information. In contrast, the MFETD-I method, which employs image modes, is more effective in classifying malicious traffic. This is because, after the network traffic data is transformed into images, the byte information of each session, as well as the temporal relationships and data distribution between sessions, is preserved. These details are represented in the images through colors and positions, enabling the model to visually capture the overall correlations and comprehensive information within the traffic.

The MFETD integrates both image modes and tabular modes, achieving 29.12% higher accuracy in detecting malicious encrypted traffic compared to methods that use only a single tabular modes. This result indicates that MFETD effectively combines the comprehensive feature-capturing capability of the image modes with the precise extraction and emphasis on key traffic features provided by the tabular modes, thereby significantly enhancing detection performance.

**Table 1.** The result of ablation experiment

| Methods | NET1-input | NET2-input | Accuracy | Precision | Recall | F1 |
|---|---|---|---|---|---|---|
| MFETD-T | / | Tabular modes | 70.88% | 71.10% | 68.80% | 69.36% |
| MFETD-I | Image modes | / | 98.36% | 98.40% | 98.10% | 98.25% |
| MFETD | Image modes | Tabular modes | 99.99% | 99.99% | 99.98% | 98.98% |

*Experimental Experiment on the Effectiveness of Multimodal Feature Fusion in Unbalanced Sample Classification.* Sample imbalance is a common challenge in real-world applications, often causing models to favor majority classes and leading to poor learning and misclassification of minority classes. This issue is critical in malicious traffic detection, as minority classes are often more covert and harmful. Failure to identify these classes can result in severe security vulnerabilities.

The experiment aims to evaluate the effectiveness of the multi-modal feature fusion approach in handling imbalanced sample data. Select 13 categories from the CICAndMal2017 dataset and 6 categories from the ISCXVPN2016 dataset for analysis. The experimental results, as shown in Fig. 6, demonstrate that MFETD exhibits significant advantages in addressing sample imbalance. Even when the sample size for a particular type of malicious traffic is small, the model still maintains high classification accuracy. This indicates that the multi-modal feature fusion approach provides the model with more comprehensive data, enabling it to more accurately capture the characteristics of malicious traffic. As a result, it significantly improves the model's ability to identify minority classes under conditions of sample imbalance (Fig. 6).

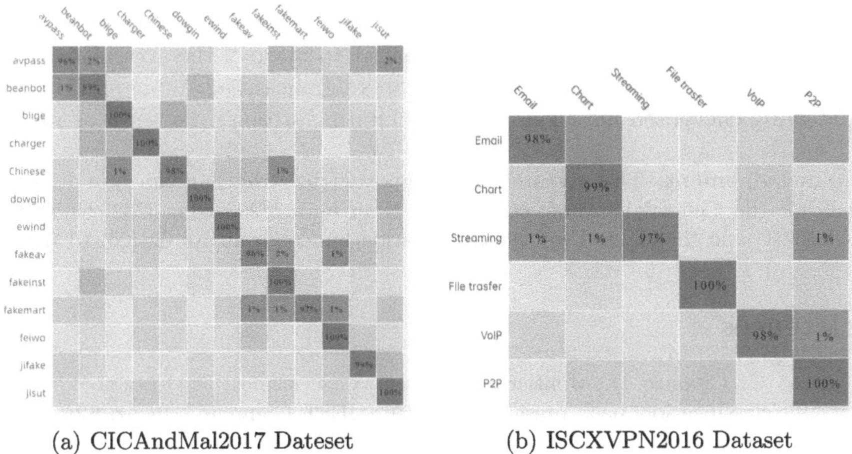


(a) CICAndMal2017 Dateset

(b) ISCXVPN2016 Dataset

**Fig. 6.** Normalized Confusion Matrix. This figure presents the normalized confusion matrix for the CICAndMal2017 dataset and ISCXVPN2016 dataset, respectively. The x-axis and y-axis each list 42 malware families. The color of each cell indicates the degree of correspondence between predicted and true labels: darker shades (red) represent higher classification error rates, while lighter shades (blue) represent higher classification accuracy. (Color figure online)

## 4 Conclusion

This paper proposes a multimodal feature fusion framework—MFETD, for detecting encrypted malicious traffic. MFETD extracts two types of features from raw encrypted network traffic: First, the image modes, where raw encrypted traffic is transformed into images, preserving the maximum amount of information from the original data. The images represent this information through color and spatial positioning, allowing the model to capture global correlations within the traffic at a visual level. Second, the tabular modes, which include structured features that retain the key characteristics of the network traffic, such as the temporal relationships between packets, TCP flags, packet length, payload, and more. This multimodal fusion approach efficiently models encrypted traffic by jointly representing it using both image and tabular modalities. It combines raw network traffic features with precise key traffic features, enabling effective modeling of encrypted traffic.

Additionally, MFETD employs a Transformer architecture to construct the classification model. After pre-training, the two modalities are converted into feature vectors that encapsulate intra-modal information. To address inter-modal dependencies, MFETD utilizes relative positional information to annotate the feature vectors. An effective mapping method is employed to ensure that the generated images can fully represent the intrinsic structure of the original data and classify malicious traffic. The effectiveness of the MFETD approach was validated on an imbalanced dataset simulating a real-world network environment. Experimental results indicate that, compared to state-of-the-art single-modal deep learning methods, MFETD demonstrates significant advantages in the task of detecting encrypted malicious traffic, exhibiting strong robustness as well.

**Acknowledgement.** This research was supported by "the Fundamental Research Funds for the Central Universities" (Grant Num ber:3282025044, 3282024050, and 3282024021) and the China University Innovation Fund (Grant No. 20221T013).

## References

1. Aceto, G., Ciuonzo, D., Montieri, A., Persico, V., Pescape, A.: AI-powered internet traffic classification: past, present, and future. IEEE Commun. Magaz. **62**(9), 168–175 (2024). https://doi.org/10.1109/MCOM.001.2300361
2. Zhao, D., Yin, Z., Cui, S., et al.: A graph-based approach for detecting malicious TLS traffic. J. Info. Sec. Res. **10**(3), 209–215 (2024)
3. Sheikh, M.S., Peng, Y.: Procedures, criteria, and machine learning techniques for network traffic classification: a survey. IEEE Access **10**, 61135–61158 (2022). https://doi.org/10.1109/ACCESS.2022.3181135
4. Tahaei, H., Afifi, F., Asemi, A., Zaki, F., Anuar, N. B.: The rise of traffic classification in IoT networks: a survey. J. Netw. Comput. Appl. **154** (2020)
5. Ramires, M., Gomes, A. S., Rito Lima, S., Carvalho, P.: Network traffic classification using ML: a comparative analysis. In: Proceedings of 2022 17th Iberian Conference on Information Systems and Technologies (CISTI), Madrid, Spain, pp. 1–6 (2022)
6. Tong, J., Chen, W., Ni, J., et al.: A noise-label detection method for encrypted malware traffic. J. Info. Sec. Res. **9**(10), 1023–1027 (2023)
7. Wang, S., et al.: TrafficAV: an effective and explainable detection of mobile malware behavior using network traffic. In: Proceedings of 24th International Symposium on Quality of Service (IWQoS), Beijing, China, pp. 1–6 (2016)
8. Zhang, L., Chen, Z., Yang, B., Jia, Z.: Research on mobile malware behavior detection method based on network traffic. China Mobile Commun. Technol. **24**, 1–6 (2016)
9. Shang, Q., Feng, L., Gao, S.: A hybrid method for traffic incident detection using random forest-recursive feature elimination and long short-term memory network with Bayesian optimization algorithm. IEEE Access **9**, 1219–1232 (2020)
10. Min, E., Long, J., Liu, Q., Cui, J., Chen, W.: TR-IDS: anomaly-based intrusion detection through text-convolutional neural network and random forest. Sec. Commun. Netw. **2018** (2018)
11. Alshammari, A., Aldribi, A.: Apply machine learning techniques to detect malicious network traffic in cloud computing. J. Big Data **8**(1) (2021)
12. Wang, W., Zhu, M., Wang, J., Zeng, X., Yang, Z.: End-to-end encrypted traffic classification with one-dimensional convolution neural networks. In: Proceedings of 2017 IEEE International Conference on Intelligence and Security Informatics (ISI), Beijing, China, pp. 43–48 (2017)

13. Lim, H., Kim, J., Heo, J., et al.: Packet-based network traffic classification using deep learning. In: Proceedings of 2019 International Conference on Artificial Intelligence in Information and Communication (ICAIIC), Okinawa, Japan, pp. 46–51 (2019)
14. Sun, B., Yang, W., Yan, M., et al.: An encrypted traffic classification method combining graph convolutional network and autoencoder. In: Proceedings of 2020 IEEE 39th International Performance Computing and Communications Conference (IPCCC), Austin, TX, USA, pp. 1–8 (2020)
15. Fu, Z., et al.: Encrypted malware traffic detection via graph-based network analysis. In: Proceedings 25th International Symposium on Research in Attacks, Intrusions and Defenses (RAID '22), Association for Computing Machinery, New York, NY, USA, pp. 495–509 (2022)
16. Ma, Q., Huang, W., Jin, Y., Mao, J.: Encrypted traffic classification based on traffic reconstruction. In: Proceedings of 2021 4th International Conference on Artificial Intelligence and Big Data (ICAIBD), Chengdu, China, pp. 572–576 (2021). https://doi.org/10.1109/ICAIBD51990.2021.9459072.

# Online Learning for Android Malware Detection Under Concept-Drift

Elif Sahin[1], Bilge Karabacak[1], Hayretdin Bahsi[2], and AbdElRahman ElSaid[1](✉)

[1] University of North Carolina Wilmington, Wilmington, NC, USA
{es5510,karabacakb,elsaida}@uncw.edu

[2] Northern Arizona University, Flagstaff, AZ, USA
Hayretdin.Bahsi@nau.edu

**Abstract.** Android malware continues to evolve rapidly, rendering traditional detection methods vulnerable to obfuscation and concept-drift. This study leverages the KronoDroid dataset—comprising over 78,000 real-device Android apps collected between 2008 and 2020—preprocessed and segmented chronologically to reflect malware evolution. We benchmark a variety of machine learning models on different feature subsets, identifying the Multilayer Perceptron (MLP) as a top performer. Building on this, we develop an online training framework using MLP, Long Short-Term Memory (LSTM), and Passive-Aggressive Classifier. Our results show that dynamic, window-based retraining achieves over 95% accuracy while effectively adapting to concept-drift. This work highlights the potential of online learning strategies to sustain malware detection accuracy in dynamic Android environments.

**Keywords:** Android Malware · Concept-drift · Online Learning · Machine Learning · Deep Learning · Cybersecurity · Real-Device Data

## 1 Introduction

The widespread adoption of Android devices, representing 86.6% of global smartphone sales in 2019 [19], has made them prime targets for sophisticated and rapidly evolving malware attacks. By early 2018, the Google Play Store hosted approximately 2 million Android applications, underscoring the platform's rapid expansion [2]. In 2016 alone, over 3.25 million Android malware applications were detected, with a new malicious app identified approximately every 10 s [12]. Traditional reactive and signature-based security methods, relying heavily on static features such as API calls, often fail to keep pace with malware evolution due to vulnerability to obfuscation and encryption [10,14].

Artificial intelligence (AI), particularly machine learning and deep learning techniques, has emerged as a proactive solution capable of analyzing extensive datasets to detect intricate malware patterns. Despite this advancement, the concept-drift phenomenon—changes in malware characteristics over time—


K.-K. R. Choo et al. (Eds.): ICDF2C 2025, LNICST 686, pp. 36–53, 2026.
https://doi.org/10.1007/978-3-032-22545-0_3

continues to challenge static AI models by rendering previously learned patterns obsolete [8].

This paper introduces a robust AI-driven framework for Android malware detection that uniquely incorporates online training strategies to dynamically adapt to concept-drift. Unlike previous studies, which largely rely on static or batch retraining approaches, our model continuously updates using sequential data intervals/windows, maintaining high accuracy and resilience against evolving threats. This novelty significantly enhances the scalability and adaptability of malware detection systems, offering a practical and dynamic defense mechanism that contributes to improved cybersecurity for Android environments.

## 2 Related Work

While earlier approaches relied on static models with fixed training sets, these methods degrade over time due to concept-drift, as shown in recent studies [3,5]. To address this, Ceschin *et al.* [3] propose evolving data stream pipelines using Adaptive Random Forests with drift detectors such as ADWIN and DDM in DREBIN and AndroZoo; their results indicate that continuous updating can recover up to 85% of the accuracy lost after six months of streaming data. Guerra-Manzanares *et al.* [9] further demonstrate that leveraging dynamic system call traces coupled with ensemble selection and anomaly detection via Isolation Forest—sustains over 92% accuracy across a seven-year time span, despite extensive code obfuscation in Android malware.

Active learning has also been proposed to reduce the human labeling burden associated with adaptive retraining. Chen *et al.* [5] introduce a pool-based uncertainty-sampling scheme that queries analysts only for the most informative samples, reducing labeling costs by roughly 70% while maintaining F1 scores above 0.90 across multiple years of evolving malware distributions. Complementary semi-supervised techniques use pseudo-labeling for high-confidence predictions and trigger full retraining only when drift detectors signal a significant distribution shift, cutting full retraining frequency to once per quarter [13].

Building on these adaptive strategies, Muzaffar *et al.*'s [15] ActDroid framework adopts an online, interval-based retraining loop to assess a variety of learners—including Random Forest, SVM, Multilayer Perceptron—and notably, a Passive-Aggressive Classifier. The Passive-Aggressive model's capacity for rapid weight updates on individual samples enables it to outperform traditional batch retraining in both speed and resilience to drift, preserving detection performance with minimal human supervision [15]. This body of work underpins our decision to design an online training framework that continuously updates the malware detection model across sequential time intervals, ensuring robust performance as threat behaviors evolve.

## 3 Dataset

This work uses the real-device subset of the KronoDroid dataset [8], which spans 2008–2020 and contains 41,382 malware and 36,755 benign apps, each annotated with timestamps to capture the evolution of malware behavior. Malware samples originate from Drebin, AMD, VirusTotal and VirusShare; benign samples from F-Droid, APKMirror and MARVIN. We restrict our experiments to the real-device files ('real_malware_v1.xlsx', 'real_legitimate_v1.xlsx'), ensuring a robust temporal context for concept-drift analysis.

All apps are represented by a 489-dimensional feature vector combining static metadata (e.g., manifest permissions, intent filters, activities, services) and dynamic traces (system-call frequencies). A compact summary of these features are given in Table 1.

**Table 1.** Data set features summary [8]

| Category | Count | Type | Description |
|---|---|---|---|
| Package Name | 1 | Categorical | App package name. |
| System Calls | 288 | Numeric | Frequency of each runtime syscall. |
| Total syscalls | 1 | Numeric | Total syscalls issued. |
| Standard Permissions | 166 | Categorical | Flags for standard Android permissions. |
| Standard Permissions Categories | 3 | Numeric | Counts of normal/dangerous/signature permissions. |
| Total Standard Perms | 1 | Numeric | Sum of standard permissions. |
| Custom Permissions | 1 | Categorical | Flag if custom permissions declared. |
| Total Custom Permissions | 1 | Numeric | Number of custom permissions. |
| Total Permissions | 1 | Numeric | Sum of all permissions. |
| SHA-256 | 1 | Categorical | APK SHA-256 hash. |
| Compressed Size | 1 | Numeric | Compressed APK size. |
| Uncompressed Size | 1 | Numeric | Uncompressed APK size. |
| Timestamps | 4 | Numeric | e.g., first/last mod., VT first seen, live first seen. |
| Files | 1 | Numeric | Files in APK. |
| HW & SW Features | 1 | List | Declared hardware/software features. |
| Activities | 1 | List | Defined activities. |
| Total Activities | 1 | Numeric | Activity count. |
| Intent Filters | 1 | List | All intent filters. |
| IF Activities | 1 | Numeric | Activities in filters. |
| IF Actions (Activities/Services/Receivers) | 1 | Numeric | Counts of filter actions. |
| Total IFs | 1 | Numeric | Filter count. |
| Services | 1 | List | Defined services. |
| Total Services | 1 | Numeric | Service count. |
| Detection Ratio | 1 | Numeric | AV detection ratio [0,1]. |
| Scan Time | 1 | Numeric | Scan timestamp. |
| Malware Family | 1 | Categorical | Predicted family. |
| Total | 489 | — | 313 Numeric, 172 Categorical, 4 List Features. |

* Features not in original dataset; see github.com/aleguma/kronodroid.

By combining static and dynamic features across a long time span, KronoDroid enables our models to learn and adapt under concept-drift, advancing the robustness of Android malware detection.

## 4 Methodology

This research focuses on building an adaptive malware detection framework using real-device data from the KronoDroid dataset. The methodology consists of three phases: (1) data preprocessing and feature engineering, (2) baseline model evaluation, and (3) the implementation of an online learning framework to simulate concept-drift-aware deployment scenarios.

### 4.1 Data Preparation and Feature Engineering

The KronoDroid dataset includes real-device Android apps labeled as benign or malicious. The raw malware and benign samples (in Excel format) were merged into a unified dataframe using `pandas`. To ensure temporal context and support concept drift analysis, the merged dataset was sorted chronologically based on the `HighestModDate` field, representing the most recent file modification timestamp [8]. To reduce dimensionality and eliminate non-informative or redundant fields, the following were removed: `'EarliestModDate'`, `'Package'`, `'sha256'`, `'MalFamily'`, `'normal'`, `'dangerous'`, `'signature'`, `'custom_yes'`, `'nr_custom'`, `'total_perm'`, `'CFileSize'`, `'UFileSize'`, `'HighestModDate'`, `'FilesInsideAPK'`, `'TimesSubmitted'`, `'NrContactedIps'`, `'Activities'`, `'NrIntServices'`, `'NrInt ServicesActions'`, `'NrIntActivities'`, `'NrIntActivitiesActions'`, `'NrInt Receivers'`, `'NrIntReceiversActions'`, `'TotalIntentFilters'`, `'NrServices'`, `'Scanners'`, `'Detection_Ratio'`, `'nr_syscalls'`, and `'nr_permissions'`. This filtering left only system call features, permission features, and the binary `Malware` label (0 for benign, 1 for malware). From this reduced dataset, three versions were created: *i)* A system calls-only dataset, *ii)* A permissions-only dataset, and *iii)* A hybrid dataset containing both. All three datasets were saved as pickle files to improve access efficiency and consistency during model training.

### 4.2 Baseline Model Evaluation

To assess the predictive value of the three dataset configurations, we applied six machine learning models: Decision Tree, Random Forest, XGBoost [4], Support Vector Machine (SVM), Logistic Regression, and Multilayer Perceptron (MLP).These models were selected based on their proven effectiveness in Android malware detection across prior studies [1,11,17,18]. Each model was trained and tested on the system calls, permissions, and hybrid datasets—both with and without dimensionality reduction using Principal Component Analysis (PCA). An 80%/20% train-test split was used, with the most recent 20% of samples reserved for testing to simulate real-world deployment on future data. The MLP architecture consisted of two hidden layers with 100 and 50 neurons respectively, trained using the Adam optimizer with ReLU activation for up to 300 iterations.

### 4.3 Online Training Framework

Following the results of baseline testing, the best-performing dataset was selected to develop a dynamic online learning framework. The KronoDroid data from 2012 to 2019 was divided into 32 non-overlapping three-month intervals to simulate sequential deployment windows. Within each interval, all feature vectors were retained while timestamps and metadata were discarded.

This structure is designed to mimic a realistic deployment scenario in which a trained model is deployed to make predictions on continuously incoming data streams.

In a real-world setting, the model would not be evaluated instantaneously on a static test set. Instead, it would process streaming data over time, and its performance would be monitored and logged during the entire deployment period. At the end of the window (e.g., three months), the average prediction accuracy would be calculated, and based on this summary performance, a decision would be made whether to retrain the model for future use.

To simulate this operational flow, we apply the model trained on interval $N$ directly to interval $N+1$, treating it as a stand-in for streamed data arriving during live deployment. No retraining occurs during the interval. Only after evaluating the average accuracy across all samples in $N+1$ do we determine whether model retraining is warranted—mirroring the way concept drift would be handled in production.

We implemented four retraining strategies to reflect different concept drift adaptation policies:

- **Case 1: Isolated Retraining**—Each interval is treated independently. The model is trained from scratch using only the current window (80% train, 20% test), with no reference to prior or future data.
- **Case 2: Cumulative Retraining**—The model is retrained from scratch using all data from the current and all preceding windows, capturing cumulative history.
- **Case 3: Threshold-Triggered Local Retraining**—The model trained on interval $N$ is deployed on $N+1$. If the average accuracy on $N+1$ drops below 90%, retraining is triggered using only the data from $N$ (80% train, 20% test).
- **Case 4: Threshold-Triggered Cumulative Retraining**—Similar to Case 3, but retraining includes all prior intervals and 80% of $N$ to incorporate both historical and recent trends.

We evaluated these strategies using three classifiers: MLP, LSTM, and a Passive-Aggressive Classifier. The LSTM was chosen for its capacity to capture temporal patterns, while the Passive-Aggressive model supports fast online updates [6]. Although LSTM performance advantages over other recurrent or Transformer-based architectures can be task-dependent, its memory mechanisms make it well-suited for scenarios with short- to medium-term dependencies [16]. Together, these methods illustrate how real-world malware detection systems can adaptively respond to evolving threats over time.

# 5 Results

All experiments were conducted on the DeepSea computing workstation, featuring 128 CPUs, 1 TB RAM, 8 TB of storage, and three NVIDIA RTX A6000 GPUs with 48 GB GDDR6 ECC memory each. The software environment was based on the Python Anaconda distribution, utilizing libraries such as Scikit-learn and TensorFlow was used. The experiments were executed in a Linux-based operating system environment.The MLP architecture dynamically adjusts across intervals, starting with a hidden layer comprising 60 ($50 + 1 \times 10$ neurons) neurons and incrementally increasing by 10 neurons with each subsequent interval (70 neurons for interval 2, 80 neurons for interval 3, and so forth). The learning rate initiates at 0.0011 and incrementally increases by 0.0001 per interval. Each MLP model is trained for a maximum of 200 iterations utilizing the Adam optimizer and ReLU activation function. This design enables the model to dynamically adapt its complexity in response to accumulating data and evolving feature distributions. The LSTM architecture adopts a similar dynamic configuration: it begins with 60 units ($50 + 1\times10$) in the LSTM layer and increases by 10 units per interval (e.g., 70 units for interval 2, 80 for interval 3, etc.). The learning rate also starts at 0.0011 and increases by 0.0001 with each new interval, mirroring the MLP schedule. Each LSTM model is trained for 200 epochs using the Adam optimizer and binary cross-entropy loss. Input sequences are reshaped into (samples, 1, features) to conform to the three-dimensional input format expected by LSTM layers. Although the input windows consist of individual static instances rather than traditional time series, this reshaping simulates a pseudo-temporal structure, allowing the model to leverage its internal memory mechanisms. This design enables the LSTM to model latent sequential dependencies and evolving relationships across features that may correlate with changes in malware behavior over time. By treating each instance as a temporal unit, the LSTM can better generalize under dynamic distributions where temporal drift may occur.

Table 2 illustrates the average training time per window/interval for each classifier and classifier (MLP, LSTM, Passive Aggressive Classifier). Window-limited updates (Cases 1 and 3), where no threshold on the output error was used, were inexpensive – less than 1 s for the Passive-Aggressive (PA) model and the MLP, and up to 16 s for the LSTM. The cumulative retraining (Cases 2 and 4) inflated the cost– for example, LSTM is roughly 10–15 min. Because Cases 2 and 4 demand much longer training times yet improve accuracy only slightly compared with Case 3, the threshold-triggered window retraining used in Case 3 offers the most efficient balance between accuracy and computational cost.

**Table 2.** Average training time per window/interval (seconds).

| Case | MLP (s) | LSTM (s) | Passive-Aggressive (s) |
|---|---|---|---|
| 1 (Window) | 0.61 | 15.75 | 0.016 |
| 2 (Cumulative) | 12.55 | 615.45 | 0.24 |
| 3 (Threshold + Window) | **0.46** | **11.00** | **0.013** |
| 4 (Threshold + Cumulative) | 13.59 | 874.02 | 0.25 |

## 5.1 Dataset Selection Results

Table 3 presents the training and test accuracies of several machine learning models applied to three dataset configurations: hybrid (system calls + permissions), permissions-only, and system calls-only. Each model was evaluated with and without dimensionality reduction using Principal Component Analysis (PCA). To ensure consistency, all models were trained as stationary classifiers using an 80%/20% train-test split.

Overall, the hybrid dataset produced the highest test accuracies across most models. In particular, the Multilayer Perceptron (MLP) achieved the best performance, with a test accuracy of 97.36% without PCA and 96.82% with PCA. Random Forest and Logistic Regression also performed well on the hybrid data, though their accuracy declined slightly when PCA was applied.

**Table 3.** Model Performance on Datasets (% Train/Test Accuracy)

| Model/Dataset | Hybrid | Permissions | Syscalls |
|---|---|---|---|
| Decision Tree | 0.9762 / 0.8846 | 0.9174 / 0.8888 | 0.9504 / 0.8261 |
| Decision Tree (PCA) | 0.9841 / 0.8622 | 0.9684 / 0.8347 | 0.9358 / 0.7753 |
| Random Forest | 0.9996 / 0.9204 | 0.9535 / 0.9042 | 0.9916 / 0.8586 |
| Random Forest (PCA) | 0.9965 / 0.9102 | 0.9597 / 0.8837 | 0.9887 / 0.8245 |
| XGBoost | 0.9762 / 0.9192 | 0.9466 / 0.8997 | 0.9321 / 0.8364 |
| XGBoost (PCA) | 0.9818 / 0.9196 | 0.9639 / 0.8931 | 0.9190 / 0.7813 |
| SVM | 0.9645 / 0.9005 | 0.9447 / 0.8692 | 0.8108 / 0.7061 |
| SVM (PCA) | 0.9603 / 0.8970 | 0.9428 / 0.8664 | 0.8088 / 0.7038 |
| Logistic Regression | 0.9474 / 0.9246 | 0.9208 / 0.8993 | 0.7999 / 0.7059 |
| Logistic Regression (PCA) | 0.9400 / 0.9087 | 0.9197 / 0.8840 | 0.7960 / 0.6997 |
| MLP | 0.9935 / **0.9736** | 0.9633 / 0.9501 | 0.9231 / 0.8978 |
| MLP (PCA) | 0.9888 / **0.9682** | 0.9631 / 0.9500 | 0.9191 / 0.8954 |

Permissions-only datasets yielded competitive results, especially for MLP (95.01% without PCA) and Random Forest. In contrast, models trained solely on system call data showed lower test performance. Logistic Regression and SVM were the weakest performers in this category, particularly when PCA was used.

These results confirm that the hybrid dataset offers the most effective feature representation for Android malware classification. Given its consistent performance across models and the particularly strong results of MLP, we selected the hybrid dataset and MLP architecture for further experimentation in our online training framework. To evaluate temporal adaptability, we extended the analysis using MLP, LSTM, and the Passive-Aggressive Classifier in the concept drift-aware experiments that follow.

## 5.2 Online Learning Results

Building on the selected hybrid dataset and top-performing models, we evaluated the effectiveness of our online training framework under simulated deployment conditions. The dataset was filtered to include samples collected between 2012-01-01 and 2019-12-31 and segmented into 32 non-overlapping three-month intervals, each representing a deployment window. We applied four retraining strategies (Cases 1 through 4) and evaluated model performance on the test set of the current interval, as well as on the datasets of the previous and subsequent intervals (when available), to simulate temporal generalization under concept drift.

By analyzing performance across all deployment windows, we were able to observe how model accuracy fluctuates over time—offering insight into which strategies exhibit robust generalization and which are more sensitive to evolving malware characteristics. This temporal analysis highlights not just average performance but also stability, adaptability, and signs of overfitting or delayed learning across intervals.

Experiments were conducted using three classifiers: Multilayer Perceptron (MLP), Long Short-Term Memory (LSTM), and Passive-Aggressive Classifier. Table 4 summarizes the average accuracies across all intervals. Baseline accuracies are provided using

**Table 4.** Average Accuracy Metrics (%) for Online Training Cases with Different Classifiers

| | MLP | | | | LSTM | | | | Passive-Aggressive | | | |
|---|---|---|---|---|---|---|---|---|---|---|---|---|
| Case | Base | Train | Prev | Next | Base | Train | Prev | Next | Base | Train | Prev | Next |
| 1 | 85.99 | 92.95 | 87.08 | 87.81 | 84.71 | 93.34 | 87.50 | 89.73 | 85.99 | 87.13 | 78.41 | 79.95 |
| 2 | 85.99 | 93.96 | 94.23 | 91.28 | 84.71 | 92.79 | 93.54 | 89.99 | 85.99 | 82.34 | 82.86 | 79.27 |
| 3 | — | — | — | 94.18 | — | — | — | 95.31 | — | — | — | 88.22 |
| 4 | — | — | — | 92.89 | — | — | — | 91.68 | — | — | — | 82.48 |

a dummy predictor that always selects the majority class, establishing a reference point for evaluating learning performance.

**MLP Results.** In Case 1 (isolated training), the MLP achieved an average accuracy of 92.95% on the current interval, but only 87.08% and 87.81% on the previous and next intervals, respectively, indicating limited temporal generalization when trained solely on the current window. Case 2 (cumulative retraining) improved current accuracy to 93.96% and substantially increased backward compatibility to 94.23% on the previous interval, while forward performance on the next interval reached 91.28%, suggesting that incorporation of historical data bolsters memory at the cost of some responsiveness to new drift. Threshold-triggered local retraining (Case 3) delivered the best forward performance, achieving 94.18% on the next interval with minimal retraining overhead, whereas threshold-triggered cumulative retraining (Case 4) produced 92.89%, reflecting a trade-off between leveraging all past data and adapting rapidly to recent changes.

**LSTM Results.** The LSTM exhibited similar baseline strength but greater resilience to drift. Under Case 1, it achieved 93.34% on the current interval, with 87.50% and 89.73% on adjacent intervals. Cumulative retraining (Case 2) produced 93.26% (current), 93.18% (previous), and 90.55% (next), demonstrating strong retention of older patterns. Case 3 again outperformed all other strategies, achieving 95.31% on the next interval, highlighting the LSTM's ability to model latent sequential dependencies when retrained on recent data, while Case 4 yielded 91.68%, underscoring the diminishing returns of excessive historical aggregation for recurrent architectures.

**Passive-Aggressive Classifier Results.** Although the Passive-Aggressive Classifier supports efficient online updates, it exhibited lower overall accuracy. In Case 1 it reached 87.13% (current), 78.41% (previous), and 79.95% (next). Case 2 marginally improved performance to 82.34%, 82.86%, and 79.27%, respectively. Case 3 achieved 88.22% on the next interval, demonstrating that windowed retraining can partially mitigate drift, while Case 4 attained only 82.48%, indicating that aggregating all prior data provides limited benefit for this algorithm's reactive update mechanism.

**Summary and Insights.** Case 3 (threshold-triggered retraining on the current interval) consistently delivered the best next-interval performance across MLP and LSTM, demonstrating its effectiveness in adapting to evolving malware patterns with minimal retraining overhead. LSTM, in particular, benefited from this setting, achieving the highest next-interval accuracy overall.

While cumulative retraining (Case 2) incorporated historical knowledge, it did not always yield better generalization, suggesting that stale data may reduce model responsiveness under concept drift. Case 4 provided a middle ground by incorporating both recent and historical context, but with slightly reduced performance compared to Case 3.

The Passive-Aggressive Classifier performed consistently below the deep learning models but still exceeded the dummy baseline and may remain useful for lightweight, latency-sensitive scenarios due to its efficiency and online learning formulation.

All classifiers significantly outperformed the baseline predictor, validating the hybrid feature set and the value of adaptive training. Moreover, the low variance observed across intervals—particularly in Cases 2 and 3—indicates robustness, which is a desirable trait in real-world deployments where data evolves gradually.

### 5.3 Visualization of Concept Drift and Model Behavior

To complement the numerical results presented earlier, we visualize model accuracy trends across deployment intervals. These plots reveal not only overall performance but also the temporal stability and adaptability of each retraining strategy in response to evolving malware patterns. By observing accuracy fluctuations across intervals, we gain insight into which approaches offer robust generalization under concept drift and which may overfit or lag in adaptation.

Figures 1, 2, and 3 plot the accuracy before training (blue) and accuracy after training (red) accuracies per interval for Case 1. The MLP and LSTM both exhibit baseline accuracy (accuracy before training) drops (notably around intervals 13 and 20–21) but recover to average trained accuracies of 92.95% and 93.34%, respectively, showing strong adaptation to concept-drift. In contrast, the Passive-Aggressive classifier peaks at only about 87.13% after training, lagging behind in responsiveness to evolving malware patterns.

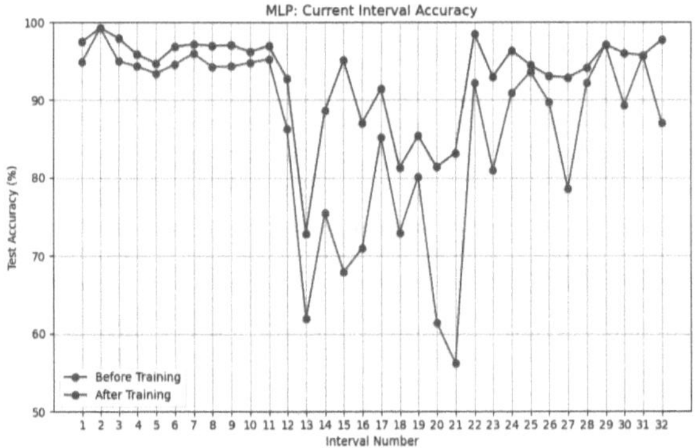


**Fig. 1.** MLP Case 1.

Figures 4, 5, and 6 plot pre-training (blue) versus post-training (red) accuracies for Case 2. Both MLP and LSTM recover baseline dips (notably around intervals 13 and 20–21) under cumulative retraining, reaching average post-training accuracies of 93.96% and 92.79%, respectively. In contrast, the Passive-Aggressive classifier peaks at just 82.34%, showing that including outdated data hinders its ability to adapt to concept-drift.

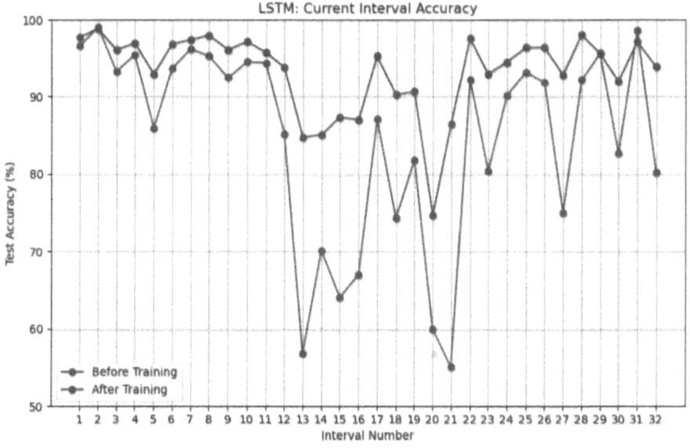


**Fig. 2.** LSTM Case 1.

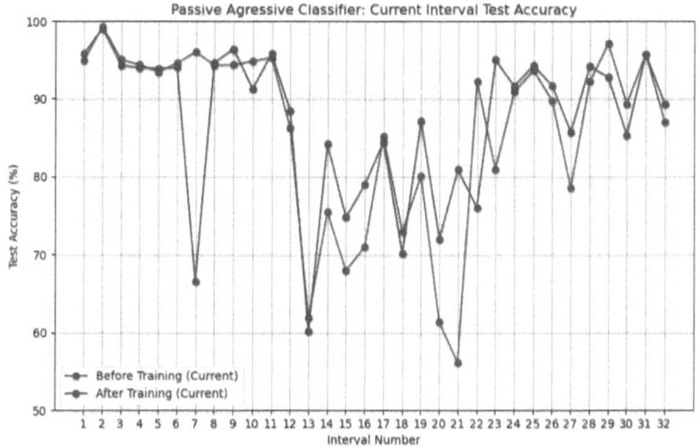


**Fig. 3.** Passive-Aggressive Classifier Case 1.

Figure 7 depicts the test accuracies on previous intervals for the MLP, LSTM, and Passive-Aggressive Classifier, when the model trained on the current interval is applied to older data. Analyzing previous interval accuracies are valuable because they measure the retaining memory of the model—that is, the degree to which a model can preserve information learned from earlier data even after training on newer data—thus offering insight into its resilience against catastrophic forgetting. For MLP, the accuracies generally hover around 87.08%—though a few intervals display sharp dips—indicating that while the MLP retains moderate backward compatibility, it still faces challenges with concept-drift. The LSTM classifier exhibits a similar overall pattern, but its recurrent architecture allows it to maintain slightly higher accuracies (near 87.5%), suggesting a marginally better ability to handle older malware patterns. By contrast, the Passive-Aggressive Classifier struggles in these previous intervals, with accuracies averaging around 78.41%. This lower resilience underscores how Passive-Aggressive models, despite their computational efficiency, are more sensitive to distributional shifts in the data, making them less effective at recognizing malware instances that diverge from the model's most recent training window.

Figure 8 shows previous-interval accuracies for Case 2 when current-interval models are applied backward. The MLP hovers around 94% (with occasional dips), indicating

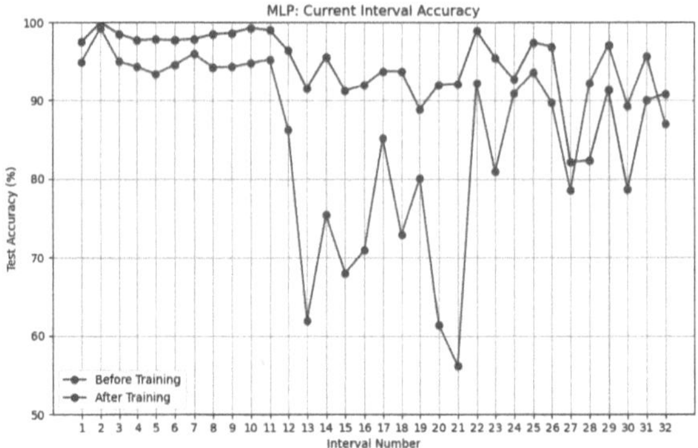


**Fig. 4.** MLP Case 2.

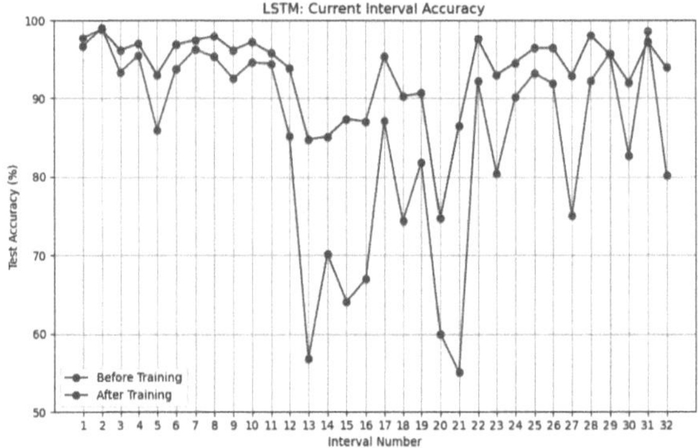


**Fig. 5.** LSTM Case 2.

strong backward compatibility despite some drift. The LSTM follows suit at roughly 93%, reflecting similar but slightly lower retention of older patterns. In contrast, the Passive-Aggressive Classifier averages only about 83%, underscoring its greater sensitivity to distributional shifts and weaker resistance to catastrophic forgetting.

Figure 9 depicts the test accuracy on the next intervals for the MLP, LSTM, and Passive-Aggressive Classifier, under the independent (Case 1) training approach. These plots provide insight into the model's ability to generalize to unseen future data—demonstrating how effectively it maintains performance despite evolving patterns introduced by concept drift. For MLP, the model achieves upper 80% to low 90% accuracy on future intervals, although occasional drops—most notably around intervals 18, 19, and 26—indicate that concept-drift can still impair generalization forward in time. The LSTM classifier exhibits a similar overall pattern achieving around 90% accuracy but tends to recover more quickly following dips, suggesting that its recurrent architecture may better anticipate short-term shifts. By contrast, the Passive-Aggressive Classifier demonstrates lower stability on next intervals, with multiple intervals slipping below 80% accuracy. This disparity across the three models highlights that, while training solely on the current interval data can achieve strong performance on the present

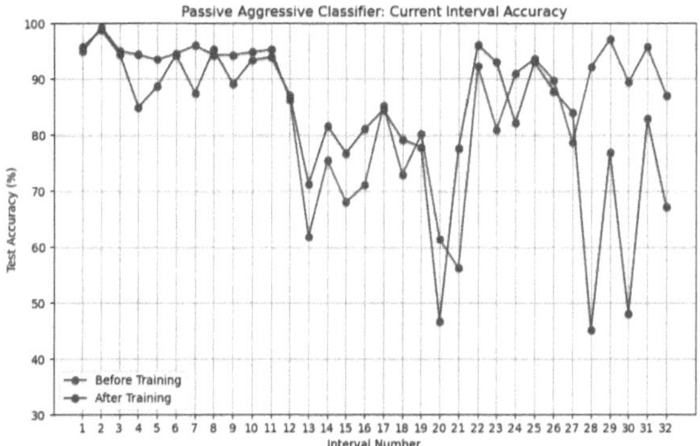


**Fig. 6.** Passive-Aggressive Classifier Case 2.

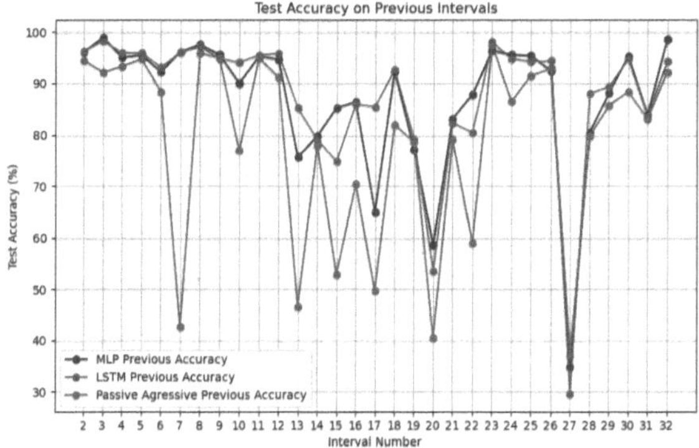


**Fig. 7.** Test Accuracy on Previous Intervals for MLP, LSTM, and Passive-Aggressive Classifier – Case1.

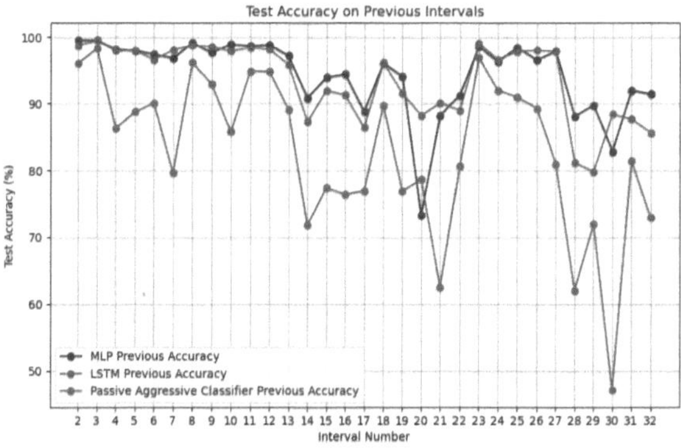


**Fig. 8.** Test Accuracy on Previous Intervals for MLP, LSTM, and Passive-Aggressive Classifier – Case 2.

window, it provides limited resilience to changes encountered in subsequent intervals, particularly for simpler or more reactive models like Passive-Aggressive Classifier.

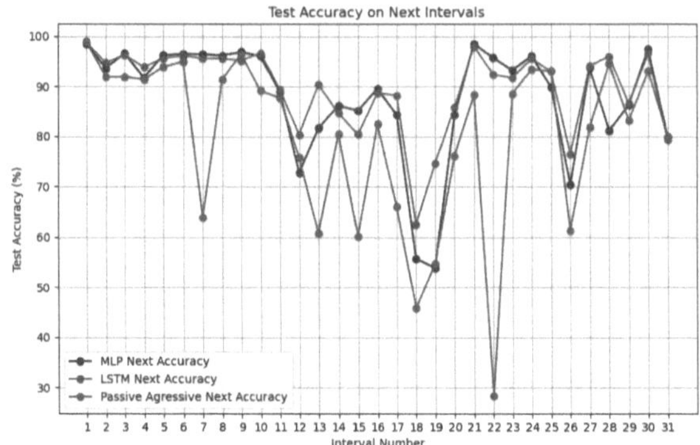


**Fig. 9.** Test Accuracy on Next Intervals for MLP, LSTM, and Passive-Aggressive Classifier – Case 1.

Figure 10 shows next-interval accuracies under the cumulative approach (Case 2). The MLP generally stays above 90% on future intervals, with occasional mid- and late-interval dips indicating residual drift. The LSTM mirrors this trend at around 90% but recovers more quickly, showcasing its recurrent advantage. In contrast, the Passive-Aggressive Classifier exhibits greater volatility and frequent drops below 80%, suggesting cumulative retraining alone is insufficient to prepare it for emerging threats.

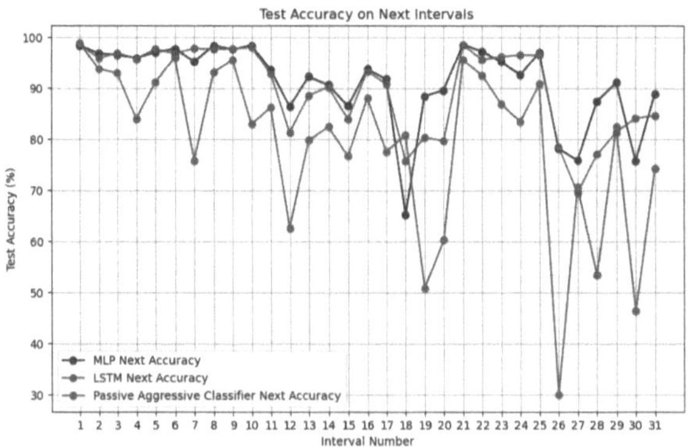


**Fig. 10.** Test Accuracy on Next Intervals for MLP, LSTM, and Passive-Aggressive Classifier – Case 2.

Figures 11, 12, and 13 illustrate the test accuracy before (blue bars) and after (red bars) retraining in the dynamic, window-based approach (Case 3) for the MLP, LSTM, and Passive-Aggressive classifiers, respectively. In the MLP figure (Fig. 11) retraining is triggered whenever the model's accuracy on the next window falls below

90%; as seen by the red bars, these retraining steps typically restore or surpass the 90% mark, yielding a final average accuracy near 94.18%. The LSTM classifier (Figure 12) benefits even more substantially from these targeted retraining events, with the red bars consistently exceeding the blue ones across the majority of windows; this is reflected in the LSTM's highest final average accuracy of 95.31%. By contrast, the Passive-Aggressive Classifier (Figure 13) shows more modest improvements upon retraining, as indicated by smaller gaps between the blue and red bars, resulting in a final accuracy of only about 88.22%. These plots confirm that while on-demand retraining with recent data (Case 3) effectively mitigates concept-drift for both MLP and LSTM models, the Passive-Aggressive Classifier remains comparatively less adept at capitalizing on retraining opportunities.

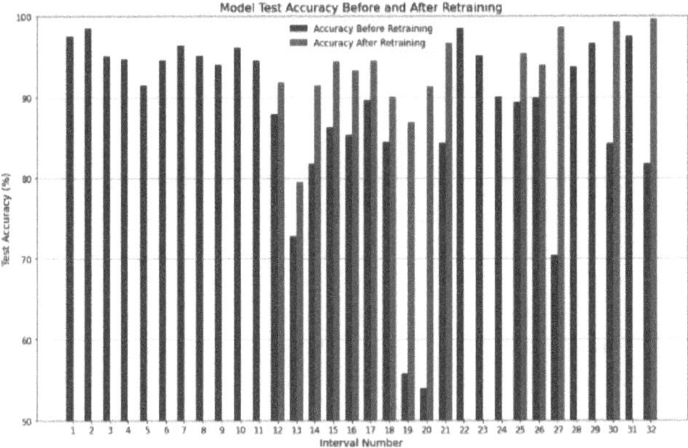


**Fig. 11.** MLP Case 3.

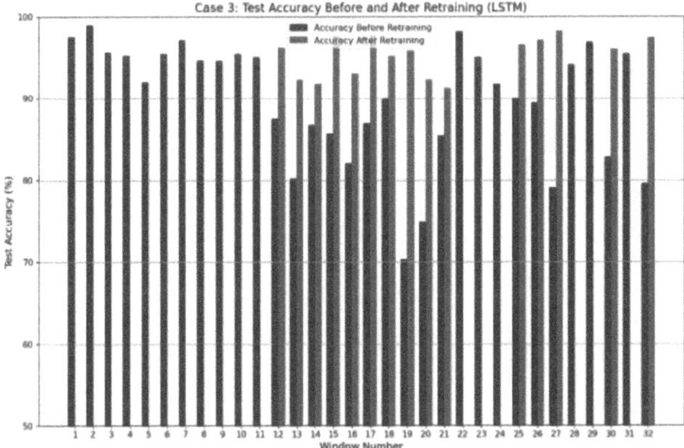


**Fig. 12.** LSTM Case 3.

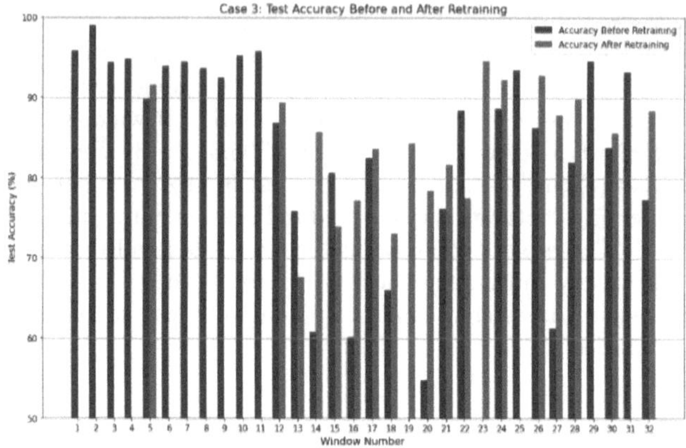


**Fig. 13.** Passive-Aggressive Classifier Case 3.

Figures 14, 15, and 16 show the test accuracy before (blue bars) and after (red bars) retraining in the aggregated approach (Case 4) for the MLP, LSTM, and Passive-Aggressive classifiers, respectively. In the MLP figure (Figure 14), retraining improves performance only modestly in many windows, resulting in a final average accuracy of about 92.89% (with pre-retraining accuracy around 91.31%). The LSTM classifier (Fig. 15) exhibits a similar pattern, but its overall accuracy appears more volatile, ultimately achieving around 91.68% in final performance (pre- and post-retraining accuracies near 89.50% and 86.98%, respectively). By contrast, the Passive-Aggressive Classifier (Figure 16) shows relatively smaller gains upon retraining, and at times even lower post-retraining accuracies, culminating in a final accuracy of roughly 82.48%. These plots indicate that while aggregating historical data can help maintain stability, it may dilute the model's adaptation to recent trends, especially for the Passive-Aggressive and LSTM classifiers.

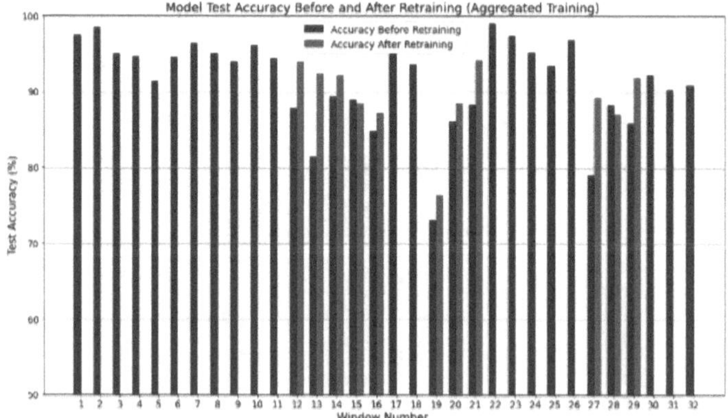


**Fig. 14.** MLP Case 4.

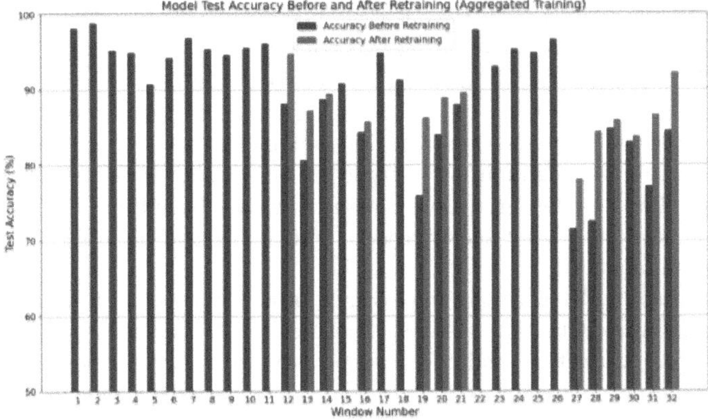


**Fig. 15.** LSTM Case 4.

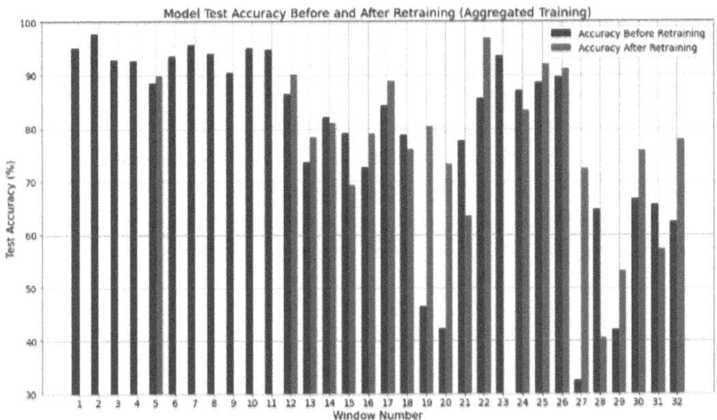


**Fig. 16.** Passive-Aggressive Classifier Case 4.

# 6 Discussion and Future Work

In this work, we introduced an online training framework for Android malware detection that continuously adapts to concept drift by partitioning a real-device, hybrid-feature dataset (KronoDroid) into sequential three-month intervals. We implemented four retraining strategies—isolated, cumulative, threshold-triggered windowed, and threshold-triggered cumulative—and evaluated them across three classifiers: MLP, LSTM, and Passive-Aggressive Classifier. By benchmarking performance on current, previous, and next intervals, we analyzed how each adaptation strategy affects both short-term accuracy and long-term generalization. A key design goal of the framework is practical deployability: the methodology is easily pipelined and automated (feature extraction $\rightarrow$ drift detection $\rightarrow$ windowing $\rightarrow$ retraining $\rightarrow$ validation $\rightarrow$ versioned release), which we view as a central contribution toward bridging research and real-world use.

Our results show that dynamic, window-based retraining (Case 3) delivers the best balance between responsiveness and stability. It achieved average final accuracies of 94.18% (MLP) and 95.31% (LSTM), and consistently outperformed other strategies in future interval prediction—demonstrating strong resilience to evolving malware patterns. In contrast, cumulative strategies that include older data (Case 4) tended to reduce adaptability, highlighting a trade-off between historical memory and current relevance. The Passive-Aggressive Classifier, while efficient and reactive, exhibited lower performance and higher sensitivity to drift, indicating its limited suitability for dynamic environments.

These findings underscore the importance of continuous, data-driven adaptation in real-time malware detection systems. Specifically, threshold-based retraining with recent data offers a practical and effective compromise between resource use and predictive power—especially when applied to neural models capable of capturing temporal structure.

However, our current framework assumes ideal retraining intervals and complete labeling, which may not hold in production environments. Future work will focus on expanding the adaptability of our framework by integrating advanced neural architecture search (NAS) and evolutionary design techniques. Specifically, we plan to incorporate CANTS [7] and EXAMM [9] for automated evolving neural architecture design capable of modeling long-term temporal dependencies.

By comparing these evolved architectures against our current models, we aim to assess their effectiveness in adapting to rapidly shifting malware patterns under concept drift. Furthermore, future work may investigate how these techniques perform in asynchronous or real-time settings, where data arrives irregularly or with noisy labels, offering a more realistic evaluation of their operational robustness.

## References

1. Arp, D., et al.: Drebin: effective and explainable detection of android malware in your pocket. In: Network and Distributed System Security Symposium (NDSS) (2014)
2. Businge, J., et al.: Studying android app popularity by cross-linking GitHub and google play store. In: 2019 IEEE 26th International Conference on Software Analysis, Evolution and Reengineering (SANER), pp. 1–12. IEEE (2019)
3. Ceschin, F., et al.: Fast and furious: on the modelling of malware detection as an evolving data stream. Expert Syst. Appl. **212**, 118590 (2023)
4. Chen, T., Guestrin, C.: XGBoost: a scalable tree boosting system. In: Proceedings of the 22nd ACM SIGKDD International Conference on Knowledge Discovery and Data Mining, pp. 785–794 (2016)
5. Chen, Y., Ding, Z., Wagner, D.: Continuous learning for android malware detection. In: 32nd USENIX Security Symposium (USENIX Security 23) (2023)
6. Crammer, K., et al.: Online passive-aggressive algorithms. J. Mach. Learn. Res. **7**, 551–585 (2006)
7. ElSaid, A., et al.: Continuous ant-based neural topology search. In: International Conference on the Applications of Evolutionary Computation (Part of EvoStar). Springer (2021)
8. Guerra-Manzanares, A., Bahsi, H., Nõmm, S.: KronoDroid: time-based hybrid-featured dataset for effective android malware detection and characterization. Comput and Sec. **110**, 102399 (2021)

9. Guerra-Manzanares, A., Luckner, M., Bahsi, H.: Android malware concept-drift using system calls: detection, characterization and challenges. Expert Syst. Appl. **206**, 117200 (2022)
10. Jusoh, R., et al.: Malware detection using static analysis in android: a review of FeCO (features, classification, and obfuscation). PeerJ Comput. Sci. **7**, e522 (2021)
11. Li, Z., Liu, M., Yang, P., He, C.: Android malware detection based on convolutional neural network. IEEE Access **9**, 135494–135503 (2021)
12. Liu, K., et al.: A review of android malware detection approaches based on machine learning. IEEE Access **8**, 124579–124607 (2020)
13. Molina-Coronado, B., et al.: Efficient concept-drift handling for batch android malware detection models. Pervasive Mob. Comput. **96**, 101849 (2023)
14. Molina-Coronado, B., et al.: Light up that droid! on the effectiveness of static analysis features against app obfuscation for android malware detection. J. Netw. Comput. Appl. **235**, 104094 (2025)
15. Muzaffar, A., et al.: ActDroid: an active learning framework for android malware detection. arXiv preprint arXiv:2401.16982 (2024)
16. Pölz, A., Blaschke, A.P., Komma, J., Farnleitner, A.H., Derx, J.: Transformer versus LSTM: a comparison of deep learning models for karst spring discharge forecasting. Water Resources Research **60**(4), e2022WR032602 (2024). https://doi.org/10.1029/2022WR032602
17. Shabtai, A., Fledel, Y., Elovici, Y.: Andromaly: a behavioral malware detection framework for android devices. J. Intell. Info. Syst. **38**(1), 161–190 (2012)
18. Tam, K.K., Feizollah, A., Anuar, N.B., Salleh, R.H., Cavallaro, L.: The evolution of android malware and android analysis techniques. ACM Comput. Surv. (CSUR) **49**(4), 1–41 (2017)
19. Tavares, B.F., et al.: Mobile applications for training plan using android devices: a systematic review and a taxonomy proposal. Information **11**(7), 343 (2020)

# Evaluating the Impact of Honeynets on Malicious Activity in Home Network Environments

Eric Edge[(✉)], James H. Jr Jones, and Kathryn Laskey

George Mason University, Fairfax, USA
eedge@gmu.edu

**Abstract.** This paper introduces a novel approach to home network security: the redirection of unsolicited traffic to a cloud-based honeynet. We hypothesize that deceiving attackers into engaging with a honeynet can deter them from targeting the home network further. We present the results of an experiment conducted on a residential network, which demonstrated a decrease in malicious connections after redirection. Although our study is subject to limitations, the observed reduction in malicious activity suggests that honeynet redirection holds promise as a supplementary security measure for home environments.

**Keywords:** Network Redirection · Honeynet · Home Networks

## 1 Introduction

Like any network connected to the internet, home networks are under constant attack, and it is important to devise effective protection for them. Home networks typically rely on basic security measures, such as firewalls and antivirus software, which are often managed by users with limited cybersecurity expertise. We propose, as an additional security measure, to redirect unsolicited network traffic to a cloud-based honeynet, thereby deterring malicious attacks. Our design is overt, thus encouraging attackers to recognize it as a honeynet and cease interaction with the associated internet protocol (IP) address. In this research we seek to determine whether the stealthy redirection of unsolicited attacks to overt honeynets can provide a measurable reduction in malicious attacks on home networks.

### 1.1 Background

Home networks present a particularly vulnerable attack surface. In contrast to corporate and government networks, which typically possess robust security infrastructures, home environments often lack the necessary resources for comprehensive protection. This vulnerability is exacerbated by the proliferation of Internet of Things (IoT) devices, many of which are inherently insecure due to limited update capabilities. Furthermore, home


K.-K. R. Choo et al. (Eds.): ICDF2C 2025, LNICST 686, pp. 54–67, 2026.
https://doi.org/10.1007/978-3-032-22545-0_4

users generally exhibit lower levels of technical proficiency, frequently neglecting system updates unless explicitly prompted. Compounding these issues, reliance on default firewall configurations provided by Internet Service Providers (ISPs) leaves home networks susceptible to malicious exploitation. These factors combine to create a significantly heightened risk profile for residential networks.

Network traffic directed at any IP address can be unsolicited by the recipient. While home users typically do not host servers and are primarily using their internet connection for outbound-initiated browsing or downloading content, they are nonetheless subject to a constant stream of unsolicited inbound network traffic. This traffic can originate from various sources, including benign scanning activities, malicious attacks, and the consequences of dynamic IP address assignment.

Although scanning for open ports and vulnerabilities is commonly associated with malicious intent, not all scanning activities are inherently harmful. Educational institutions, non-profit organizations, and businesses often conduct internet scans to enumerate services or perform health checks on IoT devices [1]. These scans, while unsolicited, are not malicious since they do not aim to gather data for an attack.

Home networks are usually assigned dynamic IP addresses, which can change at any time. An ISP is assigned a block of IP addresses which they dynamically assign to subscribers on a first-come, first-served basis. When a home network goes offline, its assigned IP address can be reclaimed and reassigned to another subscriber. This can lead to unintended consequences, such as Internet servers inadvertently directing traffic intended for the offline network to a different home network that did not initiate the communication.

Unsolicited malicious traffic, which can originate from automated malware or human actors, poses a significant security risk. This traffic often begins with scanning activities to identify open ports and running services, followed by potential exploitation attempts and password-guessing attacks. Distinguishing between malicious and benign traffic can be challenging, as the primary differentiating factor lies in the actor's intent, which is inherently difficult to ascertain.

Determining the intent of unsolicited traffic often requires consulting specialized databases that track source IP address behavior. Several such databases exist, enabling investigators to enrich their logs and differentiate between benign and malicious traffic. These databases can provide categorizations of IP addresses or assign them scores based on the likelihood of malicious activity.

These databases provide metrics that can indicate the perceived intent of an actor from a source IP address based on past behavior. These metrics, known as IP reputation scores, are used by network security practitioners to identify malicious actors and deny or degrade their ability to harm network resources. These scores do not distinguish human malicious actors from automated malware.

Typically, when unsolicited traffic reaches a home router and no service is listening on the target port, the router silently drops the traffic without sending a response. This lack of response indicates to the source IP address that no exploitable service exists at the target IP address and port. Conversely, if the target IP address responds, it may signal the presence of an active service, potentially encouraging further exploitation attempts by the source IP address, despite increased time and resource costs.

Honeytraps are designed to lure attackers and are instrumented to record the tactics, techniques, and procedures (TTPs) of the malicious actors. From the design of this experiment, the lure is the home network, which redirects unsolicited traffic into the honeynet. Once the traffic is in the honeynet, the malicious actors will engage in fruitless exploitation attempts, believing they are attacking the home network. The honeynet records the TTPs of attackers, which can then be analyzed to enhance attack awareness and develop countermeasures.

This research centers on the novel concept of employing a relay honeynet to deceive malicious actors into believing that the target home network is a honeytrap. Should the deception succeed, the expected result will be the decrease of malicious attacks on the home network. The effect of the deception will include the malicious actor expending time and resources on the deception and the recording of the TTPs. The objective is for the malicious actor to determine that the target IP address is a honeynet and blacklist the IP address from any future attacks.

In the sections that follow, we first present related work in which honeypots were used to enhance home networks. We then describe our experimental methodology and discuss our results. We conclude with an evaluation of the impact of this work and suggestions for additional work.

## 2 Related Work

This work involves using honeynets to deter attacks on home networks. In performing a literature review, we primarily encountered the use of honeypots to protect IoT networks which can exist in homes. The work that most closely relates to ours is [2]. The authors introduce Pot2DPI, a system which aims to secure IoT devices in smart homes. This system combines a honeypot with deep packet inspection (DPI) and a moving target defense mechanism. It monitors and stops attacks using a hierarchical clustering algorithm. This work will benefit home networks and could be deployed at the network perimeter to stop attacks.

In [3], the authors describe the design of low and high-interaction honeypots to enable home users to detect and monitor attacks. They were attempting to achieve timely detection of attacks and avoid the addition of home honeypots to attacker blacklists with their solution, honey@home. Their goal was to promote "large-scale deployment at low cost, while making it harder for attackers to maintain blacklists". Their work shows the observed attacks increased linearly and proportionally as the number of honey@home clients increased. They bypassed the population of attacker blacklists with honey@home honeypots by utilizing the Tor network to help anonymize users.

The YAKSHA project [4] aims to automate honeypot deployment and the full lifecycle of attack analysis, including data collection and reporting, specifically for smart home IoT environments. The work primarily outlines the project's goals and architecture.

The authors of [5] present a solution using honeypots to mitigate denial-of-service (DoS) attacks on IoT systems. This solution diverts DoS attacks away from the main IoT network. The simulation implemented in this paper describes two scenarios which involve IoT clients communicating with a server through an intrusion detection system (IDS). One redirects anomalous requests to a honeypot while the other simply blocks the request. The efficiency of communication with the server is shown to increase 55% to 60% when a honeypot is implemented.

The work presented here is different because (a) we relay all unsolicited traffic to a honeynet, and (b) we overtly expose the honeypot's nature to the attacker to dissuade them from further attack activity.

# 3 Methodology

To evaluate the effectiveness of redirecting unsolicited network traffic to a honeynet, an experiment was conducted on a residential Verizon network. We deployed a pfSense 2.7.2 firewall and collected Zeek 6.0.1 connection logs for approximately two weeks to establish a baseline of unsolicited traffic. Subsequently, firewall rulesets were configured to redirect identified unsolicited traffic to a T-Pot virtual machine (VM) hosted within the Amazon Web Services (AWS) cloud. Zeek connection logs were then collected for an additional month to observe the impact of the redirection.

For this experiment, unsolicited traffic was defined as any inbound traffic that would not match existing firewall rules, thus ultimately being caught by the DEFAULT-BLOCK rule. The DEFAULT-BLOCK rule, positioned as the final rule on the WAN interface, is configured to block all IP addresses and port numbers. To redirect this traffic, a new rule, identical in its broad matching criteria to DEFAULT-BLOCK, was placed immediately above it and modified to relay matching traffic to the AWS T-Pot VM.

The collected Zeek logs were subjected to rigorous filtering. The baseline dataset was filtered to include only network traffic that would have been rejected by the default "deny all" rule, effectively isolating unsolicited traffic. Similarly, the redirection dataset was filtered to include only traffic that was redirected to the T-Pot VM. Both datasets were filtered for only IP version four (IPv4) traffic.

To categorize unsolicited traffic, we enriched the logs with IP reputation scores from two reputable sources: AbuseIPDB and Greynoise. Initially, IP addresses identified as benign actors by Greynoise were marked accordingly. Benign categorizations from Greynoise CTI encompassed entities such as educational institutions, security research organizations, and businesses that routinely scan the internet as part of their operations. These categorizations were given precedence over AbuseIPDB categorizations, which are primarily crowdsourced and may not adequately account for the activities of these legitimate actors. Subsequently, all source IP addresses were assigned a reputation score from AbuseIPDB, ranging from 0 to 100. IP addresses with a score of 0 were categorized as benign, while those with a score of 100 were classified as malicious. Remaining IP addresses were initially categorized as "grey," unless they were previously identified as benign by Greynoise.

## 3.1 Limitations

Due to the structure of this experiment, we could not definitively attribute causality of the observations. The baseline and redirection periods were consecutive and not concurrent. We could, therefore, not rule out some time-based reason for the differences observed between these two periods. This introduces potential biases because the characteristics of network traffic experienced in one month might differ systematically from network traffic experienced in another month, making it difficult to isolate the effect of the T-Pot VM. Considering potential confounding factors and biases, we can only strongly suggest – rather than definitively conclude – that redirection to the honeynet caused the observed changes.

Additionally, there were incidents of network downtime, and the experiment duration was relatively short. Home networks are generally not subject to service level agreements (SLAs). These networks are provided on a best effort basis and have no redundancies that allow for fault tolerance during storms and power outages.

The results of this study are based on one home network and may not be generalizable across other ISPs, network configurations, or geographies.

Finally, a limitation of current IP reputation scores is their inability to distinguish between automated and human-driven attacks. While this study is expected to reveal a behavior change in malicious human actors and automated malware specifically designed to evade detection in instrumented environments, it does not definitively identify the origin (human or automated) of the traffic. Nevertheless, the study's ability to detect these behavior changes provides valuable insights into malicious activity.

## 4 Experimental Results

The baseline dataset, collected before traffic redirection was implemented, comprised over 9.1 million connection records originating from more than 20,000 unique source IP addresses. Filtering this dataset to isolate unsolicited IPv4 traffic reduced it to approximately 1.3 million connection records and over 18,000 unique source IP addresses. For analysis, the Zeek connection logs were reduced from 21 columns to six, representing the timestamp (ts) and the five-tuple identifying each connection: source IP address (id.orig_h), source port (id.orig_p), destination IP address (id.resp_h), destination port (id.resp_p), and protocol (proto). This five-tuple dataset was then enriched with IP reputation scores (specifically, abuseConfidenceScore from AbuseIPDB and category derived from Greynoise), along with additional identifying information for the source IP address, including country code (countryCode), domain (domain), internet service provider (isp), and hostnames (hostnames).

The redirection dataset, collected after implementing redirection to the honeynet, contained over 40.2 million connection records from more than 970,000 unique source IP addresses. Filtering for unsolicited IPv4 traffic yielded 9.3 million connection records and over 940,000 unique source IP addresses. This dataset was processed and enriched in the same manner as the baseline dataset, creating a comparable five-tuple enriched version. An example of the enriched data can be seen in Table 1. All data are located at https://github.com/eedge-gmu/dissertation2.

### 4.1 Analysis

The analysis aimed to determine whether redirecting unsolicited traffic to the cloud-based honeynet correlated with a reduction in malicious activity targeting the home network. The analysis focused on the enriched five-tuple datasets of unsolicited traffic.

**Table 1.** Example Dataset

| ts | id.orig_h | id.orig_ | id.resp_h | id.resp_ | proto | abuseConfidenceScor | countryCode | domain | isp | hostnames | category |
|---|---|---|---|---|---|---|---|---|---|---|---|
| 9/9/2024 3:57:55 AM | 162.244.55.20 | 5 | a.b.c.d | 1 | icmp | 0 | US | i3d.net | I3D.net B.V | ['hosted-by.i3d.net'] | benign |
| 9/9/2024 3:59:06 AM | 34.193.155.98 | 10241 | a.b.c.d | 4305 | udp | 2 | US | amazon.com | Amazon Technolog | ['ec2-34-193-155-98.com | grey |
| 9/9/2024 3:59:06 AM | 45.79.40.130 | 10241 | a.b.c.d | 1125 | udp | 0 | US | linode.com | Linode | ['lcza.chenghong.top'] | benign |
| 9/9/2024 3:59:07 AM | 170.130.200.118 | 39963 | a.b.c.d | 46931 | udp | 0 | US | serverhub.com | ServerHub Dallas | ['achestart.com'] | benign |
| 9/9/2024 3:59:07 AM | 216.244.78.82 | 37082 | a.b.c.d | 55175 | udp | 0 | US | gobsn.net | BrainStorm Networ | ['216-244-78-82-revers | benign |
| 9/9/2024 3:59:08 AM | 34.193.155.98 | 10241 | a.b.c.d | 26884 | udp | 2 | US | amazon.com | Amazon Technolog | ['ec2-34-193-155-98.com | grey |
| 9/9/2024 3:59:08 AM | 45.79.40.130 | 10241 | a.b.c.d | 1313 | udp | 0 | US | linode.com | Linode | ['lcza.chenghong.top'] | benign |
| 9/9/2024 3:59:09 AM | 108.181.62.233 | 33264 | a.b.c.d | 54362 | udp | 0 | US | psychz.net | Psychz Networks | [] | benign |
| 9/9/2024 3:59:09 AM | 108.181.55.129 | 47594 | a.b.c.d | 60979 | udp | 0 | US | psychz.net | Psychz Networks | ['unassigned.psychz.ne | benign |
| 9/9/2024 3:59:09 AM | 108.181.23.175 | 26085 | a.b.c.d | 46071 | udp | 0 | US | psychz.net | Psychz Networks | [] | benign |
| 9/9/2024 3:59:20 AM | 34.193.155.98 | 10241 | a.b.c.d | 26575 | udp | 2 | US | amazon.com | Amazon Technolog | ['ec2-34-193-155-98.co | grey |
| 9/9/2024 3:59:20 AM | 45.79.40.130 | 10241 | a.b.c.d | 44168 | udp | 0 | US | linode.com | Linode | ['lcza.chenghong.top'] | benign |
| 9/9/2024 3:59:20 AM | 108.181.55.129 | 47594 | a.b.c.d | 41261 | udp | 0 | US | psychz.net | Psychz Networks | ['unassigned.psychz.ne | benign |
| 9/9/2024 3:59:20 AM | 108.181.23.175 | 26085 | a.b.c.d | 13918 | udp | 0 | US | psychz.net | Psychz Networks | [] | benign |
| 9/9/2024 3:59:23 AM | 34.193.155.98 | 10241 | a.b.c.d | 2012 | udp | 2 | US | amazon.com | Amazon Technolog | ['ec2-34-193-155-98.co | grey |
| 9/9/2024 3:59:23 AM | 45.79.40.130 | 10241 | a.b.c.d | 30519 | udp | 0 | US | linode.com | Linode | ['lcza.chenghong.top'] | benign |
| 9/9/2024 3:59:23 AM | 172.96.164.186 | 52383 | a.b.c.d | 3679 | udp | 0 | US | dedicated.com | Dedicated.com | [] | benign |
| 9/9/2024 3:59:23 AM | 170.130.200.118 | 39963 | a.b.c.d | 18224 | udp | 0 | US | serverhub.com | ServerHub Dallas | ['achestart.com'] | benign |
| 9/9/2024 3:59:23 AM | 216.244.78.82 | 37082 | a.b.c.d | 26370 | udp | 0 | US | gobsn.net | BrainStorm Networ | ['216-244-78-82-revers | benign |
| 9/9/2024 3:59:26 AM | 108.181.62.233 | 33264 | a.b.c.d | 59025 | udp | 0 | US | psychz.net | Psychz Networks | [] | benign |
| 9/9/2024 3:59:35 AM | 34.193.155.98 | 10241 | a.b.c.d | 8985 | udp | 2 | US | amazon.com | Amazon Technolog | ['ec2-34-193-155-98.co | grey |
| 9/9/2024 3:59:35 AM | 45.79.40.130 | 10241 | a.b.c.d | 45488 | udp | 0 | US | linode.com | Linode | ['lcza.chenghong.top'] | benign |
| 9/9/2024 3:59:35 AM | 172.96.164.186 | 52383 | a.b.c.d | 4788 | udp | 0 | US | dedicated.com | Dedicated.com | [] | benign |
| 9/9/2024 3:59:35 AM | 216.244.78.82 | 37082 | a.b.c.d | 63971 | udp | 0 | US | gobsn.net | BrainStorm Networ | ['216-244-78-82-revers | benign |
| 9/9/2024 3:59:37 AM | 34.193.155.98 | 10241 | a.b.c.d | 10326 | udp | 2 | US | amazon.com | Amazon Technolog | ['ec2-34-193-155-98.co | grey |

The baseline dataset consisted of 62% UDP, 37% TCP, and 1% ICMP traffic, while the redirection dataset comprised 91% UDP, 9% TCP, and less than 1% ICMP traffic.

To visualize the data, we plotted connection counts over time (in minutes) for both the baseline (Fig. 1) and redirection (Fig. 2) datasets. Fig. 1 encompasses over 20,000 data points, with connection counts per minute ranging from 1 to 340. Figure 2 contains over 44,000 data points, with a much wider range of connections per minute 1 to 7425. This difference in the number of data points reflects the larger volume of traffic observed over the longer period in the redirection dataset.

Figures 3 and 4 present the distribution of IP reputation categories for each dataset. These categories represent the source IP address intent as calculated from AbuseIPDB and Greynoise intelligence. Using them as a benchmark, we can better determine the effectiveness of the honeynet to deter malicious traffic. While both datasets exhibit a relatively low percentage of traffic classified as malicious, the redirection dataset shows a significantly smaller proportion (less than 1%) compared to the baseline dataset (4.1%). It's important to note that the redirection dataset contains over seven times the volume of unsolicited traffic as the baseline dataset. This reduction in the percentage of malicious connections suggests a potential impact on the types of traffic observed between the two datasets.

To simplify the analysis and improve readability, the data was aggregated to daily connection counts instead of minute-by-minute counts. Figures 5 and 6 illustrate the daily connection counts for the baseline and redirection datasets, respectively, with data points categorized by IP reputation. In both figures, the malicious category initially appears as a relatively straight line due to the scale of the other categories. To better visualize the daily malicious connection counts, we zoomed in on this category, producing Figs. 7 and 8 for the baseline and redirection datasets, respectively. The baseline dataset (Fig. 7) shows daily malicious connection counts ranging from approximately 3,200 to 4,300, exhibiting relatively low day-to-day variation. In contrast, the redirection dataset (Fig. 8) reveals a greater variation, with most data points around 1,000 malicious connections per day, but with two noticeable peaks between 6,000 and 7,000 connections per day. This

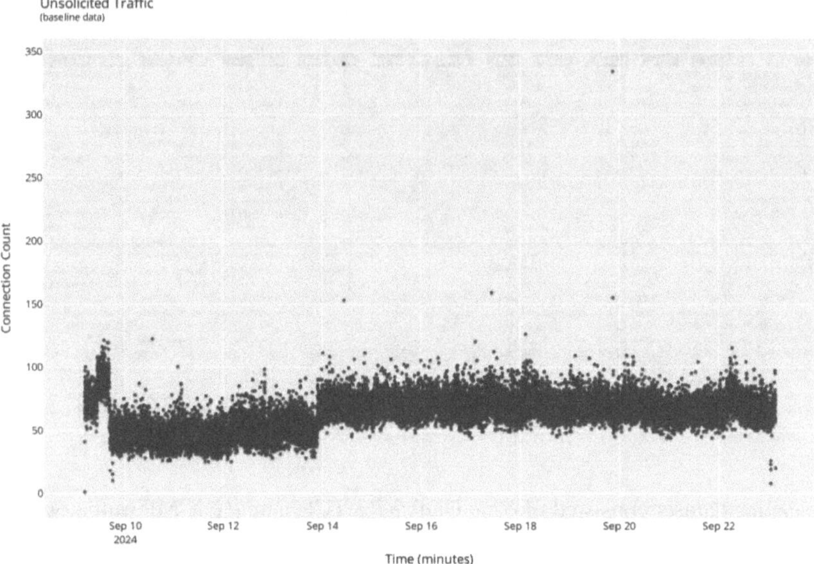


**Fig. 1.** Baseline Dataset Scatterplot of Connection Count Over Time

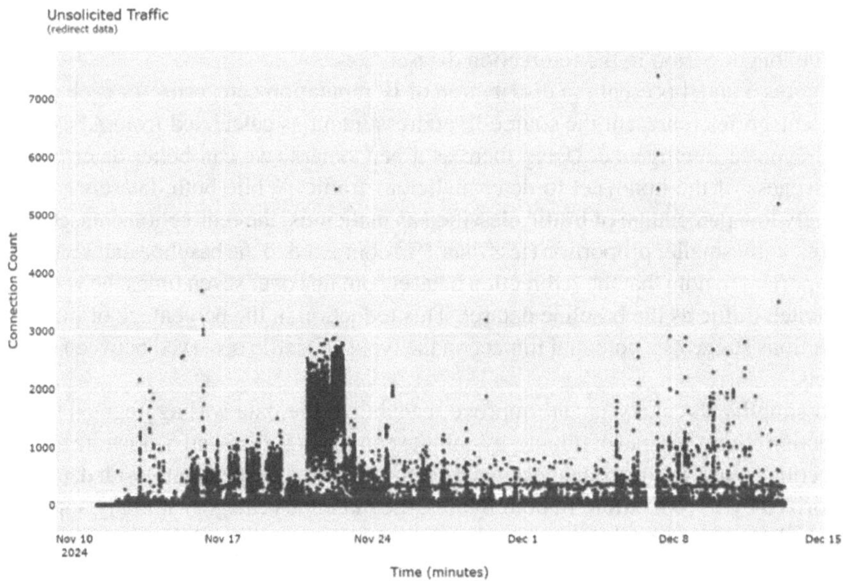


**Fig. 2.** Redirection Dataset Scatterplot of Connection Count Over Time

suggests a greater variability in daily malicious activity during the redirection period compared to the baseline period.

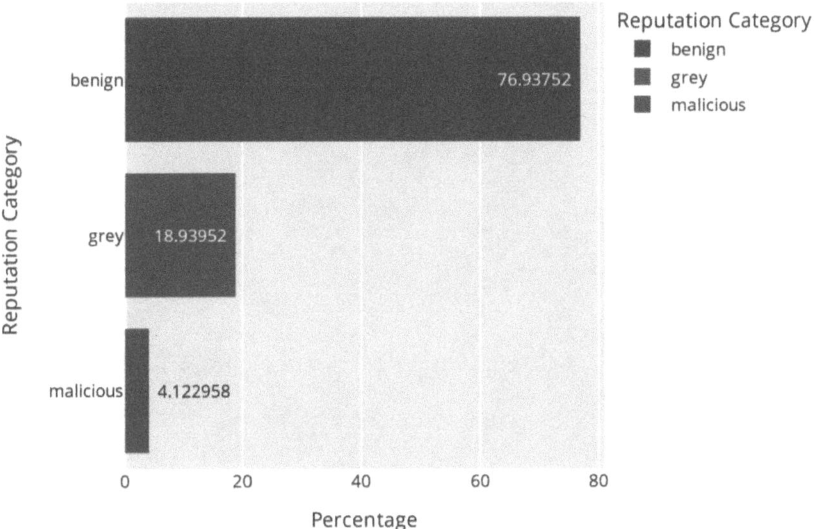


**Fig. 3.** Baseline Dataset Reputation Distribution for Unsolicited Traffic

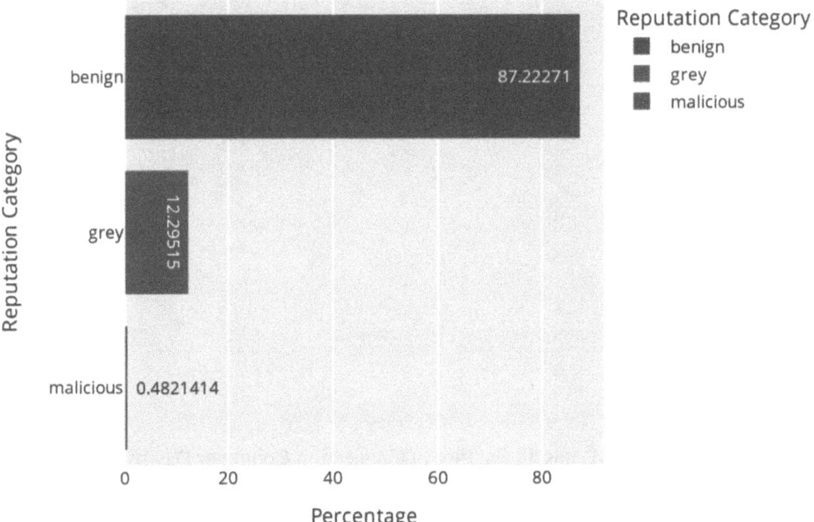


**Fig. 4.** Redirection Dataset Reputation Distribution for Unsolicited Traffic

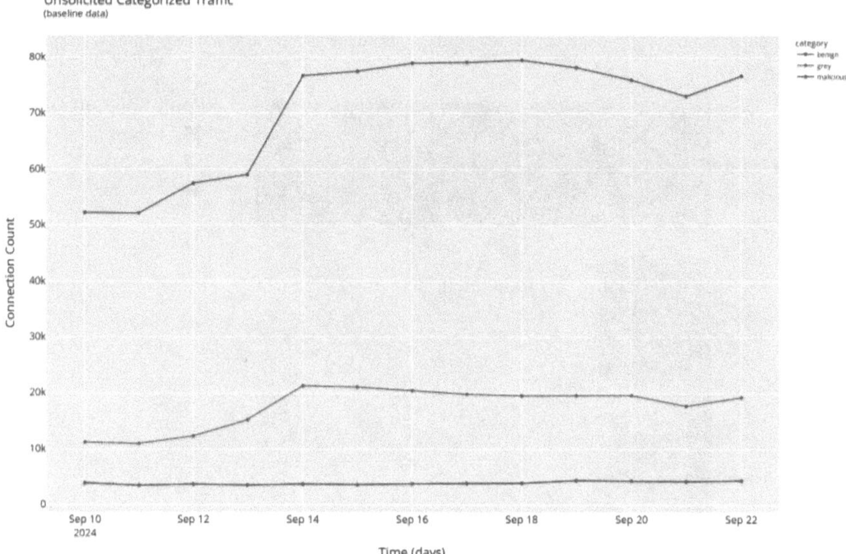


**Fig. 5.** Baseline Dataset Line Plot of Connection Count per Day by Category

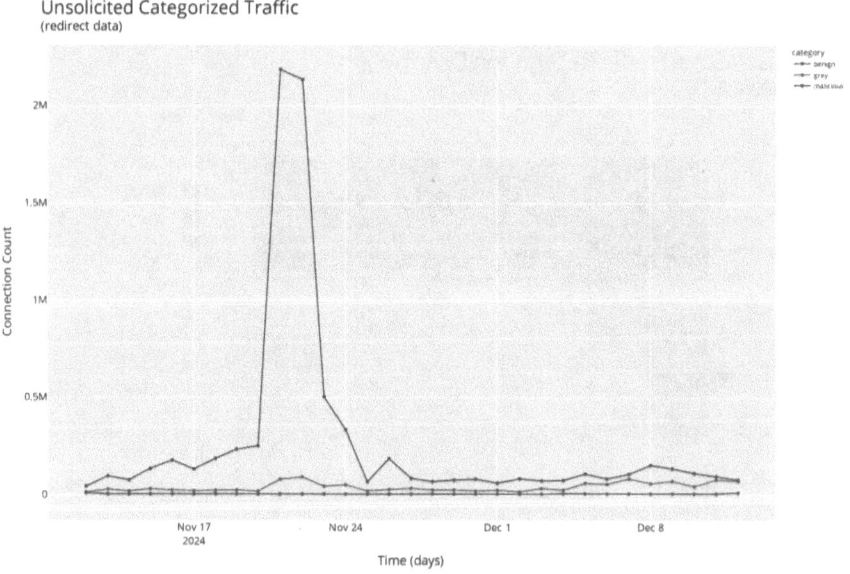


**Fig. 6.** Redirection Dataset Line Plot of Connection Count per Day by Category

We hypothesize that malicious actors, when first redirected to the honeynet, will intensify their attacks on the home network to exploit perceived vulnerabilities. However, after repeated unsuccessful attempts, they will recognize the target as a honeynet and

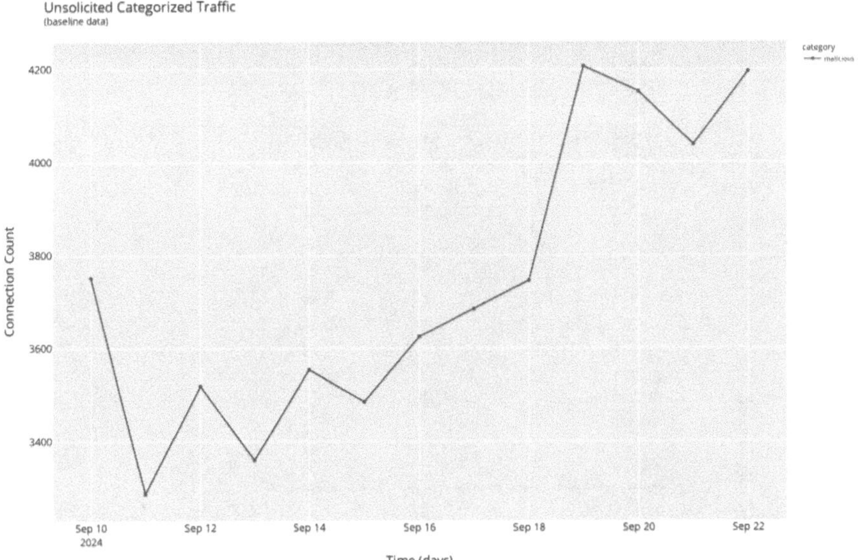


**Fig. 7.** Baseline Dataset Line Plot of Connection Count per Day by Category (zoomed in view of malicious line)

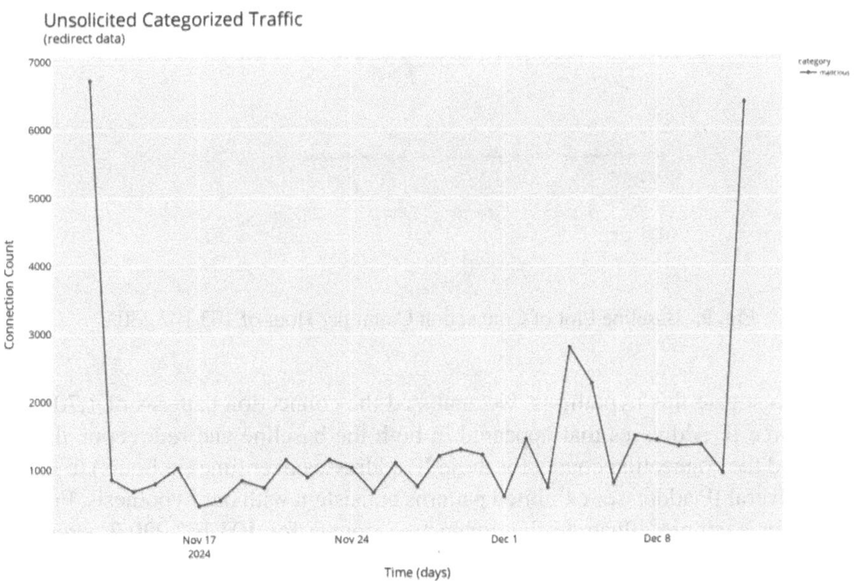


**Fig. 8.** Redirection Dataset Line Plot of Connection Count per Day by Category (zoomed in view of malicious line)

subsequently blacklist the home network's IP address, effectively removing it from their list of potential targets.

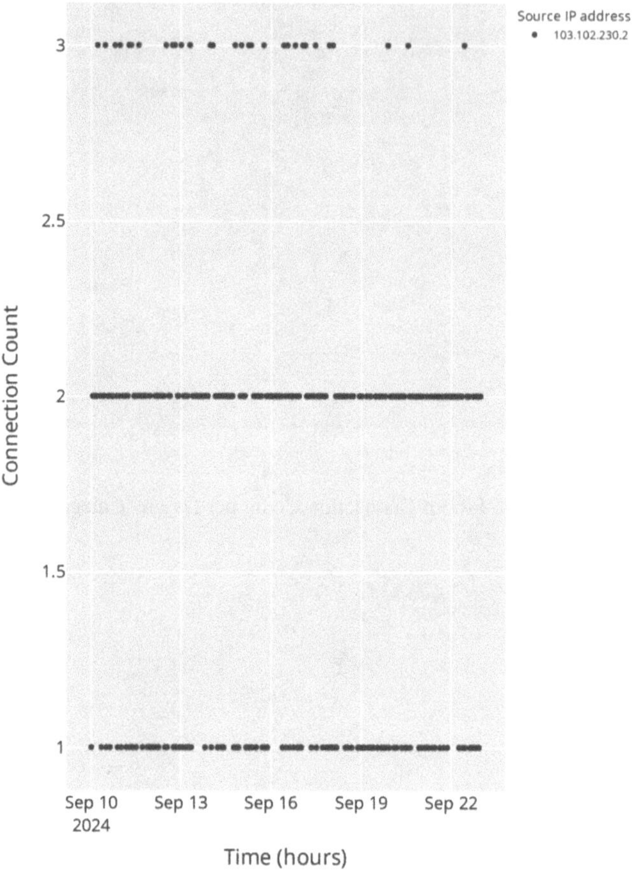


**Fig. 9.** Baseline Plot of Connection Count per Hour of 103.102.230.2

To investigate this hypothesis, we analyzed the connection patterns of 1,708 malicious source IP addresses that appeared in both the baseline and redirection datasets. We plotted the connection counts for these IP addresses over time (in hours) to identify trends. Several IP addresses exhibited patterns consistent with our hypothesis. Figures 9 and 10, for example, illustrate the connection counts for 103.102.230.2 across both datasets. Figure 9 demonstrates consistently low connection counts throughout the 13-day baseline period. Figure 10, however, shows a different pattern during the redirection period. While the full graph spans 31 days, the connection counts from this IP address are concentrated within the first five days, exhibiting higher and more intermittent activity. After this initial burst, the IP address ceases connection attempts, even though the home network continues to redirect unsolicited traffic. This behavior aligns with the expected response of a malicious actor who has identified a honeynet.

It is important to acknowledge that not all malicious connections were expected to support the hypothesis. Some malicious activity may originate from automated bots, malware, or may be the result of miscategorized traffic. While some sophisticated automated malware may be programmed to avoid honeynets after detection, other less sophisticated malware may continue exploitation attempts regardless.

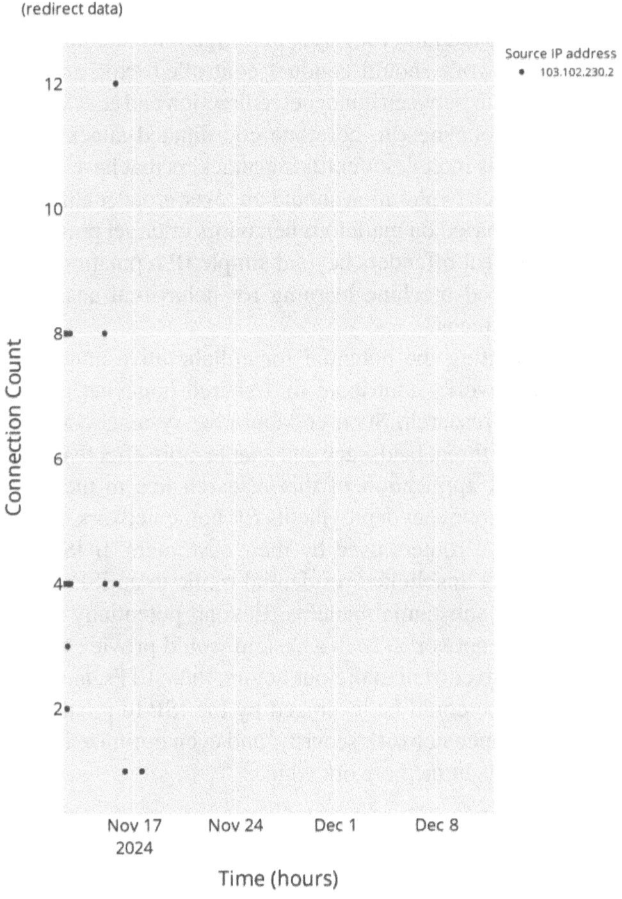


**Fig. 10.** Redirection Plot of Connection Count per Hour of 103.102.230.2

## 5 Conclusion

This research explored the potential of using a cloud-based honeynet to mitigate malicious attacks targeting home networks. By redirecting stealthy redirection of unsolicited traffic to an overt honeynet, we aimed to deter attackers and collect valuable information about their TTPs. Our analysis revealed a reduction in both the percentage and absolute number of malicious connections after implementing the redirection, suggesting a potential benefit of this approach. While further research is needed to establish causality, our findings offer promising initial evidence for the effectiveness of honeynet redirection as a supplementary security measure for home networks.

### 5.1 Future Work

This research provides a foundation for future investigations into honeynet-based home network security. Future work should conduct controlled experiments to establish a definitive causal relationship between honeynet redirection and attack reduction. Second, exploring the ability of honeynets to correlate coordinated attacks from different IP addresses is warranted. This includes identifying attackers that have had their IP address reassigned by their ISP. Such exploration should uncover broader attack patterns, lead to new attack classifications based on malicious behaviors or target ports, and help develop comprehensive lists of repeat offenders beyond simple IP reputation scores. This could involve leveraging advanced machine learning for behavioral analysis or integrating diverse threat intelligence feeds.

Additionally, investigating the potential for collaborative honeynet deployments, where multiple home networks contribute to a shared honeynet infrastructure, is an intriguing area for future research. Such collaborative systems could provide a more comprehensive view of the threat landscape and enable more effective defense strategies.

A significant practical application of this research lies in the potential for ISP-orchestrated cloud-based honeynet deployments for home network defense. Many ISPs own and manage the home routers used by their customers. If ISPs were to configure these routers to redirect unsolicited residential traffic to an ISP-owned cloud-based honeynet, this could offer substantial benefits. Beyond potentially reducing malicious traffic on individual home networks, such a system would provide the ISP with invaluable real-time visibility into current malicious actors, their TTPs, and targets of interest. This actionable intelligence could be leveraged by the ISP to proactively protect their entire customer base, enhance network security, and even optimize bandwidth usage by mitigating persistent threats at the network edge.

**Disclosure of Interests.** The authors have no competing interests to declare that are relevant to the content of this article.

## References

1. Franco, J., Aris, A., Canberk, B., Uluagac, A.S.: A survey of honeypots and Honeynets for internet of things, industrial internet of things, and cyber-physical systems. IEEE Commun Surv Tutor. **23**(4), 2351–2383 (2021). https://doi.org/10.1109/COMST.2021.3106669
2. Martin, V., Cao, Q., Benson, T.: Fending off IoT-hunting attacks at home networks. In: *Proceedings of the 2nd Workshop on Cloud-Assisted Networking*, in CAN '17, pp. 67–72. Association for Computing Machinery, New York, NY, USA (2017). https://doi.org/10.1145/3155921.3160640

3. Antonatos, S., Anagnostakis, K., Markatos, E.: Honey@home: a new approach to large-scale threat monitoring. In: *Proceedings of the 2007 ACM Workshop on Recurring Malcode*, in WORM '07, pp. 38–45. Association for Computing Machinery, New York, NY, USA (Nov. 2007). https://doi.org/10.1145/1314389.1314398
4. Kostopoulos, A., et al.: Realising honeypot-as-a-Service for Smart Home Solutions. In: 2020 5th South-East Europe Design Automation, Computer Engineering, Computer Networks and Social Media Conference (SEEDA-CECNSM), pp. 1–6 (2020). https://doi.org/10.1109/SEEDA-CECNSM49515.2020.9221787
5. Anirudh, M., Thileeban, S.A., Nallathambi, D.J.: Use of honeypots for mitigating DoS attacks targeted on IoT networks. In: 2017 International Conference on Computer, Communication and Signal Processing (ICCCSP), pp. 1–4 (2017). https://doi.org/10.1109/ICCCSP.2017.7944057

# Revealing the Intents: Malware Protocol Semantic Inference Using Large Language Models

Yuyao Huang, Hui Shu, and Fei Kang(✉)

Key Laboratory of Cyberspace Security, Ministry of Education, Beijing, China
kfminnie@163.com

**Abstract.** Inferring malware communication protocols is crucial for revealing attack intents, but the obscure binary code limits the effectiveness of existing reverse analysis methods. Advances in Large Language Models (LLMs) unlock the possibility of inferring protocol semantics based on code analysis. However, general-purpose LLMs still face challenges in semantic misfocus and insufficient domain expertise. In this paper, we propose MalExplainer, a malware protocol semantic inference framework driven by LLMs and probes. It enhances the understanding of protocol operational semantics by guiding LLMs to focus on critical code. To further elevate to high-level protocol intents, MalExplainer maps the LLM's internal semantic representations onto tactics and techniques, generating insightful descriptions. Experiments show that MalExplainer outperforms state-of-the-art models by 14%–1228% on BLEU-4, ROUGE-L, and METEOR metrics for protocol semantic inference tasks, with a techniques identification recall rate of 22.9%, surpassing CAPA. We also demonstrate its strong capabilities in protocol techniques recognition and zero-day malware detection, providing a new paradigm for intelligent threat analysis.

**Keywords:** Malware analysis · Protocol reverse engineering · Large language models · Model probes · Semantic inference

## 1 Introduction

Inferring the semantics of malware communication protocols is crucial for understanding attack intentions and building effective defenses. Statistics show that over 87.2% of malicious communications are encrypted [34], making it difficult for security analysts to parse details based on traffic analysis. Code analysis based protocol semantic inference is an effective approach that recovers protocol specifications by tracing the program message parsing process. However, existing methods can only recover basic syntactic formats and struggle to further clarify the protocol semantics. We categorize malware protocol into two levels semantics: *operational semantics*, which focus on describing the basic functionality of protocols and the operational behavior of corresponding code; and *high-level*


K.-K. R. Choo et al. (Eds.): ICDF2C 2025, LNICST 686, pp. 68–87, 2026.
https://doi.org/10.1007/978-3-032-22545-0_5

*semantics*, which reflect the underlying attack intent. Past research has primarily employed dynamic, static, or hybrid analysis methods, focusing on operational semantic recovery. Analysis of high-level semantics remains insufficient, mainly constrained by the complexity of malicious programs and heavy reliance on human expertise. For example, while existing methods can detect program semantics such as random padding, they fail to associate it with the intent of traffic obfuscation.

Recently, Large Language Models (LLMs) have made significant progress in code understanding, inspiring us to apply them to malware protocol semantic inference. However, this still faces two key challenges:

*Challenge 1: How Can LLMs Identify Key Positions That Best Reflect Core Semantics From Protocol Processing-Related Code?.* Malware typically strips function and variable symbols, resulting in the absence of high-level semantic information when analyzing protocol processing code. Large volumes of irrelevant code interfere with LLMs' ability to capture critical information, introducing understanding bias.

To address this challenge, we introduce a model probe that guides attention to key code positions based on function semantic strength detected by LLMs, enabling the model to focus on core semantics. Our insight is that neurons in LLM hidden layers exhibit differential responses to inputs—semantically rich code produces activation states distinct from ordinary code. This implies LLMs inherently recognize semantic strength in code. However, since autoregressive models are trained to generate coherent contextual sequences, they do not explicitly output code semantic strength. We locate these key positions by the probe to enhance LLMs' understanding of protocol core semantics.

*Challenge 2: How Can we Endow LLMs with Security Domain Expertise to Generate Accurate Protocol Intent Descriptions?.* General-purpose LLMs lack targeted training and sufficient expertise for inferring protocol semantics. Identifying underlying intents often requires deep experience, which existing models lack.

We posit that a semantic gap exists between protocol operational semantics and the deeper intents of malware. LLMs cannot elevate low-level semantics to high-level semantics and consequently generate hallucinated inferences. We systematically describe high-level protocol intents using tactics and techniques from the MITRE ATT&CK framework and fine-tune the LLM to enhance its domain expertise. To reduce prediction bias in the output layer, we design a classifier that connects to the hidden layers, mapping protocol semantic representations to technique categories. Finally, a retrieval-augmented mechanism enhances the reliability of intent descriptions.

This paper proposes MalExplainer, an LLM-driven malware protocol semantic inference framework that takes program execution traces as input and combines LLMs and probe techniques to generate insightful protocol intent descriptions. Specifically, MalExplainer is driven by two LLMs. The *code semantic model* aims to enhance LLMs' understanding of protocol operational semantics. We first construct a code semantics dataset to fine-tune general LLMs, improving their ability to focus on execution code semantics; meanwhile, we train a model probe that extracts function semantic strength from hidden layers and uses it to refine sliced code, ensuring more key semantics are input to the model to generate protocol semantic descriptions. The *protocol intent model* further elevates protocol operational semantics to high-level intent descriptions. We fine-tune general LLMs on constructed techniques indicators datasets and implement a classifier that maps LLM-encoded semantic representations to technique categories. Finally, a retrieval-augmented generation mechanism based on a knowledge base enhances the reliability of protocol intent descriptions, where this dataset is curated from extensive malware reports.

In summary, our contributions are as follows:

- We propose and implement MalExplainer, an LLM-driven malware protocol semantic inference framework that generates insightful protocol intent descriptions by integrating LLMs with probe techniques.
- We design a code semantic model that extracts function semantic strength from LLM hidden layers through trained probe to refine code slices, achieving better capture of protocol key semantics.
- We design a protocol intent model that generates insightful protocol descriptions through techniques classifiers built within domain-enhanced LLMs and security knowledge retrieval-augmented generation, achieving elevation from protocol operational semantics to high-level intents.
- We conduct experiments on constructed popular malware protocol datasets, validating MalExplainer's excellent performance in protocol semantic inference task. Results show that MalExplainer's BLEU-4, ROUGE-L, and METEOR metrics exceed existing state-of-the-art models by 14%–1228%, with a techniques identification recall rate of 22.9%, outperforming CAPA [24]. We also evaluate its outstanding capabilities in downstream tasks such as protocol techniques identification and zero-day malware detection, providing a new paradigm for intelligent threat analysis. We also open-source this work[1] to promote further research in LLM-assisted protocol semantic analysis.

## 2 Related Work

### 2.1 Protocol Reverse Engineering

Protocol reverse engineering (PRE) infers network protocol specifications based on traffic data or program execution traces [12], enabling applications like traffic classification [25] and malware detection [31]. Traditional PRE methods [14] recognize few field types without high-level protocol intentions. Their reliance on rules-matching also makes them ineffective for complex code like malware binaries. While other PRE tools [31] fall inaccuracy because they get distracted

[1] Available at: https://github.com/Mal-PRE/MalExplainer.

by irrelevant code context. When evaluating LLM-based tools [3], we found them tend to give superficial semantics. MalExplainer uses two domain-enhanced LLM with probe technique to facilitate malware protocol semantics inference, resulting in insightful descriptions.

### 2.2 AI-Based Binary Code Analysis

Traditional binary code analysis methods have advanced security research in many aspects [17,28], but semantic analysis of binary code still heavily relies on human experience [4,5,26]. Recent advances in LLMs for software engineering [9,22,30], provide new insights for addressing this challenge. When conducting reverse engineering on malware binaries, there is typically a lack of sufficient semantic clues, making them difficult to understand. Methods for program summarization [15], binary code similarity detection [20,27,36], and neural decompilation [11,33] have been proposed to bridge the semantic gap between binary programs and human understanding. Their work is complementary to ours. We introduce LLMs integrating with external probes for MalExplainer framework to achieve effective semantic analysis of malicious programs.

## 3 Method

Fig. 1 presents the overall workflow of MalExplainer, which first extracts code slices related to protocol processing through dynamic instrumentation of malware (Sect. 3.1). Then inputs them into a framework consisting of two models for protocol semantic inference: the *Code Semantic Model* (Sect. 3.2) refines sliced code based on function semantic strength extracted from fine-tuned LLM hidden layers and outputs protocol operational semantic descriptions; the *Protocol Intent Model* (Sect. 3.3) uses techniques classifiers and security knowledge retrieval-augmented generation (SecRAG) on fine-tuned LLMs to elevate operational semantics to high-level intent descriptions.

### 3.1 Code Slicing

To reduce interference from code obfuscation in analysis, we dynamically execute malware in a controlled environment and extract execution traces related to malware protocol message processing through program slicing techniques. Specifically, for program $P$, define the following:

**Definition 1.** *Slicing Criterion: Denoted as* $\theta = \langle f_0, i, M \rangle$, *where* $f_0$ *is the protocol message reception point in* $P$, $M$ *is the received message,* $i$ *represents the* $i$*-th field of the message,* $1 \leq i \leq |M|$.

We define the code slice $S_i$ for field $i$ as the set of basic blocks in $P$ satisfying criterion $\theta$. To separate code slices $S$ corresponding to each field, MalExplainer runs a slice extraction algorithm, as shown in Appendix A. Specifically, MalExplainer first dynamically executes the program, recording the execution

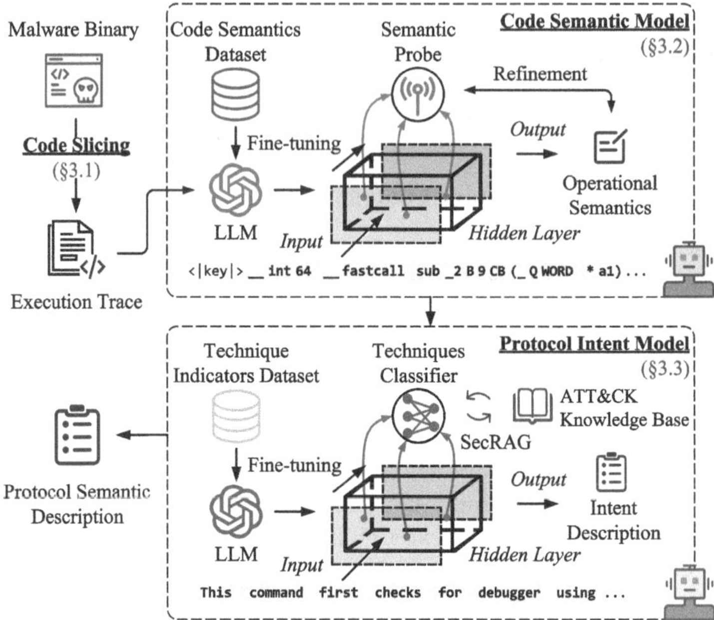


**Fig. 1.** Overall framework of MALEXPLAINER.

trace with runtime context data after receiving protocol messages. Subsequently, according to the slicing criterion, starting from $f_0$, MALEXPLAINER traverses the trace and applies taint analysis to extract basic blocks that have data flow dependencies with the $i$-th field of message $M$, finally outputting the code slice.

## 3.2 Code Semantic Model

Existing general-purpose LLMs have insufficient capability in identifying key semantics in protocol processing code. To address this, we create a code semantic model that refines code slices based on function semantic strength extracted from LLM hidden layers through probes, achieving better capture of protocol key semantics. The model creation process consists of two stages: fine-tuning and probe training, after which it processes the refined sliced code and generates protocol semantic descriptions.

*Model Fine-tuning.* We first fine-tune a general foundation model to enhance its ability to focus on execution code semantics. We construct a code semantics dataset consisting of pairs in the form "<*code snippet, semantic description*>". The "code snippet" consists of decompiled binary code, while the "semantic description" provides operational explanations for specified locations in the code. We prepend the special token `<|key|>` to mark critical execution areas, filtering out irrelevant code. The semantic descriptions comes from comments in the source code. After fine-tuning, we add special tokens at the beginning of corresponding lines in malware sliced code to explicitly point out the focused areas.

*Semantic Probe Training.* Protocol parsing processes span long program paths, and large amounts of irrelevant code occupy the input window, affecting LLMs' capture of key semantic information. Our intuition is: we should retain code that best reflect protocol core semantics to minimize interference from the irrelevant areas.

However, quantifying the semantic strength of a function is extremely challenging, even experienced reverse engineers can only provide qualitative estimates. Assuming a function's real semantics has a probability distribution of $\boldsymbol{p}$, and the LLM's predicted semantic probability distribution is $\boldsymbol{q}$, we define the model's uncertainty in predicting that function's semantics as the mathematical expectation of prediction error:

$$\mathrm{I}(\boldsymbol{q}, \boldsymbol{p}) = \mathbb{E}_{j \sim \boldsymbol{q}} \left[ (q_j - p_j)^2 \right] \tag{1}$$

where $p_j$ is the true probability of the $j$-th token, and $q_j$ is the corresponding prediction probability. We use $1 - \mathrm{I}(\boldsymbol{q}, \boldsymbol{p})$ to describe the function's semantic strength. Greater semantic strength corresponds to smaller model uncertainty in the prediction. This is consistent with our empirical observation: functions with more semantic clues (such as APIs, strings, constants, etc.) have higher probability of correct semantic inference. Inside the LLM, this appears as the difference in the activation responses of neurons to code inputs with different semantic strengths.

To leverage this inherent property of LLMs for determining code positions that best reflect protocol core semantics, we design a probe to estimate semantic strength. For the $i$-th input code, it maps the hidden layer activation state $\boldsymbol{h}^{(i)}$ to a one-dimensional value $v_\theta(\boldsymbol{h}^{(i)})$. The semantic probe is trained through the regression task, with loss in mean squared error form:

$$\mathcal{L}_{\text{probe}} = \frac{1}{N} \sum_{i=1}^{N} \left( \mathrm{I}(\boldsymbol{q}^{(i)}, \boldsymbol{p}^{(i)}) - v_\theta(\boldsymbol{h}^{(i)}) \right)^2 \tag{2}$$

where N is the number of training samples, $\boldsymbol{q}^{(i)}$ and $\boldsymbol{p}^{(i)}$ are the predicted and true distribution of the $i$-th sample respectively, and the true distribution is calculated based on the average probability output values of correct tokens in the training set. For the system prompt used for fine-tuning and probe training, see Appendix B.

*Refinement.* During inference, we use the trained code semantic model to generate semantic descriptions of the sliced protocol processing code. Given a model input window size of $W$ tokens, for an execution slice containing $k$ functions $f_1, f_2, \ldots, f_k$ with token counts $l_1, l_2, \ldots, l_k$ respectively. We extract functions $f_i$ in ascending order of semantic strength and use the model to generate their summaries $S_i$ respectively. Assuming the corresponding summary length is $d_i$

tokens ($d_i < l_i$), we replace function $f_i$ in the input with $S_i$, compressing the total input length by $l_i - d_i$ tokens. We iteratively repeat this process until the input length is less than $W$.

After the refinement process, functions with high semantic strength are retained while low semantic strength functions are compressed into brief summaries. Special tokens are added to execution code lines within retained functions that require attention. Based on this input, the model generates descriptions more focused on protocol core semantics.

### 3.3 Protocol Intent Model

This section aims to further elevate protocol operational semantics to insightful high-level intents. To our knowledge, no previous work has focused on this research area. We design a protocol intent model that combines model fine-tuning and classifier to establish mappings from LLM internal representations to the techniques, generating reliable and profound protocol intent descriptions through Security Knowledge Retrieval-Augmented Generation (SecRAG).

*Model Fine-tuning.* General-purpose LLMs lack experience in tactics and techniques inference. We first construct a technique indicators dataset and conduct supervised fine-tuning (SFT) to enhance the expertise. We align protocol high-level intent descriptions with the MITRE ATT&CK tactics and techniques framework, which is a systematic cybersecurity adversarial knowledge framework. While tactics explain attack purposes and stages, techniques explain attack methods. We primarily focus on techniques when describing protocol semantics, as they typically have more specific behavioral intents and have corresponding tactics. The dataset consists of entries in the form "<*program semantic features, technique labels*>", curated from the CAPA rule sets [24] and samples in the wild.

*Techniques Classifier.* Accurate inference of protocol intents relies on reliable technique identification. However, this poses a significant challenge for LLMs. For example, the short vocabularies like MITRE ATT&CK technique labels (typically "T" plus 4 digits, e.g., `T1055`, `T1082`) are significantly affected by the output hallucinations. Research shows [7,23] that LLMs' understanding does not necessarily increase with model layer depth, but is often affected by random sampling strategies in the output layer, resulting in "knowing but saying wrong" phenomena. To reduce technique identification bias, we design a classifier that establishes direct mappings from hidden layer representations to technique labels.

The techniques classifier $\mathcal{P} : \mathbb{R}^d \rightarrow \mathbb{R}^{\mathcal{T}}$ is essentially a model probe, with its core being a linear classification layer composed of weight matrix $\mathbf{W} \in \mathbb{R}^{\mathcal{T} \times d}$ and bias vector $\mathbf{b} \in \mathbb{R}^{\mathcal{T}}$. During training, we traverse each sample in the technique indicators dataset, obtain the activation state $h_i \in \mathbb{R}^d$ of the $k$-th hidden layer, and optimize according to the following cross-entropy minimization loss function:

$$\mathcal{L}_{\text{classifier}} = -\sum_{i=1}^{N} \log \frac{\exp(\mathbf{W}_{t_i}^{\top} h_i + \mathbf{b}_{t_i})}{\sum_{j=1}^{\mathcal{T}} \exp(\mathbf{W}_j^{\top} h_i + \mathbf{b}_j)} \tag{3}$$

where $N$ represents the total number of training samples, $i$ is the sample index, and $j$ is the technique label index. The training process freezes LLM and only optimizes classifier parameters $\mathbf{W}, \mathbf{b}$. After training, based on input protocol operational semantic description, the classifier returns technique labels with corresponding confidence scores. This avoids potential interference from the output layer. For the system prompt used for fine-tuning and classifier training, see Appendix B.

*Security Knowledge RAG.* When input protocol semantic descriptions are difficult to understand, the model may still produce plausible but incorrect results. To address this, we extract malicious behavior descriptions with corresponding techniques labels from extensive malware reports to construct an ATT&CK knowledge base, providing references for the model. During retrieval, we adopt a re-rank mechanism [19], performing vectorized queries on input semantic descriptions and returning entries with the highest similarity.

Specifically, given protocol operational semantic description input, the classifier first outputs the technique label $\hat{t}$ with its confidence $c_{\hat{t}}$. When confidence falls below our empirically set threshold $\tau = 0.7$, the SecRAG mechanism is triggered: using semantic descriptions as retrieval keys, the most semantically related text fragments are recalled from the knowledge base. If the techniques labels corresponding to text fragments match one of the predicted Top-$k$ labels, they are used as retrieval results. The final outputs integrate technique descriptions with the security knowledge, forming reliable and profound descriptions of protocol intents.

### 3.4 Implementation

We built MalExplainer with 7,600 lines of C/C++ and 1,100 lines of Python code. We use Pintool [13] and Unicorn [35] to create a code slicing platform, with IDA Pro [8] as the disassembler. We use Qwen2.5-Coder-7B [3] as foundation model and BAAI/bge-reranker-v2-m3 [6] for reranking. The decompiler and static analysis use Hex-Rays [8] and Joern [16], respectively.

All SFT process of models was conducted for 1 epoch. To prevent overfitting, we used a learning rate of 1e-6, weight decay of 0.01, and maximum gradient norm of 1.0, with a batch size of 64. For computational efficiency, we use Low-Rank Adaptation (LoRA) [10], with LoRA rank and alpha values set to 32 and 16 respectively. The model probe adopts a Multi-Layer Perceptron (MLP) structure, containing 6 hidden layers with 1024 neurons each, and the output layer uses linear activation function.

## 4 Evaluation

We aim to answer the following research questions:

- **RQ1**: How does MalExplainer perform in malware protocol semantic inference?
- **RQ2**: How does each core component of MalExplainer contribute to overall performance?
- **RQ3**: How does MalExplainer perform when applied to analyzing real-world malware?
- **RQ4**: Does MalExplainer help reverse analysts reveal deep intents of malware protocols?

### 4.1 Setup

**Datasets.** We curated four datasets for training, validation, and testing MalExplainer, detailed in Table 1.

- *Code Semantics Dataset* ($\mathcal{D}_C$): To ensure diversity of code semantics, we curated *<code snippet, semantic description>* pairs from various datasets (e.g., Bin2Summary [32], CP-BCS [37], Capybara [2]), covering programs such as coreutils, binutils, and inetutils. We expanded training samples via random crossover, keeping only single semantic descriptions and prepending tokens to corresponding code snippets.
- *Technique Indicators Dataset* ($\mathcal{D}_I$): We extracted program indicators from CAPA rule sets [24] and samples in the wild, obtaining *<program indicators, ATT&CK technique label>* pairs. Indicators descriptions are converted from YAML format to natural language expressions.
- *ATT&CK Knowledge Base* ($\mathcal{D}_K$): We extracted descriptive contents related to techniques analysis from 772 malware reports for supplementing external knowledge. The dataset covers 1,649 techniques.
- *Malware Protocol Semantics Dataset* ($\mathcal{D}_M$): Extracting ground-truth protocol descriptions from malicious binary programs is challenging. We constructed a malware benchmark from widely used red-team tools, including 6 popular families: Gh0st, Mirai, Cobalt Strike, Sliver, Revenant, and Mythic. We mannully annotated protocol semantic specifications, covering 309 field descriptions for 63 types of messages.

**Table 1.** Dataset Information

| Dataset | Component | Usage | Size |
|---|---|---|---|
| $\mathcal{D}_C$ | Code Semantic Model | Fine-tuning | 17.5k |
| $\mathcal{D}_I$ | Protocol Intent Model | Fine-tuning | 4.3k |
| $\mathcal{D}_K$ | Protocol Intent Model | SecRAG | 1.6k |
| $\mathcal{D}_M$ | Full | Evaluation | 0.3k |

**Baselines.** While prior work exists on malware summarization and protocol analysis, no unified method specifically targets malware protocol semantics descriptions. Therefore, we selected the following tools that most directly address the task:

- **CP-BCS** [37], **BinT5** [2]: Both are state-of-the-art models for generating binary code semantics. We provide IDA Pro decompiled code for CP-BCS, and Ghidra decompiled code for BinT5, consistent with their training corpora.
- **CAPA** [24]: An open-source tool for technique identification, It returns techniques with corresponding code locations in binaries. We derive its final results by intersecting identified locations with ground-truth protocol functionality.
- **Qwen2.5-Coder, CodeGemma, Code Llama**: Both are state-of-the-art open-source code LLMs. MalExplainer maintains consistency with them in foundation model size, system prompts, and hyperparameters used for inference. Due to training budget constraints, we did not use models larger than 7B.

**Metrics.** We adopt four recognized metrics for evaluation:

- **BLEU** [29]: A widely-used natural language processing (NLP) metric that evaluates how similar machine-generated text is to human-written reference text. It calculates this similarity based on overlapping sequences of words (called $k$-grams). Higher BLEU-$k$ scores mean the generated text contains more matching phrases from the reference. $k$ is usually set to 4.
- **ROUGE** [21]: Evaluates text similarity based on overlapping units such as $n$-grams, word pairs, and longest common subsequence. Particularly ROUGE-L, which simply finds the longest common subsequence (LCS) between reference and candidate texts.
- **METEOR** [18]: An advanced NLP metric that considers word order, stemming matching, and synonym matching. Similar to ROUGE-L, METEOR is recall-focused. At the sentence level, METEOR has higher correlation with human judgment than BLEU-4.
- **Recall@k**: Evaluates model accuracy in detecting ATT&CK techniques by calculating the recall proportion of true techniques in the top $k$ labels.

## 4.2 Results

**Overall Performance.** Table 2 compares the capabilities of MalExplainer and baseline methods in malware protocol semantic inference. MalExplainer achieved the best performance on all 3 NLP metrics, improving by 13.1%–41.6% compared to the foundation model Qwen2.5-Coder and by 14%–1228% compared to other baseline models. For technique identification, MalExplainer outperforms baseline models by 6.7%–10.5% (Recall@1), and when the recall count increases to Recall@5, this improvement reaches 7.6%–12.4%. Notably, MalExplainer's Recall@1 result exceeds CAPA by 8% points, highlighting MalExplainer's capability in detecting techniques in malicious code. The metrics did not reach high absolute values, which we attribute to the model's fundamental performance and the scale of external knowledge. Using models with larger parameter and expanding $\mathcal{D}_K$ could further improve the performance.

**Table 2.** Performance comparison of different methods in the protocol semantic inference task

| Method | BLEU-4 | ROUGE-L | METEOR | Recall@k (%) | |
|---|---|---|---|---|---|
| | | | | k = 1 | k = 5 |
| BinT5 | 0.74 | 1.57 | 7.23 | – | – |
| CP-BCS | 2.90 | 8.35 | 10.44 | – | – |
| CAPA † | – | – | – | 14.9 | – |
| Code Llama-7B | 5.21 | 15.39 | 13.42 | 13.3 | 24.8 |
| CodeGemma-7B | 6.58 | 17.86 | 14.52 | 12.4 | 26.7 |
| Qwen2.5-Coder-7B | 6.94 | 18.04 | 15.29 | 16.2 | 29.5 |
| MalExplainer | **9.83** | **20.41** | **19.73** | **22.9** | **37.1** |

† The detection results of CAPA have no sequence.

To gain deeper insights into MalExplainer's performance differences across samples, Table 3 shows the evaluation results on $\mathcal{D}_M$. The model achieved optimal comprehensive performance on Cobalt Strike, with BLEU-4 reaching 13.76 and ROUGE-L at 25.94, while Sliver performed weakest with BLEU-4 only 7.23, primarily because it contains only one field for transmitting shellcode data, lacking sufficient information. Gh0st and Cobalt Strike, which support numerous protocol behaviors, performed well in description generation quality, suggesting that more complex protocol structures provide more semantic clues. However, while Cobalt Strike's METEOR metric reached 24.73, mainly due to Cobalt Strike's separation of protocol parsing and behavior execution code logic, increasing the difficulty of complete tracing. In technique identification, Cobalt Strike and Mythic performed outstandingly, with Recall@1 reaching 38.4% and 24.5% respectively, benefiting from clear system call APIs in the code. Revenant's lower recall rate (16.7%) may be related to extensive self-implemented functions during execution.

**Ablation Study.** To evaluate the effectiveness of MalExplainer components, we conducted a series of ablation studies. We configured four models for comparison, each removing one important component from MalExplainer: (1) removing the fine-tuning process of the code semantic model, labeled as $\mathcal{M}_{code}$ w/o SFT; (2) removing the semantic probe mechanism, including the refinement, labeled as $\mathcal{M}_{code}$ w/o Probe; (3) removing the fine-tuning process of the protocol intent model, labeled as $\mathcal{M}_{protocol}$ w/o SFT; (4) removing the techniques classifier, labeled as $\mathcal{M}_{protocol}$ w/o Classifier, for which we did not evaluate Recall@$k$. All models were evaluated on $\mathcal{D}_M$.

**Table 3.** Evaluation Results of MALEXPLAINER on Different Malware Protocols

| Malware | Version | Fields | BLEU-4 | ROUGE-L | METEOR | Recall@k (%) | |
|---|---|---|---|---|---|---|---|
| | | | | | | **k = 1** | **k = 5** |
| Gh0st | 2019 | 41 | 10.52 | 21.67 | 20.81 | 24.2 | 38.7 |
| Mirai | 2016 | 13 | 9.17 | 19.35 | 18.92 | 21.3 | 36.3 |
| Cobalt Strike | v4.4 | 40 | 13.76 | 25.94 | 24.74 | 38.4 | 48.2 |
| Sliver | v1.5.42 | 1 | 7.23 | 16.42 | 16.17 | 12.4 | 28.4 |
| Revenant | v0.5 | 25 | 8.45 | 18.27 | 17.81 | 16.7 | 32.9 |
| Mythic | v3.3.1-rc10 | 9 | 9.86 | 20.78 | 19.95 | 24.5 | 38.2 |

**Table 4.** Performance of different model configurations.

| Component | Configuration | BLEU-4 | ROUGE-L | METEOR | Recall@k (%) | |
|---|---|---|---|---|---|---|
| | | | | | **k=1** | **k=5** |
| $\mathcal{M}_{code}$ | w/o SFT | 8.94 | 19.41 | 18.09 | 21.1 | 34.0 |
| | w/o Probe | 7.05 | 18.16 | 15.32 | 16.4 | 30.5 |
| $\mathcal{M}_{protocol}$ | w/o SFT | 9.18 | 19.73 | 18.35 | 22.3 | 35.8 |
| | w/o Classifier | 7.99 | 18.64 | 15.78 | - | - |
| MALEXPLAINER | (Full Model) | 9.83 | 20.41 | 19.73 | 22.9 | 37.1 |

Table 4 shows that removing any component affects MALEXPLAINER's performance. The results of $\mathcal{M}_{code}$ w/o Probe and $\mathcal{M}_{protocol}$ w/o Classifier indicate that the semantic probe and techniques classifier are the most important components, with their removal leading to performance decreases of 28.3% and 18.7% respectively.

To deeply evaluate the performance of semantic probe and techniques classifier, we examined their performance at different model depths (see Fig. 2). The results show that for semantic probe, as connection layer depth increases, the BLEU-4, ROUGE-L, and METEOR metrics on both Qwen2.5-Coder and Code Llama foundation models show upward trends. The METEOR of Qwen2.5-Coder reaches 20.8 at 80% layer depth, higher than direct output (100% layer depth) of 20.4, indicating that semantic probe can effectively capture code semantics in deeper layers rather than the final output. For techniques classifier, Recall@1 and Recall@3 show similar patterns, with Recall@1 reaching 24.2% at optimal depth, suggesting intermediate layers better abstract techniques. Additionally, the consistent result curve trends on Qwen2.5-Coder and Code Llama indicate that semantic probes and technique classifiers have universality across different models. We selected Qwen2.5-Coder as the foundation model for MALEXPLAINER because it outperforms Code Llama across all layer depths.

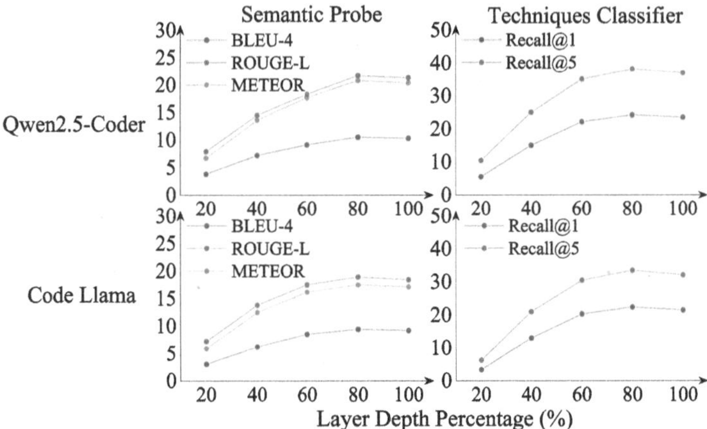


**Fig. 2.** Performance Evaluation of Semantic Probe and Techniques Classifier.

## Case Study

*Mirai Sample.* To intuitively demonstrate MalExplainer's effectiveness in protocol functionality inference, we provide an analysis example of Mirai as shown in Fig. 3. We used Qwen2.5-Coder-7B and MalExplainer respectively to analyze Mirai's "`duration`" field. The figure contains two types of markings: yellow line in the code indicate execution traces where MalExplainer prepended special token `<|key|>`; underlined markings indicate functions identified by MalExplainer with higher semantic strength, where `dword_403374[i]` resolves to `sub_73BF` at runtime. These marked positions receive more attention from the model. Comparing the generated protocol semantic descriptions, we found that Qwen2.5-Coder-7B only output operational semantics of the code, while MalExplainer's results specify the technique type and focus on the core intent of execution, namely "creating a TCP connection", which is actually for conducting TCP-based SYN attacks.

*Dataset Results Display.* To comprehensively reflect MalExplainer's capabilities, we aggregated analysis results from $\mathcal{D}_M$, as shown in Fig. 4, covering statistics of tactics, techniques, and behavioral intents. MalExplainer discovered a total of 23 techniques across 10 tactical processes, as well as 10 protocol intents categorized from them. The three main tactics are *Command and Control*, *Discovery*, and *Execution*, accounting for three-quarters of all discovered tactics, indicating that the core purpose of malware communication lies in control, information collection, and command execution. The top 5 most frequently identified techniques are `T1071`, `T1059`, `T1573`, `T1027`, and `T1083`, representing Application Layer Protocol, Command and Scripting Interpreter, Encrypted Channel, Obfuscated Files or Information, and File and Directory Discovery respectively, accounting for 60.8% of all discovered techniques. Through classified protocol intents, we can see that besides command and control, malware's main

Execution Trace
0xC50C sub_BB3C
0x2CB2 sub_2944
0x2E1F sub_2D0A
...

```
1 void sub_2D0A(...) {
2   if (fork() == 0) {
3     sleep(a1);
4     kill(getppid(), SIGKILL);
5     exit(0);
6   }
7   for (int i = 0; i < METHODS_LEN; i++) {
8     if (*(dword_403374[i] + 4) == a2) {
9       (*(void)dword_403374[i])(a3, a4, a5, a6);
10      break;
11    }
12  }
13 } …
```

**Description by Qwen:** v1 is the first 4 bytes of receive buffer a1, setting protocol timeout. This value is passed to sleep function to control maximum wait time for child process. The mechanism resembles industrial heartbeat timeout to ensure system stability. As the first field, v1's 4-byte design enables precise timeout configuration.

Execution Trace
0xC50C sub_BB3C
0x2CB2 sub_2944
0x2E1F sub_2D0A
...

```
1 void sub_2D0A(...) {
2   if (fork() == 0) {
3     sleep(a1);
4     kill(getppid(), SIGKILL);
5     exit(0);
6   }
7   for (int i = 0; i < METHODS_LEN; i++) {
8     if (*(dword_403374[i] + 4) == a2) {
9       (*(void)dword_403374[i])(a3, a4, a5, a6);
10      break;
11    }
12  }
13 } …
```

**Description by MalExplainer:** The v1 field (first 4 bytes) implements *an evasion technique using T1036.009 (adversaries may use sleep to control process termination for evasion)*. It controls process termination timing via sleep(a1), disguising as a protocol timeout while *creating a TCP connection*'s latency window. If the parent process fails to exit, the child process kills it to erase traces - effectively concealing the attack.

**Fig. 3.** Mirai Case Study Results.

intents focus on network configuration (40.9%), system operations (11.0%), and file operations (10.2%). We believe these results obtained from MalExplainer will provide targeted references for endpoint protection.

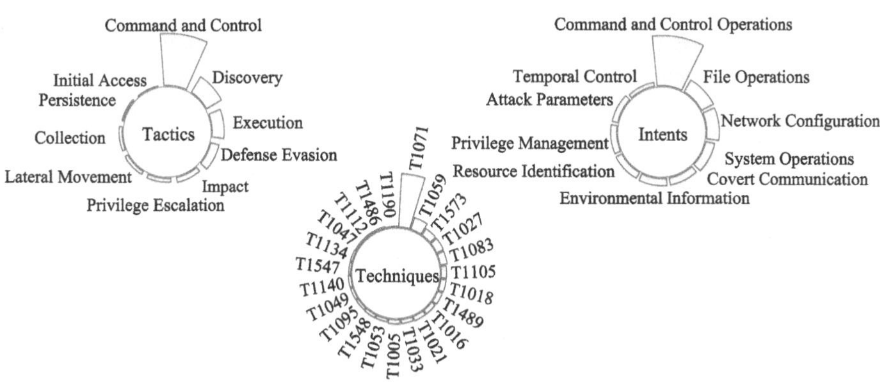


**Fig. 4.** Dataset Study Results.

*Zero-day Malware Detection.* We used MalExplainer to analyze a sample captured in the wild[2]. We selected baseline tools supporting additional detection requirement prompts (Qwen2.5-Coder, CodeGemma, Code Llama) and injected specific requirement for extracting traffic detection rules into the analysis process. Among all tool outputs, only MalExplainer performed effective analysis and correctly extracted traffic detection rules. MalExplainer's judgment is

[2] MD5: DF9344943822DE3EBCDB6A7BD27E4458.

based on two key advantages: (1) feature strings extracted from global data areas during execution, and (2) scanning data similar to feature strings matched in historical reports. The traffic rules extracted by MalExplainer have been included in the Emerging Threats (ET) Open Rulesets [1] as 2 assigned rules with severity levels marked as "Major".[3]

**User Study.** We conducted a user study to evaluate the quality of protocol semantic descriptions generated by MalExplainer. This evaluation recruited 23 participants, with 2–10 years of experience in software security analysis. We used Qwen2.5-Coder-7B as the reference model, providing participants with sample binaries with protocol semantic descriptions given by MalExplainer and the reference model. Samples were extracted from $\mathcal{D}_M$, generating a total of 516 descriptions for 129 protocol fields. Participants were asked to evaluate the descriptions according to the following questions:

1. **Accuracy**: Are the described protocol semantics consistent with the actual semantics of the malicious code?
2. **Comprehensiveness**: Do the described protocol functionalities and extracted technique labels provide comprehensive understanding?
3. **Insightfulness**: Do the protocol descriptions provide insights into the deep intents of the malware?

Each semantic description needs was scored on a 1–4 scale, with higher scores indicating better quality.When evaluating insightfulness, participants were also asked to provide additional explaining. To ensure fairness, we kept the input code and system prompts consistent for both models. Figure 5 describes the results. MalExplainer outperformed the reference model in mean scores for all three questions. For accuracy, MalExplainer achieved an average score of 2.9, showing consistency between the generated and actual semantics. In terms of comprehensiveness, MalExplainer's median was 3.0 and mean was 2.9, indicating that technique labels extracted by MalExplainer covered more extensively. Although insightfulness had the lowest average score among the three metrics, mainly due to different participants' understanding of intent depth, MalExplainer still maintained an average score of 2.7, exceeding the reference model by 0.5 points. Meanwhile, the median is above the average, showing more descriptions were considered to better reflect the intents. Based on explanations for insightfulness evaluations, we found MalExplainer's advantages concentrated in these 3 factors: (1) accurate program execution flow, (2) reliable technique mapping, and (3) professional interpretation. This indicates it is more helpful than general-purpose models in understanding the protocol intents.

[3] Rule IDs: 2058707, 2058708.

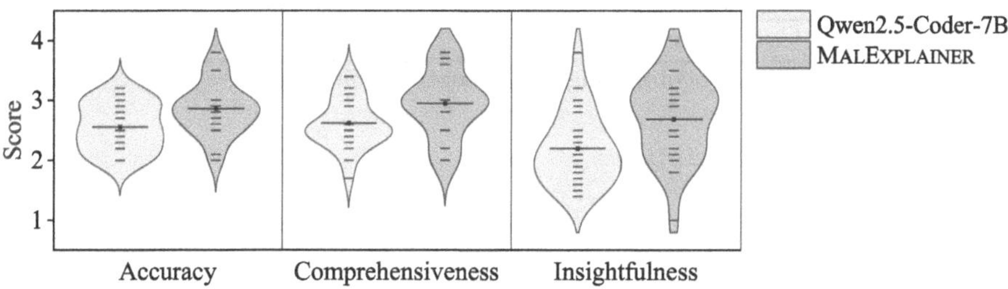


**Fig. 5.** User Study Results.

## 5 Threats to Validity

MALEXPLAINER faces several validity threats. First, our evaluation focuses on six malware families, which may not represent the full spectrum of malware communication protocols. While we selected diverse families (remote access trojans, botnets, and command-and-control frameworks), emerging malware may employ novel protocol structures not captured in our training data. Second, computational overhead may limit applicability in resource-constrained environments. Our experiments on downscaled models show performance degradation, suggesting that the approach may not scale well to lightweight deployment scenarios. Additionally, the technique identification task uses MITRE ATT&CK as ground truth, but this framework may not capture all malware behaviors, particularly novel techniques. Our actual recall rate may be lower than evaluated performance if malware employs techniques not yet catalogued in ATT&CK.

## 6 Conclusion

In this paper, we propose MALEXPLAINER, a malware protocol semantic inference framework driven by LLMs and probes in coordination. MALEXPLAINER enhances the understanding of protocol operational semantics by guiding LLMs to focus on critical code. To elevate to high-level protocol intents, MALEXPLAINER maps the representations of code semantic features within LLMs to tactics and techniques, generating insightful descriptions. Experiments, ablation studies, and user evaluations demonstrate that MALEXPLAINER surpasses existing state-of-the-art models in protocol semantic inference tasks and exhibits outstanding capabilities in downstream tasks such as protocol technique identification and zero-day malware detection, establishing a new paradigm for intelligent threat analysis.

## Appendix

## A Algorithm

The code slice extraction is described in the Algorithm 1.

**Algorithm 1:** Code Slice Extraction

```
   Input: Binary P, protocol message M, reception point f_0
   Output: Code slice set S
 1 Function TaintAnalysis(l, ctx):
 2     t ← Init(l) // Initialize the slice
 3     if t in Cache then
 4         return t
 5     SetCtx(ctx) // Set basic block context
 6     for i ← 1 to |l| do
 7         t[i] ← GetTaint(l[i]) // Get the tainted basic blocks
 8         Cache.update(t) // Cache for acceleration
 9     return t // Return the code slice
10 S ← ∅, Cache ← ∅;
11 L, ctx ← Execute(P, M, f_0) // Get execution trace L and context
12 for i ← 1 to |M| do
13     S_i ← ∅
14     for j ← 1 to |L| do
15         S_i ← S_i + TaintAnalysis(L[j], ctx[j]) // Extract tainted code
16 return S
```

# B Prompt

**Prompt for code semantic model**

Given the following code snippet, please generate a concise and comprehensive description of its semantic meaning:
`{Code with execution lines marked as <|key|>}`

**Prompt for protocol intent model**

Given the semantic description of malware protocol functionality, please identify attack techniques and infer the adversarial intent:
`{"Protocol semantic description"}`

## References


1. ET OPEN Ruleset. Download Instructions (2025). https://rules.emergingthreats.net/OPEN_download_instructions.html
2. Al-Kaswan, A., Ahmed, T., Izadi, M., Sawant, A.A., Devanbu, P., van Deursen, A.: Extending source code pre-trained language models to summarise decompiled binaries . In: 2023 IEEE International Conference on Software Analysis, Evolution and Reengineering (SANER), pp. 260–271. IEEE Computer Society, Los Alamitos, CA, USA (2023). https://doi.org/10.1109/SANER56733.2023.00033, https://doi.ieeecomputersociety.org/10.1109/SANER56733.2023.00033
3. Yang, A., Yang, B., B.H.B.Z., et al.: Qwen2 technical report. arXiv preprint arXiv:2407.10671 (2024)
4. Aonzo, S., Han, Y., Mantovani, A., Balzarotti, D.: Humans vs. machines in malware classification. In: 32nd USENIX Security Symposium (USENIX Security 23), pp. 1145–1162. USENIX Association, Anaheim, CA (2023). https://www.usenix.org/conference/usenixsecurity23/presentation/aonzo
5. Burk, K., Pagani, F., Kruegel, C., Vigna, G.: Decomperson: how humans decompile and what we can learn from it. In: 31st USENIX Security Symposium (USENIX Security 22), pp. 2765–2782. USENIX Association, Boston, MA (2022). https://www.usenix.org/conference/usenixsecurity22/presentation/burk
6. Chen, J., Xiao, S., Zhang, P., Luo, K., Lian, D., Liu, Z.: BGE M3-Embedding: multi-lingual, multi-functionality, multi-granularity text embeddings through self-knowledge distillation (2024)
7. Gekhman, Z., et al.: Inside-out: hidden factual knowledge in LLMs. arXiv preprint arXiv:2503.15299 (2025)
8. Hex-Rays: IDA Pro: a powerful disassembler, decompiler and a versatile debugger (2025). https://hex-rays.com/ida-pro. Accessed 17 Jan 2025
9. Hou, X., et al.: Large language models for software engineering: a systematic literature review. ACM Trans. Softw. Eng. Methodol. **33**(8) (2024). https://doi.org/10.1145/3695988
10. Hu, E.J., et al.: LoRA: low-rank adaptation of large language models. ICLR **1**(2), 3 (2022)
11. Hu, P., Liang, R., Chen, K.: DeGPT: optimizing decompiler output with LLM. In: Proceedings 2024 Network and Distributed System Security Symposium (2024). https://api.semanticscholar.org/CorpusID vol. 267622140 (2024)
12. Huang, Y., Shu, H., Kang, F., et al.: Protocol reverse-engineering methods and tools: a survey. Comput. Commun. **182**, 238–254 (2022)
13. Intel: Pin - a dynamic binary instrumentation framework. Online (2025). https://www.intel.com
14. Jiang, J., Zhang, X., Wan, C., Chen, H., Sun, H., Su, T.: BinPRE: enhancing field inference in binary analysis based protocol reverse engineering. In: Proceedings of the 2024 on ACM SIGSAC Conference on Computer and Communications Security. pp. 3689–3703 (2024)
15. Jin, X., Larson, J., Yang, W., Lin, Z.: Binary code summarization: benchmarking ChatGPT/GPT-4 and other large language models. arXiv preprint arXiv:2312.09601 (2023)
16. Joern: Joern - The Bug Hunter's Workbench. Online (2025). https://joern.io/
17. Kim, H., Kim, S., Lee, J., Jee, K., Cha, S.K.: Reassembly is hard: a reflection on challenges and strategies. In: 32nd USENIX Security Symposium (USENIX Security 23), pp. 1469–1486. USENIX Association, Anaheim, CA (2023). https://www.usenix.org/conference/usenixsecurity23/presentation/kim-hyungseok

18. Lavie, A., Denkowski, M.J.: The meteor metric for automatic evaluation of machine translation. Mach. Transl. **23**, 105–115 (2009)
19. Li, C., Liu, Z., Xiao, S., Shao, Y.: Making large language models a better foundation for dense retrieval (2023)
20. Li, X., Qu, Y., Yin, H.: PalmTree: learning an assembly language model for instruction embedding. In: Proceedings of the 2021 ACM SIGSAC Conference on Computer and Communications Security, pp. 3236–3251 (2021)
21. Lin, C.Y.: Rouge: a package for automatic evaluation of summaries. In: Text summarization branches out, pp. 74–81 (2004)
22. Liu, P., et al.: LLM-powered static binary taint analysis. ACM Trans. Softw. Eng. Meth. **34**(3), 1–36 (2025). https://doi.org/10.1145/3711816
23. Liu, Z., Kong, C., Liu, Y., Sun, M.: Fantastic semantics and where to find them: investigating which layers of generative LLMs reflect lexical semantics. arXiv preprint arXiv:2403.01509 (2024)
24. Mandiant FLARE Team: CAPA: Malware Behavioral Analysis Framework (2024). https://github.com/mandiant/capa
25. Antonakakis, M., Tim April, M.B., et al.: Understanding the Mirai botnet. In: 26th USENIX Security Symposium, pp. 1093–1110. Vancouver, BC (2017)
26. Mantovani, A., Aonzo, S., Fratantonio, Y., Balzarotti, D.: {RE-Mind}: a first look inside the mind of a reverse engineer. In: 31st USENIX Security Symposium (USENIX Security 22), pp. 2727–2745 (2022)
27. Marcelli, A., Graziano, M., Ugarte-Pedrero, X., et al.: How machine learning is solving the binary function similarity problem. In: 31st USENIX Security Symposium (USENIX Security 22), pp. 2099–2116 (2022)
28. Pang, C., Yu, R., Chen, Y., Koskinen, E., Portokalidis, G., Mao, B., Xu, J.: SoK: all you ever wanted to know about x86/x64 binary disassembly but were afraid to ask. In: 2021 IEEE Symposium on Security and Privacy (SP), pp. 833–851. IEEE (2021)
29. Papineni, K., Roukos, S., Ward, T., Zhu, W.J.: BLEU: a method for automatic evaluation of machine translation. In: Proceedings of the 40th annual meeting of the Association for Computational Linguistics, pp. 311–318 (2002)
30. Sha, Z., et al.: llasm: naming functions in binaries by fusing encoder-only and decoder-only LLMs. ACM Trans. Softw. Eng. Methodol. **34**(4), 1–22 (2024). https://doi.org/10.1145/3702988
31. Shi, J., Wang, Z., Feng, Z., Lan, Y., et al.: AIFORE: smart fuzzing based on automatic input format reverse engineering. In: 32nd USENIX Security Symposium (USENIX Security 23), pp. 4967–4984 (2023)
32. Song, Z., Chen, J., Zhang, K.: Bin2Summary: beyond function name prediction in stripped binaries with functionality-specific code embeddings. Proc. ACM Softw. Eng. **1**(FSE) (2024). https://doi.org/10.1145/3643729
33. Tan, H., Luo, Q., Li, J., Zhang, Y.: LLM4Decompile: decompiling binary code with large language models. arXiv preprint arXiv:2403.05286 (2024)
34. ThreatLabz, Z.: The Zscaler ThreatLabz 2024 encrypted attacks report (2024). https://www.zscaler.com/blog/threatlabz-research/encrypted-attacks-report-2024, analysis of 32.1 billion encrypted attacks blocked by Zscaler cloud (2023-2024)
35. Unicorn Engine: CPU Emulator Framework (2025). https://github.com/unicorn-engine/unicorn. Accessed 27 Jan 2025

36. Wang, H., et al.: JTrans: jump-aware transformer for binary code similarity detection. In: Proceedings of the 31st ACM SIGSOFT International Symposium on Software Testing and Analysis, pp. 1–13 (2022)
37. Ye, T., et al.: CP-BCS: binary code summarization guided by control flow graph and pseudo code. In: Bouamor, H., Pino, J., Bali, K. (eds.) Proceedings of the 2023 Conference on Empirical Methods in Natural Language Processing, pp. 14740–14752. Association for Computational Linguistics, Singapore (2023). https://doi.org/10.18653/v1/2023.emnlp-main.911

# PhishIntentionLLM: Uncovering Phishing Website Intentions Through Multi-agent Retrieval-Augmented Generation

Wenhao Li[1], Selvakumar Manickam[1(✉)], Yung-Wey Chong[2], and Shankar Karuppayah[1]

[1] Cybersecurity Research Centre, Universiti Sains Malaysia, Pulau Pinang, Malaysia
wenhaoli@ieee.org, {selva,kshankar}@usm.my
[2] School of Computer Sciences, Universiti Sains Malaysia, Pulau Pinang, Malaysia
chong@usm.my

**Abstract.** Phishing websites remain a major cybersecurity threat, yet existing methods primarily focus on detection, while the recognition of underlying malicious intentions remains largely unexplored. To address this gap, we propose *PhishIntentionLLM*, a multi-agent retrieval-augmented generation (RAG) framework that uncovers phishing intentions from website screenshots. Leveraging the visual-language capabilities of large language models (LLMs), our framework identifies four key phishing objectives: Credential Theft, Financial Fraud, Malware Distribution, and Personal Information Harvesting. We construct and release the first phishing intention ground truth dataset (~2K samples) and evaluate the framework using four commercial LLMs. Experimental results show that *PhishIntentionLLM* achieves a micro-precision of 0.7895 with GPT-4o and significantly outperforms the single-agent baseline with a ~95% improvement in micro-precision. Compared to the previous work, it achieves 0.8545 precision for credential theft, marking a ~4% improvement. Additionally, we generate a larger dataset of ~9K samples for large-scale phishing intention profiling across sectors. This work provides a scalable and interpretable solution for intention-aware phishing analysis.

**Keywords:** Cybercrime · Large Language Models (LLMs) · Phishing Website · Multi-Agent Retrieval-Augmented Generation (RAG) System

## 1 Introduction

Phishing is a dominant form of cybercrime that exploits both system vulnerabilities and human psychology to deceive users into disclosing sensitive information [1,2]. Among its various forms, phishing websites pose one of the most critical threats, using visually deceptive interfaces to impersonate trusted entities [3]. The prevalence of such attacks has continued to grow, with the Anti-Phishing Working Group (APWG) reporting 989,123 unique phishing websites in the


K.-K. R. Choo et al. (Eds.): ICDF2C 2025, LNICST 686, pp. 88–106, 2026.
https://doi.org/10.1007/978-3-032-22545-0_6

fourth quarter of 2024, compared to 888,585 in the same period of 2021 [4]. This rise is fueled by phishing-as-a-service platforms, phishing toolkits, and affordable infrastructure as well as advanced evasive techniques phishers used [5,6], making it easier for attackers to launch more long-lasting large-scale phishing campaigns. The impacts of these attacks go far beyond financial losses, including intellectual property theft and significant reputational damage [7].

To counter phishing website, a large body of research has focused on phishing website detection using heuristic-based, machine learning, and deep learning techniques that analyze features such as URLs, HTML structures, and domain metadata [8,9]. Although these studies effectively detect phishing websites, none have focused specifically on identifying the malicious intentions behind these phishing websites.

Understanding the underlying intentions behind phishing websites provides deeper insights into attacker strategies and motivations. For instance, a phishing site targeting the banking sector with a credential theft intent presents a different threat profile than one designed to harvest healthcare data. Even phishing websites impersonating the same brand can exhibit diverse malicious goals, as illustrated in Fig. 1. This level of granularity enables more precise threat intelligence, tailored defense strategies, and informed regulatory responses.

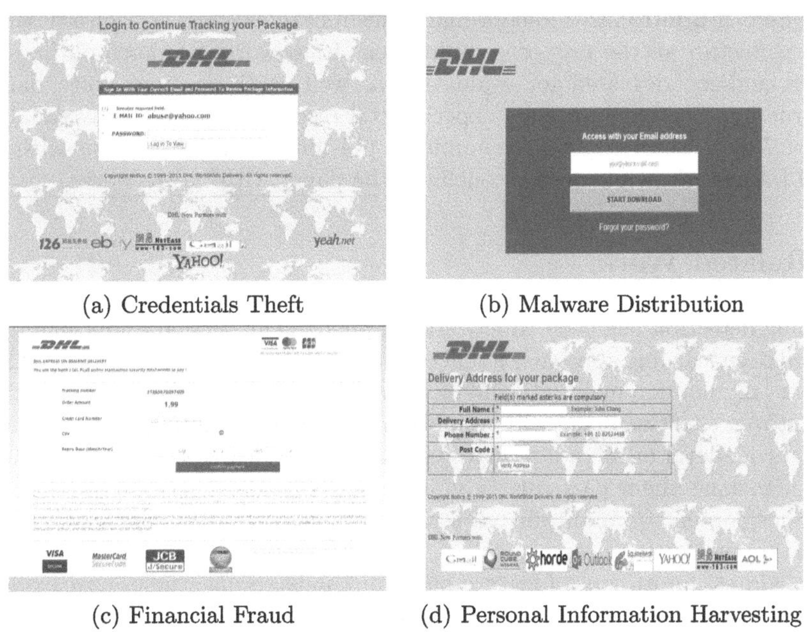


(a) Credentials Theft (b) Malware Distribution

(c) Financial Fraud (d) Personal Information Harvesting

**Fig. 1.** The Phishing DHL Websites with varied Intentions.

To bridge this gap, we propose a novel multi-agent retrieval-augmented generation (RAG) framework for identifying malicious intentions behind phishing websites through visual screenshot analysis. Our approach leverages the visual-language capabilities of large language models (LLMs) in combination with a domain-specific retrieval module to detect four primary phishing threat categories: Credential Theft, Financial Fraud, Malware Distribution, and Personal Information Harvesting.

The key contributions of this paper are as follows:

- We manually construct and publicly release the first phishing intention ground truth dataset containing ~2K phishing website samples with screenshots[1], labeled intention categories, and sectoral information.
- We propose *PhishIntentionLLM*, a novel multi-agent RAG framework that synergizes general and expert agents with knowledge bases for phishing intention detection.
- We comprehensively evaluate our framework using four commercial LLMs across multiple performance metrics, and benchmark it against a single-agent baseline and prior work focused on credential theft detection.
- We leverage our framework to detect the intention of a larger-scale phishing samples using GPT-4o and generate and publicly release a ~9K phishing intention dataset (see footnote 1), analyzing the distribution of phishing intentions and their associated sectors to uncover empirical patterns in attacker behaviors.

The remainder of this paper is organized as follows: Sect. 2 reviews related work. Section 3 introduces four primary phishing intentions. Section 4 describes the architecture of the proposed multi-agent framework. Section 5 outlines the models and metrics used for evaluation as well as the ground truth dataset construction. Section 6 presents experimental results and comparative analysis. Section 7 discusses a larger-scale empirical phishing intention analysis with proposed framework, while Sect. 8 concludes the paper with future works.

## 2 Related Work

Phishing detection has been widely studied using heuristics [10], machine learning and deep learning approaches that analyze features such as URLs [11], HTML content [12], domain metadata [13] or hybrid features [14]. While these methods have proven effective in identifying phishing websites, many of these techniques rely on code-level or metadata features that can be easily obfuscated or manipulated, making them particularly vulnerable to cloaking techniques that hide malicious content from automated scanners while displaying convincing visuals to human victims [6].

To address limitations of feature-based methods, recent studies have explored visual and multimodal analysis [15], using screenshots, layout structure, and Optical Character Recognition (OCR)-extracted text for phishing detection in addition to existing approaches [16,17]. These approaches better mimic how human users perceive websites and are naturally resilient to cloaking techniques that hide malicious content in code while keeping visual appearance intact. By

[1] Dataset: https://github.com/v1ct0rl33/PhishIntentionLLM.

focusing on visual elements, such models can generalize across phishing pages that differ at the source-code level but share deceptive front-end appearances.

However, they offer limited insights into the nature or intent of the attack. Once a phishing website is detected, understanding its specific malicious goal (e.g., credential theft vs. malware distribution) is often overlooked, leaving a critical gap in threat profiling and response strategies.

Understanding attackers' intentions has gained attention in broader cybersecurity contexts especially in the field of cybercrime [18], such as classifying types of email phishing (e.g., business email compromise vs. generic scams) [19], ransomware behavior [20], and scams and fraud campaign strategies [21]. These studies demonstrate that identifying intent is crucial for targeted mitigation, forensic analysis, and policy-making. However, such intent-focused analysis has rarely been applied to phishing websites, especially in a structured, automated manner.

To date, only one known study has attempted to detect phishing website intentions, focusing specifically on credential theft [22]. While this work represents an important step forward and demonstrates that identifying intent can aid in detecting previously unknown phishing websites, it is limited to credential theft and does not address other potential malicious phishing intention. Therefore, a more scalable and generalizable approach is required to capture the full spectrum of phishing intentions.

Recent advancements in LLMs and RAG have enabled more context-aware and interpretable solutions across various natural language processing and security tasks [23,24]. These models integrate external knowledge retrieval with language understanding, offering robust performance on complex, multi-stage tasks.

In summary, although phishing detection has advanced through traditional and deep learning methods, most approaches focus solely on binary classification, neglecting the identification of underlying malicious objectives. While visual and multimodal analysis helps address obfuscation, it has yet to be applied to phishing intention detection. Existing intent recognition efforts in cybersecurity are limited, with only one study on phishing intent that targets credential theft and lacks support for multiple intentions. Moreover, powerful tools like RAG and LLMs remain underexplored in this context. This highlights the need for a comprehensive, scalable framework that leverages visual and contextual cues to identify diverse phishing intentions.

## 3 Background

Phishing websites employ various deceptive strategies, each designed with specific malicious intentions. As illustrated in Fig. 1, our analysis of real-world phishing campaigns reveals four predominant categories of malicious intent: credential theft, malware distribution, financial fraud, and personal information harvesting. These intentions represent the primary objectives that drive phishing attacks in the current threat landscape. This section provides essential background on each category to establish a foundation for understanding the methodology presented in this study.

Credential theft, as shown in the Fig. 1(a), perhaps the most common phishing objective, involves attackers creating counterfeit websites that mimic legitimate platforms to capture user authentication credentials. These attacks typically impersonate trusted entities such as financial institutions, email providers, or corporate platforms, employing visual and structural similarities to the original sites. Once obtained, these credentials facilitate account takeovers, enabling attackers to access sensitive information, conduct unauthorized transactions, or establish footholds for further attacks.

Malware distribution phishing leverages deceptive interfaces to induce users to download malicious software, as shown in the Fig. 1(b). Such attacks frequently masquerade as software updates, security scans, media players, or document viewers. The distributed malware may include ransomware, information stealers, remote access trojans, or other malicious payloads that compromise system integrity and user privacy. These attacks typically feature prominent download buttons, alarming security warnings, or counterfeit system notifications.

Financial fraud phishing specifically targets monetary exploitation through various schemes designed to manipulate victims into financial transactions, as shown in the Fig. 1(c). These attacks employ deceptive narratives including fake investment opportunities, fraudulent merchandise sales, technical support scams, and counterfeit financial alerts. Distinguished by their emphasis on payment information collection or direct transfer solicitation, these attacks often create artificial urgency to circumvent rational decision-making processes.

Personal information harvesting, as shown in the Fig. 1(d), aims to collect comprehensive personally identifiable information beyond mere credentials. These attacks solicit sensitive data including government identification numbers, home addresses, employment details, financial information, and healthcare data, often through illegitimate forms, surveys, or registration pages. This information enables identity theft, sophisticated social engineering, or sale on underground markets for subsequent exploitation.

# 4 Methodology

This section presents the proposed methodology of this study. We describe the system's hierarchical agent architecture, knowledge retrieval mechanisms, processing pipeline. The formalized algorithm for this framework is proposed to demonstrate how these components interact to produce accurate threat classifications with supporting evidence chains, addressing the challenging task of multi-category phishing intention identification.

## 4.1 System Architecture

*PhishIntentionLLM* represents a novel multi-agent RAG framework for identifying malicious intentions behind phishing websites through screenshot analysis. Our approach leverages the visual understanding capabilities of LLMs combined with specialized RAG to detect up to four primary threat categories: Credential Theft, Financial Fraud, Malware Distribution, and Personal Information Harvesting.

The Fig. 2 presents an overview of the proposed framework. The system employs a hierarchical multi-agent architecture comprising five specialized layers, each with distinct cognitive responsibilities, working in conjunction with domain-specific knowledge bases. The Vision Analysis Agent serves as the perception layer, responsible for extracting raw data from phishing website screenshots. Using vision-language models, it identifies and organizes visual elements including textual content, interface components, page layout, and domain information when available.

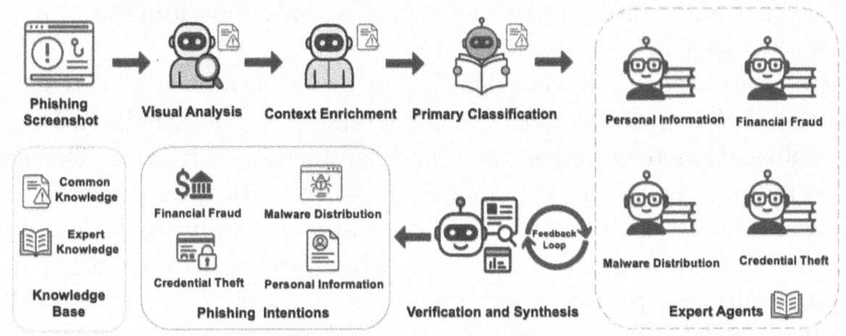


**Fig. 2.** Proposed PhishIntentionLLM Framework.

The Context Enrichment Agent functions as a semantic layer that enhances extracted elements with security-relevant context. This agent retrieves basic threat patterns from the knowledge base, tags suspicious elements with contextual information, maps visual elements to potential security implications, and generates preliminary threat hypotheses based on established patterns in phishing detection.

The Classification Agent performs multi-label classification to identify the most likely threat categories. It calculates confidence scores for each threat category, selects one to three primary threats for deeper analysis, associates evidence with each identified type, and creates an initial classification hypothesis that guides subsequent specialist analysis. The Specialist Analysis Layer contains four expert agents, each dedicated to a specific threat category. When activated based on initial classification, these specialists conduct in-depth analysis within their domains. The Credential Theft Agent evaluates login form characteristics and domain spoofing patterns, while the Financial Fraud Agent analyzes payment solicitation and unrealistic financial promises. Similarly, the Malware Distribution Agent examines download prompts and software update impersonation, and the Personal Information Agent assesses excessive data collection and privacy policy issues.

The Validation Agent integrates all previous analyses to form a comprehensive assessment. This agent combines specialist findings, resolves potential conflicts between competing hypotheses, weighs evidence based on reliability and relevance, and produces a final classification with complete evidence chains and associated confidence scores.

### 4.2 Knowledge Retrieval Architecture

*PhishIntentionLLM* incorporates a dual-layer knowledge architecture, as shown in the Definition 1, that augments agent reasoning through retrieval-augmented generation. The Basic Threat Pattern Repository contains domain-agnostic phishing indicators, including common deception patterns, visual deception elements, suspicious text patterns, and URL red flags. This knowledge supports initial detection and context enrichment phases, providing foundational patterns that transcend specific threat categories.

The Category-Specific Knowledge Repository is organized by threat type and provides detailed domain knowledge. For Credential Theft, it includes common targets, obfuscation techniques, and form submission patterns. The Financial Fraud section contains scam typologies, pressure tactics, and payment anomalies. Malware Distribution knowledge encompasses malware types, download mechanisms, and system access requests, while Personal Information resources detail data collection patterns and privacy indicators. This specialized knowledge enables expert agents to conduct nuanced analyses within their respective domains.

**Definition 1 (Knowledge Base Structures).** *The PhishIntentionLLM framework employs two complementary knowledge repositories:*

1. ***Basic Threat Pattern Repository*** *($K_B$):*

$$K_B = \{P_c, P_v, P_t\} \tag{1}$$

*where:*
- $P_c = \{p_1, p_2, \ldots, p_n\}$ *is the set of common phishing patterns*
- $P_v = \{v_1, v_2, \ldots, v_m\}$ *is the set of visual deception techniques*
- $P_t = \{t_1, t_2, \ldots, t_k\}$ *is the set of text-based manipulation patterns*

2. ***Specialist Knowledge Repository*** *($K_C$):*
*For each threat category $c \in$ {Credential Theft, Financial Fraud, Malware Distribution, Personal Information Harvesting}, we maintain:*

$$K_C^c = \{F^c, D^c\} \tag{2}$$

*where:*
- $F^c = \{f_1^c, f_2^c, \ldots, f_p^c\}$ *is the set of primary features for category $c$*
- $D^c = \{T^c, M^c, I^c\}$ *is the detailed knowledge structure, containing:*
  - $T^c = \{t_1^c, t_2^c, \ldots, t_q^c\}$*: common targets*
  - $M^c = \{m_1^c, m_2^c, \ldots, m_r^c\}$*: specialized techniques*
  - $I^c = \{i_1^c, i_2^c, \ldots, i_s^c\}$*: distinctive indicators*

### 4.3 Processing Pipeline

The *PhishIntentionLLM* processing workflow begins with image input, where the system ingests website screenshots as primary data. The Visual Analysis phase extracts text, interface elements, and page structure using vision-language capabilities. During Context Enhancement, the extracted elements are enriched with security context from the basic threat repository, establishing preliminary security implications for observed elements. Initial Classification identifies one to three primary threat categories and calculates confidence scores, determining which specialist agents to activate. In the Specialist Analysis phase, these activated agents perform in-depth examination within their respective threat domains, applying category-specific knowledge to the enriched context. Evidence Synthesis integrates all analyses to produce a cohesive final classification with complete evidence chains. When confidence falls below established thresholds, a feedback loop activates additional specialist analyses to improve certainty. This adaptive mechanism allows the system to handle ambiguous cases by gathering additional perspectives. Finally, Result Generation outputs identified threats with confidence scores and supporting evidence, providing a comprehensive assessment of phishing intentions.

```
Require: Phishing website screenshot image I
Require: Basic threat pattern knowledge base K_B
Require: Category-specific knowledge base K_C
Require: Confidence threshold τ
Ensure: Identified threat categories with evidence and confidence scores
 1: function PhishIntentionLLM(I, K_B, K_C, τ)
 2:     T ← ∅                                              ▷ Set of identified threat categories
 3:     Layer 1: Vision Analysis
 4:     E ← VisionAnalysisAgent(I)                         ▷ Extract visual elements
 5:     Layer 2: Context Enrichment
 6:     patterns ← RetrievePatterns(K_B)                   ▷ Get relevant threat patterns
 7:     E_enriched ← ContextEnrichmentAgent(E, patterns)   ▷ Add security context
 8:     Layer 3: Initial Classification
 9:     features ← RetrieveCategoryFeatures(K_C)           ▷ Get category features
10:     C, S ← ClassificationAgent(E_enriched, features)   ▷ C: categories, S: scores
11:     P ← {c_i ∈ C | Top-k(S, k = 3)}                    ▷ Select top 1-3 categories
12:     Layer 4: Specialist Analysis
13:     A ← ∅                                              ▷ Specialist analysis results
14:     for each category c ∈ P do
15:         knowledge ← RetrieveSpecialistKnowledge(K_C, c)
16:         A_c ← SpecialistAgent(E_enriched, knowledge, c)
17:         A ← A ∪ {(c, A_c)}
18:     end for
19:     Layer 5: Validation and Synthesis
20:     R, conf ← ValidationAgent(E, E_enriched, C, S, A)
21:     if conf < τ then                                   ▷ Feedback loop for low confidence
22:         categories ← {"Credential Theft", "Financial Fraud", "Malware Distribution", "Per-
    sonal Information Harvesting"}
23:         for each category c ∈ categories \ P do
24:             knowledge ← RetrieveSpecialistKnowledge(K_C, c)
25:             A_c ← SpecialistAgent(E_enriched, knowledge, c)
26:             A ← A ∪ {(c, A_c)}
27:         end for
28:         R, conf ← ValidationAgent(E, E_enriched, C, S, A)
29:     end if
30:     Result Formatting
31:     for each threat category t ∈ R do
32:         evidence ← Extract evidence from A for category t
33:         confidence ← Extract confidence from A for category t
34:         if confidence ≥ τ then
35:             T ← T ∪ {(t, evidence, confidence)}
36:         end if
37:     end for
38:     if |T| = 0 then                                    ▷ Ensure at least one category is returned
39:         t* ← arg max_{t∈R} confidence(t)
40:         evidence ← Extract evidence from A for category t*
41:         confidence ← Extract confidence from A for category t*
42:         T ← {(t*, evidence, confidence)}
43:     end if
44:     return T
45: end function
```

**Fig. 3.** The Proposed Algorithm for PhishIntentionLLM Framework.

Figure 3 demonstrates the *PhishIntentionLLM* approach through precise computational stages and decision procedures. The algorithm emphasizes the mathematical relationship between input screenshot analysis and threat categorization using set operations and conditional branches. Notable features include the top-k selection function for candidate threat categories (line 11), the union operation for specialist analysis aggregation (line 19), and the argmax function for determining the highest confidence category when necessary (line 39).

# 5 Evaluation

## 5.1 Model Selection

To evaluate the effectiveness of our framework, we selected four state-of-the-art multimodal LLMs with diverse architectures and capabilities. Qwen2.5-VL-72B-Instruct [25] is a 72B-parameter vision-language model by Alibaba Cloud, pre-trained on multilingual and multimodal datasets and known for strong visual reasoning performance. Gemini-2.0-Flash-001 [26], developed by Google DeepMind, balances efficient inference and advanced multimodal processing. GPT-4o [27], OpenAI's flagship model, integrates high-level visual understanding with robust reasoning, while GPT-4o-mini [28] offers a more lightweight alternative that retains strong multimodal capabilities. All models support API integration, ensuring compatibility with our framework and enabling comparative evaluation across computational and architectural dimensions.

## 5.2 Ground Truth Dataset

To construct the ground truth dataset for the evaluation, we randomly selected phishing website samples from three existing datasets that contain screenshots for each phishing instance and manually removed the samples with poor quality of screenshots [15,29,30]. The labeling process involved three cybersecurity engineers, each with a minimum of three years of professional experience. Two engineers independently labeled the intentions of these phishing samples based on the screenshots, while the third engineer reviewed all labeled samples to ensure consistency and accuracy. The engineers assigned one or multiple intentions to each phishing sample based on their visual content analysis.

For instance, if a phishing website solely requested username and password credentials, it was labeled as "Credential Theft." However, if the website additionally solicited telephone numbers or address information, it received dual labels of "Credential Theft" and "Personal Information Harvesting."

Through this rigorous labeling process, we constructed a multi-intention phishing dataset comprising 2,063 phishing samples from domains such as e-commerce, finance, social networking, telecommunications, and delivery services. This is one of the first phishing datasets to include explicit phishing intentions. The ground truth dataset has been publicly released.

Table 1 presents the distribution of phishing intentions identified in ground truth dataset, along with the number of records containing one, two, or three

**Table 1.** Distribution of Phishing Intentions and Number of Intentions per Record.

| Category | Type | Count |
|---|---|---|
| Phishing Intention Type | Credentials Theft | 1696 |
| | Malware Distribution | 68 |
| | Financial Fraud | 222 |
| | Personal Information Harvesting | 408 |
| Number of Intentions per Record | One Intention | 1757 |
| | Two Intentions | 281 |
| | Three Intentions | 25 |

distinct intentions. The majority of records are associated with Credentials Theft (1,696), followed by Personal Information Harvesting (408), Financial Fraud (222), and Malware Distribution (68). Additionally, most records contain only a single phishing intention (1,757), while fewer records exhibit two (281) or three (25) co-occurring intentions. No record contains four intentions.

### 5.3 Evaluation Metrics

To comprehensively evaluate this framework, various evaluation metrics are used in this study. The overall accuracy measures the proportion of correctly classified website screenshots:

$$\text{Accuracy} = \frac{|\{s \in S : \hat{Y}_s = Y_s\}|}{|S|} \tag{3}$$

where $S$ represents all samples, $Y_s$ the true intention labels, and $\hat{Y}_s$ the predicted labels for sample $s$.

Since phishing websites often exhibit multiple intentions simultaneously and some malicious phishing intentions (e.g., credential theft) are likely to occur more frequently than others (e.g., malware distribution) which leads to imbalanced classes, we employ micro-averaged metrics that aggregate contributions from all classes and reflect the actual data distribution, which is crucial in real-world scenarios:

$$\text{Precision}_{\text{micro}} = \frac{\sum_{c=1}^{C} TP_c}{\sum_{c=1}^{C} (TP_c + FP_c)} \tag{4}$$

$$\text{Recall}_{\text{micro}} = \frac{\sum_{c=1}^{C} TP_c}{\sum_{c=1}^{C} (TP_c + FN_c)} \tag{5}$$

$$\text{F1}_{\text{micro}} = \frac{2 \times \text{Precision}_{\text{micro}} \times \text{Recall}_{\text{micro}}}{\text{Precision}_{\text{micro}} + \text{Recall}_{\text{micro}}} \tag{6}$$

where $C = 4$ represents our intention classes, with $TP_c$, $FP_c$, and $FN_c$ denoting true positives, false positives, and false negatives for class $c$, respectively.

We also introduce Accuracy by Complexity ($\text{Acc}_{\text{comp}}$) to address the nuanced nature of multi-intention phishing websites:

$$\text{Acc}_{\text{comp}}(k) = \frac{|\{s \in S_k : \text{match}(Y_s, \hat{Y}_s) \geq t_k\}|}{|S_k|} \quad (7)$$

where $S_k$ represents the set of samples with exactly $k$ intentions, $\text{match}(Y_s, \hat{Y}_s)$ counts the number of correctly matched intentions, and $t_k$ is the threshold for samples with $k$ intentions, defined as:

$$t_k = \begin{cases} 1, & \text{if } k = 1 \\ 1, & \text{if } k = 2 \\ 2, & \text{if } k = 3 \end{cases} \quad (8)$$

This lies in the fact that for many phishing websites, even experienced cybersecurity experts can have slightly different understandings of the underlying intentions. Therefore, we believe partial matches provide valuable insights when evaluating multi-intention scenarios. We applied this to all above evaluations to ensure fair comparison against selected models.

For individual intention analysis, we calculate standard metrics for each class $c$ in our four phishing intention categories:

$$\text{Precision}_c = \frac{TP_c}{TP_c + FP_c} \quad \text{Recall}_c = \frac{TP_c}{TP_c + FN_c} \quad (9)$$

$$\text{F1}_c = \frac{2 \times \text{Precision}_c \times \text{Recall}_c}{\text{Precision}_c + \text{Recall}_c} \quad \text{Accuracy}_c = \frac{TP_c + TN_c}{TP_c + TN_c + FP_c + FN_c} \quad (10)$$

where $TN_c$ represents samples correctly identified as not belonging to class $c$.

# 6 Results

## 6.1 Model Performance

Table 2 and Fig. 4 present the general performance metrics of different LLMs integrated into our *PhishIntentionLLM* framework. GPT-4o achieved the highest precision (0.7895) among all evaluated models, making it particularly valuable for phishing intention detection. High precision in this context means the model correctly identifies specific phishing intentions with minimal misclassifications, providing security analysts with more accurate understanding of attackers' objectives.

While GPT-4o excels in precision, it maintains strong performance across other metrics with a micro-averaged F1 score of 0.8207 and accuracy of 0.8915. This balanced performance demonstrates GPT-4o's effectiveness as a foundation model for identifying the underlying intentions of phishing campaigns. Gemini 2.0 follows closely with slightly lower precision (0.7843) but higher recall (0.8976), resulting in the highest overall F1 score (0.8371) and accuracy (0.8987).

**Table 2.** General Performance Metrics of Selected LLMs with PhishIntentionLLM.

| Model | $\text{Precision}_{micro}$ | $\text{Recall}_{micro}$ | $\text{F1}_{micro}$ | $\text{Accuracy}_{micro}$ |
|---|---|---|---|---|
| GPT-4o | 0.7895 | 0.8544 | 0.8207 | 0.8915 |
| Gemini 2.0 | 0.7843 | 0.8976 | 0.8371 | 0.8987 |
| GPT-4o-mini | 0.6149 | 0.9744 | 0.7540 | 0.8149 |
| Qwen2.5-VL-72B | 0.4520 | 0.9428 | 0.6111 | 0.6518 |

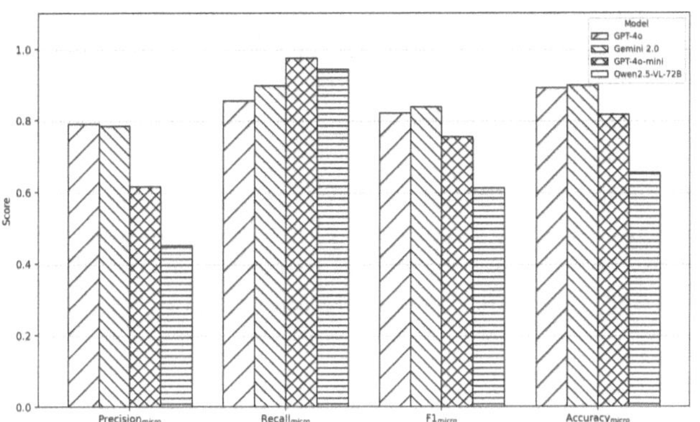


**Fig. 4.** Comparison of Selected LLMs on General Performance Metrics.

This indicates Gemini 2.0 identifies more actual phishing intentions at the expense of slightly more misattributed intentions compared to GPT-4o. GPT-4o-mini and Qwen2.5-VL-72B demonstrate significantly different performance characteristics, with extremely high recall values (0.9744 and 0.9428 respectively) but considerably lower precision scores (0.6149 and 0.4520). This suggests these models excel at capturing all potential intentions behind phishing websites but more frequently assign incorrect intentions, potentially complicating threat intelligence and response prioritization.

Table 3 provides insights into model performance across different phishing intention complexity levels. Interestingly, the performance ranking shifts when evaluated using Accuracy by Complexity ($\text{Acc}_{\text{comp}}$) metrics.

**Table 3.** Comparison of Selected LLMs on ($\text{Acc}_{\text{comp}}$) and Overall Accuracy

| Model | $\text{Acc}_{comp}$ (1 Intention) | $\text{Acc}_{comp}$ (2 Intentions) | $\text{Acc}_{comp}$ (3 Intentions) | Overall Accuracy |
|---|---|---|---|---|
| GPT-4o-mini | 0.8980 | 1.0000 | 0.9600 | 0.9130 |
| GPT-4o | 0.8996 | 0.9324 | 0.8800 | 0.9039 |
| Qwen2.5-VL-72B | 0.8953 | 0.9644 | 0.8800 | 0.9045 |
| Gemini 2.0 | 0.8750 | 0.9927 | 0.8800 | 0.8910 |

GPT-4o-mini demonstrated the highest overall accuracy (0.9130) across all complexity levels. The model achieved strong performance on single-intention phishing sites (0.8980) and notably high scores for multi-intention websites (1.0000 for two intentions and 0.9600 for three intentions).

GPT-4o maintains strong performance across complexity levels with high scores for single-intention phishing sites (0.8996), two-intention sites (0.9324), and three-intention scenarios (0.8800). This consistent performance further validates its reliability for accurately identifying diverse phishing strategies.

The $Acc_{comp}$ metrics for websites with three intentions show consistent performance across most models (0.8800), with only GPT-4o-mini achieving a higher score (0.9600). This suggests that the *PhishIntentionLLM* framework provides reliable intention identification even in the most complex phishing scenarios with multiple malicious objectives.

These results demonstrate that while GPT-4o provides the most precise identification of specific phishing intentions, all evaluated models show strong capabilities in identifying phishing intentions across various complexity levels when integrated with our *PhishIntentionLLM* framework.

### 6.2 PhishIntentionLLM Vs. Single-Agent

To further validate the effectiveness of our proposed framework, we conducted a comparative analysis between *PhishIntentionLLM* and a single-agent baseline using identical foundation model (Gemini 2.0). As shown in Table 4 and Fig. 5, the multi-agent RAG approach substantially outperforms the single-agent scenario across nearly all metrics.

**Table 4.** Comparison of PhishIntentionLLM and Single-Agent Scenario

| Metric | PhishIntentionLLM (Gemini 2.0) | Single-Agent (Gemini 2.0) |
|---|---|---|
| $Precision_{micro}$ | **0.7843** | 0.4014 |
| $Recall_{micro}$ | **0.8976** | 0.6341 |
| $F1_{micro}$ | **0.8371** | 0.4916 |
| $Accuracy_{micro}$ | **0.8987** | 0.6195 |
| Overall Accuracy | **0.8910** | 0.5870 |
| $Acc_{comp}$(1 Intention) | **0.8750** | 0.5287 |
| $Acc_{comp}$(2 Intentions) | **0.9927** | 0.9253 |
| $Acc_{comp}$(3 Intentions) | 0.8800 | 0.8800 |

The most striking improvement appears in precision, where *PhishIntention-LLM* achieves 0.7843 compared to just 0.4014 for the single-agent approach which represents a ~95% improvement. This dramatic enhancement in precision demonstrates that our hierarchical agent architecture with specialized knowledge bases significantly reduces false positive classifications, enabling much more accurate identification of specific phishing intentions.

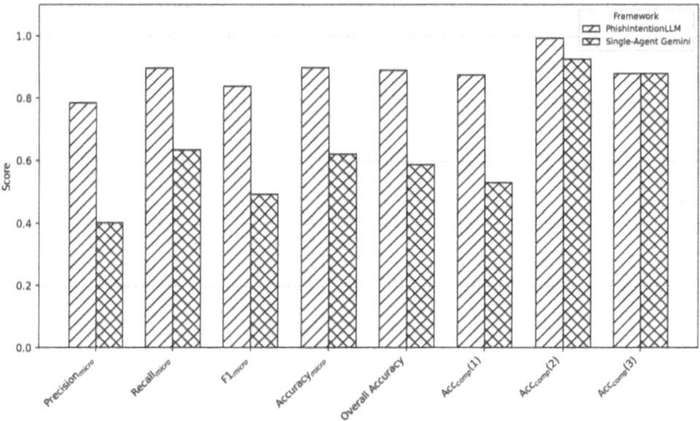


**Fig. 5.** Comparison of PhishIntentionLLM and Single-Agent Scenario.

Similarly, recall improved from 0.6341 to 0.8976 (~42% increase), indicating the multi-agent system's superior ability to identify all relevant intentions present in phishing websites. The combined improvements in precision and recall culminate in a ~70% increase in F1 score (0.8371 vs. 0.4916) and a ~45% enhancement in micro-accuracy (0.8987 vs. 0.6195).

The Accuracy by Complexity ($\text{Acc}_{\text{comp}}$) metrics reveal that our approach demonstrates particularly high effectiveness against phishing websites with single and two malicious intentions. For single-intention websites, *PhishIntentionLLM* achieves 0.8750 accuracy compared to 0.5287 for the single-agent approach with a ~65% improvement.

### 6.3 PhishIntentionLLM Vs. PhishIntention

To benchmark our framework against existing methods, we compared *PhishIntentionLLM* (GPT-4o) with PhishIntention [22], the only prior work focused on phishing intention analysis. Since PhishIntention is limited to detecting credential theft intentions only, we conducted a focused comparison on this specific intention type regarding test precision, test accuracy, F1 and recall, following PhishIntention's methodology with the same 9:1 (training:testing) ratio on our ground truth dataset.

As shown in Table 5 and Fig. 6, *PhishIntentionLLM* demonstrates superior performance across all metrics in credential theft detection. Our framework achieved a precision of 0.8545 compared to PhishIntention's 0.8206, representing a ~4% improvement in correctly identifying genuine credential theft attempts while reducing false positives.

The most dramatic improvement appears in recall, where *PhishIntentionLLM* achieved 0.9946 compared to PhishIntention's 0.7471 with a ~33% increase. This substantial enhancement in recall indicates that our multi-agent RAG framework can identify virtually all credential theft attempts (99.5%), whereas the existing approach misses approximately one-quarter of such phishing attempts.

**Table 5.** Comparison of PhishIntention and PhishIntentionLLM

| Model | Precision | Recall | F1 Score | Accuracy |
|---|---|---|---|---|
| PhishIntention [22] | 0.8206 | 0.7471 | 0.7821 | 0.6578 |
| **PhishIntentionLLM (Ours)** | **0.8545** | **0.9946** | **0.9193** | **0.8602** |

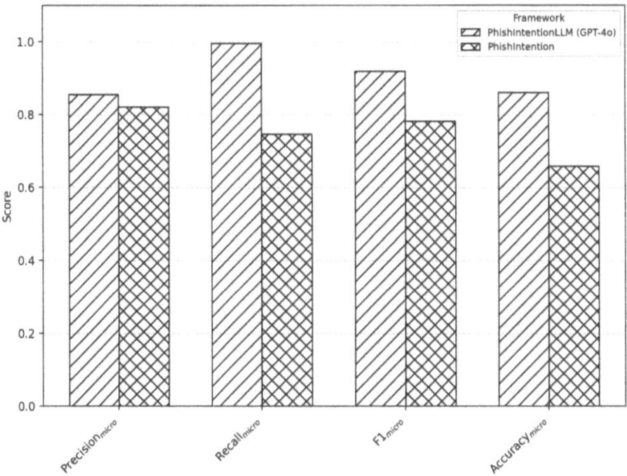


**Fig. 6.** Comparison of PhishIntention and PhishIntentionLLM on Credentials Theft Intention.

The combined improvements in precision and recall result in a significant enhancement in F1 score (0.9193 vs. 0.7821), representing an ˜18% increase over the existing approach. Additionally, overall accuracy improved from 0.6578 to 0.8602, a ˜31% enhancement that demonstrates the superior classification capabilities of our framework. PhishIntentionLLM outperforms PhishIntention by fusing visual-text understanding with RAG-driven knowledge, unlike the latter's static visual approach.

## 7 Discussion

To understand the phishing intentions in a larger scale, we use our proposed framework with GPT-4o to further evaluate 6K more phishing samples to profile their phishing intentions which results in ˜9K samples including our ground truth dataset. A sector–intention frequency matrix was constructed (see Fig. 7(a)). The matrix maps the occurrence of four major phishing intentions: Credentials Theft, Financial Fraud, Malware Distribution, and Personal Information Harvesting—across identified sectors such as financial, e-commerce, telecommunications, and government. The analysis reveals that the financial sector is the most frequently targeted, with 2,882 instances of credentials theft and 2,032 cases of personal information harvesting. Other highly targeted sectors include online/cloud service, email provider, and social networking. Notably, credentials theft and personal information harvesting followed by financial fraud are the dominant intentions across most sectors, while malware distribution remains relatively less frequent.

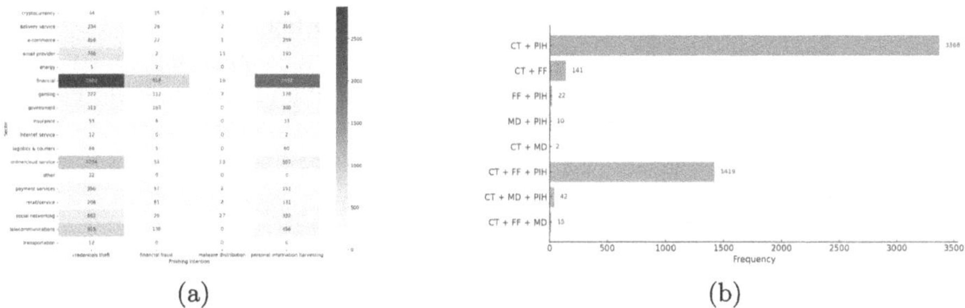


(a) (b)

**Fig. 7.** (a) shows phishing intentions across different sectors; (b) displays frequencies of two- and three-intention combinations. Two-intention combinations are in green; three-intention combinations are in orange. **Note:** (Color figure online) CT = Credentials Theft, PIH = Personal Information Harvesting, FF = Financial Fraud, MD = Malware Distribution.

We further examined records containing multiple phishing intentions to explore the strategic complexity embedded within these campaigns. Figure 7(b) shows the frequency and sectoral distribution of co-occurring phishing intentions found in samples with either two or three distinct objectives. Among the two-intention combinations, Credentials Theft + Personal Information Harvesting was by far the most prevalent, appearing in 3,368 instances, with the financial sector being the most frequently targeted (1,185 cases). This combination highlights a dual objective wherein adversaries aim not only to compromise login credentials but also to capture accompanying personal data, thereby increasing the potential for downstream exploitation. The next most common two-intention pair, Credentials Theft + Financial Fraud, appeared in 141 instances, again dominated by attacks on the financial sector (91 cases), suggesting a strong correlation between credential compromise and direct financial gain.

In records exhibiting three distinct phishing intentions, the most frequent combination was Credentials Theft + Financial Fraud + Personal Information Harvesting, found in 1,419 samples, with the financial sector again serving as the primary target (821 occurrences). This triad reflects the layered objectives of modern phishing schemes, where attackers simultaneously seek unauthorized access, financial exploitation, and user profiling. Less frequent but notable three-intention combinations included Credentials Theft + Malware Distribution + Personal Information Harvesting (42 instances, led by the social networking sector) and Credentials Theft + Financial Fraud + Malware Distribution (15 instances, with the gaming sector most affected), demonstrating that more complex phishing strategies often align with the sector-specific threat surface and user value.

The prevalence of such multi-intention combinations likely reflects an adaptive response by attackers to increasingly robust verification mechanisms used by modern systems. As single data points such as passwords or email addresses are often insufficient to gain full access to target systems—particularly those with multi-factor authentication or behavioral risk scoring—phishing campaigns have evolved to collect multiple types of sensitive information concurrently. This multi-vector approach significantly enhances the likelihood of bypassing layered defenses and achieving the attackers' ultimate goals.

## 8 Conclusion

This study presents *PhishIntentionLLM*, a novel multi-agent RAG framework for uncovering phishing website intentions through screenshot analysis. While our results demonstrate strong performance and scalability, future work can explore real-time deployment to profile phishing intentions in the wild. Additionally, the proposed approach holds potential for broader application, such as recognizing attacker intentions in phishing emails and other social engineering vectors.

## References

1. Alkhalil, Z., Hewage, C., Nawaf, L., Khan, I.: Phishing attacks: A recent comprehensive study and a new anatomy. Front. Comput. Sci. **Volume 3 - 2021** (2021). https://doi.org/10.3389/fcomp.2021.563060
2. Khonji, M., Iraqi, Y., Jones, A.: Phishing detection: a literature survey. IEEE Commun. Surv. Tutor. **15**(4), 2091–2121 (2013). https://doi.org/10.1109/SURV.2013.032213.00009
3. Lim, K., Park, J., Kim, D.: Phishing vs. legit: comparative analysis of client-side resources of phishing and target brand websites. In: Proceedings of the ACM Web Conference 2024, pp. 1756–1767. WWW '24, Association for Computing Machinery, New York, NY, USA (2024). https://doi.org/10.1145/3589334.3645535
4. Anti-Phishing Working Group (APWG): https://apwg.org/
5. Li, W., Laghari, S.U.A., Manickam, S., Chong, Y.W.: Exploration and evaluation of human-centric cloaking techniques in phishing websites. KSII Trans. Internet Inf. Syst. **19**(1), 232–258 (2025). https://doi.org/10.3837/tiis.2025.01.011
6. Li, W., Manickam, S., Laghari, S.U.A., Chong, Y.W.: Uncovering the cloak: a systematic review of techniques used to conceal phishing websites. IEEE Access **11**, 71925–71939 (2023). https://doi.org/10.1109/ACCESS.2023.3293063
7. Zieni, R., Massari, L., Calzarossa, M.C.: Phishing or not phishing? A survey on the detection of phishing websites. IEEE Access **11**, 18499–18519 (2023). https://doi.org/10.1109/ACCESS.2023.3247135
8. Li, W., Manickam, S., Chong, Y.W., Leng, W., Nanda, P.: A state-of-the-art review on phishing website detection techniques. IEEE Access **12**, 187976–188012 (2024). https://doi.org/10.1109/ACCESS.2024.3514972
9. Kulkarni, A., Balachandran, V., Das, T.: Phishing webpage detection: unveiling the threat landscape and investigating detection techniques. IEEE Commun. Surv. Tutor. **27**(2), 974–1007 (2025). https://doi.org/10.1109/COMST.2024.3441752

10. Nguyen, L.A.T., To, B.L., Nguyen, H.K., Nguyen, M.H.: A novel approach for phishing detection using URL-based heuristic. In: 2014 International Conference on Computing, Management and Telecommunications (ComManTel), pp. 298–303 (2014). https://doi.org/10.1109/ComManTel.2014.6825621
11. Sahingoz, O.K., Buber, E., Demir, O., Diri, B.: Machine learning based phishing detection from URLs. Expert Syst. Appl. **117**, 345–357 (2019). https://doi.org/10.1016/j.eswa.2018.09.029
12. Opara, C., Wei, B., Chen, Y.: HTMLPhish: enabling phishing web page detection by applying deep learning techniques on html analysis. In: 2020 International Joint Conference on Neural Networks (IJCNN), pp. 1–8 (2020)
13. Shirazi, H., Bezawada, B., Ray, I.: "kn0w thy doma1n name": unbiased phishing detection using domain name based features. In: Proceedings of the 23nd ACM on Symposium on Access Control Models and Technologies, Pp. 69–75. SACMAT '18, Association for Computing Machinery, New York, NY, USA (2018)
14. Aljofey, A., Bello, S.A., Lu, J., Xu, C.: Comprehensive phishing detection: a multi-channel approach with variants TCN fusion leveraging URL and HTML features. J. Netw. Comput. Appl. **238**, 104170 (2025). https://doi.org/10.1016/j.jnca.2025.104170
15. Lin, Y., et al.: Phishpedia: a hybrid deep learning based approach to visually identify phishing webpages. In: 30th USENIX Security Symposium (USENIX Security 21), pp. 3793–3810. USENIX Association (2021)
16. Liu, D.J., Lee, J.H.: A CNN-based SIA screenshot method to visually identify phishing websites. J. Netw. Syst. Manage. **32**(1), 8 (2024)
17. Koide, T., Nakano, H., Chiba, D.: ChatPhishDetector: detecting phishing sites using large language models. IEEE Access **12**, 154381–154400 (2024)
18. Kassa, Y.W., James, J.I., Belay, E.G.: Cybercrime intention recognition: a systematic literature review. Information **15**(5) (2024). https://doi.org/10.3390/info15050263
19. Stojnic, T., Vatsalan, D., Arachchilage, N.A.G.: Phishing email strategies: understanding cybercriminals' strategies of crafting phishing emails. Secur. Priv. **4**(5), e165 (2021). https://doi.org/10.1002/spy2.165
20. Walton, B.J., Khatun, M.E., Ghawaly, J.M., Ali-Gombe, A.: Exploring large language models for semantic analysis and categorization of android malware. In: 2024 Annual Computer Security Applications Conference Workshops (ACSAC Workshops), pp. 248–254 (2024). https://doi.org/10.1109/ACSACW65225.2024.00035
21. Kolupuri, S.V.J., Paul, A., Bhowmick, R.S., Ganguli, I.: Scams and frauds in the digital age: Ml-based detection and prevention strategies. In: Proceedings of the 26th International Conference on Distributed Computing and Networking, pp. 340–345. ICDCN '25, Association for Computing Machinery, New York, NY, USA (2025). https://doi.org/10.1145/3700838.3703672
22. Liu, R., Lin, Y., Yang, X., Ng, S.H., Divakaran, D.M., Dong, J.S.: Inferring phishing intention via webpage appearance and dynamics: a deep vision based approach. In: 31st USENIX Security Symposium (USENIX Security 22), pp. 1633–1650. USENIX Association, Boston, MA (2022)
23. Rahman, M., et al.: Retrieval Augmented Generation for Robust Cyber Defense. Tech. rep., Pacific Northwest National Laboratory (PNNL), Richland, WA (United States) (2024). https://doi.org/10.2172/2474934
24. Arikkat, D.R., et al.: IntellBot: retrieval augmented LLM chatbot for cyber threat knowledge delivery. In: 2024 IEEE 16th International Conference on Computational Intelligence and Communication Networks (CICN), pp. 644–651 (2024)

25. Bai, S., et al.: Qwen2. 5-VL technical report. arXiv preprint arXiv:2502.13923 (2025)
26. Team, G., et al.: Gemini: a family of highly capable multimodal models. arXiv preprint arXiv:2312.11805 (2023)
27. OpenAI Team: Hello GPT-4o. Tech. rep., OpenAI (2024). https://openai.com/index/hello-gpt-4o/
28. OpenAI Team: GPT-4o mini: advancing cost-efficient intelligence. Tech. rep., OpenAI (2024). https://openai.com/index/gpt-4o-mini-advancing-cost-efficient-intelligence/
29. Putra, I.K.A.A.: Phishing website dataset (2023). https://doi.org/10.5281/zenodo.8041387
30. Dalgic, F., Bozkir, A., Aydos, M.: Phish-IRIS: a new approach for vision based brand prediction of phishing web pages via compact visual descriptors. In: 2018 2nd International Symposium on Multidisciplinary Studies and Innovative Technologies (ISMSIT), pp. 1–8 (2018). https://doi.org/10.1109/ISMSIT.2018.8567299

# APT-Agent: A Training-Free, Unsupervised, LLM-Based Multi-agent Framework for Interpretable Advanced Persistent Threat Detection

Wenzhuo Cui[1,2], Yibing Hu[1,2], Zheng Liu[1,2], Jingjing Feng[1,2], Shuyi Zhang[1,2], and Yu Wen[1](✉)

[1] State Key Laboratory of Cyberspace Security Defense, Institute of Information Engineering, CAS, Beijing, China
{cuiwenzhuo,huyibing,liuzheng,fengjingjing,zhangshuyi2023,wenyu}@iie.ac.cn
[2] School of Cyber Security, University of Chinese Academy of Sciences, Beijing, China

**Abstract.** Advanced Persistent Threats (APTs)—noted for their stealth, targeting precision, and destructive impact—have become a major challenge in cybersecurity. With the progress of deep learning, deep-learning-based APT detection has emerged as the mainstream research direction. Nevertheless, current methods still face three key limitations: (1) dependence on large, labeled datasets containing attack samples and extensive domain knowledge; (2) prohibitive computational costs during training and inference, making real-world deployment difficult; and (3) a narrow focus on merely determining whether an attack exists, lacking interpretability and support for follow-up analysis.

To overcome these issues, we introduce APT-Agent, the first training-free, unsupervised LLM-based multi-agent framework dedicated to APT detection. It coordinates three agents: (1) a Dispatcher Agent that decomposes natural-language requests into subtasks, dispatches them for execution, and aggregates the results into a unified response; (2) a Detection Agent that fuses LLM reasoning with Retrieval-Augmented Generation (RAG) for efficient and accurate log detection; and (3) an Interpreter Agent that combines long-term memory with external tools to generate trustworthy explanations and mitigation advice. Evaluation results show that APT-Agent achieves outstanding detection performance across ten attack scenarios while incurring dramatically lower computational overhead than state-of-the-art APT detection methods.

**Keywords:** Advanced Persistent Threat · Large Language Model · Unsupervised Approach · Retrieval-Augmented Generation

## 1 Introduction

Advanced Persistent Threats (APTs), characterized by stealth, specificity, and destructive potential, have emerged as a critical challenge in cybersecurity [1].


K.-K. R. Choo et al. (Eds.): ICDF2C 2025, LNICST 686, pp. 107–125, 2026.
https://doi.org/10.1007/978-3-032-22545-0_7

An effective APT detection system must concurrently achieve high accuracy and a low false-positive rate while maintaining computational efficiency and minimal resource consumption.

Early studies [2–5] mainly relied on heuristic algorithms: domain experts handcrafted rules, and attacks were detected through rule matching. More recently, deep-learning-based approaches [6–18] have come to the forefront because of their capacity to automatically capture latent, complex behavioral patterns. These methods employ various neural architectures to model either APT activities or system behaviors and cast detection as a classification or anomaly-detection problem.

Despite their promise, existing methods still face several obstacles in real-world deployment: (1) Data scarcity and limited generalization. Supervised models require large volumes of labeled attack data to attain robust performance, yet high-quality training samples, particularly attack samples, are difficult to obtain; consequently, their ability to generalize to zero-day attacks is not guaranteed. (2) High computational overhead. State-of-the-art deep models, especially those based on sequential data or provenance graphs, achieve impressive accuracy but incur substantial costs during graph construction, training, and inference, hindering practical deployment. (3) Limited interpretability. Most approaches merely output whether an attack exists, offering scant explanatory evidence and leaving analysts unsure how to respond. (4) Fragmented and labor-intensive pipelines. Current frameworks typically split log preprocessing, feature extraction, and anomaly detection into stand-alone modules that must be orchestrated via expert-written scripts; this static, highly manual workflow raises the operational barrier and proves cumbersome and inefficient in practice.

Large Language Models (LLMs), endowed with superior semantic understanding, knowledge reasoning, and context-aware generation capabilities, offer a breakthrough solution for APT detection. Benefiting from the log data and attack knowledge embedded in their pre-training corpora, LLMs can deeply parse the semantic correlations in logs and identify anomalous behavioral patterns. Nevertheless, applying LLMs to APT scenarios still faces the following challenges: First, unstructured fields in raw logs (e.g., hash values and memory addresses) cause the tokenizer to emit a large number of unknown tokens (UNKs), severely damaging semantic completeness and leading to misinterpretation or even failure. Moreover, the inherent "hallucination" problem of LLMs [19] becomes more pronounced when confronting complex and covert APT attacks—because the knowledge within the LLM itself is insufficient, the model may produce seemingly plausible yet unfounded pseudo-reasoning results.

To address the above issues in existing methods and apply LLMs effectively to log analysis scenarios, we propose APT-Agent, the first training-free, unsupervised, LLM-based multi-agent framework specifically designed for APT detection. Using a dynamic task scheduling mechanism and Retrieval-Augmented Generation (RAG) technology, APT-Agent delivers a fully automated workflow that spans attack detection, result interpretation, external knowledge integration, and investigative assistance. The framework comprises three core agents:

(1) Dispatcher Agent that dynamically parses user requirements, decomposes tasks, and assigns them to designated modules; (2) Detection Agent that fuses an LLM with a knowledge base via RAG to perform reasoning and detection on logs while boosting efficiency through batching and caching; and (3) Interpreter Agent that leverages both long-term and short-term memories as well as tool collaboration to collect historical detection data and up-to-date APT intelligence, furnishing the LLM with comprehensive contextual support that yields interpretability for APT detection and subsequent investigation.

We evaluated APT-Agent in scenarios encompassing four single-host and six multi-host attack types [8]. Experiment results demonstrate that APT-Agent delivers outstanding detection performance, achieving a precision of 98.62% and a recall of 97.62%. Moreover, APT-Agent exhibits significant advantages in computational cost. Specifically, it requires no training phase and introduces only minimal operational overhead. Therefore, APT-Agent outperforms state-of-the-art approaches and demonstrates strong practical applicability.

In summary, this paper makes the following contributions:

- We propose APT-Agent, the first training-free, unsupervised LLM-based multi-agent framework for APT detection. By incorporating RAG, APT-Agent can perform fine-grained analysis and detection for APTs. Because the method relies exclusively on LLM inference through API calls—without any additional training, feature engineering, or provenance graph construction—it achieves substantially lower computational overhead and higher efficiency than existing approaches.
- By adopting an unsupervised strategy, APT-Agent removes the long-standing dependence on labeled data in APT detection. Consequently, it maintains high detection performance even in data-scarce environments and against zero-day attacks, making it particularly suitable for real-world deployments where attack samples are limited and zero-day threats are frequent.
- To address the poor interpretability of prior methods, we are the first to introduce interpretability into APT detection. By integrating long-term memory retrieval and tool invocation, APT-Agent combines historic decisions with external knowledge to generate explanations of detection results and remediation advice, enabling security analysts to understand, pinpoint, and respond to threats rapidly. Moreover, APT-Agent can automatically assign and complete tasks in response to natural-language requests, greatly enhancing ease of use in practical enterprise applications.
- We evaluate APT-Agent on widely used public datasets across four single-host and six multi-host attack scenarios. The results demonstrate that APT-Agent identifies APT attacks with superior accuracy and minimal computation, significantly outperforming state-of-the-art methods.

## 2 Related Work

**APT Detection.** Existing APT detection techniques can be broadly classified into heuristic-based and learning-based approaches. Early heuristic methods [2–5] largely relied on expert knowledge or threat intelligence to craft rules and used these rules to search for and uncover APT attacks within a system. In recent years, learning-based methods [6–18] have leveraged deep learning to model normal system behavior [7,10,14,16] or attack patterns [8,9,11–13], and have identified attacks through classification [8,12,13] or anomaly detection [9,14,16]. Among these, provenance-based methods model system entities and their interactions with graph to strengthen correlation analysis of attack activities, while log-based methods detect attacks by directly analyzing log sequences. However, current deep-learning-based methods all require model training and, in most cases, graph construction, resulting in significant computational and time costs.

**Anomaly Detection.** Anomaly detection aims to identify outliers that deviate from normal behavior. Traditional techniques include One-class SVM [20], Local Outlier Factor [21], and Isolation Forest [22]. In recent years, deep learning has been widely adopted in anomaly detection for its superior performance. For instance, DeepLog [6] leverages LSTM networks to detect abnormal behavior from system logs, while certain Transformer-based approaches (e.g., LogBERT [23] and Airtag [14]) employ more advanced Transformer embeddings to boost performance. Nevertheless, current anomaly detection methods still exhibit high false-positive rates and limited interpretability, hindering their practical adoption.

## 3 Overview of APT-Agent

APT-Agent offer an efficient, low-resource, interpretable framework for APT detection in a training-free and unsupervised manner. To this end, we propose an LLM-based multi-agent architecture (Fig. 1) consisting of three core agents—Dispatcher Agent, Detection Agent, and Interpreter Agent—to build an automated APT intrusion detection system.

The Dispatcher Agent is responsible for perceiving and parsing the user's intent, and then dynamically routing subtasks to the appropriate modules according to the task type. For log detection requests, it invokes the Detection Agent. The Detection Agent applies RAG: it embeds both the logs under inspection and the log knowledge base into vector representations, retrieves the top-$k$ relevant matches, merges the retrieved context, and submits the consolidated input to the LLM for a verdict. In addition, batch processing and cache are employed to enhance detection efficiency.

When result explanations or investigative assistance are required, the Dispatcher Agent calls the Interpreter Agent. Leveraging long-term memory, the Interpreter Agent recalls relevant historical attacks and remediation experience, and combines web search with domain-specific knowledge bases, enabling the LLM to produce trustworthy explanations and investigative guidance.

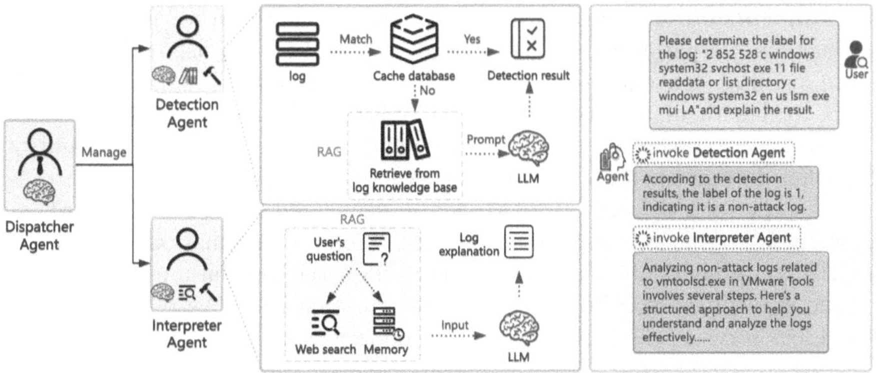


**Fig. 1.** Overview of APT-Agent pipeline.

# 4 Approach

This section describes how APT-Agent achieves efficient and accurate APT detection over massive audit logs. APT-Agent consists of the following modules.

## 4.1 Data Preprocessing

Conventional log preprocessing techniques [8,15] adopt coarse-grained abstraction, discarding a large amount of fine-grained information and thus impairing model performance. Although recent fine-grained methods [14,16] retain detailed content, common out-of-vocabulary (OOV) tokens (e.g., file path, URL, IP address, temporary file name) are still mapped to the unknown token [UNK]. This results in the loss of critical information and introduces noise, hindering the model's generalization ability. To address these issues, we design a fine-grained preprocessing scheme for logs that preserves as much information as possible while maintaining the interpretability required by downstream models.

**Log Normalization.** To mitigate the noise introduced by the large number of out-of-vocabulary (OOV) tokens in raw log streams, we apply a heuristic normalization procedure governed by three rules. First, because temporary filenames seldom carry semantic content, we abstract them by substituting their suffixes with a canonical extension such as "`.tmp`" or "`.temp`". Second, for paths residing in system directories like `/proc`—which often encode transient kernel state, most notably a process identifier (PID)—we eliminate the PID segment to remove instance-specific noise. Third, any filename that matches a well-known hash pattern (e.g., MD5 or SHA) is replaced with the placeholder "`hash value`", thereby enforcing a uniform representation.

**Domain-Specific Tokenization.** Although normalization reduces noise, entities such as file paths and URLs still contain multi-level, user-defined strings whose naming conventions differ markedly from natural language, causing LLMs to flag them as unknown tokens (`[UNK]`). To alleviate this, we design a domain-aware tokenizer that employs predefined delimiters (e.g., "." and "/") to further decompose these entities and expose their hierarchical structure. For instance, the path `C:\users\downloads` is segmented into `[C:]`, `[users]`, and `[downloads]`. This approach retains critical semantic information, improves the model's comprehension of log data, and allows the general-purpose tokenizer to process ordinary vocabulary without information loss. The resulting preprocessed logs serve as the foundation for all downstream components.

### 4.2 Dispatcher Agent

Within the APT-Agent framework, the Dispatcher Agent serves as the hub for the "decompose–dispatch–aggregate" loop. When a user submits a natural-language instruction $q$, the Dispatcher Agent first leverages the same foundational LLM, guided by the prompt $p_{\text{disp}}$, to generate a chain of thought that decomposes $q$ into a sequence of $N_t$ subtasks $\{z_i\}$:

$$z_i \leftarrow M_{\text{disp}}\big(q, p_{\text{disp}}, i = 1, \ldots, N_t\big) \tag{1}$$

Next, the Dispatcher Agent dynamically routes each $z_i$ according to a predefined semantic–capability mapping table: if a subtask concerns log-anomaly detection, it calls the Detection Agent; if it requires interpreting detection results or enriching intelligence, it delegates to the Interpreter Agent; and if it can be handled directly by the foundation model together with lightweight tools, it is executed locally. After all subtasks finish, the Dispatcher Agent structurally aggregates the returned results $\{r_i\}$ and rewrites them in natural language to yield the final answer $R_{\text{final}}$, which is also written to memory to furnish traceable context for subsequent conversations. This pipeline enables the Dispatcher Agent to decompose complex instructions on-the-fly while optimally allocating resources.

The APT-Agent framework, via the Dispatcher Agent, converts the traditional expert-script-driven and manually orchestrated multi-stage APT detection workflow into a single natural-language entry point. Security operators simply issue conversational task descriptions and the system then automatically performs log detection, result analysis, and related tasks from end to end. This design sharply reduces manual orchestration overhead and greatly improves efficiency and usability in real-world enterprise security operations.

### 4.3 APT Detection with RAG

Within APT-Agent, the Detection Agent delivers efficient log detection through a two-step approach—first building a log knowledge base, then applying RAG-assisted detection—thereby supporting the agent's log analysis and detection capabilities. The Detection Agent pipeline is illustrated in Fig. 2.

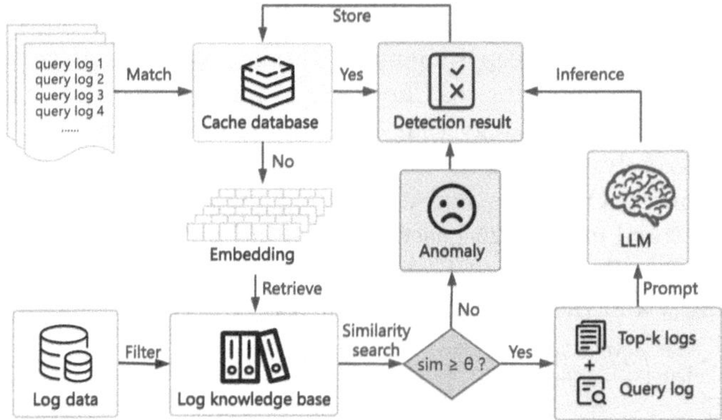


**Fig. 2.** Detection Agent pipeline.

**Log Knowledge Base Construction.** To build a normal-only log knowledge base $\mathcal{K}$ for unsupervised anomaly detection, we remove redundant log sequences using the Levenshtein distance [24]. Given two sequences $l_a$ and $l_b$, their distance $\text{lev}_{l_a,l_b}(i,j)$ is defined recursively as

$$\text{lev}_{l_a,l_b}(i,j) = \begin{cases} \max(i,j) & \text{if } \min(i,j)=0, \\ \min\begin{Bmatrix} \text{lev}_{l_a,l_b}(i-1,j)+1, \\ \text{lev}_{l_a,l_b}(i,j-1)+1, \\ \text{lev}_{l_a,l_b}(i-1,j-1)+\mathbb{1}_{(a_i \neq b_j)} \end{Bmatrix} & \text{otherwise.} \end{cases} \tag{2}$$

where $\mathbb{1}_{(a_i \neq b_j)}$ equals 1 if the two characters differ. We convert this distance to a similarity score

$$\text{sim}_{\text{LD}}(l_a,l_b) = 1 - \frac{\text{lev}(l_a,l_b)}{\max(|l_a|,|l_b|)} \tag{3}$$

and keep only one representative from any pair whose similarity exceeds a tunable threshold $\tau_K$. This procedure reduces the knowledge base to 21.8% of its original size, markedly improving retrieval speed. The remaining sequences are finally sharded by individual log entry and stored in a structured form for downstream detection.

**Log Detection with RAG.** After constructing the log knowledge base, the Detection Agent employs a RAG technique driven by semantic-similarity search. Specifically, it first retrieves the top-$k$ most similar log examples from the knowledge base, then feeds these examples—together with the query log—into the LLM as a single prompt for reasoning. Batch processing and caching are introduced to accelerate retrieval, enabling real-time attack detection.

*Hybrid Semantic-Lexical Retrieval.* Traditional lexical-only methods such as TF-IDF [25] cannot capture deep semantic relations, while pure vector retrieval may miss exact keyword cues that are critical for log forensics. Therefore, we adopt a hybrid retrieval strategy that combines semantic similarity with lexical matching. Concretely, each log record $l \in \mathcal{K}$ is (1) converted into a $d$-dimensional embedding $e_l$ using OpenAI's text-embedding model and indexed in a vector store, and (2) stored in a BM25-based inverted index [26]. At query time we run the two retrieval paths in parallel, obtaining the top-$K_{\text{sem}}$ candidates by cosine similarity $\text{sim}_{\text{sem}}$ and the top-$K_{\text{lex}}$ candidates by BM25 score $\text{sim}_{\text{lex}}$ as follows:

$$\text{sim}_{\text{lex}} = \sum_{t \in q} \log\left(\frac{N - \text{df}_t + 0.5}{\text{df}_t + 0.5}\right) \cdot \frac{(k_1 + 1)\,\text{tf}_{t,l}}{k_1((1-b) + b\,\frac{L_l}{L_{\text{avg}}}) + \text{tf}_{t,l}} \cdot \frac{(k_3 + 1)\,\text{tf}_{t,q}}{k_3 + \text{tf}_{t,q}}, \quad (4)$$

where $q$ is the query log, $l$ is a retrieved log entry, and $t$ is a query term. The two candidate sets are merged and de-duplicated; their scores are linearly fused

$$\text{sim}_{\text{hyb}} = w_1\,\text{sim}_{\text{sem}} + w_2\,\widehat{\text{sim}}_{\text{lex}}, \quad (5)$$

where $\widehat{\text{sim}}_{\text{lex}}$ is the min–max normalized BM25 score and $w_1 + w_2 = 1$. Finally, we keep the top-$k$ logs with the highest $\text{sim}_{\text{hyb}}$, forming the evidence set fed to the LLM. This hybrid design preserves the generalisation ability of semantic retrieval while retaining the precision of lexical cues, leading to more robust log anomaly detection. In our experiments, we set $w_1 = 0.7$ and $w_2 = 0.3$.

*Log Detection.* During inference, the incoming log entry $l_{\text{query}}$ is first embedded as $e_{\text{query}}$ and tokenized; the hybrid retrieval pipeline defined above is then executed, returning a candidate set $\mathcal{S}$ scored by the fused measure $\text{sim}_{\text{hyb}}$ of Eq. 5. If all candidates fall below a decision threshold $\theta$ (i.e. $\mathcal{S} = \emptyset$), the log is immediately flagged as anomalous so as to minimize false negatives. Otherwise, we sort $\mathcal{S}$ by $\text{sim}_{\text{hyb}}(l_{\text{query}}, l) \geq \theta$ and retain the top-$k$ matches $\{l_1, \ldots, l_k\}$ together with their scores $\{r_1, \ldots, r_k\}$. Finally, the query log, the $k$ retrieved exemplars and the associated hybrid scores are assembled into a prompt and fed to the LLM for verdict generation. Hyper-parameter tuning experiments show that the best performance is achieved when $k = 5$ and the similarity threshold is set to $\theta = 0.85$.

In the prompt, we explicitly instruct the LLM to account for the importance of each retrieved log example: the higher its similarity score, the greater its decision weight. The LLM must jointly reason over the query log $l_{\text{query}}$ and the provided examples $\{l_i\}$ to output the final detection result. The RAG process of the logs is shown in Fig. 3. By incorporating Retrieval Augmented Generation (RAG), we both capitalize on the LLM's reasoning power and substantially mitigate hallucinations, thereby enabling efficient and interpretable detection of previously unseen logs.

### 4.4 Improving Log Detection Efficiency

In large-scale log scenarios, earlier methods usually invoke the LLM for every single input log entry, which incurs extremely high time costs. Because the vol-

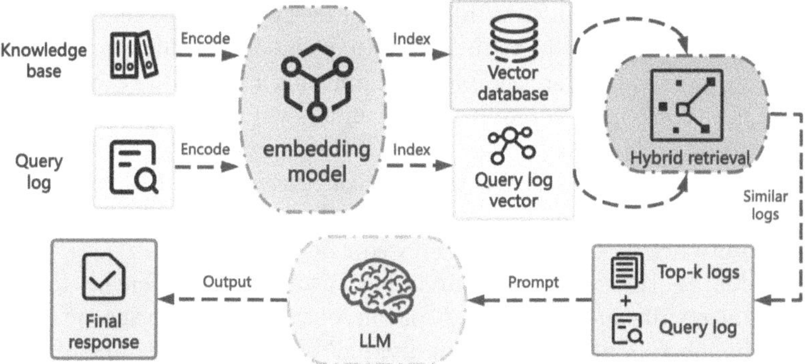


**Fig. 3.** Retrieval-Augmented Generation pipeline for logs.

ume of log data is huge, each call to the LLM requires not only knowledge-base retrieval but also a complex inference process, making log retrieval and detection highly inefficient. To solve this key problem, we propose the following optimization methods for detection efficiency, aiming to markedly improve log processing speed.

**Batch Processing.** To alleviate the overhead of repeatedly invoking the LLM during inference, we propose a prompt-based batch log–detection strategy. The method concatenates multiple log entries into a single API request and enforces both input and output formats through explicit templates. Concretely, the input-control function $F_{\text{in}}(X)$ merges $N$ log entries $X = \{x_1, \ldots, x_N\}$ into a unified request and appends the terminator token "End of log list." Formally, it is defined as follows:

$$F_{\text{in}}(X) = \texttt{There are } N \texttt{ logs:\textbackslash n } x_1\texttt{\textbackslash n } x_2\texttt{\textbackslash n } \ldots\texttt{\textbackslash n } x_N\texttt{\textbackslash n} \tag{6}$$

Accordingly, the output-control function $F_{\text{out}}(Y)$ forces the model to answer the question in a strictly aligned format, as follows:

$$F_{\text{out}}(Y) = \texttt{Organize answer as follows:\textbackslash n } y_1\texttt{\textbackslash n } y_2\texttt{\textbackslash n } \ldots\texttt{\textbackslash n } y_N\texttt{\textbackslash n} \tag{7}$$

Here, $Y = \{\text{Normal}, \text{Abnormal}\}$ and $y_i \in Y$. This design guarantees a one-to-one mapping between each log entry and its corresponding prediction, while allowing a large batch of logs to be processed in a single request. Consequently, network round-trip latency is reduced, and detection throughput is substantially improved.

**Cache-Driven Inference Acceleration.** We observe that the incoming log stream contains a large number of high-frequency duplicate entries. Performing full knowledge retrieval and LLM inference for every entry therefore incurs avoidable latency. To mitigate this, we introduce a cache-driven inference acceleration strategy. Specifically, the detection agent maintains a key-value cache that stores ⟨*log message*, *detection outcome*⟩ pairs. When a new log arrives, Detection Agent first performs an $O(1)$ lookup in the cache: if the entry is found, the cached result is returned immediately, bypassing both vector retrieval and LLM inference; otherwise, the standard pipeline is executed, and the newly generated ⟨*log*, *outcome*⟩ pair is written back to the cache for subsequent reuse.

We evaluated the combined batch log inspection and cache mechanism. Experimental results indicate a 38.7-fold acceleration in average retrieval time per log, reducing the latency for an individual entry to 0.057 s and significantly mitigating the throughput bottleneck associated with large-scale log processing.

### 4.5 Interpretable APT Detection

Within APT-Agent, the Interpreter Agent is charged with providing professional and trustworthy interpretations of detection results. By integrating a long-term memory module and a dynamic tool-invocation mechanism, the Interpreter Agent significantly improves both the interpretability of APT detection and the decision support offered for subsequent attack investigations.

**Long-Term Memory Retrieval.** Conventional conversational LLMs rely only on short-term context, making it hard to meet traceability requirements that span different time windows and scenarios. To overcome this limitation, we introduce a long-term memory module that logs prior decisions, alert contexts, and mitigation actions, giving the agent richer and more reliable information for explaining its results. This long-term memory is especially valuable for APTs, stealthy, persistent threats that unfold over extended periods. By retrieving historical attack patterns and response records, the module helps security analysts or automated detection systems quickly pinpoint the attack source, reconstruct the kill chain, and formulate effective response strategies.

The long-term memory, composed of the agent's past decisions and contextual information [27,28], is intended to retrieve task-relevant knowledge from stored memories and supply the Interpreter Agent with evidence for decision-making. At time step $t$, we collect the most recent $l$ memories $\{M_{t-1}, \ldots, M_{t-l}\}$ and match them against the current input context $c_t$. The relevance score is then computed by combining a time-decay weighting with cosine similarity. The exact formulation is as follows:

$$\underset{j}{\text{argmax}}\Big[\lambda_1\, r(t, t_j) + \lambda_2\, \text{cosim}\big(\mathcal{E}(c_t), \mathcal{E}(M_j)\big)\Big] \tag{8}$$

Here, $\mathcal{E}(\cdot)$ denotes the encoder, $r(t, t_j) = 1 - \dfrac{t - t_j}{\max_k(t - t_k)}$ is the recency score of a memory, and the coefficient $\lambda$ balances recency and relevance. The top-$k$ memories with the highest scores are injected into the LLM prompt as auxiliary context, providing factual support for explanation and investigation. By jointly considering temporal recency and semantic relevance during retrieval, APT-Agent can effectively cope with the continuously evolving nature of intrusive data. In our experiments, we retrieve the top-3 relevant long-term memory examples and balance recency and content similarity in Eq. 8 by setting $\lambda_1 = 0.4$ and $\lambda_2 = 0.6$.

**Tool Invocation and Domain-Specific Knowledge Base.** Beyond its internal memory, the Interpreter Agent can invoke external tools, enabling it to query outside data sources and further expand its knowledge horizon. During task execution, the agent may call a web Search API to scour the Internet, ensuring that its explanations remain up-to-date and authoritative. In addition, we have collected a large corpus of APT-related research papers and cyber threat intelligence (CTI) reports, segmented and vectorized them, and built a domain-specific knowledge base that supplies the LLM with specialized, trustworthy information. The detailed procedure of RAG is similar to that depicted in Fig. 3.

Benefiting from the dual enhancement of memory and tool usage—and aided by log exemplars retrieved from the log knowledge base during the detection stage—the Interpreter Agent can deliver reliable, professional, and effective explanations. This markedly improves the interpretability of APT detection and provides security analysts with dependable decision support.

## 5 Evaluation

In this section, we first describe the experimental setup and then validate the effectiveness of the proposed method through extensive experiments. We further assess its training efficiency and performance, followed by ablation studies to analyze the importance of each individual component.

### 5.1 Experimental Settings

**Dataset.** This study employs the publicly available Atlas dataset, a widely used benchmark in APT research. Atlas is constructed from detailed reports of real-world APT activities and contains ten different attack scenarios, including single-host attacks (S1–S4), multi-host attacks (M1–M6), and a variety of normal user behaviors. Specifically, scenarios S1–S4 represent single-host compromises, whereas M1–M6 simulate multi-host attacks that involve lateral movement, where the second host serves as the lateral-movement target. All attacks are executed in 32-bit Windows 7 virtual machines; each attack lasts for roughly one hour, followed by 24 h of continuous audit-log collection. In our experiments, 80% of the dataset is used to build the log knowledge base, while the remainder is reserved for testing. The portion employed to construct the knowledge base contains *only* benign samples.

**Implementation Details.** The underlying LLM for all experiments is GPT-4o. Log and text vectorization are performed with text-embedding-3-small, the most commonly used embedding model in the current GPT-4o ecosystem, both accessed via the OpenAI API. The model's initial temperature is set to 0.5, balancing richer token exploration (for stronger reasoning) against excessive randomness. All experiments run on a workstation equipped with an Intel Core i9 CPU, 64 GB of RAM, and an NVIDIA GeForce RTX 3080.

### 5.2 Main Results

**Detection Performance.** We evaluated APT-Agent's detection performance, as shown in Table 1. Across ten APT attack scenarios, APT-Agent achieved a precision of 98.62%, a recall of 97.62%, and an F1-score of 98.11%. We compared APT-Agent with the existing approaches in Table 2 and found that APT-Agent consistently outperforms them. This superiority is mainly attributable to two factors: (1) our preprocessing strategy fully exploits the richer, deeper semantic vectors of LLMs, giving log entries a more comprehensive and fine-grained representation; and (2) by integrating RAG, we harness the LLM's reasoning power while effectively mitigating its hallucination issue. These advantages enable APT-Agent to more accurately distinguish between normal and abnormal boundaries, significantly reducing false negatives and improving overall metrics.

**Table 1.** Detection performance of APT-Agent.

| ID | Symptom entity | Accuracy | Precision | Recall | F1-score |
|---|---|---|---|---|---|
| M-1 | Strategic web compromise | 99.90% | 99.15% | 96.71% | 97.91% |
| M-2 | Targeted GOV phishing | 99.69% | 99.76% | 97.79% | 98.76% |
| M-3 | Malvertising dominate | 99.88% | 99.07% | 97.09% | 98.07% |
| M-4 | Monero miner by Rig | 99.81% | 99.77% | 98.70% | 99.23% |
| M-5 | Pony campaign | 99.84% | 96.50% | 97.69% | 97.09% |
| M-6 | Spam campaign | 99.77% | 97.35% | 96.31% | 96.83% |
| S-1 | Strategic web compromise | 99.74% | 99.10% | 96.11% | 97.58% |
| S-2 | Malvertising dominate | 99.83% | 99.78% | 97.90% | 98.83% |
| S-3 | Spam campaign | 99.72% | 96.86% | 98.30% | 97.57% |
| S-4 | Pony campaign | 99.45% | 98.85% | 99.61% | 99.23% |
| **Avg.** | – | 99.76% | 98.62% | 97.62% | 98.11% |

**Practical Utility of APT-Agent's Interpretability.** The insufficient interpretability of existing methods is a major pain point in real-world enterprise applications of APT detection. To verify how effectively our approach improves interpretability in APT detection scenarios, we adopted the methodology of

**Table 2.** Comparison of APT-Agent with state-of-the-art methods.

| Method | Supervision | Precision | Recall | F1-score |
|---|---|---|---|---|
| DeepLog [6] | Supervised | 78.79% | 63.06% | 57.35% |
| Deepro [29] | Supervised | 92.55% | 89.68% | 90.61% |
| LogBert [23] | Self-supervised | 73.29% | 52.24% | 60.94% |
| Airtag [14] | Unsupervised | 59.29% | 96.72% | 73.56% |
| Logprompt [30] | Supervised | 83.86% | 88.68% | 86.30% |
| APT-Agent | Unsupervised | **98.62%** | **97.62%** | **98.11%** |

Ahmed et al. [31] and devised an evaluation framework with two dimensions—usefulness and readability (Table 3). We randomly selected 100 log entries and their corresponding model outputs, then asked five experts with extensive security-operations experience to score them on a 1–5 Likert scale. Usefulness measures how helpful the explanation is to actual analysis work in terms of detail, specificity, relevance, and logical coherence; readability focuses on grammar, clarity of expression, and professionalism. For each reviewer we recorded two indicators: the average score across all samples and the High Interpretability Proportion (HIP), defined as the percentage of samples with scores >4.

**Table 3.** Human scoring criteria for evaluating the interpretability of APT-Agent.

| Scores | Usefulness | Readability |
|---|---|---|
| 1 | Only states the predicted label; no reason for the anomaly. | Rife with grammatical errors and opaque fragments, hard to read. |
| 2 | Reasons given are irrelevant or contradict the facts. | Mostly clear, yet obvious grammar faults and vague phrases persist. |
| 3 | Supports the prediction but remains vague and short on detail. | Minor grammatical slips; some terms could be sharper. |
| 4 | Provides a focused explanation helping engineers filter false positives and dig deeper. | Clear, well-structured prose; aside from a few polishable terms, it flows smoothly. |
| 5 | Provides a thorough, relevant rationale, helping engineers filter false alarms and trace root causes. | Detailed, error-free, and professionally written for security. |

Experimental results (Table 4) show that all five reviewers gave average scores above 4 for both usefulness and readability, and the mean HIP exceeded 80%. This indicates that industry experts find most of our generated explanations helpful for understanding detection results and pinpointing issues while remaining easy to read, demonstrating that APT-Agent's interpretability is of significant practical value for enterprise applications.

**Table 4.** Human evaluation results.

| Raters | Usefulness | | Readability | |
|---|---|---|---|---|
| | Mean | HIP | Mean | HIP |
| R1 | 4.25 | 78.00% | 4.65 | 93.00% |
| R2 | 4.30 | 82.00% | 4.72 | 94.00% |
| R3 | 4.10 | 89.00% | 4.15 | 96.00% |
| R4 | 4.22 | 75.00% | 4.70 | 98.00% |
| R5 | 4.42 | 84.00% | 4.75 | 97.00% |
| **Avg.** | 4.26 | 81.60% | 4.60 | 95.60% |

**Efficiency Analysis.** Compared with existing APT detection approaches, APT-Agent offers pronounced advantages in both efficiency and resource consumption. First, APT-Agent entirely dispenses with provenance graph construction and offline model training. Contemporary deep-learning methods [8,9] require several hours to more than a full day of training even on small datasets, and the time and memory costs grow even more rapidly for the much larger data volumes typical of enterprise environments. In contrast, APT-Agent eliminates offline training and graph construction altogether, providing ready-to-use deployment with minimal offline cost. Second, APT-Agent is training-free, and its inference phase only involves invoking the OpenAI API. As a result, it can run on CPU with a peak memory footprint of just 90.4 MB. Its requirements for both GPU and system memory are therefore much lower than those of existing deep-learning-based APT detection methods, enabling lightweight deployment on laptops and even edge devices and making APT detection feasible for individuals and small enterprises. Moreover, the RAG knowledge base can be updated in real time, enabling rapid adaptation to attackers' evolving tactics and preventing the significant losses caused by detection lag.

### 5.3 Ablation Study

We evaluated APT-Agent in a wider range of scenarios and examined the factors that might influence its performance.

**Impact of RAG on Detection Performance.** To quantitatively assess how the RAG module affects detection performance, we set up a controlled experiment. In the complete configuration (with RAG), our method first builds a log knowledge base; during detection, it retrieves similar logs, merges them, and feeds the resulting prompt to the LLM for inference. In the control group (no RAG), the retrieval step is omitted—the LLM receives only the log to be analyzed along with a fixed task prompt and relies solely on its own knowledge for inference.

The results are summarized in Table 5. With RAG enabled, the model achieves a precision of 98.62%, a recall of 97.62%, and an F1-score of 98.11%.

**Table 5.** Impact of the RAG on detection performance of APT-Agent.

| Methods | Accuracy | Precision | Recall | F1-score |
|---|---|---|---|---|
| APT-Agent no RAG | 92.09% | 52.48% | 75.18% | 61.82% |
| APT-Agent with RAG | **99.76%** | **98.62%** | **97.62%** | **98.11%** |
| Improvement $\Delta$ | **+7.67%** | **+46.14%** | **+22.44%** | **+36.29%** |

Relative to the configuration without RAG, these metrics improve by 46.14%, 22.44%, and 36.29%, respectively. By supplying similar logs, the RAG module fills knowledge gaps in the LLM and effectively mitigates hallucinations, markedly increasing both precision and recall in anomaly detection and demonstrating its effectiveness.

**Impact of Data Preprocessing.** To quantitatively evaluate the impact of our log-normalization and domain-specific tokenization preprocessing pipeline on detection performance, we conducted a controlled experiment in which all other settings were kept identical. As shown in Table 6, applying our preprocessing yields improvements of 14.5%, 11.93%, and 13.19% in precision, recall, and F1-score, respectively. These findings indicate that the proposed preprocessing method effectively reduces the noise caused by out-of-vocabulary (OOV) tokens in the logs and significantly enhances the model's overall detection performance and generalization capability.

**Table 6.** Impact of the data preprocessing of APT-Agent.

| Method | Accuracy | Precision | Recall | F1-score |
|---|---|---|---|---|
| APT-Agent no Preprocessing | 98.48% | 84.12% | 85.69% | 84.92% |
| APT-Agent with Preprocessing | **99.76%** | **98.62%** | **97.62%** | **98.11%** |
| Improvement $\Delta$ | **+1.28%** | **+14.50%** | **+11.93%** | **+13.19%** |

**Impact of Cache and Batch Processing.** To quantify the impact of the cache mechanism and batch detection on efficiency, we compared detection times of the Detection Agent under three configurations: no cache and no batching (baseline), cache enabled only (with cache), and both cache and batching enabled (with cache + batching). The experimental results are presented in Table 7.

Enabling the cache mechanism reduced the average detection time per log entry to only 23.7% of the original value, shrinking the average time from 2.225 s to 0.529 s. After further introducing the batch detection strategy, the detection time dropped to 0.057 s, yielding an overall speed-up of roughly 39×. These results indicate that our cache mechanism and batch detection strategy markedly

**Table 7.** Impact of the cache and batching on inference time.

| Methods | Time | Speed - up |
|---|---|---|
| Baseline | 2.225 s | 1× |
| APT-Agent with Cache | 0.529 s | 4.2× |
| APT-Agent with Cache + Batching | **0.057 s** | **38.7**× |

decrease the number of model–inference calls, respond rapidly to highly repetitive logs, and avoid a large volume of redundant LLM invocations. Hence, the cache mechanism proposed in this work is a key component for ensuring detection efficiency.

It should be noted that the improvement from 0.529 s to 0.057 s is observed for a single LLM API endpoint. If $n$ LLM endpoints are invoked in parallel, the overall inference latency can theoretically converge further as $O(1/n)$ and approach the lower bound imposed by the network round-trip time. Moreover, because only lightweight routing and result aggregation are performed locally, computational overhead scarcely increases. The extremely low resource consumption and excellent processing efficiency make APT-Agent a viable choice for individual users and small businesses.

**Impact of Prompt Design.** During our experiments, we found that format constraints within the prompt are critical to the usability of LLM-based detection. In the absence of an explicit output template, the model is prone to returning results with inconsistent formats or irrelevant information, leading to parsing failures. Consequently, we designed two control functions to standardize the answer format for each input log. With all other factors held constant, introducing this format constraint increased the parsing success rate of structured outputs from 82.32% to 99.98% (Table 8). This confirms that well-designed prompts can virtually eliminate misclassifications caused by output inconsistencies.

**Table 8.** Impact of format constraints on parsing success.

| Prompt Setting | Parsing Rate | $\Delta$ Improvement |
|---|---|---|
| No-control prompt | 82.32% | — |
| Format-control prompt | **99.98%** | **+17.66%** |

### 5.4 Conclusion

We present APT-Agent, the first training-free, unsupervised LLM-based multi-agent framework for automated and interpretable APT detection. A dispatcher agent, a RAG-enhanced detection agent, and a long-term memory interpreter agent work in concert to deliver fine-grained anomaly detection and human-readable reasoning without any offline training or provenance graphs. We evaluated APT-Agent on ten attack scenarios, and the results show that it delivers superior detection performance, and significantly outperforms existing state-of-the-art methods in both resource use and efficiency.

## References


1. Alshamrani, A., Myneni, S., Chowdhary, A., Huang, D.: A survey on advanced persistent threats: techniques, solutions, challenges, and research opportunities. IEEE Commun. Surv. Tut. **21**(2), 1851–1877 (2019)
2. Milajerdi, S.M., Gjomemo, R., Eshete, B., Sekar, R., Venkatakrishnan, V.: HOLMES: real-time apt detection through correlation of suspicious information flows. In: 2019 IEEE Symposium on Security and Privacy (SP), pp. 1137–1152. IEEE (2019)
3. Hossain, M.N., et al.: SLEUTH: real-time attack scenario reconstruction from cots audit data. In: 26th USENIX Security Symposium (USENIX Security 17), pp. 487–504 (2017)
4. Hassan, W.U., Bates, A., Marino, D.: Tactical provenance analysis for endpoint detection and response systems. In: 2020 IEEE Symposium on Security and Privacy (SP), pp. 1172–1189. IEEE (2020)
5. Milajerdi, S.M., Eshete, B., Gjomemo, R., Venkatakrishnan, V.: POIROT: aligning attack behavior with kernel audit records for cyber threat hunting. In: Proceedings of the 2019 ACM SIGSAC Conference on Computer and Communications Security, pp. 1795–1812 (2019)
6. Du, M., Li, F., Zheng, G., Srikumar, V.: DeepLog: anomaly detection and diagnosis from system logs through deep learning. In: Proceedings of the 2017 ACM SIGSAC Conference on Computer and Communications Security, pp. 1285–1298 (2017)
7. Han, X., Pasquier, T., Bates, A., Mickens, J., Seltzer, M.: UNICORN: runtime provenance-based detector for advanced persistent threats. arXiv preprint arXiv:2001.01525 (2020)
8. Alsaheel, A., et al.: ATLAS: a sequence-based learning approach for attack investigation. In: 30th USENIX Security Symposium (USENIX Security 21), pp. 3005–3022 (2021)
9. Zengy, J., et al.: SHADEWATCHER: recommendation-guided cyber threat analysis using system audit records. In: 2022 IEEE Symposium on Security and Privacy (SP), pp. 489–506. IEEE (2022)
10. Wang, S.: threaTrace: detecting and tracing host-based threats in node level through provenance graph learning. IEEE Trans. Inf. Forensics Secur. **17**, 3972–3987 (2022)
11. Liu, F., Wen, Y., Zhang, D., Jiang, X., Xing, X., Meng, D.: Log2vec: a heterogeneous graph embedding based approach for detecting cyber threats within enterprise. In: Proceedings of the 2019 ACM SIGSAC Conference on Computer and Communications Security, pp. 1777–1794 (2019)

12. Li, Z., Cheng, X., Sun, L., Zhang, J., Chen, B.: A hierarchical approach for advanced persistent threat detection with attention-based graph neural networks. Secur. Commun. Netw. **2021**(1), 9961342 (2021)
13. Kapoor, M., Melton, J., Ridenhour, M., Krishnan, S., Moyer, T.: PROV-GEM: automated provenance analysis framework using graph embeddings. In: 2021 20th IEEE International Conference on Machine Learning and Applications (ICMLA), pp. 1720–1727. IEEE (2021)
14. Ding, H., Zhai, J., Nan, Y., Ma, S.: AIRTAG: towards automated attack investigation by unsupervised learning with log texts. In: 32nd USENIX Security Symposium (USENIX Security 23), pp. 373–390 (2023)
15. Xu, Z., Fang, P., Liu, C., Xiao, X., Wen, Y., Meng, D.: DEPCOMM: graph summarization on system audit logs for attack investigation. In: 2022 IEEE Symposium on Security and Privacy (SP), pp. 540–557. IEEE (2022)
16. Rehman, M.U., Ahmadi, H., Hassan, W.U.: Flash: a comprehensive approach to intrusion detection via provenance graph representation learning. In: 2024 IEEE Symposium on Security and Privacy (SP), pp. 3552–3570. IEEE (2024)
17. Sharif, M., et al.: DrSec: flexible distributed representations for efficient endpoint security. In: 2024 IEEE Symposium on Security and Privacy (SP), pp. 3609–3624. IEEE (2024)
18. Jia, Z., Xiong, Y., Nan, Y., Zhang, Y., Zhao, J., Wen, M.: MAGIC: detecting advanced persistent threats via masked graph representation learning. In: 33rd USENIX Security Symposium (USENIX Security 24), pp. 5197–5214 (2024)
19. Huang, L., et al.: A survey on hallucination in large language models: principles, taxonomy, challenges, and open questions. ACM Trans. Inf. Syst. **43**(2), 1–55 (2025)
20. Manevitz, L.M., Yousef, M.: One-class SVMs for document classification. J. Mach. Learn. Res. **2**, 139–154 (2001)
21. Breunig, M.M., Kriegel, H.P., Ng, R.T., Sander, J.: LOF: identifying density-based local outliers. In: Proceedings of the 2000 ACM SIGMOD International Conference on Management of Data, pp. 93–104 (2000)
22. Liu, F.T., Ting, K.M., Zhou, Z.H.: Isolation forest. In: 2008 Eighth IEEE International Conference on Data Mining, pp. 413–422. IEEE (2008)
23. Guo, H., Yuan, S., Wu, X.: LogBERT: log anomaly detection via BERT. In: 2021 International Joint Conference on Neural Networks (IJCNN), pp. 1–8. IEEE (2021)
24. Beijering, K., Gooskens, C., Heeringa, W.: Predicting intelligibility and perceived linguistic distance by means of the Levenshtein algorithm. Linguist. Netherlands **25**(1), 13–24 (2008)
25. Sparck Jones, K.: A statistical interpretation of term specificity and its application in retrieval. J. Documentation **28**(1), 11–21 (1972)
26. Robertson, S., Zaragoza, H., et al.: The probabilistic relevance framework: BM25 and beyond. Found. Trends Inf. Retrieval **3**(4), 333–389 (2009)
27. Wang, W., et al.: Augmenting language models with long-term memory. Adv. Neural. Inf. Process. Syst. **36**, 74530–74543 (2023)
28. Zhong, W., Guo, L., Gao, Q., Ye, H., Wang, Y.: MemoryBank: enhancing large language models with long-term memory. In: Proceedings of the AAAI Conference on Artificial Intelligence, vol. 38, pp. 19724–19731 (2024)
29. Yan, N., et al.: Deepro: Provenance-based APT campaigns detection via GNN. In: 2022 IEEE International Conference on Trust, Security and Privacy in Computing and Communications (TrustCom), pp. 747–758. IEEE (2022)

30. Liu, Y., Tao, S., Meng, W., Yao, F., Zhao, X., Yang, H.: LogPrompt: prompt engineering towards zero-shot and interpretable log analysis. In: Proceedings of the 2024 IEEE/ACM 46th International Conference on Software Engineering: Companion Proceedings, pp. 364–365 (2024)
31. Ahmed, T., Ghosh, S., Bansal, C., Zimmermann, T., Zhang, X., Rajmohan, S.: Recommending root-cause and mitigation steps for cloud incidents using large language models. In: 2023 IEEE/ACM 45th International Conference on Software Engineering (ICSE), pp. 1737–1749. IEEE (2023)

# Digital Evidence Management, Blockchain, and Privacy: Addressing Blockchain Forensics, Data Provenance, and Privacy-Preserving Computation

# Blockchain-Based vs. SQL Database Systems for Digital Twin Evidence Management: A Comparative Forensic Analysis

Boyd Franken, Hong-Hanh Nguyen-Le, and Nhien-An Le-Khac(✉)

University College Dublin, Dublin, Ireland
{boyd.franken,hong-hanh.nguyen-le}@ucdconnect.ie, an.lekhac@ucd.ie

**Abstract.** Digital forensics faces unprecedented challenges with the emergence of digital twins and metaverse technologies. This paper presents the first comparative analysis between blockchain-based and traditional database systems for managing digital twin evidence in forensic investigations. We conducted controlled experiments comparing the Ethereum blockchain with IPFS storage against traditional SQL databases for digital twin evidence management. Our findings reveal that while blockchain provides superior data integrity and immutability, crucial for forensic applications, traditional databases offer better performance consistency. The blockchain implementation showed faster average storage times but higher variability in retrieval operations. Both systems maintained forensic integrity through hash verification, though blockchain's immutable nature provides additional security guarantees essential for legal proceedings. This research contributes to the development of robust digital forensic methodologies for emerging technologies in the metaverse era.

**Keywords:** Blockchain · Digital Twins · Evidence Management · Digital Forensics

## 1 Introduction

The rapid evolution of digital twins and blockchain technologies has fundamentally transformed the landscape of criminal investigations and digital forensics. Digital twins [20], sophisticated virtual replicas of physical entities, processes, or systems, enable comprehensive modeling and simulation of real-world scenarios through advanced sensor data integration and computational analysis. Blockchain technology [28] is a distributed ledger that maintains cryptographically secured and immutable transaction records across a decentralized network. The emergence of these technologies [23] presents a powerful tool for managing digital evidence and maintaining evidence integrity.

In digital forensic contexts, digital twins can serve as comprehensive evidence repositories that capture not only static data but also dynamic interactions and


K.-K. R. Choo et al. (Eds.): ICDF2C 2025, LNICST 686, pp. 129–143, 2026.
https://doi.org/10.1007/978-3-032-22545-0_8

environmental conditions [10]. This capability has potential in legal proceedings, which can be used in the courtroom as a copy of the physical evidence and the possibility of making detailed examinations of complex scenarios. The integration of blockchain technology with digital twins promises to enhance evidence handling by providing a decentralized, immutable, and transparent ledger for recording interactions and metadata associated with digital twin evidence. Particularly, blockchain technology enables digital evidence to be encrypted and stored online with metadata in a private manner and avoid unauthorized access [23,26]. However, the practical performance implications of using blockchain-based systems for managing potentially large and complex digital twin data, compared to traditional database systems [22], remain underexplored in digital forensic contexts.

This paper addresses this gap by conducting a comparative analysis of blockchain-based versus traditional SQL database systems for the storage and retrieval of digital twin evidence. To achieve this, we develop two parallel environments: a private Ethereum blockchain [11] with InterPlanetary File System (IPFS) storage [5] versus a traditional MySQL database system. We evaluate the efficiency, which is defined as the time taken for storage (POST) and retrieval (GET) operations, for digital twins of varying sizes (i.e., ranging from 1MB to 200MB) across both systems. Furthermore, we assessed the forensic utility of each approach, primarily by verifying the integrity of the evidence via hash value comparisons. A web interface using the A-Frame framework is also developed to enable interactive 3D visualization of digital twin evidence, supporting forensic analysis workflows. In experiments, we employ Cohen's d [13] for effect size determination and linear regression for scalability assessment.

**Contribution.** Our contributions are summarized as follows:

- **A quantitative performance comparison**: We first provide a quantitative comparison of blockchain-based and traditional SQL database systems, specifically for digital twin evidence management in forensic applications.
- **An assessment of forensic integrity mechanisms**: We evaluate the forensic soundness of both systems by implementing and verifying hash-based integrity checks. This includes leveraging the immutable nature of blockchain for recording IPFS hashes and comparing them with hash storage and verification in a SQL database.
- **Implementation of experimental frameworks**: We provide a detailed design and implementation of two controlled experimental environments, including the integration of Ethereum, Solidity smart contracts, IPFS, a MySQL database, and a unified Python-based web application featuring an A-Frame interface for interaction and 3D visualization.
- **An analysis of scalability and performance-integrity trade-offs**: We offer insights into the scalability implications and performance-integrity trade-offs inherent in each system. This provides guidelines for practitioners and researchers when selecting or designing systems for digital twin evidence management.

# 2 Related Works

## 2.1 Blockchain in Digital Forensics

Recent research has extensively explored blockchain's potential for enhancing digital forensics capabilities. Li et al. [19] developed a blockchain-based framework for Internet-of-Things (IoT) forensics, namely IoT-fog-cloud (IoTFC), which addresses challenges of evidence authenticity and traceability in dynamic environments. With this framework, the transparent audit trails are provided to enhance trust between investigative entities. Gopalan et al. [14] demonstrated how the decentralized and tamper-proof nature of blockchain can be adopted to assure maintenance of evidence integrity and purity. Their proposed blockchain-based system hashes the data and stores it in blocks, ensuring that digital evidence is kept free from unauthorized changes or deletions. Another study has provided a detailed analysis of how blockchain technology can be applied to improve control over the chain of custody in forensic science, particularly physical evidence [9]. Alqahtany and Syed et al. [7] introduced ForensicTrans-Monitor, a comprehensive blockchain approach for forensic transaction and evidence preservation. Their system leverages blockchain's immutability to ensure evidence integrity while providing automated verification mechanisms through smart contracts. This means that all activities within the forensic process are recorded as verifiable transactions on the blockchain.

The application of blockchain for provenance management has shown promising results in scientific data management. Ramachandran and Kantarcioglu et [21] developed DataProv, which uses blockchain's distributed nature to prevent unauthorized modifications while implementing smart contracts for automated verification. Their system demonstrated effectiveness in tracking clinical drug trials and agricultural supply chains, highlighting blockchain's versatility in maintaining data integrity across various domains.

## 2.2 Applications of Digital Twins

Digital twins have emerged as powerful tools for industrial IoTs. Attaran et al. [8] explored the relationship between digital twins and industrial IoT. The article identifies some applications of digital twins in manufacturing by developing exact replicas of physical systems, which can be used to monitor them in real-time and also for predictive maintenance. Artificial intelligence (AI) algorithms have been leveraged to improve the prediction or automation capabilities of the digital twins. A modular approach is introduced by Zhang et al. [27] proposed an intelligent multi-objective optimization algorithm which allows the digital twin to not only simulate the production line but also to optimize its design and dynamic execution. Sun et al. [24] utilized models like CNNs, RNNs, and PCNNs to process and structure complex, multi-source data, including images, noise, and 3D point clouds from the assembly process. This approach helps enhance the assembly-commissioning process and autonomous decision-making.

The integration of digital twins with cyber-physical-social systems has shown particular promise for security applications. Han et al. [15] introduced ParaDefender, a scenario-driven parallel architecture that uses digital twins to enhance metaverse security. Their system demonstrates how digital twins can be used for a real-world use case.

### 2.3 Metaverse Digital Forensics

The emergence of metaverse technologies has created new forensic challenges requiring specialized tools and methodologies. Kim et al. [18] outlined approaches for extracting and analyzing data from Head-Mounted Displays (HMDs). This work highlights the unique aspects of metaverse forensics where evidence exists both on physical devices and within virtual environments. Huynh-The et al. [17] examined blockchain's role in metaverse security, emphasizing how distributed ledgers can support data integrity and non-repudiation in virtual environments. Their research identifies the convergence of Virtual Reality (VR) and blockchain technologies as creating new dimensions for forensic investigations, where digital interactions must be verifiable and auditable.

**Research Gaps Identified from Previous Works.** Research gaps identified in the literature include (i) the lack of comprehensive performance comparisons between blockchain and traditional database systems for forensic applications, (ii) limited evaluation of hybrid storage approaches, and (iii) insufficient investigation of blockchain's impact on forensic workflow efficiency.

## 3 Problem Statement and Forensic Approach

### 3.1 Motivations

Current evidence management systems in digital forensics rely heavily on centralized databases and traditional storage architectures that present significant vulnerabilities in terms of data integrity, chain of custody maintenance, and cross-jurisdictional evidence sharing. The centralized nature of these systems requires complex trust relationships between investigating agencies, particularly in international collaborations where evidence authenticity and tamper-proofing become critical legal considerations [16]. The integration of blockchain technology with digital twins in legal spheres represents opportunities:

- A detailed and accurate representation of crime scenes or incidents can be done by digital twins, which will enable investigators to collect comprehensive forensic data. VR equipment can be used for immersive analysis, allowing forensic experts to walk through virtual environments with all the tiny details.
- The hash of digital twins is stored on a private Ethereum blockchain while the actual digital twin is stored on the IPFS network. This improves the security and integrity of the data because Blockchain will ensure that evidence has not been tampered with, while IPFS guarantees efficient as well as secure storage and retrieval of these files.
- Blockchain technology guarantees transparency in recording all transactions and changes that digital twins undergo.

### 3.2 Forensic Methodology

This work investigates the efficacy of blockchain-based and traditional SQL database systems in managing digital twin models through a quantitative comparative analysis, focusing on the efficiency of both systems. To achieve this analysis, two parallel controlled environments are implemented to systematically assess the performance, integrity, and forensic utility of each approach.

In our methodology, digital twins are treated as forensic artifacts that may represent:

- Crime scene reconstructions with spatial and temporal data
- 3D models of physical evidence (weapons, vehicles, or other objects)
- Environmental conditions and their evolution over time
- Virtual reconstructions of incidents based on multiple data sources

Each digital twin undergoes cryptographic hashing (MD5) upon submission to ensure integrity verification throughout the evidence lifecycle. The hash values are stored alongside the evidence in both systems, enabling forensic examiners to verify that digital twins have not been altered or corrupted during storage or transmission.

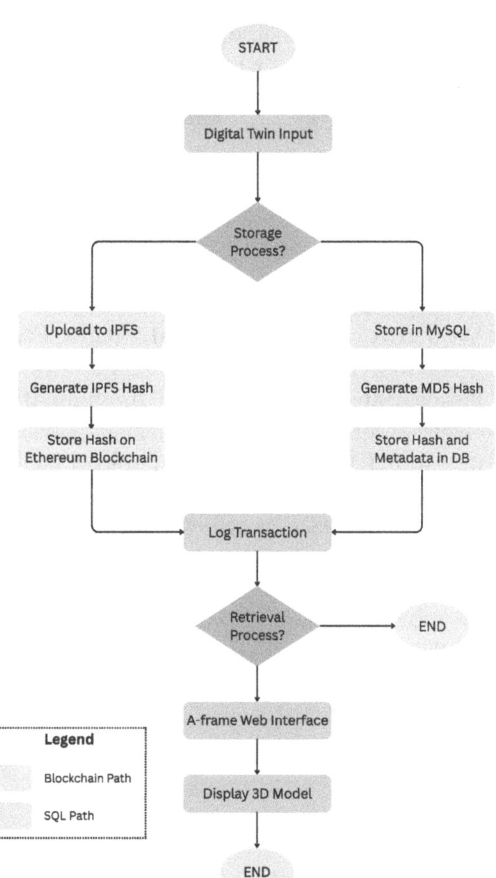


**Fig. 1.** Flow chart of adopted forensic approach.

**Controlled Environments Implementation.** We establish two distinct forensic evidence management systems:

**Blockchain-Based System:** A private Ethereum blockchain network [11] integrated with the InterPlanetary File System (IPFS) [5] for decentralized storage. Smart contracts, developed in Solidity [25], manage the interaction with the blockchain. The digital twin files are stored on the IPFS via the Pinata.cloud pinning service [6]. The core idea is to store the large digital twin files off-chain on IPFS and record only their immutable IPFS hash and associated metadata on the blockchain.

**Traditional SQL Database System:** A standard MySQL database is employed, which is hosted on the Aiven.com cloud service [2]. In this environment, digital twin files are stored directly as binary large objects (BLOBs) along with their associated metadata and MD5 hash values within the SQL database.

Both environments are accessed through a unified Python-based backend that standardizes the storage and retrieval operations, ensuring fair comparison between the two approaches.

**Storage and Retrieval Processes.** Figure 1 illustrates two primary processes of our forensic methodology.

**Storage Process (POST):** For the blockchain system, when digital evidence in the form of a digital twin is submitted to the system, it is uploaded to IPFS. The IPFS then returns a unique content identifier, which is then recorded on the Ethereum blockchain along with the file's MD5 hash through a smart contract transaction. Regarding the SQL system, the digital twin file is directly stored in the database along with its computed MD5 hash and associated metadata.

**Retrieval Process (GET):** This process is conducted when forensic investigators need to access evidence. For the blockchain system, the smart contract is queried using the block number to retrieve the IPFS hash, which is then used to fetch the digital twin from the IPFS network. In contrast, a direct database query is performed in the SQL system to retrieve the digital twin based on its unique identifier.

**Web Interface and Visualization Framework.** To facilitate forensic analysis and evidence examination, we develop a web-based interface using the A-Frame framework [1], which provides immersive 3D visualization capabilities essential for digital twin evidence analysis. There are two main purposes of this interface: (i) Investigators can upload digital twin models through a standardized web form, initiating the storage process in either the blockchain or SQL system; (ii) The interface provides an analysis environment for investigators to interact with 3D digital twin models in real-time, examine evidence from multiple angles, and compare evidence across different time periods or versions. Figure 2 illustrates the digital twin file shown on the web application.

The web application maintains system-agnostic functionality, seamlessly retrieving and displaying digital twins regardless of whether they are stored via blockchain/IPFS or traditional SQL database. Moreover, it also ensures consistent forensic analysis capabilities across both storage paradigms.

Fig. 2. An example of the retrieved digital twin in the web application.

# 4 Experiments

## 4.1 Tools

Tools used to build the blockchain-based system, the traditional SQL database system, and the A-frame webpage are summarized in Table 1.

## 4.2 Datasets

To conduct our analysis, we collect a dataset of digital twin models sourced from publicly available 3D model repositories. Because of the inherent sensitivity of actual case data, utilizing public sources provided an ethical means to acquire diverse models for testing. Our dataset consists of 10 distinct 3D models, selected to reflect potential digital twin evidence scenarios, such as vehicle reconstructions. These models are specifically selected to cover a range from 1MB to 200MB.

## 4.3 Configuration for Storage and Retrieval Operations

**Ethereum Blockchain Configuration:** The blockchain environment utilized a private Ethereum network (Ganache) with the following specifications:

**Table 1.** Summarization of tools used in our experiments.

| Tool | Category | Version | Role/Purpose in the Experiment |
|---|---|---|---|
| Ganache [3] | Blockchain environment | v2.7.1 | Served as the private blockchain system for controlled testing environment |
| Pinata [6] | Blockchain environment | API v1 | Decentralized IPFS file storage for digital twin models |
| Solidity [4] | Blockchain environment | v0.8.19 | Smart contract development for evidence management logic |
| MySQL | Database environment | v8.0 | Relational database for traditional evidence storage |
| Aiven [2] | Database environment | Custom | Cloud database hosting service |
| PyMySQL | Database environment | v1.0.3 | Python MySQL database connector |
| A-Frame | User interface and visualization | v1.5.0 | Web-based VR framework for 3D model visualization |
| Flask | User interface and visualization | v2.3.2 | Python web framework for application backend |
| HTML5/CSS3/ JavaScript | User interface and visualization | ES6+ | Frontend technologies for web interface |
| Python | Development and analysis tools | v3.9+ | Primary programming language for system implementation |
| SPSS | Development and analysis tools | v29.0 | Statistical analysis and hypothesis testing |

- Network ID: Private testnet for controlled experimentation.
- Smart contract deployment using Solidity for evidence management.
- IPFS integration through Pinata service (1GB free tier).
- Web3.py library for blockchain interaction.
- JSON configuration file containing blockchain URLs, contract addresses, and API credentials.

**SQL Database Configuration:** The SQL environment employed MySQL with the following setup:

- Aiven cloud hosting service (5 GB free tier). The configuration includes host address, port number, authentication credentials, and database name.
- Direct file storage with metadata tables.
- PyMySQL driver for database connectivity.
- Additional parameters such as character set (utf8mb4) and timeout values for connection, read, and write operations are set to 10 s each to ensure reliable database operations.

**Table 2.** Experimental variables and their characteristics.

| Variable | Type | Description | Range/Values |
|---|---|---|---|
| File size | Independent (Continuous) | Size of digital twin evidence files | 1–200 MB |
| Storage method | Independent (Categorical) | Type of storage system | Blockchain/IPFS, SQL |
| Internet speed | Independent (Continuous) | Network bandwidth | 100/100 Mbps |
| Execution time | Dependent | Time for POST/GET operations | Measured in seconds |
| Forensic integrity | Dependent | Hash verification success | Boolean (Pass/Fail) |

### 4.4 Key Variables

Table 2 summarizes the key variables in our experimental design. File size serves as an independent continuous variable ranging from 1 to 200 MB, representing various sizes of digital twin evidence files. Storage method is an independent categorical variable with two levels: blockchain with IPFS and traditional SQL database. Internet speed is a continuous independent variable, which is controlled at 100/100 Mbps to maintain consistent network conditions. Execution time, measured in seconds, serves as the primary dependent variable for both POST and GET operations. Forensic integrity is assessed as a binary dependent variable indicating successful hash verification.

### 4.5 Metrics for Evaluation

To evaluate the performance and forensic utility of both the blockchain-based and traditional SQL database systems for digital twin evidence management, we employ a set of quantitative and qualitative metrics.

**Efficiency Analysis.** The primary metric for efficiency is the execution time (in seconds) required for both storage (POST) and retrieval (GET) operations. For each transaction, we calculate the mean execution time:

$$\bar{T} = \frac{1}{n} \sum_{i=1}^{n} T_i, \tag{1}$$

where $n$ is the number of files and $T_i$ is the execution time for the $i$-th transaction: $T_i = T_{i_{\text{end}}} - T_{i_{\text{start}}}$.

To quantify the magnitude of the difference in performance between the two systems, we calculated Cohen's D [13], which is computed as follows:

$$D = \frac{\bar{T}_{\text{blockchain}} - \bar{T}_{\text{SQL}}}{\sigma_{\text{pooled}}}, \tag{2}$$

where $\bar{T}_{\text{blockchain}}$ and $\bar{T}_{\text{SQL}}$ are the means of execution time of blockchain-based and traditional SQL database systems, respectively; and $\sigma_{\text{pooled}}$ is the pooled standard deviation, which is computed as $\sigma_{\text{pooled}} = \frac{\sigma^2_{\text{blockchain}} + \sigma^2_{\text{SQL}}}{2}$. This effect size measure helps in understanding the practical significance of the observed differences beyond statistical significance.

**Scalability Analysis.** To assess how each system performs as the size of the digital twin files increases, we conducted a *linear regression analysis* [12]. This helps in understanding the relationship between file size (independent variable) and execution time (dependent variable). We fit separate regression models for each storage method and operation type. The general model is:

$$\text{ExecutionTime} = \beta_0 + \beta_1 \times \text{FileSize} + \epsilon, \tag{3}$$

where $\beta_0$ is the intercept, $\beta_1$ is the coefficient representing the change in time per unit increase in file size, and $\epsilon$ is the error term.

**Forensic Integrity Assessment.** Forensic integrity is evaluated as a binary outcome (Pass/Fail) based on hash value verification. Upon retrieval, the MD5 hash of the digital twin file is recalculated and compared against the hash value stored during the initial storage operation.

## 5 Description of Results

In this section, we present results and findings from our comparative experiments. We focus on the efficiency and forensic integrity of managing digital twin evidence using both the blockchain-based and traditional SQL database systems.

### 5.1 Descriptive Statistics

We conduct controlled experiments to analyze the execution times for storing and retrieving 10 digital twin models ($n = 10$) of varying sizes (i.e., ranging from 1MB to 200MB). The experimental results from both blockchain and traditional SQL database systems reveal significant performance differences across storage and retrieval operations. Table 3 presents the descriptive statistics for both storage

**Table 3.** Descriptive statistics of experimental results.

| Operation Type | Storage Method | Mean Time (s) | Std Dev (s) | Min Time (s) | Max Time (s) |
|---|---|---|---|---|---|
| Storage (POST) | Blockchain | 16.43 | 9.43 | 4.08 | 30.97 |
| Storage (POST) | SQL Database | 25.36 | 16.85 | 2.56 | 51.77 |
| Retrieval (GET) | Blockchain | 15.95 | 10.65 | 3.36 | 23.59 |
| Retrieval (GET) | SQL Database | 11.01 | 7.21 | 1.13 | 22.59 |

(POST) and retrieval (GET) operations across blockchain-based and traditional SQL database systems.

From Table 3, we can observe that blockchain systems achieved faster average performance for storage operations (16.43s vs 25.36s) while SQL database outperforms the blockchain system (11.01s vs 15.95s) in terms of retrieval operations.

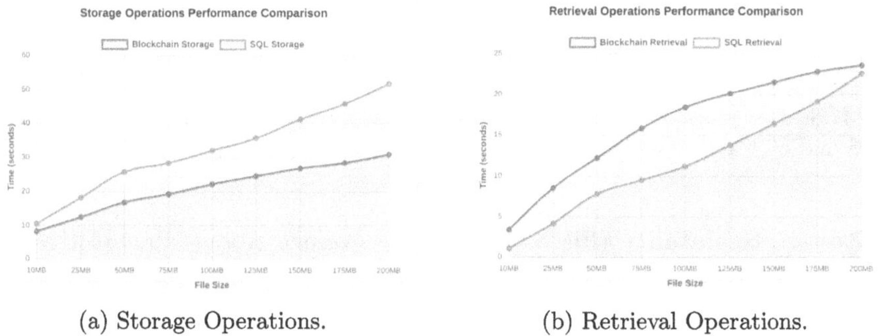


(a) Storage Operations.

(b) Retrieval Operations.

**Fig. 3.** Comparison of storage and retrieval operations of blockchain-based and SQL database systems.

## 5.2 Performance Analysis by File Size

We analyzed the execution times for storing and retrieving 10 digital twin models on two systems. Figure 3a illustrates the relationship between file size and storage execution time for both systems. The blockchain-based system demonstrates superior storage performance with 35% faster average times compared to SQL databases. This result suggests that the blockchain/IPFS hybrid architecture benefits from batch processing efficiencies and distributed storage mechanisms when handling larger files.

In contrast, regarding retrieval operations, Fig. 3b reveals that SQL databases maintain more consistent performance across varying file sizes, with 31% faster average times. However, when the file size increases to 200MB, the difference in retrieval execution time between the two systems becomes lower. This indicates that the blockchain-based system might be effective for larger files compared to the SQL database system.

## 5.3 Scalability Analysis

To understand how each storage system handles increasing data loads, we analyzed the relationship between digital twin file size and execution time using linear regression.

The regression analysis (illustrated in Fig. 4) reveals important scalability characteristics:

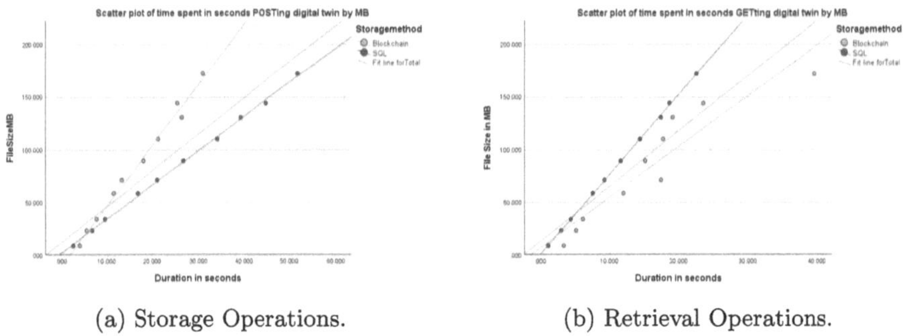


(a) Storage Operations.

(b) Retrieval Operations.

**Fig. 4.** Scatter plots of times spent for storage and retrieval operations of lockchain-based and SQL database systems.

- **Storage Scalability** (Fig. 4a): While the average storage time of the SQL database system is higher, the trend line shows a more linear increase in time with file size. Although exhibiting more variability, the trend line for blockchain storage is less steep than SQL's. This suggests that as file sizes grow, the increase in storage time is less pronounced for the blockchain system, implying potentially better scalability for storage operations.
- **Retrieval Scalability** (Fig. 4b): The trend line for SQL retrieval was less steep and more linear. This indicates that SQL retrieval times increase at a slower and more predictable rate as the file size grows, suggesting better scalability for retrieval operations. In contrast, the time required for retrieval operations of the blockchain system grows more rapidly with larger file sizes, indicating potential scalability challenges for handling bigger datasets during retrieval.

### 5.4 Forensic Integrity Analysis

We assess the data integrity of two systems by verifying hash values. During the evaluation, we compare the hash values stored in both systems against the original MD5 hashes generated when the data was first created. The result demonstrates that both systems successfully maintained forensic soundness, as all hash values correctly match the originals. This confirms that both systems can provide a verifiable record that the digital twin evidence is not altered. However, the inherent immutability and decentralized nature of the blockchain provide an additional layer of security and trust, which is particularly valuable for legal proceedings where proving non-tampering is essential.

## 6 Discussion of Results

Our comparative analysis between blockchain-based (Ethereum/IPFS) and traditional SQL database systems for managing digital twin evidence has revealed significant insights into their respective strengths and weaknesses within a digital forensics context. The results highlight a crucial trade-off between performance efficiency and the robustness of data integrity guarantees.

First, our experiments show that the blockchain-based system is faster for storing digital twin evidence, suggesting efficiency in handling large files. However, the SQL database system outperforms for the retrieval operation.

Second, the results indicate a scalability trade-off: SQL appears more scalable for consistent and efficient retrieval of digital twins, while the blockchain/IPFS approach shows promise for more scalable storage in this specific experiment, despite its inherent performance variability.

Crucially, while both systems maintain forensic integrity through hash verification, blockchain's inherent immutability and decentralization provide a significantly higher level of security. This is vital for legal proceedings where proving evidence has not been tampered with is essential.

Therefore, the choice depends on priorities. For rapid and consistent access, SQL remains strong. For cases demanding the highest level of verifiable integrity and trust, blockchain offers compelling advantages, despite its current performance overheads.

## 7 Conclusion

This work provides the first comparative analysis of blockchain-based and traditional database systems for digital twin evidence management in forensic contexts. Through controlled experiments, we evaluated performance based on storage (POST) and retrieval (GET) times for files ranging from 1 MB to 200 MB, alongside a crucial assessment of forensic integrity. Our findings underscore performance-integrity trade-offs: (i) The blockchain-based system is faster for the storage operation, while the SQL database system outperforms for the retrieval operation; and (ii) The inherent immutability and decentralized trust model of blockchain offer higher security guarantees. Future work should focus on optimizing blockchain performance and exploring hybrid models of blockchain and SQL database systems to harness the best of both paradigms.

**Acknowledgement.** This research is partially funded by UCD ASEADOS Lab and UCD School of Computer Science.

## References

1. A-Frame – Make WebVR — aframe.io. https://aframe.io/. Accessed 26 May 2025
2. Aiven - Your AI-ready Open Source Data Platform — aiven.io. https://aiven.io/. Accessed 26 May 2025
3. Ganache - Truffle Suite — archive.trufflesuite.com. https://archive.trufflesuite.com/ganache/. Accessed 26 May 2025

4. Introduction to Smart Contracts — Solidity 0.8.31 documentation — docs.soliditylang.org. https://docs.soliditylang.org/en/latest/introduction-to-smart-contracts.html. Accessed 26 May 2025
5. IPFS Documentation | IPFS Docs — docs.ipfs.tech. https://docs.ipfs.tech/. Accessed 25 May 2025
6. Pinning Service API - Pinata Docs — docs.pinata.cloud. https://docs.pinata.cloud/api-reference/pinning-service-api. Accessed 26 May 2025
7. Alqahtany, S.S., Syed, T.A.: ForensicTransMonitor: a comprehensive blockchain approach to reinvent digital forensics and evidence management. Information **15**(2), 109 (2024)
8. Attaran, S., Attaran, M., Celik, B.G.: Digital twins and industrial internet of things: uncovering operational intelligence in Industry 4.0. Decis. Anal. J. **10**, 100398 (2024)
9. Batista, D., et al.: Exploring blockchain technology for chain of custody control in physical evidence: a systematic literature review. J. Risk Financ. Manage. **16**(8), 360 (2023)
10. Becker, S., Fritzsch, T.H., Labuddc, D.: The role of a digital twin in supporting criminal investigations-a case report about a possible abuse. Forensic Sci. Med. Pathol., 1–10 (2024)
11. Buterin, V., et al.: Ethereum white paper. GitHub repository **1**(22-23), 5–7 (2013)
12. DeVore, C., Kaukis, N.: Linear regression analysis. Stat **3013**(11/16), 15 (2003)
13. Diener, M.J.: Cohen's d. In: The Corsini Encyclopedia of Psychology, p. 1 (2010)
14. Gopalan, S.H., Suba, S.A., Ashmithashree, C., Gayathri, A., Andrews, V.J.: Digital forensics using blockchain. Int. J. Recent Technol. Eng. **8**(2), 182–184 (2019)
15. Han, J., et al.: ParaDefender: a scenario-driven parallel system for defending metaverses. IEEE Trans. Syst. Man Cybern. Syst. **53**(4), 2118–2127 (2022)
16. Hofmeister, U., Martin, S.S., Villalobos, C., Padilla, J., Finegan, O.: The ICRC AM/PM database: challenges in forensic data management in the humanitarian sphere. Forensic Sci. Int. **279**, 1–7 (2017)
17. Huynh-The, T.: Blockchain for the metaverse: a review. Futur. Gener. Comput. Syst. **143**, 401–419 (2023)
18. Kim, D., Oh, S., Shon, T.: Digital forensic approaches for metaverse ecosystems. Forensic Sci. Int. Digit. Invest. **46**, 301608 (2023)
19. Li, S., Qin, T., Min, G.: Blockchain-based digital forensics investigation framework in the internet of things and social systems. IEEE Trans. Comput. Soc. Syst. **6**(6), 1433–1441 (2019)
20. Mihai, S.: Digital twins: A survey on enabling technologies, challenges, trends and future prospects. IEEE Commun. Surv. Tut. **24**(4), 2255–2291 (2022)
21. Ramachandran, A., Kantarcioglu, D.M.: Using blockchain and smart contracts for secure data provenance management. arXiv preprint arXiv:1709.10000 (2017)
22. Silva, Y.N., Almeida, I., Queiroz, M.: SQL: from traditional databases to Big Data. In: Proceedings of the 47th ACM Technical Symposium on Computing Science Education, pp. 413–418 (2016)
23. Suhail, S., Hussain, R., Jurdak, R., Oracevic, A., Salah, K., Hong, C.S., Matulevičius, R.: Blockchain-based digital twins: research trends, issues, and future challenges. ACM Comput. Surv. (CSUR) **54**(11s), 1–34 (2022)
24. Sun, X., Bao, J., Li, J., Zhang, Y., Liu, S., Zhou, B.: A digital twin-driven approach for the assembly-commissioning of high precision products. Robot. Comput. Integr. Manuf. **61**, 101839 (2020)

25. Wohrer, M., Zdun, U.: Smart contracts: security patterns in the Ethereum ecosystem and solidity. In: 2018 International Workshop on Blockchain Oriented Software Engineering (IWBOSE), pp. 2–8. IEEE (2018)
26. Yaqoob, I., Salah, K., Uddin, M., Jayaraman, R., Omar, M., Imran, M.: Blockchain for digital twins: recent advances and future research challenges. IEEE Netw. **34**(5), 290–298 (2020)
27. Zhang, H., Liu, Q., Chen, X., Zhang, D., Leng, J.: A digital twin-based approach for designing and multi-objective optimization of hollow glass production line. IEEE Access **5**, 26901–26911 (2017)
28. Zheng, Z., Xie, S., Dai, H.N., Chen, X., Wang, H.: Blockchain challenges and opportunities: a survey. Int. J. Web Grid Serv. **14**(4), 352–375 (2018)

# FAIR-MPC: Secure and Auditable SMPC for Anonymous Financial Collaboration

Tao Bai, Yuanqing Feng, Zhi Lu, and Songfeng Lu(✉)

School of Cyber Science and Engineering, Huazhong University of Science and Technology, Wuhan, China
{d201980943,yuanqing_feng,luzhi,lusongfeng}@hust.edu.cn

**Abstract.** In the context of increasingly stringent data privacy regulations and the growing demand for cross-institutional collaboration, we propose FAIR-MPC, a privacy-preserving computing framework specifically designed for collaborative financial analysis. The FAIR-MPC framework provides robust privacy guarantees under malicious attacks, making it suitable for privacy-sensitive regulatory analysis, fraud detection, and inter-bank cooperation. FAIR-MPC enables multiple financial institutions to jointly train user credit scoring models through Secure Multi-Party Computation (SMPC) without disclosing their own data. Our design introduces two key enhancements on top of the standard SMPC framework. First, we propose an anonymous authentication mechanism based on Schnorr protocol, which allows institutions to prove their eligibility to participate in the computation while remaining anonymous. Second, we develop a cryptographic input auditing scheme that ensures the validity and well-formedness of each party's input without disclosing the inputs themselves. This is achieved by combining bulletproof range proofs with homomorphic commitment consistency checks. Finally, based on the FAIR-MPC framework, we implement a privacy-preserving decision tree training protocol among financial institutions, which enables the training of a decision tree model to determine user risk without disclosing local institutional data. Experimental results show that our approach is both practical and effective.

**Keywords:** Malicious-Secure Multi-Party Computation · Anonymous · Zero-Knowledge Proofs · Input Auditing · Financial Risk Analysis

## 1 Introduction

For decades, the financial industry has heavily relied on data-driven decision-making for tasks such as credit assessment, fraud detection, and risk-based pricing. However, the flow of sensitive personal data across and within financial institutions is subject to increasingly stringent regulatory oversight. Legal frameworks such as the European Union's General Data Protection Regulation [11], the California Consumer Privacy Act [6], and other regional data protection laws


K.-K. R. Choo et al. (Eds.): ICDF2C 2025, LNICST 686, pp. 144–159, 2026.
https://doi.org/10.1007/978-3-032-22545-0_9

impose strict rules on the collection, sharing, and processing of personal information. These regulations aim to safeguard individual privacy while allowing institutions to leverage data in a legally compliant manner for business operations and risk management.

To address this tension, privacy-preserving computing technologies have garnered significant attention in recent years [9,12,32]. These techniques allow computations to be performed on encrypted or obfuscated data, enabling organizations to jointly analyze or learn from sensitive datasets without revealing the underlying information.

Despite their promise, applying privacy-preserving computation in real-world financial settings presents several challenges [1,16,24]. One of the most pressing concerns is the quality and integrity of encrypted data. Predictive models in finance are highly sensitive to input accuracy, and once data is encrypted or anonymized, verifying its validity without compromising confidentiality becomes non-trivial. If the data is incomplete, incorrect, or malformed, the resulting model may yield unreliable or biased decisions.

Moreover, in collaborative financial analytics, secure computation alone is insufficient to meet the high standards of regulatory accountability and auditability. Two critical challenges must also be addressed: first, participating institutions must be able to prove their eligibility to join the collaboration without disclosing their real-world identities; second, the encrypted input data provided by each party must be validated to ensure it lies within acceptable numeric ranges and is structurally well-formed. These issues are particularly crucial in adversarial environments where participants may behave maliciously or inject invalid data, thereby compromising the integrity of the computation.

To tackle these challenges, we propose a novel framework FAIR-MPC tailored for secure and auditable collaboration among financial institutions. The proposed system enables privacy-preserving computation without revealing raw data or institutional identities. Specifically, we demonstrate how multiple institutions can jointly train a decision tree model for user risk assessment in a manner that ensures cryptographic input validity, structural integrity, and participant anonymity, while maintaining model accuracy and regulatory compliance. The framework incorporates several key innovations:

- Anonymous authentication based on Schnorr zero-knowledge proofs, enabling institutions to prove eligibility without revealing identity. The additional overhead introduced by anonymity is negligible;
- Encrypted input auditing, combining Bulletproofs and Pedersen commitments to ensure input validity and well-formedness. The additional overhead introduced by auditing is negligible;
- Privacy-preserving decision tree training, supporting efficient, interpretable risk modeling across institutions under full data confidentiality.

## 2 Related Work

**MPC with Malicious Adversaries.** Implementing a secure multi-party computation (MPC) protocol that can operate under a malicious security model is challenging, and as a result, there are relatively few such protocols. Keller et al. proposed MASCOT [18], an MPC protocol that supports an arbitrary number of participants and is based on Oblivious Transfer. Subsequently, Keller and colleagues introduced Overdrive [19], an improvement over MASCOT, by replacing Oblivious Transfer with homomorphic encryption. Ronald Cramer et al. also proposed spdz2k [7], an efficient ring-based MPC protocol. Payman Mohassel et al. introduced ABY3 [23], which also supports the malicious security model, but is limited to three-party computations. Other protocols that support malicious security include [4,8,20,30].

**Privacy-Preserving Decision Trees.** Adi Akavia et al. [1] implemented a privacy-preserving decision tree algorithm using fully homomorphic encryption (FHE). However, the overhead introduced by homomorphic encryption is significant, making their scheme time-consuming. Similarly, Shin et al. [28] used homomorphic encryption to train decision trees, and their scheme also requires considerable time. Wang et al. [31] employed GPU acceleration for decision tree training, but their approach only supports three-party computations. Robin Berger et al. [3] proposed a two-party privacy-preserving decision tree training algorithm, which similarly faces limitations due to the participant count restriction. Earlier related works include [10,21,29].

# 3 Preliminaries

We use $|D|$ to denote the size of dataset $D$, $F_{MPC}$ to represent the function of MPC, $[x]$ to denote the secret sharing of data $x$.

## 3.1 Secure Multi-party Computation

Secure Multi-Party Computation (SMPC) enables multiple parties to collaboratively compute a function without disclosing their private inputs. SMPC primarily supports two security models: the semi-honest security model and the malicious security model. In the semi-honest model, participants follow the protocol but may attempt to infer additional information. In the malicious model, participants may attempt to deviate from the protocol. However, existing SMPC techniques support collaborative computation under the malicious security model. When honest participants detect a malicious participant violating the protocol, they can terminate the protocol. Therefore, SMPC supporting the malicious security model provides *abort security*. In this paper, we implement a privacy-preserving decision tree training algorithm using SMPC techniques that support the malicious security model.

## 3.2 Zero-Knowledge Proofs

A zero-knowledge proof (ZKP) [14] is a cryptographic protocol enabling a prover to convince a verifier of the truth of a statement without revealing any information beyond its validity. Formally, let $L$ be a language in $\mathsf{NP}$ with a relation $R$

such that:

$$x \in L \iff \exists w \text{ such that } (x, w) \in R,$$

a ZKP proves knowledge of a witness $w$ for public input $x$, without disclosing $w$. A ZKP must satisfy the following properties:

- **Completeness:** Honest provers convince honest verifiers if the statement is true.
- **Soundness:** False statements cannot be proven, except with negligible probability.
- **Zero-Knowledge:** Verifiers learn nothing beyond the validity of the statement; a simulator can replicate the view without the witness.

In our setting, ZKPs ensure that secret-shared inputs in a maliciously secure SMPC protocol satisfy public constraints (e.g., $x_i < B$) without revealing the private values $x_i$. Each party generates a non-interactive ZKP that is broadcast and verified before the inputs are accepted.

We utilize efficient non-interactive ZK proof systems suitable for arithmetic statements, including Bulletproofs [5] and zk-SNARKs [2,15,25], which are particularly well-suited for proving range constraints and structured input validity in privacy-preserving financial applications.

### 3.3 Decision Tree Training with Gini Index

A *decision tree* is a supervised machine learning algorithm used for both classification and regression tasks. It models a decision-making process by recursively splitting the data based on the most significant feature at each node, resulting in a tree-like structure. Each internal node represents a decision based on a specific feature, and each leaf node represents the outcome (or label) of the decision.

The construction of a decision tree involves choosing the best feature to split the data at each step. This is typically done using criteria such as *Gini impurity*, *information gain*, or *mean squared error*, depending on whether the task is classification or regression. The Gini Index is a widely used impurity measure for constructing decision trees, particularly in the CART (Classification and Regression Trees) algorithm. The training process involves recursive binary partitioning of the feature space based on the Gini impurity reduction.

**Gini Impurity Definition.** For a dataset $D$ with $K$ classes, the Gini impurity is calculated as $\text{Gini}(D) = 1 - \sum_{k=1}^{K} p_k^2$, where $p_k$ is the proportion of class $k$ instances in $D$. Here the value of $K$ is $0, 1$.

**Splitting Criterion.** At each node, the algorithm selects the feature $A$ and split point that maximizes the Gini gain:

$$\Delta\text{Gini}(A) = \text{Gini}(D) - \sum_{v \in \text{Values}(A)} \frac{|D_v|}{|D|} \text{Gini}(D_v),$$

where $D_v$ represents the subset of instances where feature $A$ takes value $v$.

**Recursive Training Algorithm.** The complete training procedure follows these steps:

1. Start with the entire dataset at the root node.
2. For each candidate feature $A$ and possible split:
   - Calculate the weighted Gini impurity for the resulting partitions
   - Compute the Gini gain $\Delta \text{Gini}(A)$
3. Select the feature and split point with maximum Gini gain
4. Partition the data into child nodes according to the selected split
5. Repeat recursively for each non-pure child node until:
   - All instances in a node belong to the same class (Gini $= 0$)
   - Maximum tree depth is reached
   - Minimum samples per node threshold is met

## 4 System Overview

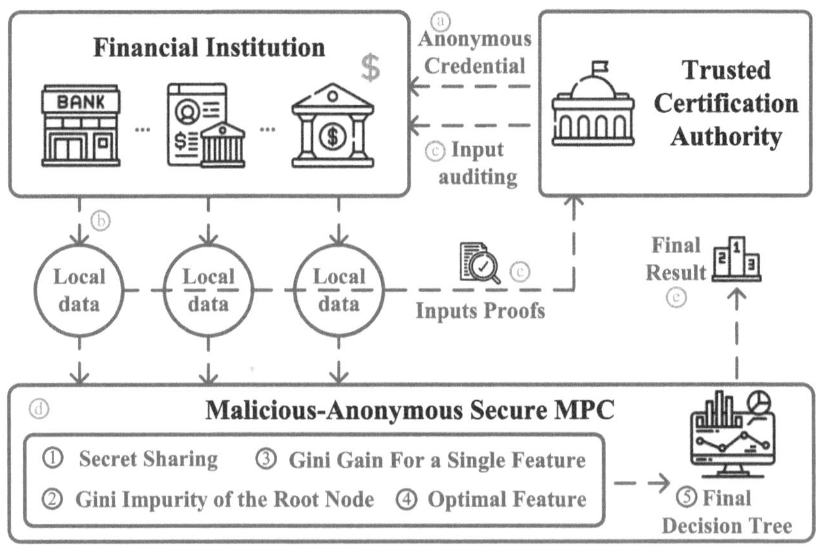


**Fig. 1.** FAIR-MPC's System Overview.

The **FAIR-MPC** framework enables multiple financial institutions to jointly conduct privacy-preserving analytics—such as credit scoring and fraud detection—without disclosing sensitive data or institutional identities. The system architecture, illustrated in Fig. 1, comprises four core components: participating institutions, a trusted certification authority (CA), the malicious-secure SMPC engine, and the analytical model.

Each financial institution (e.g., banks, credit agencies, fintech companies) holds local data about users. Before participating in any collaborative computation, the institution must obtain a credential from a CA—typically a regulatory agency or certified consortium. This authority verifies the legitimacy of the institution and issues a digitally signed anonymous credential.

During computation setup, each institution uses a zero-knowledge proof to anonymously prove that it holds a valid credential from the CA, without revealing its identity. This ensures that only qualified entities can participate, while preserving unlinkability and deniability.

Once verified, the institution prepares its input data vector (e.g., user financial features), and uses additive secret sharing to divide the input into shares distributed to all other participants. To ensure the correctness of the encrypted input, each party generates:

- A **range proof** using Bulletproofs to show the inputs lie within predefined acceptable ranges;
- A **well-formedness proof** based on Pedersen commitments, proving that the distributed shares are consistent with a committed original value.

All other parties verify these zero-knowledge proofs before admitting the input into the joint computation.

The core secure computation is performed using a maliciously secure SMPC protocol over arithmetic circuits. As a representative analytical task, we focus on decision tree training and evaluation—commonly used in financial risk assessment. The computation includes secure splitting, Gini impurity calculations, and decision path evaluations under encryption, without leaking private inputs or intermediate states.

Final outputs (e.g., high-risk user flags or scoring thresholds) are selectively revealed to authorized verifiers. All intermediate data remains protected. This architecture ensures regulatory compliance, verifiability, and institutional privacy, making **FAIR-MPC** suitable for practical deployment in collaborative financial forensics and analytics.

# 5 Privacy-Preserving Decision Tree Training Algorithm

## 5.1 Secret Sharing

We denote the secret sharing function as $F_{MPC}^{SS}$. Each participant inputs their raw data into $F_{MPC}^{SS}$, which uses secret sharing techniques to share the raw data in a secret form with the other participants. During the execution of the secure multi-party computation function, all participants input secret shares of the data. The secret sharing process is shown in Algorithm 1.

## 5.2 Computing the Gini Impurity of the Root Node

The Gini impurity is computed using $\mathrm{Gini}(D) = 1 - \sum_{i=0}^{1} p_i^2$.

**Algorithm 1:** Secret Sharing.$\Pi_{\mathrm{SS}}$

**Input:** $P_i$ inputs $x$.
**Output:** All parties get a secret share of $x$.
1 $P_i$ randomly selects $n-1$ numbers uniformly from the ring, denoted as $\{x_1, \ldots, x_{i-1}, x_{i+1}, \ldots, x_n\}$.
2 $P_i$ computes $x_i = x - \sum_{j=1, j\neq i}^{n} x_j$.
3 $P_i$ then distributes $x_j$ to $P_j$.

We need to calculate $p_i$ under the secret sharing state. In the secret sharing state, the actual classification of the data is unknown. However, we can design an algorithm based on the plaintext classification to compute $p_i$. For instance, if the data classification $y$ is represented as 0 or 1 in the plaintext, and we need to calculate $p_1$, we can sum all the data points corresponding to the class and then divide by the total number of data points. This gives us: $p_1 = \frac{1}{n}\sum_{j=1}^{n} y_j$

Thus, $p_0 = 1 - p_1$. Finally, we can compute the Gini impurity using Formula ??. The detailed algorithm is presented in Algorithm 2.

**Algorithm 2:** Computing the Gini Impurity of the Root Node. $\Pi_{\mathrm{Gini_R}}$

**Input:** $P_i$ inputs $[y]$, where $[y]$ is the classification of the data in the ciphertext state.
**Output:** $P_i$ obtains the secret share of $Gini(D)$.
1 **All parties** compute locally: $[num] = \sum_{i=1}^{|D|}[y]$.
2 **All parties** invoke the secure division protocol to compute and obtain:$[p_1] = F_{MPC}^{Div}([num], |D|)$.
3 **All parties** compute locally: $[p_0] = [1] - [p_1]$.
4 **All parties** invoke the secure multiplication protocol to compute: $[p_1^2] = F_{MPC}^{Mul}([p_1], [p_1]), \quad [p_0^2] = F_{MPC}^{Mul}([p_0], [p_0])$.
5 **All parties** compute locally: $[Gini(D)] = [1] - [p_0^2] - [p_1^2]$.

### 5.3 Calculating the Gini Gain for a Single Feature

A single feature may correspond to many types, denoted typically as {0, 1, 2, ...}. However, in the secret sharing state, parties do not know the specific type of the feature for the data, but the types of the features are public information. Therefore, we can use a secure comparison algorithm (denoted as $F_{MPC}^{CMP}$) to classify the data and compute the Gini gain for a single feature. Note that the result obtained from $F_{MPC}^{CMP}$ will be shared as secret shares with all participants, meaning that no participant knows the comparison result, but only gets a share of the comparison result. We divide the computation of the Gini gain for a single feature into four steps.

**Step 1: Counting the Number of Data Points in Each Class.** We use $F_{MPC}^{CMP}$ to determine whether data point $x$ belongs to class $k$, and count how many data points belong to this class. This is represented as: $\text{num}_k = \text{num}_k + F_{MPC}^{CMP}(x == k)$.

---

**Algorithm 3:** Calculating the Gini Gain for a Single Feature.$\Pi_{\text{Gini}_\text{F}}$

---

**Input:** $P_i$ input the feature data $[x]$, the class labels $[y]$, and the Gini impurity of the root node $[Gini(D)]$.

**Output:** Each party receives $[\Delta Gini]$.

1 **for** $i = 1$ *to* $|D|$ **do**
2     **for** $j = 1$ *to* $k$ **do**
3         $[num_j] = [num_j] + F_{MPC}^{CMP}([x_i] == j)$
4         $[sum_j] = [sum_j] + F_{MPC}^{Mul}(F_{MPC}^{CMP}([x_i] == j), [y])$
5     **end**
6 **end**
7 **for** $j = 1$ *to* $k$ **do**
8     $[d_{j1}] = F_{MPC}^{Div}(1, [num_j])$
9     $[p_{j1}] = F_{MPC}^{Mul}([d_{j1}], [sum_j])$
10     $[p_{j0}] = [1] - [p_{j1}]$
11     $[Gini(D_j)] = [1] - F_{MPC}^{Mul}([p_{j0}], [p_{j0}]) - F_{MPC}^{Mul}([p_{j1}], [p_{j1}])$
12     $[sum] = [sum] + [sum_j]$
13 **end**
14 $[d] = F_{MPC}^{Div}(1, [sum])$
15 **for** $j = 1$ *to* $k$ **do**
16     $[Gini_d] = [Gini_d] + F_{MPC}^{Mul}(F_{MPC}^{Mul}([d], [num_j]), [Gini(D_j)])$
17 **end**
18 $[\Delta Gini] = [Gini(D)] - [Gini_d]$

---

**Step 2: Calculating the Gini Gain for Each Class.** We follow a similar approach as in Algorithm 2, but with an additional condition: the data must belong to the $k$-th class. Specifically, we compute: $p_1 = \frac{1}{\text{num}_k} \sum_{i=1}^{|D|} F_{MPC}^{CMP}(x == k) \cdot y$. Then we can compute $p_0 = 1 - p_1$. Finally, we compute the Gini impurity for class $k$ as: $\text{Gini}(D_k) = 1 - \sum_{i=0}^{1} p_i^2$

**Step 3: Calculating the Weighted Gini Impurity for the Feature.** We calculate the weighted Gini impurity for the feature using the following formula: $\text{Gini}_d = \sum_{i=1}^{k} \frac{\text{num}_k}{|D|} \cdot \text{Gini}(D_k)$

**Step 4: Calculating the Gini Gain for the Feature.** The final step is to calculate the Gini gain for the feature using the following formula: $\Delta\text{Gini} = \text{Gini}(D) - \text{Gini}_d$

The overall algorithm is presented in Algorithm 3.

### 5.4 Selecting the Optimal Feature

---

**Algorithm 4:** Selecting the Optimal Feature.$\Pi_{\mathrm{SF}}$

---

**Input:** $P_i$ input $\{[Gini_1], [Gini_2], \ldots, [Gini_t]\}$.

**Output:** Each party receives the optimal feature selected in this round.

1 $[idx] = [1]$

2 $[Gini_{max}] = [Gini_1]$

3 **for** $i = 1$ *to* $t$ **do**

4 $\quad [cmp] = F_{MPC}^{CMP}([Gini_{max}] >= [Gini_i])$

5 $\quad [Gini_{max}] = F_{MPC}^{Mul}([cmp], [Gini_{max}]) + F_{MPC}^{Mul}([1] - [cmp], [Gini_i])$

6 $\quad [idx] = F_{MPC}^{Mul}([cmp], [idx]) + F_{MPC}^{Mul}([1] - [cmp], i)$

7 **end**

8 Each party reconstructs the index $idx$ to obtain the optimal feature.

---

After calculating the Gini gain for all features, we need to select the optimal feature, i.e., the feature with the highest Gini gain, which will serve as the root node's splitting feature for this round. We use Algorithm 4 to select the optimal feature while ensuring that the privacy of individual features is not leaked. In Algorithm 4, we also utilize the $F_{MPC}^{CMP}$ function to compare the sizes of two data points.

### 5.5 Constructing the Final Decision Tree

The process of constructing the decision tree follows the same steps as the algorithm for the plaintext case. First, we calculate the Gini impurity of the root node. Then, we iterate over all features and split points, selecting the splitting feature that maximizes the Gini decrease as a child node. Finally, we repeat this process for the child nodes until the decision tree is fully constructed. The detailed process is shown in Algorithm 5.

---

**Algorithm 5:** Constructing the Decision Tree

---

1 Each party invokes $\Pi_{\mathrm{SF}}$ to share the private dataset with the other parties through secret sharing.

2 Each party invokes $\Pi_{\mathrm{Gini_R}}$ to compute the Gini impurity of the root node.

3 Each party invokes $\Pi_{\mathrm{Gini_F}}$ to compute the Gini gain for all features.

4 Each party invokes $\Pi_{\mathrm{SF}}$ to select the optimal feature for the current round, and subsequently updates the decision tree.

5 The process repeats steps 3-4 until all features are computed.

---

# 6 Auditing of Anonymous Identity and Input

## 6.1 Auditing of Anonymous Identity

To ensure that only authorized entities participate in the SMPC protocol while preserving their anonymity, we introduce a Schnorr-based zero-knowledge proof mechanism [27]. This protocol allows each participant to prove possession of a certified private key without revealing their actual identity, enabling anonymous yet verifiable participation.

We assume that each eligible institution has registered with a trusted certification authority (CA), which issues a signature on their public key. Formally, each participant $P_i$ holds a key pair $(sk_i, pk_i)$, where $pk_i = sk_i \cdot G$ under a cyclic group $\mathbb{G}$ of prime order $q$, and a corresponding CA signature $\sigma_i = \mathcal{CA}.\mathsf{Sign}(pk_i)$. The protocol, denoted as $\Pi_{\text{Auth}}$, proceeds as shown in Algorithm 6:

Participant $P_i$ selects a fresh random nonce $\rho_i$ and computes a pseudonymous identity $\mathsf{anonID}_i = \mathsf{Hash}(pk_i \parallel \rho_i)$, which serves as their unlinkable identifier throughout the SMPC protocol. To prove ownership of $sk_i$ corresponding to $pk_i$ without revealing $sk_i$, $P_i$ generates a Schnorr proof of knowledge. This involves sampling a random scalar $r \in \mathbb{Z}_q$, computing $t = r \cdot G$, deriving a challenge value $c = \mathsf{Hash}(t \parallel pk_i \parallel \mathsf{anonID}_i)$, and then computing the response $s = r + c \cdot sk_i$. The proof is the pair $\pi_i = (t, s)$. $P_i$ broadcasts the tuple $(\mathsf{anonID}_i, pk_i, \sigma_i, \pi_i)$ to all participants. Each receiving party verifies: The CA's signature $\sigma_i$ is valid for $pk_i$: $\mathcal{CA}.\mathsf{Verify}(pk_i, \sigma_i) = 1$; The Schnorr [27] proof satisfies the verification equation: $s \cdot G \stackrel{?}{=} t + c \cdot pk_i$. If both checks succeed, $\mathsf{anonID}_i$ is accepted as a valid anonymous participant. Otherwise, $P_i$ is excluded from the protocol.

**Algorithm 6:** Anonymous Identity Authentication Protocol $\Pi_{\text{Auth}}$

**Input:** Each participant $P_i$ holds $(sk_i, pk_i)$ and an authorization signature $\sigma_i$ issued by a certification authority $\mathcal{CA}$.

**Output:** All parties verify that $P_i$ is a valid participant without revealing $P_i$'s identity.

1. $P_i$ samples a random nonce $\rho_i \leftarrow \mathbb{Z}_q$ and computes: $\mathsf{anonID}_i = \mathsf{Hash}(pk_i \parallel \rho_i)$;
2. $P_i$ generates a Schnorr zero-knowledge proof of knowledge of $sk_i$ as follows: $r \leftarrow \mathbb{Z}_q$, $t = r \cdot G$, $c = \mathsf{Hash}(t \parallel pk_i \parallel \mathsf{anonID}_i)$, $s = r + c \cdot sk_i$.
3. $P_i$ broadcasts $(\mathsf{anonID}_i, pk_i, \sigma_i, \pi_i = (t, s))$ to all other parties;
4. $P_i$ verifies other participants $P_j$'s proofs: $\mathcal{CA}.\mathsf{Verify}(pk_j, \sigma_j) \stackrel{?}{=} 1$, $c = \mathsf{Hash}(t \parallel pk_j \parallel \mathsf{anonID}_j)$, $s \cdot G \stackrel{?}{=} t + c \cdot pk_j$
5. If both checks pass, then $P_i$ is accepted as a valid anonymous participant with identifier $\mathsf{anonID}_i$.

## 6.2 Auditing of Encrypted Identity

To ensure that each participant submits a valid and honest input to the SMPC protocol, our design enforces two cryptographic guarantees:

**Algorithm 7:** Secure Input Auditing Protocol $\Pi_{\text{InputAudit}}$

**Input:** User $P_i$ holds private input $x_i$, and shares $\{x_{ij}\}_{j=1}^n$.
**Output:** All parties are convinced that $x_i < B$ and $\sum_j x_{ij} = x_i$, without learning $x_i$.

1 **Step 1: Range Validity Proof**
2 $P_i$ samples random $r_i \in \mathbb{Z}_q$ and computes Pedersen commitment: $\mathsf{com}_i = x_i \cdot G + r_i \cdot H$.
3 $P_i$ generates Bulletproof range proof: $\pi_i^{\text{range}} = \mathsf{Bulletproof}(x_i, r_i, B)$.
4 **Step 2: Secret Sharing and Commitments**
5 $P_i$ samples random values $\{r_{ij}\}_{j=1}^n$ with $\sum_j r_{ij} = r_i$;
6 $P_i$ computes commitments: $\mathsf{com}_{ij} = x_{ij} \cdot G + r_{ij} \cdot H$, for each $j$.
7 **Step 3: Broadcast and Verification**
8 $P_i$ broadcasts $(\mathsf{com}_i, \pi_i^{\text{range}}, \{\mathsf{com}_{ij}\}_{j=1}^n)$.
9 **Each party** verifies:
10 **Range Proof:** Accept if $\mathsf{Verify}(\mathsf{com}_i, \pi_i^{\text{range}}, B) = 1$;;
11 **Well-Formedness:** Accept if $\sum_{j=1}^n \mathsf{com}_{ij} \stackrel{?}{=} \mathsf{com}_i$;;
12 If both checks pass, accept $P_i$'s input as valid and correctly shared.

- **Range validity:** The private input $x_i$ of each user must lie in a publicly known range, specifically $x_i < B$.
- **Well-formedness:** The secret-shared values $[x_{ij}]_{j=1}^n$ that user $P_i$ distributes to others must reconstruct to $x_i$, i.e., $\sum_j x_{ij} = x_i$.

We achieve both goals using zero-knowledge proofs, without leaking any information about $x_i$.

**Range Proof.** Each participant $P_i$ first computes a Pedersen commitment [26] to their input $\mathsf{com}_i = x_i \cdot G + r_i \cdot H$, where $r_i \in \mathbb{Z}_q$ is a random blinding factor, and $G, H$ are fixed generators of a cyclic group with unknown discrete log relation [22].

To prove that $x_i < B$, $P_i$ constructs a Bulletproofs range proof [5] $\pi_i^{\text{range}}$ with the idea of Gentry et al. [13] to reduce communication overhead and shorten acceleration time for the following statement: There exists $x_i, r_i$ such that $\mathsf{com}_i = x_i G + r_i H$ and $x_i < B$. The pair $(\mathsf{com}_i, \pi_i^{\text{range}})$ is then broadcast to all other parties, who verify the proof locally.

**Well-Formedness Proof.** After generating secret shares $[x_{ij}]_{j=1}^n$ of $x_i$ such that $\sum_j x_{ij} = x_i$, the participant commits to each share: $\mathsf{com}_{ij} = x_{ij} \cdot G + r_{ij} \cdot H$, where $r_{ij} \in \mathbb{Z}_q$ are fresh random values for each share. To ensure consistency between the committed input and the distributed shares, $P_i$ sets: $r_i = \sum_{j=1}^n r_{ij}$, which guarantees the homomorphic relation: $\mathsf{com}_i = \sum_{j=1}^n \mathsf{com}_{ij}$. The set $\{\mathsf{com}_{ij}\}_{j=1}^n$ and $\mathsf{com}_i$ are broadcast alongside the range proof. All parties verify the well-formedness by checking: $\sum_{j=1}^n \mathsf{com}_{ij} \stackrel{?}{=} \mathsf{com}_i$. This confirms that the shared values reconstruct to the same $x_i$ previously committed in the range proof, thereby ensuring structural correctness of the input.

This two-tier proof mechanism guarantees that each participant submits a bounded, valid, and honest input without revealing the value itself. The verification is fully non-interactive and can be executed locally by each party. The detailed process is shown in Algorithm 7.

# 7 Experiment

## 7.1 Experiment Setup

Our experimental environment is as follows: the operating system is Ubuntu 22.04, the local network bandwidth is 30 Gbps, and the network latency is 0.1 ms. We implemented the algorithm using the malicious Shamir protocol and the malicious spdz2k protocol from MP-SPDZ [17].

## 7.2 Experiment Result

**Table 1.** Comparison with [1].

| Framework | Protocol | Parties | Feature | Data | Time (min) |
|---|---|---|---|---|---|
| [1] | Homomorphic Encryption | 2 | 15 | 1000 | 364 |
| Ours | malicious Shamir | 3 | 15 | 1000 | 7 |

We first compare our work with that of Akavia et al., who used a dataset containing 1,000 data points, each with 15 features. Akavia et al. [1] employed a homomorphic encryption technique and proposed a two-party training scheme. In contrast, our approach is based on a malicious Shamir-based MPC protocol. The experimental results, as shown in Table 1, demonstrate that, under the same conditions, our scheme achieves a 50× improvement in efficiency.

Furthermore, to validate the scalability of our approach, we conducted three sets of experiments evaluating the system under varying computational and data parameters.

First, we varied the number of participating institutions from 3 to 7 and compared two underlying malicious MPC protocols: *mal-shamir* and *spdz2k*. As shown in Fig. 2, both the computation time and communication overhead increase with the number of parties, which is consistent with the expected growth in round complexity and message passing in secret-sharing–based protocols. Notably, *spdz2k* demonstrated better communication efficiency at larger scales, making it a favorable option for wide-scale deployments involving many financial institutions.

Second, we evaluated the impact of input dimensionality, i.e., the number of features per input record. In this setting, we increased the feature dimension

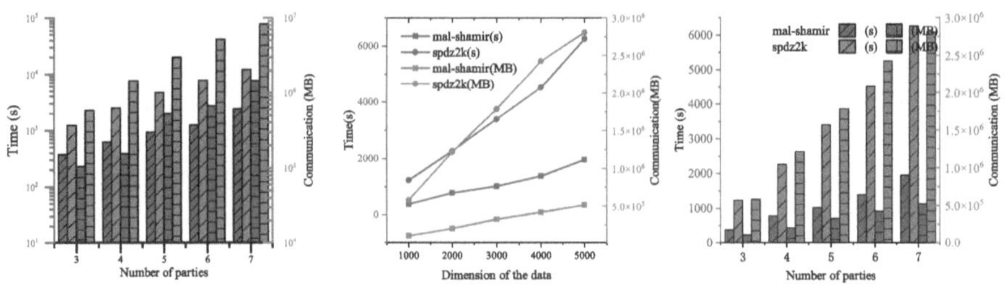


**Fig. 2.** Overhead variation of FAIR-MPC as the number of parties, data's dimension and number change. The default parties are 3. The default data's dimension and number are 15 and 1000.

from 1 to 7 to simulate real-world financial scoring models. As shown in Fig. 2, both time and communication grew approximately linearly with dimensionality for both protocols. While *mal-shamir* had slightly lower runtime at lower dimensions, *spdz2k* became more efficient in communication as the feature space expanded.

Lastly, we assessed how the framework handles growing data volume by increasing the number of input records while keeping dimensionality fixed. The results in Fig. 2 show that both protocols scale linearly in runtime and communication with respect to dataset size. Again, *spdz2k* maintained better communication performance, especially under large-batch input scenarios.

From Figs. 2, we conclude that our framework exhibits strong scalability and flexibility across various deployment settings, with minimal overhead introduced by our auditing and anonymity-preserving mechanisms.

# 8 Conclusion

In this work, we presented **FAIR-MPC**, a privacy-preserving and malicious-secure computation framework tailored for collaborative financial analysis among multiple institutions. The framework enables secure decision tree training for credit scoring without exposing sensitive institutional data. To ensure privacy, accountability, and compliance, we introduced two key cryptographic components: an anonymous authentication mechanism based on Schnorr zero-knowledge proofs, and an encrypted input auditing protocol that verifies both range validity and share consistency. These features make FAIR-MPC well-suited for privacy-preserving regulatory analytics, fraud detection, and secure interbank collaboration. We believe FAIR-MPC offers a promising technical foundation for secure and auditable computation in financial forensics and cybercrime analysis—areas of growing interest in both industry and academia. In future work, we plan to extend the framework to support broader classes of machine learning models and to explore integration with decentralized identity and forensic traceability mechanisms.

**Acknowledgment.** This work is supported by the Major Research Plan of Hubei Province under Grant/Award NO. 2023BAA027, Changsha Key Science and Technology Project under the "Unveiling and Commanding" Initiative under Grant No. kq2503009, the project of Science, Technology and Innovation Commission of Shenzhen Municipality of China under Grant No. GJHZ20240218114659027 and the Key Research & Development Plan of Hubei Province of China under Grant No. 2024BAB049.

## References


1. Akavia, A., Leibovich, M., Resheff, Y.S., Ron, R., Shahar, M., Vald, M.: Privacy-preserving decision trees training and prediction. ACM Trans. Priv. Secur. **25**(3) (2022). https://doi.org/10.1145/3517197
2. Ben-Sasson, E., Chiesa, A., Spooner, N., Virza, M.: Zkproofs: foundations, applications, and open problems. Proc. IEEE **109**, 1043–1061 (2021)
3. Berger, R., Dörre, F., Koch, A.: Two-party decision tree training from updatable order-revealing encryption. In: Applied Cryptography and Network Security: 22nd International Conference, ACNS 2024, Abu Dhabi, United Arab Emirates, 5–8 March 2024, Proceedings, Part I, pp. 288–317. Springer, Heidelberg (2024). https://doi.org/10.1007/978-3-031-54770-6_12
4. Boyle, E., Gilboa, N., Ishai, Y., Nof, A.: Practical fully secure three-party computation via sublinear distributed zero-knowledge proofs. In: Proceedings of the 2019 ACM SIGSAC Conference on Computer and Communications Security, CCS '19, pp. 869–886. Association for Computing Machinery, New York, NY, USA (2019). https://doi.org/10.1145/3319535.3363227
5. Bünz, B., Bootle, J., Boneh, D., Poelstra, A., Wuille, P., Maxwell, G.: Bulletproofs: short proofs for confidential transactions and more. In: 2018 IEEE Symposium on Security and Privacy, SP 2018, Proceedings, 21–23 May 2018, San Francisco, California, USA, pp. 315–334. IEEE Computer Society (2018). https://doi.org/10.1109/SP.2018.00020
6. CCPA: California consumer privacy act (2023). https://oag.ca.gov/privacy/ccpa
7. Cramer, R., Damgård, I., Escudero, D., Scholl, P., Xing, C.: SPDZ2k: efficient MPC mod 2k for dishonest majority. In: Shacham, H., Boldyreva, A. (eds.) Advances in Cryptology - CRYPTO 2018, pp. 769–798. Springer, Cham (2018)
8. Dalskov, A., Escudero, D., Keller, M.: Fantastic four: honest-majority four-party secure computation with malicious security. Cryptology ePrint Archive, Paper 2020/1330 (2020). https://eprint.iacr.org/2020/1330
9. Dwork, C.: Differential privacy. In: Encyclopedia of Cryptography and Security, pp. 338–340. Springer, Boston (2006). https://doi.org/10.1007/978-1-4419-5906-5_752
10. Emekci, F., Sahin, O., Agrawal, D., El Abbadi, A.: Privacy preserving decision tree learning over multiple parties. Data Knowl. Eng. **63**(2), 348–361 (2007). https://doi.org/10.1016/j.datak.2007.02.004, https://www.sciencedirect.com/science/article/pii/S0169023X07000365
11. GDPR: General data protection regulation (2024). https://eur-lex.europa.eu/TodayOJ/
12. Gentry, C.: Fully homomorphic encryption using ideal lattices. In: Proceedings of the Forty-First Annual ACM Symposium on Theory of Computing, STOC '09, pp. 169–178. Association for Computing Machinery, New York, NY, USA (2009). https://doi.org/10.1145/1536414.1536440

13. Gentry, C., Halevi, S., Lyubashevsky, V.: Practical non-interactive publicly verifiable secret sharing with thousands of parties. In: Dunkelman, O., Dziembowski, S. (eds.) Advances in Cryptology - EUROCRYPT 2022 - 41st Annual International Conference on the Theory and Applications of Cryptographic Techniques, Trondheim, Norway, 30 May–3 June 2022, Proceedings, Part I. LNCS, vol. 13275, pp. 458–487. Springer, Cham (2022). https://doi.org/10.1007/978-3-031-06944-4_16
14. Goldwasser, S., Micali, S., Rackoff, C.: The knowledge complexity of interactive proof systems. SIAM J. Comput. **18**(1), 186–208 (1989). https://doi.org/10.1137/0218012
15. Groth, J.: On the size of pairing-based non-interactive arguments. In: Fischlin, M., Coron, J. (eds.) Advances in Cryptology - EUROCRYPT 2016 - 35th Annual International Conference on the Theory and Applications of Cryptographic Techniques, Vienna, Austria, 8–12 May 2016, Proceedings, Part II. LNCS, vol. 9666, pp. 305–326. Springer, Heidelberg (2016). https://doi.org/10.1007/978-3-662-49896-5_11
16. Haseeb, A., Ekerete, I., Moore, S.: A privacy-preserving federated learning framework for financial crime. In: Bravo, J., Nugent, C., Cleland, I. (eds.) Proceedings of the International Conference on Ubiquitous Computing and Ambient Intelligence (UCAmI 2024), pp. 743–754. Springer, Cham (2024). https://doi.org/10.1007/978-3-031-77571-0_70
17. Keller, M.: MP-SPDZ: a versatile framework for multi-party computation. In: Proceedings of the 2020 ACM SIGSAC Conference on Computer and Communications Security, CCS '20, pp. 1575–1590. Association for Computing Machinery, New York, NY, USA (2020). https://doi.org/10.1145/3372297.3417872
18. Keller, M., Orsini, E., Scholl, P.: MASCOT: faster malicious arithmetic secure computation with oblivious transfer. In: Proceedings of the 2016 ACM SIGSAC Conference on Computer and Communications Security, CCS '16, pp. 830–842. Association for Computing Machinery, New York, NY, USA (2016). https://doi.org/10.1145/2976749.2978357
19. Keller, M., Pastro, V., Rotaru, D.: Overdrive: making SPDZ great again. In: Nielsen, J.B., Rijmen, V. (eds.) Advances in Cryptology - EUROCRYPT 2018, pp. 158–189. Springer, Cham (2018). https://doi.org/10.1007/978-3-319-78372-7_6
20. Koti, N., Kukkala, V.B., Patra, A., Raj Gopal, B.: PentaGOD: stepping beyond traditional god with five parties. In: Proceedings of the 2022 ACM SIGSAC Conference on Computer and Communications Security, CCS '22, pp. 1843–1856. Association for Computing Machinery, New York, NY, USA (2022). https://doi.org/10.1145/3548606.3559369
21. Lory, P.: Enhancing the efficiency in privacy preserving learning of decision trees in partitioned databases. In: Domingo-Ferrer, J., Tinnirello, I. (eds.) Privacy in Statistical Databases. LNCS, pp. 322–335. Springer, Heidelberg (2012). https://doi.org/10.1007/978-3-642-33627-0_25
22. Menezes, A., van Oorschot, P.C., Vanstone, S.A.: Handbook of Applied Cryptography. CRC Press (1996). https://doi.org/10.1201/9781439821916, http://cacr.uwaterloo.ca/hac/
23. Mohassel, P., Rindal, P.: ABY3: a mixed protocol framework for machine learning. In: Proceedings of the 2018 ACM SIGSAC Conference on Computer and Communications Security (2018)
24. Naresh, Vankamamidi S.D, A.: PPDNN-CRP: privacy-preserving deep neural network processing for credit risk prediction in cloud: a homomorphic encryption-based approach. J. Cloud Comput. **13** (2024). https://doi.org/10.1186/s13677-024-00711-y

25. Parno, B., Howell, J., Gentry, C., Raykova, M.: Pinocchio: nearly practical verifiable computation. In: 2013 IEEE Symposium on Security and Privacy, SP 2013, Berkeley, CA, USA, 19–22 May 2013, pp. 238–252. IEEE Computer Society (2013). https://doi.org/10.1109/SP.2013.47
26. Pedersen, T.P.: Non-interactive and information-theoretic secure verifiable secret sharing. In: Feigenbaum, J. (ed.) Advances in Cryptology - CRYPTO '91, 11th Annual International Cryptology Conference, Proceedings, Santa Barbara, California, USA, 11–15 August 1991. LNCS, vol. 576, pp. 129–140. Springer, Heidelberg (1991). https://doi.org/10.1007/3-540-46766-1_9
27. Schnorr, C.: Efficient identification and signatures for smart cards. In: Brassard, G. (ed.) Advances in Cryptology - CRYPTO '89, Proceedings, 9th Annual International Cryptology Conference, Santa Barbara, California, USA, 20–24 August 1989. Lecture Notes in Computer Science, vol. 435, pp. 239–252. Springer, Heidelberg (1989). https://doi.org/10.1007/0-387-34805-0_22
28. Shin, H., Choi, J., Lee, D., Kim, K., Lee, Y.: Fully homomorphic training and inference on binary decision tree and random forest. In: Garcia-Alfaro, J., Kozik, R., Choraś, M., Katsikas, S. (eds.) Computer Security – ESORICS 2024, pp. 217–237. Springer, Heidelberg (2024). https://doi.org/10.1007/978-3-031-70896-1_11
29. Vaidya, J., Clifton, C., Kantarcioglu, M., Patterson, A.S.: Privacy-preserving decision trees over vertically partitioned data. ACM Trans. Knowl. Discov. Data **2**(3) (2008). https://doi.org/10.1145/1409620.1409624
30. Wagh, S., Tople, S., Benhamouda, F., Kushilevitz, E., Mittal, P., Rabin, T.: FALCON: honest-majority maliciously secure framework for private deep learning. In: Privacy Enhancing Technologies Symposium, vol. 2021, pp. 188–208 (2021). https://doi.org/10.2478/popets-2021-0011
31. Wang, Q., et al.: GTree: GPU-friendly privacy-preserving decision tree training and inference. In: 2024 IEEE 23rd International Conference on Trust, Security and Privacy in Computing and Communications (TrustCom), pp. 775–785 (2024). https://doi.org/10.1109/TrustCom63139.2024.00118
32. Yao, A.C.: Protocols for secure computations. In: 23rd Annual Symposium on Foundations of Computer Science, SFCS 1982, pp. 160–164 (1982). https://doi.org/10.1109/SFCS.1982.38

# Privacy-Preserving $k$-Bitruss Community Query over Encrypted Bipartite Graphs

Xiaoxian Liu[1], Chen Chen[2](✉), Xueqiao Liu[2], and Xiaoyang Wang[1]

[1] University of New South Wales, Sydney, NSW 2033, Australia
{xiaoxian.liu,xiaoyang.wang1}@unsw.edu.au
[2] University of Wollongong, Wollongong, NSW 2500, Australia
{chenc,xueqiao_liu}@uow.edu.au

**Abstract.** Bipartite graphs are widely used to model user–item interactions in domains such as e-commerce and cybersecurity, including fraud detection and recommendation. However, outsourcing such graphs to public clouds introduces privacy risks, including topology inference and access-pattern leakage. We propose the first privacy-preserving $k$-bitruss community query framework over encrypted bipartite graphs, designed under a semi-honest, non-colluding threat model. Our scheme integrates the BiT-BU decomposition into a butterfly-cohesion-preserving encrypted index and introduces two orthogonal privacy mechanisms: dummy-row insertion for structural obfuscation and $\epsilon$-differentially private dummy-query injection to mask access behavior. Encrypted query tokens carry cryptographically indistinguishable flags that indicate real or dummy identity, enabling post-execution filtering by the proxy without revealing query intent. The protocol achieves simulation-based security under IND-CPA encryption and formal $\epsilon$-DP query protection, with structural indistinguishability bounded by Theorem 3. Experiments on real-world graphs demonstrate linear scalability, sub-200s query latency on 50K-edge datasets, and a core recovery success rate under 0.0025%. Our work enables secure and efficient encrypted community detection in outsourced bipartite graph analytics.

**Keywords:** Privacy-preserving query · Bipartite graphs · $k$-Bitruss community · Homomorphic encryption · Differential privacy · Encrypted index

## 1 Introduction

Bipartite graphs model critical relationships between two distinct entity types, and are widely used in domains such as fraud detection in e-commerce [18], contagion modeling [17], and smart city analytics [13]. Such graphs often exhibit sparse global structure with dense local regions—e.g., fraud rings or viral spreaders—that signal coordinated behaviors. The $k$-bitruss community, defined via butterfly-based structural cohesion, captures these dense substructures and supports applications such as recommendation, anomaly detection, and influence analysis [20]. However, outsourcing graphs to public clouds risks disclosing


K.-K. R. Choo et al. (Eds.): ICDF2C 2025, LNICST 686, pp. 160–175, 2026.
https://doi.org/10.1007/978-3-032-22545-0_10

sensitive bipartite interactions, such as user–product or account–IP linkages.

Unipartite projection of bipartite graphs can amplify local density and cause edge explosion [14], making the $k$TCQ framework [7], originally designed for unipartite $k$-truss queries, ill-suited for bipartite settings. Its indexing strategy deterministically encodes butterfly structures and leaks partition membership of center nodes, revealing symmetric roles of $U$ and $V$. Moreover, $k$TCQ lacks structural and behavioral obfuscation, making it vulnerable to core exposure, frequency analysis, and neighborhood fingerprinting. While symmetric homomorphic encryption (SHE) enables secure graph computation, its ciphertext cost limits large-scale deployments. Recent studies have developed SHE-based optimizations for tasks like shortest-path search [1], spectral analysis [15], and encrypted GCN inference [12], showing the potential of domain-specific designs in encrypted graph analytics. Butterfly counting over encrypted bipartite graphs has also been studied [10], but such methods return only global counts and lack support for center-based community queries. Moreover, PSI-based protocols incur high computational and communication overhead.

To address these limitations, we propose the first privacy-preserving $k$-bitruss community query scheme over encrypted bipartite graphs. Our contributions are:

- We extends the $k$TCQ framework by incorporating the BiT-BU algorithm [16] into a bottom-up encrypted index generation process that avoids unipartite projection and mitigates edge explosion. This ensures high scalability on large and sparse bipartite graphs while preserving structural cohesion information.
- We propose a composable dual-layer privacy protection mechanism: (i) *Static layer*: dummy-row insertion with index shuffling disrupts topology–identifier dependencies; (ii) *Dynamic layer*: $\varepsilon$-DP dummy-query injection with cryptographic indistinguishability obfuscates access patterns.
- We design an *automatic slice optimization algorithm* that heuristically selects the optimal block partition size to minimize total index rows and padding, improving both storage and query efficiency.
- Extensive experiments on real-world bipartite graphs validate the scheme's effectiveness in preserving structural access privacy and achieving low query latency under a proxy–cloud architecture.

## 2 Preliminaries

### 2.1 Bipartite Graphs and $k$-Bitruss Communities

Let $G = (U, V, E)$ be a bipartite graph, where $U$ and $V$ are disjoint vertex sets and $E \subseteq \{U \times V\}$ is the edge set. We denote $n = |U| + |V|$ as the total number of nodes, and $e = |E|$ as the total number of edges. A fundamental cohesive structure in bipartite graphs is the *butterfly*.

**Definition 1 (Butterfly).** *A* butterfly *in $G$ is a $(2, 2)$-biclique formed by vertices $u, w \in U$ and $v, x \in V$ such that all edges $(u, v)$, $(u, x)$, $(w, v)$, and $(w, x)$ exist in $E$.*

A $k$-bitruss is a maximal edge-induced subgraph in which every edge is contained in at least $k$ butterflies. We now define the local variant centered around a query vertex.

**Definition 2 ($k$-bitruss Community [20]).** *Given a query vertex $q \in \{U \cup V\}$, a subgraph $C(q) \subseteq G$ is a $k$-*bitruss community *if it is a maximal connected subgraph containing $q$ such that*

$$\forall e \in E(C(q)),\ bs(e) \geq k,$$

*where $bs(e)$ denotes the butterfly support of edge $e$.*

### 2.2 SHE-Based Logic Operators

We adopt six encrypted operations (OP1–OP6) introduced in [7] to support privacy-preserving graph query processing. All operations are performed over bitwise ciphertexts under a SHE scheme. Specifically, OP1 performs equality testing between encrypted integers (e.g., encrypted node IDs); OP2 compares encrypted values against encrypted thresholds; OP3 conditionally increments encrypted counters without decryption; OP4 provides a fully encrypted queue with oblivious enqueue/dequeue logic; OP5 checks encrypted set membership (e.g., encrypted edge ID lookup); OP6 updates encrypted visited flags using logic gates over ciphertexts. These operators together support secure control flow and state tracking entirely over encrypted graph data.

### 2.3 Differential Privacy and Laplace Mechanism)

Differential privacy (DP) [4] is a rigorous privacy model that ensures the output distribution of a randomized algorithm remains nearly unchanged when a single individual's data is modified. A mechanism $\mathcal{M}$ satisfies $\varepsilon$-DP if for any neighboring datasets $D_1$ and $D_2$ differing in one element, and for any output $o$:

$$\Pr[\mathcal{M}(D_1) = o] \leq e^{\varepsilon} \cdot \Pr[\mathcal{M}(D_2) = o].$$

A common instantiation is the Laplace mechanism, which adds noise drawn from the Laplace distribution $\mathrm{Lap}(\Delta/\varepsilon)$ to the output of a real-valued function $f$. Here, $\Delta$ denotes the $\ell_1$ sensitivity of $f$, measuring the maximum output change due to a single input difference.

## 3 System Model and Design Goals

### 3.1 System and Threat Model

Our protocol involves four parties under a **semi-honest, non-colluding** adversary model, as illustrated in the system architecture (Fig. 1).

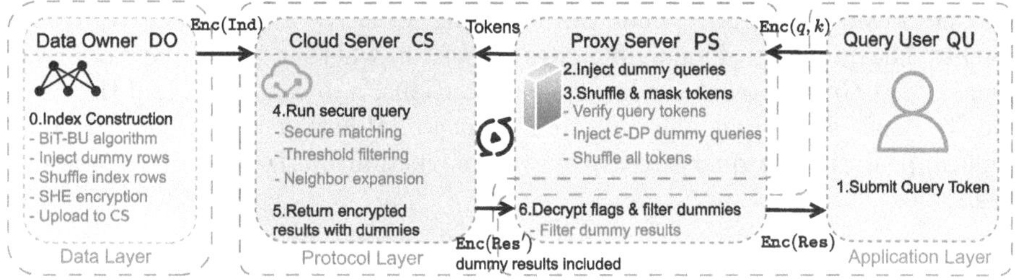


**Fig. 1.** System overview for privacy-preserving $k$-bitruss community query over encrypted bipartite graphs.

- Data Owner DO : DO constructs the encrypted index using BiT-BU decomposition, injects dummy rows at ratio $\rho$ (optimized in Sect. 6.3) with out-of-range node IDs to obfuscate structural patterns, randomly shuffles all rows to eliminate layout correlation, and encrypts each index field using SHE before outsourcing to the cloud.
- Cloud Server CS : CS stores the encrypted index and performs oblivious query evaluation using SHE-based logic gate operators (OP1–OP6). Due to ciphertext-level masking and index shuffling, CS cannot distinguish between real and dummy rows or queries.
- Proxy Server PS : PS issues $\varepsilon$-DP dummy queries by perturbing the query count using Laplace noise with base scale $\delta_{\text{base}} = 2$, ensuring differential privacy over query participation. It also decrypts selection flags output from homomorphic comparison circuits to assist CS filter results securely. Non-collusion between the PS and CS is essential to preserve access privacy.
- Query User QU : QU generates encrypted query tokens $\texttt{Enc}(q, k)$, where both the node ID and threshold $k$ are encrypted using SHE, preventing CS from learning their values. Queries are submitted to the PS for privacy-preserving injection into the index traversal process.

**3.1.1 Threat Assumptions** We assume a standard **semi-honest, non-colluding adversary** [5], where the cloud server (CS) and the proxy server (PS) are managed by independent parties and do not collude. Each party follows the protocol faithfully but attempts to infer additional information from the data they observe. This setting reflects practical deployments [7,19] and enables query and structural privacy without incurring the high cost of fully oblivious computation. We assume that the adversary can compromise either the cloud server (CS) or the proxy server (PS), but not both. During query execution, a compromised server may observe: (i) Encrypted index access patterns (e.g., which rows are accessed), which may leak graph structure information [8]; (ii) The number and frequency of submitted queries $\gamma$, enabling statistical inference attacks such as frequency analysis [2]; (iii) The size of the encrypted result set $|\texttt{Enc}(\texttt{Res})|$, which can reveal query selectivity; (iv) Proxy-decrypted selection flags, if PS is compromised; (v) Timing and latency signals, which may optionally be exploited via side-channel analysis.

The adversary aims to infer the following sensitive information: (i) *Query Intent:* The identity of queried nodes $(q, k)$, or whether a specific node was queried; (ii) *Graph Structure:* Degree distributions, hub centrality, and the presence of dense subgraphs; (iii) *Result Disclosure:* Whether a particular edge or node appears in the query result, or reconstruction of the overall community size.

### 3.2 Design Goals

Our protocol is designed to support privacy-preserving $k$-bitruss community queries over encrypted bipartite graphs. Under the semi-honest threat model described in Sect. 3.1.1, the system aims to achieve the following goals:

- Query Privacy: Provide $\varepsilon$-differential privacy [4] for query participation, preventing node/threshold inference
- Structural Privacy: Rely on IND-CPA secure SHE [9] for data confidentiality, use dummy rows to prevent topology inference
- Access Pattern Privacy: Prevent leakage of token-to-target mappings and query traversal paths
- Result Confidentiality: Conceal community membership and size in the encrypted result set, resist size-based disclosure with noise injection
- Scalability: Ensure sublinear query latency with respect to graph size via index slicing and filtering
- Correctness: Guarantee that the output exactly matches the plaintext $k$-bitruss community of the original graph

These goals are addressed through a combination of encrypted index construction, dummy query and row injection, and secure query evaluation protocols.

## 4 Our Solution

Building on the $k$TCQ [7] framework, we extend its encrypted query design to support $k$-bitruss community search over bipartite graphs. Our scheme incorporates two lightweight privacy mechanisms: dummy rows with index-level shuffling for structural obfuscation, and differentially private dummy queries for access pattern protection. We now describe the encrypted index structure, detail the privacy mechanisms, present the secure query protocol, and conclude with a semantic correctness analysis.

### 4.1 Encrypted BE-Index Construction

To support privacy-preserving $k$-bitruss community queries on bipartite graphs, we construct an encrypted index structure based on the BiT-BU algorithm [16]. It is currently the most efficient method for capturing local butterfly cohesion in bipartite graphs, especially those with globally sparse yet locally dense connectivity patterns.

- Index Layout. Each index row corresponds to a center node $x \in U \cup V$ and contains a metadata field `max` followed by $\omega$ fixed-size neighbor blocks. Each neighbor block stores a neighbor ID $y$, the edge support value $\hat{k}$ for edge $(x, y)$, and the edge ID `eid`.
- ID Assignment and Slicing. We assign unique node IDs by indexing all $V$-type vertices after the $U$-type vertices. To minimize padding, we evaluate all possible slice sizes $\omega \in [1, d_{\max}]$ and select the one that minimizes total row count and padding overhead.
- Bitstream Encoding. Each field is encoded as a fixed-length binary segment. Node IDs use $l_n = \lceil \log_2(n+1) \rceil + 2$ bits, with 2-bit redundancy reserved for node IDs and dummy encoding; edge IDs use $l_e = \lceil \log_2(|E|+1) \rceil + 2$ bits, with 2-bit redundancy reserved for edge IDs and dummy encoding; support values use $l_{\hat{k}} = \lceil \log_2(\hat{k}_{\max}+1) \rceil$ bits. Each neighbor block thus becomes a triplet $(y, \hat{k}, \texttt{eid})$ of bit length $(l_n, l_{\hat{k}}, l_e)$.
- Row Flattening. Each index row is serialized as one center node ID $(l_n)$, one `max` field $(l_{\hat{k}})$, and $\omega$ neighbor blocks. The resulting bitstream has uniform length across all rows, facilitating compact storage and parallel processing.
- Encryption. Each bitstream is encrypted using randomized symmetric homomorphic encryption (SHE), producing uniformly structured ciphertext rows. These encrypted rows support privacy-preserving traversal without revealing structural details such as degrees or neighborhood patterns.

## 4.2 Privacy Enhancements

To protect both access patterns and structural information during query execution, we incorporate two lightweight and orthogonal privacy mechanisms: dummy-row insertion and differentially private dummy-query injection. These mechanisms address leakage risks at both the storage and runtime levels through complementary design principles.

### 4.2.1 Structural Obfuscation via Dummy Rows

Bipartite graphs typically exhibit highly skewed degree distributions, where structural patterns (e.g., hub concentration) may be inferred from index layout even under encryption. To disrupt such correlations, we apply the following obfuscation strategies during index construction:

- Inject dummy rows with node and edge IDs sampled from an out-of-range domain $[n, 2^{\ell_n} - 1]$;
- Set all support values (e.g., `max`, $\hat{k}$) to zero to eliminate informative signals;
- Randomly shuffle all rows after encryption to remove positional bias.

This approach aims to: (i) Decouple node degree from row density patterns; (ii) Create a uniform index footprint resistant to structural inference; (iii) Provide plausible targets for runtime dummy queries. The insertion ratio $\rho$ is selected to achieve a practical balance between privacy strength and index size overhead. The effectiveness of this design is formally analyzed in Sect. 5.

### 4.2.2 Access Pattern Protection via DP Dummy Queries

Query traversal paths may reveal sensitive information about the queried node and community structure. To mitigate this, we adopt a differential privacy framework based on Laplace noise injection:

$$\delta \sim \text{Lap}(1/\varepsilon), \quad \delta_{\text{dummy}} = \max(0, \delta_{\text{base}} + \delta)$$

Two types of dummy queries are generated:

- Valid-target dummies: Sampled from $[0, n-1]$ to emulate real queries.
- Path dummies: Directed to the out-of-range domain $[n, 2^{\ell_n} - 1]$ to disrupt query locality.

All tokens are cryptographically indistinguishable after encryption and shuffling. Each token includes an additional 1-bit ciphertext—set by the proxy during query construction—to indicate whether it is a real or dummy query. This encrypted indicator is preserved throughout the entire traversal and is propagated to all newly enqueued tokens derived from the current token. It is also appended to any result edge produced during the expansion, enabling proxy-side filtering without revealing its value to the cloud. This strategy is designed to: (i) Provide $\varepsilon$-differential privacy for query participation; (ii) Inject uncertainty into access paths through contextual noise; (iii) Preserve query semantics via post-execution filtering. The parameter $\varepsilon$ governs the privacy–efficiency tradeoff, and its impact is formally analyzed in Sect. 5.

### 4.2.3 Synergistic Protection

The two mechanisms operate orthogonally but produce multiplicative effects when combined. Static–Dynamic Decoupling: Dummy rows perturb the storage layout, while dummy queries disrupt access patterns, jointly resisting cross-layer correlation attacks. Shared Obfuscation Domain: The out-of-range domain $[n, 2^{\ell_n} - 1]$ serves a dual role: (i) As structural noise in the index (dummy rows); (ii) As behavioral noise in runtime queries (path dummies), enabling plausible interaction points between storage and access layers. Dummy query tokens are flagged during construction, and their encrypted indicators are propagated during query execution. When result edges are added, these indicators are appended by the cloud and later decrypted by the proxy to filter out dummy-query results. This ensures that privacy mechanisms do not interfere with query correctness or result semantics.

## 4.3 Secure Query Protocol

Our encrypted query protocol extends the $k$TCQ traversal logic with structure-preserving modifications to support privacy-preserving $k$-bitruss community queries over bipartite graphs. The entire process is collaboratively executed by CS and PS, with clearly separated responsibilities.

The execution begins with the queue initialization step. As detailed in Sect. 4.2.2, the encrypted query queue includes one real and several dummy tokens, all indistinguishable and each carrying an encrypted indicator. CS initializes the queue with all unvisited tokens and proceeds with secure traversal. When CS dequeues a token representing a potential center node, it immediately marks it as visited by updating its encrypted state. This design is intended to ensure each node is expanded at most once, thereby avoiding redundant traversal and limiting access-pattern leakage.

- Secure Matching. To locate the index row(s) corresponding to the dequeued token, CS performs encrypted equality tests between the pointer and the encrypted center node fields ($\texttt{Enc}(x)$) in each index row. These comparisons are performed using $k$TCQ [7] secure equal operator (OP1).
- Row Filtering. For each matched row, CS determines whether the encrypted support field $\texttt{Enc}(\texttt{max})$ meets the encrypted query threshold $\texttt{Enc}(k)$. These comparisons are performed using homomorphic comparison circuits. The result of each comparison is an encrypted bit, which is decrypted by PS to decide whether the row should be retained for neighbor expansion or safely discarded.
- Neighbor Evaluation. If a row passes filtering, CS enters the neighbor evaluation phase. It iterates over the $\omega$ neighbor blocks in the row. For each block, CS checks whether the support value $\texttt{Enc}(\hat{k})$ meets the threshold $\texttt{Enc}(k)$. If so, it verifies whether the pair consisting of the encrypted edge identifier $\texttt{Enc}(\texttt{eid})$ and the token's encrypted indicator has already been marked as visited. If not, the encrypted edge $\texttt{Enc}(\texttt{eid})$ with the token's encrypted indicator is added to the encrypted result set $\texttt{Enc}(\texttt{Res}')$, and the pair is marked visited. If the neighbor node is unvisited, its pointer with the token's encrypted indicator is combined as the new token and enqueued for future expansion. The expansion continues until no new pointers remain in the queue. At that point, CS concludes the traversal and outputs the encrypted result set.
- Result Post-processing. After traversal completes, PS filters out any dummy entries from the result set. This is achieved by attaching a 1-bit indicator to each query token during construction. When an edge identifier is added to the result set, CS appends the corresponding indicator. Upon decryption, PS uses the indicator to filter out any entries originating from dummy queries, without learning edge contents. These indicators enable PS to identify and discard dummy-derived results, with the aim of preserving output authenticity without revealing query intent.

This protocol ensures that CS learns nothing about the graph structure or query intent. All sensitive operations—including pointer equality, threshold filtering, and visited state tracking—are executed via homomorphic computation. Proxy involvement is limited to decrypting binary flags, enabling post-execution filtering without leaking semantic information. Once traversal completes, the resulting encrypted set is forwarded to PS, which performs the final decryption and filtering based on the embedded indicators.

### 4.4 Correctness Guarantee

The protocol is designed to preserve the semantics of plaintext $k$-bitruss community discovery, even under encryption and obfuscation. To support this semantic preservation, all key operations—such as node expansion, threshold filtering, and neighbor propagation—are implemented using homomorphic circuits over encrypted data. During expansion, the design attaches the encrypted indicator of the corresponding query token to each edge added to the encrypted result set. The proxy decrypts these indicators to retain only those results originating from real queries, with the aim of preserving the correctness of the result without revealing the token identity. Dummy rows are designed to remain unmatched by real queries, though they may be accessed by dummy queries that target the out-of-range domain. These accesses act as contextual noise by design, and are intended to be filtered during post-processing using encrypted flags. These design choices collectively aim to preserve the soundness and completeness of the final result, aligning it with the expected $k$-bitruss community semantics under plaintext.

# 5 Privacy and Security Analysis

Our simulation-based security analysis extends the standard semi-honest model [5] by incorporating structured leakage profiling and privacy-preserving query abstractions. Specifically, we draw inspiration from leakage-resilient searchable encryption [3], oblivious RAM techniques for hiding access patterns [6], and differential privacy principles for query obfuscation [4]. Recent work on differentially oblivious queries [11] demonstrates that combining DP-based perturbation with controlled access patterns provides a practical alternative to full obliviousness, which motivates our dual-layer design.

## 5.1 Simulation-Based Security Model

We first show that the protocol reveals only minimal, well-defined leakage under IND-CPA security, and that both cloud and proxy views are simulatable without knowledge of plaintext data.

**Theorem 1 (Simulation-Based Security).** *Let $\Pi$ be an IND-CPA secure SHE scheme. Then the protocol leaks only the following:*

- *To the* $\mathtt{CS}$ *: The size of the encrypted index* $|\mathtt{Enc}(\mathtt{Ind})|$*, the total number of accessed index rows* $T$ *(one per dequeued token), and the result size* $|\mathtt{Enc}(\mathtt{Res}')|$*, which includes dummy results from dummy queries. The dummy portion is designed to behave as Laplace-like noise to obscure the true result size.*
- *To the* $\mathtt{PS}$ *: Real query count* $\tau$ *and dummy query count* $\gamma$*, the number of decrypted selection flags from homomorphic equality or comparison circuits, and* $|\mathtt{Enc}(\mathtt{Res})|$*.*

*No information beyond these leakage functions is revealed. In particular, the final result content remains hidden—only its size* $|\mathtt{Enc}(\mathtt{Res})|$ *is observable. But* $\mathtt{PS}$ *cannot link it to graph topology without collusion with* $\mathtt{CS}$*.*

*Under the IND-CPA security of* $\Pi$*, there exist polynomial-time simulators* $(Sim_{\mathtt{CS}}, Sim_{\mathtt{PS}})$ *such that:*

$$\{\mathcal{V}_{\mathcal{CS}}^{REAL}\} \approx_c \{Sim_{\mathcal{CS}}(|\mathit{Enc}(\mathit{Ind})|, T, |\mathit{Enc}(\mathit{Res}')|)\},$$

$$\{\mathcal{V}_{\mathcal{PS}}^{REAL}\} \approx_c \{Sim_{\mathcal{PS}}(\tau, \gamma, \#_{flags}, |\mathit{Enc}(\mathit{Res})|)\}.$$

*Proof (Sketch).* For CS: The view includes only encrypted operations on ciphertexts (e.g., homomorphic comparisons, queue updates), and the number of rows accessed. $\mathrm{Sim}_{\mathcal{CS}}$ simulates ciphertexts and access traces of length $T$ consistent with the leakage. For PS: It sees decrypted binary flags and which are set to 1. $\mathrm{Sim}_{\mathcal{PS}}$ samples a flag vector of length $\#_{\mathtt{flags}}$, with exactly $|\mathtt{Enc}(\mathtt{Res})|$ flags set. Since all plaintexts remain hidden, the simulated view is indistinguishable.

### 5.2 Formal Privacy Guarantees

#### Differential Privacy via Dummy Queries

**Theorem 2 (Formal $\varepsilon$-DP Guarantee).** *Let $\mathcal{Q}$ be a set of real query tokens. Define two neighboring query sets $\mathcal{Q}$ and $\mathcal{Q}'$ such that $|\mathcal{Q} \oplus \mathcal{Q}'| = 1$ (differ by one real query token). The dummy query injection mechanism $\mathcal{M}$ satisfies $\varepsilon$-differential privacy:*

$$\frac{\Pr[\mathcal{M}(\mathcal{Q}) \in \mathcal{O}]}{\Pr[\mathcal{M}(\mathcal{Q}') \in \mathcal{O}]} \leq e^{\varepsilon} \quad \forall \mathcal{O} \subseteq Range(\mathcal{M})$$

*where $\mathcal{M}$ operates as follows: (i) Compute noise: $\delta \sim \mathrm{Lap}(1/\varepsilon)$ (ii) Set dummy count: $\delta_{dummy} = \max(0, \delta_{base} + \delta)$ (iii) Generate $\delta_{dummy}$ dummy queries consisting of: $\alpha \cdot \delta_{dummy}$ valid-target dummies: sampled uniformly from $[0, n-1]$ with random $k > 0$; $(1-\alpha) \cdot \delta_{dummy}$ path dummies: sampled uniformly from $[n, 2^{\ell_n} - 1]$ with $k = 0$ (iv) Combine with real queries, apply SHE encryption and random shuffling This ensures: Query Privacy: $\varepsilon$-DP for real query participation Access Pattern Privacy: All queries are cryptographically indistinguishable to $\mathcal{CS}$.*

*Proof (Proof Sketch).* Part 1 (DP Guarantee): The Laplace mechanism with sensitivity $\Delta = 1$ (single query difference) and scale $1/\varepsilon$ satisfies $\varepsilon$-DP by definition. Part 2 (Indistinguishability): After processing: (i) All tokens encrypted with IND-CPA secure SHE; (ii) Query batch randomly shuffled; (iii) Valid/path dummies have identical ciphertext distributions. Thus no PPT adversary can distinguish token types with non-negligible advantage.

This DP protection remains effective even if structural obfuscation (via dummy row injection) is partially compromised, ensuring layered defense.

#### Structural Obfuscation via Dummy Rows

**Theorem 3 (Structural Obfuscation Guarantee).** *Let the encrypted index contain $d = \rho n$ dummy rows ($\rho > 0$) with: (i) Node IDs sampled uniformly from $[n, 2^{\ell_n} - 1]$; (ii) All support values set to 0; (iii) Random row permutation after encryption. Then for any PPT adversary $\mathcal{A}$ knowing global statistics $(n, e, \deg_{avg})$ but not per-node topology:*

$$\mathtt{Adv}_{\mathcal{A}}^{struct} \leq \frac{1}{(1+\rho)n} + \mathcal{O}\left(\frac{\sigma_{\deg}}{n}\right) + \mathtt{negl}(\lambda)$$

*where $\sigma_{\deg}$ is the standard deviation of node degrees.*

*Proof (Proof Sketch).* The bound combines: (i) Combinatorial term: Probability of random guess $\frac{1}{(1+\rho)n}$; (ii) Statistical leakage: $\mathcal{O}(\sigma_{\text{deg}}/n)$ from known degree distribution; (iii) Crypto indistinguishability: $\mathtt{negl}(\lambda)$ from IND-CPA security; *Empirical success rates (e.g., 9.1% in Sect.* 6.3*) include system-side channels beyond this model.*

### 5.3 Privacy Summary

Our protocol establishes comprehensive privacy guarantees through two orthogonal defense layers: (i) Dynamic Protection: $\varepsilon$-DP dummy queries (Theorem 2) safeguard query participation and access patterns; (ii) Static Protection: Dummy row injection (Theorem 3) obfuscates graph topology and node correlations. The key guarantees include: (i) End-to-End Protection: Secures query intent, graph structure, and result content; (ii) Layered Resilience: Compromising one layer does not break the other (Sect. 4.2.3); (iii) Composable Security: Formal guarantees hold under semi-honest, non-colluding model.

## 6 Experimental Evaluation

We empirically evaluate our protocol with respect to the design goals stated in Sect. 3.2, focusing on the following aspects:

- Scalability and Efficiency: We assess how query latency and encrypted index size scale with increasing dataset sizes (Sect. 6.2), validating sublinear query performance.
- Access Pattern Privacy: We analyze the impact of the differential privacy budget $\varepsilon$ on query participation leakage and processing overhead (Sect. 6.3.2).
- Structural Privacy: We examine how varying the dummy row ratio affects structural obfuscation and index-level indistinguishability (Sect. 6.3.1).
- Parameter Sensitivity: We explore how query correctness and system overhead respond to changes in the bitruss threshold $k$ and slice size $\omega$, to understand robustness and tunability (Sect. 6.4).

Together, these experiments support the protocol's ability to protect query privacy, mask structural signals, and scale efficiently while preserving functional correctness.

### 6.1 Setup and Datasets

We evaluate our protocol using user–movie bipartite graphs from the IMDB dataset[1]. To simulate varying scales, we construct five edge-induced subgraphs ($i_1$–$i_5$) with 10K–50K edges; summary statistics are in Appendix Table 4. Following our design in Sects. 4.2.1 and 4.2.2, we inject dummy rows at a configurable ratio $\rho$, and apply dummy query injection with token shuffling. Index

[1] http://konect.cc/networks/komarix-imdb/.

fields are bit-encoded and encrypted using SHE with parameters $(k_0, k_1, k_2) = (1024, 20, 80)$. We use $\omega = 1$ as the default slice size, computed by our optimization strategy to minimize padding on these datasets. Experiments are implemented in Rust with `rayon`, and executed on a Windows 10 machine (Intel i7 CPU, 16 GB RAM). Index scalability and $\omega$ sensitivity are analyzed in Sects. 6.2 and 6.4. While we use a user–movie graph for evaluation, the protocol is structure-driven and applicable to bipartite graphs with similar butterfly cohesion. Future work will explore datasets with diverse $k$-bitruss distributions.

### 6.2 Scalability with Increasing Dataset Size

We fix the bitruss threshold at $k = 3$, the slice size at $\omega = 1$ (as determined by our initialization strategy), and the privacy budget at $\varepsilon = 1$, and evaluate protocol performance on five datasets ($i_1$–$i_5$) with 10K to 50K edges. As shown in Fig. 2 and Table 1, both the average query time and encrypted index size increase nearly linearly with dataset size, consistent with our design for scalable encrypted slicing and traversal. Encryption time grows with input size due to bitstream encoding and dummy row injection, reflecting a tradeoff between structural privacy and preprocessing cost.

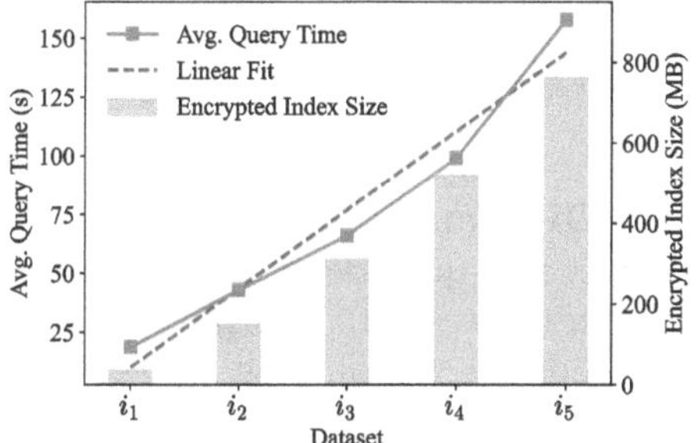


**Fig. 2.** Query performance over datasets $i_1$–$i_5$ with increasing edge count.

**Table 1.** Summary of query latency and index size across datasets.

| Dataset | Query Time (s) | Enc. Size (MB) |
|---|---|---|
| $i_1$ | 18.80 | 42.23 |
| $i_2$ | 42.91 | 154.98 |
| $i_3$ | 66.14 | 316.45 |
| $i_4$ | 99.10 | 525.71 |
| $i_5$ | 158.02 | 768.01 |

### 6.3 Privacy–Utility Tradeoff with Risk-Mitigating Obfuscation

#### 6.3.1 Structural Obfuscation via Dummy Rows

We analyze the impact of dummy row injection on index-level structural privacy. Unlike dummy queries, dummy rows are injected during index construction (Sect. 4.2.1), interleaved with real rows at a configurable ratio $\rho$. Each dummy row uses an invalid node ID and $k = 0$, and is structurally indistinguishable from real entries after encryption. Using dataset $i_5$ and $\omega = 1$, we vary $\rho \in \{5\%, 10\%, 15\%, 20\%\}$ and report: (i) encrypted index size in MB, (ii) encryption time, (iii) total row count, and (iv) theoretical attacker success rate $1/(n+d)$. As shown in Table 2, increasing $\rho$ linearly increases storage and precomputation cost, while reducing adversarial distinguishability. For example, with

$\rho = 10\%$, the theoretical attacker success rate drops to $1/(n + d) \approx 0.0025\%$, illustrating the concrete strength of index-level obfuscation. This empirically supports Theorem 3, which bounds the success probability of identifying real rows by $\leq \frac{1}{(1+\rho)n} + \mathcal{O}(\sigma_{\text{deg}}/n)$. Because dummy rows are layout-randomized and encrypted, they remain indistinguishable from real rows, providing static structural privacy regardless of $\varepsilon$ or query behavior. Together with the dynamic protection offered by DP dummy queries (Sect. 6.3.2), our scheme achieves orthogonal privacy guarantees for both topology and access patterns.

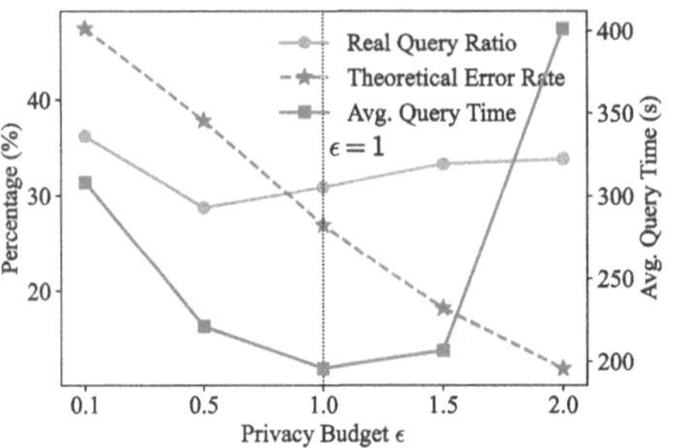


**Fig. 3.** Privacy–latency tradeoff under varying $\varepsilon$.

**Table 2.** Impact of dummy row ratio $\rho$ on index overhead and structural inference bound.

| $\rho$ (%) | Enc. Size (MB) | Enc. Time (s) | Row Count | Attacker Success (%) |
|---|---|---|---|---|
| 5 | 733.11 | 8.23 | 38246 | 0.00262 |
| 10 | 768.01 | 8.87 | 40067 | 0.00250 |
| 15 | 802.92 | 9.08 | 41888 | 0.00239 |
| 20 | 837.82 | 9.58 | 43709 | 0.00229 |

### 6.3.2 Access Pattern Protection via DP Dummy Queries

We evaluate the impact of the privacy budget $\varepsilon$ on query-level anonymity under our randomized dummy injection mechanism (Sect. 4.2.2). The protocol injects $\delta_{\text{dummy}}$ dummy queries sampled from the Laplace distribution $\mathcal{L}(1/\varepsilon)$. These are divided into two types: (i) $\alpha \cdot \delta_{\text{dummy}}$ *valid-target dummies*, sampled from node ID range $[0, n-1]$ with random $k > 0$, used to obfuscate token–target mappings during traversal; (ii) $(1-\alpha) \cdot \delta_{\text{dummy}}$ *path dummies*, sampled from non-node range $[n, 2^{\ell_n}-1]$ with $k = 0$, used to ensure $\varepsilon$-differential privacy for query participation. We empirically evaluated several $\alpha$ settings, including $\{0.9, 0.85, 0.8, 0.75, 0.7\}$, and found that $\alpha = 0.8$ yields the best balance between query latency and access indistinguishability. This setting is used throughout our evaluation unless otherwise stated. We fix $k = 5$ and $\omega = 1$, and vary $\varepsilon \in \{0.1, 0.5, 1.0, 1.5, 2.0\}$. Metrics include: (i) Real Query Ratio: proportion of real tokens among total queries; (ii) Avg. Query Time: end-to-end latency; (iii) Theoretical Error Rate: $1/(1 + e^{\varepsilon})$, representing the adversary's best guess under $\varepsilon$-DP. As shown in Fig. 3, increasing $\varepsilon$ reduces dummy query volume and increases the real query ratio from 28.77% to 33.87%. Latency exhibits a non-monotonic pattern, minimized near $\varepsilon = 1.0$, reflecting the privacy–efficiency tradeoff. Empirical results closely follow the expected theoretical trend, supporting the consistency of our randomized injection mechanism with Theorem 2. Although CS observes the total number of tokens $\tau + \gamma$, the combination of encrypted token shuffling (via $\alpha$ fraction) and uniformly distributed dummy paths prevents meaningful token–target inference. Even under high $\varepsilon$, access patterns remain indistinguishable.

### 6.4 Parameter Sensitivity

We evaluate how two key parameters—the bitruss threshold $k$ and the slice size $\omega$—affect the query performance and encryption overhead ($i_5$, $\varepsilon = 1.0$).

**Effect of Bitruss Threshold $k$.** Figure 4 shows the impact of varying $k$ from 3 to 15 under fixed $\omega = 1$. As $k$ increases, both the average query time and the number of visited index rows grow steadily, due to deeper structural exploration. Meanwhile, the result size |Res| stabilizes as $k$ increases, due to the sparse–dense nature of bipartite graphs: higher bitruss communities tend to concentrate around a small number of structurally dense regions.

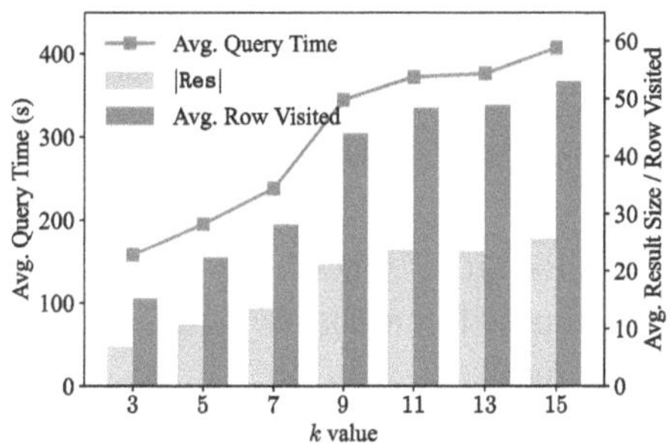


**Fig. 4.** Impact of $k$ on query latency and traversal ($i_5$, $\omega = 1$, $\varepsilon = 1$).

**Table 3.** Impact of $\omega$ on index size and query cost ($i_5$, $k = 5$, $\varepsilon = 1$).

| $\omega$ | Enc(Ind) (MB) | Enc. Time (s) | Row Count | Padding (%) | Query Time (s) |
|---|---|---|---|---|---|
| 1 | 768.01 | 8.87 | 40066 | 0.000 | 195.77 |
| 2 | 918.17 | 10.32 | 29374 | 31.80 | 210.22 |
| 3 | 1196.68 | 13.55 | 27608 | 51.63 | 170.49 |
| 4 | 1507.31 | 17.41 | 27192 | 63.16 | 188.87 |
| 5 | 1830.35 | 22.20 | 27109 | 70.23 | 199.95 |

**Effect of Slice Size $\omega$.** We also vary the slice size $\omega \in \{1, 2, 3, 4, 5\}$ under fixed $k = 5$ and observe its impact on encryption overhead and query time. Query latency, however, does not follow a monotonic trend: it reaches the lowest value at $\omega = 3$ in our experiments. This suggests that $\omega = 3$ offers a sweet spot where the index granularity aligns well with the query distribution and flag evaluation cost. Still, the optimal $\omega$ for query time depends heavily on graph structure and query targets. While the optimal $\omega$ for minimizing query latency varies with the graph structure and query distribution, our initialization strategy selects the slice size that minimizes the total number of index rows and padding overhead. This structure-driven choice ensures compact encrypted storage, but does not guarantee optimal query performance. Detailed results are listed in Table 3.

## 7 Conclusion

We presented a privacy-preserving framework for $k$-bitruss community queries over encrypted bipartite graphs. Our protocol combines bipartite-aware index construction (BiT-BU) with orthogonal obfuscation mechanisms—dummy rows and $\varepsilon$-DP dummy queries— achieving strong privacy guarantees: the theoretical attacker success rate for identifying real index rows drops below 0.0025% (Table 2), while query-level anonymity under DP injection limits inference accuracy to 26.9% (Fig. 3). At the same time, the protocol demonstrates linear scalability with dataset size (Sect. 6.2), supporting secure analysis of dense interaction patterns—such as coordinated fraud—in real-world bipartite settings like e-commerce and social networks. Current limitations include the semi-honest threat model and the reliance on exact $k$-bitruss semantics. Future directions include approximate query support via probabilistic encryption and adaptive privacy budgeting for dynamic or evolving bipartite graphs.

## Appendix

### Supplementary Dataset Statistics and Query Performance

**Table 4.** Dataset statistics of sampled IMDB bipartite graphs.

| Dataset | $\|U\|$ | $\|V\|$ | $n$ | $e$ | $\hat{k}_{\max}$ | $\hat{k}_{\text{avg}}$ |
|---|---|---|---|---|---|---|
| $i_1$ | 9491 | 9483 | 18974 | 10000 | 6 | 0.113 |
| $i_2$ | 18178 | 18026 | 36204 | 20000 | 14 | 0.245 |
| $i_3$ | 26231 | 25891 | 52122 | 30000 | 18 | 0.353 |
| $i_4$ | 33793 | 33039 | 66832 | 40000 | 15 | 0.463 |
| $i_5$ | 40908 | 39703 | 80611 | 50000 | 22 | 0.571 |

## References

1. Bramm, G., Schütte, J.: CipherPath: efficient traversals over homomorphically encrypted paths, vol. 3, pp. 271–278 (2020)
2. Cao, X., Liu, J., Shen, Y., Ye, X., Ren, K.: Frequency-revealing attacks against frequency-hiding order-preserving encryption. Cryptology ePrint Archive (2023)
3. Curtmola, R., Garay, J., Kamara, S., Ostrovsky, R.: Searchable symmetric encryption: improved definitions and efficient constructions. In: Proceedings of the 13th ACM Conference on Computer and Communications Security, pp. 79–88 (2006)
4. Dwork, C., McSherry, F., Nissim, K., Smith, A.: Calibrating noise to sensitivity in private data analysis. In: TCC, pp. 265–284. Springer, Heidelberg (2006). https://doi.org/10.1007/11681878_14
5. Goldreich, O.: General cryptographic protocols. In: Foundations of Cryptography, vol. 2, pp. 599–764. Cambridge University Press (2004)
6. Goldreich, O., Ostrovsky, R.: Software protection and simulation on oblivious RAMs. J. ACM **43**(3), 431–473 (1996)
7. Guan, Y., Lu, R., Zhang, S., Zheng, Y., Shao, J., Wei, G.: $k$TCQ: achieving privacy-preserving $k$-truss community queries over outsourced data. IEEE Trans. Dependable Secure Comput. **21**(4), 2750–2765 (2024)

8. Islam, M.S., Kuzu, M., Kantarcioglu, M.: Access pattern disclosure on searchable encryption: ramification, attack and mitigation. In: NDSS, vol. 20, pp. 12. Citeseer (2012)
9. Katz, J., Lindell, Y.: Introduction to Modern Cryptography, 2nd edn. Chapman & Hall/CRC (2014)
10. Pang, X., Chen, L.: Efficient and privacy-preserving butterfly counting on encrypted bipartite graphs. J. Inf. Secur. Appl. **89**, 103952 (2025)
11. Qiu, L., Kellaris, G., Mamoulis, N., Nissim, K., Kollios, G.: Doquet: differentially oblivious range and join queries with private data structures. Proc. VLDB Endow. **16**(13) (2023)
12. Ran, R., Wang, W., Gang, Q., Yin, J., Xu, N., Wen, W.: CryptoGCN: fast and scalable homomorphically encrypted graph convolutional network inference. Adv. Neural. Inf. Process. Syst. **35**, 37676–37689 (2022)
13. von Richthofen, A., Tomarchio, L., Costa, A.: Identifying communities within the smart-cultural city of Singapore: a network analysis approach. Smart Cities **2**(1), 66–81 (2019)
14. Sarıyüce, A.E., Pinar, A.: Peeling bipartite networks for dense subgraph discovery. In: Proceedings of the Eleventh ACM International Conference on Web Search and Data Mining, pp. 504–512 (2018)
15. Selvaraj, D., Sankar, S.U., Dhinakaran, D., Anish, T.: Outsourced analysis of encrypted graphs in the cloud with privacy protection. SSRG Int. J. Electr. Electron. Eng. **10**(1), 53–62 (2023)
16. Wang, K., Lin, X., Qin, L., Zhang, W., Zhang, Y.: Efficient bitruss decomposition for large-scale bipartite graphs. In: 2020 IEEE 36th International Conference on Data Engineering (ICDE), pp. 661–672. IEEE (2020)
17. Yu, J., Zhang, X., Wang, H., Wang, X., Zhang, W., Zhang, Y.: FPGN: follower prediction framework for infectious disease prevention. World Wide Web **26**, 3795–3814 (2023)
18. Yu, W., et al.: MRFS: mining rating fraud subgraph in bipartite graph for users and products. IEEE Trans. Comput. Soc. Syst. (2023)
19. Zhang, S.: Performance enhanced secure spatial keyword similarity query with arbitrary spatial ranges. IEEE Trans. Inf. Forensics Secur. **19**, 5272–5285 (2024)
20. Zhang, Z., Li, H., Huang, K., Jiang, Y.: k-bitruss-attributed weighted community search on attributed weighted bipartite graphs. In: 2023 IEEE International Conference on Big Data (BigData), pp. 562–567. IEEE (2023)

# Towards Regulated and Accountable Privacy-Preserving Retrieval for Digital Forensics: A Cryptographic Design Framework

Jie Song[1,2,3], Zhen Xu[2], Yan Zhang[2,3](✉), and Hong Miao[1]

[1] Intelligent Policing Key Laboratory of Sichuan Province, Sichuan Police College, Luzhou, China

[2] Institute of Information Engineering, Chinese Academy of Sciences, Beijing, China
{songjie,xuzhen,zhangyan}@iie.ac.cn

[3] School of Cyber Security, University of Chinese Academy of Sciences, Beijing, China

**Abstract.** As digital evidence becomes increasingly central to modern law enforcement, a core challenge has emerged in balancing lawful investigative needs with rigorous privacy safeguards. Traditional forensic mechanisms often assume honest behavior from both investigators and data holders, leaving systems vulnerable in adversarial settings. Two critical threats remain unaddressed: data holders could infer investigation targets by monitoring query patterns, compromising case confidentiality; while investigators might exploit broad access privileges to harvest extraneous personal data. To address this, we propose a regulated and accountable privacy-preserving retrieval framework that integrates Private Information Retrieval (PIR) with blockchain-based accountability, enabling investigators to query forensic datasets without revealing search intent, while ensuring all queries are cryptographically authorized, publicly auditable, and subject to oversight by supervisory entities. Data holders can verify the legitimacy of queries without learning their content, and all actions are logged immutably for auditability and dispute resolution. We formally specify the protocol's architecture and phases, analyze its security and compliance properties, and discuss its applicability to real-world forensic environments. The framework provides a foundational step toward reconciling privacy, accountability, and legal oversight in forensic data access.

**Keywords:** Privacy-preserving Retrieval · Digital Forensics · Auditable · Supervised

## 1 Introduction

In the digital era, vast volumes of personal and organizational data reside across cloud services, online platforms, and edge devices. As criminal activity increasingly leverages these digital infrastructures, digital forensics has become indispensable for public security agencies in evidence acquisition and case resolution.


K.-K. R. Choo et al. (Eds.): ICDF2C 2025, LNICST 686, pp. 176–196, 2026.
https://doi.org/10.1007/978-3-032-22545-0_11

However, collecting evidence from third-party platforms (e.g., social media, cloud storage, IoT environments) presents two enduring challenges: preserving privacy and ensuring the accountability of all participants in the data access process.

Traditional forensic practices typically rely on subpoenas or administrative requests issued to data custodians such as cloud providers or communication platforms. These approaches risk two-fold exposure: they may violate individual privacy through overcollection of irrelevant data, while simultaneously leaking investigative intentions to compromised or adversarial data custodians. This creates a trust vacuum: citizens lack verifiable assurance of law enforcement compliance with privacy constraints, whereas investigators face heightened risks of alerting suspects through potential collusion with compromised data custodians.

Recent research has explored the use of cryptographic protocols such as Private Information Retrieval (PIR) [1–4] to enable query privacy. PIR allows a querier to retrieve an item from a database without revealing which item is being retrieved. However, while PIR protects the privacy of law enforcement personnel during investigation, it lacks mechanisms to ensure legal compliance, proper authorization, and post-hoc accountability, all of which are crucial in the forensic context. Moreover, we adopt a modular PIR layer that can be replaced with alternative schemes without affecting the authorization and audit infrastructure.

To address these limitations, we propose a novel privacy-preserving forensic query framework tailored to the needs of public security investigations. The framework incorporates a blockchain-based supervisory mechanism that enables fine-grained auditability, traceability, and accountability of forensic search operations, while safeguarding the confidentiality of investigative intentions and preventing the exposure of unrelated individuals' personal data. Our design assumes a multi-party ecosystem involving three primary actors, the investigator, the data holder, and a supervisory committee.

The protocol of the framework proceeds in four phases: (i) database commitment, (ii) supervised PIR query authorization, (iii) result verification, and (iv) dispute resolution-each carefully crafted to harmonize privacy preservation, legal compliance, and verifiable accountability. It significantly enhances the trustworthiness of digital forensic processes, particularly in high-stakes environments where the correctness and legitimacy of evidence are paramount. Moreover, our system allows organizations to comply with data protection regulations while supporting lawful criminal investigations.

In summary, we make the following contributions:

- We identify key limitations in existing forensic data retrieval practices and formulate the design goals for privacy-preserving supervised queries.
- We present a modular cryptographic framework that combines PIR, verifiable commitments, threshold authorization, and blockchain-based auditing in a cohesive design.
- We provide a comprehensive analysis of the protocol's security and performance properties, and outline a prototype architecture to illustrate its applicability.

# 2 Background and Related Work

## 2.1 Privacy Challenges in Digital Forensics

As digital technologies become embedded in daily life, digital forensics has become a key investigative tool in combating crime. Law enforcement agencies routinely seek evidence from mobile devices, cloud storage, messaging apps, and IoT platforms. However, these sources often contain highly sensitive or unrelated personal information, raising serious concerns about privacy intrusions during data collection.

Traditional forensic procedures operate on a "full access" model, where data is copied wholesale from seized devices or servers for offline analysis. This model risks overcollection- acquiring data beyond the authorized investigative scope—and may violate legal limits or user privacy expectations [5–7]. These risks are exacerbated in the absence of strong oversight or transparency, potentially undermining public trust.

In response, modern privacy regulations, such as the European Union's General Data Protection Regulation (GDPR) [8], emphasize principles of data minimization and purpose limitation. Similarly, China's Personal Information Protection Law (PIPL) [9] mandates that public authorities handling personal information for statutory obligations must strictly observe necessity requirements (Article 34). These regulations, though not originally designed for law enforcement, increasingly influence public sector data practices and create pressure for reform in digital forensic methodology [10].

## 2.2 Existing Approaches to Privacy-Preserving Retrieval

To align forensic practice with privacy regulations and societal expectations, privacy-preserving retrieval techniques have been introduced. One primary approach is searchable encryption (SE) [11,12], which enables keyword-based search over encrypted data without revealing its plaintext contents. However, SE schemes are typically designed under the assumption that encrypted data is stored on untrusted servers but the query execution is performed by a trusted data provider. This assumption does not always hold in forensic scenarios where the data holder may be semi-honest or untrusted. Furthermore, although the data is stored in encrypted form, SE protocols may reveal leakage such as access patterns (which records are returned) and query patterns (whether two queries are the same) [13,14]. Mitigating these leakages requires additional obfuscation techniques, which are computationally heavy and hard to scale.

By contrast, Private Information Retrieval (PIR) provides strong privacy guarantees without leaking the query or access pattern to the data holder, even if the holder is curious or untrusted. This makes PIR particularly suitable for forensic data access settings that demand minimal trust assumptions while preserving query confidentiality. Classic PIR schemes include information-theoretic approaches [1] and more practical computational schemes using homomorphic encryption [15–18]. Keyword PIR extends PIR to key-value lookups, which is more suitable for forensic databases.

Recent advancements such as Constant-weight PIR (cw-PIR) [2], SparsePIR [3], and PIRANA [4] achieve improved efficiency while preserving strong query privacy. However, these schemes typically focus on privacy alone and do not enforce legal authorization or enable post-hoc auditability.

In the forensic context, these privacy-preserving mechanisms allow investigators to query evidence repositories without exposing their targets or intents to the data holders, who may be neutral third parties or under different jurisdictions. Yet, they do not inherently provide guarantees of accountability or authorize lawful access control, which are critical in law enforcement settings.

### 2.3 Blockchain-Based Accountability in Forensics

To address the gap in accountability and traceability, researchers have explored the integration of blockchain technology into forensic systems. Blockchains provide an immutable, append-only ledger that enables transparent and verifiable recordkeeping of data access and processing events.

For example, [19] proposed using blockchain to record the chain of custody of digital evidence, ensuring tamper-proof logging of evidence handling. [20] designed Forensic-Chain, a blockchain-based framework implemented in Hyperledger Composer to preserve the integrity and auditability of digital evidence during cybercrime investigations. In the context of IoT environments, [21] introduced BEvPF-IoT, a blockchain-based multimedia evidence preservation framework that ensures the integrity and transparency of digital artifacts collected from smart devices. Expanding the scope beyond evidence logging, [22] developed LEChain, a comprehensive lawful evidence management system that spans from data collection to court trial stages. LEChain incorporates witness and juror privacy protection using anonymous signatures and secure voting mechanisms, alongside fine-grained access control enforced through attribute-based encryption.

However, most existing blockchain-forensics applications focus on integrity preservation and event logging. They rarely address privacy concerns such as investigator query protection, or allow fine-grained control of data visibility, making them insufficient for scenarios that demand both privacy and accountability. Our work builds upon these prior approaches by integrating cryptographic query privacy (via PIR) with blockchain-based supervision and authorization, thus enabling privacy preserving yet auditable forensic queries.

### 2.4 Towards a Regulated and Accountable Privacy-Preserving Forensic Framework

Our work bridges these two lines of research, privacy preserving retrieval and blockchain-based auditability, by proposing a regulated forensic protocol that combines PIR-based private search with blockchain-enforced legal supervision.

In this framework, investigators issue encrypted queries using keyword PIR, concealing their search targets from the data holder. At the same time, all query requests and corresponding authorizations are logged on a permissioned blockchain, ensuring traceability and tamper resistance.

Critically, access to sensitive data is mediated by a multi-party threshold signature scheme. Investigators must obtain cryptographic approval from both their commanding officer and an independent auditor before a query is executed.

This approach balances the confidentiality of investigative interests with the need for procedural accountability. Compared to prior works that focus solely on privacy or auditability, our framework integrates both dimensions. It aligns with growing policy consensus around the need for proportionate, transparent, and supervised use of investigative technologies [8,9], offering a privacy-aware and legally compliant forensic infrastructure.

## 3 Preliminaries

To enable a privacy-preserving yet supervised forensic data retrieval protocol, our design integrates multiple cryptographic primitives and decentralized enforcement tools. These foundations are carefully selected to achieve three critical goals: confidentiality of investigators' search interests, integrity and verifiability of data holder responses, and enforceable auditability and accountability through supervision and blockchain anchoring. This section introduces the essential technologies underpinning our framework.

### 3.1 Private Information Retrieval

Private information retrieval (PIR) [23] enables users to retrieve data from servers without revealing which item is being queried. In forensic investigations, this ensures that investigators can perform sensitive queries without exposing their investigative interests to the data holder.

Traditional PIR schemes assume index-based access, i.e., retrieving the $i$-th entry from a database of $n$ items without revealing $i$. However, forensic databases are often structured as keyword-value pairs. Keyword PIR [2,24–26] is better suited here: the client retrieves the value associated with a keyword without revealing the keyword to the server.

In our protocol, we employ constant-weight PIR (cw-PIR) [2], a keyword PIR variant where each query is encoded as a binary vector $\mathbf{cw}_k \in \{0,1\}^d$ of fixed Hamming weight. This encoding supports efficient homomorphic matching, enabling data holder to perform encrypted keyword searches without knowing the query.

### 3.2 Homomorphic Encryption

Homomorphic encryption (HE) enables computation on encrypted data, producing encrypted results that correspond to operations on the underlying plaintexts. Applying HE to PIR is a productive initiative [15–18]. Client sends encrypted queries to the server, which processes them using homomorphic encryption and returns encrypted results. It is easier to deploy on a single server and has lower communication costs.

The cw-PIR scheme adopt the BFV scheme [27], a leveled homomorphic encryption scheme that supports both addition and multiplication on encrypted integers. Like most HE schemes, BFV is based on the Ring Learning with Errors (RLWE) problem [28,29], offering both security and efficiency.

In our context, the investigator sends an encrypted constant-weight vector as a query. The data holder performs homomorphic equality testing $\mathsf{HE.Equal}(\cdot,\cdot)$ between this query and all entries in its CW-encoded database, then computes a masked sum over encrypted values. The result is an encrypted payload $R$ that investigator can decrypt to learn the response—without any information leakage to data holder.

### 3.3 Merkle Trees and Authenticated Commitments

To ensure the authenticity and verifiability of responses, our protocol leverages Merkle trees [30], which allow efficient commitments to large datasets and support succinct inclusion proofs.

A Merkle tree is a binary tree where each leaf node contains the hash of a committed value, and each internal node is the hash of its two children: $h_{\text{parent}} = H(h_{\text{left}} \| h_{\text{right}})$. The Merkle root $\mathsf{root}$ commits to the entire database. To prove that a particular value $h_i$ is part of the committed dataset, a Merkle proof $\pi$ is used. A Merkle proof is a sequence of sibling hashes along the path from a given leaf to the root, which enables efficient reconstruction and verification of the root hash.

The verification procedure checks whether $\mathcal{M}.\mathsf{VerifyProof}(h_i, \pi, \mathsf{root}) \rightarrow \{\mathsf{true}, \mathsf{false}\}$. Merkle proofs are logarithmic in the number of database entries, making them highly efficient for verifiable audit in large-scale datasets.

### 3.4 Threshold Signatures and Authorization

To enforce supervised access control while maintaining decentralization and fault tolerance, our protocol employs a threshold signature scheme to authorize forensic queries. This mechanism ensures that no single supervisory entity can unilaterally approve a data retrieval request—rather, a quorum of supervisory nodes must jointly authorize the query.

Given $n_{\text{sup}}$ supervisor nodes, any subset of $t_{\text{sup}}$ nodes can jointly generate a signature $\tau$ on a message $msg$. Initially, $n_{\text{sup}}$ supervisor nodes generate a collective public key $pk_{\text{sup}}$ and private key shares $\{sk_{\text{sup}}^{(j)}\}_{j=1}^{n_{\text{sup}}}$ through $\left(pk_{\text{sup}}, \{sk_{\text{sup}}^{(j)}\}\right) \leftarrow \mathsf{BLS.KeyGen}(1^{\lambda}, t_{\text{sup}}, n_{\text{sup}})$, where $\lambda$ is the security parameter, $t_{\text{sup}}$ is the authorization threshold, and $n_{\text{sup}}$ is the total supervisor nodes. This ensures no single node controls authorization.

To authorize a message, each SUP node $j$ computes a partial signature over a message $\sigma_j \leftarrow \mathsf{BLS.PartialSign}\left(sk_{\text{sup}}^{(j)}, msg\right)$.

Once $t_{\text{sup}}$ partial signatures $\{\sigma_j\}_{j \in S}$ (with $|S| \geq t_{\text{sup}}$) are collected, they are aggregated into a single signature $\tau \leftarrow \mathsf{BLS.SignCombine}(\{\sigma_j\}_{j \in S})$. And verification checks validity via $\mathsf{BLS.Verify}(pk_{\text{sup}}, msg, \tau) \stackrel{?}{=} \mathsf{true}$, ensuring integrity and threshold approval.

### 3.5 Blockchain and Consortium Chain

To ensure auditability and enforce supervision in forensic data access, our protocol integrates a permissioned blockchain, or consortium chain, as a tamper-resistant log for access control and dispute resolution. Blockchains provide an immutable ledger where each block contains a cryptographic hash of the previous block, a timestamp, and a set of transactions, forming a secure and append-only structure [31,32].

In our setting, the consortium chain is jointly maintained by supervisory nodes from legally authorized institutions. Unlike public blockchains, consortium chains [33] offer higher throughput and controlled access, making them suitable for regulated environments such as law enforcement and judicial oversight.

All authorized query requests are recorded on-chain as transactions. This ensures that each data request is transparently logged and publicly auditable within the consortium.

Additionally, to avoid storing large volumes of private forensic data on-chain, our protocol can use content-addressable storage to store ciphertexts off-chain while anchoring their hashes on-chain. This allows integrity verification without burdening the blockchain with bulky data.

## 4 Framework Design

### 4.1 System Model and Design Goals

This framework is designed for digital forensic collaboration under judicial supervision. It involves four major parties: the Data Holder (DH), the Investigation Authority (INV), a set of decentralized Supervisory Nodes (SUP), and a tamper-evident Blockchain Network.

The system adopts the following role definitions:

(i) The DH stores forensic records in a structured database indexed by keywords. These keywords are encoded into constant-weight binary vectors and embedded as plaintext RLWE polynomials. The database remains in plaintext form to allow efficient homomorphic equality testing.

(ii) The INV is a legally authorized actor who generates encrypted queries over keywords of interest. The query is constructed as a constant-weight RLWE ciphertext, which hides the target keyword from the data holder.

(iii) The SUP-nodes form a decentralized supervisory committee that verifies whether a query is within the scope of authorized investigations. They collectively sign and publish query authorizations, serving as legally accountable intermediaries.

(iv) The Blockchain Network serves as a verifiable and tamper-resistant ledger to record commitments, e.g., Merkle roots, query authorizations, and audit evidence. This ensures traceability and accountability in the absence of cryptographic proofs.

The design of the framework is guided by the following goals:
**Privacy-Preserving Query Capability.** The framework should allow investigators to retrieve data matching a keyword without disclosing the keyword to the data holder or unauthorized entities. This is achieved using a constant-weight PIR technique built on RLWE-based homomorphic encryption.
**Auditability.** The framework achieves a legally enforceable assurance through verifiable audit trails, index commitments, and supervisory authorization records logged on the blockchain network.
**Decentralized Supervision and Legal Accountability.** SUP-nodes collectively ensure that each query is within the authorized investigative scope. Authorization decisions are signed and recorded, enabling investigators to prove their access rights and enabling external auditors or courts to verify compliance post-hoc.
**Integrity and Accountability of Responses:** The response of data holder to a query can be demonstrated through a Merkle based proof that includes all matching records. These proofs can be publicly verified against a committed root hash recorded on-chain, deterring dishonest or malicious behavior.
**Framework Flexibility and Modularity.** Although the framework exemplifies cw-PIR as the privacy layer, the framework is modular and can accommodate alternative PIR schemes depending on practical requirements. The supervisory and audit components are abstracted from the PIR scheme itself.
**Resistance to Abuse and Misuse.** By enforcing mandatory supervision, recording all query authorizations, and verification of results, the framework provides strong deterrence against unauthorized access, misbehavior by the data holder, or overreach by investigators.

In essence, the framework strikes a deliberate balance between privacy, efficiency, and legal verifiability. Rather than relying on cryptographic guarantees alone, it builds an accountable ecosystem where data access is governed, monitored, and auditable under decentralized legal oversight.

### 4.2 Protocol Workflow

We have built a protocol to instantiated the framework, the protocol consists of four main phases:

**Phase 1: Constant-Weight Encoding and Commitment Initialization.** In this phase, a forensic keyword dataset is prepared for privacy-preserving queries by encoding each keyword into a constant-weight binary representation and committing the entire database to a verifiable Merkle structure.

**Keyword Encoding Process.** Let the forensic database consist of key-value pairs $\mathcal{D} = \{(w_1, v_1), \ldots, (w_N, v_N)\}$, where each $w_i$ is a unique searchable keyword, and $v_i$ is the associated private data payload.

Each keyword $w_i$ is deterministically encoded into a constant-weight binary vector $\mathbf{cw}_i \in \{0,1\}^\ell$ using the function: $\mathbf{cw}_i = \mathsf{CWEncode}(w_i, \ell, t_{\mathrm{cw}})$. Here, $\ell$ is the fixed vector length, and $t_{\mathrm{cw}}$ denotes the hamming weight, i.e., number of 1 s in the encoded vector. These system parameters govern the resolution and collision resistance of the PIR matching process. The resulting vectors $\{\mathbf{cw}_i\}$ serve as inputs to the constant-weight PIR protocol [2], where homomorphic matching is performed over encrypted vectors.

**Commitment Construction.** To ensure that the DH cannot alter the database after publication, each entry $(\mathbf{cw}_i, v_i)$ is committed via a Merkle tree. For each $i$, the value payload $v_i$ is first hashed to obtain a short commitment $c_i = H(v_i)$ Then, the Merkle leaf digest is computed as $h_i = H(\mathbf{cw}_i \parallel c_i)$. This construction binds each encoded keyword to its associated data payload while preserving confidentiality.

The set of leaf digests $\{h_i\}_{i=1}^N$ is used to build a binary Merkle tree $\mathcal{M}$, where each internal node is computed as $H(h_L \parallel h_R)$ from its child digests. The resulting Merkle root $\mathsf{root} = \mathcal{M}.\mathrm{root}()$ serves as a compact, tamper-evident fingerprint of the database and is published on-chain. The algorithm for phase 1 is described in detail in Appendix A.1.

**Verification Setup.** To enable decentralized supervision, a set of $n_{\mathrm{sup}}$ supervisory nodes SUP-nodes collaboratively execute a threshold key generation protocol [34,35]: $(pk_{\mathrm{sup}}, \{sk_{\mathrm{sup}}^{(j)}\}) \leftarrow \mathsf{BLS.KeyGen}(1^\lambda, t_{\mathrm{sup}}, n_{\mathrm{sup}})$. Here, $t_{\mathrm{sup}}$ is the decryption threshold, each $sk_{\mathrm{sup}}^{(j)}$ is a partial share of the decryption key.

All public parameters—including $\mathsf{root}$, encoding parameters $(\ell, t_{\mathrm{cw}})$, encryption parameters such as polynomial degree and plaintext modulus are immutably recorded on the blockchain.

**Phase 2: Query with Constant-Weight PIR.** This phase allows an investigator to perform a privacy-preserving search for a keyword $w_k$ in the forensic dataset, under the supervision and authorization of supervisory nodes. It integrates constant-weight encoding, homomorphic encryption, and digital attestation to ensure privacy, auditability, and policy compliance.

**Investigator Authorization and Query Submission.** To initiate a search, the investigator locally generates a BFV encryption key (symmetric mode to reduce ciphertext size) $sk_{\mathrm{inv}}$ for query encryption and result decryption. The INV then prepares the target keyword $w_k$, a digitally signed judicial warrant $\mathcal{W}$, case metadata, e.g., $m = (\mathsf{warrantID}, \mathsf{caseType}, \mathsf{targetDH})$, timestamp $\mathsf{ts}$ indicating the time of the request, and investigator identity $ID_{\mathrm{inv}}$.

The keyword $w_k$ is deterministically encoded into a constant-weight vector $\mathbf{cw}_k = \mathsf{CWEncode}(w_k, \ell, t_{\text{cw}})$, and then encrypts this vector using its BFV key: $q_{\text{enc}} = \mathsf{BFV.Enc}_{sk_{\text{inv}}}(\mathbf{cw}_k)$.

The investigator sends the tuple $(\mathcal{W}, m, \mathsf{ts}, ID_{\text{inv}}, \mathbf{cw}_k, q_{\text{enc}})$ to the SUP-node committee for validation. The encrypted query $q_{\text{enc}}$ can be stored off-chain with an on-chain hash index.

**SUP Authorization and Signature Generation.** Upon receiving the request, SUP-nodes perform the following steps:
*Step 1* Validate the authenticity and jurisdiction of the warrant $\mathcal{W}$.
*Step 2* Check that $w_k$ satisfies policy constraints. If $w_k \in \Gamma_{\text{legal}} \wedge \mathsf{ValidWarrant}(m.\mathsf{warrantID})$, then $\mathsf{Authorize}(w_k, m) = \text{true}$, otherwise $\mathsf{Authorize}(w_k, m) = \text{false}$, where $\Gamma_{\text{legal}}$ is a set of policy-approved keywords.
*Step 3* If authorized, each SUP-node $j$ generates a partial signature $\sigma_j \leftarrow \mathsf{BLS.PartialSign}(sk_{\text{sup}}^{(j)}, H(q_{\text{enc}} \parallel ID_{\text{inv}} \parallel \mathsf{ts}))$.
*Step 4* Once at least $t_{\text{sup}}$ valid partial signatures $\sigma_j$ are collected, they are combined $\tau \leftarrow \mathsf{BLS.SignCombine}(\{\sigma_j\}_{j \in S})$.
*Step 5* The SUP committee returns the threshold signature $\tau$ to both INV and DH, and publishes it on-chain for auditability.

After receiving the threshold signature $\tau$ from the SUP-nodes, the investigator forwards the encrypted query $q_{\text{enc}}$ along with the signature $\tau$, $ID_{\text{inv}}$ and $\mathsf{ts}$ to the data holder. The DH verifies the validity of $\tau$ against the signed message components $(q_{\text{enc}}, ID_{\text{inv}}, \mathsf{ts})$ before proceeding with the homomorphic query evaluation. This ensures that only SUP-authorized queries are served by DH, preserving access policy compliance and enabling accountability. The algorithm for phase 1 is shown in Algorithm A.2.

**Phase 3: Query Response and Result Verification.** At this stage, the DH responds to the query results and enables the investigator (INV) to verify the correctness of the homomorphic search results returned by the data holder (DH) under the supervision of the SUP node. It ensures that the returned encrypted payload corresponds to a committed entry in the Merkle-authenticated database, without revealing the queried keyword or the matching index.

**Homomorphic Query Evaluation by DH.** Upon receiving a query package $Q = (q\_\text{enc}, ID\_\text{inv}, \tau, \mathsf{ts})$ from INV, the data holder (DH) performs authorization verification by checking the threshold signature $\tau$ from SUP: $\mathsf{Verify}_{\text{sup}}(\tau, H(q_{\text{enc}} \parallel ID_{\text{inv}} \parallel \mathsf{ts})) \stackrel{?}{=} \text{true}$. If the signature is valid, DH proceeds to evaluate the homomorphic constant-weight PIR query. Let $\mathcal{CW} = \mathbf{cw}_1, \ldots, \mathbf{cw}_N$ be the CW-encoded database vectors and $v_1, \ldots, v_N$ the corresponding payloads. DH computes $r_i = \mathsf{HE.Equal}(q_{\text{enc}}, \mathbf{cw}_i), \quad \forall i \in [N]$. Here, $\mathsf{HE.Equal}(\cdot, \cdot)$ is homomorphic equality operator (see 2.4 in cw-PIR [2]) that evaluates to an encrypted 0/1 mask indicating whether $q_{\text{enc}}$ matches $\mathbf{cw}_i$. Next, calculate the inner product between the mask and the payload: $R = \sum_{i=1}^{N} r_i \cdot v_i$. The resulting ciphertext $R$ is the encrypted payload corresponding to the matched keyword (or 0 if unmatched), which DH returns to INV.

**Payload Decryption and Hash Proof by INV.** After receiving $R$, the investigator decrypts the payload using their secret key, $v_k = \mathsf{BFV.Dec}_{sk_{\text{inv}}}(R)$. Then, the INV computes a hash of the decrypted result $c_k = H(v_k)$.

The INV provides the previously submitted CW-encoded query $\mathbf{cw}_k$ and $c_k$ to the SUP. The SUP verifies whether $\mathbf{cw}_k$ is consistent with the previous submission, and verifies whether the following digest exists in the Merkle tree committed by the DH in Phase 1: $h_k = H(\mathbf{cw}_k \parallel c_k)$. If a valid Merkle inclusion proof for $h_k$ is found in the tree $\mathcal{M}$ (with respect to on-chain root $\mathsf{root}$), this confirms that $v_k$ is an authentic result matching the committed database. Otherwise, the integrity of DH's response is challenged.

**Proof Validation by SUP.** The INV submits $\mathbf{cw}_k$, $c_k = H(v_k)$ to SUP. SUP verifies: $\mathcal{M}.\mathsf{VerifyProof}(h_k = H(\mathbf{cw}_k \parallel c_k), \pi, \mathsf{root}) \stackrel{?}{=} \text{true}$.

If the verification passes, SUP accepts that $R$ was correctly computed by DH with respect to the query $q_{\text{enc}}$ and the committed database. SUP then publishes a signed audit statement attesting to the correctness of the retrieval, thus finalizing the forensic query. Phase 3 workflow is shown in Algorithm A.3.

**Phase 4: Dispute Resolution and Result Revocation.** This phase is triggered when the supervisory node fails to validate the query result against the committed Merkle root during Phase 3. The goal of dispute resolution is to determine whether the fault lies with the investigator, who may have submitted an inconsistent query or forged payload hash, or with the data holder, who may have returned a malformed or incorrect result.

**Triggering Condition and Arbitration Request.** If the Merkle verification of $h_k = H(\mathbf{cw}_k \parallel H(v_k))$ fails $\mathcal{M}.\mathsf{VerifyProof}(h_k, \pi, \mathsf{root}) = \mathsf{false}$, then SUP initiates a dispute resolution procedure. The investigator is required to submit their secret key $sk_{\text{inv}}$ along with the original query package $Q = (q_{\text{enc}}, ID_{\text{inv}}, \tau, \mathsf{ts})$ to SUP. This enables SUP to independently decrypt the query ciphertext and check for consistency.

**SUP Arbitration Logic.** SUP performs two main checks:
*Query-Authorization Consistency Check.* SUP verifies that the query ciphertext $q_{\text{enc}}$ corresponds to the same $\mathbf{cw}_k$ that was used for result verification, and that $\tau$ is a valid SUP-issued signature over the query metadata: $\mathsf{Verify}_{\mathsf{sup}}(\tau, H(q_{\text{enc}} \parallel ID_{\text{inv}} \parallel \mathsf{ts})) \stackrel{?}{=} \text{true}$. SUP decrypts $q_{\text{enc}}$ using $sk_{\text{inv}}$ to recover the original query vector: $\mathbf{cw}'_k = \mathsf{BFV.Dec}_{sk_{\text{inv}}}(q_{\text{enc}})$. If $\mathbf{cw}'_k \neq \mathbf{cw}_k$, then INV submitted an inconsistent or manipulated result and is held accountable.

*DH Response Validation.* If the decrypted $\mathbf{cw}'_k$ matches the previously submitted $\mathbf{cw}_k$, then SUP concludes that DH must have returned an incorrect response $R$ that fails Merkle verification. In this case, DH is found at fault, and a revocation or penalty is triggered.

**Result Revocation and Audit Logging.** Upon determining fault, SUP publishes the arbitration verdict to the blockchain for transparency and logs a result revocation event. This ensures accountability and enables forensic traceability of misbehavior by either party. Algorithm A.4 shows the workflow of Phase4.

This final phase guarantees accountability for both parties: any attempt by INV to tamper with query records or falsify verification inputs is detectable, and any deviation by DH from the committed database is provably punishable. The transparency of the SUP-verified arbitration process enhances the credibility and legal admissibility of forensic search outcomes.

# 5 Analysis

In this section, we analyze how the proposed forensic query protocol satisfies its design goals of privacy preservation, legal compliance, and auditability, while also discussing potential limitations.

## 5.1 Security and Privacy Guarantees

The protocol ensures that investigators can perform forensic keyword searches without revealing the query target to the data holder or supervisory nodes, thus preventing data profiling or leakage of investigative intent:

**Keyword Privacy.** The investigator encrypts the search keyword using BFV homomorphic encryption [27] to generate $q_{\text{enc}}$. This ensures that neither the DH nor the supervisory nodes learn the plaintext keyword without the $sk_{\text{inv}}$. The DH cannot distinguish which keyword is being queried. Even repeated queries over the same keyword produce unlinkable ciphertexts due to semantic security.

**Query Result Privacy.** The DH performs homomorphic equality checks between $q_{\text{enc}}$ and encoded keys $\mathbf{cw}_i$without decrypting $q_{\text{enc}}$. The inner product result $R$ is returned in ciphertext form, ensuring that the payload $v$ remains hidden from any third party except INV.

**Access Control Integrity.** Only investigators with valid judicial warrants can obtain threshold-signed tokens $\tau$ from the SUP committee. These tokens are cryptographically bound to the request and timestamp, preventing reuse, forgery, or token sharing. The SUP committee use threshold BLS signatures to generate authorization $\tau$. This requires a quorum of SUP nodes to collaborate, preventing unilateral access to sensitive data.

## 5.2 Legal Compliance and Supervision

The protocol integrates verifiable authorization and supervisory control into the query process to ensure all forensic activities conform to regulatory mandates.

**Decentralized Authorization and Supervision.** Each query must be endorsed by SUP through a threshold signature $\tau$, which binds the investigator's identity and timestamp to the encrypted query. Unauthorized queries are automatically rejected by DH. In addition to the authorization process requiring threshold consensus between SUP nodes, dispute resolution also requires SUP consensus, so no node can authorize illegal queries or bypass compliance checks. This agreement essentially resists collusion and centralized abuse of power.

**Auditable Metadata Binding.** Every authorized query request is recorded on-chain, including the hash of the warrant, investigator identity, timestamp, and policy decision, providing a legally admissible trail of authorization, consistent with real-world forensic chain-of-custody requirements. This ensures future accountability and enables retrospective investigation.

### 5.3 Auditability and Traceability

The protocol ensures auditability and traceability across all stages of the forensic query lifecycle by combining authenticated data structures with blockchain-based publication.

**Immutable Commitment to Evidence Database.** The data holder commits to its entire encoded keyword-value database by constructing a Merkle tree and publishing its root $\mathsf{root}$ to the blockchain. This root acts as a tamper-evident commitment to the state of the database at the time of query initiation, preventing any post-hoc modification of evidence records.

**Proof Verification.** The SUP receives $(\mathbf{cw}_k, H(v_k))$ from the investigator. Holding the full Merkle tree, SUP reconstructs the inclusion proof $\pi_k$ and verifies that $H(\mathbf{cw}_k \parallel H(v_k))$ is contained in the committed root.

**On-chain Audit Trail.** SUP publishes signed verdicts and arbitration outcomes to the blockchain, providing external auditors and courts with a verifiable log of access requests, result validations, and detected misbehaviors.

### 5.4 Performance and Cost Analysis

As this work presents a cryptographic design framework rather than an implemented system, our analysis focuses on the theoretical resource requirements and structural efficiency of the framework components. The goal is to assess the feasibility and design-level trade-offs of the proposed protocol, rather than reporting empirical benchmarks. Specifically, we examine the computational complexity, bandwidth usage, and blockchain-related load, focusing on non-PIR components.

The PIR module is designed to be pluggable, meaning different keyword PIR schemes can be substituted depending on the deployment context and performance needs. Therefore, the following analysis assumes the PIR selection is fixed externally and concentrates on evaluating the remaining cryptographic and system-level components, particularly those related to commitment, verification, and audit processes.

**Cryptographic Assumptions.** The following analysis assumes standard post-quantum cryptographic primitives and complexity bounds. Specifically, commitment schemes are instantiated using collision-resistant hash functions (e.g., SHA-3 with 256-bit output), and Merkle trees are binary with depth $\log_2 N$. Merkle proof size scales logarithmically with $N$ as $|\pi| = \mathcal{O}(\log N \cdot |h|)$. Constant-weight vectors are treated as opaque objects of fixed size $\ell$, and homomorphic ciphertexts are assumed to be represented under the BFV scheme. While precise encoding sizes and encryption parameters are deployment-dependent, the analysis focuses on asymptotic behaviors rather than concrete runtime or bandwidth figures.

**Investigator (INV).** The investigator initiates the query, decrypts the result, and engages in result verification. Computational burden on the investigator is lightweight across all phases.

In *Phase 2*, INV constructs the PIR query and packages it with metadata including a SUP-issued threshold signature. As the PIR module is treated externally, the query ciphertext is considered precomputed. The additional metadata and packaging operations are minimal.

During *Phase 3*, INV decrypts the homomorphic result and hashes the resulting plaintext. These operations involve standard polynomial arithmetic and a hash evaluation, both of which are efficient. INV then sends a short verification tuple to SUP, consisting of the CW vector and hash. Since the CW vector is small, communication cost is negligible.

If a dispute arises in *Phase 4*, INV discloses their decryption key to SUP. This step requires no heavy computation unless enhanced privacy-preserving dispute resolution mechanisms are introduced. The overall overhead for INV remains low throughout the protocol.

**Data Holder (DH).** The data holder bears the most substantial computational cost due to the database commitment and PIR response generation.

In *Phase 1*, the data holder generates hash commitments for each database entry by computing $h_i = H(\mathbf{cw}_i \parallel H(v_i))$ and constructs a Merkle tree over the $N$ resulting hashes. The computation cost scales linearly with $N$, both for hashing the leaves and computing internal nodes. In addition to posting the Merkle root on-chain, DH transmits the full Merkle tree (or equivalent authentication paths) to the SUP to enable independent path verification. This communication cost is linear in $N$, and its volume size is acceptable (≈4 MB for $N = 2^{16}$). The commitment process can be efficiently parallelized or precomputed offline.

In *Phase 3*, DH evaluates the PIR query. The main cost of this step comes from within PIR, which involves applying homomorphic operations—primarily multiplications and additions—across the entire dataset. The bandwidth cost is independent of $N$ due to the returned response is fixed at one ciphertext, but the computation is linear in database size and dominated by PIR arithmetic.

**Supervisory Node (SUP).** SUP oversees the query process and performs lightweight cryptographic verification.

In *Phase 2*, SUP verifies the threshold signature on the query metadata using standard signature schemes. This verification involves a single curve operation and is computationally trivial.

In *Phase 3*, SUP receives a short verification tuple $(\mathbf{cw}_k, c_k)$ from INV, reconstructs the commitment hash $h_k = H(\mathbf{cw}_k \parallel c_k)$, and verifies Merkle inclusion under the committed root. This verification involves $\mathcal{O}(\log N)$ hash evaluations, which are efficient even for large databases. If validation succeeds, SUP signs and posts a verdict on-chain.

In *Phase 4*, if a dispute is triggered, SUP decrypts the query ciphertext using the investigator's disclosed key and recomputes the corresponding CW vector. SUP then verifies the recomputed hash against the Merkle tree and previous records. These steps involve a single decryption and $\mathcal{O}(\log N)$ hash operations, incurring negligible computation but requiring SUP to post an auditable dispute record on-chain.

**Blockchain Interaction Overhead.** The proposed protocol is designed for deployment over a permissioned blockchain (consortium chain) maintained by authorized stakeholders such as forensic labs, courts, and regulatory bodies. Unlike public blockchains, consortium chains do not rely on permissionless consensus or fee-based gas models. Therefore, chain interactions are not subject to volatile cost estimation in gas units but are instead governed by deterministic consensus schedules and throughput constraints.

Blockchain interactions are sparse and lightweight, limited to one-time Merkle root commitment and Merkle tree by DH in Phase 1, query registration with hash anchor in Phase 2, and audit verdict publication in Phase 3 or Phase 4.

All on-chain payloads are fixed-size cryptographic digests or signatures. As a result, the overall chain storage complexity per query is $\mathcal{O}(1)$, and the write frequency is independent of the database size. This makes the framework compatible with private and semi-private blockchain infrastructures, such as Hyperledger Fabric [33], where controlled write access and optimized ledger throughput are available.

Across all phases, the heaviest load falls on the DH in the form of cryptographic preprocessing and query evaluation. SUP and INV perform only verification and lightweight messaging. The modularity of the design allows the PIR backend to evolve independently, while maintaining a constant and predictable non-PIR overhead profile.

Table 1 demonstrates the cost breakdown of our protocol framework, where the most computationally and bandwidth-intensive operation occurs in Phase 3 when DH performs homomorphic computations - operations inherent to the PIR scheme. Thus, our protocol framework achieves its design objectives while introducing only minimal additional overhead beyond the intrinsic computational costs of PIR.

**Table 1.** Theoretical Cost Breakdown

| Phase | Role | Operation | Time Complexity | Bandwidth | Chain Load |
|---|---|---|---|---|---|
| Phase 1 | DH | Build Merkle tree over $(\mathbf{cw}_i \| H(v_i))$ | $\mathcal{O}(N)$ | $\mathcal{O}(N)$ | - |
| | DH | Commit Merkle root to chain | $\mathcal{O}(1)$ | - | $\mathcal{O}(1)$ |
| Phase 2 | INV | Encrypt query $q_{\text{enc}}$ and send $Q$ to DH | $\mathcal{O}(1)$ | $\mathcal{O}(\|Q\|)$ | - |
| | INV | Post $H(q_{\text{enc}})$ to chain for audit trace | $\mathcal{O}(1)$ | - | $\mathcal{O}(1)$ |
| | SUP | Threshold sign query metadata | $\mathcal{O}(t_{sup})$ | $\mathcal{O}(t_{sup} \cdot \|\tau\|)$ | - |
| | SUP | Store authorization record to chain | $\mathcal{O}(1)$ | - | $\mathcal{O}(\|QueryAuthRecord\|)$ |
| Phase 3 | DH | Compute $r_i = \mathsf{HE.Equal}(q_{\text{enc}}, \mathbf{cw}_i)$ and $R = \sum r_i \cdot v_i$ | $\mathcal{O}(N)$ (PIR) | $\mathcal{O}(\|R\|)$ | - |
| | DH | Post commitment of $R$ to chain | $\mathcal{O}(1)$ | - | $\mathcal{O}(1)$ |
| | INV | Decrypt $R$ and compute $H(v_k)$ | $\mathcal{O}(1)$ | $\mathcal{O}(\|\mathbf{cw}_k\| + \|H(v_k)\|)$ | - |
| | SUP | Verify Merkle proof $(\pi, h_k)$ and publish result | $\mathcal{O}(\log N)$ | - | $\mathcal{O}(\|Verdict\|)$ |
| Phase 4 | INV | Reveal $sk_{\text{inv}}$ for dispute audit | $\mathcal{O}(1)$ | $\mathcal{O}(\|sk_{\text{inv}}\|)$ | - |
| | SUP | Decrypt $q_{\text{enc}}$, determine responsibility | $\mathcal{O}(1)$ | - | $\mathcal{O}(\|DisputeRecord\|)$ |

### 5.5 Limitations

While the protocol offers strong privacy and accountability guarantees, it relies on several assumptions and introduces certain limitations:

**Honest-but-Curious SUP Model.** All supervisory nodes are assumed to behave honestly in protocol execution, while possibly being curious about metadata. Stronger adversarial models—e.g., actively malicious SUPs—would require zero-knowledge or multi-party computation extensions, which come with increased cost.

**BFV Performance Overhead.** Homomorphic equality and inner product operations in CW-PIR are computationally intensive, potentially affecting real-time search responsiveness. Hardware acceleration or scheme optimizations may be needed for large-scale deployments. Fortunately, the PIR scheme is plugin based, and other more efficient PIR schemes can be chosen within the framework.

**INV Key Disclosure in Arbitration.** During dispute resolution, the investigator must reveal their decryption key (or key share), which may raise operational or legal concerns. One-time encapsulated keys for each query and immediately destroy them after arbitration could mitigate this.

**Keyword Granularity.** The current protocol supports only exact keyword match queries. Extending support to range query, boolean predicate, or similarity search requires non-trivial modifications and remains an open area. We are working on tackling this challenging problem in another work.

## 6 Conclusion

We have presented a supervised, privacy-preserving forensic query protocol that integrates Constant-weight PIR, cryptographic commitments, and blockchain-based auditing to enable legally compliant access to sensitive digital evidence. By combining PIR mechanisms with on-chain compliance enforcement, our framework ensures that investigative queries remain unlinkable and hidden from data holders, while still subject to strict judicial oversight.

The modular design supports pluggable PIR backends, allowing performance to be tuned to application needs without weakening the compliance and audit guarantees. Through detailed analysis, we demonstrate that the protocol satisfies its design goals: legal accountability, query privacy, retrieval correctness, and traceable auditing. Theoretical cost models show that, outside the PIR core, the overhead remains low and scales logarithmically with database size in critical components such as Merkle proofs.

Nonetheless, certain limitations remain. The reliance on BFV-based PIR implies computational overhead on the server side, especially for large-scale deployments. Additionally, real-world integration with legal systems and court-issued digital warrants introduces non-technical challenges in policy standardization and governance.

Future work includes exploring more efficient PIR variants, and expanding to multi-keyword or range queries. Our framework lays a privacy-preserving, auditable foundation for lawful digital forensics in the era of decentralized and cloud-based evidence storage.

**Acknowledgements.** This work was supported by the Intelligent Policing Key Laboratory of Sichuan Province under Grant ZNJW2022ZZQN004.

## Appendix A: Protocol Algorithms

**Algorithm A.1: Keyword Encoding and Merkle Commitment**

**Input:** Keyword set $\{(w_i, v_i)\}_{i=1}^{N}$, encoding parameters $(\ell, t_{\text{cw}})$
**Output:** Encoded vectors $\{\mathbf{cw}_i\}$, Merkle root $\mathsf{root}$
1: **for** each $(w_i, v_i)$ in the dataset **do**
2: $\quad \mathbf{cw}_i \leftarrow \mathsf{CWEncode}(w_i, \ell, t_{\text{cw}})$
3: $\quad c_i \leftarrow H(v_i)$ ▷ Payload commitment
4: $\quad h_i \leftarrow H(\mathbf{cw}_i \parallel c_i)$ ▷ Merkle leaf
5: **end for**
6: Build Merkle tree $\mathcal{M}$ from leaves $\{h_1, \ldots, h_N\}$
7: Send $\mathcal{M}$ to SUP
8: $\mathsf{root} \leftarrow \mathcal{M}.\mathsf{root}()$
9: **return** $\{\mathbf{cw}_i\}, \mathsf{root}$

**Algorithm A.2: CWPIR Query Construction and Authorization**

**Input:** Keyword $w_k$, warrant $\mathcal{W}$, metadata $m$, investigator ID $ID_{\text{inv}}$
**Output:** Authorized query package $Q = (q_{\text{enc}}, \tau, \mathsf{ts})$

*Performed by Investigator (INV)*

1: $sk_{\text{inv}} \leftarrow \mathsf{BFV.KeyGen}(1^\lambda)$
2: $\mathbf{cw}_k \leftarrow \mathsf{CWEncode}(w_k, \ell, t_{\text{cw}})$
3: $q_{\text{enc}} \leftarrow \mathsf{BFV.Enc}_{sk_{\text{inv}}}(\mathbf{cw}_k)$
4: $\mathsf{ts} \leftarrow \mathsf{GetCurrentTimestamp}()$
5: Anchor $q_{\text{enc}}$ to blockchain
6: Submit $(\mathcal{W}, m, ID_{\text{inv}}, \mathsf{ts}, \mathbf{cw}_k, q_{\text{enc}})$ to SUP-nodes

*Performed by Supervisory Nodes (SUP)*

7: **if** $\neg\mathsf{VerifyWrt}(\mathcal{W}) \vee \neg\mathsf{ValidWrt}(m.\mathsf{warrantID})$ **then**
8: Abort query (invalid warrant)
9: **end if**
10: **if** $w_k \notin \Gamma_{\text{legal}}$ **then**
11: Abort query (keyword not permitted)
12: **end if**
13: $M \leftarrow q_{\text{enc}} \parallel ID_{\text{inv}} \parallel \mathsf{ts}$
14: $h \leftarrow H(M)$
15: $\tau \leftarrow \mathsf{BLS.Sign}_{\mathsf{sup}}(h)$
16: Upload $\tau$ to blockchain

*Output by SUP*

17: $Q \leftarrow (q_{\text{enc}}, ID_{\text{inv}}, \tau, \mathsf{ts})$
18: **return** $Q$

**Algorithm A.3: Query Response and Result Verification**

**Input:** Query ciphertext $q_{\text{enc}}$, Merkle root root, encrypted database $\{(\mathbf{cw}_i, v_i)\}_{i=1}^N$, decryption key $sk_{\text{inv}}$
**Output:** Audit decision Verdict $\in \{\mathsf{Valid}, \mathsf{Invalid}\}$

*Performed by Data Holder (DH)*

1: **for** $i = 1$ **to** $N$ **do**
2: $r_i \leftarrow \mathsf{HE.Equal}(q_{\text{enc}}, \mathbf{cw}_i)$
3: **end for**
4: $R \leftarrow \sum_{i=1}^N r_i \cdot v_i$
5: Send $R$ to INV

*Performed by Investigator (INV)*

6: $v_k \leftarrow \mathsf{BFV.Dec}_{sk_{\text{inv}}}(R)$
7: $c_k \leftarrow H(v_k)$
8: Submit $(\mathbf{cw}_k, c_k)$ to SUP

*Performed by Supervisory Nodes (SUP)*

9: $h_k \leftarrow H(\mathbf{cw}_k \parallel c_k)$
10: $\pi \leftarrow \mathsf{MerklePath}(h_k)$
11: **if** $\mathcal{M}.\mathsf{VerifyProof}(h_k, \pi, \mathsf{root}) = \mathsf{true}$ **then**
12: Verdict ← Valid
13: Sign and publish audit result to blockchain
14: **else**
15: Verdict ← Invalid
16: Trigger Phase 4 (Dispute Resolution)
17: **end if**
18: **return** Verdict

**Algorithm A.4: Dispute Resolution and Result Revocation**

**Input:** Query package $Q = (q_{\text{enc}}, ID\_\text{inv}, \tau, \mathsf{ts})$, submitted $\mathbf{cw}_k$, hash digest $c_k = H(v_k)$, Merkle root root, decryption key $sk_{\text{inv}}$
**Output:** Arbitration verdict $\mathsf{Blame} \in \mathsf{INV}, \mathsf{DH}$

*Performed by Supervisory Nodes (SUP)*

1: Verify authorization signature:
2: **if** $\mathsf{Verify}_{\mathsf{sup}}(\tau, H(q_{\text{enc}} \parallel ID\_\text{inv} \parallel \mathsf{ts})) \neq \mathsf{true}$ **then**
3: Blame ← INV ▷ Invalid authorization
4: Publish arbitration log to blockchain
5: **return** Blame
6: **end if**
7: Decrypt query ciphertext: $\mathbf{cw}'_k \leftarrow \mathsf{BFV.Dec}_{sk_{\text{inv}}}(q_{\text{enc}})$
8: Compare decrypted query with submitted $\mathbf{cw}_k$:
9: **if** $\mathbf{cw}'_k \neq \mathbf{cw\_}k$ **then**
10: Blame ← INV ▷ Query mismatch
11: Publish arbitration log to blockchain
12: **else**
13: Blame ← DH ▷ DH returned incorrect result
14: Revoke result $R$ and publish revocation to blockchain
15: **end if**
16: **return** Blame

## References


1. Chor, B., Goldreich, O., Kushilevitz, E., Sudan, M.: Private information retrieval. In: Proceedings of the 36th Annual Symposium on Foundations of Computer Science (FOCS), pp. 41–50. IEEE (1995)
2. Mahdavi, R.A., Kerschbaum, F.: Constant-weight {PIR}: single-round keyword {PIR} via constant-weight equality operators. In: 31st USENIX Security Symposium (USENIX Security 22), pp. 1723–1740 (2022)

3. Bienstock, A., Patel, S., Seo, J.Y., Yeo, K.: Batch PIR and labeled PSI with oblivious ciphertext compression. In: 33rd USENIX Security Symposium (USENIX Security 24), August 2024, pp. 5949–5966 (2024)
4. Liu, J., Li, J., Wu, D., Ren, K.: PIRANA: faster multi-query pir via constant-weight codes. In: 2024 IEEE Symposium on Security and Privacy (SP), pp. 4315–4330. IEEE (2024)
5. Dehghantanha, A., Franke, K.: Privacy-respecting digital investigation. In: 2014 Twelfth Annual International Conference on Privacy, Security and Trust, pp. 129–138. IEEE (2014)
6. Park, S., Akatyev, N., Jang, Y., Hwang, J., Kim, D., Yu, W., Shin, H., Han, C., Kim, J.: A comparative study on data protection legislations and government standards to implement digital forensic readiness as mandatory requirement. Digit. Investig. **24**, S93–S100 (2018)
7. Casino, F., et al.: Research trends, challenges, and emerging topics in digital forensics: a review of reviews. IEEE Access **10**, 25464–25493 (2022)
8. General data protection regulation (2020). https://gdpr.eu/
9. Personal information protection law of the People's Republic of China (2021). https://www.chinalawtranslate.com/en/Personal-Information-Protection-Law
10. Horsman, G.: Defining principles for preserving privacy in digital forensic examinations. Forensic Sci. Int. Digit. Invest. **40**, 301350 (2022)
11. Song, D.X., Wagner, D., Perrig, A.: Practical techniques for searches on encrypted data. In: IEEE Symposium on Security and Privacy, pp. 44–55 (2000)
12. Cash, D., Grubbs, P., Perry, J., Ristenpart, T.: Dynamic searchable encryption in very-large databases: data structures and implementation. In: Network and Distributed System Security Symposium (NDSS) (2014)
13. Song, Q., Liu, Z., Cao, J., Sun, K., Li, Q., Wang, C.: SAP-SSE: protecting search patterns and access patterns in searchable symmetric encryption. IEEE Trans. Inf. Forensics Secur. **16**, 1795–1809 (2021)
14. Oya, S., Kerschbaum, F.: Hiding the access pattern is not enough: exploiting search pattern leakage in searchable encryption. In: 30th USENIX Security Symposium (USENIX Security 21), pp. 127–142 (2021)
15. Aguilar Melchor, C., Barrier, J., Fousse, L., Killijian, M.O.: XPIR: private information retrieval for everyone. Proc. Priv. Enhanc. Technol. (avril) **2016**, 155–174 (2016)
16. Angel, S., Chen, H., Laine, K., Setty, S.: PIR with compressed queries and amortized query processing. In: 2018 IEEE Symposium on Security and Privacy (SP), May 2018, pp. 962–979 (2018)
17. Mughees, M.H., Chen, H., Ren, L.: OnionPIR: response efficient single-server PIR. In: Proceedings of the 2021 ACM SIGSAC Conference on Computer and Communications Security, CCS '21, November 2021, pp. 2292–2306. Association for Computing Machinery, New York (2021)
18. Menon, S.J., Wu, D.J.: SPIRAL: fast, high-rate single-server PIR via FHE composition. In: 2022 IEEE Symposium on Security and Privacy (SP), May 2022, pp. 930–947 (2022)
19. Al-Khateeb, H., Epiphaniou, G., Daly, H.: Blockchain for modern digital forensics: the chain-of-custody as a distributed ledger. In: Blockchain and Clinical Trial: Securing Patient Data, pp. 149–168 (2019)
20. Lone, A.H., Mir, R.N.: Forensic-chain: blockchain based digital forensics chain of custody with PoC in hyperledger composer. Digit. Investig. **28**, 44–55 (2019)

21. Malik, A., Sharma, A.K., et al.: Blockchain-based digital chain of custody multimedia evidence preservation framework for internet-of-things. J. Inf. Secur. Appl. **77**, 103579 (2023)
22. Li, M., Lal, C., Conti, M., Hu, D.: LEChain: a blockchain-based lawful evidence management scheme for digital forensics. Futur. Gener. Comput. Syst. **115**, 406–420 (2021)
23. Chor, B., Goldreich, O., Kushilevitz, E., Sudan, M.: Private information retrieval. In: Proceedings of IEEE 36th Annual Foundations of Computer Science, October 1995, pp. 41–50 (1995)
24. Chor, B., Gilboa, N., Naor, M.: Private information retrieval by keywords (1997)
25. Ali, A., et al.: {Communication–Computation} trade-offs in {PIR}. In: 30th USENIX Security Symposium (USENIX Security 21), pp. 1811–1828 (2021)
26. Patel, S., Seo, J.Y., Yeo, K.: {Don't} be dense: efficient keyword {PIR} for sparse databases. In: 32nd USENIX Security Symposium (USENIX Security 23), pp. 3853–3870 (2023)
27. Fan, J., Vercauteren, F.: Somewhat practical fully homomorphic encryption. Cryptology ePrint Archive (2012)
28. Lyubashevsky, V., Peikert, C., Regev, O.: On ideal lattices and learning with errors over rings. In: Gilbert, H. (ed.) EUROCRYPT 2010. LNCS, vol. 6110, pp. 1–23. Springer, Heidelberg (2010). https://doi.org/10.1007/978-3-642-13190-5_1
29. Brakerski, Z., Vaikuntanathan, V.: Fully homomorphic encryption from ring-LWE and security for key dependent messages. In: Rogaway, P. (ed.) CRYPTO 2011. LNCS, vol. 6841, pp. 505–524. Springer, Heidelberg (2011). https://doi.org/10.1007/978-3-642-22792-9_29
30. Liu, H., Luo, X., Liu, H., Xia, X.: Merkle tree: a fundamental component of blockchains. In: 2021 International Conference on Electronic Information Engineering and Computer Science (EIECS), pp. 556–561. IEEE (2021)
31. Nakamoto, S., Bitcoin, A.: A peer-to-peer electronic cash system. Bitcoin **4**(2), 15 (2008). https://bitcoin.org/bitcoin.pdf
32. Wood, G., et al.: Ethereum: a secure decentralised generalised transaction ledger. Ethereum project yellow paper **151**(2014), 1–32 (2014)
33. Androulaki, E., et al.: Hyperledger fabric: a distributed operating system for permissioned blockchains. In: Proceedings of the Thirteenth EuroSys Conference, pp. 1–15 (2018)
34. Boneh, D., Lynn, B., Shacham, H.: Short signatures from the weil pairing. In: Boyd, C. (ed.) ASIACRYPT 2001. LNCS, vol. 2248, pp. 514–532. Springer, Heidelberg (2001). https://doi.org/10.1007/3-540-45682-1_30
35. Boldyreva, A.: Threshold signatures, multisignatures and blind signatures based on the Gap-Diffie-Hellman-group signature scheme. In: Desmedt, Y.G. (ed.) PKC 2003. LNCS, vol. 2567, pp. 31–46. Springer, Heidelberg (2003). https://doi.org/10.1007/3-540-36288-6_3

# Automatic Recovery of Cryptowallets from Mnemonic Seed Phrases

Abhishek Bhattarai(✉), Carlos Imery, and Kemal Akkaya

Florida International University, 11200 SW 8th St, Miami, FL 33199, USA
{abhat031,cimer001,kakkaya}@fiu.edu

**Abstract.** Crypto wallets are software tools that allow individuals to manage their cryptocurrencies from a secure and easily accessible platform. Seed mnemonics are strings of words that, once put together, can allow the user to gain access to the wallets they belong to. As cryptocurrencies are increasingly being used for illicit activities, cryptowallets have started to receive close attention from digital forensics researchers. These wallets may contain critical information that can be used as evidence in criminal investigations. To this end, one of the challenges faced is to identify the cryptowallet type from the obtained seed mnemonics and retrieve the information within the wallet. In this paper, we present a framework for forensic investigators to gather all necessary information within a crypto wallet by using only the wallet's associated mnemonics. Using a comprehensive approach, we design and evaluate methods for mnemonic-type identification, address seed reconstruction, private and public key reconstruction, and wallet address generation. Evaluation results show that our framework can quickly and accurately identify the type of wallet the mnemonics belong to and then generate potential private key addresses corresponding to this wallet owner.

**Keywords:** Seed Mnemonics · Crypto Wallets · Wallet Forensics · Blockchain Forensics · Bitcoin · Ethereum · Digital Forensics

## 1 Introduction

The launch of cryptocurrencies (e.g., Bitcoin, Ethereum, etc.) has revolutionized digital assets ownership due to a decentralized infrastructure, state-of-the-art security & privacy, along with verifiability and lower costs. These cryptocurrencies are used in transactions through a peer-to-peer exchange system using cryptographic methods [1]. Transaction data is hashed into consecutive blocks and stored in distributed ledgers called a Blockchain. These blocks are linked together as a chain, verified by consensus protocols such as *Proof-of-work (PoW)*, and maintain synchronization among the blocks [2]. Blockchain technologies provide foundational means to record all cryptocurrency transactions as immutable data.

The gateway to bridge the cryptocurrencies, blockchain, and user is *cryptowallet* applications, which enable users to make transactions with a user-friendly UI. Nevertheless, a cryptowallet does not store the cryptocurrencies;


K.-K. R. Choo et al. (Eds.): ICDF2C 2025, LNICST 686, pp. 197–212, 2026.
https://doi.org/10.1007/978-3-032-22545-0_12

rather, it stores the private keys that enable users to send, receive, and manage funds securely. These wallets rely on *mnemonics phrases* for securely accessing and recovering the cryptocurrencies. The mnemonics seed phrases are a sequence of randomly selected words from a list specified by technical design documents introduced by the cryptocurrency community, such as Bitcoin Improvement Proposal (BIP), SLIP (SatoshiLabs Improvement Proposal), EIP (Electrum Improvements Proposal) protocol [3], Cardano, etc. Thus, knowing the mnemonic phrases can give one access to the user's account if they forget their private keys.

As criminals frequently choose cryptocurrencies for activities such as tax evasion, currency theft, money laundering, purchasing illegal goods, and facilitating kidnappings [4], accessing the contents of a cryptowallet became crucial for law enforcement to fight against these crimes. Specifically, law enforcement must get access to digital assets faster to generate evidence for various cases if they locate any mnemonic phrases in a confiscated phone's gallery, note applications, etc. While there has been an increasing interest in researching and developing tools on cryptocurrency forensics [5–9], tools fall short when it comes to mnemonics-based analysis. In the case involving the UK's Crown Prosecution Service in July 2023, the law enforcement seized about £750,000 associated with the cryptowallet mnemonic seed phrase. However, in this investigation, they had to manually test the process to recover the assets [10,11]. This shows that they either lack the features for automating the wallet information extraction from the mnemonic phrases, or even if they trace the mnemonic phrases, they still require considerable manual effort from the investigators. As such, there is a dire need for comprehensive digital forensics frameworks or tools to automatically trace the information associated with the crypto wallets using seed mnemonic phrases.

Our proposed framework in this paper aims to fill this gap by automatically recovering the crypto wallet from the mnemonic seed phrases. We navigate the engineering behind the generation of the seed phrases and eventually help extract the information from the blockchain. Our approach is based on a comprehensive framework: It first takes a mnemonics phrase as input and validates its protocols using word lists and checksum. The cryptographic algorithms are then applied to the validated seed phrases to obtain an address known as the master seed. This address is the foundation for deriving child private addresses. All the information associated with a child private key is finally extracted from the blockchain ledger using a third-party API.

We implemented and tested this approach extensively. We demonstrated that our approach successfully decrypts the address of mnemonic seed phrases created with any of our supported protocols without any manual effort. This automation reduces the investigation time as our approach successfully extracts wallet information at an average of 3 min per 30 addresses.

The rest of the paper is organized as follows: Next, we discuss the related work on crypto seeds, private keys, address generation, and current trends in forensics investigation in Sect. 2 and present some background information in Sect. 3. The framework for the recovery of the wallet from seed phrases is presented in Sect. 4

while the experiment results are discussed in Sect. 5. Finally, we provide our conclusions in Sect. 6.

## 2 Related Work

The work of Kovalcik highlighted private keys of the wallet to be the crucial artifacts for any wallet application, which helps to identify the user associated with it [12]. The mnemonic phrases are the security foundation of the hierarchical deterministic (HD) wallet that recovers all the keys ever created. Similarly, the work by Mirza et al. analyses web3 wallet applications in Android and iOS, which mentions the importance of seed phrases that may reveal valuable information [13]. Zollner et al. proposed an automated live forensics and post-mortem analysis tool to trace all the crypto artifacts from the phone, including any mnemonic phrases, but only to mention its importance and not focusing on decrypting the seed phrases [7]. The work by Bhattarai et al. used machine learning and neural networks to trace the seed phrases from smartphones and check if the words belong to the BIP wordlist or not [14] [15] [16]. However, it does not recover and reconstruct the wallet from the acquired mnemonic seed phrases.

Some works have focused on mnemonic identification. For instance, Kao proposed an NLP-driven approach to identify the mnemonics phrase to tackle the challenges posed by the traditional Mnemonic Library Matching method [17]. The work achieved high accuracy in the identification of the mnemonic phrase but it does not reconstruct the wallet from the seed phrases. Using the mnemonics phrases, Sans et al. backed up the decentralized mnemonics phrase and reconstructed it with the help of email [18]. In the work of [19], the author recovers the mobile device share with key generation and derivation for blockchain access to mitigate the vulnerabilities by combining cryptographic and hardware-level authentication. A tool such as Mnemonic code converter[1] does construct the wallet addresses from the seed phrases but the identification and extraction of information from the blockchain is not available.

As can be seen, despite the advancements in cryptocurrency forensics, automatically recovering the seed phrases remains a complex task demanding a careful evaluation of methodologies. To bridge this gap of acquiring the seed phrases and constructing the wallet, our proposed framework addresses this issue and provide a comprehensive solution that would automate the identification, generation of address, and extraction of information from the blockchain efficiently with a high accuracy.

## 3 Background

**Blockchain Transactions:** Blockchain is used to send and receive transactions that involve cryptocurrencies. These transactions are stored in a data structure called *block* (i.e., an element in a blockchain) that contains multiple transaction data. When a transaction is started, it is broadcast to all the nodes in the

[1] https://iancoleman.io/bip39/.

peer-to-peer network and will be added to a new block. A node is a component in the network maintaining records of cryptocurrency transactions [20]. A block contains five fields: *fixed magic number, block size, block header (contains the hash of the previous block, time stamps, version number, hash and nonce), transaction counter*, and *set of transactions* added by the nodes. The hash is a transformation function that takes the input data and generates a fixed-length output [21]. The nonce is a random number usually used once in the algorithmic process and discarded [22]. The validated transactions are grouped by miners and through running a consensus mechanism such as *Proof of Work (PoW)*, it is agreed upon whether the block should be added to the blockchain or not. Once the consensus is reached, the block is added to the blockchain, making it immutable. This ensures secure, transparent, and attack-proof processing across the decentralized network. With the cryptowallet and its private addresses, we can access the block and its information in the blockchain.

**Mnemonics Phrase:** After the release of Bitcoin, mnemonic phrases were introduced as part of the Bitcoin Improvement Proposal (BIP) protocol in 2013. The objective was to simplify the backup and recovery process for cryptocurrency wallets while maintaining a high level of security. There are various methods, or protocols, that exist to generate mnemonics for different types of wallets.

The protocols are foundational rules and standards set with blockchain consensus on how the cryptocurrency system operates. They ensure the updates to the blockchain network are secure and reliable [23–25]. Major protocols used in current crypto wallet standards are BIP, SLIP, EIP, and more [26]. These protocols define the mnemonic phrase as a sequence of words selected from a set of predefined words for the generation of a deterministic wallet using protocol methods like BIP039 or similar [27]. It is more convenient than relying on a backup file to save the recovery method.

**Protocols Mnemonic Generation:** Most cryptocurrency wallets use mnemonic phrases to deterministically derive seeds. These protocols typically follow four steps: generating entropy, computing and appending a checksum, splitting the result into fixed-size chunks, mapping them to words, and deriving a final seed using a key-stretching function. Variations exist in wordlist size, chunk size, derivation method, and encoding. **BIP39, Electrum 2.0, Cardano, and Algorand** all use the same 2048-word list but differ in derivation logic.

**BIP39** uses 11-bit chunks with entropy sizes from 128–256 bits (12–24 words); **Electrum 2.0** generates mnemonics from 132-bit entropy; **Cardano** applies `PBKDF2-HMAC-SHA512` with 2048 iterations and custom salt to generate a 96-byte seed, it then applies hardened `Ed25519-bip32` derivation, using the path `m/1852'/1815'/account'/role/address`; **Algorand** generates a 25-word mnemonic (the last word as checksum); **SLIP0039** uses a 1024-word list and Shamir's Secret Sharing to split entropy into shares formed from 10-bit chunks; Finally, **Monero** uses a unique 1626-word list (Table 1).

**Table 1.** Comparison of Mnemonic Seed Generation Protocols

| Protocol | Wordlist Size | Key Derivation | Checksum | Compatible? | Unique Features |
|---|---|---|---|---|---|
| BIP39 | 2048 | PBKDF2-HMAC-SHA512 (2048x) | SHA-256 | Yes | Standard HD derivation, 1224 words |
| Cardano | 2048 | PBKDF2-HMAC-SHA512 (2048x) | SHA-256 | No | Ed25519 hardened derivation, Icarus/Daedalus logic |
| Algorand | 2048 | Direct reversible encoding | 25th word | No | Mnemonic = private key; uses SHA-512/256 |
| SLIP0039 | 1024 | Shamir Secret Sharing | N/A | No | Threshold recovery, 10-bit chunks, share metadata |
| Electrum 2.0 | 2048 | PBKDF2-HMAC-SHA512 (2048x) | N/A | No | 132-bit entropy, embedded version prefix |
| Monero | 1626 | Keccak, Ed25519, CRC32 | CRC32 | No | Subaddresses, Base58, deterministic accounts |

**Derivation Paths for Wallet Addresses:** Derivation paths are structured sequences, essentially a list of variables, that define how keys and addresses are generated from a high-entropy random master seed in a hierarchical deterministic (HD) wallet [28]. HD wallets were introduced to simplify the management of multiple private keys [29]. BIP32 describes the HD wallets as a chain of key pairs derived from the master (or root) seed. HD wallet is widely adopted by BIP39 mnemonics generation, which allows for the generation and management of an entire hierarchical tree of private and public keys, simplifying their backups and recovery process. Before HD wallets, each transaction and coin required generating new and unrelated keys, which had to be manually backed up.

Each cryptocurrency or protocol (if necessary) follows a specific derivation path. To enhance security and prevent brute-force attacks, HD wallets use cryptographic algorithms to derive private keys in a deterministic yet secure manner [30]. These derived addresses are called child private keys and are used to access the funds from the blockchain [31]. An example of a derivation path structure would be: *m/44'/0'/0'/0'/0'*, where $m$ is the master key, *44'* is the coin standard (e.g. BIP44), the first *0'* specifies the coin type (e.g. Bitcoin), the second *0'* represents the account index, the third *0'* represents the change type (internal or external), and the last *0'* represents the address to generate.

**Cryptocurrencies Address Format:** The address structures of cryptocurrencies vary depending on their inherent transaction model and derivation approach. **Bitcoin, Litecoin, Bitcoin Cash, Cardano, and Dogecoin** are all UTXO-based, relying on HD wallets to generate multiple addresses with similar hashing and encoding methods. UTXO is a chunk of cryptocurrency that is received from a previous transaction that hasn't been spent yet. **Ethereum and Algorand** use an account-based model. The account-based model tracks balances by maintaining a single balance for each account, like a bank account. **Monero** is unique with its privacy-focused design, using the CryptoNote protocol, dual public keys, and deterministic sub-address generation. Table 2 holds a detailed breakdown of each currency's address format.

**Table 2.** Cryptocurrency Address Format Comparison

| Currency | Model | Address Type(s) | Prefix(es) | Encoding | Derivation Path |
|---|---|---|---|---|---|
| Bitcoin (BTC) | UTXO | Legacy, SegWit, Native SegWit | 1, 3, bc1 | Base58Check, Bech32 | m/44'/0'/0'/0/ index |
| Litecoin (LTC) | UTXO | Legacy, SegWit, Native SegWit | L, M, 3, ltc1 | Base58Check, Bech32 | m/44'/2'/0'/0/ index |
| Dogecoin (DOGE) | UTXO | Legacy-style | D | Base58Check | m/44'/3'/0'/0/ index |
| Bitcoin Cash (BCH) | UTXO | Legacy, CashAddr | 1, bitco-incash, q | Base58Check, Bech32-like | m/44'/145'/0'/0/ index |
| Ethereum (ETH) | Account | Single format | 0x | Hex (Keccak) | m/44'/60'/0'/0/ index |
| Algorand (ALGO) | Account | Single address | A-Z base32 | Base32 | direct from private key |
| Cardano (ADA) | Account | Base, Enterprise, etc. | addr1, DdzFF | Bech32/Base58 | m/1852'/1815'/ account'/role/index |
| Monero (XMR) | Account | Standard, Subaddress | 4, 8... | Custom Base58 | Derived from master seed |

## 4 Proposed Framework

In this section, we present our framework for the automation of the recovery of wallets from crypto mnemonic seeds. The overall framework is shown in Fig. 1. We show details of each step of this framework in the following subsections.

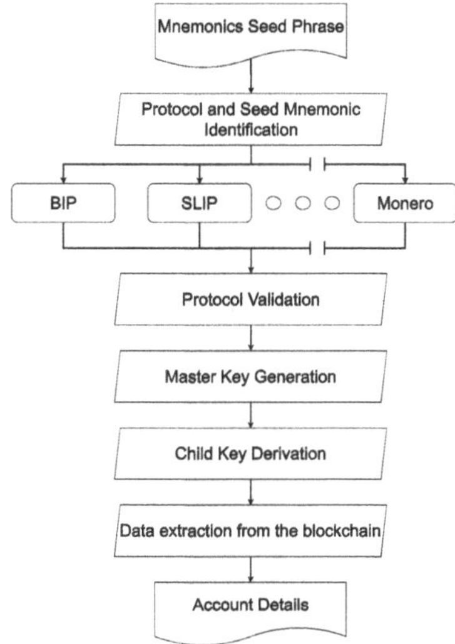


**Fig. 1.** Seed address generation framework

### 4.1 Protocol and Seed Mnemonics Identification

The first step in automating wallet recovery from crypto seeds is to identify the protocol type for the acquired seed phrases, as it is required for accurate address querying. Once the protocol type has been identified, we can start deriving the private addresses from it.

First, we validate the number of words present in the seed phrases, either 12, 15, 18, 20, 21, 24, 25, or 33 words, which is the standard sequence for phrases. Once the words have the correct number of counts, we check each word in the word list to narrow down the selection of the protocol. Each protocol has its distinct feature in the wordlist. For instance, some words are exclusive to a given mnemonic type. Some of the differentiations are shown in Table 3. The mnemonic phrase words should match their corresponding word list before we move to the next step.

**Table 3.** Simplified Wordlist differences

| Feature | BIP | SLIP | Monero |
|---|---|---|---|
| Word Count | 2048 | 1024 | 1626 |
| Structure | 48 chars, uniq 4-prefix, no word repetition | Uniq 4-prefix, word repetition | Uniq 3-prefix, word repetition, checksum supported |

To validate the selected protocol, we generate the checksum and check whether the generated checksum is valid, as Fig. 2. Each protocol has different ways to validate the checksum as shown in Table 4.

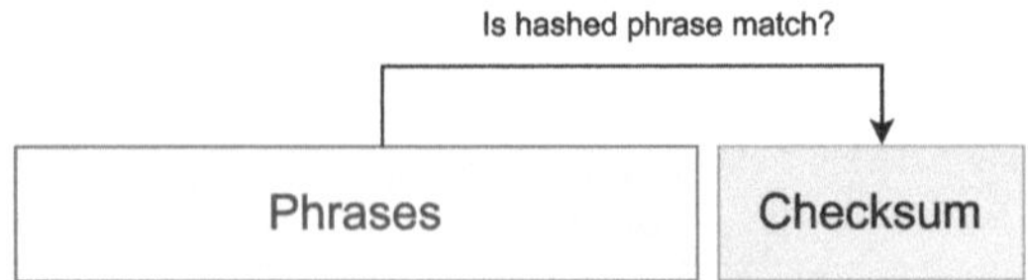


**Fig. 2.** Phrase validation with checksum

**Table 4.** Checksum Validation Methods by Protocol

| Protocol | Checksum Description |
|---|---|
| **BIP39** | Computes a SHA-256 hash of the entropy and appends the first $\frac{\text{ENT}}{32}$ as a checksum before mapping to mnemonic words. *Formula:* BIPCS = SHA256(Entropy)[: ENT/32] |
| **SLIP0039** | Employs a (27,24) Reed-Solomon code over $GF(1024)$ with the last 3 words as parity symbols detecting <= 3 errors [32] *Formula:* $p(x) = m(x) \cdot x^{n-k} \bmod g(x), \quad g(x) = \prod_{i=1}^{n-k}(x - \alpha^i)$ |
| **Electrum 2.0** | SHA-512 hashes the seed, using the first byte (e.g., `0x01`, `0x100`), as a version code validated against known constants. |
| **Cardano** | Embeds CRC32 checksum into CBOR-serialized entropy and metadata, using BIP39 wordlist with distinct validation. |
| **Algorand** | Converts 25 BIP39 words to a 32-byte key, validating the 25th word as a hash-derived index checksum. |
| **Monero** | Converts 25 words (1626-word list) to entropy, with CRC32 checksum of first 24 words validating the 25th. |

The verification step ensures our selected protocol is compatible with our phrase. Algorithm 1 summarizes the pseudo-code for our approach.

## 4.2 Master Key Generation

To generate the master seed from a given set of mnemonics, our algorithm takes two inputs: the mnemonic phrase and a password (which can be empty). If the mnemonic isn't generated by a recognized protocol, our approach will display a warning and not generate a master seed.

Once the mnemonic type is verified and the corresponding protocol is selected, the master seed generation process begins. However, different protocols have varying processes of derivation; as such, we require distinct calculations and derivations for each given protocol.

For BIP39, the mnemonic phrase is converted into a binary seed using the Password-Based Key Derivation Function 2 (PBKDF2)[2] function [33], which uses HMAC-SHA512 as the pseudo-random function, shown in Eq. 1.

[2] *PBKDF2* is a strong key generation algorithm which secures the passwords by deriving the encryption from the password.

**Algorithm 1.** Comprehensive Mnemonic Protocol Detection and Validation

**Require:** $\mathcal{M}$: Input mnemonic (string or list of shares)
**Ensure:** $\mathcal{P}$: Set of valid matching protocols
1: $\mathcal{P} \leftarrow \emptyset$ {Initialize detected protocols}
2: **if** isString($\mathcal{M}$) **then**
3:   **for all** protocol $\pi \in \Pi$ **do**
4:     $n \leftarrow$ wordCount($\mathcal{M}$)
5:     $L \leftarrow$ validLengths($\pi$)
6:     **if** $n \in L$ **then**
7:       $wordlistCheck \leftarrow$ allWordsInWordlist($\mathcal{M}, \pi$)
8:       **if** $wordlistCheck$ = true **then**
9:         $cs \leftarrow$ validateChecksum($\mathcal{M}, \pi$)
10:         **if** $cs$ = true **then**
11:           $\mathcal{P} \leftarrow \mathcal{P} \cup \{\pi\}$
12: **else if** isList($\mathcal{M}$) **then**
13:   $\mathcal{S} \leftarrow$ combineShares($\mathcal{M}$)
14:   $cs \leftarrow$ validateSLIPChecksum($\mathcal{S}$)
15:   **if** $cs$ = true **then**
16:     $\mathcal{P} \leftarrow \mathcal{P} \cup \{$`SLIP0039`$\}$
17:   **else**
18:     **error:** Invalid SLIP0039 checksum
19: **else**
20:   **error:** Invalid mnemonic input format
21: **if** $\mathcal{P} = \emptyset$ **then**
22:   **warning:** No valid protocol detected
23: **return** $\mathcal{P}$

An optional passphrase can be included as additional input, acting as a "`salt`" for the derivation process, rather than being appended as an extra word to the mnemonic phrase itself.

$$DK = PBKDF2(PRF, Password, Salt, c, dkLen) \tag{1}$$

Here, *PRF* is the pseudorandom function, *Password* is the master password, *Salt* is the random or unique value added to input data before hashing, $c$ is the number of iterations, *dklen* is the bit-length.

For SLIP0039, the seed reconstruction relies on Lagrange interpolation over finite fields, implemented as part of Shamir's Secret Sharing Scheme[3] [34]. This scheme splits the master seed into multiple shares, requiring a threshold number of shares to recover the original seed.

Likewise, for Electrum 2.0, the master seed is derived using a custom HMAC-SHA512 implementation prepended with 'electrum' and uses the passphrase (if any) as salt. For Cardano, the master seed is derived using PBDKF2-HMAC-SHA512 and the salt 'mnemonic' concatenated with the passphrase (if any). For Algorand, the mnemonic is directly encoded into a raw 32-byte private key,

[3] *Shamir's secret sharing* is a cryptographic method that split a secret $S$ into $n$ parts, known as *shares*, ensuring that no single shares can reveal the secret by itself.

meaning a single Algorand mnemonic can only have a single Algorand address. For Monero, the mnemonic is decoded into raw entropy from which a 32-byte seed is reconstructed without the need to rely on PBDKF2 or any salt.

### 4.3 Child Key Derivation

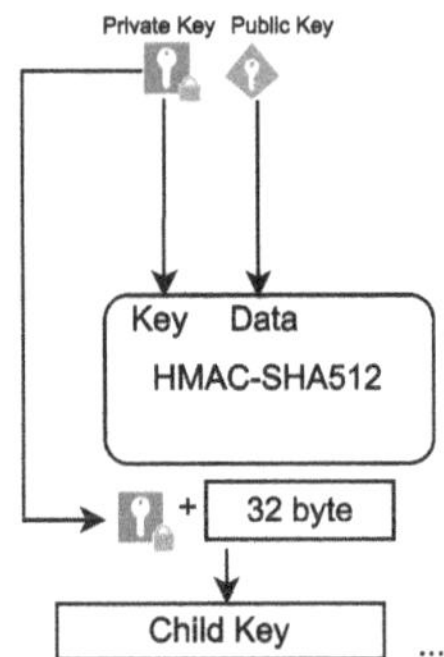


**Fig. 3.** Child key generation

After generating the extended master key from a mnemonic, we derive child private keys and public addresses following the protocol-specific derivation path. These paths describe the hierarchical structure of keys using a standardized format (e.g., BIP44), or custom logic in non-BIP wallets. The key derivation for BIP is shown in Fig. 3.

Each supported protocol defines a distinct derivation path format and address encoding method, summarized in Table 5.

### 4.4 Data Extraction from the Blockchain

Gathering information from the blockchain involves interacting with APIs for the blockchain to fetch on-chain metadata. APIs enable access to information such as transaction history, balances, transaction dates, and other critical pieces of information that may aid investigators.

We use blockchain APIs that are publicly available to extract the information associated with our generated addresses. However, in general, a gap limit[4] is set while creating the wallet application, which sets how many addresses from the HD wallet will be checked for the transaction. Any wallet that may have funds beyond the set gap limit shows no funds in the corresponding wallet. Hence, we set our derived addresses until 30, which is beyond the standard limit. After the set limit of 30, we check if two consecutive accounts after the 30th address hold any values. If not, we stop the address generation. We use *Blockchair API, Etherscan API, and Algonode* to retrieve data for supported cryptocurrencies by querying each with a given address and parsing the JSON response.

[4] https://learnmeabitcoin.com/technical/keys/hd-wallets/derivation-paths/#bip44.

**Table 5.** Derivation Path and Encoding by Protocol

| Protocol | Derivation Path Format | Address Encoding |
|---|---|---|
| BIP39 (BTC) | `m/44'/0'/0'/0/i` (Legacy), `49'`, `84'` | Base58Check, Bech32 |
| BIP39 (ETH) | `m/44'/60'/0'/0/i` | Keccak-256, Checksum Hex |
| SLIP0039 | Threshold seed reconstruction → BIP32/BIP44 derivation | Keccak-256 |
| Electrum 2.0 | `m/0/k` or `m/1/k` | Base58 (P2PKH), Bech32 (P2WPKH) |
| Cardano | `m/1852'/1815'/acc'/chain/i` | CBOR + Bech32 (addr1) |
| Monero | 256b spend key → view key (Keccak-256) → EC public keys; $(a, i)$-indexed subaddresses | Monero Base58 |
| Algorand | None (fixed root address) | Raw public key encoding |

# 5 Evaluation

In this section, we will execute the experiment and evaluate the results of the recovery of the wallet using various metrics.

## 5.1 Experiment Setup

To validate our framework, we generated the mnemonic phrases from commercially available wallets across all supported protocols as shown in Table 6. A total of 230 mnemonics were generated and saved securely for testing. Some wallets had some currencies to test the transaction information extracted via the APIs. Transactions were conducted for each protocol type—BIP, SLIP, Electrum, Cardano, and Algorand—while most wallet mnemonics remained unused and had no transaction history. For Monero, no funds were loaded because its blockchain is private and cannot be queried; therefore, only address derivation was verified.

**Table 6.** Wallet Applications Used in Testing

| Protocol | Wallet Name | Account created | Platform |
|---|---|---|---|
| BIP39 (BTC/ETH) | Blockchain.com, Trust, Coinomi, MetaMask | 40 | Android, iOS |
| SLIP0039 | Sparrow Wallet | 40 | Desktop, Mobile |
| Electrum 2.0 | Electrum CLI/GUI v4.5.8 | 20 | Windows 10 |
| Cardano | Yoroi Wallet | 40 | iOS |
| Algorand | Pera Algo Wallet | 40 | iOS |
| Monero | MyMonero, CakeWallet | 20 | iOS |

For each protocol that we performed transactions, we followed these steps: **(1)** Created a new account and recorded its mnemonic, **(2)** Added a small amount of funds (between $0.10 and $3 in the equivalent cryptocurrency), **(3)** Performed at least two transactions, and **(4)** logged both sender and receiver addresses for validation.

In another note, seed phrases may exist in notes, SMS, images, or messaging apps, saved or shared by users, but identifying them in these formats is outside our current scope.

### 5.2 Performance Metrics

We consider the following metrics in assessing the performance of our framework:

- *Address Generation Speed*: How fast can we generate a given number of addresses?
- *Address Accuracy*: How accurate were the addresses we generated compared to the actual addresses?
- *Blockchain Querying Speed*: How fast can we gather information about the given addresses from the blockchain?

### 5.3 Seed Phrase and Protocol Identification

We begin the experiment by passing the mnemonics through the algorithm. The algorithm successfully categorized 100% of the mnemonics. Some were identified as belonging to multiple protocols due to the shared/similar wordlist. To tackle this overlap, we allowed for multiple protocol detection. As a result, the script checked for each detected protocol. Some invalid mnemonics occasionally matched certain protocols because each protocol has different rules for what's considered valid—so a mnemonic that's invalid for one might still be valid for another. Any mnemonics that don't meet a protocol's requirements will simply be ignored. We compiled the results of protocol validation identification in Table 7.

**Table 7.** Result of mnemonics identification

| Protocol | # Tested | # Detected | Double Match? |
|---|---|---|---|
| BIP | 40 | 40 | Yes, with Cardano |
| SLIP | 40 | 40 | No |
| New Electrum (V2) | 20 | 20 | No |
| Cardano | 40 | 40 | Yes, with BIP |
| Algorand | 40 | 40 | No |
| Monero | 20 | 20 | No |
| Invalid | 30 | 26 | N/A |

### 5.4 Master and Child Seed Key Generation

To validate the accuracy of our implementation, we manually tested address generation across major wallet protocols by using publicly known tools and wallet applications. For each protocol, we passed a sample mnemonic into both our algorithm and the corresponding wallet application. All protocols returned a 100% match for the master keys and derived addresses between our algorithm and the test tools. A seed address sample from the wallet is shown in Table 8.

**Table 8.** Seed and Root key of BIP39

| | |
|---|---|
| Seed Address | ea523c3fe922003627467460 4d219028fb55d538a0c4cb267d8275bce6f 3b21c273b23798f966570ed16b601eb647fc37f749b7aa577bbe1ca5f8 f61bd1a4e80 |
| BIP32 Root key | zprvAWgYBBk7JR8GmCAnkomLLiZEfo3CUmtfcCDxyTEEu TJGEWqCCtSh3Aih765HQafVyiWJEDVCqXMXYzx29YvuBTk JtXKtveEfzoBR2kiX6Hs |

### 5.5 Blockchain Query

After deriving the private keys and addresses from each mnemonic, we retrieved blockchain data primarily using the previously mentioned APIs. We did not perform blockchain queries for Monero, as its privacy features prevent access to the required information.

Due to API rate limits, we tested only seven real mnemonics: three BIP-39, one SLIP-0039, one Algorand, one Electrum, and one Cardano. For each, we searched addresses beyond the gap limit (set to 30) and checked for confirmed transactions or balances. BIP-based wallets returned cryptocurrency data across various address types, while SLIP-0039 and Electrum yielded similar results—though both are limited to Bitcoin support. Summary of the blockchain query is shown in Table 9.

### 5.6 Discussion

Based on the defined metrics, Table 10 summarizes the performance of our framework. The average address generation speed for generating one address across all experiments was 0.02 s, and the average information querying for one address was 5.73 s. The following experiment shows that the speed of extracting the information from the mnemonic phrases depends on how many addresses users want to generate, as it is directly proportional to the address count. The runtime complexity for our algorithm is $O(n + a * d)$, where $n$ is mnemonic length, $a$ is the number of accounts, and $d$ is the address count per account. Additionally, we are utilizing a third-party API whose speed may be affected by network

**Table 9.** Blockchain Query Test Results by Protocol

| Protocol | Address Queried | Query Result |
|---|---|---|
| BIP39 (BTC) | bc1q4hx... | 0.00003 BTC ($3.04) |
| BIP39 (ETH) | 0x4D23...9765 | 0.00002997 ETH ($0.10) |
| SLIP0039 | bc1... | 2 transactions found |
| Electrum v2 | bc1qx2n...352n | 0.0000053 BTC ($0.59) |
| Cardano | addr1q9p7...kgx | 10 ADA ($7.54) |
| Algorand | ZMDSTR...VIQIY | 5.03 ALGO ($1.21) |
| Monero | N/A | Not Queried due to privacy |

latency, server processing, or the API design of the provider. In the event of an API restriction, law enforcement may need to employ traditional investigative methods, such as requesting records from service providers.

**Table 10.** Performance metrics for querying

| Mnemonic Phrases | Address Count | Address Generation(in sec) | Address Generation and Query(in Sec) |
|---|---|---|---|
| Phrase 1 (BIP) | 1 | 0.05 | 27.93 |
| | 10 | 0.37 | 49.35 |
| | 50 | 1.78 | 136.31 |
| Phrase 2 (SLIP) | 1 | 0.05 | 20.12 |
| | 10 | 0.39 | 32.68 |
| | 50 | 1.89 | 95.13 |
| Phrase 3 (Electrum) | 1 | 0.02 | 19.96 |
| | 10 | 0.12 | 165.0 |
| | 50 | 0.57 | 817.70 |

# 6 Conclusion

We introduced a comprehensive framework to streamline automated wallet recovery forensics from seed phrases, which facilitates investigations by reducing their crucial time and effort. We targeted known limitations of modern tools and resources to build a robust approach capable of providing practical and effective solutions for investigators tasked with tackling crypto-related crimes.

In conclusion, the results of our study demonstrate that our framework can expedite the investigation by automatically retrieving information from the blockchain using only the provided mnemonic phrase, thereby reducing the need for manual efforts. Our approach successfully identified protocols, generated master and child private keys, and retrieved information from the blockchain with high efficiency and accuracy, demonstrating its potential as a reliable and effective tool for cryptocurrency forensics. Our current approach limitation is the potential security risk, like unauthorized access and seed phrase exposure in recovered wallets. Future work will enhance wallet security by preventing these risks and securely managing cryptographic data to build trust and safeguard assets.

## References


1. Farell, R.: An analysis of the cryptocurrency industry. Wharton Res. Scholars **130**, 1–23 (2015)
2. Nofer, M., et al.: Blockchain. Bus. Inf. Syst. Eng. **59**, 183–187 (2017)
3. Shaik, C.: Securing cryptocurrency wallet seed phrase digitally with blind key encryption. Int. J. Crypt. Inf. Secur. (IJCIS) **10**(4) (2020)
4. Kethineni, S., Cao, Y.: The rise in popularity of cryptocurrency and associated criminal activity. Int. Crim. Justice Rev. **30**(3), 325–344 (2020)
5. Montanez, A.: Investigation of cryptocurrency wallets on iOS and Android mobile devices for potential forensic artifacts. In: Department Forensic Science, Marshall University: Huntington, WV, USA (2014)
6. Nabi, A.G.: Analytic Study on Android-based Crypto-Currency Wallets (2018)
7. Zollner, S., Raymond Choo, K.-K., Le-Khac, N.-A.: An automated live forensic and postmortem analysis tool for bitcoin on windows systems. In: IEEE Access **7**, 158250–158263 (2019)
8. Chang, E., et al.: Forensic artefact discovery and attribution from android cryptocurrency wallet applications. In: arXiv preprint arXiv:2205.14611 (2022)
9. Park, A.-H., et al.: Forensic investigation framework for cryptocurrency wallet in the end device. Comput. Secur. **133**, 103392 (2023)
10. Huge cryptocurrency wallet retrieved after hacker found guilty of blackmail (2023). https://www.cps.gov.uk/cps/news/huge-cryptocurrency-wallet-retrieved-after-hacker-found-guilty-blackmail
11. Chainalysis Team. Identifying, Seizing Illicit Crypto Assets with Chainalysis Investigations (2024). https://www.chainalysis.com/blog/identifying-and-seizing-illicit-crypto-assets/
12. Kovalcik, T.: Digital forensics of cryptocurrency wallets (2022)
13. Mirza, M.M., Ozer, A., Karabiyik, U.: Mobile cyber forensic investigations of Web3 wallets on Android and iOS. In: Appl. Sci. **12**(21), 11180 (2022)
14. Bhattarai, A., et al.: Crypto wallet artifact detection on android devices using advanced machine learning techniques. In: International Conference on Digital Forensics and Cyber Crime, pp. 111–132. Springer (2022)
15. Bhattarai, A., et al.: Systems and methods for detecting cryptocurrency wallet artifacts in a file system. US Patent 11,755,958 (2023)
16. Bhattarai, A., et al.: Cryptocurrency forensics automation: a deep learning and NLP-based approach for mobile platforms. Discover Comput. **28**(1), 123 (2025)
17. Kao, H.-H.: Accelerating multilingual cryptocurrency forensics: an NLP-driven approach for efficient mnemonic identification. IEEE Access (2025)
18. Sans, T., Liu, Z., Oh, K.: A decentralized mnemonic backup system for non-custodial cryptocurrency wallets. In: International Symposium on Foundations and Practice of Security, pp. 355–370. Springer (2022)
19. Khade, A.V., Patel, H.R., Modi, C.: Mnemonic phrase management and SIM based two-factor authentication (2FA) for mobile wallets in blockchain. In: 2023 IEEE International Conference on Blockchain and Distributed Systems Security (ICBDS), pp. 1–6. IEEE (2023)

20. Ho, K.-H., Chiu, W.-H., Li. C.: A network analysis of the cryptocurrency market. In: 2020 IEEE Symposium Series on Computational Intelligence (SSCI), pp. 2178–2185. IEEE (2020)
21. Kuznetsov, A., et al.: Performance of hash algorithms on GPUS for use in blockchain. In: 2019 IEEE International Conference on Advanced Trends in Information Theory (ATIT), pp. 166–170. IEEE (2019)
22. Raju, R., SaiVignesh, M., Infant Arun Prasad, K.: A study of current cryptocurrency systems. In: 2018 International Conference on Computation of Power, Energy, Information and Communication (ICCPEIC), pp. 203–209. IEEE (2018)
23. Bitcoin Cash. "Bitcoin cash". In: Development, 2 (2019)
24. Nguyen-Dinh, T., et al.: A hierarchical deterministic wallet using Ed25519 digital signature scheme. In: International Conference on Future Data and Security Engineering, pp. 240–257. Springer (2022)
25. Mingxiao, D., et al.: A review on consensus algorithm of blockchain. In: 2017 IEEE International Conference on Systems, Man, and Cybernetics (SMC), pp. 2567–2572. IEEE (2017)
26. Van Der Horst, L., Raymond Choo, K.-K., Le-Khac, N.-A.: Process memory investigation of the bitcoin clients electrum and bitcoin core. In: IEEE Access **5**, 22385–22398 (2017)
27. Reitenbach, M.: Using secret sharing to store cryptocurrency. PRIMUS **34**(1), 32–40 (2024)
28. Wuille, P.: Bip-0032.Mediawiki at master · bitcoin/bips. en. https://github.com/bitcoin/bips/blob/master/bip-0032.mediawiki
29. Chuang, C.Y., Hsu, I.H., Lee, T.F.: A two-party hierarchical deterministic wallets in practice. Cryptol. ePrint Arch. (2023)
30. De La Semilla, M.L.S.: Enhancing the security of the bitcoin wallet master seed (2019)
31. Gutoski, G., Stebila, D.: Hierarchical deterministic bitcoin wallets that tolerate key leakage. In: International Conference on Financial Cryptography and Data Security, pp. 497–504. Springer (2015)
32. Sheu, J.-P.: Reed-Solomon Codes Lecture Notes (2008). Accessed May 2025. http://hscc.cs.nthu.edu.tw/~sheujp/lecture_note/rs.pdf
33. Ertaul, L., Kaur, M., Kumar, V.A., Gudise, R.: Implementation and performance analysis of PBKDF2, Bcrypt, Scrypt algorithms. In: Proceedings of the international conference on wireless networks (ICWN). The Steering Committee of The World Congress in Computer Science, Computer... , p. 66 (2016)
34. Gupta, K.D., et al.: Shamir's secret sharing for authentication without reconstructing password. In: 2020 10th Annual Computing and Communication Workshop and Conference (CCWC), pp. 0958–0963. IEEE (2020)

# AnchorMark: Real-World Anchor-Based Watermarking for Digital Content Authentication and Manipulation Detection

Xinyun Liu[1], Ronghua Xu[1](✉), and Yu Chen[2]

[1] Michigan Technological University, Houghton, MI 49931, USA
{xinyunl,ronghuax}@mtu.edu
[2] Binghamton University, SUNY, Binghamton, NY 13902, USA
ychen@binghamton.edu

**Abstract.** With the rapid advancement in artificial intelligence (AI) and deepfake techniques, determining the authenticity and provenance of digital content in cyberspace has become increasingly complex. However, existing forensics solutions are limited to identifying artifacts left by deepfake manipulations or tracing the source of digital content generated by specific AI models. Thus, they struggle to ensure the authenticity and traceability of digital content without a ground-truth reference. In this work, we propose AnchorMark, a real-world anchor-based watermarking framework for digital content authentication and manipulation detection. A binary AnchorMark meta-structure (AMM) is designed to record verifiable locators that link to physical Electrical Network Frequency (ENF) signals as the ground truth reference. In addition, we introduce GaWRI, a **G**enerative **a**dversarial network (GAN) based **W**atermarking framework with the **R**obustness and **I**mperceptibility for embedding AMM as multi-bit watermarks in multimedia (image or video). Therefore, investigators can extract AMM from watermarked content and use it to verify authenticity and provenance using a trusted physical anchor fabric. The experimental results demonstrate AnchorMark's superior performance in terms of effectiveness and robustness in ensuring image authentication and manipulation detection under various attacks and baselines.

**Keywords:** Digital Forensics · Digital Twins · Real World Anchor · Digital Watermarking · Generative Adversarial Network (GAN)

## 1 Introduction

The exponential growth of digital content, driven by advances in artificial intelligence (AI), immersive technologies, and high-speed communication networks, has significantly transformed the digital landscape. This transformation has led to the emergence of intelligent digital ecosystems, where physical and digital elements are deeply integrated to support business operations, innovation, and economic value [4]. Central to this evolution are technologies such as Digital


K.-K. R. Choo et al. (Eds.): ICDF2C 2025, LNICST 686, pp. 213–230, 2026.
https://doi.org/10.1007/978-3-032-22545-0_13

Twins (DT), the Internet of Things (IoT), Virtual Reality (VR), and Artificial Intelligence Generated Content (AIGC) [10]. DTs establish bidirectional real-time links between physical assets and their virtual counterparts, enabling simulation, monitoring, and predictive analytics in sectors such as healthcare, manufacturing, and smart cities [27]. Similarly, IoT networks support adaptive decision-making through continuous data collection from distributed sensors, while VR technologies provide immersive environments that include high-value digital assets, such as 3D models and spatial interaction data [5]. At the same time, AIGC systems, powered by large-scale generative models, can automatically produce high-quality text, images, videos, audio, and 3D content [6]. This improves production efficiency and leads to the creation of a new category of AI-generated digital assets.

Although these technological advancements contribute to the development of seamless services and realistic digital media, supporting innovations such as Smart Cities and the Metaverse [32], they also present significant challenges for digital forensics in the age of increasingly accessible and widespread digital manipulation. The rise of fake AIGC (FAIGC) through the abuse of AI technologies to create deceptive and Deepfake content has dramatically challenged investigators to determine the authenticity and integrity of digital content [38]. To counter Deepfake antiforensics, ongoing research efforts are focused on detection, attribution, and characterization [22]. Detection solutions are based on identifiable artifacts, such as inconsistencies, abrupt changes, or unnatural details, to differentiate human-generated content (HGC) and AIGC [11]. However, as AI techniques and generative models have evolved, existing detection methods are becoming less effective and more easily circumvented. By embedding identifiable patterns into AI models through parameter adjustments or architectural modifications, attribution mechanisms allow content verification during inference or after analysis [23]. However, these methods need access to the original training data and internal model configurations. This dependency can compromise security, impair performance, and hinder the adaptability of detection systems across various application domains. Thus, there is a growing demand for exploring methods to verify authenticity and trace the origin and history of digital content, AIGC or not, in cyberspace.

Digital content, such as images and videos, typically has metadata (e.g., device settings, location, and date and time) attached by physical devices or processing programs. However, this metadata can be easily viewed and modified with standard programs and easily removed from original files during publication on social media sites or transmission via messaging platforms. Due to key characteristics such as invisibility and resilience, digital watermarking technology (DWT) offers a potential robust and reliable solution to address the challenges of data authenticity [25,26]. By embedding imperceptible and unique signals (watermarks) within digital content, DWT allows investigators to detect unauthorized modifications [35] or verify the origin of data generated by AI models [40]. Thus, these hidden but consistent watermarks can serve as verifiable markers that include useful reference information to establish authenticity and provenance in contexts such as scientific investigations or legal proceedings [36].

In this work, we propose AnchorMark, a robust framework for digital content authentication and manipulation detection. Unlike passive learning-based forensic techniques that focus on detecting fake multimedia based on vulnerability or artifacts of deep-faked methods [15], AnchorMark aims for a proactive solution that binds physical-world information with digital content to enhance authenticity and traceability. Specifically, we introduce GaWRI, a **G**enerative Adversarial Network (GAN) based **W**atermarking framework with the **R**obustness and **I**mperceptibility for embedding multi-bit watermarks into images or videos. Unlike existing model watermarking-based forensic approaches for detecting and tracking AIGC [38], GaWRI is decoupled from generative AI model tasks, thereby not requiring access to training data, internal parameters, or inference processes. Thus, GaWRI is a unified and transferable watermarking framework for the authenticity of digital content (both AIGC and HGC).

In contrast to deepfake detection solutions that use the metadata of digital content to save authentication information [33], our AnchorMark relies on real-world anchor information as a reference for effective forensic analysis in the digital ecosystem. Specifically, the Anchormark meta (AMM) structure is designed to record verifiable locators that link to physical Electrical Network Frequency (ENF) signals managed by a trust anchor fabric. The owner can request AMM based on current ENF signals from the anchor fabric and then use GaWRI to embed AMM into images or videos before publishing them. Upon suspicious digital content, investigators can recover AMM from watermarked images or videos and then compare them with ground truths. They can determine whether the data originates from unknown sources or has been tampered with in any way, such as by modifying metadata or content. Therefore, our AnchorMark promises to enhance the reliability and effectiveness of digital forensics in complex cyberspace. The key contributions of this work are summarized below:

1) We propose the AnchorMark framework, which consists of two key sub-frameworks: (i) GaWRI, a GAN-driven watermarking model designed to embed and retrieve AMM data tied to digital assets; and (ii) a trust physical anchor framework that manages the ENF ground truth database and provides AMM generation and verification.
2) We introduce the GaWRI model, which utilizes the Feature Refinement Module (FRM) and the Attention-Guided Module (AGM) to enhance robustness and imperceptibility during the watermarking process.
3) We evaluate the performance of the GaWRI model and analyze its robustness against various attacks and minimal visual distortion.

The remainder of this paper is structured as follows. Section 2 provides a brief overview of existing ENF-based solutions for digital multimedia forensics. We also briefly describe deep learning-based methods for multimedia forensics. Section 3 presents the AnchorMark system architecture, highlighting the synergistic integration of the GaWRI framework and the physical anchor fabric for the authentication of images and videos in metaverse applications. Specifically, we illustrate the GaWRI model and the design of FRM and AGM. Section 4 describes the prototype implementation and shows the experimental results to verify the effectiveness of AnchorMark. Finally, Sect. 5 concludes this paper with a summary and discussion of future directions.

# 2 Background and Related Work

## 2.1 Digital Multimedia Forensics Using ENF Analysis

The Electric Network Frequency (ENF) is represented as the nominal frequency (typically 50 or 60 Hz) of the alternating current in power grids, which exhibits minor but characteristic fluctuations over time due to changes in power supply and demand. These fluctuations are globally synchronized within a power grid and can be unintentionally embedded in audio and video recordings through electrically powered devices such as microphones, cameras, and lighting systems. Due to properties such as randomness and spatial-temporal sensitivity, ENF analysis has emerged as a powerful forensic tool in the domain of digital multimedia authentication. Early work by Grigoras [12] demonstrated that ENF fluctuations could be detected in digital audio recordings and used to verify the authenticity and timestamp of the recordings. This foundational idea was extended by Cooper et al. [9], who developed techniques to extract ENF traces from video recordings by analyzing the flickering patterns of light sources powered by mains electricity. These studies showed that ENF-based analysis could be a reliable indicator of temporal integrity and authenticity.

In recent years, ENF-based digital multimedia forensics has shown significant promise in authenticating the time, source, and integrity of audiovisual content [31]. For multimedia forensics in smart surveillance systems, Defakepro [30] uses ENF signals embedded in video recordings to identify malicious injection of fake frames, replays, and deepfake attacks. For images and videos uploaded to social networks, DEMA [29] built the ground truth of the electricity grid for verifying metadata. Thus, investigators can use extracted ENF signals to easily verify time and location in media metadata that may have been tampered with during content distribution. To ensure the authenticity and trustworthiness of virtual representations in Metaverse applications, Anchor-Gird [13] relies on ENF signals as real-world anchors to detect Deepfaked DTs of grid components in smart grid systems. However, the aforementioned ENF-based solutions cannot ensure the authenticity of AIGC or HGC, which do not contain ENF signals or other environmental fingerprints. Our AnchorMark can remedy this limitation by embedding ENF locators as watermarks within multimedia.

## 2.2 Deep Watermarking for Multimedia Forensics

Image watermarking has been widely used to protect multimedia in digital networks, such as verifying the authenticity of digital content and establishing ownership rights [2]. In recent years, deep learning-based models have been investigated in image watermarking due to higher imperceptibility and stronger robustness [15]. As the first end-to-end learning framework for robust watermarking, HiDDeN [42] uses three CNNs to hide data in the image. It also integrated noise layers with an encoder-decoder framework to achieve robustness given different noisy transmissions. ReDMark [3] is a deep end-to-end diffusion watermarking framework that uses two fully connected CNNs with residual structure to embed and extract watermarks. However, these CNN-based solutions are susceptible to adversarial attacks, which are subtle and malicious perturbations that can diminish or completely remove the watermark [14].

In contrast to traditional CNN-based image watermarking techniques, GAN-based methods provide enhanced robustness, invisibility, and flexibility. GAN-based watermarking leverages adversarial training to embed watermarks in a data-driven fashion [17]. As a result, watermarked images remain visually faithful while being resilient to various distortions such as compression, cropping, and noise. By randomly selecting the noise layer from real JPEG, simulated JPEG, and noise-free layer for each mini-batch, MBRS [20] guarantees optimized robustness and decoding accuracy while preserving video quality. By applying the attention mechanism to the encoder-decoder watermarking framework, ABDH [37] utilizes the attention mask to identify inconspicuous areas for embedding watermarks in host images or videos, thus enhancing robustness.

Recent developments in robust and invisible watermarking have significantly advanced proactive forensics for multimedia, such as copyright protection, source tracing, and content authentication [38,40]. To achieve both deepfaked content detection and source tracing tasks, SepMark [34] is a multi-embedding framework consisting of fragile watermarks and robust marks. A single encoder embeds one watermark into the image, while two separable decoders (a detector and a tracker) can extract the fragile watermark and the robust watermark separately. Detector decides if an image has been tampered with, while the tracker verifies if a reliable source generated it. To address issues in localizing malicious tampering in the era of AIGC, EditGuard [39] is a unified framework for copyright protection and tamper-agnostic localization. Like SepMark, EditGuard utilizes a dual-watermark encoder to embed both a localization watermark and a copyright watermark in the original images. Then the tamper locator and copyright extractor can accurately recover dual watermarks at the verification stage. As a scalable and robust framework for deepfake detection, DeepMark [33] extracts visual features of a video and saves them in the metadata fields of the video file. Then it uses MBRS to embed locators linked to visual features into video frames as watermarks. Thus, anyone can extract watermarks as the ground truth and compare them with stored visual features to identify manipulations.

## 3 AnchorMark: System Architecture and Design

### 3.1 Threat Models

The AnchorMark framework aims to ensure the authenticity and provenance of digital entities in a metaverse-driven digital ecosystem, such as Metaverse [32] and Anchor-Gird [13]. In this virtual space, individuals utilize their digital representations, known as avatars, to interact with one another. Digital content can be generated by physical devices like wearable sensors or VR headsets, or it can be outputs of AIGC tools or any programs in virtual space. The diverse types of digital content, including images and videos, support core functions and virtual environment settings for metaverse applications. Regarding adversary knowledge and capabilities, we assume that: i) the adversary cannot access watermarking models and embedding and extraction procedures; ii) the adversary cannot control ground truth reference management and verification due to a trusted authority.

However, attacks can compromise communications between participants and directly access digital content in metaverse applications, as shown in Fig. 1. An adversary can manipulate original images or videos, such as altering time and location metadata or modifying content data using deepfake techniques, and then distribute tampered versions to disrupt normal operations. In addition, an adversary seeks to create fake images and videos and attach fake watermarks. As a result, malicious actors can break the timeline of criminal activities or attribute fake content to specific individuals, potentially compromising trust and reliability in forensic scenarios. AnchorMark relies on a robust watermarking model to ensure security, thus, we define two adversarial objectives: i) watermark removal attack; ii) watermark forge attack.

### 3.2 The AnchorMark Architecture

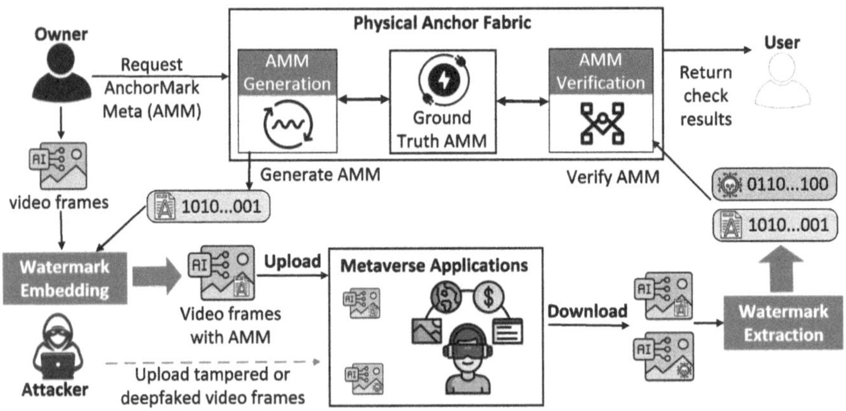


**Fig. 1.** AnchorMark System Overview.

To address the aforementioned issues in the digital ecosystem, AnchorMark is a secure-by-design framework that consists of two sub-frameworks: i) a physical anchor fabric that manages ground truth reference and provides AnchorMark meta (AMM) data generation and verification; ii) a GAN-based watermarking framework that embeds AMM into images or videos and extracts them upon the digital content verification stage. Figure 1 illustrates the video distribution workflow in the AnchorMark framework.

Each owner can upload the video to a hosting service in metaverse applications (e.g., DT entities, Virtual Environments). To prevent adversaries from tampering with it or creating fake digital content and then uploading it to the same or other hosting services for illegal purposes, a physical anchor fabric can generate verifiable AMM associated with external ground references for authenticity and integrity assurance. Currently, we choose DEMA [29] as an ENF ground truth database example used by the physical anchor fabric. Figure 2 shows a DEMA infrastructure based on North American power transmission grid. Each regional power grid relies on a dedicated server to store and manage ground truth ENF data within its network. The DEMA system allows for regional ENF source search given time and location. Thus, it provides physical ground truths to support video authentication in cyberspace.

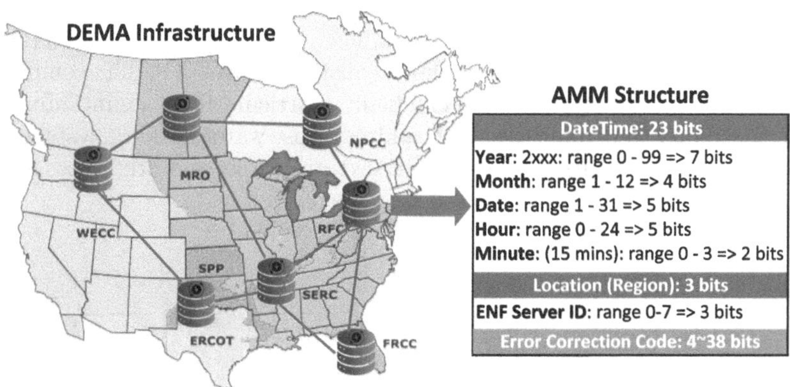


**Fig. 2.** AMM Data Structure and DEMA Infrastructure.

Before uploading the video $M$ to Metaverse applications, the owner contacts the physical anchor fabric to request an AMM data $A_M$ associated with the metadata of $M$, such as created time and location. Figure 2 illustrates the AMM data structure that combines time and location to construct environmental identifiers linking ground truth sources from DEMA. The data structure of $A_M$ is defined as a binary string of length $s$, which has three main fields: time range $t$, location range $l$, and error correction code (ECC) $e$. Studies show that the length of the test recording is preferred to be 8 min or longer for higher forensic matching accuracy [18,31]. Therefore, we choose 15 min as the minimal duration for the date time $t$ that represents 23 bits. The location $l$ records the ENF server ID, which needs 3 bits to index 8 regional servers. After completion of the AMM generation procedures, a secure watermark embedding process embeds $A_M$ in the original content $M$ and produces a watermark $M_A$ that can be uploaded and distributed throughout the metaverse application network.

On the designation side, a user (or investigator) downloads a video $M^{'}$ and verifies its authenticity by using AMM. At first, the watermark extraction process attempts to recover $A_M$ and then sends it to AMM verification in the physical anchor fabric. In the verification stage, an ENF signal $E_{(t^{'},l^{'})}$ is re-tested using created time $t^{'}$ and location $l^{'}$ saved in metadata of $M^{'}$. Although a ground truth ENF signal $E_{(t,l)}$ is estimated using the time range $t$ and location range $l$ recorded in $A_M$. The verification procedure then checks the condition that satisfies $similar(E^O_{(t,l)}, E_{(t,l)}) \geq \theta$ where $\theta$ indicates the minimum viable similarity factor. If the calculated similarity factor is greater than a threshold of $\theta$, a pass result is returned, indicating that the video $M^{'}$ is authentic and published by its owner. Otherwise, the video is considered tampered with or faked.

### 3.3 The Watermarking Model

Images and videos in the Metaverse application often feature highly diverse and synthetic visual content, including stylized avatars, virtual environments, and dynamic lighting conditions, which introduce challenges such as domain variability, graphical artifacts, and nonphotorealistic textures [41]. The complexities make embedding watermarks more difficult, particularly in maintaining both visual invisibility and robustness. To address this, watermarking systems must flexibly respond to localized variations in texture, shape, and brightness for optimal performance.

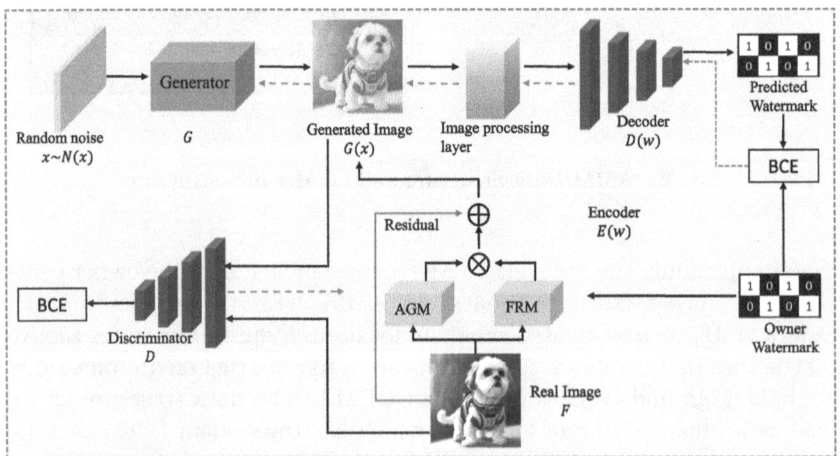


**Fig. 3.** Overview of our GaWRI watermarking model.

In this paper, we introduce a robust GAN-based framework that incorporates feature refinement and attention-guided strategies to embed watermarks within metaverse images. The overall architecture of the system is illustrated in Fig. 3, where we begin by describing the two fundamental components of the GAN: the generator $G$ and the discriminator $D$. The generator $G$ is trained to synthesize realistic images $G(x)$ from input noise $x$ and incorporate a hidden watermark in each output. To enable this, we structure $G$ so that applying a specialized decoder $D_w$ to $G(x)$ yields an accurate recovery of the watermark $w$, where $w \in 0, 1^N$ denotes a sequence of bits $N$ that uniquely verifies the ownership of the model. A noise vector $x$ sampled from a normal distribution $x \sim N(x)$ is input into $G$, which transforms it into a realistic image that aligns with the target domain. Simultaneously, a discriminator $D$ is trained to differentiate between real samples $F$ and the generated outputs $G(x)$. The discriminator's loss is minimized through the following objective:

$$L_D(D, G) = -\mathbb{E}_{F \sim p_{data}(F)}[\log D(F)] - \mathbb{E}_{x \sim P(x)}[\log(1 - D(G(x)))] \quad (1)$$

where $p_{data}$ refers to the real data distribution, and the generator's loss function can be written as follows:

$$L_G(D, G) = \mathbb{E}_{x \sim P(x)}[\log(1 - D(G(x)))] \quad (2)$$

Our GAN-based watermarking model adopts an encoder-decoder architecture, where $E_w$ denotes the encoder and $D_w$ the decoder. The encoder $E_w$ is responsible for producing the watermarked image, as illustrated in the green middle region of Fig. 3, while the decoder $D_w$ is trained to retrieve the embedded watermark. In the embedding process, $E_w$ extracts essential features from the input image and integrates them with the watermark information. The FRM increases the system's robustness by combining the watermark with image characteristics. At the same time, the AGM selectively focuses on embedding the watermark in less perceptually sensitive areas to reduce visible distortion. These areas typically include regions of high redundancy or low texture to enhance imperceptibility. During training, both $E_w$ and $D_w$ are optimized together by minimizing the following loss function:

$$L_w = \sum_{i=1}^{n} MSE(F_i, E_w(F_i, w)) + \lambda BCE(w, D_w(F_{w,i})) \quad (3)$$

where $F_i$ refers to the original input image, while $F_{w,i}$ indicates the encoder's output, the image containing the embedded watermark. The variable $n$ represents the total number of training instances. In Eq. 3, the first component aims to minimize the deviation between $F$ and $F_w$, thus preserving image quality with minimal distortion. The second component aims to reduce the error between the embedded watermark and the version retrieved by the decoder $D_w$. The coefficient $\lambda$ regulates the combined loss, effectively balancing visual fidelity and the accuracy of watermark recovery. As illustrated in Fig. 3, the forward propagation paths are shown in black, while the red arrows highlight the backpropagation process. The terms $MSE$ and $BCE$ correspond to the Mean Squared Error and Binary Cross Entropy (BCE) loss functions, respectively.

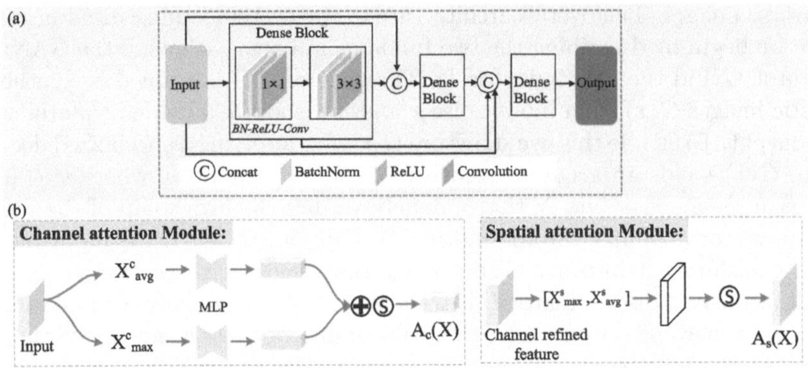


**Fig. 4.** (a) The details of DenseNet. (b) Overview of attention models.

Figure 4 illustrates the encoder, which integrates two fundamental components: the feature refinement module (FRM) and the attention-guided module (AGM). The FRM leverages the DenseNet architecture, known for its dense layer connectivity that links each layer to all previous layers that share the same feature map size [16]. As depicted in Fig. 4(a), this structure enables each layer to access the accumulated feature maps of previous layers, thus enhancing the transmission of gradients and facilitating the sharing of characteristics. Each dense block is composed of a series of batch normalization (BN), ReLU activations, and convolution layers. These densely connected layers significantly increase the encoder's effectiveness in extracting complex features from metaverse images $F_i$.

The FRM addresses the limitation of exclusively depending on surface-level image features, which often fail to ensure the robustness of watermarks. By extracting and merging shallow and deep features from various convolutional layers, the FRM builds a more detailed and holistic representation of features, capturing intricate aspects of the image's texture and structure. This enriched integration improves the encoder's ability to embed watermarks with greater precision and robustness. Because watermark performance varies according to the embedding location, where low-texture zones favor minimal distortion and high-texture regions support stronger robustness, we propose the AGM to strike a balance, as shown in Fig. 4(b). By applying an attention mask, the AGM dynamically regulates the watermark strength across different image areas, minimizing interference in smooth, sensitive areas and intensifying it in more inconspicuous regions. This leads to a watermarking strategy that achieves strong resistance to distortion while maintaining high visual fidelity.

Finally, the adversarial training process enables the discriminator to steer the encoder toward creating watermarked images that balance two key objectives: i) remaining undetectable to the human eye while withstanding distortions; ii) permitting accurate watermark recovery. This collaboration ensures exceptional visual quality, as the watermark is embedded in a way that is both imperceptible and durable, without degrading the original image. Additionally, the decoder is essential for reliably extracting the watermark, even under challenging conditions like compression artifacts, noise interference, or intentional manipulation.

# 4 Experimental Study

## 4.1 Implementation Details

The proposed GaWRI watermarking model was evaluated using publicly available datasets, including the COCO (Common Objects in Context) dataset [1], built by Microsoft and contains more than 330,000 images with complex everyday scenes and object-level annotations in 80 categories, and the FFHQ (Flickr-Faces-HQ) dataset [19], created by NVIDIA researchers, which consists of 70,000 high-quality human face images at 1024×1024 resolution, covering a wide range of age, ethnicity, and image conditions. These datasets were selected to ensure comprehensive testing in various visual contexts, supporting a robust evaluation of the model performance and its applicability to metaverse environments. GaWRI is implemented by PyTorch and runs on a NVIDIA Tesla V100 GPU. To maintain consistency, all input images were resized to $512 \times 512 \times 3$.

**Evaluation Metrics.** The imperceptibility of the watermarked images was evaluated using both subjective visual quality checks and quantitative indicators, such as the Peak Signal-to-Noise Ratio (PSNR) and the Structural Similarity Index Metric (SSIM). For a reliable assessment, a five-fold cross-validation approach was used, with the mean results of all folds being reported. For the robustness test, the average bit accuracy (BA) is utilized as the default evaluation metric. Here, BA is defined as the average proportion of watermark bits accurately recovered from the distorted images relative to the original watermark.

## 4.2 Imperceptibility Analysis

To improve the imperceptibility of the watermark, we optimize the loss function in Equation (3) during training of the GaWRI model. This refinement helps minimize discrepancies between the original and watermarked images, resulting in a low visual distortion. Figure 5 presents this effect by presenting both original images and watermarked images. As shown in panels (a) and (b). The encoded images closely resemble the originals, indicating that the watermark has been embedded in a way that is virtually imperceptible to the human eye.

The objective visual quality of the GaWRI watermarking model is evaluated using PSNR and SSIM, which assess the similarity between the original images and the watermark images. Table 1 presents the average results obtained by evaluating 1,000 watermarked images from the COCO data set using three state-of-the-art watermarking methods, HiDDeN [42], MBRS [20], and ReDMark [3], for benchmarking purposes. To ensure consistency and fairness in the comparison, each method embedded binary watermarks of lengths $w$=30 bits and $w$=64 bits. Our proposed GaWRI model outperforms all three baseline techniques in terms

**Fig. 5.** Subjective visual quality of GaWRI watermarking model. (**a**) Original images. (**b**) Watermarked images.

of both PSNR and SSIM. Specifically, the GaWRI encoder still achieves an average PSNR of 45.29 dB and an SSIM of 0.9903 when the watermark length is 64, indicating optimal image fidelity after embedding a large size of watermarks. This shows the effectiveness of using GaWRI to embed AMM data as invisible watermarks in images for authentication.

**Table 1.** Comparison of different models on COCO dataset.

| Model | PSNR ($w$=30) | SSIM ($w$=30) | PSNR ($w$=64) | SSIM ($w$=64) |
|---|---|---|---|---|
| HiDDeN [42] | 32.02 | 0.9143 | 31.94 | 0.9138 |
| MBRS [20] | 33.28 | 0.9021 | 33.05 | 0.9026 |
| ReDMark [3] | 37.65 | 0.9682 | 37.27 | 0.9679 |
| **GaWRI** | 45.37 | 0.9904 | 45.29 | 0.9903 |

### 4.3 Robustness Analysis

Watermarked images and videos are inevitably subjected to different attacks during transmission and storage. As a robust watermarking model, our GaWRI ensures that embedded watermarks, AMM, can be extracted and recovered despite undergoing various types of attacks, including compression, noise, color, filtering, and geometric attacks. Thus, we used the average BA to evaluate the robustness. Typically, a higher BA value indicates stronger extraction reliability.

As shown in Table 2, our GaWRI model significantly outperforms the HiDDeN model in terms of robustness in different simulated attacks. When Gaussian noise with a variance of 0.10 was applied, GaWRI retained a high BA of 96.36%, whereas HiDDeN's accuracy dropped considerably to 76.54%. The different quality factors (QF) used by JPEG compression aim to improve transmission efficiency at the cost of reduced image quality. In the case of JPEG compression (QF = 10), GaWRI demonstrated significantly better performance, maintaining an accuracy that was 20.73% higher than HiDDeN. Considering color attacks

**Table 2.** Evaluating the robustness of the proposed GaWRI model.

| Attack | Noise Density | HiDDeN [.%] | GaWRI [.%] $w$=30 | GaWRI [.%] $w$=64 |
|---|---|---|---|---|
| Gaussian Noise | 0.001 | 83.15 | 100.00 | 100.00 |
| | 0.05 | 80.36 | 98.18 | 99.41 |
| | 0.10 | 76.54 | 96.36 | 97.83 |
| JPEG Compression | QF = 10 | 73.69 | 94.42 | 96.78 |
| | QF = 50 | 76.72 | 98.55 | 98.02 |
| | QF = 90 | 92.05 | 99.43 | 99.54 |
| Cropping | [20, 20, 420, 420] | 79.21 | 98.32 | 99.01 |
| Dropout | 0.3 | 86.84 | 99.12 | 99.32 |
| Salt and Pepper | 0.001 | 89.91 | 99.33 | 99.56 |
| | 0.05 | 82.47 | 98.26 | 98.03 |
| | 0.1 | 79.23 | 97.59 | 98.79 |
| Rotation | 45° | 78.52 | 97.94 | 98.64 |
| | 90° | 75.61 | 96.75 | 98.17 |
| Median Filter | [2, 2] | 88.25 | 98.81 | 99.08 |
| | [3, 3] | 80.73 | 97.40 | 98.35 |
| Adjust Brightness | 1.1 | 92.08 | 98.92 | 99.04 |
| | 1.3 | 83.45 | 97.17 | 98.77 |
| Adjust Contrast | 1.0 | 84.63 | 97.09 | 97.81 |
| | 2.0 | 77.52 | 96.65 | 97.12 |
| Image Scaling | 0.5 | 76.38 | 98.53 | 99.09 |
| | 2 | 81.44 | 96.79 | 96.65 |
| Shearing Attack | [0.4, 0.4] | 80.61 | 98.68 | 99.03 |
| Histogram Equalization | 1.0 | 86.17 | 98.92 | 99.11 |

(salt and pepper, adjusting brightness and contrast, and histogram equalization) and geometric attacks (cropping, scaling, rotation, shearing), our GaWRI also shows higher BA values than HiDDeN. Furthermore, the BA values of GaWRI are almost stable as the watermark length is increased to 64 bits for capacity improvements. These numerical results indicate that GaWRI can achieve trade-offs between impeccability, robustness, and capacity in data hiding for AMM.

Figure 6 illustrates the robustness evaluation of four watermarking methods, HiDDeN, MBRS, ReDMark, and the proposed AnchorMark, under various image distortions and attacks. Across all types of attacks, the proposed method (represented by the red solid line) consistently outperforms the other three baselines, maintaining a high decoding accuracy of nearly 1.00. ReDMark (green dashed line) outperforms HiDDeN and yields competitive results under certain distortions, such as cropping and image scaling; however, its overall accuracy

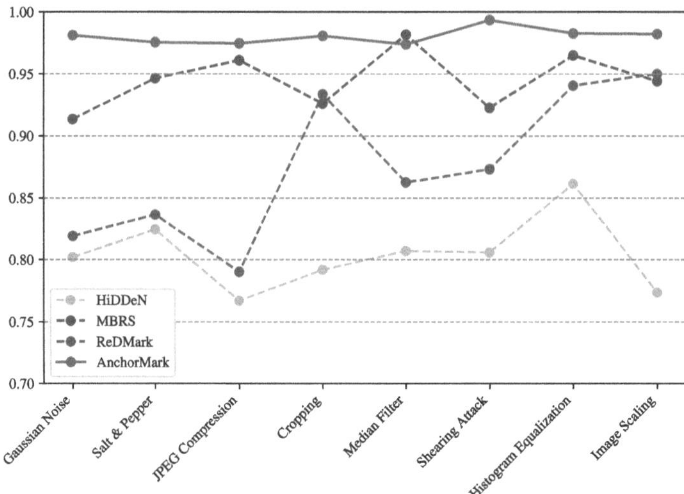


**Fig. 6.** Comparative analysis of proposed AnchorMark with HiDDeN [42], MBRS [20], ReDMark [3]. The vertical axis represents bit accuracy.

is less stable compared to the proposed work. These results highlight the superior robustness of GaWRI in preserving the integrity of the watermark against a wide range of image processing attacks. These results highlight the superior robustness of GaWRI in preserving the integrity of the watermark against a wide range of image processing attacks. Therefore, this indicates the effectiveness of applying AnchorMark for image authentication.

### 4.4 Discussions

For digital content authentication and manipulation detection, there are three key enabling technologies: metadata, fingerprinting, and watermarking [8]. Metadata can provide details on digital content when it is created, but it can be easily removed and modified during the storage and transmission stages. In this work, AnchorMark introduces AMM data as identifiers to link external physical ENF signals as the ground truth source. Unlike metadata that is saved in digital content, ground-truth ENF sources are stored and managed by a trusted physical anchor fabric. Thus, it is difficult to modify the physical anchor information, thereby improving security. However, AMM generation and verification depend on secure and reliable access to DEAM infrastructure, which inevitably incurs performance challenges. In addition, the current AnchorMark is limited to certain scenarios where ENF analysis may not be applicable, such as images and videos generated in outdoor environments or by battery-powered devices. Therefore, AnchorMark will extend the physical anchor fabric by cooperating with more environmental factors. We leave it to future efforts.

By binding extracted features of content as verifiable information, fingerprint technology is widely used for content identification, copyright protection, and retrieval applications [7]. Unlike passive fingerprinting methods, AnchorMark adopts an active approach that uses a robust GaWRI model to embed AMM data into original images and videos before distribution. Using AMM to locate external information as a cross-reference, AnchorMark can verify the authenticity of digital content and track its distribution and life cycles. Due to available technology, the current AnchorMark prototype focuses on image and video, and it cannot be generalized to other modalities like text and audio. Unlike images and videos, texts have strict syntactic or formatting requirements. Thus, low-entropy text content leads to a small watermark capacity, making it harder for text watermark generation [24]. More research is required on practical text watermarking frameworks to handle challenges in terms of integrity, information availability, and preservation of originality [21]. Future endeavors could extend the watermarking model to text and audio data and support multimodal watermarks such as images containing texts and video & audio recordings.

The proposed AnchorMark uses watermarking technology to ensure authentication and provenance of digital content in cyberspace. However, it also raises concerns about potential privacy risks and ethical implications. Watermarks can be used for surveillance purposes without users' consent. By tracking and monitoring watermarks, an adversary can learn the multimedia purchases and usage patterns of users. In addition, unauthorized third parties may compromise watermark extraction and then access personally identifiable information (PII) saved in watermarks. Therefore, privacy-by-design should be considered in the implementation of the watermarking framework. Our AnchorMark will integrate zero-knowledge proof (ZKP) protocols [28] with the AMM generation and verification stages to ensure the preservation of privacy for the authentication and provenance of digital content.

## 5 Conclusions

In this work, we propose a robust watermarking framework, namely AnchorMark, to address the growing challenges in authentication and detection for digital manipulations based on AIGC and HGC. The design of AMM allows the owner to use real-world anchors (ENF signals) as the ground truth to verify the authenticity of digital content. As a robust watermarking model, GaWRI integrates FRM and AGM to ensure imperceptibility and robustness as it embeds AMM data into images. The experimental results demonstrate that AnchorMark can effectively conceal binary AMM strings within high-quality images. Additionally, our AnchorMark can effectively retrieve AMM data from watermarked images under various simulated attacks. By combining a robust GaWRI watermarking model and a trusting physical anchor fabric, AnchorMark demonstrates the potential to enhance the authenticity and provenance of digital content in forensic scenarios.

However, several limitations and unresolved issues exist before the current version of AnchorMark can be adopted in real-world applications. Firstly, the current AnchorMark remains nascent without implementing AMM data structures and authentication procedures based on the ENF ground truth. Additionally, using public datasets to evaluate the GaWRI model may not accurately reflect the actual performance of embedding and extracting AMM in practical data-driven systems or metaverse applications. Moreover, the robustness is not evaluated by using real-world attacks on the GaWRI model, such as screen-shooting and watermark removal. Therefore, we will develop a secure AMM-based authentication framework and then build a complete version of the AnchorMark. A comprehensive experiment will be conducted to evaluate system performance and security in real-world scenarios.

## References

1. COCO. https://cocodataset.org/#download/ (2018)
2. Aberna, P., Agilandeeswari, L.: Digital image and video watermarking: methodologies, attacks, applications, and future directions. Multimedia Tools Appl. **83**(2), 5531–5591 (2024)
3. Ahmadi, M., Norouzi, A., Karimi, N., Samavi, S., Emami, A.: ReDMark: framework for residual diffusion watermarking based on deep networks. Expert Syst. Appl. **146**, 113157 (2020)
4. Alcaraz, C., Lopez, J.: Digital Twin: a comprehensive survey of security threats. IEEE Commun. Surv. Tutorials **24**(3), 1475–1503 (2022)
5. Alwahedi, F., Aldhaheri, A., Ferrag, M.A., Battah, A., Tihanyi, N.: Machine learning techniques for IoT security: current research and future vision with generative AI and large language models. Internet of Things Cyber-Phys. Syst. **4**, 167–185 (2024)
6. Cao, Y., Li, S., Liu, Y., Yan, Z., Dai, Y., Yu, P., Sun, L.: A survey of AI-generated content (AIGC). ACM Comput. Surv. **57**(5), 1–38 (2025)
7. Chen, W., Gan, W., Yu, P.S.: Digital fingerprinting on multimedia: a survey. arXiv preprint arXiv:2408.14155 (2024)
8. Collomosse, J., Parsons, A.: To authenticity, and beyond! building safe and fair generative AI upon the three pillars of provenance. IEEE Comput. Graph. Appl. **3**, 82–90 (2024)
9. Cooper, A., Grigoras, C., et al.: Forensic authentication of digital video recordings using the electric network frequency signal. In: Proceedings of the AES 39th International Conference (2010)
10. Dwivedi, Y.K., et al.: Metaverse beyond the hype: multidisciplinary perspectives on emerging challenges, opportunities, and agenda for research, practice and policy. Int. J. Inf. Manage. **66**, 102542 (2022)
11. Ghiurău, D., Popescu, D.E.: Distinguishing reality from AI: approaches for detecting synthetic content. Computers **14**(1), 1 (2024)
12. Grigoras, C.: Digital audio recording analysis: the electric network frequency criterion. Int. J. Speech Lang. Law **12**(1), 63–76 (2005)
13. Hatami, M., Qu, Q., Chen, Y., Mohammadi, J., Blasch, E., Ardiles-Cruz, E.: Anchor-grid: authenticating smart grid digital twins using real-world anchors. Sensors **25**(10), 2969 (2025)
14. Hosny, K.M., Magdi, A., ElKomy, O., Hamza, H.M.: Digital image watermarking using deep learning: a survey. Comput. Sci. Rev. **53**, 100662 (2024)

15. Hu, K., Wang, M., Ma, X., Chen, J., Wang, X., Wang, X.: Learning-based image steganography and watermarking: a survey. Expert Syst. Appl., 123715 (2024)
16. Huang, G., Liu, Z., Van Der Maaten, L., Weinberger, K.Q.: Densely connected convolutional networks. In: Proceedings of the IEEE Conference on Computer Vision and Pattern Recognition, pp. 4700–4708 (2017)
17. Huang, J., Luo, T., Li, L., Yang, G., Xu, H., Chang, C.C.: ARWGAN: attention-guided robust image watermarking model based on GAN. IEEE Trans. Instrum. Meas. **72**, 1–17 (2023)
18. Huijbregtse, M., Geradts, Z.: Using the ENF criterion for determining the time of recording of short digital audio recordings. In: International Workshop on Computational Forensics, pp. 116–124. Springer (2009)
19. jannehellsten: FFHQ. https://github.com/NVlabs/ffhq-dataset?tab=readme-ov-file/ (2020)
20. Jia, Z., Fang, H., Zhang, W.: MBRS: enhancing robustness of DNN-based watermarking by mini-batch of real and simulated jpeg compression. In: Proceedings of the 29th ACM International Conference on Multimedia, pp. 41–49 (2021)
21. Kamaruddin, N.S., Kamsin, A., Por, L.Y., Rahman, H.: A review of text watermarking: theory, methods, and applications. IEEE Access **6**, 8011–8028 (2018)
22. Kumarage, T., et al.: A survey of ai-generated text forensic systems: detection, attribution, and characterization. arXiv preprint arXiv:2403.01152 (2024)
23. Liang, Y., Xiao, J., Gan, W., Yu, P.S.: Watermarking techniques for large language models: a survey. arXiv preprint arXiv:2409.00089 (2024)
24. Liu, A., Pan, L., Lu, Y., Li, J., Hu, X., Zhang, X., Wen, L., King, I., Xiong, H., Yu, P.: A survey of text watermarking in the era of large language models. ACM Comput. Surv. **57**(2), 1–36 (2024)
25. Liu, X., Xu, R., Chen, Y.: A decentralized digital watermarking framework for secure and auditable video data in smart vehicular networks. Future Internet **16**(11) (2024)
26. Liu, X., Xu, R., Zhao, C.: AGFI-GAN: an attention-guided and feature-integrated watermarking model based on generative adversarial network framework for secure and auditable medical imaging application. Electronics **14**(1), 86 (2024)
27. Mazzetto, S.: A review of urban digital twins integration, challenges, and future directions in smart city development. Sustainability **16**(19), 8337 (2024)
28. Morais, E., Koens, T., Van Wijk, C., Koren, A.: A survey on zero knowledge range proofs and applications. SN Appl. Sci. **1**, 1–17 (2019)
29. Nagothu, D., Xu, R., Chen, Y.: Dema: decentralized electrical network frequency map for social media authentication. In: Disruptive Technologies in Information Sciences VII, vol. 12542, pp. 57–72. SPIE (2023)
30. Nagothu, D., Xu, R., Chen, Y., Blasch, E., Aved, A.: DeFakePro: decentralized deepfake attacks detection using ENF authentication. IT Professional **24**(5), 46–52 (2022)
31. Ngharamike, E., Ang, L.M., Seng, K.P., Wang, M.: ENF based digital multimedia forensics: survey, application, challenges and future work. IEEE Access **11**, 101241–101272 (2023)
32. Qu, Q., et al.: The microverse: a task-oriented edge-scale metaverse. Future Internet **16**(2), 60 (2024)
33. Tang, L., Ye, Q., Hu, H., Xue, Q., Xiao, Y., Li, J.: DeepMark: a scalable and robust framework for deepfake video detection. ACM Trans. Priv. Secur. **27**(1), 1–26 (2024)

34. Wu, X., Liao, X., Ou, B.: SepMark: deep separable watermarking for unified source tracing and deepfake detection. In: Proceedings of the 31st ACM International Conference on Multimedia, pp. 1190–1201 (2023)
35. Xia, X., Zhang, S., Wang, K., Gao, T.: A novel color image tampering detection and self-recovery based on fragile watermarking. J. Inf. Secur. Appl. **78**, 103619 (2023)
36. Xu, R., Liu, X., Nagothu, D., Qu, Q., Chen, Y.: Detecting manipulated digital entities through real-world anchors. In: International Conference on Advanced Information Networking and Applications, pp. 450–461. Springer (2025)
37. Yu, C.: Attention based data hiding with generative adversarial networks. In: Proceedings of the AAAI Conference on Artificial Intelligence, vol. 34, pp. 1120–1128 (2020)
38. Yu, X., et al.: Fake artificial intelligence generated contents (FAIGC): a survey of theories, detection methods, and opportunities. arXiv preprint arXiv:2405.00711 (2024)
39. Zhang, X., Li, R., Yu, J., Xu, Y., Li, W., Zhang, J.: EditGuard: versatile image watermarking for tamper localization and copyright protection. In: Proceedings of the IEEE/CVF Conference on Computer Vision and Pattern Recognition, pp. 11964–11974 (2024)
40. Zhao, X., et al.: Sok: Watermarking for ai-generated content. arXiv preprint arXiv:2411.18479 (2024)
41. Zhao, Y., et al.: Metaverse: Perspectives from graphics, interactions and visualization. Vis. Inform. **6**(1), 56–67 (2022)
42. Zhu, J., Kaplan, R., Johnson, J., Fei-Fei, L.: Hidden: hiding data with deep networks. In: Proceedings of the European Conference on Computer Vision (ECCV), pp. 657–672 (2018)

# Critical Infrastructure and Cyber-Physical Security: Cyber Resilience in Physical and Industrial Systems, Including IoT, Satellites, and SCADA

# Resilient Satellite Cybersecurity: Integrating NIST and AI Governance

Kimberly A. Cornell(✉) and Li Huang

University at Albany, Albany 12222, USA
{kacornell,lhuang9}@albany.edu

**Abstract.** The growing dependence on commercial satellite networks during military conflicts and humanitarian crises has exposed critical cybersecurity gaps. While frameworks like the NIST Cybersecurity Framework (CSF) and the NIST AI Risk Management Framework (RMF) offer structured guidance, they remain underutilized in satellite ecosystems. This paper proposes a unified, multi-layered cybersecurity framework that adapts these standards to the unique needs of commercial space assets. We address technical vulnerabilities and organizational misalignments across public, private, and military domains, emphasizing AI system transparency, risk governance, and stakeholder alignment.

Through case studies such as the Viasat KA-SAT attack and Starlink's operations in Ukraine, we demonstrate how this approach enhances resilience, accountability, and cross-sector cooperation. Our contribution is a layered defense model that integrates technical and policy solutions, strengthens collaboration, and ensures secure, resilient satellite operations in high-risk scenarios. By bridging policy and technical domains, this framework supports a robust and trusted public-private satellite cyber ecosystem.

**Keywords:** Satellite security · AI governance · NIST CSF · Cyber resilience · Public-private cooperation

## 1 Introduction

Commercial satellite systems have become a critical backbone for global communications, intelligence gathering, disaster response, and military operations. As of 2024, over 7,500 satellites are operational [32], with projections nearing 100,000 by 2030 [30]. A growing number of these assets are privately owned, particularly by companies such as SpaceX, Amazon, and Viasat. This evolution raises an urgent question: How can the public sector rely on privately owned satellite infrastructure while ensuring robust and resilient cybersecurity?

The integration of private assets into national and global communication systems has introduced significant cybersecurity challenges. These include legacy encryption, opaque protocol standards, conflicting commercial and governmental priorities, and the increasing use of generative artificial intelligence (AI) by both


K.-K. R. Choo et al. (Eds.): ICDF2C 2025, LNICST 686, pp. 233–247, 2026.
https://doi.org/10.1007/978-3-032-22545-0_14

attackers and defenders. Recent events, such as the 2022 Viasat cyberattack attributed to Russian threat actors [4,21,34], have shown how adversaries can target commercial infrastructure during active conflicts, disrupting both military operations and civilian services.

In response, this paper proposes a structured framework for improving the cybersecurity of commercial satellite systems through cross-sector collaboration. Drawing upon the National Institute of Standards and Technology (NIST) Cybersecurity Framework [22] and its 2024 AI Risk Management Framework [26], we develop a technical roadmap for integrating public and private cybersecurity efforts. Our key contribution is adapting these standards to the unique constraints of the space domain, including misaligned economic incentives, AI model deployment risks, and limited system-level visibility. By analyzing existing technical standards, threat models, and real-world events, we argue for a multi-layered cybersecurity framework that promotes resilience, transparency, and coordination across stakeholders. Our study is grounded in both technical and policy perspectives, aiming to support researchers and decision-makers in designing a secure and adaptable satellite cyber ecosystem.

## 2 Related Work

Research on satellite cybersecurity has expanded in response to the growing interdependence between terrestrial and space-based systems. Prior studies have identified a wide range of vulnerabilities in both communication protocols and hardware components of satellite systems. Bardin outlines the various attack surfaces, including ground stations, telemetry, and command links, emphasizing the susceptibility of satellite infrastructure to spoofing, jamming, and unauthorized access [2]. More recent works, such as Carlo and Obergfaell, examine how cyber attacks on critical infrastructure increasingly target commercial satellites, particularly during conflicts or humanitarian operations [5].

A significant body of research also focuses on integrating encryption standards, such as AES, and end-to-end encryption for secure data transmission over satellite links [7,18]. Su et al. discuss broadband Low Earth Orbit (LEO) satellite architectures and highlight challenges in securely managing dynamic constellations [33]. However, few studies explore how cybersecurity standards, particularly from NIST, can be systematically applied to satellite ecosystems.

As AI becomes a dual-use technology, its impact on satellite security has drawn scholarly attention. Wang et al. demonstrate how anomaly detection using AI models can improve monitoring of LEO networks [35]. Conversely, Fang et al. and Maguire warn that generative AI systems can be weaponized to automate reconnaissance, discover vulnerabilities, or execute misinformation campaigns through space assets [13,19]. Despite these advances, research on AI governance and risk management for space systems remains underdeveloped.

An absence from the literature is a unified framework that adapts cybersecurity standards, such as the NIST Cybersecurity Framework (CSF) [22] and the AI Risk Management Framework (AI RMF) [26], to commercial satellite contexts.

While NIST IRs, such as IR 8270 (spacecraft systems) [23], IR 8401 (terrestrial infrastructure) [24], and IR 8441 (hybrid satellite networks) [25], offering relevant guidance, academic efforts to synthesize and operationalize these insights in multi-stakeholder, real-world environments are rare.

This paper aims to fill that gap by presenting a multi-layered cybersecurity framework designed for commercial satellite operations. It integrates NIST's structured risk-based approach with policy-driven insights into public-private collaboration and proposes mechanisms to address interest alignment, protocol transparency, and AI safety.

While several NIST publications offer guidance relevant to satellite cybersecurity, including IR 8270 for spacecraft, IR 8401 for ground infrastructure, and IR 8441 for hybrid satellite networks, these documents often remain siloed and lack explicit integration with AI risk governance. Moreover, none offer a comprehensive model that spans orbital, ground, and data infrastructure layers while aligning public, private, and military responsibilities. To our knowledge, no prior work has synthesized NIST CSF and AI RMF in a way that is operationally viable for commercial satellite systems. This work addresses the gap.

Table 1 summarizes the scope and limitations of the NIST frameworks and demonstrates how our approach expands upon them to address multi-layered threats, AI governance, and cross-sector coordination in high-stakes satellite operations. The comparisons presented in this table form the basis for our multi-layered defense framework, detailed in Sect. 4. This framework translates these standards into practical applications through role-based mappings, implementation strategies, and governance mechanisms designed to enhance real-world resilience.

## 3 Cyber Threat Landscape and Systemic Challenges

Commercial satellites are increasingly exposed to complex cyber threats due to their dual-use nature and integration into both civilian and military operations. These threats emerge across the entire satellite communication chain, from orbital assets to ground control to end-user terminals, and are amplified during geopolitical crises and natural disasters. This section identifies key technical and organizational vulnerabilities and highlights the growing influence of AI in both offensive and defensive operations.

### 3.1 Multi-vector Cyber Threats in Satellite Ecosystems

Satellite systems face unique cyber attack vectors that are distinct from traditional Information Technology (IT) infrastructure:

- **Uplink/Downlink Interception** [2,10]
  Unauthorized access to command and telemetry channels can enable adversaries to issue false commands or deny legitimate access.

**Table 1.** Comparison of NIST Guidance & Contribution of This Paper

| NIST Guidance | Scope | Limitations in Satellite Context | Extension in This Paper |
|---|---|---|---|
| NIST CSF [22] | General IT/OT systems | Not tailored for space systems or AI governance | Adapted to satellite-specific operational layers; mapped to actor roles |
| NIST IR 8270 [23] | Spacecraft systems | Lacks AI governance and public-private mapping | Integrates AI RMF and adds layered governance for commercial and public actors |
| NIST IR 8401 [24] | Ground control systems | Lacks economic or regulatory coordination mechanisms | Adds commercial incentive structures and policy-driven security alignment |
| NIST IR 8441 [25] | Hybrid satellite networks | Limited threat modeling for complex attack surfaces; no guidance on AI-specific risks or mitigation strategies | Adds layered anomaly detection and introduces a centralized AI model registry for satellite systems |
| NIST AI RMF [27] | General AI risk management | Lacks adaptation for satellite protocols or layered space system architectures | Applied to signal routing, intrusion detection, load balancing, and fallback mechanisms |

- **Jamming and Spoofing** [9]
  Signal jamming can disable communications, while spoofing can mislead satellite navigation or positioning systems, affecting both military and civil operations.
- **Ground Segment Vulnerabilities** [5]
  Ground stations are typically less protected than satellites in orbit. They are vulnerable to lateral movement from compromised IT systems, firmware exploitation, and physical breaches.
- **Supply Chain Risks** [28]
  Satellite components sourced from global suppliers introduce attack surfaces through insecure firmware, counterfeit parts, or compromised software updates.
- **Cloud-Connected Interfaces** [8]
  Modern satellite networks rely on cloud systems for data analytics and service orchestration, expanding the attack surface to include platform-as-a-service (PaaS) and software-as-a-service (SaaS) vulnerabilities.

Recent events exemplify these risks. In 2022, Russian actors executed a cyberattack on Viasat's KA-SAT system, disrupting connectivity for Ukrainian military units and causing collateral outages across Europe [11,32]. This attack exploited vulnerable modem firmware, highlighting the cascading effects of poor endpoint security in satellite networks.

### 3.2 The Role of AI in Cyber Offense and Defense

The integration of AI into cyber operations has intensified the threat environment:

- **Generative AI Threat** [13]
  Attackers are using generative AI models (e.g., large language models, LLMs) to autonomously scan satellite protocols, identify zero-day vulnerabilities, and simulate intrusion paths [35]. Reports from U.S. intelligence indicate that groups such as Fancy Bear have deployed AI to interfere with satellite-based radar and positioning systems during active conflicts.
- **AI-Enabled Spoofing and Signal Manipulation** [20]
  Generative models can craft signals or commands that imitate legitimate satellite communications. These spoofed transmissions can deceive navigation systems or ground operators, with potentially catastrophic results.
- **Model Drift and Data Poisoning** [3]
  Defensive AI systems themselves are vulnerable. Malicious actors can exploit weaknesses in training data to induce biased or unpredictable model behavior over time.

Despite these threats, AI also offers defensive potential. For example, two-stage anomaly detection algorithms can identify subtle deviations in satellite telemetry and communication flows [35]. However, most AI defenses rely on access to high-quality data, a persistent challenge due to proprietary protocols and fragmented system ownership.

### 3.3 Systemic Challenges in Public-Private Defense

- **Misaligned Incentives** [1,29]
  Private companies prioritize uptime and profitability, often at odds with public mandates for transparency, resilience, and compliance with regulations. Without regulatory pressure or shared risk frameworks, security investment is deprioritized. For instance, reports suggest that Starlink limited Ukrainian access to terminals in 2023 due to funding concerns, illustrating how corporate decision-making can impact national defense operations.
- **Opaque Protocols and Limited Standardization** [17]
  Most commercial satellite systems use proprietary communication protocols, which impede security auditing, protocol verification, and AI risk management. The lack of shared standards hinders interoperability and complicates efforts to deploy NIST-aligned defense strategies.
- **AI Transparency and Accountability Gaps** [14,15,31]
  While the NIST AI Risk Management Framework (AI RMF) emphasizes documentation, testing, and monitoring, few commercial actors currently apply these principles to space systems. There is no requirement to disclose how AI models are trained, what data they use, or how adversarial robustness is ensured, leaving both technical and regulatory blind spots.

## 4 Proposed Framework: A Multi-Layered Model

In response to the growing cyber threat landscape and systemic governance challenges in satellite communications, we propose a multi-layered defense framework grounded in NIST's Cybersecurity Framework and the 2024 AI Risk Management Framework (AI RMF). Table 2 presents the core structure and components of the proposed model. It adapts traditional cybersecurity controls to the technical and organizational realities of commercial satellite operations, emphasizing risk-based prioritization, cross-sector coordination, and transparency in AI deployment.

**Table 2.** Core Structure & Components

| Function | Satellite Context | Examples |
|---|---|---|
| Identify | Risk classification across space assets and operators | Catalog commercial satellites, classify AI-enabled systems, assess supply chain exposure |
| Protect | Secure architecture, encryption, access controls | Implement resilient protocols, enforce endpoint security on ground stations |
| Detect | Real-time anomaly monitoring across orbit and ground | Deploy AI-based anomaly detection on satellite telemetry streams |
| Respond | Cross-sector incident response coordination | Integrate commercial providers into national response protocols, joint tabletop exercises |
| Recover | Post-incident reconstitution and improvement | Secure reboot protocols, forensics, lessons-learned databases |

To further illustrate the practical application of our proposed framework, Table 3 provides a detailed overlay of NIST CSF functions and AI RMF components across the satellite stack, showcasing specific examples of implementation for each layer.

**Table 3.** AI Risk Management Integration Across Satellite System Layers

| Layer | CSF Function | AI RMF Integration | Example Implementation |
|---|---|---|---|
| Orbital | Detect, Protect | Map (AI-assisted routing, radar, etc.) | AI telemetry anomaly detection; zero-trust endpoint hardening |
| Ground | Identify, Respond | Measure (robustness, adversarial risk) | Firmware audits; AI model stress testing; satellite registry |
| Data Infrastructure (Cloud/PaaS) | Recover, Protect | Manage (model documentation, fallback) | Red-teaming model prioritization and fallback strategies; AI registry; encryption standards |

### 4.1 Core Structure and Components

Our framework extends the five functional domains of the NIST CSF (Identify, Protect, Detect, Respond, Recover) and maps each to specific actors, actions, and assets in the satellite ecosystem.

Unlike general CSF applications, our framework introduces a role-mapping layer that distinguishes between public, private, and military responsibilities for each function. For example, the "Respond" function involves private operators (e.g., satellite owners), public regulators (e.g., the FCC, CISA), and defense stakeholders (e.g., the Space Force) acting in a synchronized manner, with pre-defined communication protocols and contingency plans.

### 4.2 Incorporating AI Risk Management

To address the use and misuse of AI in satellite systems, our framework integrates core principles of the AI RMF, including:

1. **Map**: define where AI is used across the satellite communication lifecycle, e.g., signal routing, orbital traffic management, intrusion detection systems.
2. **Measure**: evaluate model robustness, input/output behavior, and adversarial risk. Require black-box and white-box testing prior to deployment.
3. **Manage**: implement governance mechanisms such as third-party audits, documentation of training data, model lineage tracking, and fallback procedures.

We advocate for a centralized AI risk registry to facilitate transparency, cross-sector collaboration, and AI risk governance in critical space systems. A centralized registry identifies both models used in critical communications functions and levels of exposure to adversarial manipulation [12]. It also outlines transparency scores based on disclosure of training methods, model scope, and red-teaming practices [14]. By centralizing AI system information, regulators and trusted partners would gain real-time visibility into the deployment and security posture of critical space assets, enabling faster incident response.

### 4.3 Interest Alignment Mechanisms

We have discussed in Sect. 3.3 that one of the central challenges in securing commercial satellite infrastructure is the misalignment of interests between private operators, public regulators, and military users. To bridge the gap between public objectives and private constraints, our framework introduces a set of mechanisms designed to incentivize collaboration without compromising operational independence. First, we propose that participation in national defense or emergency response contracts should align with demonstrable cybersecurity compliance, such as measuring against NIST standards and verifying through periodic audits. This creates economic incentives for private companies to prioritize security investments. Second, we recommend the creation of dual-use risk-sharing models, such as pooled cyber insurance, which distribute the financial burden of cyber incidents across stakeholders. These models acknowledge the shared nature of satellite infrastructure in modern conflict and crisis response. Finally, we suggest embedding cybersecurity liaison officers within major commercial providers, akin to the DHS's existing public-private programs for critical infrastructure. These embedded roles would improve coordination, reduce ambiguity during cyber incidents, and foster continuous knowledge exchange between sectors. Collectively, these mechanisms promote a more resilient and collaborative satellite cybersecurity ecosystem by aligning economic, strategic, and operational incentives.

These mechanisms are designed to address misaligned interests and promote shared ownership of risk, creating accountability without stifling innovation.

### 4.4 Summary

As shown in Fig. 1, the proposed layered defense model is organized into three distinct operational domains: orbital, ground, and data infrastructure. We illustrate how the five core functions of the NIST Cybersecurity Framework (Identify, Protect, Detect, Respond, and Recover) apply across all operational layers of a satellite system, from space assets to terrestrial control centers and cloud-based analytics platforms. The framework also incorporates the NIST AI Risk Management Framework (AI RMF), highlighting how AI-related activities such as mapping use contexts, measuring risks, and managing governance processes are embedded within each layer of operation. The framework emphasizes the roles of key stakeholders, private sector entities, public regulators, and military or defense agencies, demonstrating how responsibilities and coordination mechanisms are distributed across the system. This structure emphasizes the importance of multi-layered defense and joint accountability, while also serving as a practical reference for policymakers, engineers, and cybersecurity professionals working at the intersection of space and AI. By integrating technical controls with governance, the framework promotes a unified and transparent approach to securing satellite infrastructure in an increasingly complex digital environment.

# 5 Case Study: Applying the Framework in Real-World Incidents

The growing use of commercial satellite networks in conflict and crisis scenarios demands structured, risk-informed approaches to cybersecurity. This section focuses on two incidents, Viasat's KA-SAT hack and Starlink's operational ambiguity in Ukraine, to demonstrate how the proposed framework could have mitigated risks and supported resilient outcomes.

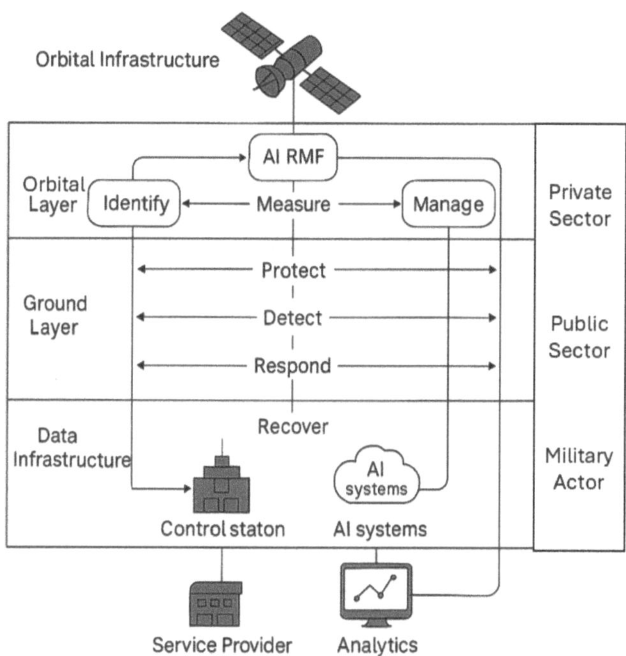


**Fig. 1.** Multi-layered Cybersecurity Model

## 5.1 Viasat KA-SAT Hack (February 2022)

On the day of Russia's invasion of Ukraine, a cyberattack targeted Viasat's KA-SAT satellite broadband service [16]. Attackers exploited a vulnerability in ground-based modems, disabling thousands of terminals used by the Ukrainian military and civilian customers across Europe. The attack chain proceeded as follows:

- Reconnaissance: Threat actors scanned publicly accessible interfaces and harvested version data for firmware running on KA-SAT ground terminals.
- Access: Exploitation of a misconfigured VPN appliance allowed lateral movement into the network management segment.
- Exploitation: Attackers deployed a wiper payload that corrupted flash memory in modems, making them inoperable.
- Delayed Response: Coordination between Viasat, NATO, and Ukrainian authorities occurred post-impact, extending downtime to multiple days.

As shown in Table 4, there are some key failures:

1. Firmware updates were insufficiently protected.
2. No anomaly detection flagged the abnormal network activity before the widespread outage.
3. There were delays in coordinated response between Viasat, NATO allies, and Ukrainian partners.

**Table 4.** Framework Mapping

| Function | What Wrong | Recommendation |
|---|---|---|
| Identify | No detailed asset-level threat classification across satellite endpoints | Conduct regular risk mapping for all commercial terminals used in national infrastructure |
| Protect | Firmware not cryptographically signed or verified | Enforce mandatory cryptographic validation of all over-the-air updates |
| Detect | No proactive monitoring for abnormal modem behavior | Deploy machine-learning-based intrusion detection at the edge (modem/ground station) |
| Respond | Delayed multi-party coordination | Develop joint incident response protocols among public-private stakeholders |
| Recover | Recovery required physical replacement of devices | Integrate secure fallback procedures (e.g., factory resets or secondary channels) |

This event shows the cost of not implementing an AI-augmented detect-and-respond cycle. With our proposed framework, anomaly detection models and cross-sector drills could have reduced downtime and prevented cascading effects.

### 5.2 Starlink in Ukraine: Operational Benefits and Strategic Ambiguity

Elon Musk's SpaceX deployed Starlink services to Ukraine in 2022, ensuring continued civilian and military connectivity amidst kinetic and cyber warfare

[6]. However, decisions over coverage, prioritization, and withdrawal remained under SpaceX's control, raising ethical and strategic concerns. In Table 5, we map some key observations:

1. Ukrainian forces had no binding service-level agreement (SLA) with SpaceX.
2. Network coverage decisions (e.g., cutting access during offensive operations) were made unilaterally by the provider.
3. The AI-based load-balancing and prioritization algorithms were opaque to both regulators and users.

**Table 5.** NIST & AI RMF

| Function | Risk | Recommended Application |
|---|---|---|
| Map (AI RMF) | Unknown AI decision boundaries | Require providers to disclose AI-assisted network management roles |
| Manage (AI RMF) | No oversight on service denials | Establish red teaming, model documentation, and rollback options |
| Identify / Align | Conflicting profit and defense motives | Create regulatory-military partnerships with embedded cybersecurity liaisons |
| Respond / Govern | Lack of predefined policy for service disruption | Include commercial satellite providers in national cyber drills and disaster contingency plans |

This example reveals a structural gap in governance. While technically secure, the service operated outside a cohesive public cybersecurity and response framework. Our model requires transparency and AI auditing for mission-critical infrastructure, even when it is delivered by private entities.

## 6 Discussion and Future Work

The case studies above highlight a growing strategic paradox: while commercial satellite infrastructure is indispensable to modern military and humanitarian operations, it is largely governed by private decision-making and proprietary technologies. Without a cohesive framework, this environment becomes vulnerable to misalignment, exploitation, and strategic uncertainty.

### 6.1 Implications for Research and Practice

The proposed framework contributes to both cybersecurity practice and academic literature by offering a structured, NIST standards-based approach to securing commercial satellite systems. It bridges the technical rigor of the NIST Cybersecurity Framework with the adaptive governance of the NIST AI Risk Management Framework, creating a comprehensive model for managing cybersecurity in dual-use space infrastructure. Practically, this framework provides stakeholders with a scalable template for aligning technical controls and operational roles across private, public, and defense sectors. For researchers, it introduces new avenues for exploring cross-sector collaboration, AI accountability, and layered security in emerging technology ecosystems. This integration of cybersecurity engineering, AI risk governance, and strategic coordination addresses a growing need for actionable models that reflect the hybrid nature of modern satellite networks.

Furthermore, the implementation of this framework offers an opportunity to formalize cybersecurity expectations for commercial satellite operators through regulatory mechanisms. By requiring evidence of NIST-aligned practices and AI transparency in contract awards or orbital frequency allocations, governments can drive accountability without imposing overly prescriptive controls. Additionally, this framework supports the standardization of technical language and expectations across jurisdictions, which is critical for international coordination in responding to cross-border cyber threats. Enforcing commercial satellite providers into national or multinational cyber response protocols would further ensure continuity of operations during high-impact events. Ultimately, the framework can help shift cybersecurity from a discretionary investment to a baseline requirement, shaping the next generation of space policy and cyber norm development.

### 6.2 Future Research

This work has several directions for future research. One promising area involves simulating and empirically validating AI-assisted anomaly detection systems in satellite telemetry, which could assess the effectiveness of real-time defensive responses across various orbital scenarios. We will use publicly available satellite telemetry logs with MATLAB and ns-3 to model satellite system behaviors and emulate network conditions, attack scenarios, and defense responses. Another area includes the formal verification of proprietary satellite communication protocols, particularly to evaluate cryptographic strength and resistance to spoofing or jamming. There is also a need to study the ethical and operational boundaries of autonomous AI systems in prioritizing satellite resources during conflict, as these decisions may affect both strategic outcomes and humanitarian access.

Moreover, comparative analysis of national AI governance models could inform the creation of interoperable registries or red-teaming strategies tailored to space infrastructure. These directions would not only extend the technical depth of the framework but also expand its relevance in a rapidly evolving technological landscape.

### 6.3 Validation Concept: Governance-Driven Response Simulation

A practical direction for future work involves simulating how governance-aligned cybersecurity frameworks affect operational response during satellite-related incidents. Rather than focusing on model performance, this validation would assess how applying role-based responsibilities (e.g., operator alerts, escalation paths, regulatory logging) can improve coordination and recovery times during simulated cyber incidents. These simulations could use mock telemetry logs, scenario-based tabletop exercises, or open-source orbital system datasets to emulate governance and incident response behavior. The goal is to evaluate whether aligning actions with the proposed NIST CSF and Artificial Intelligence Risk Management Framework (AI RMF) functions leads to better resilience, accountability, and communication across stakeholders during real-time disruption scenarios.

## 7 Conclusion

The increasing militarization and humanitarian reliance on commercial satellite communications have exposed critical vulnerabilities in current cybersecurity governance. This paper presents a multi-layered framework grounded in the NIST Cybersecurity Framework and AI Risk Management Framework, designed to address the unique operational, technical, and political complexities of space-based systems.

By integrating cybersecurity best practices with AI-specific governance tools and role-based collaboration between private, public, and military stakeholders, our model fills a gap in existing literature and practice. Case studies of the Viasat cyberattack and Starlink's strategic ambiguity in Ukraine highlight the urgent need for shared technical standards, coordinated response protocols, and transparency mechanisms for AI in space operations.

As satellite constellations expand and AI becomes increasingly embedded in cyber and space operations, it is essential to align national security, commercial innovation, and public benefit within a cohesive cybersecurity defense strategy. Our framework provides a way to achieve this alignment through structured governance, robust technical controls, and cross-sector cooperation.

**Acknowledgments.** The authors would like to thank the University at Albany for its institutional support and the Cybersecurity & Cryptography Lab at the University at Albany for providing resources and support.

**Disclosure of Interests.** The authors have no competing interests to declare that are relevant to the content of this article.

## References

1. Anderson, R., Moore, T.: The economics of information security. Science **314**(5799), 610–613 (2006)
2. Bardin, J.: Satellite cyber attack search and destroy. In: Computer and Information Security Handbook, pp. 1173–1181. Elsevier (2013)
3. Breda, P., Markova, R., Abdin, A., Jha, D., Carlo, A., et al.: Cyber vulnerabilities and risks of AI technologies in space applications. In: 73Rd International Astronautical Congress (IAC). International Astronautical Congress, Paris, France (2022), ffhal-03908014
4. Brewster, T.: Bombs and hackers are battering Ukraine'S internet providers. 'Hidden Heroes' risk their lives to keep their country online (2022). https://www.forbes.com/sites/thomasbrewster/2022/03/15/internet-technicians-are-the-hidden-heroes-of-the-russia-ukraine-war/?sh=6c18b1902884
5. Carlo, A., Obergfaell, K.: Cyber attacks on critical infrastructures and satellite communications. Int. J. Crit. Infrastruct. Prot. **46**, 100701 (2024)
6. Spacex limited ukraine's use of starlink, report says. https://www.cnn.com/2022/11/04/politics/spacex-ukraine-elon-musk-starlink-internet-outage (2022). cNN, published 2022-11-04. Accessed 22 Nov 2022
7. Cruickshank, H.: A security system for satellite networks. In: Fifth International Conference On Satellite Systems For Mobile Communications and Navigation, pp. 187–190. IET (1996)
8. Deloitte: New Deloitte Report Addresses Increasing Danger Of Cyber Threats In Space. Industrial Cyber (2024). https://industrialcyber.co/reports/new-deloitte-report-addresses-increasing-danger-of-cyber-threats-in-space-issues-call-to-action/
9. Egozi, A.: New protections deployed against attacks on navigation systems. Aviation International News (2024). https://www.ainonline.com/aviation-news/air-transport/2024-07-16/new-protections-deployed-against-attacks-navigation-systems
10. Elbert, B.R.: The Satellite Communication Applications Handbook. Artech House (2004)
11. Erkel, D.: The Success of Emerging Space Actors: Effective Strategies in the Newspace Era. Ph.D. thesis, Massachusetts Institute of Technology (2023)
12. European Commission: Proposal for a Regulation laying down harmonised rules on Artificial Intelligence (Artificial Intelligence Act) (2021). https://op.europa.eu/en/publication-detail/-/publication/e0649735-a372-11eb-9585-01aa75ed71a1, cOM(2021) 206 final
13. Fang, R., Bindu, R., Gupta, A., Kang, D.: LLM agents can autonomously exploit one-day vulnerabilities. arXiv preprint arXiv:2404.08144 (2024)
14. Felzmann, H., Villaronga, E.F., Lutz, C., Tamò-Larrieux, A.: Transparency you can trust: transparency requirements for artificial intelligence between legal norms and contextual concerns. Big Data Soc. **6**(1), 2053951719860542 (2019)
15. Feuerriegel, S., Hartmann, J., Janiesch, C., Zschech, P.: Generative AI. Bus. Inf. Syst. Eng. **66**(1), 111–126 (2024)
16. Greig, J.: NSA, Viasat Say 2022 hack was two incidents; Russian sanctions resulted from investigation. https://therecord.media/viasat-hack-was-two-incidents-and-resulted-in-sanctions (2024). Accessed 13 Jun 2024
17. Jobin, A., Ienca, M., Vayena, E.: The global landscape of AI ethics guidelines. Nat. Mach. Intell. **1**(9), 389–399 (2019)

18. Landau, S.: Communications security for the twenty-first century: the advanced encryption standard. Not. AMS **47**(4), 450–459 (2000)
19. Maguire, P.: AI at the crossroads of cybersecurity, space and national security in the digital age. https://spacenews.com/ai-crossroads-cybersecurity-space-national-security-digital-age/ (2024)
20. Metta, S., Chang, I., Parker, J., Roman, M.P., Ehuan, A.F.: Generative AI in Cybersecurity. arXiv preprint arXiv:2405.01674 (2024)
21. Miller, M.: Ukraine'S largest telecom stands against Russian cyberattacks (2022). https://www.politico.com/news/2022/09/07/hackers-ukraine-telecom-00055060
22. National institute of standards and technology: cybersecurity framework (2014). https://www.nist.gov/cyberframework
23. National institute of standards and technology: applying the cybersecurity framework to commercial satellite operations. Tech. Rep. IR 8270, NIST (2022)
24. National institute of standards and technology: satellite ground segment: applying the cybersecurity framework to satellite command and control (2022). https://csrc.nist.gov/pubs/ir/8401/final
25. National institute of standards and technology: cybersecurity framework profile for hybrid satellite networks (HSN). Tech. Rep. IR 8441, NIST (2023)
26. National institute of standards and technology: AI risk management framework (2024). https://www.nist.gov/itl/ai-risk-management-framework
27. National institute of standards and technology: AI Risk Management Framework (AI RMF). Tech. rep., NIST (2024). https://www.nist.gov/itl/ai-risk-management-framework
28. Protik, R.C.: Updated standard for secure satellite communications: analysis of satellites, attack vectors, existing standards, and enterprise and security architectures. arXiv preprint arXiv:2310.19105 (2023)
29. Quach, S., Thaichon, P., Martin, K.D., Weaven, S., Palmatier, R.W.: Digital technologies: tensions in privacy and data. J. Acad. Mark. Sci. **50**(6), 1299–1323 (2022)
30. Scharping, N.: The future of satellites lies in the constellations (2021). https://astronomy.com/news/2021/06/the-future-of-satellites-lies-in-giant-constellations
31. Scherer, M.U.: Regulating artificial intelligence systems: risks, challenges, competencies and strategies. Harv. J. Law Tech. **29**, 353 (2015)
32. Sebastian, K.A.: Union Of Concerned Scientists (UCS) Satellite Database. https://www.ucsusa.org/resources/satellite-database (2024). Accessed 21 Nov 2022
33. Su, Y., Liu, Y., Zhou, Y., Yuan, J., Cao, H., Shi, J.: Broadband LEO satellite communications: architectures and key technologies. IEEE Wirel. Commun. **26**(2), 55–61 (2019)
34. Turak, N., Fabbro, R.: 10 Million Ukrainians Without Power, Kyiv Says; evidence of "Gross Sabotage" found at nord stream blast site (2022). https://www.cnbc.com/2022/11/18/russia-ukraine-live-updates.html
35. Wang, Y., et al.: Two-stage anomaly detection in LEO satellite network. In: Science of Cyber Security, pp. 423–438. Springer (2023)

# An Enhanced Federated Machine Learning Approach for Decentralized Water Contamination Detection

Raja Kumar[1](✉), Jayesh Soni[1], and Himanshu Upadhyay[2]

[1] Applied Research Center, Florida International University, Miami, USA
{rkuma024,jsoni}@fiu.edu

[2] Department of Electrical and Computer Engineering, Florida International University, Miami, USA
upadhyay@fiu.edu

**Abstract.** Water contamination anomaly detection is a challenging task due to heterogeneous sensor data and stringent privacy constraints. In this paper, we propose a federated approach to the detection of water contamination anomalies that addresses both technical and organizational challenges in water monitoring utilizing open-source water quality data from the city of Austin. The model applies various data-related techniques to build a high-performance contamination detection system by using long-short-term memory (LSTM) networks. This approach ensures data-knowledge distillation from various water quality datasets without centralized environmental monitoring data, creating a paradigm for data utility and privacy protection as a critical infrastructure process. Experimental results show that our FedAvg-based federated learning approach achieves a test-set MSE of 0.07—substantially lower than the best traditional LSTM algorithm with a MSE of 0.13, while preserving data privacy.

**Keywords:** Federated learning · Anomaly detection · Water contamination · Deep Learning · LSTM · Privacy preservation

## 1 Introduction

The global challenge of ensuring safe drinking water has reached unprecedented levels of complexity in the 21st century. With the advent of industrialization, agricultural intensification, and climate change as major factors of water contamination, water resources are constantly threatened from a wide variety of pollutants. As stated by the United Nations, around 80% of the wastewater all over the globe goes untreated and is released directly into the environment which ultimately affects drinking water resources. The traditional water quality examination methods are primarily based on lab analysis of individual samples, a methodological approach that causes temporary lapses in detection capabilities and introduces numerous problems in identification of irregular contamination


K.-K. R. Choo et al. (Eds.): ICDF2C 2025, LNICST 686, pp. 248–263, 2026.
https://doi.org/10.1007/978-3-032-22545-0_15

events [1]. These demerits are of great importance to public health, as the pollution events may be unnoticed for several days or weeks, and in that time, the population can be exposed to toxic substances.

The combination of sensor technologies and IoT devices with water distribution networks has made it possible to continuously monitor multitude water parameters. Nowadays sensor arrays are remarkably advanced and can detect several water quality parameters simultaneously such as pH, turbidity, chlorine levels, electrical conductivity, temperature, and dissolved oxygen, thus producing streams of multivariate data continuously [2]. The right use of this data for the detection of contamination points to significant challenges. Water quality parameters have temporal patterns that are affected by seasonal changes, user behaviors, treatment processes, and environmental effects. Predicting anomalies that may be caused by contamination from normal scenarios throughout the operational process requires sophisticated machine learning techniques that can cope with these intricate patterns [3].

Anomaly detection, utilizing traditional machine learning [4,5] has shown a high degree of efficiency in numerous domains; however, detection of water contamination faces unique barriers. Water monitoring networks are traditionally distributed systems with a vast number of sensors located in disparate geographical areas, operated by autonomous utilitarians or controlled by different organizations. Water utilities, municipalities, environmental agencies, and research institutes each have their own data repository, and thus, the data landscape is fragmented [6]. Attempting to centralize this data is very difficult to overcome, such as the existence of proprietary systems, discrepancies in data formats, legal issues, and worries about critical infrastructure data being shared.

Federated Learning (FL) is a revolutionary paradigm that tackles issues related to data sharing and privacy preservation. FL enables distributed training without the direct exchange of data between clients, allowing each entity to completely control sensitive data on its own water quality. Through the exchange of model updates rather than raw data, FL effectively maintains privacy while promoting the development of robust anomaly detection capabilities derived from diverse training experiences across different water systems [7].

In this paper, we propose a federated learning architecture for water contamination anomaly detection that addresses both technical and organizational challenges in water monitoring utilizing open-source water quality data from the city of Austin. Our approach leverages recent advances in deep learning for time series analysis, particularly LSTM [8,9] combined with secure federated optimization techniques. We applied a suite of federated learning algorithms, including FedAvg [10], FedAvgM [11], FedAdam - FedYogi [12], and QFedAvg [13] to collaboratively train anomaly detection models across distributed clients. Each client represents an individual site, and within these clients, we employed Long Short-Term Memory (LSTM) networks both locally and globally to capture temporal dependencies inherent in water quality time series data. Additionally, each well within the clients was modeled individually using LSTM to ensure granularity in anomaly detection [14].

Our experimental results demonstrated that the federated approach had slightly worse performance metrics, it still proved to be highly competitive on the corresponding loss values and detection robustness. Most importantly, this performance is achievable without trading data privacy and thus makes a compelling and privacy preserving alternative. The approach described in this paper presents a federated methodology that not only improves detection reliability but also satisfies the practical constraints that real world water utilities face, e.g., resource constraints and heterogeneous data distribution across monitoring sites.

## 2 Literature Review

Recent advances in artificial intelligence have transformed water quality surveillance, with federated machine learning (FL) emerging as a pivotal paradigm for contamination anomaly detection - an inherently complex task due to heterogeneous sensor data and stringent privacy constraints. Contemporary studies have introduced sophisticated FL strategies that augment deep sequence models such as LSTMs with privacypreserving optimization (e.g., FedAvgM, FedAdam, FedYogi), enabling them to scale across diverse utilities and outperform conventional centralized or heuristic approaches.

Chen, Zheliang, et al. [15] introduced the FedLGAN model, which integrates Generative Adversarial Networks (GAN) with Federated Learning (FL) and a bidirectional Long Short-Term Memory (LSTM) network enhanced by an attention mechanism to address anomaly detection and data repair in hydrological telemetry data. Employing a discriminator for anomaly detection and a generator for data repair, the model effectively handles temporal data features while ensuring data privacy. Tested on data from four hydrological telemetry devices, the FedLGAN model demonstrates improved performance and preservation of privacy, highlighting the potential for future improvements in handling heterogeneity of data and operational efficiency.

Yan, Yuhang, et al. [16] presents a federated learning-based, lightweight anomaly detection method for environmental sensor networks. Sensor nodes convert data into symbolic sequences for local threshold training. A global threshold, derived through an energy-weighted method, updates node thresholds for autonomous anomaly detection. Demonstrated in indoor monitoring, the method offers enhanced detection accuracy and energy efficiency, suitable for resource-constrained edge nodes. Future work aims to extend this approach to multimodal environmental parameters for improved performance.

Park, Soohyun, et al. [17] develops a novel network model for predicting green tide phenomena using smart sensor-based federated learning, which utilizes distributed data from geographically separated models. The study introduces an optimal scheduling algorithm that enhances the efficiency of data usage and prediction performance by managing real-time big data arrivals. Experiments with real water quality data confirm the benefits of the proposed system in accurately predicting green tide occurrences and optimizing network system operations. Future work will explore the impact of sensor positioning, data distribution ratios, and communication quality on the system's performance, expanding experiments to cover a broader geographic scope.

Rejula, M. Anline, et al. [18] introduces a federated learning approach with recurrent neural networks (RNNs), specifically Long Short-Term Memory (LSTM) networks, for decentralized water quality monitoring. By avoiding the transfer of sensitive data and capturing temporal trends in water quality parameters like pH and dissolved oxygen, this methodology achieves a 92.3% classification accuracy. The results underscore improvements in data confidentiality and scalability, making it a viable solution for secure and collaborative environmental monitoring across remote locations.

# 3 Methodology

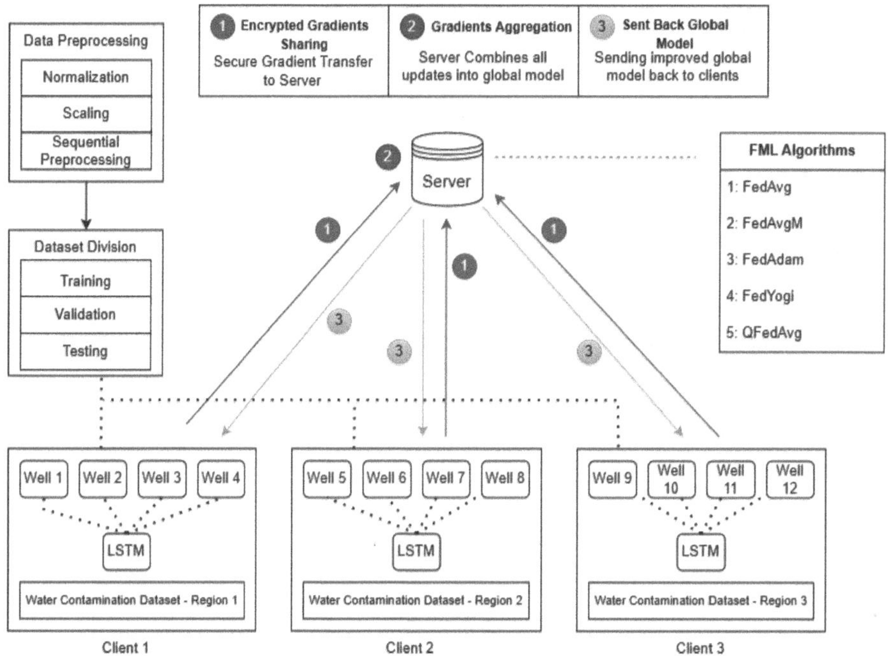


**Fig. 1.** Proposed Methodology Framework.

The proposed methodological framework introduces a federated approach to the detection of water contamination anomalies based on federated learning principles over distributed geographical monitoring networks. The privacy-preserving model fosters the development of collaborative models while protecting the privacy of individual client data. The model applies various data-related techniques, such as data preprocessing, sequential partitioning protocols, secure gradient transmission, and innovative federated aggregation algorithms, to build a high-performance contamination detection system by using long-short-term memory (LSTM) networks. This approach ensures data-knowledge distillation from various water quality datasets without centralized environmental monitoring data, creating a paradigm for data utility and privacy protection as a critical infrastructure process (Fig. 1).

### 3.1 Dataset

**Austin City Water Dataset:** The dataset sourced from the data.gov website, contains raw data used to evaluate water quality conditions in natural creeks, aquifers, and lakes across the Austin area. The dataset includes information about sample locations, collection dates, and various water quality parameters. Key columns include:

- SAMPLE SITE NO: Identifies specific sampling sites.
- LAT-DD-WGS84 and LON-DD-WGS84: Provide the geographic coordinates of the sampling locations.
- SAMPLE DATE: Records the date of sample collection.
- PARAM TYPE: Specifies the type of water quality parameter measured.
- RESULT: Indicates the measurement value.

The PARAM TYPE column contains parameters such as color, conductance, dissolved ammonia, dissolved arsenic, dissolved boron, total alkalinity, total organic carbon, turbidity, UV absorption, and pH. For our experiments, we choose pH as a target value.

The dataset includes samples from multiple wells. For each client, we selected four wells whose sampling locations exhibited the smallest pairwise Haversine distances—thereby ensuring high spatial similarity among the wells. Consequently, each client's dataset consists of samples from exactly four wells.

The sample distribution for each client is as follows:

- **Client 1**: Well 1 (505 samples), Well 2 (426 samples), Well 3 (200 samples), Well 4 (198 samples); total = 1329 samples.
- **Client 2**: Well 1 (193 samples), Well 2 (225 samples), Well 3 (291 samples), Well 4 (234 samples); total = 943 samples.
- **Client 3**: Well 1 (419 samples), Well 2 (143 samples), Well 3 (136 samples), Well 4 (965 samples); total = 1663 samples.

### 3.2 Data PreProcessing

The initial phase of our methodological approach includes comprehensive data preprocessing such as Normalization & Scaling, Sequential Preprocessing protocols to ensure optimal model performance.

**Sequential Preprocessing:** The sequential preprocessing component implements a sliding window approach optimized for time series water quality data, structuring monitoring data into fixed-length input-output pairs. This method involves the creation of overlapping windows in which past observations are considered as input and the corresponding future values are regarded as targets. According to the contamination propagation characteristics (e.g., 72 h), calibrated window sizes are used. Each input window consists of water quality parameters from a specific time frame, with the targets being subsequent anomaly indicators. The window moves ahead with set increments, thus laying temporal data in format that fits supervised learning, particularly the LSTM architectures, which are then used to find contamination patterns that occur at the diverse hydrogeological conditions. In our experiments, we set the sliding window input value to 3.

### 3.3 Federated Learning Architecture

The core of our methodology comprises a three-phase federated learning cycle (Fig. 2).

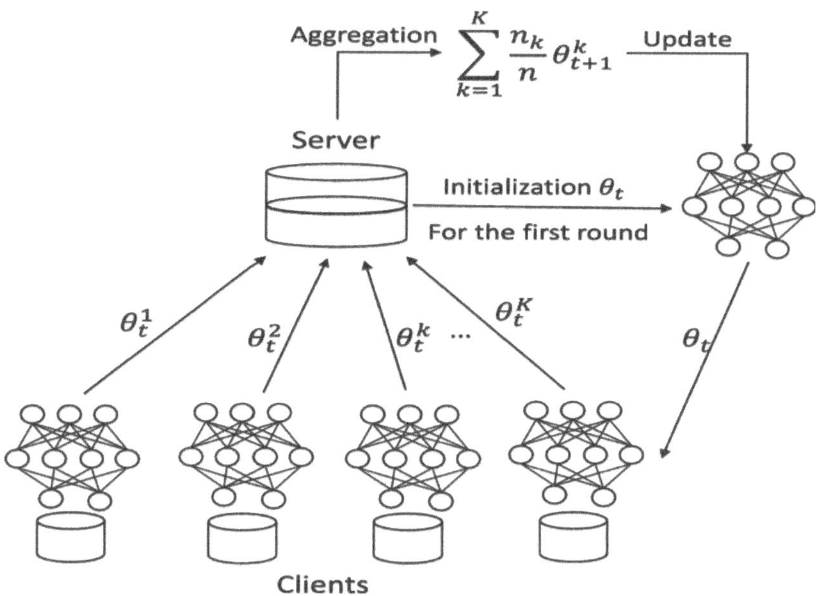


**Fig. 2.** Federated Learning Architecture.

**Encrypted Gradients Sharing:** This mechanism sets up the secure gradient transfer protocols through which each client (region 1–3 & each with multi-wells), exchanges model updates based on local LSTM training without exposing raw water quality data. This phase consists of cryptographic mechanisms that ensure the sensitive pollution indicators remain confidential while the global model still receives the benefits of model improvement.

**Gradient Aggregating:** The global server deals with complex aggregation of the encrypted updates amassed by all the participating clients. This aggregation step unites knowledge from diverse water systems to create a universal model that diagnoses contamination using the experience of multi-regions to their advantage.

**Global Model Distribution:** The Global model which is rectified is transmitted to back all clients in a secure manner thereby also boosting the local detection in each region without relinquishing data sovereignty.

**LSTM:** Long Short-Term Memory networks have emerged as the optimal architectural configuration for the detection of time series anomalies mainly, they have the potential to learn the temporal dependencies at different time scales from the data.

**Long Short-Term Memory (LSTM) Cell** At each time step $t$, given input $x_t$, previous hidden state $h_{t-1}$ and cell state $c_{t-1}$, the LSTM cell computes:

$$i_t = \sigma\big(W_i x_t + U_i h_{t-1} + b_i\big), \tag{1}$$
$$f_t = \sigma\big(W_f x_t + U_f h_{t-1} + b_f\big), \tag{2}$$
$$o_t = \sigma\big(W_o x_t + U_o h_{t-1} + b_o\big), \tag{3}$$
$$\tilde{c}_t = \tanh\big(W_c x_t + U_c h_{t-1} + b_c\big), \tag{4}$$
$$c_t = f_t \odot c_{t-1} \ + \ i_t \odot \tilde{c}_t, \tag{5}$$
$$h_t = o_t \odot \tanh(c_t). \tag{6}$$

Each client employs Long Short-Term Memory networks specifically configured for time-series analysis of water contamination indicators:

- Well-Specific Modeling: Individual LSTM models are deployed for each monitoring well (Wells 1–12 across three regions), accommodating localized contamination patterns and hydrogeological variations.
- Regional Integration: The federated approach enables integration of knowledge across geographically distinct water systems while preserving the integrity of region-specific detection characteristics.

**FML Algorithms:** We integrated five federated machinelearning algorithms—FedAvg, FedProx, SCAFFOLD, FedYogi, and QFedAvg—to drive the threephase training cycle.

### 3.4 Results

**Evaluation Metrics.** The models are evalauted using Mean Square Error (MSE), Root Mean Square Error (RMSE), Mean Absolute Error (MAE) and Mean Absolute Percentage Error (MAPE).

**Centralized Evaluation:** In centralized evaluation [22], the clients send their locally trained model updates to a central server which will then apply the aggregated global model to a hold-out validation data set processed on the server side. Using a unified dataset which is a representative of the overall population—or a carefully curated sample dataset, the global server computes performance metrics such as MSE, loss, or MAE in a consistent environment. This method makes it easy to compare communication rounds and manage metrics. However, it relies on the presence of centralized validation data which may conflict with stringent privacy measures and introduce potential biases if the held-out set does not accurately reflect the difference in client data distributions.

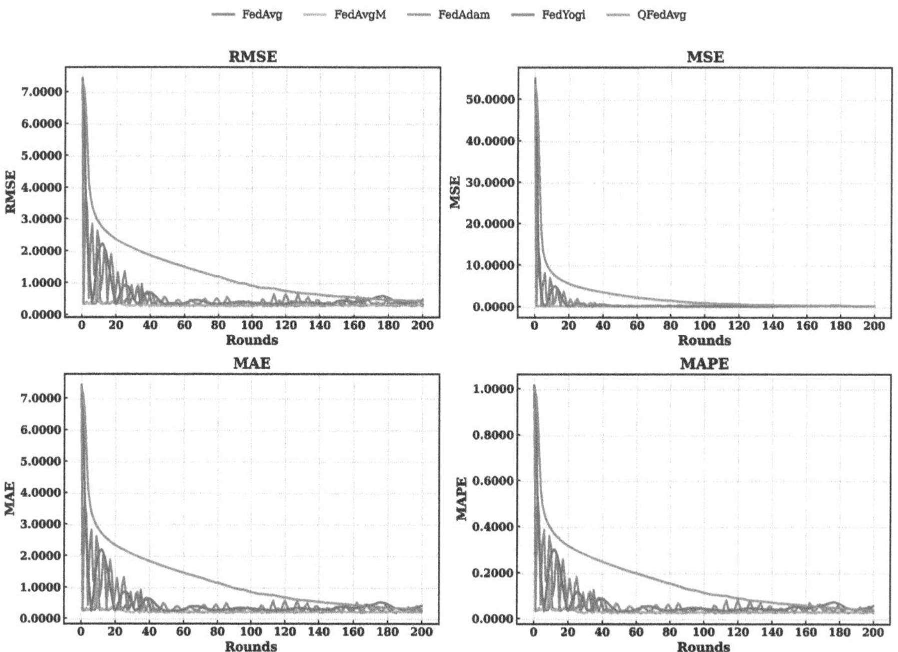


**Fig. 3.** Centralized Evaluation.

Figure 3 shows the metrics across 200 federated training rounds. FedAvg and FedAvgM (blue and orange) deliver the most stable learning curves: After an initial drop in the first 30 rounds, the four error metrics (RMSE, MSE, MAE, MAPE) flatten near the lower bound with very little variance. FedYogi (red) begins erratically, especially in MSE and MAE, where it spikes around rounds 50–150, but then decays sharply and eventually matches or slightly outperforms FedAvg at the end of training. FedAdam (green) is consistently the noisiest: its errors fluctuate by one to two orders of magnitude throughout, never settling into the low-error band, which suggests poor hyperparameter robustness on this task. QFedAvg (purple) shows the smoothest descent but converges more slowly; although its metrics improve monotonically, they plateau above FedAvg/FedAvgM/FedYogi. Overall, the figure indicates that simple momentum-based FedAvg variants achieve fast and reliable convergence, FedYogi offers competitive late-stage accuracy after an unstable warm-up, FedAdam struggles with stability, and QFedAvg trades speed for stability, but finishes with higher residual error.

**Table 1.** Best-MSE Wise Error Metrics for Federated Learning Algorithms (200 Rounds)

| FML Algorithms | Best MSE | RMSE | MAE | MAPE | Round |
|---|---|---|---|---|---|
| FedAvg | 0.07 | 0.27 | 0.18 | 0.02 | 185 |
| FedAvgM | 0.07 | 0.26 | 0.18 | 0.02 | 34 |
| FedAdam | 0.11 | 0.33 | 0.25 | 0.03 | 125 |
| FedYogi | 0.11 | 0.33 | 0.25 | 0.03 | 20 |
| QFedAvg | 0.18 | 0.42 | 0.31 | 0.03 | 200 |
| Vanilla LSTM | 0.13 | 0.36 | 0.31 | 0.04 | — |

Table 1 reports the best-achieved performance of each federated learning algorithm over 200 communication rounds. For each method, the round with the minimum MSE was first identified; the accompanying RMSE, MAE, and MAPE values of that same round were recorded to give a coherent 'best snapshot'. Both FedAvg and FedAvgM reach the lowest observed MSE of 0.07, but they do so on markedly different schedules. FedAvgM attains its optimum as early as round 34, whereas FedAvg requires 34 rounds. FedAdam, FedYogi and QFedAvg converge to higher error levels 0.11, 0.11 and 0.18 respectively suggesting that their adaptive optimization schemes were less effective on this task. Finally, the centralized Vanilla LSTM baseline performs worst in all metrics, underscoring the advantage of federated training, especially the simple FedAvg family, in minimizing predictive error while preserving privacy.

**Distributed Evaluation:** In distributed evaluation [22], each client is responsible for validating the global model on its individual private hold-out dataset.

After receiving the updated global parameters, clients compute local performance statistics (like local loss, MSE, MAE) and return only summary metrics back to the server. The server aggregates the reported statistics, usually weighing them by the size of each client's data set, to estimate the overall performance of the model.rmance of the model. By not having evaluation data outside the client's premises, the scheme holds data privacy and agreements with privacy constraints existing in federated learning. The difference in the quality and size of local data can cause the difference in metrics, making it hard to interpret and potentially slow down the convergence time if clients have a big influence on the aggregating parameters. The results are presented by best performing FML algorithm fedavg. The local metrics are basically predictions by locally trained model on each on its local data. The global metrics are predictions by global model on each round by global aggregated model.

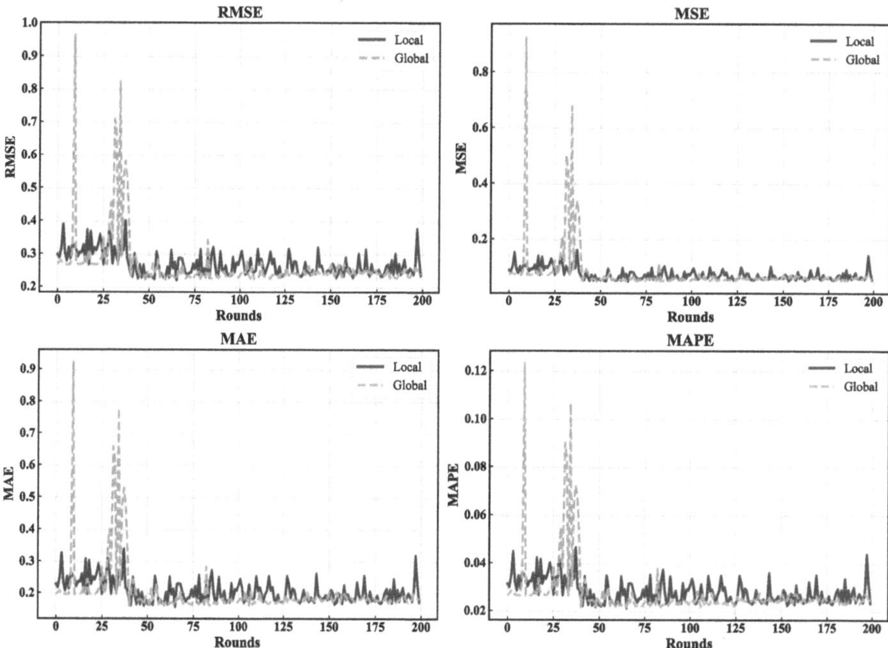


**Fig. 4.** Client 1 - Distributed Evaluation.

The figure:4 presents a side-by-side comparison of four error metrics—RMSE (top-left), MSE (top-right), MAE (bottom-left) and MAPE (bottom-right)—over 200 training rounds for both the local model (blue) and the global model (orange). In each subplot, both curves follow the same overall trajectory: large fluctuations during the early rounds give way to more stable values as the model converges. For RMSE, both models settle into the 0.26–0.32 range, with the local model showing slightly higher spikes. The MSE plot mirrors this behavior on a smaller scale (around 0.06–0.12), again with a bit more volatility in the local updates. MAE values remain between roughly 0.17 and 0.30, whereas MAPE hovers between 0.03% and 0.042%, with the global model smoothing out some of the sharp local oscillations. Overall, the close alignment of the two lines in each panel indicates that the global aggregation preserves nearly the same predictive accuracy as the local model while reducing its noise.

Table 2 provides a detailed analysis each algorithm's behaviour by reporting the minimum, mean, and maximum error attained over the entire test horizon for Client 1. Two patterns stand out immediately. First, global aggregation consistently lowers the average error relative to the corresponding local model. For example, FedAvg's mean RMSE drops from 0.268 to 0.261 after federated averaging, and its mean MSE falls from 0.197 to 0.192; similar though slightly smaller gains appear for FedAvgM, FedAdam, and FedYogi. Second, the FedAvg family not only achieves the lowest central tendency but also the tightest error spread. FedAvg and FedAvgM record minimum MSEs of 0.157 and 0.162, with maxima below 0.050 in the global view—roughly half the worst-case values observed for FedAdam and an order of magnitude below the extreme spikes seen in QFedAvg (max RMSE ¿ 7). FedAdam shows moderate improvement after aggregation but retains a broader error range, indicating residual instability. FedYogi narrows its mean errors under the global model yet still exhibits high peaks (max RMSE 5), while QFedAvg remains the least reliable, posting both the highest means and the largest maxima across all four metrics. Taken together, these statistics confirm that simple averaging (FedAvg/FedAvgM) delivers the most accurate and stable predictions for this client, and that federated aggregation generally dampens the large error excursions that individual local models can experience.

**Table 2.** Summary Statistics (Min, Mean, Max) of Error Metrics for Client 1

| Algorithm | Model | RMSE | | | MSE | | | MAE | | | MAPE (%) | | |
|---|---|---|---|---|---|---|---|---|---|---|---|---|---|
| | | Min | Mean | Max | Min | Mean | Max | Min | Mean | Max | Min | Mean | Max |
| FedAvg | Local | 0.219 | 0.268 | 0.399 | 0.048 | 0.073 | 0.159 | 0.157 | 0.205 | 0.333 | 0.021 | 0.027 | 0.046 |
| | Global | 0.220 | 0.264 | 0.962 | 0.048 | 0.078 | 0.927 | 0.159 | 0.202 | 0.921 | 0.021 | 0.027 | 0.123 |
| FedAvgM | Local | 0.218 | 0.268 | 0.396 | 0.047 | 0.072 | 0.157 | 0.154 | 0.205 | 0.333 | 0.020 | 0.027 | 0.045 |
| | Global | 0.224 | 0.260 | 1.286 | 0.050 | 0.073 | 1.65 | 0.160 | 0.197 | 1.25 | 0.021 | 0.026 | 0.171 |
| FedAdam | Local | 0.266 | 0.314 | 0.461 | 0.071 | 0.100 | 0.212 | 0.195 | 0.245 | 0.403 | 0.026 | 0.033 | 0.055 |
| | Global | 0.266 | 0.480 | 3.72 | 0.071 | 0.485 | 13.86 | 0.195 | 0.416 | 3.71 | 0.026 | 0.056 | 0.50 |
| FedYogi | Local | 0.266 | 0.311 | 0.472 | 0.071 | 0.099 | 0.222 | 0.195 | 0.242 | 0.415 | 0.026 | 0.033 | 0.057 |
| | Global | 0.266 | 0.479 | 7.05 | 0.071 | 0.655 | 49.75 | 0.195 | 0.415 | 7.04 | 0.026 | 0.056 | 0.949 |
| QFedAvg | Local | 0.266 | 0.306 | 0.467 | 0.071 | 0.095 | 0.218 | 0.195 | 0.237 | 0.410 | 0.026 | 0.032 | 0.056 |
| | Global | 0.464 | 1.32 | 7.22 | 0.215 | 2.73 | 52.24 | 0.406 | 1.29 | 7.22 | 0.053 | 0.173 | 0.973 |

### 3.5 Anomaly Detection:

Anomaly detection refers to the identification of unusual observations or patterns that significantly deviate from expected or normal behavior in data. To detect anomalies in this study, we employed a statistical-residual approach, computing the absolute residual errors ($|y_{\text{true}} - y_{\text{pred}}|$) between observed and predicted pH values. An adaptive threshold was then defined as the mean ($\mu$) of these residuals plus 1.5 times their standard deviation ($\sigma$). Any residual surpassing this threshold ($\mu + 1.5\sigma$) was flagged as an anomaly. This straightforward yet robust method effectively identifies isolated spikes and sustained deviations without being overly sensitive to regular fluctuations. All resulting anomaly visualizations presented in this work are generated using the **FedAvg** model, as it consistently demonstrated superior predictive accuracy compared to other federated learning algorithms evaluated.

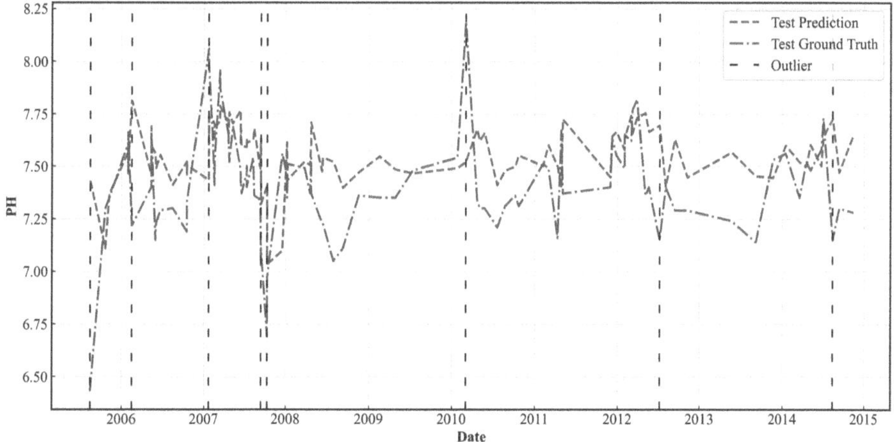


**Fig. 5.** Client 1 - Anomaly Detection.

Figure 5 displays a time-series comparison between predicted (red dashed line) and actual (green dash-dotted line) PH values, highlighting outlier events marked by vertical dashed black lines. Over the entire test period from approximately 2006 to 2020, predictions closely follow actual measurements, with both curves generally remaining within a similar range ( 6.8 to 7.8). However, notable discrepancies occur at specific intervals, particularly around early 2007, mid-2012, and late 2018, indicating transient divergence between the predicted and actual PH values. These periods align precisely with the flagged anomalies, suggesting that the model effectively identifies periods of abnormal behavior. Despite these outliers, the overall trajectory of the predicted values remains stable and consistent with observed data, underscoring the robustness of the model's forecasting performance. The presence of fewer dramatic deviations after 2015

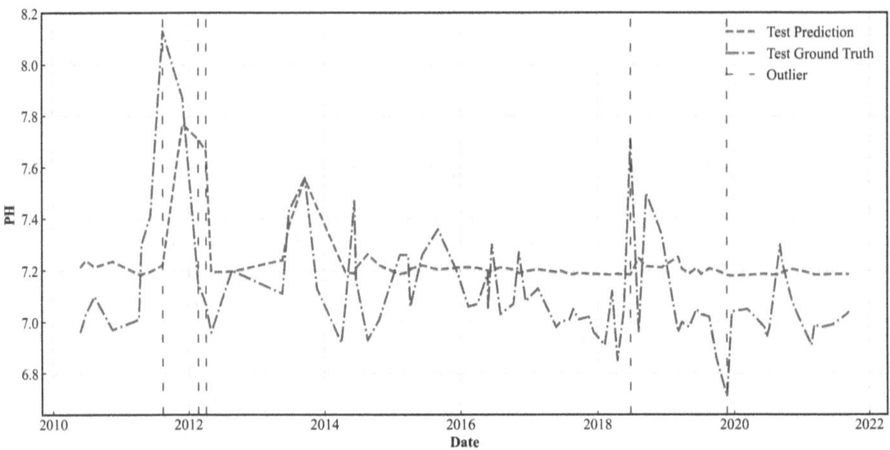


**Fig. 6.** Client 2 - Anomaly Detection.

illustrates increased model stability over time, reflecting an improvement in predictive consistency in later years.

Figure 6 compares predicted (red dashed line) and actual (green dash-dotted line) PH measurements over a test period spanning roughly from 2010 to 2020. Vertical dashed gray lines indicate anomalies identified by the model. Initially, both prediction and ground truth closely align within a stable range ( 7.1 to 7.4), although significant divergences are observed around late 2011, mid-2018, and notably in 2020. At these points, actual measurements exhibit sharp peaks and drops, clearly deviating from the more stable prediction line. The anomalies flagged by vertical lines accurately pinpoint these deviations, including the previously overlooked outlier event in 2020, demonstrating the model's effectiveness in identifying genuine abnormal occurrences. Overall, the model predictions remain robust and stable, highlighting critical deviations in actual measurements effectively.

Figure 7 illustrates the comparison between predicted (red dashed line) and actual (green dash-dotted line) PH measurements across a testing period from approximately 2009 to 2017, with vertical dashed gray lines highlighting anomaly events. Throughout this period, the predicted values consistently remain within a relatively narrow band ( 7.0–7.3), indicating stable model behavior. In contrast, the actual PH measurements exhibit frequent sharp fluctuations, especially notable around late 2012 to early 2014 and again prominently in mid-to-late 2017. These large divergences between predictions and actual observations correspond closely with the marked anomaly lines, demonstrating the model's efficacy at detecting and flagging abnormal events. The multiple anomalies clustered around 2013 particularly highlight a turbulent period of erratic PH fluctuations. Overall, the model maintains steady predictions despite significant volatility in the ground truth, accurately flagging periods of genuine anomalies and underscoring its robust anomaly detection capabilities.

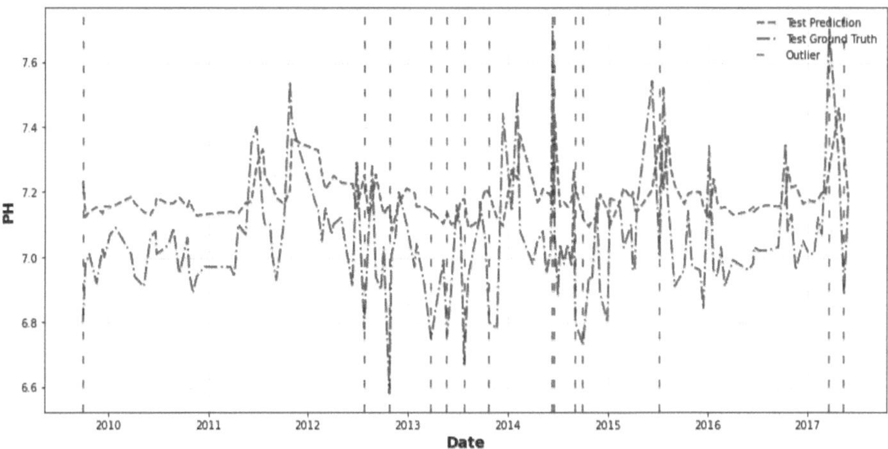


**Fig. 7.** Client 3 - Anomaly Detection.

# 4 Conclusion

This work has introduced a privacy-preserving, federated learning (FL) framework for the detection of water-contamination anomalies across geographically dispersed monitoring wells. Leveraging open-access data from the City of Austin, we trained well–specific LSTM predictors on three independent clients and collaboratively refined them via five state-of-the-art FL optimisers (FedAvg, FedAvgM, FedAdam, FedYogi and QFedAvg). Comprehensive centralised and distributed evaluations demonstrated that **simple averaging remains the most reliable strategy**: FedAvg achieved the lowest test-set MSE of 0.07—outperforming the best traditional, centralised LSTM baseline (MSE = 0.13)—while simultaneously damping high-frequency error spikes that appeared in local models. Momentum-augmented FedAvgM offered comparable accuracy and faster early-round convergence, whereas adaptive or fairness-oriented schemes (FedAdam, FedYogi, QFedAvg) exhibited pronounced instability and, for certain clients, amplified worst-case errors by up to two orders of magnitude.

The client-wise analyses reveal the impact of data heterogeneity on FL performance. For Client 1, global aggregation consistently reduced both mean error and error spread, confirming the classical benefit of knowledge sharing. Client 2 gained only marginally from federation, suggesting that its local data already captured most predictive variance. Client 3 highlighted a potential limitation: aggressive optimisers (e.g. QFedAvg) severely magnified outlier behaviour when confronted with extreme, non-IID residuals. Nonetheless, the proposed statistical-residual anomaly detector—using a dynamic $\mu + 1.5\sigma$ threshold—successfully flagged genuine contamination events across all clients, with the clearest visual separation obtained from the FedAvg predictions.

## References

1. Ahmed, U., et al.: Water quality monitoring: from conventional to emerging technologies. Water Supply **20**(1), 28–45 (2020)
2. Zainurin, S.N., et al.: Advancements in monitoring water quality based on various sensing methods: a systematic review. Int. J. Environ. Res. Public Health **19**(21), 14080 (2022)
3. Omol, E., Mburu, L., Onyango, D.: Anomaly detection in IoT sensor data using machine learning techniques for predictive maintenance in smart grids. Int. J. Sci. Technol. Manage. **5**(1), 201–210 (2024)
4. Dharwadkar, N.V., Dixit, A.A., Kannur, A.K., Kadampur, M.A., Joshi, S.: Identification of reasons behind infant crying using acoustic signal processing and deep neural network for neonatal intensive care unit. Int. J. Inf. Retrieval Res. (IJIRR) **12**(1), 1–17 (2022)
5. Dharwadkar, N.V., Shingan, G.G., Mane, S.U., Joshi, S.: Enhanced parallel-particle swarm optimization (EP-PSO) approach for solving nurse rostering problem: enhanced parallel-particle swarm optimization (EP-PSO) algorithm. Int. J. Swarm Intell. Res. (IJSIR) **13**(1), 1–17 (2022)
6. Gallaher, S., Heikkila, T.: Challenges and opportunities for collecting and sharing data on water governance institutions. J. Contemp. Water Res. Educ. **153**(1), 66–78 (2014)
7. Li, Q., et al.: A survey on federated learning systems: vision, hype and reality for data privacy and protection. IEEE Trans. Knowl. Data Eng. **35**(4), 3347–3366 (2021)
8. Soni, J., Prabakar, N.: KeyNet: enhancing cybersecurity with deep learning-based LSTM on keystroke dynamics for authentication. In: International Conference on Intelligent Human Computer Interaction, pp. 761–771. Springer International Publishing, Cham (2021)
9. Soni, J., Prabakar, N., Upadhyay, H.: Deep learning approach to detect malicious attacks at system level: poster. In: Proceedings of the 12th Conference on Security and Privacy in Wireless and Mobile Networks, pp. 314–315 (2019)
10. McMahan, B., et al.: Communication-efficient learning of deep networks from decentralized data. Artif. Intell. Stat. PMLR (2017)
11. Hsu, T.-M.H., Qi, H., Brown, M.: Measuring the effects of non-identical data distribution for federated visual classification. arXiv preprint arXiv:1909.06335 (2019)
12. Reddi, S., et al.: Adaptive federated optimization. arXiv preprint arXiv:2003.00295 (2020)
13. Li, T., et al.: Fair resource allocation in federated learning. arXiv preprint arXiv:1905.10497 (2019)
14. Soni, J., Prabakar, N., Upadhyay, H.: Comparative analysis of LSTM sequence-sequence and auto encoder for real-time anomaly detection using system call sequences. Int. J. Innov. Res. Comput. Commun. Eng. **7**, 4225–30 (2019)
15. Chen, Z., et al.: FedLGAN: a method for anomaly detection and repair of hydrological telemetry data based on federated learning. PeerJ Comput. Sci. **9**, e1664 (2023)
16. Yan, Y., et al.: Federated learning-based anomaly detection for environment monitoring sensor networks. IEEE Sens. Lett. (2024)
17. Park, S., et al.: Large-scale water quality prediction using federated sensing and learning: a case study with real-world sensing big-data. Sensors **21**(4), 1462 (2021)

18. Rejula, M.A., et al.: Decentralized water quality classification using federated learning with recurrent neural networks. Water Quality Res. J. **60**(1), 135–150 (2025)
19. Laridi, S., Palmer, G., Mark Tam, K.-M.: Enhanced federated anomaly detection through autoencoders using summary statistics-based thresholding. Sci. Rep. **14**(1), 26704 (2024)
20. Vellingiri, J., et al.: Strategies for classifying water quality in the Cauvery River using a federated learning technique. Int. J. Cogn. Comput. Eng. **4**, 187–193 (2023)
21. Zhang, K., et al.: Federated variational learning for anomaly detection in multivariate time series. In: 2021 IEEE International Performance, Computing, and Communications Conference (IPCCC). IEEE (2021)
22. Nilsson, A., et al.: A performance evaluation of federated learning algorithms. In: Proceedings of the Second Workshop on Distributed Infrastructures for Deep Learning (2018)

# DepFieldGen: Research on Dependent Field Generation for Secure ICS Protocols

Zhanwei Song[1,2], Dongliang Fang[1,2], Yaowen Zheng[1,2], Shichao Lv[1,2(✉)], Xin Chen[1,2], Shuaizong Si[1,2], Zhi Li[1,2], and Limin Sun[1,2]

[1] Institute of Information Engineering, Chinese Academy of Sciences, Beijing, China
{songzhanwei,fangdongliang,zhengyaowen,lvshichao, chenxin1990,sishuaizong,lizhi,sunlimin}@iie.ac.cn

[2] School of Cyber Security, University of Chinese Academy of Sciences, Beijing, China

**Abstract.** Industrial Control Systems (ICS) constitute critical infrastructure, and their security directly affects national security. In recent years, attackers exploiting protocol vulnerabilities have surged significantly, prompting ICS vendors to adopt protocol security enhancements. However, existing fuzzing tools frequently fail to generate dependent fields, such as authentication field and integrity checksum field. This limitation prevents numerous test cases from circumventing security mechanisms, thereby inducing repeatability failure and substantially degrading testing efficiency. To address this challenge, we propose DepFieldGen, a method for generating fields with strong dependencies in protocol messages. We further extend AFLNet to form DepAFLNet, a fuzzing framework for security-enhanced ICS protocols. We evaluated the dependency identification performance of DepFieldGen on the Transport Layer Security (TLS) protocol, which achieved 53.56% average precision and 54.43% average recall improvement over the Angr framework. Furthermore, we assessed the fuzzing effectiveness of DepAFLNet on three typical secure ICS protocols–MMS, IEC104, and Modbus, demonstrating an average code coverage enhancement of 39.8% over AFLNet. Notably, our approach demonstrates the capability to circumvent security mechanisms and trigger exploitable vulnerabilities in protocols. Experimental results validate the accuracy and effectiveness of our methodology.

**Keywords:** Industrial Control Systems · Secure Protocol · Data Dependency Graph · Dependent Field · Fuzzing

## 1 Introduction

Industrial Control Systems (ICS) are computerized control systems designed to monitor and manage industrial processes in manufacturing, production, distribution, and critical infrastructure domains. These systems constitute critical infrastructure, and their security directly affects national security. In recent years, Attackers, including **Stuxnet** [13] in 2010, **Industroyer** [6] in 2017, and


K.-K. R. Choo et al. (Eds.): ICDF2C 2025, LNICST 686, pp. 264–279, 2026.
https://doi.org/10.1007/978-3-032-22545-0_16

**Industroyer2** [5] in 2022, precisely tampered with and forged ICS protocols, such as S7, IEC 60870-5-104 (IEC104), and IEC 61850 MMS (MMS), to target nuclear power plants and power systems. These attacks caused delays in Iran's nuclear program and triggered large-scale blackouts in Ukraine.

Fuzz testing (also known as fuzzing) has been proven to be an effective technique for vulnerability discovery and is widely employed in the testing of various systems and software. The American Fuzzy Lop (AFL) [8] is one of the most popular fuzzing tools. Researchers have extended AFL through methods such as AFLNet [12] and StateAFL [3]. These extensions characterize the state space of a program by leveraging response codes from communication packets and the memory states of long-lived variables. However, these approaches require manual patching to eliminate randomness, thereby ensuring the repeatability of individual test cases. For instance, when fuzzing the live555 server of RTSP protocol using AFLNet, it is necessary to modify the server's source code to fix the session ID to a constant value. Meanwhile, AFLFast [4] and $\text{Havoc}_{MAB}$ [19] focus on optimizing the generation of random mutations. However, these methods lack the recovery of dependencies between fields, authentication and integrity checksum. For ICS protocols, the majority are proprietary, with server-side programs running on embedded devices with diverse architectures. These characteristics make it extremely challenging to eliminate randomness through source code modifications to address field dependencies in messages. For client-side programs running on host platforms like Windows and Linux, current mainstream symbolic execution-based program analysis engines, such as Angr [14], face path explosion challenges when analyzing complex program logic. Meanwhile, manual reverse engineering approaches heavily depend on expert knowledge, resulting in severely inefficient recovery of protocol field constraint relationships.

To address these challenges, we present DepFieldGen, an automated approach for generating protocol message fields with strong interdependencies. We observe that protocol client programs in ICS typically operate on general platforms such as Windows and Linux, and these programs inherently possess the ability to construct fields with strong dependencies. Based on this fact, we consider identifying and extracting segments for generating fields with strong dependencies from client programs. These segments can be used in the fuzz testing of ICS protocols to generate test cases that meet strong dependency constraints, thereby passing the security checks and achieving effective testing of the business functions of server programs.

We evaluated the performance of Enhanced data dependency graph (EDDG) generation on the Transport Layer Security (TLS) protocol, achieving 53.56% average precision and 54.43% average recall improvement compared to Angr's DDG (AngrDDG). Furthermore, we assessed the fuzzing effectiveness of DepAFLNet on three typical secure ICS protocols, demonstrating an average code coverage enhancement of 39.8% over AFLNet. Notably, our approach demonstrates the capability to circumvent security mechanisms and trigger exploitable vulnerabilities in protocols. Experimental results validate the accuracy and effectiveness of our methodology.

**Contributions.** Our main contributions are outlined below:

- We have provided a novel method DepFieldGen for restoring secure interactions, addressing a fundamental issue in fuzz testing: The generated test cases must be repeatable.
- We implemented DepFieldGen as an effective framework for secure ICS protocols based on IDA Pro [9], Angr [14] and Qiling [20].
- We evaluated DepFieldGen on TLS protocol and assessed DepAFLNet on three typical secure ICS protocols. The EDDG showed higher accuracy than AngrDDG. DepAFLNet significantly increased coverage compared to AFLNet, and discovered all known vulnerabilities in protocols.

## 2 Background

**Fig. 1.** Connection Process of MMS with TLS.

Industrial control protocols are crucial components of industrial control systems, primarily used for communication between host computer software and industrial control devices such as PLCs and RTUs. Among them, the protocols used for core functions such as parameter configuration, device control, and programming debugging of industrial control devices are usually proprietary industrial control protocols of vendors, such as AB's CIP protocol, GE's SRTP protocol, and Mitsubishi's Melsoft protocol.

At the same time, to enhance the security of industrial control devices, many proprietary industrial control protocols have added security mechanisms such as authentication, encryption, and verification. These security mechanisms are typically implemented in the security interaction process before the business function communication. As shown in the communication process of the MMS with TLS protocol in Fig. 1, the client and server first execute steps such as random number sending, signature authentication, and key exchange in the security interaction process. Then, based on the negotiated results, the actual data used for business functions are encrypted for communication. In this process, protocol fields such as random numbers, signatures, keys, and checksums have close and complex dependencies with other fields or data packets, which are difficult to identify through communication traffic analysis alone.

# 3 Approach

## 3.1 Overview

Modern ICS protocols predominantly employ security-enhanced proprietary designs, where client request messages contain strongly interdependent fields generated through complex program logic. These fields, such as authentication field and integrity checksum field, exhibit dependencies on either randomized fields in server responses or operational data fields within the request payloads. When fuzz testing ICS devices that use security-enhanced private protocols, existing fuzz testing, such as AFLNet, cannot construct test cases that can be replayed and tampered with business data, resulting in most test cases failing to pass the initial security check and failing to touch business functions. When analyzing complex program logic (e.g., signature, encryption, verification), the current mainstream symbolic execution-based program analysis engines, such as Angr, have the problem of path explosion, and the manual reverse engineering method relies heavily on expert knowledge, which leads to extremely low efficiency in recovering the protocol field constraint relationship.

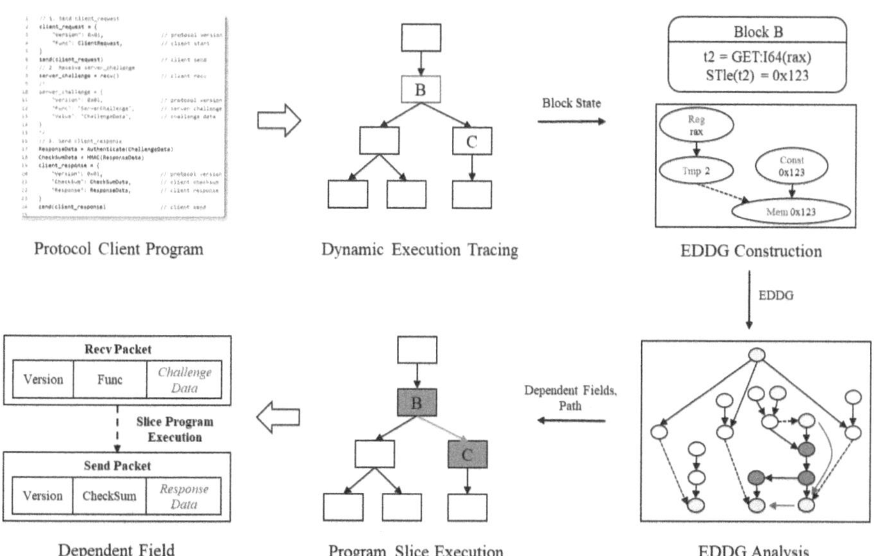


**Fig. 2.** Main Workflow of Dependent Field Generation.

To solve the above problems, we propose a dependent field generation method DepFieldGen, which can correctly identify and restore strongly dependent fields, as show in Fig. 2. This method mainly consists of four stages: Dynamic Execution Tracing, EDDG Construction, Constraint-Aware EDDG Analysis, and Program Slice Execution. Below, we will provide an overview of the technical approaches for each stage.

**Dynamic Execution Tracing.** We observe that communication protocols have a layered nature, with security interactions and business communications being relatively independent. Different business communication processes occur after the same security interaction process. For example, in the MMS protocol with TLS, business communication processes such as GetNameList, Read, and Write all take place after the same TLS interaction process. Therefore, we adopt a method of conducting dynamic execution analysis on a single interaction process on the client side to identify the security interaction process that can be repeatedly applied to different business communications. Meanwhile, the concrete execution approach avoids issues faced by static data dependency analysis, such as path explosion and redundant dependencies, and retains strong dependencies in the interaction process.

**EDDG Construction.** The DDG often contains a large number of redundant nodes caused by symbolic values, making it difficult to determine whether memory read/write addresses fall within the range of send/receive buffers. This hampers the accurate identification and inference of field dependencies within and between messages. Based on the results of dynamic execution analysis, we significantly reduce the size of the data dependency graph. Meanwhile, we introduce the execution count of data definition instructions and the set of values for memory and register data into the DDG to form the EDDG, thereby effectively improving the accuracy of field dependency identification.

**EDDG Analysis.** Based on the EDDG, we perform backward traversal to trace address source nodes and data source nodes, and forward traversal to track address-based memory reads. By combining memory operation ranges, we accurately identify the dependencies between fields in send and receive data packets. Additionally, we leverage the statistical characteristics of data values, such as the randomness of fields between messages, to infer the types of field dependencies, including authentication, validation, and encryption.

**Program Slice Execution.** We extract instruction sequences based on dependent field data nodes and connected paths, recording the starting instruction according to the execution order and saving the initial program state for subsequent efficient execution of program snippets. Compared to whole-program hooking execution, program snippet simulation execution offers significant advantages. Specifically, the instruction sequence represents the minimal set for field generation, resulting in a substantial compression rate compared to the total number of instructions executed in the entire program. This approach achieves efficient generation of field data.

### 3.2 Dynamic Execution Tracing

**Security Interaction Code Region Localization.** Client-side programs generally consist of multiple components, such as protocol implementation, user input handling, and business logic execution, and are typically large in scale. The protocol implementation, which is the focus of our study, mainly involves packet construction and transmission as well as packet reception and parsing. To initially identify the code region associated with protocol implementation, we pinpoint the call sites of the *Send* and *Recv* functions. Further, leveraging the characteristic of communication protocols that security interaction logic is relatively independent of business interaction logic and that different business functionalities share the same security functions, we dynamically execute various business functionalities to generate multiple execution sequences. By comparing the similarities among these sequences, we are able to precisely locate the code region that encompasses the security interaction logic.

**Execution State Synchronization and Process Control.** To conduct dependency analysis and construct the EDDG, we collect program information during the dynamic execution process. Therefore, at the beginning of each basic block, we synchronize the data values of registers and memory. Specifically, we read the values of all registers during each synchronization to minimize the number of interactions between the client program and the dynamic analysis program. Memory synchronization, on the other hand, is performed on-demand only when the analysis program encounters a memory read instruction, based on the actual memory read range, to reduce storage space occupation and improve synchronization efficiency. During the dynamic execution process, identification of system library functions occurs solely at the conclusion of each basic block, with the option to execute or skip them as needed. For instance, by default, the execution of the system library function $malloc$ and $sprintf$ is skipped.

### 3.3 EDDG Construction

**Formal Definition of EDDG.** The $EDDG=(V,E)$ represents definition-use relationships between program variables, where $V$ denotes the set of nodes representing program variables, and $E$ defines dependency relations between nodes. Each node $v \in V$ is structured as $v = (ID, Type, CodeAddr, Times, ValueSet)$, where $ID$ uniquely identifies the variable, $Type$ specifies its category (e.g., register or memory), $CodeAddr$ denotes the definition location comprising the instruction address, basic block address, and VEX statement index, $Times$ records the execution count of the defining instruction, and $ValueSet$ captures distinct concrete values assigned during execution.

The EDDG categorizes nodes into four types: Register, Memory, Temporary Variable, and Constant, distinguished as follows: Register nodes ($Type = Reg$) are identified by a composite $ID$ comprising the register number and bit-width; Memory nodes ($Type = Mem$) feature an $ID$ combining the base memory address and data size in bytes; Temporary Variable nodes ($Type = Tmp$) are assigned a unique numerical $ID$, while their $Times$ and $ValueSet$ are omitted due to their transient nature as intermediate artifacts during VEX IR translation; Constant nodes ($Type = Const$) inherently lack mutable states, resulting in null values for $ID$, $Times$, and $ValueSet$, since their values remain immutable during execution.

The edge $e \in E$ is structured as $e = (Type, Source, Destination)$, where $Type$ indicates the dependency category: $General$ for dependencies among registers, temporary variables, and constants; $MemData$ for dependencies between memory data; and $MemAddr$ for dependencies between memory address variables and the memory space variables they reference. $Source$ and $Destination$ specify the edge's originating and terminating nodes, respectively.

**Construction of EDDG.** We introduce VEX intermediate representation to unify the execution semantics of programs across architectures. Each VEX statement is decomposed into discrete operations including read operations, write operations, and computation operations, which interact with four data node types: Register, Memory, Temporary Variable, and Constant (the latter being inherently immutable). Data dependency edges, encompassing data assignment and memory address dereferencing, are then constructed via def-use relationship analysis.

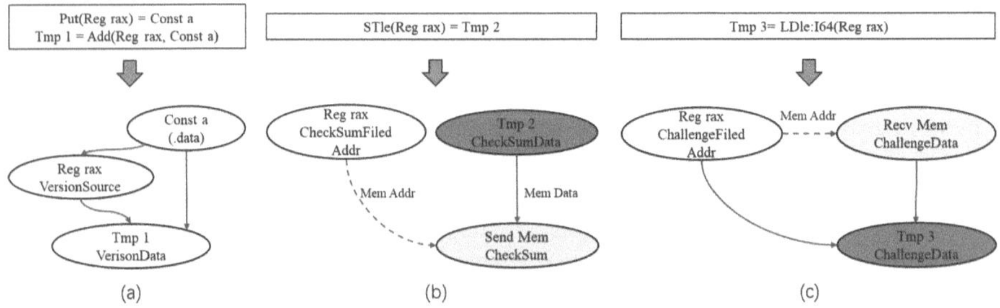


**Fig. 3.** Example of Handle VEX Statement.

To detail the analysis workflow, we examine representative VEX statements extracted from the client-side program of the challenge-response protocol. As illustrated in Fig. 3, subfigure (a) shows the assignment of constant data Const $a$ to register data Reg $rax$, followed by an addition operation that assigns the result to temporary variable data Tmp 1. The first statement establishes a dependency between the constant data node Const $a$ and the register data node Reg $rax$. The second statement, involving an addition operation, creates dependencies between both the constant data node Const $a$ and the register data node Reg $rax$ with the temporary variable data node Tmp 1. Since registers and temporary variables can be referenced using fixed identification numbers, and constant data (immediate values in instructions) can be referenced directly using fixed instruction addresses, the edges representing dependencies between temporary variable data and constant data are classified as general edges (*General*). These edges do not require separate address information for identification.

Subfigure (b) illustrates a memory write operation, where temporary variable data Tmp 2 is assigned to a memory region Send Mem pointed to by register data Reg $rax$. Although the instruction only specifies the source data and address data, the memory region Send Mem can be explicitly identified based on the address value and the size of the source data. Consequently, a memory data node Send Mem is created in the dependency graph, establishing a data dependency between the temporary variable data node Tmp 2 and the memory data node Send Mem. In the dependency graph, the dashed line between the register data node Reg $rax$ and the memory data node Send Mem represents an address-pointing relationship, indicating that Reg $rax$ points to the memory region Send Mem rather than representing a data dependency. During dependency graph traversal, the analysis is strictly confined to data dependencies, explicitly excluding address-pointing relationships.

Subfigure (c) depicts a memory read operation, where the value from a memory region Recv Mem, pointed to by register data Reg $rax$, is assigned to temporary variable data Tmp 3. Similar to the memory write operation, the memory region Recv Mem can be identified based on the address value and the number of bits read (e.g., I64). Therefore, a memory data node Recv Mem is created in the dependency graph, forming a data dependency between the memory data node Recv Mem and the temporary variable data node Tmp 3. The dashed line between the register data node Reg $rax$ and the memory data node Recv Mem indicates an address-pointing relationship, while the solid line between the register data node Reg $rax$ and the temporary variable data node represents an address dependency rather than a data dependency. This address dependency is inferred in conjunction with the address-pointing relationship between Reg $rax$ and Recv Mem. In contrast, the dependency between the constant data node Const $a$ and the register data node Reg $rax$ in subfigure (a) represents a data dependency, which is different from the address dependency in subfigure (c). Therefore, all three dependencies in subfigure (a) are data dependencies.

### 3.4 EDDG Analysis

EDDG Analysis is primarily used for the identification and analysis of dependent fields, with the process illustrated in Fig. 4. Prior to analysis, we incorporate predefined data dependency models into the EDDG. These models are constructed specifically for system library functions to eliminate redundant invocation analysis.

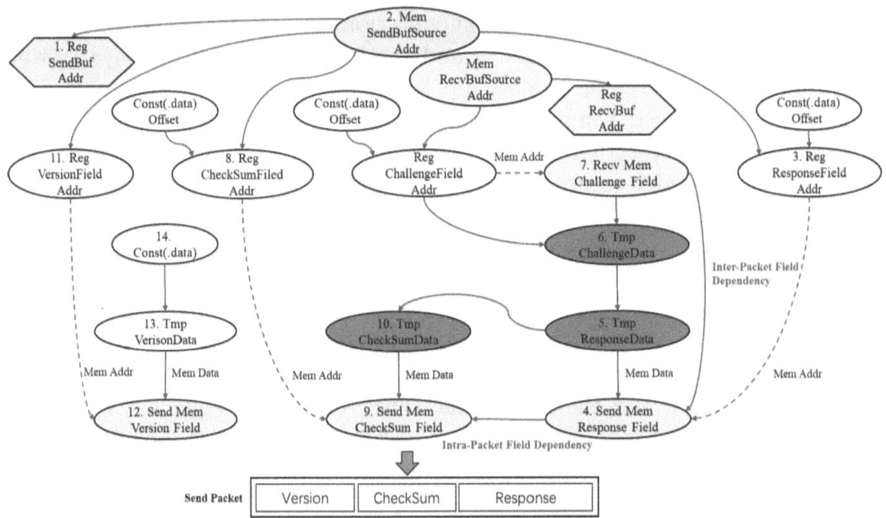


**Fig. 4.** Identification and Analysis of Dependent Field.

First, we initiate a backward traversal of the EDDG from the register parameters of the *send* functions (node 1) to identify the source nodes of the address data (node 2). These source nodes are typically memory addresses allocated dynamically by the *malloc* function or defined by global array declarations. Since the address data source nodes are the definition locations of address ranges and contain the address ranges for sending packets, forward traversal from these nodes can identify the locations where the fields of the outgoing message are generated.

Next, we perform a forward traversal from the address source nodes to identify nodes that propagate the address data as memory write operations, such as nodes 3 and 4 for version field, nodes 8 and 9 for checksum field, nodes 11 and 12 for response field. Then, we continue the backward traversal from the memory write operations to identify the source nodes of data generation, such as node 7 for data of protocol client program, node 14 for data of received packet from server), constructing dependency paths for data generation (4->5->6->7, 9->10->5->6->7, 12->13->14).

Finally, we analyze the overlap of data dependency paths to identify dependencies between fields within the outgoing message, that is, intra-packet field dependencies. By judging whether the data of a source node comes from the received packet based on the memory address range of the data source node, we detect dependencies between fields across different packets, that is, inter-packet field dependencies. When the data dependency path constitutes an intra-packet field dependency, where the $ValueSet$ of the source node contains randomized data and its cardinality equals the value of $Times$, the field is categorized as a strong dependency field requiring reconstruction, such as integrity checksum field. For example, the dependency paths (4->5 and 9->10->5) reveal strong interdependencies between the checksum field and response field within send data packets. Similarly, fields derived from received packet data sources demonstrating randomized values, such as authentication field, are classified as critical dependencies requiring discovery. As shown in Fig. 4, the dependency path (4->5->6->7) demonstrates interdependencies between the response field and challenge field exhibiting inherent randomness within response packets.

### 3.5 Program Slice Execution

Given the need to accurately generate fields with strong dependencies in the data packets of the security interaction process, a straightforward approach is to execute only the instruction code related to the generation of these fields. Therefore, based on the EDDG, we start from the nodes corresponding to the data of fields with strong dependencies in the data packet and traverse all nodes along the data dependency path to obtain their instruction addresses, thereby forming a program slice. Meanwhile, during the actual execution of the client program, we capture the program state information such as registers and memory at the starting instruction of this slice, forming the initial state for slice execution. Finally, through a simulation execution framework, we execute the program slice to generate the values of fields with strong dependencies.

## 4 Implementation

The proposed DepAFLNet architecture, as depicted in Fig. 5, constitutes a hybrid system incorporating the dependent field generation capability of DepFieldGen within the AFLNet fuzzing framework. The framework DepFieldGen for generating dependent fields was primarily developed in Python and provides an interface for dependent field generation, facilitating its application in fuzz testing. In DepFieldGen, we integrated dynamic execution with IDA Pro [9], the VEX statement analysis engine of Angr [14], and simulation execution based on the Qiling [20] architecture. The specific versions of the tools used are 7.5, Angr 9.2.102, and Qiling 1.4.6.

To evaluate the effectiveness of dependent field recovery in fuzz testing, we combined the fuzz testing tool AFLNet. We added a dependent field replacement plugin, namely the DepFiledReplace Plugin, to the seed mutation module of the AFLNet framework. This plugin interacts with AFLNet via inter-process communication using pipes. Specifically, the mutated test data is first sent to the plugin via a pipe. Subsequently, the plugin utilizes DepFieldGen to regenerate the dependent field data, which is then feedback into the seed mutation module. If the plugin determines that there are no restorable fields, it returns the data directly. This plug-and-play extension approach facilitates better comparative analysis of the application effectiveness of dependent field generation.

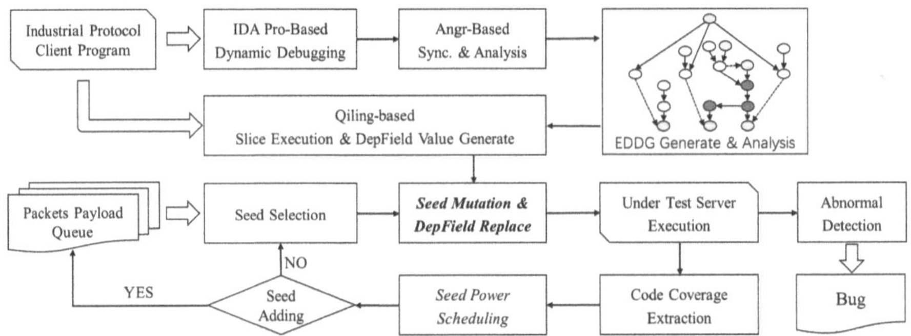


**Fig. 5.** Architecture of DepAFLNet with DepFieldGen and AFLNet.

## 5 Evaluation

**Testing Targets.** We validate the accuracy of DepFieldGen by comparing its EDDG generation with AngrDDG generation on TLS protocol dependency identification. Furthermore, we evaluate the practical utility of DepAFLNet against AFLNet through fuzz testing, measuring code coverage and crash count on three ICS protocols (MMS, IEC104, Modbus). These protocols are widely used in real-world industrial applications and are thus representative choices for evaluation.

**Experiment Setup.** For experimental validation, we selected the following open-source implementations as protocol testbeds: mbedtls v2.16.12 (TLS) [18], lib61850 v1.4.0 (MMS) [2], lib60870 v2.3.1 (IEC104) [1], and libmdbus v3.1.6 (Modbus) [16]. For the MMS and IEC104 protocols, TLS security enhancement was enabled through the $WITH\_MBEDTLS = 1$ compilation option. Building upon the TLS security enhancement mechanisms implemented in MMS and IEC104 protocols, we developed and activated TLS-enabled security features for the Modbus protocol. The evaluation was conducted on an Ubuntu 20.04 desktop equipped with a 2.60 GHz Intel Xeon Platinum 8358P processor, 128 GB of memory, and a 100 GB SSD.

**Evaluation Metrics.** We systematically evaluated two methods: For EDDG with TLS protocol, measured execution time, precision, and recall; For DepAFLNet using secure ICS protocols, analyzed code coverage and crash count.

**Time.** This metric measures the time taken to generate the EDDG and DDG for the same code. It is used to evaluate the efficiency of data dependency graph generation. A shorter time indicates higher generation efficiency.

**Precision and Recall.** Since the generation of EDDG and DDG relies on program basic block transitions, their precision and recall can be calculated by extracting and analyzing these transitions from the graphs. Specifically, the ratio of correctly identified transitions to all identified transitions indicates the precision, while the ratio of correctly identified transitions to all actual correct transitions indicates the recall.

**Coverage and Crash.** The performance of DepAFLNet and AFLNet was comparatively evaluated using standard metrics, including code coverage and crash count, to quantify their effectiveness in vulnerability discovery.

### 5.1 Evaluation of EDDG

The TLS protocol communication primarily consists of two phases: the handshake and data transfer. We selected the functions *ssl_write_client_hello* and *mbedtls_ssl_write_certificate* during the handshake phase, along with the function *mbedtls_ssl_write* from the data transfer phase, to assess the performance of EDDG against Angr's DDG.

**Table 1.** Performance Comparison between EDDG and AngrDDG

| Tested Function | EDDG | | | AngrDDG | | |
|---|---|---|---|---|---|---|
| | Time (s) | Precision | Recall | Time (s) | Precision | Recall |
| ssl_write_client_hello | 551 | 93.6% | 85.6% | 435 | 34.2% | 26.3% |
| mbedtls_ssl_write_certificate | 557 | 87.3% | 79.7% | 461 | 38.5% | 31.4% |
| mbedtls_ssl_write | 444 | 81.17% | 80.2% | 236 | 29.7% | 25.3% |

As shown in Table 1, the generation of EDDG demonstrates higher precision and recall in all tested functions, indicating that the EDDG is more accurate and better restored, which can greatly assist subsequent dependency analysis and recovery.

Specifically, in the *ssl_write_client_hello* function, the precision and recall of EDDG are 59.4% and 59.3% higher than those of AngrDDG, respectively. In the *mbedtls_ssl_write_certificate* function, the precision and recall of EDDG are 48.8% and 48.3% higher than those of AngrDDG, respectively. In the *mbedtls_ssl_write* function, the precision and recall of EDDG are 51.47% and 54.9% higher than those of AngrDDG, respectively. Although EDDG generally consumes more time than AngrDDG, its advantages in precision and recall are significant.

In the Angr framework, the *call_depth* parameter controlling symbolic execution's function call depth was empirically set to 3. When $call\_depth \geq 4$, deep invocations trigger cryptographic algorithms and complex logic, exponentially expanding the symbolic state space. Such expansion induces path explosion during symbolic execution, ultimately forcing Angr to terminate prematurely due to StopIteration exceptions. The limited *call_depth* value induced substantial missing data dependencies in AngrDDG, yielding an average recall of 27.7%, while symbolic execution incurred significant false positives during indirect call inference, resulting in an average precision of 34.1%.

The proposed DepFieldGen method achieves precise indirect call recovery through dynamic execution-synchronized basic block tracking. To mitigate redundant analysis of system library functions, we construct pre-defined data dependency models for such functions or user-specified ones, enabling comprehensive data flow establishment during EDDG analysis. While bypassing the analysis of these functions during EDDG generation reduces average precision and recall by 12.6% and 18.2% respectively, this trade-off preserves the integrity of subsequent dependent field generation.

## 5.2 Evaluation of DepAFLNet

We conducted fuzzing tests on three TLS-enhanced ICS protocols to validate DepFieldGen's effectiveness in protocol fuzzing.

**Table 2.** Code Coverage by AFLNet and DepAFLNet

| Tool Name | MMS | IEC104 | Modbus |
|---|---|---|---|
| AFLNet | 6966 | 4692 | 4591 |
| DepAFLNet | 12370 | 5871 | 5355 |

The experimental results demonstrate that, within a 24-h testing period, DepAFLNet outperforms the traditional AFLNet in terms of code coverage. As indicated in the Table 2, DepAFLNet demonstrates code coverage improvements of 77.6%, 25.1%, and 16.6% over AFLNet for the MMS, IEC104, and Modbus protocols, respectively.

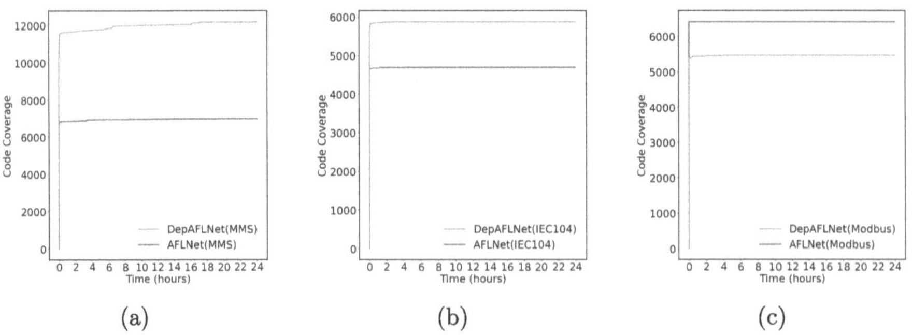


**Fig. 6.** Code Coverage Trends for AFLNet and DepAFLNet.

DepAFLNet exhibits statistically equivalent code coverage trends to AFLNet, but achieves significantly higher final coverage counts, as shown in Fig. 6. This is because we only added the DepFieldReplace Plugin to AFLNet without changing the seed mutation method and scheduling strategy. This plugin utilizes DepFieldGen to regenerate the dependent field data, which allows the test case to reach the business processing area through the security interaction layer. The limited gains in IEC104 and Modbus are attributed to their structural simplicity compared to TLS protocols, where the increased line count constitutes a negligible proportion relative to the TLS protocol's codebase.

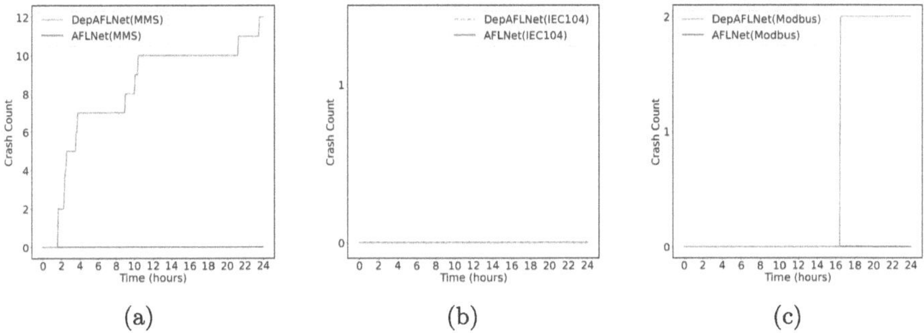


**Fig. 7.** Crash Count Trends for AFLNet and DepAFLNet.

The experimental results demonstrate that, within a 24-h testing period, DepAFLNet outperforms the traditional AFLNet in terms of crash count. As shown in Fig. 7, on MMS, it triggered 12 crashes compared to 0 by AFLNet; on IEC104, neither method triggers a crash; on Modbus, it triggered 2 crashes compared to 0 by AFLNet. This is because AFLNet failed to bypass the secure interaction and did not trigger any crashes in the business function communication. In contrast, DepAFLNet, which can recover dependent fields to bypass TLS, triggered 12 crashes in MMS and 2 crashes in Modbus. Due to the limitations of AFLNet's mutation method and scheduling strategy, we only discovered all known vulnerabilities. In the future, we will continue to optimize fuzz testing to mine unknown vulnerabilities.

## 6 Related Work

In blackbox fuzzing, IPSpex [17] extracts message field semantics from network traffic, collects execution traces from network packet construction, and extracts message formats using backward data flow tracking and sequence alignment algorithms. Blackbox fuzzing relies strictly on protocol templates and is unable to perform testing beyond what is specified in the templates. For example, $ICS^3$Fuzzer [7] uses existing tool(i.e., Netzob) to infer the protocol format, and then generates inputs by mutating each filed one by one.

In coverage-guided fuzzing, there are several works that enhance fuzzing by improving performance. FirmAFL [22] integrates system mode simulation with user mode simulation to enhance process simulation, achieving high compatibility and high throughput. One Fuzzing Strategy [19] updates the Havoc random mutation strategy. ICS Protocol Fuzzing [10] captures valuable seeds that trigger new paths and extracts reusable field data for mutation-based generation. ICSP-Fuzzer [15] improves ICS Protocol fuzzing via protocol-aware seed mutation and energy scheduling, leveraging structural features including identifiers, function codes, path depth, and dangerous operations.

The method presented in this paper optimizes fuzz testing for security-enhanced protocols but still has limitations in efficiency and performance. For example, dynamic analysis of multiple processes and threads to extract data dependencies, and optimize fuzz testing to mine unknown vulnerabilities. Future work aims to explore the use of Large Language Model (LLM)-based fuzzing [11,21] to address these limitation.

## 7 Conclusion

This paper proposes DepFieldGen, a novel method for generating dependent fields. Compared with AngrDDG, we construct an enhanced DDG, which improves the precision by 53.56% and the recall by 54.43% on average. In fuzz testing applications, DepAFLNet achieves an average increase of 39.8% in code coverage compared to the original tool AFLNet, and discover all known vulnerabilities in MMS and Modbus protocol. DepFieldGen and DepAFLNet demonstrate the capability to circumvent security mechanisms and trigger exploitable vulnerabilities in protocols. Experimental results validate the accuracy and effectiveness of our methodology.

**Acknowledgements.** This research is supported by the National Natural Science Foundation of China (Grant No.62472302), and the National Natural Science Foundation of China (Grant No. 92467201).

## References

1. MZ Automation: IEC104 library (2021). https://github.com/mz-automation/lib60870
2. MZ Automation: IEC61850 library (2019). https://github.com/mz-automation/libiec61850/
3. Ba, J., et al.: Stateful greybox fuzzing. In: 31st USENIX Security Symposium (USENIX Security 22), pp. 3255–3272 (2022)
4. Böhme, M., Pham, V.-T., Roychoudhury, A.: Coverage-based greybox fuzzing as Markov chain. IEEE Trans. Softw. Eng. **45**(5), 489–506 (2017). https://doi.org/10.1109/tse.2017.2785841
5. CERT-UA: Cyberattack by the Sandworm group on Ukrainian energy facilities using the malware (2022). https://cert.gov.ua/article/39518
6. ESET: WIN32/INDUSTROYER A new threat for industrial control systems (2017). https://web-assets.esetstatic.com/wls/2017/06/Win32_Industroyer.pdf

7. Fang, D., et al.: ICS3Fuzzer: a framework for discovering protocol implementation bugs in ICS supervisory software by fuzzing. In: Proceedings of the 37th Annual Computer Security Applications Conference, pp. 849–860 (2021)
8. Google: American Fuzzy Lop (2020). https://github.com/google/AFL
9. Hex-Rays: IDA Pro (2020). https://hex-rays.com/ida-pro
10. Luo, Z.: ICS protocol fuzzing: coverage guided packet crack and generation. In: 57th ACM/IEEE Design Automation Conference (DAC), 2020, pp. 1–6. IEEE (2020)
11. Meng, R., et al.: Large language model guided protocol fuzzing. In: Proceedings of the 31st Annual Network and Distributed System Security Symposium (NDSS) (2024)
12. Pham, V.-T., Böhme, M., Roychoudhury, A.: AFLNet: a greybox fuzzer for network protocols. In: 2020 IEEE 13th International Conference on Software Testing, Validation and Verification (ICST), pp. 460–465. IEEE (2020)
13. Symantec Security Response: Stuxnet Dossier (2011). https://docs.broadcom.com/docs/security-response-w32-stuxnet-dossier-11-en
14. Shoshitaishvili, Y., et al.: SoK: (State of) the art of war: offensive techniques in binary analysis. In: IEEE Symposium on Security and Privacy (2016)
15. Song, Z., et al.: ICSPFuzzer: an efficient fuzzing technique for ICS protocols. In: Cai, Z., et al. (eds.) Wireless Artificial Intelligent Computing Systems and Applications, pp. 369–380. Springer, Singapore (2025). ISBN: 978-981-96-8728-2. https://doi.org/10.1007/978-981-96-8728-2_30
16. Stephane. Modbus library (2024). https://libmodbus.org/
17. Sun, Y., et al.: IPSpex: enabling efficient fuzzing via specification extraction on ICS protocol. In: Ateniese, G., Venturi, D. (eds.) International Conference on Applied Cryptography and Network Security, ACNS 2022, pp. 356–375. Springer, Cham (2022). https://doi.org/10.1007/978-3-031-09234-3_18
18. Mbed TLS: TLS library (2021). https://github.com/Mbed-TLS/mbedtls/
19. Wu, M., et al.: One fuzzing strategy to rule them all. In: Proceedings of the 44th International Conference on Software Engineering, pp. 1634–1645 (2022)
20. xwings. Qiling Framework (2023). https://qiling.io/
21. Yao, Y., et al.: A survey on large language model (LLM) security and privacy: the good, the bad, and the ugly. High Confidence Comput. **4**(2), 100211 (2024). ISSN: 2667-2952. https://doi.org/10.1016/j.hcc.2024.100211, https://www.sciencedirect.com/science/article/pii/S266729522400014X
22. Zheng, Y., et al.: FIRM-AFL: high-throughput greybox fuzzing of IoT firmware via augmented process emulation. In: 28th USENIX Security Symposium (USENIX Security 19), pp. 1099–1114 (2019)

# A ROSI-Based Framework with Zero Trust Architecture: Interdependent Risks and Cybersecurity Investment

Li Huang and Kimberly A. Cornell(✉)

University at Albany, Albany 12222, USA
{lhuang9,kacornell}@albany.edu

**Abstract.** In today's interconnected digital ecosystems, cybersecurity investment decisions must consider both internal risks and the vulnerabilities of connected entities. Traditional models often overlook these external factors. This paper proposes a new framework that combines Return on Security Investment (ROSI) with Zero Trust Architecture (ZTA) to assess cybersecurity investments in interdependent risk conditions. Our model quantifies direct and cascading risk exposure while accounting for security architecture maturity and insurer incentives. We develop expressions for breach probability and residual loss based on security investment and ZTA adoption, including a cyber insurance pricing component for compliance-driven premium adjustments. Using industry-informed parameters, we demonstrate how optimal investment strategies vary by architectural maturity and insurer behavior. Our case study on small-to-medium enterprises (SMEs) in supply chain networks shows that ZTA implementation enhances ROSI and leads to better insurance terms. Overall, our findings suggest that integrating ZTA with ROSI-based planning offers an effective approach to cyber risk management in interconnected environments, contributing to the discourse on economically rational security architecture.

**Keywords:** Cybersecurity · Zero Trust Architecture · Cyber Insurance · Return on Security Investment · Interdependent Systems

## 1 Introduction

In today's hyperconnected digital landscape, organizations increasingly face complex and costly cybersecurity threats. Interconnected networks make an entity's cyber risks contagious to others within the same system. When one entity is hacked, others in the same network also suffer losses. Thus, a firm's losses include direct cyber attacks and costs from interdependence. The rise of ransomware, supply chain compromises, and state-sponsored attacks underscores the critical need for effective and efficient cybersecurity investment strategies. The interconnected network may mitigate the efficiency of protection for a single entity that represents all firms in this network. A company's self-protection not only


K.-K. R. Choo et al. (Eds.): ICDF2C 2025, LNICST 686, pp. 280–294, 2026.
https://doi.org/10.1007/978-3-032-22545-0_17

reduces the probability of data breaches [8,17,24] but also benefit other firms through improved network security. Interdependence in security generates externalities that affect a firm's security effort. Organizations must decide not only how much to invest in protection, but also which strategies to adopt, especially in environments where their risk is partially determined by the security posture of others in their ecosystem.

Traditional models of cybersecurity investment have largely assumed independent risks and focused on decision-making frameworks such as expected utility theory. However, these approaches often overlook operational realities: organizations operate within interdependent networks, insurers require baseline security practices before coverage, and emerging paradigms such as Zero Trust Architecture are fundamentally reshaping the threat landscape. Scholars have found that externalities impact security investments in a networked economy [24,41]. Some firms may take advantage of a free ride, investing less in security protection, while others overinvest to achieve their expected goals. Thus, interdependence results in security investment inefficiency (below or above socially optimal level) [40]. To address the complexity of cyber risk management, various investment strategies have been developed, each with its own strengths and weaknesses, but the core is to reduce and maintain cyber risks at an acceptable level [18,23].

This paper investigates how organizations can optimize their cybersecurity investments under interdependent risks by leveraging ROSI metrics and adopting Zero Trust principles. We model the tradeoffs between direct investments in self-protection and the use of cyber insurance, while accounting for the increasing need to satisfy insurer and regulatory requirements. We develop a network-aware ROSI-based framework that captures the compounding impact of both internal and external security postures.

Our contributions are threefold: first, we propose a ROSI-based decision model that incorporates interdependent risks across organizations and simulates the return on investing in Zero Trust security controls. Second, we demonstrate how insurance availability and pricing are influenced by a firm's security maturity and the maturity of its partners. Third, we provide a numerical case study based on real-world supply chain risk data, showing how ROSI shifts under different interdependence levels and security architectures.

## 2 Literature Review

Information security in the networked ecosystem has received significant attention. Existing literature explores developing and improving technical security solutions to prevent information breaches, such as intrusion detection systems, firewalls, anti-virus software, and encryption. Studies provide insights into the evolution of security techniques and their principles [13,15,22,26,32,34,36,37]. With widespread Internet and digital device usage, concerns about network vulnerabilities and endpoint protection have increased. Various cybersecurity mechanisms, like honeypots, VPNs, and multi-factor verification, are employed to protect information assets and mitigate unauthorized access risks. Researchers have discussed the effectiveness of these tools in reducing the likelihood and severity of security breaches [28,33,35]. Despite advancements, cyber incidents persist, highlighting that information security is not solely a technical issue.

Some scholars examine economic perspectives on cybersecurity management [8,17]. Gatzlaff and McCullough [16] found that data breaches significantly decrease a firm's wealth due to negative market reactions. Campbell et al. [12] found that breaches involving customer confidential information have more adverse impacts than other types of data incidents. Other studies analyze how security expenditure reduces breach-related costs. Demetz and Bachlechner [14] assessed economic models of security investment, revealing that while such investments do not generate monetary gains, they reduce costs by preventing breaches and increasing trustworthiness. Neuhaus and Plattner [29] found that the impact of security investment varies based on real-life contexts and information asset characteristics. Researchers also use financial methods such as Cost-Benefit Analysis to measure cybersecurity risk management benefits and costs. Arora et al. [9] estimated risk-based Return on Investment to evaluate protection measures' viability, emphasizing effective resource allocation to reduce cyber risks. As cyber attacks become more sophisticated, the importance of cybersecurity investment grows.

However, organizations struggle to understand how cybersecurity investments correlate with risk levels due to interdependence externalities. Kunreuther & Heal [24] identified positive and negative externalities in network security. Positive externalities occur when a firm's self-protection benefits others, while negative externalities arise when it makes others less safe. For example, strong protection in one firm can reduce virus transmission to partners, but attackers may target less protected entities. These externalities complicate IT management decisions, often leading to inefficient investment. Positive externalities can lead to underinvestment, while negative externalities can result in overinvestment. Gordon et al. [18] found that interdependent risks lead to underinvestment as firms free-ride on others' investments. Ogut & Raghunathan [30] confirmed that interconnected firms often transfer cyber risks, resulting in suboptimal security investment. Hofmann & Ramaj [21] concluded that cybersecurity protection levels in a community are below optimal due to interdependent risks.

Scholars develop models to internalize externalities and address investment inefficiency. Heal and Kunreuther [19] used a game-theoretical model to show how expectations about others' choices can influence risk management investments, often leading to suboptimal outcomes. Ogut et al. [31] argue that imposing liability for financial losses from cyber incidents can internalize externalities. Hofmann [20] demonstrated that proper contract design can optimize security investments by internalizing loss prevention externalities. Some researchers suggest using cyber insurance to address externality issues, balancing expenditures between self-protection and insurance coverage [11].

Cybersecurity investment has traditionally been approached through frameworks such as cost-benefit analysis, game theory, and expected utility theory. However, practical decision-making in enterprise settings often relies on more quantifiable and intuitive metrics, such as the Return on Security Investment (ROSI). ROSI calculates the net benefit of security controls by comparing the anticipated cost of incidents with and without security measures in place. Yaqoob et al. [39] proposed a comprehensive framework for calculating ROSI tailored to security-oriented organizations. Their model emphasized integrating loss expectancy, control effectiveness, and residual risk. Similarly, Lee [25] and Demetz & Bachlechner [14] highlighted the challenges of quantifying security value, especially when risks are dynamic and externally influenced.

In addition to ROSI, Zero Trust Security Architectures have emerged as a dominant model for reducing interdependent risks. ZTA is built on the principle of "never trust, always verify,âĂİ assuming all users and devices, internal or external, must be authenticated and continuously monitored [1,4,7]. By isolating assets and minimizing trust zones, ZTA limits the lateral movement of threats across an organization's ecosystem, making it particularly relevant in networked environments where partner vulnerabilities pose significant risks.

Despite these advancements, current literature has not sufficiently addressed how ROSI can be applied to evaluate network-wide risk impacts under Zero Trust frameworks, or how insurance dynamics respond to these architectures. Our work bridges this gap by integrating ROSI and Zero Trust into a cohesive model that accounts for interdependent risks, compliance-driven insurance incentives, and attacker diversity.

# 3 Theoretical Framework

In an interdependent cyber ecosystem, the value of an organization's security investments is not determined solely by its own efforts. The security posture of its partners, vendors, and other connected entities plays a critical role in shaping risk exposure. Traditional cost-benefit models often fail to capture these network externalities. We propose a framework based on ROSI integrated with principles of Zero Trust Architecture to assess optimal investment decisions under interdependent risks.

## 3.1 Return on Security Investment with Interdependence

ROSI is a metric used to assess the financial return of security investments by comparing the expected loss reduction due to security controls against the cost of implementing those controls. In a simplified form:

$$ROSI = \frac{(ALE\_baseline - ALE\_residual) - Cost\_control}{Cost\_control}$$

Where

- $ALE\_baseline$: Annual Loss Expectancy without control.
- $ALE\_residual$: Annual Loss Expectancy with control.
- $Cost\_control$: Cost of implementing the security control.

To adapt $ROSI$ for interdependent risk, we decompose $ALE$ into components:

- Direct loss $L_i$: From breaches targeting firm $i$.
- Indirect loss $L_j$: From partner firm $j$'s breach cascading to firm $i$.
- Probability of loss: a function of both internal control effectiveness and external trust level.

While this traditional ROSI formulation provides a baseline for evaluating the benefits of internal security investments, it does not fully account for the complexities of today's interconnected digital environments. In such settings, a firm's risk is not determined solely by its own defenses but also by the security posture of its partners and peers. Therefore, to better reflect the realities of interdependent risks, we decompose the expected annual loss into both direct and indirect components, the former resulting from attacks targeting the firm itself and the latter arising from cyber incidents at connected organizations that cascade through the network.

Let:
- $p_i(x_i)$: Breach probability for firm $i$ based on internal investment $x_i$.
- $q_{ij}$: Interdependence factor with firm $j$ (how much firm $j$'s breach affects firm $i$).
- $p_j$: Breach probability of firm $j$.

Total expected loss for firm $i$:

$$ALE_i = p_i(x_i) * L_i + \sum_{j \neq i} q_{ij} * p_j x_j * L_i$$

Where:
- $p_i(x_i) = \alpha_i * e^{-\beta_i x_i}$
- The reduction in $ALE_i$ due to increased $x_i$ gives us the $ROSI$ numerator.

## 3.2 Incorporating Zero Trust Architecture

Zero Trust principles alter the security landscape by reducing interdependence risks. Rather than relying on perimeter-based controls, ZTA continuously verifies trust at every layer: device, user, application, and data.

Define a ZTA maturity score $z_i \in [0, 1]$, where:

- $z_i = 0$: No Zero Trust adoption,
- $z_i = 1$: Full implementation of Zero Trust controls.

Zero Trust reduces:

1. The effectiveness of lateral movement by attackers (lowering $q_{ij}$).
2. The firm's own breach probability (enhancing $\beta_i$).

We modify the breach probability and interdependence factor accordingly:

$$p_i(x_i, z_i) = \alpha_i * e^{-\beta_i(1+\gamma z_i)x_i}$$

and

$$q_{ij}(z_i, z_j) = q_{ij}^0 * (1 - \delta z_i)(1 - \delta z_j)$$

Where:

- $\gamma$ captures ZTA's enhancement to internal control efficiency
- $\delta$ measures ZTA's dampening effect on risk spillover

Thus, ZTA reduces both internal and external risks, and its ROSI impact is dual-layered:

1. Higher return from local breach reduction
2. Reduced exposure to interdependent risk

### 3.3 Role of Cyber Insurance

Most cyber insurers today require minimum security standards, often aligned with ZTA principles (e.g., MFA, network segmentation, continuous monitoring). Insurance premiums are sensitive to the organization's:

- Internal controls $x_i$
- Zero Trust maturity $z_i$
- Ecosystem maturity (aggregate $z_j$)

Premium $\pi_i$ function:

$$\pi_i = (1 + \lambda) * ALE_i(x_i, z_i, z_{-i})$$

Where $\lambda$ reflects market inefficiency or loading factor.

Therefore, cyber insurance is not just a risk transfer mechanism, but also a compliance and incentive structure. The combination of strong self-protection, ZTA adoption, and risk-aware insurance can generate optimal investment outcomes.

### 3.4 Optimal Decision Strategy

Each firm aims to maximize its net benefit:

$$\max_{x_i, z_i}[ROSI(x_i, z_i) - \pi_i(x_i, z_i)]$$

Subject to:

- Budget constraint: $x_i + c(z_i) \leq B_i$
- Compliance requirements: $z_i \geq z_{min}$ to qualify for insurance

This framework allows firms to dynamically balance the followings:

1. Technical controls: these are direct security investments like endpoint protection, access controls, firewalls, encryption, etc. They reduce a firm's own breach probability $p_i(x_i)$.
2. Architecture maturity: it influences how deeply a firm has implemented Zero Trust Architecture ($z_i$ from 0 to 1). A mature ZTA will enhance the effectiveness of internal controls (improving $\beta_i$) and reduce spillover from other firms (lowering contagion $q_{ij}$)
3. Risk transfer mechanisms: a firm can transfer residual risk to insurers, but only if they meet security and ZTA maturity thresholds. Premiums are based on a function of ALE and ZTA maturity.

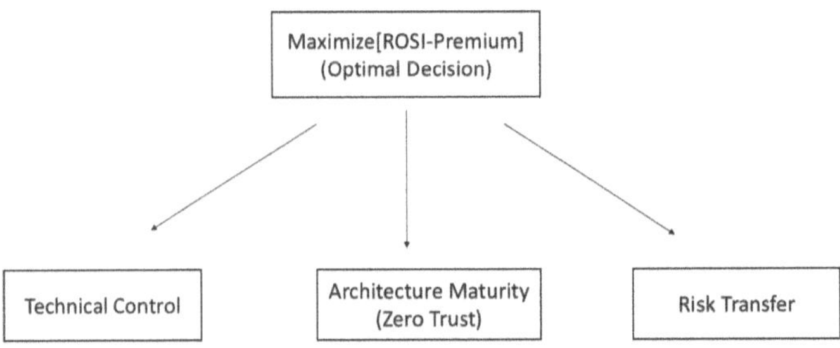


**Fig. 1.** Optimal Cybersecurity Investment Framework

Figure 1 indicates a dynamic of making an integrated decision that allocates a limited budget across three core aspects for maximum net security and economic benefit. In environments with limited budgets and interdependent cyber risks, a firm's optimal decision strategy should prioritize marginal returns across three perspectives: first, increasing control effectiveness to directly reduce breach probability. Second, investing in Zero Trust Architecture to reduce both internal and external exposure. Third, satisfying insurer criteria to access affordable risk transfer. This optimization strategy ensures that cyber investments are not isolated but synergistically aligned to achieve maximal economic protection.

## 4 Case Study

In this case study, we examine an SME within a supply chain network, focusing on how investments in internal controls and Zero Trust Architecture influence the ROSI and overall risk exposure. SMEs are particularly vulnerable to cyber threats, with 61% of cyberattacks aimed at them, and 48% experiencing a cybersecurity incident between 2022 and 2023 [6].

We cite the data from a NAVEX's article titled "The State of Cybersecurity for Small and Medium Businesses" [6]. This article provides insights into cybersecurity challenges faced by SMBs. The specific statistics include:

- In 2023, 61% of cyberattacks were aimed at SMBs [6].
- Between 2022 and 2023, 48% of SMBs experienced a cybersecurity incident [6].
- The average data breach cost for companies with fewer than 500 employees was $3.31 million in 2023 [6].

### 4.1 Model Setup

Consider a SME with 300 employees that collaborates with two supply chain partners. The SME is contemplating investments in:

1. Internal Controls Investment ($x$): Allocated budget for cybersecurity measures like endpoint protection and access management.
2. Zero Trust Maturity Level ($z$): Degree of ZTA implementation, ranging from 0 (none) to 1 (fully implemented).

We assume the parameters as follows:

- Base Breach Probability ($\alpha$): 0.30
- Investment Efficiency ($\beta$): 0.10
- ZTA Effectiveness ($\gamma$): 0.50
- Interdependence Factor ($q_{ij}^0$): 0.06
- ZTA Interdependence Reduction ($\delta$): 0.70
- Average Cost per Breach ($L$): $3.31 million (average cost for companies with fewer than 500 employees)
- ZTA Implementation Cost ($c(z)$):$10,000*$z$
- Total Security Budget ($B$): $100,000

The justifications for parameter assumption are given in Table 1.

### 4.2 Numerical Analysis

Assuming the SME allocates its $100,000 security budget between internal controls and ZTA implementation, we analyze three scenarios:

1. No ZTA Implementation ($z = 0$)
   - Investment in Controls ($x$): $100000
   - Resulting Breach Probability ($p_i$): $0.30 * e^{-0.10*100000} \approx 0$
   - Interdependence Impact ($q_{ij}$): 0.06
   - ALE: In this scenario, internal risk is negligible, while interdependent risk dominates.
2. Partial ZTA Implementation ($z = 0.5$):
   - Investment in Controls ($x$): In this scenario, investment in controls refers to the remaining budget after ZTA costs, $100000 - 100000 * 0.5 = 95000$
   - Resulting Breach Probability ($p_i$): $0.30 * e^{-0.10*1.25*95000} \approx 0$
   - Interdependence Impact ($q_ij$): $0.06 * (1 - 0.7 * 0.5)^2 \approx 0.027$
   - ALE: Reduced interdependent risk due to partial ZTA.
3. Full ZTA Implementation ($z = 1$):

**Table 1.** Justification for Parameter Assumption

| Parameter | Value | Source |
|---|---|---|
| $\alpha = 0.30$ | 30% base breach probability | Reflects average likelihood of a cyber incident in SMEs without meaningful controls. NAVEX [6] reports 48% of SMBs were hit over 2 years, mapping to ≈30% annualized risk. |
| $\beta = 0.10$ | Control effectiveness factor | Similar convex decay functions used in prior models (e.g., Ogut & Raghunathan [31], Yaqoob et al. [39]), $\beta$ reflects diminishing returns on security investment. |
| $\gamma = 0.5$ | ZTA impact on control efficiency | This scaling factor increases the effect of internal investments when ZTA is in place. Based on NIST 800-207 [7]. |
| $q_{ij}^0 = 0.06$ | Base interdependence risk | From NetDiligence report [5]: 6% of claims involve supply chain incidents. |
| $\delta = 0.7$ | ZTA reduction of interdependent risk | Reflects that ZTA significantly reduces lateral movement risk, basing on MITRE Zero Trust [4] and Forrester [1]. |
| $L = \$3.31$ million | Expected breach loss for SMB | Cited from NAVEX 2023 [6] for firms with < 500 employees. |
| $c(z) = 10000 * z$ | ZTA implementation cost | Simplified linear model: $10K per maturity tier is conservative for SMEs [3]. |
| $B = 100000$ | Firm's cybersecurity budget | Realistic number for SMBs allocating IT security annually, aligned with survey reports [2]. |
| $\lambda = 0.2$ | Insurance loading factor | Reflects market imperfection; premiums typically 10–30% above expected loss. Based on BÃűhme [10] and Woods et al. [38]. |

- Investment in Controls ($x$): the remaining budget after ZTA costs, $100000 - 100000 * 1 = 90000$
- Resulting Breach Probability ($p_i$): $0.30 * e^{(-0.10*1.5*90000)} \approx 0$
- Interdependence Impact ($q_{ij}$): $0.06 * (1 - 0.7 * 1)^2 \approx 0.0054$
- Minimal interdependent risk

We summarize the ROSI outcomes in Table 2, which shows that the increase in ZTA optimizes the outcome of investment return.

**Table 2.** ROSI Outcomes with ZTA

| Scenario | Outcome |
|---|---|
| No ZTA | Higher interdependent risk leads to lower ROSI. |
| Partial ZTA | Balanced investment reduces interdependent risk, improving ROSI. |
| Full ZTA | Optimal reduction in both internal and interdependent risks, maximizing ROSI. |

### 4.3 Cyber Insurance Consideration

To assess the role of cyber insurance under varying Zero Trust maturity levels, we analyze how insurance eligibility and premiums respond to changes in organizational security posture. Cyber insurance often requires a minimum ZTA maturity level for coverage eligibility [27]. Thus, the minimum ZTA for cyber insurance $z \gneqq 0$, reflecting a common trend in current underwriting practices that emphasize compliance with modern cybersecurity standards. We analyze three scenarios:

1. No ZTA Implementation ($z = 0$): In this scenario, the firm is not eligible for insurance, regardless of investment in traditional controls. This reflects an underwriting constraint and underscores the critical role of architecture maturity in qualifying for risk transfer mechanisms.
2. Partial ZTA Implementation ($0 < z < 1$): The firm becomes eligible for insurance, and the expected loss drops significantly due to reduced interdependent risk. However, the premium remains moderately high, suggesting that while eligibility is met, full efficiency is not yet achieved.
3. Full ZTA Implementation ($z = 1$): When fully implementing ZTA, the company not only qualifies for insurance but does so with the lowest ALE and premium. The combined effect of reduced direct breach probability and interdependent exposure translates into the most cost-effective security strategy.

These results emphasize that ZTA is not only a technical upgrade but also a financial lever: firms that mature their security architectures benefit from both improved ROSI and lower insurance premiums.

## 5 Discussion

This paper has developed a novel framework for cybersecurity investments by integrating a ROSI approach with Zero Trust Architecture principles in an interdependent risk environment. Our framework departs from traditional expected utility models by explicitly quantifying how internal security investments and Zero Trust adoption affect both direct breach probabilities and the interdependent risk arising from supply chain relationships.

Our key findings include the following:

1. The numerical analysis shows that even moderate increases in Zero Trust maturity significantly improve ROSI. This result is primarily due to the dual

effect of ZTA in reducing the internal breach probability and mitigating the risk transferred from interconnected partners.
2. By adjusting the interdependence factor based on ZTA maturity, our model demonstrates that organizations can achieve a substantial reduction in overall risk exposure. As a result, the expected annual loss (ALE) decreases, improving both the financial justification for investments and the attractiveness of cyber insurance.
3. The framework confirms that insurers increasingly require minimum security standards, consistent with ZTA principles, for eligibility. With full ZTA implementation, organizations can secure favorable insurance premiums, which further enhances the overall cost-benefit balance of cybersecurity investments.

The case study, based on recent data from NAVEX 2023 SMB Cybersecurity Report [6] and supported by parameters grounded in contemporary industry and academic literature (e.g., NIST SP 800-207 [7], Yaqoob et al. [39]), illustrates that integrating Zero Trust not only improves technical control effectiveness but also generates tangible financial benefits. This dual benefit reinforces the idea that cybersecurity strategies should extend beyond isolated technical investments to include comprehensive architectural shifts.

To assist practitioners in applying the proposed framework, we outline a step-by-step method for operationalization.

1. Assess Current Risk Posture: Determine the organization's baseline breach probability using internal incident history or industry reports, and quantify interdependence risk by evaluating the security posture of key partners or supply chain members.
2. Estimate ZTA Costs and Gains: For each Zero Trust component (e.g., identity verification, network segmentation, continuous monitoring), estimate both the implementation cost and the expected maturity gain.
3. Calculate ROSI for Investment Options: Apply the model to compute ROSI under different combinations of internal control investments and ZTA maturity levels, considering both direct and interdependent risk reductions.
4. Compare Against Cyber Insurance Premium Effects: Evaluate how each investment combination affects insurance eligibility and premium reductions, and identify strategies that yield the highest net financial benefit.
5. Adapt for Limited Data Environments: For small firms lacking detailed internal data, apply industry averages or sector benchmarks for initial parameter estimation, and refine inputs as more data becomes available.

This structured approach enables practitioners to translate the theoretical framework into a practical risk management tool, ensuring that security investments are both economically justified and operationally feasible.

## 6 Limitations and Future Work

While the proposed framework offers an innovative perspective, several limitations indicate further investigation:

1. Parameter Uncertainty: Although the parameter assumptions are based on the latest reports and academic studies, future work should incorporate empirical sensitivity analyses and validation with real-world datasets across different industries.
2. Dynamic Investment Decisions: Our model currently considers a single-period static decision-making framework. Extending the analysis to multi-period settings or dynamic investment models would capture evolving threat landscapes and investment returns over time.
3. Broader Ecosystem Effects: Further research could incorporate behavioral aspects and competitive dynamics among interconnected organizations, including the effects of regulatory requirements and evolving insurer practices.

Future work could also explore integrating additional metrics (e.g., incident response costs, reputational damage) into the ROSI framework and examine the impact of emerging technologies (e.g., Artificial Intelligence, Machine Learning, etc.) on cyber risk interdependencies.

## 7 Conclusion

In conclusion, this study presents an alternative perspective on cybersecurity investment by leveraging a ROSI framework incorporated with Zero Trust principles. Our approach addresses key criticisms of traditional models by:

1. Quantitatively linking cybersecurity investment decisions to both direct and interdependent risks.
2. Demonstrating how Zero Trust adoption reduces risk propagation and enhances overall security posture.
3. Highlighting the role of cyber insurance as both a risk transfer mechanism and a compliance incentive.

The findings suggest that a balanced strategy, combining robust internal controls with a mature Zero Trust architecture, can yield higher returns on security investments and lower overall risk exposure, particularly for small and medium enterprises operating in interdependent networks.

Beyond theoretical modeling, this work provides practical insights for practitioners. For SMEs, the framework provides a structured method to allocate limited security budgets by quantifying the benefits of both internal controls and architectural upgrades. Particularly in resource-constrained environments, the model helps justify investments in Zero Trust not merely as a technical enhancement but as a financially optimal strategy. In addition, cyber insurers can use these insights to better price risk and incentivize client behavior through premium adjustments linked to ZTA maturity.

This research also contributes to the broader literature on cyber economics by integrating architectural maturity into interdependence-aware risk modeling. By incorporating compliance-driven incentives and risk spillover dynamics, our model aligns with real-world decision-making conditions more closely than conventional utility-based approaches. The dual-layered effect of ZTA, improving both internal efficiency and external insulation, presents a more holistic investment rationale that can guide future security architecture design.

From a policy standpoint, our findings support initiatives that encourage Zero Trust adoption, especially among firms within critical infrastructure and supply chains. Public-private partnerships, tax credits, or industry standards that promote architectural maturity could help internalize externalities and reduce systemic cyber risk.

By advancing this framework, we provide decision-makers and policymakers with actionable insights into optimizing cybersecurity investments in an era of rapid digital transformation and increasing interconnectedness. Future work will further refine these models, enhancing their practical relevance and applicability across diverse organizational contexts.

**Acknowledgments.** We would like to thank the University at Albany for its institutional support.

**Disclosure of Interests.** The authors have no competing interests to declare that are relevant to the content of this article.

## References

1. The business of zero trust security. https://www.forrester.com/zero-trust/. Accessed 19 May 2025
2. CrowdStrike state of SMB cybersecurity survey. https://www.crowdstrike.com/en-us/resources/reports/state-of-smb-cybersecurity-survey/. Accessed 20 May 2025
3. The European small business finance outlook. https://www.eif.org/news_centre/publications/eif_working_paper_2023_96.pdf. Accessed 20 May 2025
4. Mitre zero trust framework. https://www.mitre.org/sites/default/files/2021-12/pr-21-1273-zero-trust-architectures-are-we-there-yet.pdf. Accessed 19 May 2025
5. NetDiligence 2020 annual report. https://netdiligence.com/cyber-claims-study-2020-report/. Accessed 19 Dec 2024
6. The state of cybersecurity for small and medium businesses. https://www.navex.com/en-us/blog/article/the-state-of-cybersecurity-for-small-and-medium-businesses/. Accessed 21 May 2025
7. Zero trust architecture. https://nvlpubs.nist.gov/nistpubs/specialpublications/NIST.SP.800-207.pdf. Accessed 19 May 2025
8. Anderson, R., Moore, T.: The economics of information security. science **314**(5799), 610–613 (2006)
9. Arora, A., Hall, D., Piato, C., Ramsey, D., Telang, R.: Measuring the risk-based value of it security solutions. IT Prof. **6**(6), 35–42 (2004)
10. Böhme, R., Schwartz, G., et al.: Modeling cyber-insurance: towards a unifying framework. In: WEIS (2010)
11. Bolot, J., Lelarge, M.: Cyber insurance as an incentive for internet security. In: Managing Information Risk and the Economics of Security, pp. 269–290 (2009)

12. Campbell, K., Gordon, L.A., Loeb, M.P., Zhou, L.: The economic cost of publicly announced information security breaches: empirical evidence from the stock market. J. Comput. Secur. **11**(3), 431–448 (2003)
13. Chapman, D.B., Zwicky, E.D.: Building Internet Firewalls. O'Reilly & Associates Inc. (1995)
14. Demetz, L., Bachlechner, D.: To invest or not to invest? Assessing the economic viability of a policy and security configuration management tool. In: Böhme, R. (ed.) The Economics of Information Security and Privacy, pp. 25–47. Springer, Heidelberg (2013). https://doi.org/10.1007/978-3-642-39498-0_2
15. Denning, D.E.: An intrusion-detection model. IEEE Trans. Softw. Eng. **2**, 222–232 (1987)
16. Gatzlaff, K.M., McCullough, K.A.: The effect of data breaches on shareholder wealth. Risk Manage. Insur. Rev. **13**(1), 61–83 (2010)
17. Gordon, L.A., Loeb, M.P.: The economics of information security investment. ACM Trans. Inf. Syst. Secur. (TISSEC) **5**(4), 438–457 (2002)
18. Gordon, L.A., Loeb, M.P., Sohail, T.: A framework for using insurance for cyber-risk management. Commun. ACM **46**(3), 81–85 (2003)
19. Heal, G., Kunreuther, H.: Modeling interdependent risks. Risk Anal. Int. J. **27**(3), 621–634 (2007)
20. Hofmann, A.: Internalizing externalities of loss prevention through insurance monopoly: an analysis of interdependent risks. Geneva Risk Insur. Rev. **32**, 91–111 (2007)
21. Hofmann, A., Ramaj, H.: Interdependent risk networks: the threat of cyber attack. Int. J. Manag. Decis. Mak. **11**(5–6), 312–323 (2011)
22. Joan, D., Vincent, R.: The Design of Rijndael: AES-The Advanced Encryption Standard. Information Security and Cryptography (2002)
23. Kejwang, B.: Effect of cybersecurity risk management practices on performance of insurance sector: a review of literature. Int. J. Res. Bus. Soc. Sci. (2147-4478) **11**(6), 334–340 (2022)
24. Kunreuther, H., Heal, G.: Interdependent security. J. Risk Uncertain. **26**, 231–249 (2003)
25. Lee, I.: Cybersecurity: risk management framework and investment cost analysis. Bus. Horiz. **64**(5), 659–671 (2021)
26. Liao, H.J., Lin, C.H.R., Lin, Y.C., Tung, K.Y.: Intrusion detection system: a comprehensive review. J. Netw. Comput. Appl. **36**(1), 16–24 (2013)
27. Marsh McLennan: Using data to prioritize cybersecurity investments. https://www.marsh.com/en/services/cyber-risk/insights/using-cybersecurity-analytics-to-prioritize-cybersecurity-investments.html. Accessed 21 Nov 2024
28. Mitchell, R., Chen, I.R.: A survey of intrusion detection techniques for cyber-physical systems. ACM Comput. Surv. (CSUR) **46**(4), 1–29 (2014)
29. Neuhaus, S., Plattner, B.: Software security economics: theory, in practice. In: Böhme, R. (ed.) The Economics of Information Security and Privacy, pp. 75–92. Springer, Heidelberg (2013). https://doi.org/10.1007/978-3-642-39498-0_4
30. Ogut, H., Raghunathan, S.: Cyber insurance and it security investment: Impact of interdependent risk (2005)
31. Ogut, H., Raghunathan, S., Menon, N.M.: Information security risk management through self-protection and insurance. The University of Texas at Dallas (2005)
32. Roesch, M.: Snort: Lightweight intrusion detection for networks. In: Proceedings of the 13th USENIX Conference on System Administration (LISA '99), pp. 229–238. USENIX Association (1999)

33. Rowe, N.C.: Measuring the effectiveness of honeypot counter-counter deception. In: Proceedings of the 39th Annual Hawaii International Conference on System Sciences (HICSS'06), vol. 6, p. 129c. IEEE (2006)
34. Schneier, B.: Applied Cryptography: Protocols, Algorithms, and Source Code in C. Wiley (2007)
35. Shah, S., Mehtre, B.M.: An overview of vulnerability assessment and penetration testing techniques. J. Comput. Virol. Hacking Tech. **11**, 27–49 (2015)
36. Stamp, M.: Information Security: Principles and Practice. Wiley (2011)
37. Wagner, D., Dean, R.: Intrusion detection via static analysis. In: Proceedings 2001 IEEE Symposium on Security and Privacy, S&P 2001, pp. 156–168. IEEE (2000)
38. Woods, D., Simpson, A.: Policy measures and cyber insurance: a framework. J. Cyber Policy **2**(2), 209–226 (2017)
39. Yaqoob, T., Arshad, A., Abbas, H., Amjad, M.F., Shafqat, N.: Framework for calculating return on security investment (ROSI) for security-oriented organizations. Futur. Gener. Comput. Syst. **95**, 754–763 (2019)
40. Zhao, X.: Economic analysis on information security and risk management. Ph.D. thesis, The University of Texas at Austin (2007)
41. Zhao, X., Xue, L., Whinston, A.B.: Managing interdependent information security risks: cyberinsurance, managed security services, and risk pooling arrangements. J. Manag. Inf. Syst. **30**(1), 123–152 (2013)

# Accelerating Criminal Investigations with TRACY

Pradeep Rangappa[1], Petr Motlicek[1,2(✉)], Dairazalia Sanchez-Cortes[1], Alejandra Sanchez Lara[1], Michaela Antonopoulou[3], Ioannis Fourfouris[3], Nikos Avgerinos[3], and Manolis Tsangaris[3]

[1] Idiap Research Institute, Martigny, Switzerland
{pradeep.rangappa,petr.motlicek,dairazalia.sanchez-cortes, alejandra.sanchezlara}@idiap.ch
[2] Brno University of Technology, Brno, Czech Republic
[3] Performance Technologies, Anonymos Etairia Pliroforikis, Athens, Greece
{michaela.antonopoulou,giannis.fourfouris, nikos.avgerinos,manolis.tsangaris}@performance.gr

**Abstract.** Effective investigation of criminal cases increasingly depends on the ability to correlate both content data (e.g., call audio, text messages, or email bodies) and non-content data (NCD)—metadata such as subscriber details, traffic/logs, and location information—with supporting evidence like surveillance footage and witness testimonies. This reliance aligns with and is underscored by the European Commission's ongoing efforts to regulate and study the retention of NCD, recognizing its critical role in law enforcement and public safety. A primary challenge for Law Enforcement Agencies (LEAs) is processing the massive volumes of data lawfully obtained from Communication Service Providers (CSPs). Even when constrained in time and space (e.g., a 4-h window within a $2 \times 2$km area), mobile signaling records can exceed one million entries. To address this, we propose TRACY, a framework that scans large-scale signaling communication logs to identify terminals located near key evidence points during a crime, relying solely on encrypted terminal identifiers. We propose three core analytical methods within TRACY: (Method-1) scoring individuals based on spatiotemporal proximity to evidence, (Method-2) detection of co-located individuals within short time intervals to infer potential coordination, and (Method-3) network analysis of communication data to assess individual influence and connectivity. These methods are combined through a final scoring mechanism that robustly ranks suspects by integrating both spatial-temporal and behavioral indicators. To further enhance suspect discovery, TRACY Canvas, an in-house developed tool, provides an interactive platform to visualize suspect relationships and explore supporting evidence. It allows investigators to interpret data-driven findings more intuitively and investigate connections between individuals identified through TRACY's analytical pipeline. We deployed the integration on realistic data and evaluated it through two synthetic case studies: (1) a demo robbery in Athens and (2) a Zurich drug-related scenario involving three suspects from ROXANNE Simulated Data (ROXSD). Results showthat combining spatial-


K.-K. R. Choo et al. (Eds.): ICDF2C 2025, LNICST 686, pp. 295–310, 2026.
https://doi.org/10.1007/978-3-032-22545-0_18

temporal inference and communication behavior significantly improves detection rates, revealing suspects initially missed by physical presence inference alone. The system demonstrates high hit rates in identifying true suspects and accelerates investigations while complying with European privacy regulations.

**Keywords:** TRACY · Non-Content data · Law Enforcement Agencies · Suspect Detection · Mobile Signaling Data · ROXANNE

## 1 Introduction

The rapid growth of digital communications has significantly transformed the landscape of criminal investigations. Law Enforcement Agencies (LEAs) can nowadays lawfully request and access vast amounts of data (for a limited time) from Communication Service Providers (CSPs), which offers new opportunities for more effective investigation of criminal cases [5]. However, the large volume and complexity of this data present a substantial challenge. Investigators are tasked with sifting through massive datasets that include Call Detail Record (CDR): including metadata about phone calls (CALLs) or messages (SMS), and Data Usage Detail Record (DDR): metadata about mobile data sessions, such as internet usage, app activity, and IP sessions over mobile networks. Both CDR and DDR can be used to track a terminal's overall communications activity (voice and data) and location patterns based on cell tower information, allowing to uncover meaningful patterns of behavior and lead to suspect identification. The motivation for this paper stems from the need to speed up criminal investigations by considering both content and non-content communication data, and correlating it with additional surveillance evidence such as Closed-Circuit Television (CCTV) footage and witness testimonies. Specifically, our focus is on addressing the complexities of processing large amounts of data that is both time and location-restricted—often limited to small windows of time and specific geographic areas (e.g., a 4-h window within a $2 \times 2$ km area surrounding a crime scene) [21].

In this context, TRACY[1] (A bigdata analyTics from base-stations Registrations And Cdrs e-evidence sYstem) stands out as a solution that analyzes mobile signaling datasets to pinpoint devices that were located near crime scenes at the time of the incident. It operates without needing access to call content, instead utilizing encrypted terminal identifiers and mobile network topology to draw insights. By processing massive amounts of non-content CDR and DDR metadata, TRACY significantly speeds up the process of identifying relevant (and potentially suspect) terminals during criminal investigations.

Although content is unavailable, valuable metadata such as cell ID, timestamp, and tower geolocation is retained. For privacy preservation, this information is aggregated into $2 \times 2,$km spatial grid cells. The dataset is dominated

[1] https://www.tracy-project.eu/.

by DDR signaling records (approximately 95%), with CDR (CALL and SMS) contributing 5%. To quantify the terminal's relevance to a case, we introduce a scoring mechanism based on evidence intervals-time windows as reported by LEAs when the crime is believed to have occurred. An evidence point is a specific location and time where a key event occurred or was captured (e.g., crime scene, CCTV footage). It helps track when and where something happened and can be marked as critical or non-critical based on its importance.

Prior work in behavioral analysis and mobile data mining has explored the use of geo-positional and communication patterns to understand human behavior [4,18,20]. However, our work stands apart by integrating spatial-temporal heuristics with behavioral scoring in a unified system aimed at real-world criminal investigation scenarios.

We propose three core methods within the TRACY framework to identify and rank suspects from large-scale mobile signaling data collected near crime events. TRACY Method-1 scores individuals based on their spatio-temporal proximity to key evidence points—locations and times where a crime-related event occurred (e.g., crime scenes, CCTV detections). This method identifies terminals frequently or closely present at these evidence points during the critical window. Following the individual-level suspect scoring of TRACY Method-1, TRACY Method-2 [17] shifts the focus to relational analysis—identifying concurrent pairs of individuals who appear together at the same location within a one-minute interval, using synthetic terminal data. Such patterns help infer possible coordination or group activity among individuals. TRACY Method-3 builds on the successful application of network analysis features from the ROXANNE[2] project on real content data [23,24], evaluating each terminal's connectivity and influence within the broader communication graph. Building upon the AUTOCRIME [13] platform developed under the ROXANNE project, we also present TRACY Canvas [12], a visualization tool developed entirely using open-source technologies to render complex communication networks. Through dynamic filtering, visual timelines, and geospatial mapping, TRACY Canvas helps bridge the gap between raw metadata and investigative reasoning. Investigators can visualize clusters of co-located individuals, inspect communication patterns, and cross-reference metadata with external evidence such as surveillance video timestamps. Together, these methods enable a comprehensive ranking mechanism that integrates spatial, temporal, and behavioral signals to prioritize individuals for investigation. The final suspect list is not only based on presence near evidence points, but also on their behavioral proximity to others involved, and their strategic position in the communication network. This fusion of physical and digital traces enables more robust suspect identification compared to traditional spatial-only filtering approaches.

Due to the inherent sensitivity and restricted access of real-world data related to criminal scenarios, the use of synthetic data has become indispensable in contemporary forensic research [3,7,13,14,17]. All data processing within the TRACY project is conducted in strict adherence to European privacy regula-

[2] https://www.roxanne-euproject.org/.

tions, thereby ensuring both legal compliance and the ethical handling of personal information in the context of criminal investigations. Notably, our study relies exclusively on synthetic non-content data to uphold these standards.

In this paper, we evaluated TRACY through synthetic case studies that simulate real-world investigative scenarios. These case studies, derived from the ROXANNE Simulated Dataset (ROXSD) [14], demonstrate how TRACY surfaces suspects overlooked by traditional spatiotemporal filters alone. In both scenarios—a street robbery in Athens and a drug trafficking case in Zurich—TRACY achieved high detection accuracy, successfully correlating location, co-presence, and behavioral indicators to identify suspects. These results underscore TRACY's potential to enhance digital investigations by accelerating suspect triage while preserving data privacy and regulatory compliance.

## 2 Prior Work

Mobile phone data has been widely used to analyze human behavior across land use, public health, transportation, and social networks [1,9,11,25]. Since 2010, location-sharing apps like Foursquare, Yelp, and Gowalla have enabled users to check-in, promote venues, and express identity through location [6,19].

Trajectory records are also used for pathfinding and travel recommendations based on GPS/WiFi data [25]. Co-occurrence in movement patterns often reflects latent social or contextual links. Such geolocation corpora have also supported synthetic mobility data generation [1,9].

Smartphones act as rich forensic evidence sources, offering data across multiple sensors [16]. Leveraging this data, ML techniques applied to sensor data (e.g., accelerometer, gyroscope) show potential in classifying criminal activity [15]. However, such methods require physical access to devices, which is often infeasible in daily law enforcement.

Alternatively, mobile metadata offers valuable insight into population dynamics and criminal behavior. Cell tower logs and CDRs have been used to forecast crimes using models like random forests and regression, linking mobility patterns to crime rates [2,22].

Nevertheless, access to real-world law enforcement data is restricted due to legal and privacy concerns [8,10], hindering large-scale validation. Hence, synthetic data are essential in recent research. It mimics real-world complexity without exposing sensitive information and allows the design of scalable forensic tools.

Notably, Rangappa *et al.* [17] emphasize tracing suspect movements using Non-Content Data (NCD), integrating multiple sources. The TRACY project's use of synthetic NCD supports scalable, privacy-compliant investigation pipelines aligned with real evidence.

## 3 Problem Statement

### 3.1 Background and Motivation

Understanding human behavior in urban areas is key to urban planning and safety. Previous work has used mobile phone metadata to study this across cities and times [9,11]. Despite dataset differences, the main challenge remains: how to analyze human presence and movement from coarse spatio-temporal data?

### 3.2 Limitations of Existing Approaches

Suspect identification often uses historical signaling records but faces issues:

1. **Spatial Resolution**: Location is approximated by CELL IDs, causing uncertainty from hundreds of meters near towers to kilometers in rural zones.
2. **Temporal Constraints**: Sparse and irregular signaling events hinder accurate mobility reconstruction.
3. **Prior Investigations**: Projects like TRACY show potential for criminal analysis but struggle to narrow suspects due to data imprecision.

### 3.3 The Challenge

We study a crime in a 2 × 2 km urban area with an initial suspect list from filtering. Refinement is needed within spatial (2 km) and narrow temporal bounds around the event.

**How to accurately identify suspects using coarse mobile signaling data constrained by spatial and temporal proximity?**

This is critical in urban surveillance, where millions interact with infrastructure continuously.

### 3.4 Spatio-temporal Evidence and Simulation Scenario

Identifying suspects near a crime scene using geolocated timestamps is key. We simulate this with four evidence points tagged by location and time.

Given millions of potential paths taken by individuals (simplified as black lines in Fig. 1), the core objective is to identify suspects or potential perpetrators whose movement paths intersect with the reported evidence points, both spatially and temporally. For example, the green path corresponds to a suspect intersecting all four evidence points, while the red path intersects only two, suggesting varying levels of suspicion.

This problem extends further into:

1. Detecting and ranking suspects based on how closely their movement paths align with evidence points during the specified time intervals.
2. Enhancing spatial-temporal analysis with behavioral signals (e.g., call logs, device metadata) to improve identification through multimodal correlation.
3. Visualizing terminal networks and mobility graphs to detect interaction zones, frequently visited places, and possible accomplice links.

Our work proposes a framework to simulate, visualize, and analyze such scenarios, laying the groundwork for scalable, automated suspect identification systems in real-world surveillance contexts.

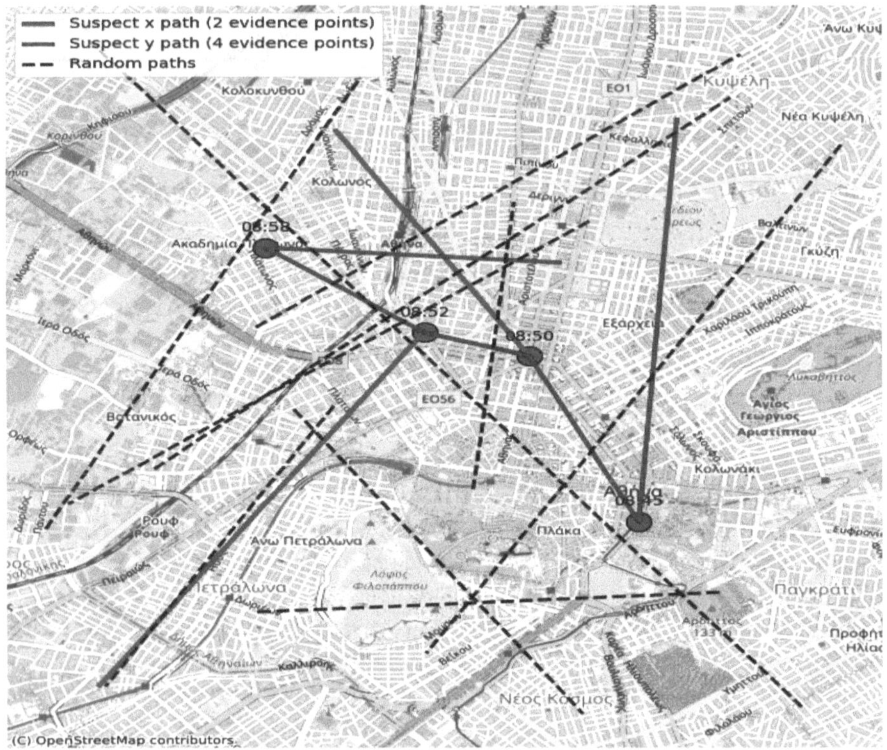


**Fig. 1.** Paths of mobile terminals as 2D (geolocation) and time sequences. We plot paths of random and suspected terminals.

## 4 Legal

The operational use of TRACY brings forth important legal considerations related to data retention, access, and the scope of data requests. Law enforcement agencies (LEAs) may need to request large amounts of data to identify relevant devices, and the main legal issue is whether national laws allow such broad access, especially for live data. National laws also govern the procedure, including safeguards like judicial approval or emergency access through prosecutors. An important consideration is what types of crimes justify requesting location data, as the Court of Justice of the European Union (CJEU) has ruled that such data can reveal private information and should be limited to serious crimes or national security cases. National laws vary in interpreting this rule, which involves both targeted data retention and access. TRACY could also be useful for reviewing past cases, meaning access to historical data is important. A practical challenge is the lack of standard formats for data provided by operators, which can delay LEAs in using the data efficiently.

# 5 Dataset Description

## 5.1 Non-Content Data (NCD)

NCD refers to metadata related to communication events, excluding actual content. It includes:

- **Subscriber Data**: Identifiers like name, address, phone number.
- **Traffic Data**: Communication type, time, and participants.
- **Location Data**: E.g., Cell ID, used to infer geographic position via:
  - *OpenCelliD*: Public global cell tower database.
  - *CellMapper*: Crowd-sourced mobile infrastructure mapping.

## 5.2 Realistic Dataset (Athens)

Collected during a pilot in Athens on Jan 27, 2025 (13:00–16:00), this dataset includes 1,156 call/SMS/data events from 46 anonymized users. Though GPS is unavailable, cell-ID-based location tracking enables spatial-temporal analysis.

## 5.3 Synthetic Dataset: Athens (SAEX1)

Simulated data from July 28, 2023, spans 6.9M events from 32,485 terminals in a 2 km × 2 km area over 4 h. After filtering for activity near Kerameikos, 1.5M records from 30,703 users remained. Records are categorized as:

- **CDR**: Voice/SMS, includes start/end times (calls), Cell ID (caller only).
- **DDR**: Internet usage, with start time and Cell ID.

Ground truth includes crime details (e.g., perpetrator ID: 5000000), CCTV sightings, and primary suspect IDs.

## 5.4 Synthetic Dataset: Zurich

This dataset simulates 9,000 terminals over 8 h using Swiss open-access antenna data. Terminals and antennas are used to generate mobility paths (filtered via haversine distance). Events include 10% calls, 5% SMS, and 85% DDR, close to realistic durations.

Three additional suspect paths were manually created (linked to ROXSD), ensuring overlaps in antenna connections and CDR events. Ground truth includes a reported drug transaction and multiple eyewitness and CCTV observations. Primary suspect IDs: `ru05M_T`, `ru06F_T`, `cs04M_T`.

# 6 TRACY Workflow

TRACY uses heuristics and machine learning to make ongoing predictions, flagging terminals that exhibit behavioral patterns similar to those observed in case analyses. In this section, we describe how TRACY processes large volumes of data, identifies suspects, and extracts key insights through a combination of spatial, temporal, and network-based methods.

### 6.1 System Architecture

Figure 2 represents the workflow of TRACY, which integrates content and non-content data along with evidence points to identify potential suspects. TRACY Method 1 scores individuals based on their proximity to evidence-related locations and corresponding time intervals. The top-$k$ candidates are then examined by TRACY Method 2, which detects concurrent pairs—individuals who co-occur within a one-minute window across sites—revealing possible coordination. In parallel, TRACY Method 3 performs graph analytics on the communication network, combining PageRank, degree centrality, and a frequency-weighted interaction score into a Network Analysis (NA) score. The outputs from all methods feed into the TRACY Canvas, a visualization tool for interpreting suspect rankings. More details of the methods and the visualization tool are discussed in the subsequent sections.

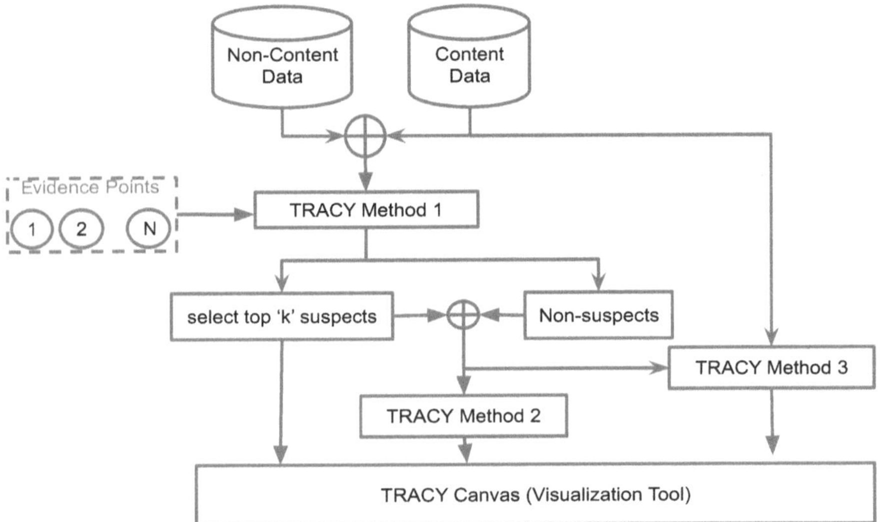


**Fig. 2.** System architecture illustrating the workflow of TRACY.

- **Data Sources**
  The system ingests two main categories of data: *Non-Content Data* and *Content Data.*
- **Evidence Points**
  Evidence points are defined by a specific location and time interval, indicating where and when a key event occurred—such as a crime scene, the time a crime took place, or the availability of CCTV footage. These points serve as reference anchors to identify suspects in the data.

- **TRACY Method 1**
  The TRACY Method 1 is the core analytical engine that takes both the merged data (Content + Non-Content) and the evidence points as input. A set of *Evidence Points*, indexed from 1 to $N$, is provided as an additional input to the TRACY Method 1. Scoring the individuals are based on spatiotemporal proximity to evidence. More details are discussed in 6.2
- **Suspect Selection**
  Based on the output from the TRACY Method 1, we select the top-$k$ most relevant or suspicious entities. These are considered potential suspects for further investigation or visualization.
- **Non-Suspects and Integration**
  The remaining entities classified as *non-suspects* are not discarded but are instead routed to the Autocrime Platform. This ensures that even non-suspects are preserved for contextual understanding or secondary analysis.
- **TRACY Canvas**
  The final results, including both the selected suspects and insights from the Autocrime Platform, are compiled and visualized. This enables LEA's or downstream systems to interpret the findings and make informed decisions.

### 6.2 TRACY Method 1

**The summary of TRACY Method 1 is as follows:**

- **Input Dataset:** Contains person IDs, latitude/longitude, and timestamps; loaded into a dataframe.
- **Grouping by Terminal ID:** Data is organized per terminal to enable focused analysis.
- **Evidence Points:** Time-bound events reported by police, serving as query points.
- **Time Window Extraction:** Time frames are derived from evidence entries.
- **Matching and Scoring:** Terminal records overlapping with evidence windows are scored.
- **Suspect List Generation:** Terminals are ranked based on scores and returned.

### 6.3 TRACY Method 2: Concurrent Pair Detection

Building on TRACY Method 1, Method 2 focuses on identifying pairs of individuals co-located within the same area during a one-minute interval using synthetic terminal data. A concurrent pair is defined as two terminals present at the same cell location within this short window.

Expanding on prior work [17], we applied a spatio-temporal co-occurrence approach using TRACY's synthetic dataset, which includes person IDs, cell coordinates, and timestamps. The timeline was divided into 1-minute slots, and individuals at each location were grouped into all possible pairs to detect co-location events.

For each pair, we tracked meeting frequency, shared locations, and cumulative distance traveled—computed using the Haversine formula for geographic distance estimation. This process, repeated across all time slots (e.g., 240 between 08:00 and 12:00), produced a dictionary of co-occurring pairs sorted by total joint distance, helping to reveal strong physical meeting edges.

### 6.4 TRACY Method 3

TRACY Method 3 performs graph analytics on the communication network by combining PageRank, degree centrality, and a frequency-weighted interaction score into a Network Analysis (NA) score. The details of TRACY Method 3 are provided after the introduction of the network analysis section (see Sect. 7.3).

## 7 Interpretation of Evidence

This section explains how evidence derived from TRACY Method 1 and Method 2 is interpreted and presented using visual techniques. It focuses on the analysis of CDR and DDR data through graph-based methods. We also introduce the TRACY Canvas, an open-source visualization tool developed to support and enhance network-based analysis. The key components are described in below sub-sections.

### 7.1 TRACY Canvas: Visualization Through the Network

As part of the TRACY project, we developed the TRACY Canvas, an open-source visualization tool designed to interpret results from TRACY methods. Building upon the ROXANNE project, more technical details are available in the accompanying report[3].

Call Detail Records (CDR) are visualized as networks, where nodes represent terminal IDs and edges indicate communication (calls or SMS). Device Detection Records (DDR), lacking terminal-to-terminal links, do not form meaningful networks. TRACY Method 1 annotates the CDR network with crime scene presence per terminal. TRACY Method 2 adds co-location data to support analysis of physical proximity.

Figure 3 shows the **Network of Terminals**, where:

- Nodes = terminals; red = suspects, grey = others.
- Edges = communication events: grey (calls), orange (SMS).

Arrows show direction, edge color indicates type. This helps reveal clusters, suspect interactions, and potential collaborators.

Figure 4 shows the **Network of Individuals with Physical Concurrent Edge**, combining communication with co-location (green edges). These concurrent edges, derived from Method 2, highlight overlapping physical presence, revealing potential in-person meetings and coordinated activity.

[3] See technical report for full details.

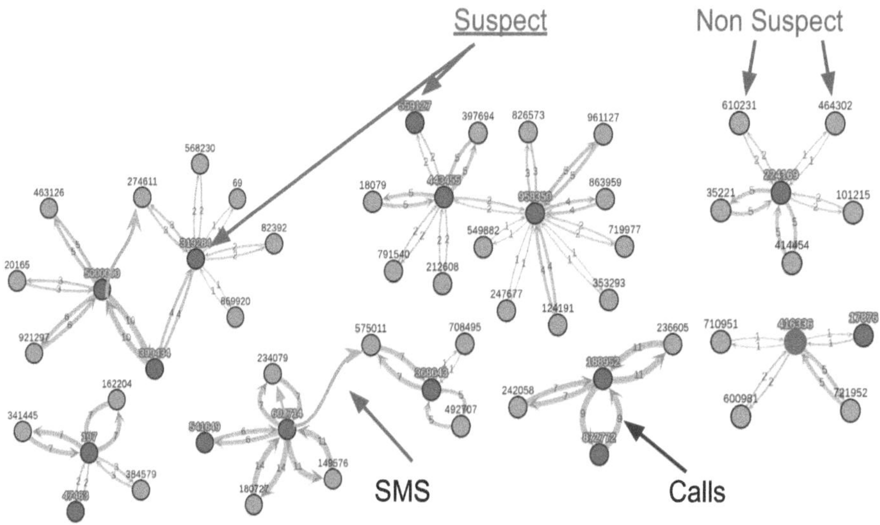


**Fig. 3.** Network of Terminals.

### 7.2 Network Analysis

While the TRACY Canvas primarily serves as a tool for visualizing the outcomes of the TRACY Method 1 and Method 2, network analysis adds an essential layer of interpretation on top of these visualizations. It does more than just display the data—it helps uncover hidden patterns and relationships within large-scale CDR. By applying unsupervised methods based on graph structure, we extract insights such as:

- Visualizing CALL and SMS links between terminals in a clear, structured graph
- Identifying cohesive groups that are not easy to see from big CDRs files (e.g., main network and their clans).
- Focusing on more influential node (terminal) and its interacting neighbors.
- Spotting outliers—nodes with little or unusual activity
- This analytical layer transforms the TRACY Canvas from a static visual display into a powerful investigative tool for LEA.

### 7.3 TRACY Method 3: Scoring Based on Network and Communication Patterns

TRACY Method 3 applies network analysis to the call detail records (CDR) graph, incorporating metrics like PageRank and degree centrality to assess the influence and connectivity of individuals. It also computes a communication-based score to capture suspicious behavioral patterns.

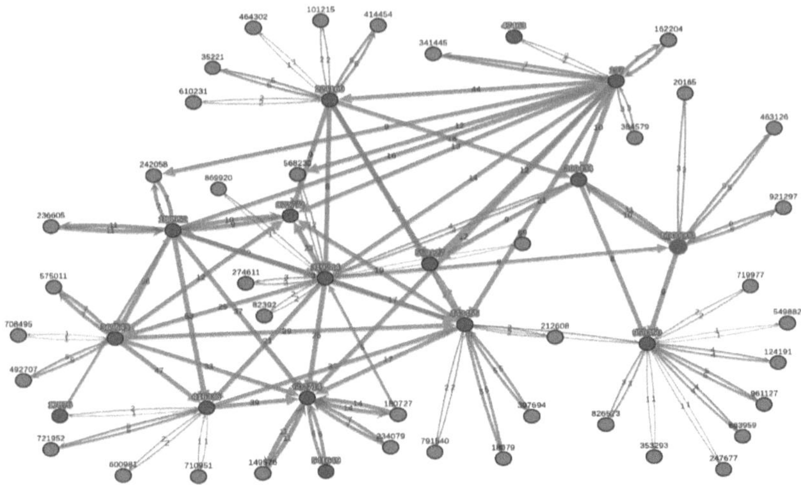


**Fig. 4.** Network of Individuals with Physical Concurrent Edge.

A directed graph is constructed where each node represents a phone number and edges indicate suspicious interactions, weighted by base suspicion scores. Two primary graph-based features are used:

- **Degree Centrality (DC):** Measures how strongly a node influences others through outgoing weighted edges.
- **PageRank (PR):** Reflects both direct and indirect influence based on the overall network structure.

For the communication score (CS), features such as number of calls near the crime scene, call durations, and call counts are normalized using Min-Max scaling. The final communication score is a weighted sum of these normalized features:

$$\text{Communication Score} = \sum_{i=1}^{n} w_i \cdot x_i, \quad \text{where} \quad \sum_{i=1}^{n} w_i = 1,\ w_i \geq 0 \tag{1}$$

The TRACY Method 3 score is then computed as a weighted combination of the three components:

$$\text{TRACY\_Method\_3\_Score} = \beta_1 \cdot \text{PR} + \beta_2 \cdot \text{DC} + \beta_3 \cdot \text{CS} \tag{2}$$

with constraints:

$$\beta_1 + \beta_2 + \beta_3 = 1, \quad \beta_i \geq 0 \tag{3}$$

This score effectively integrates both network structure and communication behavior to enhance suspect identification.

## 8 Evaluation of TRACY Methods

To evaluate the performance of the proposed TRACY methods, we calculate the 'Hit Rate'. It measures the number of true suspects that appear in the top-$k$ ranked predictions. A "hit" occurs when a ground-truth suspect is found within the top-$k$ list.

Table 1 reports the Top-$k$ suspect identification hit rates for various feature sets across different platforms (TRACY Method 1, TRACY Method 3 and TRACY Final score). The hit rate at a particular threshold $k$ where $k$ is defined as the number of unique ground-truth suspects correctly identified within the top-$k$ ranked predictions, divided by the total number of ground-truth suspects. A prediction is considered a hit if a suspect from the ground-truth set appears in the top-$k$ list sorted by feature-based scores. The ranking scores are computed as weighted combinations of different feature values (e.g., degree centrality, call proximity to crime, call duration), and multiple weight configurations are evaluated. This approach allows measuring how effectively each feature or combination of features helps surface true suspects early in the ranked list. Notably, features like Distance to Evidence and combinations such as A1 + A2 + A3 show consistently higher hit rates, especially at broader thresholds (e.g., Top-10 or Top-20), indicating strong discriminatory power.

**Table 1.** Suspect Identification Rate for Different Features Across Various Top-$k$ Thresholds Across Platforms. This measures the Top-$k$ Suspect Identification Rates Across Platforms and Feature Categories

| Scoring Systems | Category of Features | Normalised Feature | Hit Rate @1 | Hit Rate @5 | Hit Rate @10 | Hit Rate @20 |
|---|---|---|---|---|---|---|
| TRACY Method 1 | Evidence Based | Spatio Temporal | 0.00 | 0.33 | 0.33 | 0.67 |
| TRACY Method 3 | Network Based | Degree Centrality (N1) | 0.00 | 0.33 | 0.33 | 0.67 |
| | | Page Rank (N2) | 0.00 | 0.00 | 0.33 | 0.67 |
| | | N1 + N2 | 0.00 | 0.00 | 0.67 | 0.67 |
| | Call Based | Calls Near Crime (A1) | 0.00 | 0.33 | 0.67 | 0.67 |
| | | Avg Call Duration (A2) | 0.00 | 0.00 | 0.00 | 0.33 |
| | | Distance To Evidence (A3) | 0.33 | 0.67 | 1.00 | 1.00 |
| | | A1 + A2 + A3 | 0.00 | 0.33 | 0.67 | 1.00 |
| TRACY Final | Graph Based | N1 + N2 | 0.000 | 0.33 | 0.67 | 0.67 |
| | Call Based | A1 + A2 + A3 | 0.00 | 0.33 | 0.67 | 1.00 |

## 9 Visualization of Suspects

Figure 5 shows the network after applying the TRACY Method 1. Each **node** represents an individual, with **edges** indicating communication interactions, including content and non-content data. Red nodes mark suspects, while gray nodes are non-suspects. Edge **thickness** reflects interaction frequency—thicker edges mean more frequent communications or physical contact.

Two areas stand out: region **(a)** features suspect node 5000000 with many strong connections, indicating a central role, while region **(b)** shows non-suspect

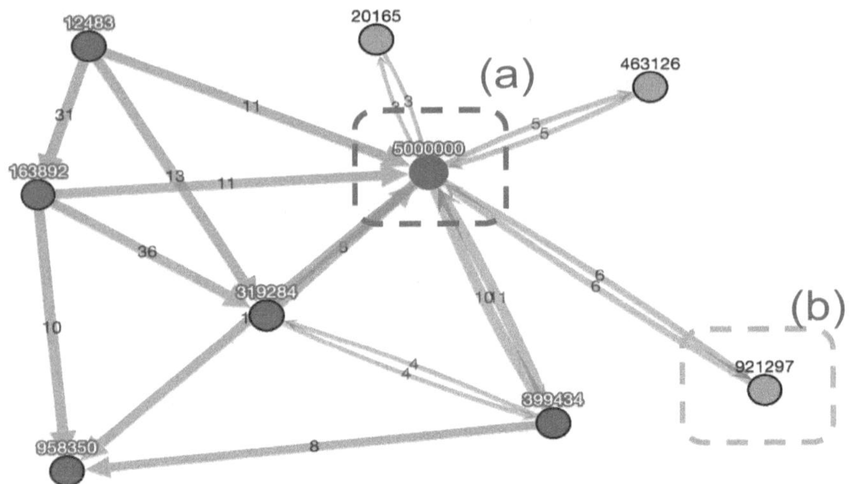


**Fig. 5.** Spotlight Visualization of CDR for terminal 500000 from TRACY Canvas.

node 921297 with fewer, weaker ties. This highlights TRACY's effectiveness in identifying key suspicious individuals within the network.

## 10 Conclusions

In this paper, we present TRACY, a significant advancement in leveraging non-content communication data to support criminal investigations. By integrating spatial-temporal proximity analysis, co-location detection, and network analysis into a unified scoring system, TRACY effectively identifies and prioritizes suspects. The three proposed core methods are combined into a comprehensive scoring mechanism: Method-1, assesses individual proximity to evidence points; Method-2, detects co-located pairs to infer coordination; and Method-3, employs network analysis to evaluate influence and connectivity. This robust approach enables investigators to prioritize suspects based on both physical movement and digital communication patterns. Complementing these analytical methods, the TRACY Canvas visualization tool provides an intuitive platform for exploring suspect relationships and integrating multiple evidence views, thereby facilitating easier interpretation and decision-making. Evaluation results on synthetic case studies demonstrate that TRACY reliably detects true suspects with high accuracy, with detection rates significantly improving when multiple features are combined. Overall, TRACY proves to be a practical and effective solution that accelerates investigative processes while respecting legal privacy standards.

**Acknowledgements.** This work was supported by the European Health and Digital Executive Agency (HADEA) under the Commission Digital Europe Programme (DIGITAL) with grant agreement No. 101102641 (project TRACY - a big-data analyTics from base-stations Registrations And Cdrs e-evidence sYstem, 2023–2025).

## References


1. Amiri, H., Yang, R., Züfle, A.: GeoLife+: large-scale simulated trajectory datasets calibrated to the GeoLife dataset. In: Proceedings of the 7th ACM SIGSPATIAL International Workshop on GeoSpatial Simulation, pp. 25–28 (2024)
2. Arnold, L., Hollick, M., Classen, J.: Catch you cause i can: busting rogue base stations using cellguard and the apple cell location database. In: Proceedings of the 27th International Symposium on Research in Attacks, Intrusions and Defenses, RAID 2024, pp. 613–629. Association for Computing Machinery, New York, NY, USA (2024). https://doi.org/10.1145/3678890.3678898
3. Du, X., Hargreaves, C., Sheppard, J., Scanlon, M.: TraceGen: user activity emulation for digital forensic test image generation. Forensic Sci. Int. Digit. Invest. **38**, 301133 (2021)
4. Eagle, N., Pentland, A.S., Lazer, D.: Inferring friendship network structure by using mobile phone data. Proc. Natl. Acad. Sci. **106**(36), 15274–15278 (2009)
5. Faubert, C., Décary-Hétu, D., Malm, A., Ratcliffe, J., Dupont, B.: Law enforcement and disruption of offline and online activities: a review of contemporary challenges. In: Cybercrime in Context: The Human Factor in Victimization, Offending, and Policing, pp. 351–370 (2021)
6. Frith, J.: Communicating through location: the understood meaning of the foursquare check-in. J. Comput. Mediat. Commun. **19**(4), 890–905 (2014)
7. Göbel, T., Breitinger, F., Baier, H.: Optimising data set creation in the cybersecurity landscape with a special focus on digital forensics: principles, characteristics, and use cases. Forensic Sci. Int. Digit. Invest. **52**, 301882 (2025)
8. Guild, E., Kuskonmaz, E., Mitsilegas, V., Vavoula, N., et al.: Data retention and the future of large-scale surveillance: the evolution and contestation of judicial benchmarks. Queen Mary Law Research Paper (372) (2021)
9. Kapp, A., Hansmeyer, J., Mihaljević, H.: Generative models for synthetic urban mobility data: a systematic literature review. ACM Comput. Surv. **56**(4), 1–37 (2023)
10. Karagiannis, C., Vergidis, K.: Digital evidence and cloud forensics: contemporary legal challenges and the power of disposal. Information **12**(5), 181 (2021)
11. Kiukkonen, N., Blom, J., Dousse, O., Gatica-Perez, D., Laurila, J.: Towards rich mobile phone datasets: Lausanne data collection campaign. In: Proceedings of the ICPS, Berlin, vol. 68, no. 7 (2010)
12. Lara, A.S., Motlicek, P., Sanchez-Cortes, D., Rangappa, P., Madikeri, S., Khalil, D.: Tracy canvas: a criminal network visualization tool. Idiap-RR Idiap-RR-03-2025, Idiap, May 2025. https://publications.idiap.ch/publications/show/5598
13. Madikeri, S., et al.: Autocrime-open multimodal platform for combating organized crime. Forensic Sci. Int. Digit. Invest. **54**, 301937 (2025)
14. Motlicek, P., et al.: ROXSD: the ROXANNE multimodal and simulated dataset for advancing criminal investigations. In: The Speaker and Language Recognition Workshop (Odyssey 2024), pp. 17–24 (2024). https://doi.org/10.21437/odyssey.2024-3
15. Moubarak, N.N.I., Omar, N.M.M., Youssef, V.N.: Smartphone-sensor-based human activities classification for forensics: a machine learning approach. J. Electr. Syst. Inf. Technol. **11**(1), 33 (2024)
16. Mylonas, A., Meletiadis, V., Tsoumas, B., Mitrou, L., Gritzalis, D.: Smartphone forensics: a proactive investigation scheme for evidence acquisition. In: Gritzalis, D., Furnell, S., Theoharidou, M. (eds.) SEC 2012. IAICT, vol. 376, pp. 249–260. Springer, Heidelberg (2012). https://doi.org/10.1007/978-3-642-30436-1_21

17. Rangappa, P., et al.: Detecting criminal networks via non-content communication data analysis techniques from the TRACY project. In: Goel, S., Uzun, E., Xie, M., Sarkar, S. (eds.) Digital Forensics and Cyber Crime, ICDF2C 2024. Lecture Notes of the Institute for Computer Sciences, Social Informatics and Telecommunications Engineering, vol 613. Springer, Cham (2025). https://doi.org/10.1007/978-3-031-89363-6_20
18. Ratti, C., Pulselli, R.M., Williams, S., Frenchman, D.: Mobile landscapes: using location data from cell phones for urban analysis. Environ. Plann. B. Plann. Des. **33**(5), 727–748 (2006)
19. Salt, S.: Social Location Marketing: Outshining Your Competitors on Foursquare, Gowalla, Yelp & Other Location Sharing Sites. Pearson Education (2011)
20. Song, C., Qu, Z., Blumm, N., Barabási, A.L.: Limits of predictability in human mobility. Science **327**(5968), 1018–1021 (2010)
21. Spaulding, J.S.: Spatio-Temporal Analysis of Crime Incidents for Forensic Investigation. West Virginia University (2020)
22. Wu, J., Abrar, S.M., Awasthi, N., Frias-Martinez, E., Frias-Martinez, V.: Enhancing short-term crime prediction with human mobility flows and deep learning architectures. EPJ Data Sci. **11**(1), 53 (2022)
23. Zhang, J., Luo, Y.: Degree centrality, betweenness centrality, and closeness centrality in social network. In: 2017 2nd International Conference on Modelling, Simulation and Applied Mathematics (MSAM2017), pp. 300–303. Atlantis Press (2017)
24. Zhang, P., Wang, T., Yan, J.: PageRank centrality and algorithms for weighted, directed networks. XXPhys. A **586**, 126438 (2022)
25. Zheng, Y., Xie, X., Ma, W.Y., et al.: GeoLife: a collaborative social networking service among user, location and trajectory. IEEE Data Eng. Bull. **33**(2), 32–39 (2010)

# Legal, Policy, and AI Governance in Digital Forensics: Studies Bridging AI Governance, Digital Law, Compliance, and Socio-technical Policy

# Retrospective Analysis of Legal Documents Using Hybrid AI - A Preliminary Empirical Study of Historical Search Warrant Processing

Md. Ashiqur Rahman[1](✉), Gokila Dorai[1], Thomas E. Kadri[2], Dane R. Thorley[3], John B. Meixner Jr.[2], Miguel de Figueiredo[4], and Gagan Agrawal[2]

[1] Augusta University, Augusta, USA
{mdrahman,gdorai}@augusta.edu
[2] University of Georgia, Athens, USA
{tek,John.Meixner,gagrawal}@uga.edu
[3] Brigham Young University, Provo, USA
thorleyd@law.byu.edu
[4] University of Connecticut, Mansfield, USA
miguel.defigueiredo@uconn.edu

**Abstract.** This study presents *iDX*: Intelligent Data Extraction, a hybrid AI framework which is an early-stage proof-of-concept, combining Regular Expression techniques with Large Language Models for automated search warrant analysis. Using 123 expert-annotated search warrant cases from Utah's E-Warrants system (2013–2020), we evaluated multiple extraction methodologies including base and fine-tuned LLAMA3.1 and PHI4 models where we are extracting data elements for retrospective empirical legal research. The extraction targets include warrant scope indicators, digital search determinations, and document structural elements. Automation is important because manual analysis of thousands of historical warrants is impractical for researchers studying patterns in judicial practices over time. The framework processes 94 queries across objective and subjective legal analysis tasks. The *iDX* framework employs majority voting to select optimal extraction methods, achieving 86.25% accuracy on objective factual extraction tasks and 81.10 BERT F1-score on subjective legal analysis tasks outperforming individual baseline models. Human evaluation preferences aligned with *iDX* automated selections in approximately 40% of cases. This research provides preliminary empirical evidence for hybrid AI approaches in retrospective legal document processing, offering a methodology for empirical legal research and historical warrant analysis.

**Keywords:** AI in Government · Legal Document Processing · Search Warrants · Digital Government · Natural Language Processing · Judicial AI


K.-K. R. Choo et al. (Eds.): ICDF2C 2025, LNICST 686, pp. 313–332, 2026.
https://doi.org/10.1007/978-3-032-22545-0_19

## 1 Introduction

Large Language Models (LLMs) have emerged as transformative technologies for government operations, offering unprecedented opportunities to modernize public sector document processing and enhance decision-support systems [36]. As government agencies face mounting pressures to deliver efficient services with constrained resources, AI technologies present viable pathways for improving operational capabilities while maintaining public trust and democratic accountability [45]. LLMs demonstrate exceptional performance in language processing tasks including translation, summarization, and analysis, yet their application in government contexts requires careful consideration of unique public sector requirements including transparency, statutory compliance, and data sovereignty. However, successful implementation in sensitive government domains remains limited by challenges specific to public administration and democratic governance.

Legal document processing presents particularly complex challenges for LLM implementation, where standard AI approaches often fail to meet the precision and reliability standards required for retrospective legal analysis. Although LLMs excel at general text processing, their performance diminishes when they are confronted with specialized legal document analysis. This limitation is especially pronounced in historical document analysis for empirical legal research, where constitutional protections and precise interpretation of legal standards including probable cause and Fourth Amendment requirements must be accurately extracted from historical records. Addressing these challenges requires specialized approaches that integrate domain-specific knowledge while maintaining the transparency and accountability essential for empirical legal research.

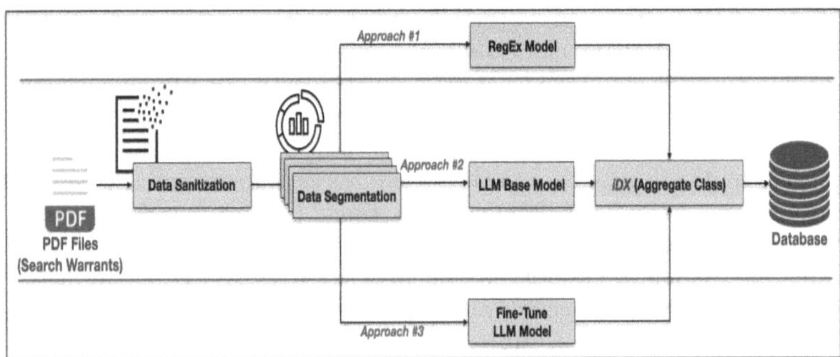


**Fig. 1.** *iDX* Architecture.

This research addresses critical gaps in the search warrant process within increasingly complex digital environments, where vast data must be balanced against precise legal boundaries. Prior studies reveal systemic shortcomings: [44], found infrequent warrant rejections, reliance on unsworn anonymous tips, and minimal judicial limitation of search scope; [12], highlighted the routine use of boilerplate language over concrete facts despite efforts to corroborate tips; [31], demonstrated that while judicial ideology does not affect wiretap approvals, African

American judges receive significantly fewer applications, suggesting structural bias; and [18], revealed that 98% of warrant applications are approved, often within minutes, indicating superficial judicial review. These findings question the effectiveness of the current review system and highlight the need for more robust safeguards. This study proposes a digitally managed, locally deployed corpus of search warrants to uncover latent trends such as the breadth of digital evidence requests. The proposed hybrid methodology integrates domain-specific legal knowledge while preserving the transparency and auditability required for judicial processes. This research focuses on retrospective analysis of historical warrant practices rather than prospective judicial assistance tools.

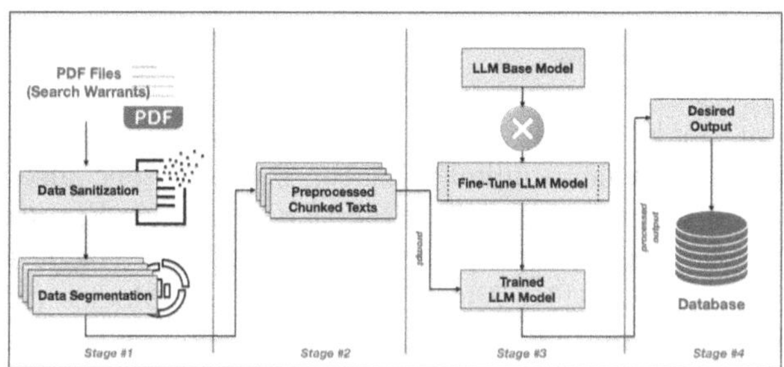


(a) Local Deployment of Base and Fine-Tune LLM models

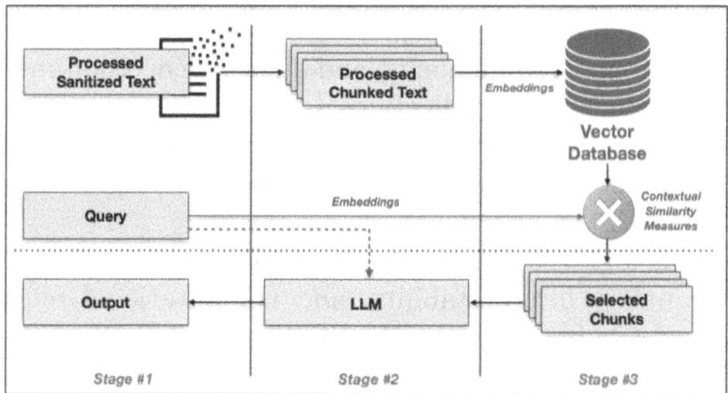


(b) Chunk Embeddings

**Fig. 2.** System Architecture Components.

This paper introduces *iDX* - Intelligent Data Extraction (Fig. 1), a hybrid framework designed for search warrant analysis for automating the extraction and analysis of warrant patterns for studying historical judicial practices and to enable large-scale empirical research on warrant approval patterns and digital evidence trends. The hybrid approach combines Regular Expression (RegEx) reliability for structured elements with Large Language Models (LLMs) contextual understanding for legal language interpretation, enabling researchers to analyze both factual and interpretive elements across large historical documents. *iDX* integrates multiple extraction methodologies including base LLAMA3.1, fine-tuned LLAMA3.1, base PHI4, and fine-tuned PHI4 variants that leverage contextual reasoning capabilities. *iDX* employs a majority-voting mechanism to select the optimal data extraction method for each query. *iDX* achieves 86.25% accuracy on objective factual extraction queries and 81.10 BERT F1-score on subjective legal analysis tasks compared to 79.63% and 73.29% for baseline LLMs.

The remainder of this paper is organized as follows: Sect. 2 reviews related work in legal document processing and AI applications. Section 3 examines search warrant analysis challenges and requirements. Section 4 presents the preliminaries, while Sect. 5 discusses the details of *iDX* architecture. Section 6 presents the emprical analysis, limitations and implications; then we conclude with Sect. 7.

## 2 Literature Review

Legal document analysis has evolved from keyword search to sophisticated automated systems, yet faces unique challenges due to specialized terminology and constitutional requirements [22]. Traditional Regular Expression (RegEx) approaches provide deterministic pattern matching but struggle with semantic nuances in legal language [11]. While Large Language Models (LLMs) demonstrate potential for contextual understanding and domain-specific terminology processing [19], their application in judicial contexts requires careful consideration of accuracy, interpretability, and consistency standards [40].

Government AI implementation presents distinct challenges including data sovereignty, transparency requirements, and auditable decision-making processes that differ from commercial applications [13]. Judicial systems demand both technical precision and constitutional compliance, particularly in search warrant processing where Fourth Amendment protections require precise probable cause analysis [28,33].

Hybrid methodologies combining multiple AI techniques have shown promise in balancing accuracy, interpretability, and computational efficiency [14,24]. The integration of rule-based methods with machine learning approaches offers advantages for legal document processing by providing both deterministic reliability and contextual reasoning flexibility [16]. These hybrid approaches are particularly relevant for government applications requiring explainable AI systems and transparent decision mechanisms.

## 3 Application Scenario and Challenges

Legal document analysis presents unique challenges due to specialized terminology, complex linguistic structures, and jurisdictional variations that distinguish legal texts from general domain applications [21]. Search warrants exemplify these complexities through their integration of procedural requirements, statutory references, and constitutional standards. [43] reveals that individual warrants frequently cite multiple Utah Code provisions, including Sects. 76-6-602 (retail theft), 76-6-408 (possession of stolen property), 58-37-8 (drug possession), and 41-6A-502 (driving under the influence). Standard language models

**Table 1.** Sample Queries (Questions 1–94) (detailed in [9]).

| sl. | Query Types | Query | Mapped Searching Space |
|---|---|---|---|
| 1 | Objective | EXTRACT THE 'AFFIDAVIT' PORTION FROM THE TEXT. | Entire Text |
| 2 | | EXTRACT THE 'SEARCH WARRANT' PORTION FROM THE TEXT. | Entire Text |
| 3 | | EXTRACT THE 'RETURN' PORTION FROM THE TEXT. | Entire Text |
| 4 | | WHAT IS THE AFFIDAVIT SUBMISSION TIME IN YYYY-MM-DD:HH:MM FORMAT? | Affidavit |
| 5 | | WHAT IS THE NAME OF THE 'COUNTY' MENTIONED IN THE TEXT? | Affidavit |
| 6 | | WHAT IS THE RANK OF THE AFFIANT? | Affidavit |
| 7 | | WHAT ORGANIZATION DOES THE AFFIANT WORK FOR? | Affidavit |
| 8 | | WHAT IS THE NAME OF THE AFFIANT IN THE FORM OF FIRST NAME, MIDDLE NAME, LAST NAME? | Affidavit |
| ... | | | |
| 40 | Subjective | IS THIS AFFIDAVIT 'DIGITAL' OR 'NOT DIGITAL'? IF THIS AFFIDAVIT REQUESTS TO SEARCH OR SEIZE ANY 'DIGITAL' ITEMS, THEN THE WARRANT IS 'DIGITAL'. | Affidavit |
| 41 | | IF THE AFFIDAVIT SEEKS TO SEARCH SOMETHING DIGITAL, DOES IT SEEK TO SEARCH DATA FROM A DEVICE? | Affidavit |
| 42 | | IF THE AFFIDAVIT SEEKS TO SEARCH SOMETHING DIGITAL, DOES IT SEEK TO SEARCH A USER'S DATA STORED BY A THIRD-PARTY INTERMEDIARY? | Affidavit |
| ... | | | |
| 65 | Objective | WHAT IS THE ITEM OR ITEMS REQUESTED TO BE SEARCHED IN THE 'WARRANT'? | Search Warrant |
| 66 | Subjective | IS THIS WARRANT 'DIGITAL' OR 'NOT DIGITAL'? IF THIS WARRANT REQUESTS TO SEARCH OR SEIZE ANY 'DIGITAL' ITEMS, THEN THE WARRANT IS 'DIGITAL'. | Search Warrant |
| 67 | | IF THE WARRANT SEEKS TO SEARCH SOMETHING DIGITAL, DOES IT SEEK TO SEARCH DATA FROM A DEVICE? | Search Warrant |
| ... | | | |

require domain-specific adaptation to handle legal precision requirements, statutory citation patterns, and constitutional language governing warrant validity.

This preliminary study examines historical search warrants as the primary case study for evaluating *iDX* capabilities in retrospective legal analysis. Search warrants represent fundamental law enforcement tools governed by Fourth Amendment protections against unreasonable searches and seizures [1]. Legal warrants require judicial determination of probable cause, defined as a reasonable likelihood that sought evidence exists at the specified location [2,3], and must satisfy the particularity requirement by specifying the place to be searched and items to be seized [1,4].

Courts recognize that warrants containing digital devices raise unique Fourth Amendment concerns regarding scope and particularity [5]. This makes digital warrants compelling for automated analysis. The warrant process generates three document types: the *Affidavit* (sworn statement establishing probable cause), the

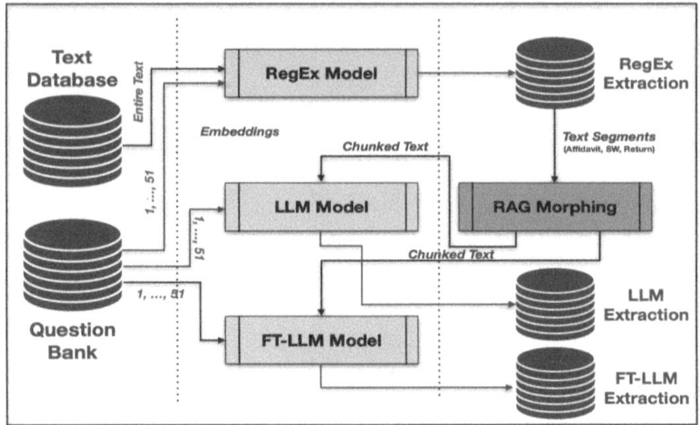


**Fig. 3.** RegEx Segmentations used to Reduce Search Domains.

*Search Warrant* (judicial authorization), and the *Return* (execution documentation).

This research utilizes Utah's E-Warrants system, which provides comprehensive electronic warrant documentation [18]. The system enables digital submission, judicial review, and approval processes through structured forms, generating the legal documents analyzed by the *iDX* system while maintaining traditional procedural requirements. In summary, this research analyzes historical search warrant documents from Utah's E-Warrants system (2013–2020) to identify empirical patterns in digital evidence request trends, warrant document structures, warrant scope, characteristics, and judicial approval processes over time.

### 3.1 Dataset and Training Set

The study employs warrant documents from Utah's Xchange database spanning December 1, 2013, to January 29, 2020, comprising approximately 30,000 approved warrants with affidavits ranging from 279 to 18,511 words (median: 979) [42]. The dataset encompasses violent, property, drug, and motor vehicle offenses, with motor vehicle cases representing the most frequent category. Metadata including warrant numbers, investigating officers, agencies, court locations, and processing dates were obtained from the Utah Department of Public Safety for validation purposes.

From this corpus, 123 complete warrant sets were selected for analysis, labeled and hand-coded by academic experts in law, with 70 cases allocated for LLAMA3.1 and PHI4 model training and 35 reserved for testing. Moreover, 18 case files are considered for human evaluation. Training data employed the Alpaca and Parquet prompt format with paraphrased queries to address linguistic variation [10,38]. Extraction targets and query specifications are detailed in Sect. 3.2.

### 3.2 Queries

The evaluation framework comprises 94 queries categorized as objective (factual extraction) or subjective (summarization and analysis), as detailed in Table 1. The term 'objective' refers to questions that prompt the model to directly extract information from the warrant without requiring contextual interpretation. In contrast, 'subjective' questions involve a degree of analytical reasoning over the warrant's content. For example, "WHAT IS THE ITEM OR ITEMS REQUESTED TO BE SEARCHED IN THE 'WARRANT'?" is a typical objective question, as it seeks straightforward information. Conversely, "IS THIS AFFIDAVIT 'DIGITAL' OR 'NOT DIGITAL'?" is a subjective question, requiring interpretation to determine whether the requested items are digital in nature. Each query targets specific document sections to optimize search efficiency. To assess generalization, additional evaluation metrics (BERT, BLEU, ROUGE) are reported [9]. Query dependencies were identified to support chain-of-thought reasoning, as expressed in Eqs. 1–21. These relationships enable sequential question processing where prior responses inform subsequent queries through chat prompts, maintaining logical consistency across related extractions.

$$Q_{39} \leftarrow Q_{40} \cdots (1) \quad Q_{65} \leftarrow Q_{66} \cdots (8) \quad Q_{87} \leftarrow Q_{88} \cdots (15)$$
$$Q_{40} \leftarrow Q_{41} \cdots (2) \quad Q_{66} \leftarrow Q_{67} \cdots (9) \quad Q_{88} \leftarrow Q_{89} \cdots (16)$$
$$Q_{41} \leftarrow Q_{42} \cdots (3) \quad Q_{67} \leftarrow Q_{68} \cdots (10) \quad Q_{89} \leftarrow Q_{90} \cdots (17)$$
$$Q_{39} \leftarrow Q_{43} \cdots (4) \quad Q_{65} \leftarrow Q_{69} \cdots (11) \quad Q_{87} \leftarrow Q_{91} \cdots (18)$$
$$Q_{39} \leftarrow Q_{44} \cdots (5) \quad Q_{65} \leftarrow Q_{70} \cdots (12) \quad Q_{87} \leftarrow Q_{92} \cdots (19)$$
$$Q_{41} \leftarrow Q_{45} \cdots (6) \quad Q_{67} \leftarrow Q_{71} \cdots (13) \quad Q_{89} \leftarrow Q_{93} \cdots (20)$$
$$Q_{45} \leftarrow Q_{46} \cdots (7) \quad Q_{71} \leftarrow Q_{72} \cdots (14) \quad Q_{93} \leftarrow Q_{94} \cdots (21)$$

## 4 Preliminaries

***Large Language Model (LLM):*** This research employs LLAMA3.1 and PHI4 for local deployment to ensure data sovereignty and minimize security risks when processing sensitive legal information [6,30,39,45]. Local deployment addresses confidentiality requirements inherent in warrant data containing personal identifiers, investigative details, and law enforcement information. The approach leverages the models' contextual reasoning capabilities for legal document analysis while maintaining complete control over data processing environments, as illustrated in Fig. 2a. OLLAMA [34] provides an additional isolation layer for local LLAMA3.1 and PHI4 deployment, ensuring warrant data processing occurs within controlled environments. This architecture maintains data sovereignty while enabling advanced language model capabilities for legal document analysis.

***Embeddings:*** The framework employs *nomic-embed-text* embeddings with an 8192-token context length, which demonstrates superior performance compared to OpenAI's *Ada-002* and *text-embedding-3-small* on both short and long context tasks [7,32]. Input texts are embedded without modification to preserve original legal language and maintain semantic accuracy throughout the analysis process.

***Fine-Tuning LLMs:*** The LLAMA3.1(8B) Instruct model and PHI4(14B) undergoes fine-tuning using QLoRA on a 24GB consumer GPU to incorporate legal domain knowledge [23]. The approach employs 16-bit quantization to balance computational efficiency with accuracy requirements for legal document analysis. This configuration captures domain-specific legal terminology and warrant analysis patterns while maintaining practical deployment constraints.

***Retrieval-Augmented Generation (RAG):*** enhances language model performance by combining parametric and non-parametric memory components [27]. The implementation focuses search scope on relevant document sections while incorporating domain-specific legal knowledge, improving extraction accuracy for warrant analysis tasks.

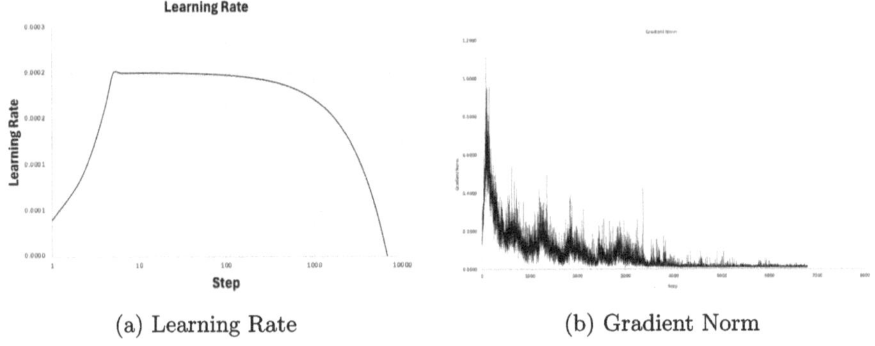


(a) Learning Rate (b) Gradient Norm

**Fig. 4.** Training Learning Rate and Gradient Norm of LLAMA3.1.

***Prompt Engineering:*** The implementation uses both LLAMA3.1 and PHI4's native prompt syntax with "Chain-of-Thought" reasoning for complex queries [15,37]. The parameters included *temperature* is set to 0 for deterministic output, context length is maximized at 8192 tokens, and responses are limited to 200 tokens for objective queries, while the maximum limit is assigned for subjective analysis. Fixed *seed* values ensure reproducible results throughout the training and inference phases. The chat template is organized using *system*, *user*, and *assistant* roles to align with specific experimental conditions. Context, descriptions, and prompts are formatted as *user* messages, while corresponding predefined responses are assigned to the *assistant* role. The *system* role sets the tone of responses, the *user* role presents the input content and queries, and the *assistant* role is designated exclusively for use in the dry-run experiment.

# 5 *iDX* – Intelligent Data Extraction

Search warrant documents are segmented into chunks of 10 sentences with single-sentence overlap to maintain contextual continuity. Chunk embeddings are stored in ChromaDB for vector-based retrieval during inference [8], as illustrated in

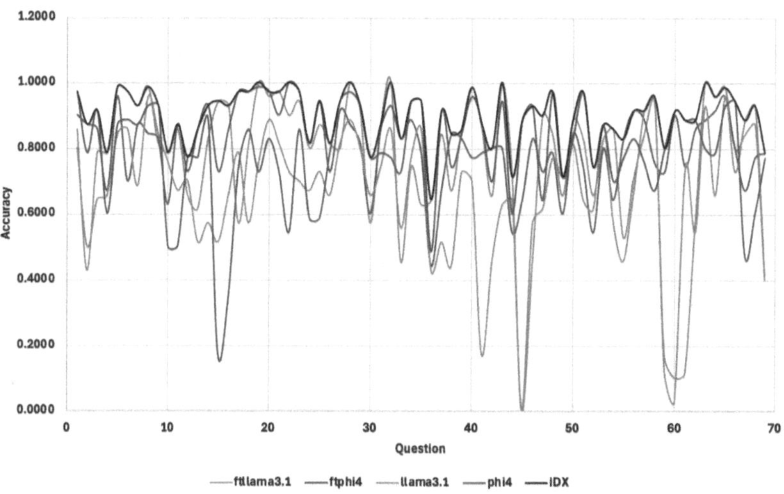


**Fig. 5.** Training Accuracy (Objective).

Fig. 2b. The system selects the 10 most relevant chunks using cosine similarity between chunk embeddings and query representations. When the accumulated chunks exceed token limits, the selection count is reduced iteratively using $\lceil(\text{chunk count})/2\rceil$ until constraints are satisfied, as detailed in Algorithm 1. The *iDX* framework integrates five extraction methodologies: RegEx, LLAMA3.1, Fine-tuned LLAMA3.1, PHI4, Fine-tuned PHI4 with chain-of-thought reasoning capabilities. The system employs majority voting to select the optimal extraction method for each query, with implementation details provided in Sect. 6.

***RegEx Data Extraction:*** Regular Expression extraction captures data between specified markers using seven patterns designed for the 94-query evaluation framework. The approach identified three consistent patterns for Questions #1–3, achieving 100% accuracy with minimal computational overhead. Extracted data serve as input for subsequent methodologies. [9], details the regular expressions employed in this research. Figure 3 illustrates the domain reduction framework. Although the warrant structure remains consistent, variations in the writing style from 2013 to 2019 introduce processing complexity; the performance analysis is presented in Sect. 6.

***LLMs Data Extraction:*** LLAMA3.1 (Meta-Llama-3.1-8B-Instruct) and PHI4 (14B) provide contextual reasoning capabilities that address RegEx limitations in unstructured text processing. The implementation incorporates Retrieval-Augmented Generation to refine search domains and optimize computational efficiency for both objective and subjective queries. Chain-of-thought reasoning proves particularly effective for questions 41–48, 66–72, 75–76, and 88–94, enhancing accuracy for subjective analysis tasks. Performance evaluation is detailed in Sect. 6.

***Fine-Tuned LLMs Data Extraction:*** Fine-tuned LLAMA3.1 and Fine-tuned PHI4 addresses domain-specific limitations in legal document analysis, particularly for concepts related to warrant scope. The model underwent few-shot learning using 70 annotated warrant cases. Training data included manual extractions for all 94 evaluation questions, with subjective queries supplemented by definitional context and analogical examples. Confidentiality constraints prevent public dataset release. Dry-run addresses potential hallucination and linguistic inconsistencies in text generation. The approach employs 14 pre-labeled warrant cases (two per year, 2013–2019). These cases provide exemplar *assistant* responses to establish appropriate linguistic tone and reasoning patterns before inference.

**Algorithm 1 : Text Compression**

```
// number of chunks to be selected (m = 10)
// number of chunks selected m
1: Input: text chunks C = {c_1, c_2, c_3, ..., c_n}
2: for each chunk c_i in C do
3:     rank_i ← cosine_similarity(c_i, prompt)
4: end for
5: S ← sort_chunk_by_rank(C)
6: while m > 1 do
7:     selected chunk Ŝ ← top(S, m)
8:     transient text T ← concat(Ŝ)    [Ŝ = {ŝ_1, ŝ_2, ..., ŝ_m}]
9:     token count t ← count(T)
10:    if t ≤ LLM token limit then
11:        break
12:    else
13:        m ← max(1, ⌈m/2⌉)
14:    end if
15: end while
16: return m
```

***iDX* - Methodology:** The *iDX* framework integrates RegEx techniques with the contextual reasoning capabilities of LLM through a hybrid aggregator approach (Fig. 1). The system evaluates the accuracy of the extraction methodologies per query and employs majority voting to select optimal approaches, as detailed in Algorithm 2. Evaluation metrics include accuracy scores for objective queries and BERT scores for subjective queries [46]. BLEU and ROUGE-L scores assess the quality of text generation between models and increase the reliability of the proposed methodology [20,26,35]. Performance comparisons between the training and inference phases are presented in Figs. 6 and 8.

The semantic consistency between the LLM responses ($S$) and the input text ($T$) ensures the validity of the extracted information. The *iDX* framework employs majority voting based on computational metrics (accuracy for objective queries, BERT scores for subjective queries) to automatically select the optimal model for each question. This automated selection operates independently from human evaluation, which serves purely as a validation check to assess whether computational metrics align with expert judgment. Table 2 summarizes the *iDX* selection process based on the accuracy (acc) and precision (prc) scores. While all methodologies employ RAG, only FT-LLAMA3.1 and FT-PHI4 require robust training.

## 6 Empirical Analysis

***Evaluation Metrics:*** The evaluation employed 94 queries (69 objective, 25 subjective) from the test set. The evaluation framework employs distinct metrics tailored to question types. For objective queries requiring factual extraction, *accuracy* measures the percentage of model responses that perfectly match labeled ground truth, as these questions have definitive correct answers. For subjective queries involving interpretation or analytical reasoning, we used BERT F1-scores to measure semantic similarity between responses and reference answers, as exact matching is inappropriate for open-ended analysis tasks. The evaluation also employs human reviewers (authors of this work). The human reviewers rate model responses using a five-point Likert scale for accuracy and precision. The Likert scale included five levels: Very Good (VG) for responses that are entirely accurate and highly precise; Good (G) for fully accurate responses with minor verbosity or imprecision; Moderate (M) for mostly accurate responses with minor factual gaps or redundancy; Bad (B) for partially accurate responses with noticeable errors or lack of clarity; and Very Bad (VB) for responses that are largely or entirely inaccurate, misleading, or incoherent. Because the Likert scores are assigned by human coders using relatively subjective measures (accuracy and precision), the cumulative scores presented below should be seen as a robustness check for the primary evaluation framework as opposed to a direct comparison to the primary outcomes.

**Algorithm 2** : *iDX*

1: **Input:** *prompt*: the question number
2: **Input:** *case_number*: the search warrant number
3: **procedure** *iDX*(prompt, case_number)
4: **if** the *prompt* is objective **then**
5: *accuracy_scores* ← calculate_accuracy(responses of all methodologies, manual_labels)
6: *selective_method* ← according to the highest *accuracy_scores* and *response_time*
7: **else if** the *prompt* is subjective **then**
8: *bert_scores* ← calculate_bert_score(responses of all methodologies, associated_input)
9: *selective_method* ← according to the highest *bert_scores* and *response_time*
10: **end if**
11: *master_base* ← data_extract(*case_number*, *input_text*, *prompt*, *selective_method*)
12: **end procedure**

***Quantitative Analysis:*** Fine-tuning employed a CloudLab computing system with dual 16-core AMD processors (3.00 GHz), 128 GB ECC RAM, and a 24 GB Nvidia Ampere A30 GPU [17]. Inference testing utilized an Apple M3 Pro system with 11-core CPU, 14-core integrated GPU, and 18 GB RAM. Training data comprised 16 MB JSON and Parquet files containing text-only warrant information. Training completed 3 epochs over 72 h, encompassing 11367 steps

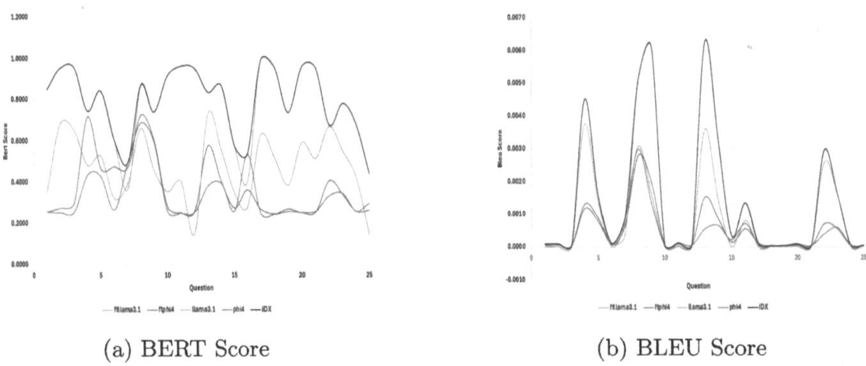

(a) BERT Score (b) BLEU Score

**Fig. 6.** Training BERT, and BLEU Score (Subjective).

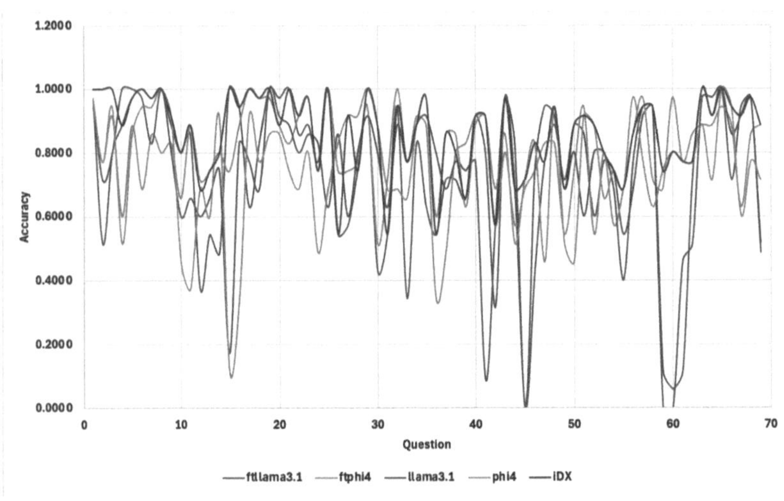


**Fig. 7.** Inferencing Accuracy (Objective).

using 16-bit QLoRA with ADAMW optimization [23,29]. The model employed 16-bit quantization for local deployable models with a learning rate of 0.00002. Figure 4 shows the declination of learning rate over training steps (logarithmic scale), with down sloped gradient norm evolution, indicating successful convergence. Mean Square Error (MSE) was employed as the training loss metric during fine-tuning, yielding final error scores of 0.003700 for FT-LLAMA3.1 and 0.004200 for FT-PHI4 after 11,367 optimization steps. The accuracy scores of the objective questions on training are shown in Fig. 5, with BERT, and BLEU scores for subjective questions are in Figs. 6. Results demonstrate FT-LLAMA3.1 superiority over baseline LLMs for objective tasks.

Testing used 35 case files with 94 queries (69 objective, 25 subjective) aligned with available metadata. Figures 7 and 8 present inference accuracy

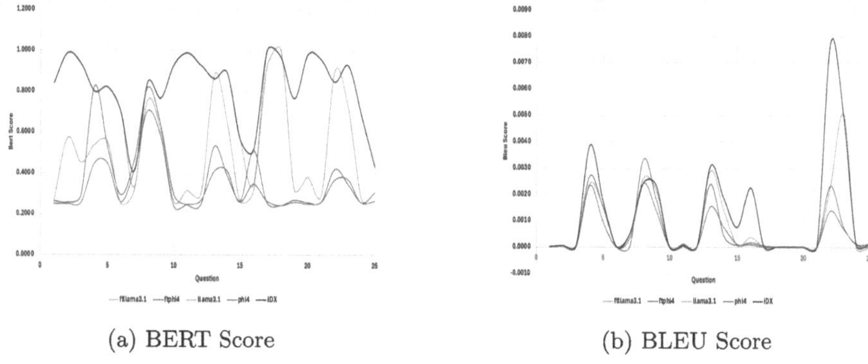


(a) BERT Score (b) BLEU Score

**Fig. 8.** Inferencing BERT, and BLEU Score (Subjective).

and reasoning performance. While objective extraction shows comparable performance across methods, FT-LLAMA3.1 achieves superior subjective analysis with enhanced legal linguistic accuracy. RegEx extraction proves highly effective for questions #1–3, achieving consistent pattern matching despite writing style variations from 2013–2019. Document structural markers remain stable, though content complexity limits RegEx applicability beyond these initial queries. Table 2 summarizes *iDX* analysis results with accuracy (acc) and precision (prc) metrics. Figure 10 presents average computational time for document chunk retrieval associated with average response time. RAG implementation reduces processing time from approximately 4 h to significantly shorter durations, demonstrating computational efficiency gains for the extraction pipeline. Evaluations revealed hallucination tendencies across LLM variants that compromise extraction reliability. While fine-tuned LLMs exhibit improved hallucination resistance, response length occasionally exceeds token constraints. The framework implements token limits and selection mechanisms to mitigate these issues, though human verification remains essential for quality assurance.

Table 2 presents cumulative accuracy results across all models and query types. The *iDX* majority voting mechanism selects optimal extraction methods based on accuracy and text generation quality metrics for each specific query. The consolidated experimental results for training and testing are illustrated in Fig. 9.

***Human Evaluation:*** To validate model performance beyond automated metrics, we conducted human evaluation involving the authors (law and computer science expertise) of this paper. Each of the 18 documents was evaluated by one evaluator among the authors in a blinded review process, with model identities concealed from evaluators to prevent bias. For each question, participants rated outputs from all four models (LLAMA3.1, FT-LLAMA3.1, PHI4, FT-PHI4) using a five-point Likert scale discussed previously. Average scores were calculated for each model per question across all participants, with the minimum possible average being 1 and the maximum possible average being 5. The

**Table 2.** textitiDX: methodology selection; textit'acc' is 'accuracy', and textit'prc' is 'precision'

| SL# | PID | type | RegEx | ftllama3.1 | | | | | | | ftphi4 | | | | | | | llama3.1 | | | | | | | phi4 | | | | | | | IDX_Model |
|---|---|---|---|---|---|---|---|---|---|---|---|---|---|---|---|---|---|---|---|---|---|---|---|---|---|---|---|---|---|---|---|---|
| | | | acc | acc | bert | | bleu | rouge-l | | | acc | bert | | bleu | rouge-l | | | acc | bert | | bleu | rouge-l | | | acc | bert | | bleu | rouge-l | | | |
| | | | | | F1 | pre | | F1 | pre | | | F1 | pre | | F1 | pre | | | F1 | pre | | F1 | pre | | | F1 | pre | | F1 | pre | | |
| 1 | 1 | | **1.0000** | 0.8571 | 0.6762 | 0.7090 | 0.0012 | 0.6762 | 0.8281 | | 0.9000 | 0.7685 | 0.7942 | 0.0011 | 0.7695 | 0.8992 | | 0.8000 | 0.6134 | 0.6736 | 0.0021 | 0.6134 | 0.7003 | | 0.9714 | 0.7507 | 0.7748 | 0.0009 | 0.7507 | 0.8934 | | **RegEx** |
| 2 | 2 | obj | **1.0000** | 0.4286 | 0.5855 | 0.7562 | 0.0420 | 0.5855 | 0.8372 | | 0.8714 | 0.6995 | 0.7966 | 0.0016 | 0.6995 | 0.7894 | | 0.5000 | 0.6000 | 0.7058 | 0.0054 | 0.6000 | 0.7794 | | 0.7857 | 0.7370 | 0.7913 | 0.0012 | 0.7370 | 0.8456 | | **RegEx** |
| 3 | 3 | | **1.0000** | 0.7857 | 0.8243 | 0.8480 | 0.0024 | 0.8243 | 0.8210 | | 0.8571 | 0.7261 | 0.7792 | 0.0021 | 0.7261 | 0.7387 | | 0.6429 | 0.6118 | 0.7375 | 0.0056 | 0.6118 | 0.8027 | | 0.9143 | 0.7741 | 0.8177 | 0.0021 | 0.7741 | 0.7892 | | **RegEx** |
| 7 | 7 | | 0.0000 | **0.9286** | 0.8753 | 0.8487 | 0.0024 | 0.8753 | 0.7946 | | 0.8714 | 0.5354 | 0.4427 | 0.0014 | 0.5354 | 0.2452 | | 0.6857 | 0.6237 | 0.5817 | 0.0028 | 0.6237 | 0.4703 | | 0.8714 | 0.6803 | 0.6372 | 0.0017 | 0.6803 | 0.5125 | | **ftllama3.1** |
| 8 | 8 | obj | 0.0000 | **0.9857** | 0.9725 | 0.9746 | 0.0144 | 0.9725 | 0.9714 | | 0.8429 | 0.6246 | 0.5739 | 0.0102 | 0.6246 | 0.4015 | | 0.9571 | 0.8854 | 0.9012 | 0.0199 | 0.8854 | 0.9214 | | 0.9286 | 0.3175 | 0.2166 | 0.0012 | 0.3175 | 0.0302 | | **ftllama3.1** |
| 41 | 41 | | 0.0000 | 0.9857 | **0.9538** | 0.9538 | 0.0000 | 0.9538 | 0.8143 | | 0.8714 | 0.2739 | 0.2155 | 0.0001 | 0.2739 | 0.0061 | | 0.8714 | 0.6856 | 0.6579 | 0.0000 | 0.6856 | 0.5071 | | 0.8286 | 0.2509 | 0.2009 | 0.0001 | 0.2509 | 0.0003 | | ftllama3.1 |
| 42 | 42 | sub | 0.0000 | 0.9857 | **0.9538** | 0.9538 | 0.0000 | 0.9538 | 0.8143 | | 0.7857 | 0.3008 | 0.2518 | 0.0000 | 0.3008 | 0.0026 | | 0.7286 | 0.6500 | 0.6141 | 0.0000 | 0.6500 | 0.4961 | | 0.8857 | 0.2544 | 0.1977 | 0.0000 | 0.2544 | 0.0012 | | ftllama3.1 |
| 50 | 50 | | 0.0000 | 0.8571 | 0.9248 | 0.9217 | 0.0016 | 0.9248 | 0.8952 | | 0.7857 | 0.8333 | 0.8189 | 0.0001 | 0.8333 | 0.7283 | | 0.1714 | 0.4394 | 0.4192 | 0.0016 | 0.4384 | 0.1774 | | **0.8714** | 0.6697 | 0.6461 | 0.0002 | 0.6697 | 0.5485 | | phi4 |
| 51 | 51 | obj | 0.0000 | 0.6571 | 0.5456 | 0.5136 | 0.0067 | 0.5456 | 0.3348 | | **0.8000** | 0.4482 | 0.3721 | 0.0018 | 0.4482 | 0.1474 | | 0.4571 | 0.3736 | 0.3315 | 0.0030 | 0.3736 | 0.1056 | | 0.7000 | 0.4103 | 0.3421 | 0.0019 | 0.4103 | 0.1230 | | ftphi4 |
| 90 | 90 | | 0.0000 | 1.0000 | **0.9493** | 0.9493 | 0.0000 | 0.9493 | 0.7857 | | 0.7286 | 0.2526 | 0.1977 | 0.0000 | 0.2526 | 0.0004 | | 0.7857 | 0.5125 | 0.4734 | 0.0000 | 0.5125 | 0.3365 | | 0.9000 | 0.2573 | 0.2018 | 0.0000 | 0.2573 | 0.0001 | | ftllama3.1 |
| 91 | 91 | sub | 0.0000 | 0.6000 | **0.6739** | 0.6643 | 0.0029 | 0.6739 | 0.5066 | | 0.7000 | 0.4050 | 0.3211 | 0.0007 | 0.4050 | 0.1232 | | 0.7000 | 0.6666 | 0.6597 | 0.0026 | 0.6666 | 0.4944 | | 0.7714 | 0.3326 | 0.2342 | 0.0004 | 0.3326 | 0.0292 | | ftllama3.1 |

model achieving the highest average score for each question was selected and compared with the *iDX*'s preference for that specific query, implementing a human-validated majority voting mechanism.

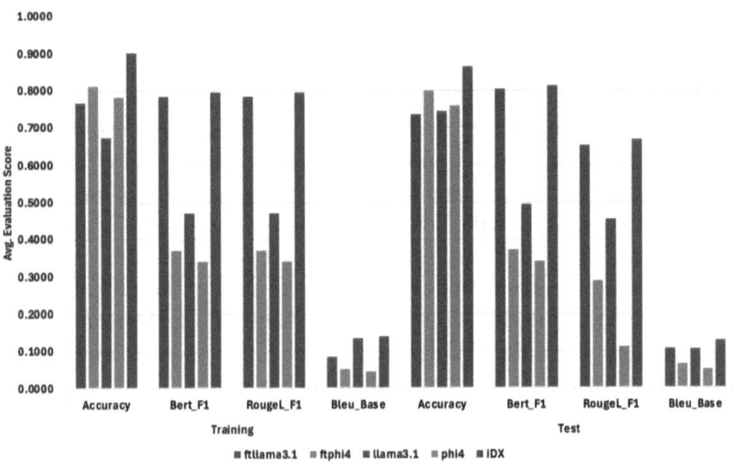


**Fig. 9.** Average Evaluation Scores.

Figure 11 presents the question-wise average human evaluation scores, with cumulative means of 3.73 for LLAMA3.1, 3.98 for FT-LLAMA3.1, 2.17 for PHI4, and 3.29 for FT-PHI4, indicating that FTLLAMA3.1 performs most satisfactorily among individual models. The *iDX* framework, which selects the best response across all models, achieves an average of 3.56 - slightly higher than the "Moderate" threshold on the Likert scale. Statistical analysis using the Kruskal-Wallis [25] test yields an H-statistic of 1136.64 with a p-value of 4.092e−246, confirming significant differences in average human evaluation scores across models. Additionally, Fig. 12 displays model averages as rated by each participant, with a Kruskal-Wallis H-statistic of 231.18 and a p-value of 5.975e−48, indicating significant variation across participants while affirming consistent model rankings.

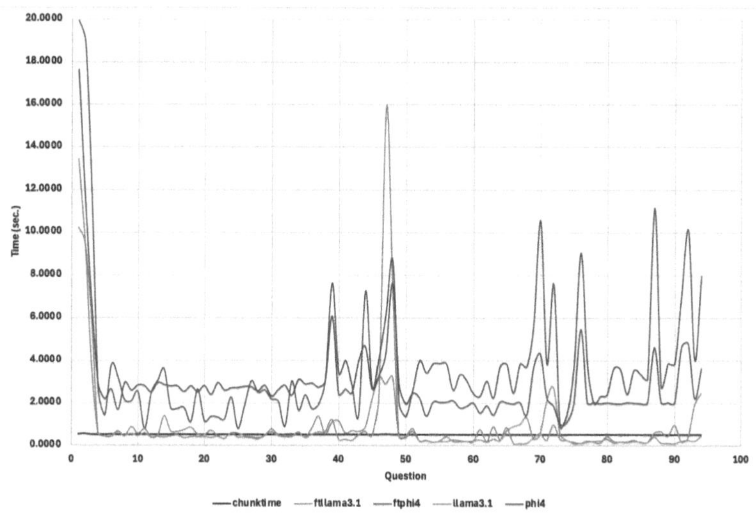


**Fig. 10.** Chunk Retrieval vs Average Response Time by LLMs.

***Results:*** The *iDX* framework achieved 86.25% accuracy on 69 objective queries, significantly outperforming baseline LLAMA3.1 and PHI4. For 25 subjective queries, the framework obtained an average BERT F1-score of 81.10. Human evaluation preferences aligned with *iDX* automated selections in 37 of 94 cases (39.4%), with mismatches occurring in 57 cases (60.6%). This finding highlights the importance of human validation in legal document processing, where automated performance metrics may not fully represent the practical utility and accuracy requirements valued by domain experts. The 60.6% mismatch rate between human preferences and automated selection underscores the complexity of evaluating AI performance in legal contexts, where factors beyond computational accuracy - such as legal precision, contextual appropriateness, and interpretive nuance - influence quality assessments.

### 6.1 Limitations

We acknowledge several methodological limitations. Specifically, multiple questions contained minor inaccuracies about which document should be analyzed (e.g., questions seeking to extract the target's identity from the warrant instead referenced the target's identity in the affidavit), potentially creating measurement bias in the assessment of extraction capabilities. Future work will address through refined query design and validation protocols. Human validation relied

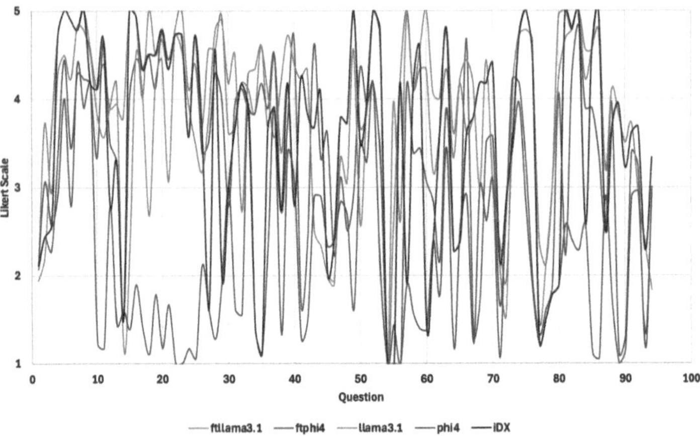


**Fig. 11.** Avg. Human Evaluation by Questions.

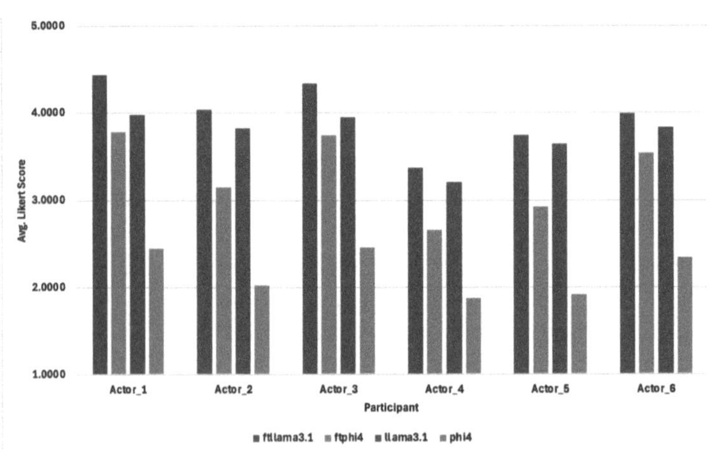


**Fig. 12.** Avg. Human Evaluation by Participants.

on authors of this paper, introducing some confirmation bias in performance assessment. The study's focus on Utah warrant data limits generalizability to other jurisdictions with different legal frameworks and document structures. These limitations affect the interpretation of accuracy claims and practical applicability, underscoring the need for rigorous query validation and independent expert review in future legal document AI research. The substantial disagreement between human evaluation and automated selection (60.6% of queries) represents a significant limitation, suggesting that current automated metrics may inadequately capture the quality dimensions most relevant for legal document analysis.

### 6.2 Implications for Practice and Research

This exploratory work represents an initial investigation into computational approaches for legal document analysis. While the *iDX* framework demonstrates technical feasibility, significant barriers exist for real-world implementation, including legitimate concerns about AI reliability in judicial contexts, data privacy and security requirements, and questions about the appropriate role of automated tools in legal decision-making processes. The local deployment architecture attempts to address some data sovereignty concerns, though acceptance of such technologies within judicial systems would be unwise at this time. Any practical application would require extensive stakeholder engagement, regulatory approval, and validation studies before consideration. The current work primarily serves as a research contribution to understanding the potential and limitations of computational methods in legal document processing, rather than advocating for immediate adoption. Substantial additional research and legal review would be prerequisites for any future implementation. While this preliminary study examines hybrid AI approaches for document processing using limited labeled data, future research might investigate cross-domain applications, though significant validation challenges remain regarding AI acceptability in judicial contexts. Finally, this work demonstrates the limitations of automated model selection in legal contexts, providing empirical evidence about the challenges of developing AI systems that align with expert judgment in legal document processing.

## 7 Conclusion

While this work establishes a methodology for retrospective analysis of historical warrant practices that can inform evidence-based legal research, the findings emphasize that human oversight remains essential in legal document analysis applications, particularly where accuracy and constitutional compliance are paramount. Future research should investigate improved metrics that better align with expert judgment and explore the appropriate boundaries for AI assistance in legal contexts.

**Acknowledgement.** The authors thank CloudLab [17] for providing computational resources and acknowledge the Utah judges, law enforcement officers, and administrators for facilitating data access. This work was supported in part by NSF grants CNS-2131509 [41].

## References

1. U.S. constitution, fourth amendment (1789). Ratified in 1791. https://www.archives.gov/founding-docs/constitution-transcript
2. Brinegar v. United States, 338 U.S. 160 (1949). https://supreme.justia.com/cases/federal/us/338/160/

3. Illinois v. Gates, 462 U.S. 213 (1983). https://supreme.justia.com/cases/federal/us/462/213/
4. Groh v. Ramirez, 540 U.S. 551 (2004). https://supreme.justia.com/cases/federal/us/540/551/
5. Riley v. California, 573 U.S. 373 (2014). https://supreme.justia.com/cases/federal/us/573/373/
6. Abdin, M., et al.: Phi-4 technical report. arXiv preprint arXiv:2412.08905 (2024)
7. Almeida, F., Xexéo, G.: Word embeddings: a survey. arXiv preprint arXiv:1901.09069 (2023)
8. An, C., et al.: Training-free long-context scaling of large language models. arXiv preprint arXiv:2402.17463 (2024)
9. Anonymous: iDX repo (2025). https://github.com/anonymous-repo25/idx
10. Apache Software Foundation: Apache parquet. https://parquet.apache.org/ (2025). Accessed 13 Mar 2025
11. Bartoli, A., De Lorenzo, A., Medvet, E., Tarlao, F.: Inference of regular expressions for text extraction from examples. IEEE Trans. Knowl. Data Eng. **28**(5), 1217–1230 (2016). https://doi.org/10.1109/TKDE.2016.2515587
12. Benner, L.A., Samarkos, C.T.: Searching for narcotics in San Diego: preliminary findings from the San Diego search warrant project. California Western Law Rev. **36**(2) (2000). https://scholarlycommons.law.cwsl.edu/cwlr/vol36/iss2/3
13. Bui, D.D.A., Del Fiol, G., Hurdle, J.F., Jonnalagadda, S.: Extractive text summarization system to aid data extraction from full text in systematic review development. J. Biomed. Inform. **64**, 265–272 (2016). https://doi.org/10.1016/j.jbi.2016.10.014
14. Chapman, C., Stolee, K.T.: Exploring regular expression usage and context in Python. In: Proceedings of the 2016 International Symposium on Software Testing and Analysis (ISSTA 2016), pp. 282–293. Association for Computing Machinery, New York, NY, USA (2016). https://doi.org/10.1145/2931037.2931073
15. Chen, B., Zhang, Z., Langrené, N., Zhu, S.: Unleashing the potential of prompt engineering in large language models: a comprehensive review. arXiv preprint arXiv:2310.14735 (2024)
16. Cho, J., Rajagopalan, S.: A fast regular expression indexing engine. In: Proceedings of the 18th International Conference on Data Engineering, pp. 419–430. IEEE (2002). https://doi.org/10.1109/ICDE.2002.994755
17. CloudLab: Cloudlab (2025). https://www.cloudlab.us/#team. Accessed 30 Jan 2025
18. De Figueiredo, M., Hashimoto, T.B., Thorley, D.: Unwarranted warrants? An empirical examination of the search and seizure process. Harvard Law Rev. **138** (2025, forthcoming)
19. Dunn, A., et al.: Structured information extraction from complex scientific text with fine-tuned large language models. arXiv preprint arXiv:2212.05238 (2022)
20. Fernandez, F.C.: LLM summarization metrics. https://www.holisticai.com/blog/ (2024). Accessed 17 Aug 2024
21. Gibbons, J., Turell, M.T.: Dimensions of Forensic Linguistics, 1st edn. AILA Applied Linguistics Series, vol. 5. John Benjamins Publishing Company, The Netherlands (2008)
22. Hearst, M.A.: Untangling text data mining. In: Proceedings of the 37th Annual Meeting of the Association for Computational Linguistics, pp. 3–10. Association for Computational Linguistics, USA (1999). https://doi.org/10.3115/1034678.1034679
23. Hu, E.J., et al.: LoRA: low-rank adaptation of large language models. arXiv preprint arXiv:2106.09685 (2021)

24. Kao, A., Poteet, S.R.: Natural Language Processing and Text Mining. Springer, London (2007). https://doi.org/10.1007/978-1-84628-754-1
25. Kruskal, W.H., Wallis, A.W.: Use of ranks in one-criterion variance analysis. J. Am. Stat. Assoc. **47**(260), 583–621 (1952). https://doi.org/10.1080/01621459.1952.10483441, https://www.tandfonline.com/doi/abs/10.1080/01621459.1952.10483441
26. Lee, S., et al.: A survey on evaluation metrics for machine translation. Mathematics **11**(4), 1006 (2023). https://doi.org/10.3390/math11041006
27. Lewis, P., et al.: Retrieval-augmented generation for knowledge-intensive NLP tasks. arXiv preprint arXiv:2005.11401 (2021)
28. Li, J., Chiu, B., Feng, S., Wang, H.: Few-shot named entity recognition via meta-learning. In: 2020 IEEE 36th International Conference on Data Engineering (ICDE), pp. 4245–4256 (2020). https://doi.org/10.1109/TKDE.2020.3038670
29. Loshchilov, I., Hutter, F.: Decoupled weight decay regularization. arXiv preprint arXiv:1711.05101 (2019)
30. Meta: Llama3.1 (2024). https://www.llama.com/models/llama-3/. Accessed 17 Aug 2024
31. Miles, T.J.: Racial disparities in wiretap applications before federal judges. J. Legal Stud. **41**, 419–451 (2012). https://doi.org/10.1086/669607
32. Nomic Team: Introducing nomic embed: a truly open embedding model (2024). https://www.nomic.ai/blog/posts/nomic-embed-text-v1. Accessed 17 Aug 2024
33. Olivetti, E.A., et al.: Data-driven materials research enabled by natural language processing and information extraction. Appl. Phys. Rev. **7**(4), 041317 (2020)
34. Ollama Team: Ollama (2024). https://github.com/ollama/ollama. Accessed 17 Aug 2024
35. Papineni, K., Roukos, S., Ward, T., Zhu, W.J.: BLEU: a method for automatic evaluation of machine translation. In: Proceedings of the 40th Annual Meeting on Association for Computational Linguistics, pp. 311–318. Association for Computational Linguistics (2002). https://doi.org/10.3115/1073083.1073135
36. Radford, A., Wu, J., Child, R., Luan, D., Amodei, D., Sutskever, I.: Language models are unsupervised multitask learners. In: OpenAI Blog (2019)
37. Sahoo, P., Singh, A.K., Saha, S., Jain, V., Mondal, S., Chadha, A.: A systematic survey of prompt engineering in large language models: Techniques and applications. arXiv preprint arXiv:2402.07927 (2024)
38. Taori, R., et al.: Alpaca: a strong, replicable instruction-following model (2023). https://crfm.stanford.edu/2023/03/13/alpaca.html. Accessed 17 Aug 2024
39. Touvron, H., et al.: LLaMA: open and efficient foundation language models. arXiv preprint arXiv:2302.13971 (2023)
40. Trewartha, A., et al.: Quantifying the advantage of domain-specific pre-training on named entity recognition tasks in materials science. Patterns **3**(4), 100488 (2022). https://doi.org/10.1016/j.patter.2022.100488
41. U.S. National Science Foundation: U.S. National Science Foundation (2025). https://new.nsf.gov/. Accessed 30 Jan 2025
42. Utah Courts: Xchange: Public case search (2020). https://www.utcourts.gov/en/court-records-publications/records/xchange.html. Accessed 30 Jan 2020
43. Utah State Legislature: Utah code (2025). https://le.utah.gov/xcode/code.html
44. Van Duizend, R., Sutton, L.P., Carter, C.A.: The Search Warrant Process: Preconceptions, Perceptions, Practices, National Center for State Courts (1985)

45. Vaswani, A., et al.: Attention is all you need. arXiv preprint arXiv:1706.03762 (2023)
46. Zhang, T., Kishore, V., Wu, F., Weinberger, K.Q., Artzi, Y.: BERTScore: evaluating text generation with BERT. arXiv preprint arXiv:1904.09675 (2020)

# Where the Money Is: Shadow AI Risks to Family Offices and the Wealth Management Sector

Brian H. Nussbaum and Kimberly A. Cornell(✉)

University at Albany, Albany 12222, USA
{bnussbaum,kacornell}@albany.edu

**Abstract.** Family offices are private financial institutions that manage the wealth, and sometimes lives, of high-net-worth individuals and families; by some estimates, they manage more wealth than the hedge fund industry. This growing and increasingly important sector is also rapidly introducing many varieties of technology to analyze data, support investment decisions, automate operations, and perform various other tasks. The introduction of information technology to any organization introduces "shadow information technology (SIT)" – unapproved, unsanctioned, or unvetted hardware and software on the network, which brings important technological risks. So too, does the introduction of artificial intelligence (both into the organization, but also into the more general computing environment) create the possibility of "shadow AI (SAI)" – employees or principals using artificial intelligence models or tools in ways that could result in data leakage, inaccurate decision support, or various other risks. Family office decisions around the adoption of AI, and mitigations of AI-related risks, have many parallels to other organizations in the wealth management and financial sectors, but given their unusual focus on families and the broad variety of tasks they undertake on behalf of those families, there are some unique challenges they face. Our paper discusses some of these challenges, suggests mitigation strategies, and points to areas of multidisciplinary future work to help this at-risk group.

**Keywords:** Cybersecurity · Cyber Risk · Family Offices · Wealth Management · Shadow AI · Shadow IT

## 1 Introduction

When asked why he robbed banks, notorious gentleman bandit Willie Sutton reportedly said "Because that is where the money is." [15] This too might explain why cybercriminals, scammers, fraudsters, and others might target family offices, as well as other wealth managers [30]. Are family offices indeed "where the money is"? Well, Bloomberg reports that "A 2019 estimate by researcher Campden Wealth put the figure at almost $6 trillion globally—larger than the entire hedge


K.-K. R. Choo et al. (Eds.): ICDF2C 2025, LNICST 686, pp. 333–344, 2026.
https://doi.org/10.1007/978-3-032-22545-0_20

fund industry." [44] By assets under management then, they do seem to be where the money is.

Any cybersecurity or technological risks faced by family offices are then consequential in dollar terms, if perhaps not necessarily in systemic financial terms. Family offices, by their nature, do not typically accept external investments; as such, they are sometimes not subject to the same regulatory and disclosure requirements that financial firms of comparable size that invest external client wealth are. For example, single-family offices (those that invest the assets of just one family) are not required to register under the 1940 Investment Advisers Act by the Securities and Exchange Commission (SEC), because they do not invest "outside capital." [4].

Family offices are a huge sector of the financial industry, by some estimates larger than the hedge fund industry [33], that has lower regulatory and disclosure requirements, is highly secretive, and serves as an important, but understudied and not well understood, locus of cyber and technological risk. All this while the wealth management industry writ large, and the family office sector in particular, are rapidly technologizing and informatizing their operations. According to one survey of family offices, the top technological needs were 1) data analytics, 2) artificial intelligence, and 3) cybersecurity - three items that obviously overlap in many important ways [43]. In that same survey, the number one technical challenge they face is cybersecurity, number three is keeping pace with technological change, with number four being data privacy. Again, overlapping issues of data security [43].

There have been some limited and preliminary attempts to study the cybercrime-related risk of this sector [30], but there are other types of technological risk in this area that have not yet been addressed. One important challenge is insider threats - including malicious insiders, as well as accidental and unintentional insider threats; one particularly interesting version of unintentional (or perhaps more precisely, reckless) insider threat is "shadow Artificial Intelligence" or SAI.

## 2 Shadow IT

Shadow IT (SIT) is "...all hardware, software, or any other solutions used by employees inside of the organisational ecosystem which have not received any formal IT department approval." [38] That is to say, it is anything added to the network or IT ecosystem that has not been put in place through official procedures, or with official approval. This can range from hardware (personal devices connected to the network, work-related devices acquired without IT approval) to software (social networking apps downloaded onto work mobile devices, gaming software run on workstations, etc.), it can be on premises or in the cloud, and comes in many variations. What all of the variations have in common is that they introduce new, and potentially unknown, attack surfaces and vulnerabilities into the organization's IT environment, and sometimes, because they are not known to the IT staff, they are not seen or monitored in the way official IT is. Scholars have noted numerous types of problems that result from shadow IT. Unsanctioned hardware and software make it "difficult to support and maintain" systems during incidents, are often run with an "absence of security controls" and because they are not approved and supported are subject to failure resulting from the informal installer ("original sponsor of the SIT solution") of the hardware or software leaving the firm. [26] How common is shadow IT? "...41% of employees have acquired, modified or created technology without the oversight of IT departments, according to a Gartner report, which predicts that figure will hit 75% by 2027." [14]

Shadow IT is not a new or unknown phenomenon, and there are a series of tools (both technical tools and process tools) designed to assess and respond to shadow IT-related risk. Scholars have proposed various models and process tools to evaluate such risks. [35] Major technology providers ranging from Microsoft [28] to Splunk [41] (and many others) offer tools and approaches to helping organizations manage these risks. Shadow IT is not merely a traditional and generic organizational problem, but one with unique challenges in particular fields. In fields ranging from utilities, to academia, to hospitality, shadow IT has been seen as a challenge [26]. Finance is no different. Scholars have tied different approaches to shadow IT risks to financial executives in different countries [12], as well as understanding the various shadow IT problems in finance as an "antecedent to internal data security breaches" [12].

## 3 Shadow AI

Shadow AI is like shadow IT, insofar as it is about the use of AI within the organization, but without formal approvals. It is also an informal adoption or usage by employees, but outside organizational planning, risk management, data protection, and IT support processes. No less an authority than IBM describes shadow AI as "...the unsanctioned use of any artificial intelligence (AI) tool or application by employees or end users without the formal approval or oversight of the information technology (IT) department." [20]

Researchers have suggested that "most companies are dangerously naïve about their GenAI usage – a phenomenon termed shadow AI." [10] The potential impacts of shadow AI for organizations include data exfiltration, leaks of customer data, trade secrets not being protected, copyright infringement, and the ability of bad actors to conduct reconnaissance on the organization [10]. Additionally, many of these initial problems have the potential to lead to regulatory concerns for organizations [23]. There is also the potential for reputational damage – "Unauthorized AI use might also contradict a company's quality standards and undermine consumer trust. Consider the backlash when Sports Illustrated was exposed for publishing articles written by AI-generated authors or when Uber Eats was called out for using AI-generated food images." [20]

Shadow AI also crosses boundaries like sector, industry, and firm size. Several examples of concerns about shadow AI have emerged from the public sector [21,34], however the majority of the coverage of the problem tends to focus on private firms [13]. There is some coverage that ties shadow AI to the finance industry [2,39], but less than might be imagined given the risks. That said, the scholarly coverage of shadow AI is thin because of how new the problem is, and the industrial and analytic coverage is often relatively generic, with limited sector and industry-specific analysis of shadow AI risks. There are some examples of approaches or measures that can be used to manage shadow AI risk. Campbell and Jovanovic suggest AI usage policies, training, platform sanctioning, AI coaching, access restrictions, as well as the use of proprietary AI models [10].

In addition to information directly entered into generative AI models by employees, such software often collects extensive data about the user's computer systems as well as user behavior, both of which have the potential to cause privacy or identifiability concerns. For example, the high profile Chinese generative AI model DeepSeek makes clear in its terms of service that it collects technical information like operating system, language settings, device model, and IP address, but also - importantly - things like "keystroke patterns or rhythms" which are more like biometric data on individual users [6]. Such data collection is not uncommon in various software and application contexts; however, any holistic assessment of the privacy and data security implications of shadow AI needs to include these additional issues.

Shadow AI is already a serious global challenge for companies and organizations. The firm Salesforce surveyed "14,000 global workers across 14 countries" and found that 28% of them were using generative AI tools at work [37]. Of these workers using generative AI tools at work, more than half of them (55%) use tools that are not approved by their employers, and importantly, a large number (40%) are using generative AI tools that are explicitly banned for work [37]. Additionally, 64% of those using generative AI admitted passing off the work of generative AI tools as their own work [37]. Notably, "nearly 7 in 10 global workers have never completed or received training on how to use generative AI safely and ethically at work." [37]

## 4 Family Offices and Artificial Intelligence

Family offices are clearly engaging with artificial intelligence in at least two ways, one as an area of investment focus, and one as a set of tools to improve their operations. The first is unsurprising, as there has been a lot of investment in AI-related technologies, including a lot outside of public markets, where family offices often focus their investing. According to Campden Wealth and the Royal Bank of Canada's 2024 The North America Family Office Report, 72% of "private equity owning family offices" have already invested in artificial intelligence, higher than any other technology sector except healthcare technology [50]. In Europe, the numbers are slightly lower, but still quite high; there Campden Wealth and HSBC see 61% of "private equity owning family offices" have already invested in artificial intelligence [49]. In Europe, this number is lower than healthcare or automation and robotics, but still higher than the percentage of family offices invested in clean technology or climate solutions, data centers, biotech, or renewable energy [49]. In their 2024 survey, Citi Private Banking found more than half of the family offices they talked to had investments in AI, and "another 26% are considering it." [50]. Family offices are certainly aware of artificial intelligence technologies, and are making moves to leverage AI investments.

They are also, with various levels of speed and depth, beginning to leverage artificial intelligence to improve their operations. While Citi notes "It has yet to be widely adopted for operational purposes" they did note that a minority of family offices were using such technologies, and what they were using them for. "Less than 15% of respondents said they were deploying AI for the likes of task automation, presentation building or forecasting." [5] "About one in ten" were using the technologies for automating business processes, but notably "Another quarter or so are exploring various related possibilities." [5]. Though these numbers, of course, represent the known and approved usage of AI tools, rather than any shadow AI.

In addition to using AI to automate operations, there are other areas that are being explored. Plante Moran suggest that in addition to using AI to improve operations - to "streamline administrative tasks and reduce manual errors" [29] - it can also be used for portfolio management, improved risk management, and for "identifying opportunities" [29] and evaluating alternative investments [29]. Here they are talking not just about simplifying operational and administrative tasks, but about family office investment decisions being guided (or even run) by artificial intelligence systems [29]. Among family offices using artificial intelligence, using software that relies on it, or exploring such software, there is a clear sense of concern about these issues. "Family offices also often queried their service providers about the security and reliability of AI, where their data was being processed, and, simply, if they should be using AI in light of these concerns." [43]

According to Morgan Stanley's The Future Ready Family Office, there are at least five ways in which family offices are likely to incorporate artificial intelligence into their operations; using AI for "Analyzing financial data," "Summarizing earnings calls and market commentaries," "Incorporating private markets performance data," "Automating communications," and "Streamlining the onboarding process." [42] Though Morgan Stanley does include an important disclaimer about AI and family office operations - "Artificial intelligence (AI) is subject to limitations, and you should be aware that any output from an AI-supported tool or service made available by the Firm for your use is subject to such limitations, including but not limited to inaccuracy, incompleteness, or embedded bias. You should always verify the results of any AI-generated output." [42]

According to the UBS 2025 Family Office Report, more than 60% of family offices worldwide envision using AI in the next five years for financial reporting and data visualization, text analysis, and portfolio analysis; and more than half envision using it for content creation [46]. Fewer than one in ten family offices (6%) believe they will not use AI at all in the next five years (though there is some regional variation, the numbers do go up to 12% in Switzerland and North Asia) [46]. But clearly, even most family offices that do not currently use AI extensively believe they are likely to in the relatively near term.

## 5 Shadow AI Risks In Family Offices

Adoption of AI is a complicated set of choices and tradeoffs in any organization, but there are reasons that it is even more complicated for family offices. As Eton Solutions notes, "The tradition of privacy in the family office sector, especially now related to data security, brings nuance to the sector in determining which AI technologies to adopt immediately and which require further development." [43] In any privacy-focused enterprise or organization, the question of how new tools and software present risk must be weighed more heavily.

Family offices are fundamentally investment firms that operate on behalf of a single family (or several families), and so they face many of the same Shadow AI challenges that traditional investment firms and firms more generally face. Additionally, the face some unusual and specific challenges tied to things like reputational risk for family principals, that differ somewhat from traditional investment and wealth management firms. The leakage or theft of information can potentially be used in numerous ways; it can be made public to cause reputational damage or regulatory scrutiny, it can be used to trade on material non-public information, it can be used to negotiate against a firm in various kinds of transactions, as well as myriad other uses that could damage the short or long-term interests of a family office.

Wealth managers expect that AI will be changing what they do and how they do it. In a 2022 study, Accenture surveyed 500 financial advisors in North America. Of the surveyed advisors, 98% agreed with the statement "AI is transforming how advice is created for, delivered to, and consumed by clients today" and 99% agreed that "AI plays a role in the future of financial advice (e.g., the role of technology to power/enhance the client-advisor relationship)" [1]. In its 2024 document "How AI Can Be Good for Wealth Managers" KPMG described a series of areas in which AI can help wealth managers across a process model of the tasks that such managers undertake, from prospecting new clients, to onboarding clients, to planning and advising, implementation and servicing, and reviewing and reporting [22]. In each step of this process, there are some tasks which KPMG suggests that AI will be of assistance, and some where it may be less useful [22].

While family offices, or at least many of them, may not be prospecting for new clients and onboarding them the way traditional wealth managers do; the remaining steps are all central to family office operations. If indeed staff at family offices begin using AI tools for these tasks, there is potential for various kinds of data leakage. The document does describe some short-term risks resulting from these changes, including "data quality," "regulatory compliance," "explainability," and "human expertise." [22] The lack of the inclusion of data leakage and related shadow AI risks may be based on the idea that the usage of AI will be done according to organizational rules and best practices; but that is a substantial assumption, and one that the history of shadow IT does not offer much confidence in. Information that could find its way into Shadow AI (for example, from a staff member using Large Language Models or other tools):

- Deal Flow: Information about prospective deals and acquisitions, ranging from due diligence information to research topics and offer or price information, could all potentially be compromised.
- Investment Choices and Allocations: Information about investments, ranging from broad portfolio allocations or risk tolerances to detailed information about particular investments in controversial firms, industries, or commodities, could be compromised.
- Future Plans and Perspectives: Information about a Family Office's macro-level outlooks, key sectoral or industry interests, and economic expectations could potentially be compromised.
- Intellectual Property: Information about patents, trademarks, copyrights, and various kinds of proprietary processes has the potential to be compromised.
- Family Office Process and Operations Information: Information about organizational processes beyond investment selection has the potential to be compromised, and these have the potential to be used to inform or enable sophisticated cybercrime or fraud like Business Email Compromise (BEC).
- Family and Staff Personally Identifiable Information (PII) and Logistical Information: Information about family members, stakeholders, partners, and staff could all potentially be compromised. These present different risks. While the compromise of family member information – from addresses to travel information to professional activity – has the potential to create privacy reputational risks, information about family members and staff could be used to inform or enable fraud or crime.

## 6 Solutions and Mitigations

There are some standard solutions to cybersecurity concerns that are becoming something like an industry standard. "To safeguard their data, family offices are investing in advanced security measures, including encryption, multi-factor authentication, and intrusion detection systems. Regular security audits, staff training, and the adoption of best practices in data protection are also essential to mitigate risks and ensure the privacy of family information." [43]. Part of the reason for the proliferation of technologies like multifactor authentication is that they have become requirements for purchasing cybersecurity insurance policies, a growing method of cyber risk management [7,19].

Some organizations try to minimize risk by avoiding centralized cloud APIs and instead rely on large language models that operate offline or locally. While this approach can reduce certain vulnerabilities, such as the risk of external API breaches, it does not offer a complete solution. Offline models may still interact with the internet through hybrid retrieval systems or plugins; for example, LlamaIndex's RemoteReader allows even a locally hosted model to fetch and parse live URLs[1] [25]. This capability can diminish the security advantages of purely local deployment [3,24]. Moreover, if external services or upstream logging are involved, user queries might inadvertently be included in future training data, sometimes without full transparency [11,32].

One effective countermeasure is to operate systems or virtual machines entirely offline, ensuring strict network isolation. However, this approach requires careful planning to keep offline models updated, particularly when access to recent data or capabilities is essential. This challenge is especially significant in contexts where AI is applied to tasks like those discussed in Sect. 4, such as portfolio management, alternative investment analysis, and investment decision-making [29]. In these cases, secure periodic updates, like vetted financial data imports, may be necessary to balance isolation with the need for timely and relevant information.

Beyond technical controls, comprehensive governance policies play a crucial role in mitigating organizational AI risks. Organizations should establish clear guidelines on which AI tools may be used and strictly regulate the types of data allowed for input [31,47]. They must also review accepted technologies frequently, as previously approved enterprise software is increasingly integrating generative AI features. For example, Microsoft 365 now includes Copilot, which can interact with and analyze content stored in OneDrive, SharePoint, and Teams [27]. Similar integrations are also appearing in tools like Google Workspace's Duet AI and Salesforce Einstein GPT [18,36]. Rigorous employee training programs are equally important to address shadow AI usage, disinformation risks, and to encourage appropriate reporting of incidents [8,17]. Additionally, proactive monitoring, such as prompt logging, anomaly detection, and forensic audits, can deter insider threats and support investigations when incidents occur [48].

While not a shadow AI risk per se, one key AI-related risk facing family offices and others in the wealth management industry are increasingly complex and sophisticated scams that leverage AI-generated "deepfake" audio or video to engage in social engineering attacks like business email compromise (BEC). In such attacks, like one that targeted an executive at the carmaker Ferrari, someone purports to be a senior executive and seeks to initiate a fraudulent financial transaction through a phone call or message with audio that appeared realistic [16]. The targeting of high net worth individuals and families for such attacks has become common enough [40,45], that those in the wealth management industry are beginning to suggest some of the same solutions that are more common in the traditional efforts to counter such scams in other sectors - including out of band communication to ensure requests are legitimate, multi-factor authentication, and the use of code words "...known only to key personnel, as a third factor of authentication to enhance security against AI replication of voices and images." [9]

[1] In LlamaIndex's RemoteReader, the line urlopen(req) indicates that offline models can connect to online resources [25].

Geography remains a central concern for family offices, not just for regulatory and taxation environments, but such concerns are also central to decision-making about technology and cybersecurity. One professional services provider for family offices describes regional cybersecurity threats, such as family offices in Singapore facing "sophisticated phishing attacks," as well as family offices opting to use cloud solutions based in reliable countries like Switzerland [43]. The flexibility of family offices, their ability to move capital across borders, to hire professional services globally, and to find locales that best fit their goals, is a central theme that informs both investment activities, but also technological choices. Understanding family office decision-making around technological risks requires understanding that they are often global and mobile.

## 7 Conclusion and Future Work

It is increasingly clear that family offices are evaluating AI not just as an investment theme, but increasingly as a set of tools to improve operations, planning, asset allocation, and to otherwise improve their performance. This choice will entail various types of technological risk related to data privacy, security, compliance, and other needs. Beyond the proactive choice to employ AI in the enterprise though, family offices will need to take seriously additional technological risks that stem not from approved and adopted AI tools, but from shadow AI tools used by their employees (as well as the members of the family themselves) in ways that will not be immediately apparent, and likely will not comport with policies, rules, and their expectations. The nature of the shadow AI risk is that it often remains unseen until the consequences of it begin to be noticed. These consequences are potentially serious: leaked or spilled data, lost intellectual property, decreases in the quality or profitability of investments, and information about operations or family members being made public.

Further research is needed in several areas to improve the ability of family offices to assess the relevant risks. Much more research on shadow AI in general is needed, but especially in the financial sector and wealth management industries, areas which would potentially have more direct bearing on the risks in family offices. Further research on the nature of family office adoption of not just explicitly AI-focused software, but also on the increasing adoption of AI and related computational technologies into more standard software packages and tools, though this kind of research will no doubt be challenging given the secretive nature of these organizations. Finally, it seems clear that additional research is needed, especially academic research rather than white papers by professional services providers such as banks, on the unique technological risks facing high-net-worth individuals, their families, family offices, and other unusual at-risk populations. Together, these types of research have the potential to inform better threat and risk assessment, as well as improve the kinds of mitigation and response strategies that family offices can undertake.

**Acknowledgments.** We would like to thank the University at Albany for its institutional support.

**Disclosure of Interests.** The authors have no competing interests to declare that are relevant to the content of this article.

## References


1. Accenture: AI in wealth management: a financial advisor study (2022). https://www.accenture.com/content/dam/accenture/final/a-com-migration/r3-3/pdf/pdf-178/accenture-wealth-management-ai-all-systems-go.pdf
2. Adams, M.: The innovative role of AI in finance operations and reporting (2024). https://www.financialexecutives.org/Network/Chapters/Dallas/Files/FEI-Dallas-Moss-Adams-September-2024-PD-Session.aspx
3. AI, M.: Llama-index documentation (2024). https://gpt-index.readthedocs.io/en/latest/guides/primer/index.html#remote-querying
4. Asencio, K.: The family office rule: a re-examination. J. Legislation **46**(40), 55 (2019)
5. Banking, C.P.: Global family office: 2024 survey insights (2024). https://www.privatebank.citibank.com/insights/the-family-office-survey. Accessed 22 May 2025
6. Barrabi, T.: Deepseek AI collects, stores us user data in China – sparking eerily similar national security concerns that forced Tiktok crackdown (2025). https://www.msn.com/en-us/money/other/deepseek-ai-collects-stores-us-user-data-in-china-sparking-eerily-similar-national-security-concerns-that-forced-tiktok-crackdown/ar-AA1y1v4B, mSN Today
7. Bruce, A.: Why insurers are requiring MFA for cyber insurance (2023). https://securenvoy.com/blog/mfa-cyber-insurance/ securEnvoy. Accessed 30 June 2025
8. Brundage, M., et al.: Toward trustworthy AI development: mechanisms for supporting verifiable claims. arXiv preprint arXiv:2004.07213 (2020)
9. Buckner, D., van der Linde, I.: From risk to resilience: strategies for cybersecurity in family offices. Family Wealth Report (2024). https://www.familywealthreport.com/article.php/From-Risk-To-Resilience%3A-Strategies-For-Cybersecurity-In-Family-Offices. Accessed 30 June 2025
10. Campbell, M., Jovanović, M.: Disinfecting AI: mitigating generative AI's top risks. Computer **57**(5), 111–116 (2024)
11. Carlini, N., Zhang, E., Brundage, M., Leike, J.: Poisoning web-scale training datasets is practical. arXiv preprint arXiv:2310.05914 (2023)
12. Castellano, N.G., Felden, C., Pinsker, R.E.: Shadow it behavior of financial executives in Germany and Italy as an antecedent to internal data security breaches. In: Hawaii International Conference on System Sciences (HICSS), pp. 1–11 (2022)
13. Curry, R.: Shadow AI in the 'dark corners' of work is becoming a big problem for companies (2024). https://www.cnbc.com/2024/02/07/shadow-ai-in-the-dark-corners-of-work-is-a-big-problem-for-companies.html, cNBC
14. Ernst, Y.: Why the family office of the future needs refreshed operating models (2024). https://www.ey.com/content/dam/ey-unified-site/ey-com/en-us/insights/family-enterprise/documents/ey-why-family-offices-need-refreshed-operating-models.pdf. Accessed 22 May 2025
15. Federal Bureau of Investigation: History: Willie sutton (nd). https://www.fbi.gov/history/famous-cases/willie-sutton, Accessed 22 May 2025
16. Galletti, S., Pani, M.: How Ferrari hit the brakes on a deepfake CEO. MIT Sloan Management Review (2025). https://sloanreview.mit.edu/article/how-ferrari-hit-the-brakes-on-a-deepfake-ceo/. Accessed 30 June 2025

17. Gartner: Toolkit: Establish an AI TRiSM program (trust, risk, and security management) (2023). https://www.gartner.com/en/documents/4007165
18. Google: Duet AI for google workspace (2023). https://workspace.google.com/blog/product-announcements/duet-ai-in-google-workspace. Accessed June 2025
19. Huang, L., Cornell, K.A.: Cyber protection strategies: balancing insurance and security. In: Proceedings of the 20th International Conference on Cyber Warfare and Security (ICCWS 2025), pp. 151–159. Academic Conferences International Limited (2025). https://doi.org/10.34190/iccws.20.1.3218
20. IBM: What is shadow AI? (2024). https://www.ibm.com/think/topics/shadow-ai
21. Kanowitz, S.: Shining a light on shadow AI. Route 50 (2024)
22. KPMG: How AI can be good for wealth managers (2024). https://kpmg.com/kpmg-us/content/dam/kpmg/pdf/2024/ai-good-news-wealth-managers.pdf
23. Kwan, T.W.: Navigating the risks of shadow AI. ITNOW **66**(2), 42–43 (2024)
24. Lewis, P., et al.: Retrieval-augmented generation for knowledge-intensive NLP tasks. arXiv preprint arXiv:2005.11401 (2020)
25. LlamaIndex Development Team: Remotereader – general reader for any remote page or file (2025). Demonstrates how hybrid retrieval setups can perform live online queries even with local LLMs. https://docs.llamaindex.ai/en/stable/api_reference/readers/remote/
26. Magunduni, J., Chigona, W.: Revisiting shadow it research: what we already know, what we still need to know, and how do we get there? In: 2018 Conference on Information Communications Technology and Society (ICTAS), pp. 1–6. IEEE (2018)
27. Microsoft: Introducing Microsoft 365 copilot—your copilot for work (2023). https://www.microsoft.com/en-us/microsoft-365/copilot. Accessed June 2025
28. Microsoft: Discover and identify shadow it with Microsoft defender for cloud apps. https://learn.microsoft.com/en-us/defender-cloud-apps/tutorial-shadow-it (nd)
29. Moran, P.: Family office answer book (2024). https://go.plantemoran.com/rs/946-CTY-601/images/WM_Family_office_answer_book_landscape_2024.pdf?version=0. Accessed 22 May 2025
30. Nussbaum, B.H., Cornell, K.A., Huang, L.: The perfect victim? Family offices as targets for cybercriminals. In: Adi, K., et al. (eds.) Foundations and Practice of Security, pp. 3–17. Springer, Cham (2025). https://doi.org/10.1007/978-3-031-87499-4_1
31. OECD: OECD framework for the classification of AI systems (2023). https://www.oecd.org/going-digital/ai/classification/
32. OpenAI: Terms of use (2024). https://openai.com/policies/terms-of-use
33. Osnos, E.: The Getty family's trust issues. The New Yorker (2023). https://www.newyorker.com/magazine/2023/01/23/the-getty-familys-trust-issues Accessed 08 July 2025
34. Ray, S.: Combating shadow AI: Implementing controls for government use of AI. Gov. Technol. **37**(6) (2024)
35. Rentrop, C., Zimmermann, S.: Shadow it evaluation model. In: 2012 Federated Conference on Computer Science and Information Systems (FedCSIS), pp. 1023–1027. IEEE (2012)
36. Salesforce: Introducing Einstein GPT: The world's first generative AI for CRM (2023). https://www.salesforce.com/news/stories/introducing-einstein-gpt-the-worlds-first-generative-ai-for-crm/. Accessed June 2025
37. Salesforce: More than half of generative AI adopters use unapproved tools at work (2023). https://www.salesforce.com/news/stories/ai-at-work-research/

38. Silic, M., Back, A.: Shadow it–a view from behind the curtain. Comput. Secur. **45**, 274–283 (2014)
39. Smarsh: Financial services and generative AI: navigating a new era of innovation (2024). https://www.smarsh.com/media/financial-services-and-generative-ai-ebook.pdf
40. Snape, G.: From AI deepfakes to wire transfer fraud, cyber risks are growing for high-net-worth individuals. Insurance Business (2025). https://www.insurancebusinessmag.com/us/news/cyber/from-ai-deepfakes-to-wire-transfer-fraud-cyber-risks-are-growing-for-highnetworth-individuals-533768.aspx. Accessed 30 June 2025
41. Splunk: What is shadow it? (nd). https://www.splunk.com/en_us/blog/learn/shadow-it.html
42. Stanley, M.: The future-ready family office: evolving with purpose (2024). https://www.morganstanley.com/content/dam/msdotcom/en/wealth-management/msfo/1335542-4891049-MSFO-Future-Ready-Family-Office-White-Paper-FINAL.pdf. Accessed 22 May 2025
43. Struthers, D., Botha, F.: Family office software and technology report 2024. Technical report, Simple. Eton Solutions (2024). https://eton-solutions.com/wp-content/uploads/2025/06/682711b19f734fcbf642b2c9_Software-Technology-Report_2024.pdf. Accessed 30 June 2025
44. Stupples, B.: How new wealth, few rules fuel family office boom (2023). https://www.bloomberg.com/news/articles/2023-09-01/how-new-wealth-few-rules-fuel-family-office-boom. Accessed 22 May 2025
45. Tobentkin, D.: Cyber attacks tailored to individuals. The Edge (2024). https://www.leadersedge.com/p-c/cyber-attacks-tailored-to-individuals. Accessed 30 June 2025
46. UBS Global Wealth Management: Global family office report 2025. Technical report, UBS AG (2025). https://advisors.ubs.com/mediahandler/media/708880/UBS-Global-Family-Office-Report-2025-Final-Single-Pages.pdf, based on a survey of 317 family offices across more than 30 markets
47. Vaishnav, L., Singh, S., Cornell, K.A.: Transparency, security, and workplace training and awareness in the age of generative AI. arXiv preprint arXiv:2501.10389 (2024)
48. Vaishnav, L., Singh, S., Cornell, K.A.: The hidden dangers of publicly accessible LLMs: a case study on gab ai. In: Goel, S., Uzun, E., Xie, M., Sarkar, S. (eds.) Digital Forensics and Cyber Crime. ICDF2C 2024. Lecture Notes of the Institute for Computer Sciences, Social Informatics and Telecommunications Engineering, vol. 613, pp. 312–330. Springer, Cham (2025). https://doi.org/10.1007/978-3-031-89363-6_18
49. Wealth, C., Banking, H.P.: The European family office report (2024). https://www.privatebanking.hsbc.com/content/dam/privatebanking/gpb/uhnw/mena-family-office/HSBC%20Global%20Provate%20Banking%20-%20European%20Family%20Office%20Report%202024.pdf. Accessed 22 May 2025
50. RBC Wealth Management of Canada: The North America family office report (2024). https://www.rbcwealthmanagement.com/en-us/campaign/the-north-america-family-office-report. Accessed 22 May 2025

# Chances and Challenges of the Model Context Protocol in Digital Forensics and Incident Response

Jan-Niclas Hilgert, Carlo Jakobs, Michael Külper(✉), Martin Lambertz, Axel Mahr, and Elmar Padilla

Fraunhofer FKIE, Zanderstr. 5, 53177 Bonn, Germany
{jan-niclas.hilgert,carlo.jakobs,michael.kuelper,martin.lambertz, axel.mahr,elmar.padilla}@fkie.fraunhofer.de

**Abstract.** Large language models hold considerable promise for supporting forensic investigations, but their widespread adoption is hindered by a lack of transparency, explainability, and reproducibility. This paper explores how the emerging Model Context Protocol can address these challenges and support the meaningful use of LLMs in digital forensics. Through a theoretical analysis, we examine how MCP can be integrated across various forensic scenarios—ranging from artifact analysis to the generation of interpretable reports. We also outline both technical and conceptual considerations for deploying an MCP server in forensic environments. Our analysis reveals a wide range of use cases in which MCP not only strengthens existing forensic workflows but also facilitates the application of LLMs to areas of forensics where their use was previously limited. Furthermore, we introduce the concept of the inference constraint level—a way of characterizing how specific MCP design choices can deliberately constrain model behavior, thereby enhancing both auditability and traceability. Our insights demonstrate that MCP has significant potential as a foundational component for developing LLM-assisted forensic workflows that are not only more transparent, reproducible, and legally defensible, but also represent a step toward increased automation in digital forensic analysis. However, we also highlight potential challenges that the adoption of MCP may pose for digital forensics in the future.

**Keywords:** Model Context Protocol · MCP · Artificial Intelligence · Large Language Models · Digital Forensics

## 1 Introduction

Over the past few years, large language models (LLMs) have emerged as a breakthrough in artificial intelligence, demonstrating impressive capabilities in language understanding, reasoning, and tool use. Their rapid evolution and integration have prompted researchers and practitioners to explore their potential well beyond traditional Natural Language Processing tasks—including applications


K.-K. R. Choo et al. (Eds.): ICDF2C 2025, LNICST 686, pp. 345–362, 2026.
https://doi.org/10.1007/978-3-032-22545-0_21

in digital forensics and incident response. Several studies highlight AI's growing role in digital forensics, with some demonstrating its potential to automate evidence analysis [3], and others exploring explainable AI to enhance the transparency and reliability of forensic triage and artifact extraction [7]. An expanding line of research [12,15] underscores the increasing interest in leveraging LLMs and other AI methods for digital forensic applications including artifact identification, anomaly detection, script generation, incident analysis, and educational support in forensic training scenarios. LLMs are considered promising in digital forensics due to their capacity to interpret natural language prompts, simulate procedural reasoning, and assist with both technical and explanatory tasks across investigative contexts [14]. Wickramasekara et al. [17] argue that LLMs are increasingly considered in digital forensics to help address investigation backlogs by enhancing efficiency, improving traceability, and lowering technical and legal barriers across multiple phases of the forensic process.

Despite their potential, LLMs currently face several significant barriers to autonomous use in digital forensics. Their "black box" nature raises critical concerns around transparency, accountability, and explainability—attributes essential to maintaining trust and evidentiary integrity in legal and investigative contexts. In addition, LLMs may hallucinate facts, misinterpret evidence, or produce incomplete or unverifiable reasoning chains, all of which undermine the reliability of their outputs. Furthermore, LLMs often lack domain-specific knowledge required to accurately interpret low-level forensic artifacts, making them prone to incorrect assumptions when working with unfamiliar data structures or tool outputs. Adding to these limitations, making relevant forensic data available to an LLM in a structured and usable form is itself a complex task.

In November 2024, Anthropic introduced the Model Context Protocol (MCP), a standardized framework designed to connect LLMs *"to the systems where data lives"*[1]. MCP enables LLMs to interact with external tools and data sources through so-called *MCP servers*, which expose well-defined functions for tasks such as data retrieval or tool execution. Since its release, MCP has quickly gained recognition as a foundational component in the evolving AI ecosystem. Adoption by major organizations is accelerating this momentum: OpenAI has integrated MCP into its Agents SDK and has announced plans to support it in the Responses API[2] and the ChatGPT desktop application. Microsoft has introduced native MCP support in Windows 11[3], alongside a dedicated C# SDK, enabling tighter integration with the Windows architecture and tools like Copilot Studio. Google DeepMind has also confirmed its intention to adopt MCP within its Gemini model ecosystem[4], recognizing it as a rapidly emerging open standard for AI-agent connectivity.

[1] https://www.anthropic.com/news/model-context-protocol.
[2] https://openai.com/index/new-tools-and-features-in-the-responses-api/.
[3] https://blogs.windows.com/windowsexperience/2025/05/19/securing-the-model-context-protocol-building-a-safer-agentic-future-on-windows/.
[4] https://blog.google/technology/google-deepmind/google-gemini-updates-io-2025/#performance.

While MCP presents considerable potential, as a relatively recent innovation, it has received limited attention in the literature to date. The most comprehensive analysis so far is provided by Hou et al. [10] who examine the protocol's architecture, security risks, and broader adoption in general AI contexts. While their work provides a foundational understanding of MCP at the systems level, it does not explore its potential in domain-specific settings such as digital forensics—where many of MCP's strengths directly address the core challenges of applying LLMs, including limited tool access, lack of domain context, and the need for transparent and verifiable reasoning.

This paper addresses this gap by exploring the emerging role of MCP in digital forensics and incident response. We present several use cases demonstrating how MCP can support a variety of tasks, ranging from artifact analysis to the generation of comprehensible reports and outline important considerations for deploying MCP servers within forensic workflows. In addition to these aspects, we also highlight potential challenges that may arise as MCP becomes more widely adopted. By doing so, this work aims to raise awareness of both the benefits and limitations of MCP, and its potential impact on the future of digital forensics and incident response.

## 2 Model Context Protocol

MCP is an open standard designed to provide a unified interface for connecting LLM applications with external tools and resources. Unlike traditional integrations that depend on hardcoded API connections, MCP enables LLMs to independently locate, choose, and interact with services and data sources based on the given task context. It also incorporates human-in-the-loop capabilities, allowing users to contribute data or validate actions when necessary. The following sections outline the structure of MCP, based on its official specification [1].

### 2.1 Architecture

MCP employs a client-server architecture, where one host application can establish connections with several MCP servers. Figure 1 gives an exemplary overview. The architecture consists of the following core components:

- **MCP Host:** The MCP host is the LLM-enabled application (e.g. VS Code, Claude Desktop) that seeks to interact with a resource. It separately coordinates the integration of the LLM and of one or more MCP clients.
- **MCP Client:** The MCP client is a component within the MCP host and sends requests to an MCP server. Each MCP client maintains a dedicated one-to-one connection with an MCP server. The MCP specification provides that a separate client-server pair is used for each type of resource. For example, one pair may be used to interface with MySQL databases, while another may handle interaction with IDA Pro.

- **MCP Server:** The MCP server is the main component of interest for practitioners and needs to be implemented for dedicated access to the corresponding resource. It connects to the actual resource, either locally (via direct access) or remotely (via a Web API), and exposes its functionalities to the corresponding MCP client.

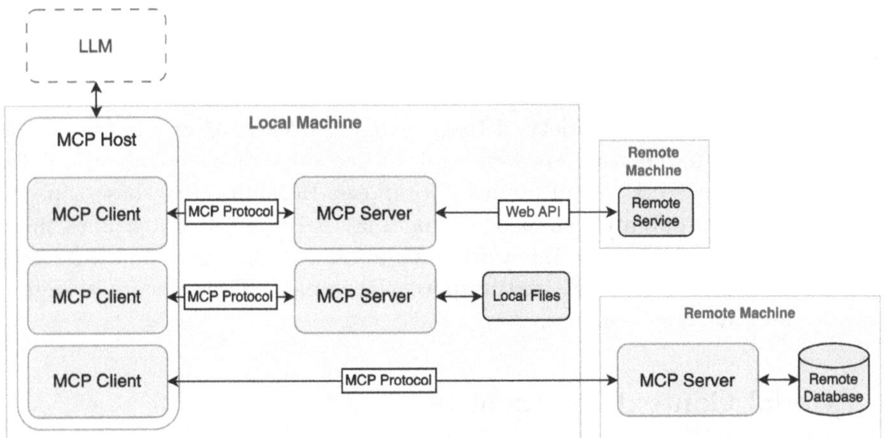


**Fig. 1.** Overview of the MCP architecture, illustrating interactions with both local and remote resources. Depending on the specific host configuration, the LLM may also run locally.

## 2.2 Capabilities

In addition to the communicating parties, the MCP specification defines so-called *capabilities* which constitute (partly mandatory) extensions to the raw message exchange between MCP client and server and can be configured by either side.

- **Roots:** Defined by the MCP client, roots specify the files and directories that the MCP server is permitted to access. They are represented as URIs, which may point to local file paths, directories, or remote API endpoints.
- **Resources:** This capability represents the data sources accessed by the MCP server. These may include persistent data stored in files, such content from databases, images, or log files, as well as transient text or binary data handled by a connected service. Depending on the MCP client implementation, the client may autonomously select which resources to access within the defined roots.
- **Tools:** Defined by the MCP server, tools represent the specific functionalities it provides to the client—ranging from simple data retrieval to complex operations. Each tool is identified by a name and accompanied by a description

of its functionality. The choice of which tool to invoke is delegated to the LLM. Furthermore, MCP supports *dynamic tool discovery*, allowing clients to query available tools at any time, while enabling the server to update or modify tools at runtime.

- **Sampling:** When the MCP server requires additional information outside its scope of expertise, it can submit queries back to the LLM via the MCP client. These queries must be reviewed and approved by the user before being passed to the LLM. The LLM's response is then returned to the server through the client, again subject to user review.
- **Prompts:** This capability allows the MCP server to provide reusable prompt templates, which are exposed to the MCP client and can be selected by the user. These prompts may include resource-specific dynamic content and can be chained together to support entire workflows.
- **Logging:** Defined by the MCP server, this defines the log message level for log messages sent to the client and may let the client adjust it.
- **Experimental:** This capability serves as a wildcard for custom, application-specific features that may be implemented by either the MCP client or server.

### 2.3 Procedure

MCP uses JSON-RPC as the underlying protocol for message exchange between the client and server. Messages can be transmitted via stdin/stdout when the client and server run on the same system, or via HTTP POST for network-based communication. For HTTP-based interactions, MCP optionally supports OAuth 2.1 for authorization, to be implemented by both the client and server as needed.

MCP defines three primary message types: request, response and notification. All three message types have a predefined JSON-RPC format and can be initiated by both the client and the server. Notifications are one-way messages and used to signal events such as task cancellation or to report task progress.

The typical use of MCP is structured into three phases:

1. **Initialization:** MCP client and server exchange and negotiate capabilities, and agree on a protocol version.
2. **Operation:** The client and server exchange messages according to the negotiated capabilities. A typical interaction starts with a user prompt, which the LLM converts into a sequence of MCP requests containing capability-specific calls. These requests, which may be batched, are sent to the server. Depending on the capability and logging strategy, the server may trigger additional nested message exchanges and LLM interactions. The final result is returned to the MCP host.
3. **Shutdown:** The connection is closed gracefully, with the shutdown procedure differing based on the chosen transport method (stdio or HTTP).

### 2.4 Current Implementations

There are already thousands of MCP server implementations available, covering a wide range of use cases, including database integration, file system operations, software development and application automation, image and video processing, blockchain interaction, and more. A comprehensive and regularly updated list can be found on the Glama website[5].

To support the development of MCP-based systems, several codebases are available for implementing MCP clients and servers. Official SDKs provided by Anthropic include support for Python, TypeScript, C#, Java, Kotlin, and Swift. In addition, community-driven projects offer implementations in other languages such as Go and Rust, as well as a widely adopted, feature-rich Python implementation known as *fastmcp*[6].

## 3 Use Cases in Digital Forensics and Incident Response

AI, in general, and LLMs, in particular, offer significant potential to support forensic investigations. However, for such technologies to be adopted on a broad scale and especially admissible in court, several critical challenges must be addressed. One central point of criticism, which continues to foster skepticism, is the lack of transparency in the outputs generated by AI methods [5]. Even modern reasoning models, capable of providing a chain of thought, do not yet meet the reproducibility and explainability required for their unreserved use in investigative contexts. One contributing factor is that the way an LLM interprets data and formulates conclusions is often difficult for humans to comprehend. As the model is granted greater freedom to analyze information and generate its inferences, the transparency of its reasoning diminishes. This increased freedom makes it harder for humans to trace or validate the model's logic and increases the risk of misinterpretation and hallucinations. We refer to the extent of an LLM's independent reasoning as its *inference freedom level.*

This shortcoming affects not only parties, such as judges or attorneys, but also the investigators themselves. Investigators and independent experts must be able to present their conclusions in a manner that is comprehensible and verifiable in a legal setting, which is not feasible if AI models are applied in a black-box manner [7,15]. An essential requirement in this context is auditability. The use of AI systems in forensic investigations must be accompanied by robust logging and documentation mechanisms that enable the reconstruction of each step in the analytical process. This documentation includes the input data, model versions, prompt formulations, and generated outputs. Only with such traceable and verifiable records can investigators and expert witnesses credibly justify their conclusions, and can courts evaluate the reliability and admissibility of AI-assisted findings.

[5] https://glama.ai/mcp/servers.
[6] https://github.com/jlowin/fastmcp.

From our perspective, MCP servers can contribute to resolving or at least mitigating many of the aforementioned issues. In particular, they enable an assessment of the AI methods employed, which in turn can be used to evaluate their admissibility in forensic investigations. For traditional forensic tools, a range of requirements must be met in order to conform to established best practices. Daniel and Daniel state that "*[f]or any tool to be forensically sound, it must be definable, predictable, repeatable, and verifiable*" [4] and Horsman emphasizes the need for rigorous tool testing [9]. MCP servers as building blocks for larger AI-based workflows can fulfill these requirements, as they can be assessed and tested separately from the LLM orchestrating them. They can significantly promote the traceability and comprehensibility of the results produced by an LLM, helping to reduce the black-box nature that poses significant challenges in forensic and legal contexts [5,17]. However, this does not occur automatically. Since an MCP server can essentially implement arbitrary functionalities, including querying other LLMs, it is important to assess a server's functionality concerning its suitability for forensic purposes.

We argue that MCP servers can be classified based on how much they allow the LLM discretion in interpreting the data returned. For example, to determine the group membership of a user account, an MCP server might return only the contents of the Windows registry in plain text to the controlling LLM. In this case, the LLM is responsible for correctly parsing the data and correlating values from the relevant registry keys. The MCP server merely provides the data in a format readable by the LLM, while all interpretation is left entirely to the LLM.

At the other end of the spectrum is an MCP server that directly provides the functionality to return the group membership of accounts. The corresponding logic, i.e., parsing the registry and linking the relevant keys, can be implemented within the MCP server in a transparent and auditable manner. In this scenario, the LLM has no interpretive discretion when answering whether a given account belongs to a specific group. Naturally, intermediate levels also exist—for instance, when the Windows registry data has already been preprocessed or filtered.

We call this spectrum the *inference constraint level* of an MCP server. This level describes how much an MCP server constrains the inference freedom level. The inference constraint level of an MCP server is inversely proportional to the inference freedom level of an LLM. As constraint increases, the model's capacity for interpretive deviation decreases, ensuring greater alignment with forensic standards. Figure 2 illustrates this concept on a schematic level.

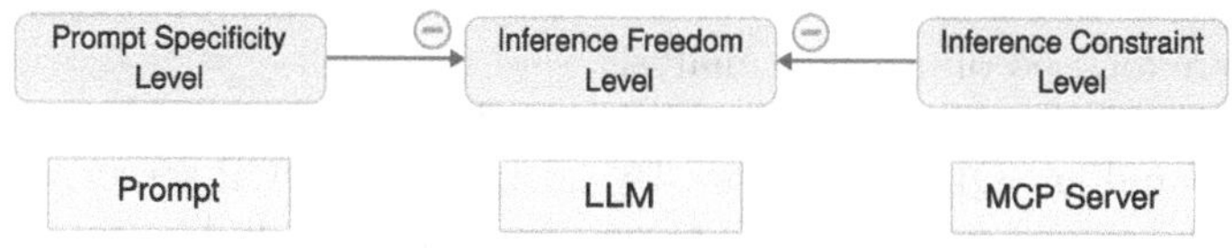


**Fig. 2.** Relation between prompt specificity level, inference constraint level, and the inference freedom level.

Figure 2 also illustrates that the inference freedom level is not limited solely by the inference constraint level; the prompt also influences it. The prompt may be highly specific, e.g., prescribing the execution of certain MCP functions in a defined order, or it may be abstract and generic. Accordingly, we define the *prompt specificity level* as the variable that captures this dimension.

An MCP server's appropriate inference constraint level depends heavily on its intended use. For artifact analysis, a very high level is required. The MCP server should provide only transparent and verifiable functionality in such cases. In contrast, when an MCP server is used to generate guesses for password cracking, it may employ arbitrary or non-explainable methods, as the individual guesses are available for inspection afterward.

The following sections present various applications that benefit from integrating MCP servers to constrain the inference freedom level of LLMs. These use cases span digital forensic investigations, incident response scenarios, test data generation, and the development of knowledge bases.

### 3.1 Knowledge Database

One use case of an MCP server within forensic workflows is to enable an LLM to access and query knowledge databases. These may include scientific papers, technical specifications, documentation, or dedicated forensic knowledge bases such as SOLVE-IT [8]. This approach also addresses a limitation noted by Scanlon et al. [14], who observed that LLMs may lack information on recent artifacts due to the static nature of their training data. In contrast, MCP servers could query the internet or fall back to maintained data sources.

The MCP server can present the LLM with varying levels of structured data depending on the implementation. In its simplest form, it supplies raw, unformatted content directly retrieved from the knowledge sources. In more advanced setups, it can enrich this input with contextual metadata—such as source reliability, publication date, document type, or cross-references to related materials. This added structure helps the LLM reason more effectively about the information it receives.

By enabling the LLM to access structured forensic knowledge, the MCP server supports forensic processes in multiple ways. At its simplest, it allows investigators to retrieve relevant information more easily and quickly by expressing their queries in natural language. Beyond that, the MCP server can help extract detailed guidance—for example, where to find a specific artifact, how to parse it, or how to interpret it. This capability can also be combined with other MCP servers focused on artifact analysis.

For example, consider an investigator analyzing a mobile device that contains an unfamiliar SQLite database. By querying the MCP server with a natural language question such as "What does the msg_store.db file from WhatsApp contain, and how can I extract message timestamps?", the LLM can access structured knowledge from relevant documentation, prior case analyses, or published forensic research.

### 3.2 Artifact Analysis

Digital forensic investigations often involve analyzing data from application- or operating system-specific sources. Common examples include SQL or SQLite databases used by messaging apps and other mobile applications, though a wide variety of formats may be encountered. Before such data can be examined, it typically must be parsed into a structured, human-readable format. A common approach is to extract and convert the contents into plain text, which is then passed to an LLM for analysis. MCP simplifies this process by enabling LLMs to interact directly with databases or other data sources. For instance, official MCP servers for PostgreSQL and SQLite already support such direct access[7].

While this approach simplifies data ingestion, it presents two key limitations: (i) it remains generic, requiring the LLM to interpret and analyze the raw data itself, and (ii) it often involves transmitting large volumes of data, constrained by the LLM's context window. To overcome these issues, we propose the use of *application-specific and context-aware MCP servers*. MCP can act as a *semantic layer* between the LLM and data sources, e.g. including databases, log files, or application-specific formats, without requiring the model to directly parse or understand the underlying structure, thus reducing its inference freedom level. By exposing well-defined tools with meaningful names and descriptions, the MCP server allows the LLM to select appropriate operations based on what it is trying to accomplish in response to the user's query. The MCP server then performs targeted, domain-specific tasks and returns only the relevant results. This not only increases the accuracy and efficiency of the analysis, but also significantly reduces context window usage by avoiding unnecessary data transfer.

*Forensic Tool Use.* One example of this approach is the use of an MCP server to enable LLMs to interact with arbitrary forensic applications and tools. In digital forensics, this opens the door for LLMs to use established forensic utilities rather than reproducing functionality that existing tools already implement. MCP can interface with anything from basic command-line tools like `file` or `strings` to advanced frameworks such as Volatility or The Sleuth Kit (TSK), and even GUI-based software—provided the MCP server manages the interaction appropriately.

However, as discussed before, the inference freedom level of an LLM when interacting with forensic tools depends heavily on how the corresponding MCP server is implemented. In a minimal setup, the MCP server may act as a thin wrapper that simply allows the LLM to execute a tool and return its raw output. While this approach can be effective when the prompt is explicit, it poses several challenges for more general or ambiguous instructions: the LLM may fail to recognize which tool is appropriate, lack the necessary knowledge to construct correct command-line arguments, or misinterpret the tool's output.

To illustrate these limitations, consider the prompt: *"List all deleted files of the file system on disk.dd."*

[7] https://github.com/modelcontextprotocol/servers/.

In this scenario, the LLM is granted access to a basic MCP server that exposes a tool called `run_tsk_command()`, allowing execution of arbitrary commands from TSK. This tool requires the LLM to specify the exact command and its parameters—such as invoking `fls` with the appropriate flags. As a result, the LLM must (i) identify that TSK is the appropriate toolkit, (ii) construct the correct command syntax, and (iii) correctly interpret the output. This setup leaves significant room for error. Without sufficient context, the LLM may hallucinate commands, misuse tool arguments, or misread results—ultimately compromising the quality and reliability of the response.

In a more advanced implementation, the MCP server might expose a dedicated tool such as `get_fls_output()`. This abstraction makes it easier for the LLM to invoke the underlying functionality without constructing the full command manually. However, it still assumes that the LLM understands that `fls` is the appropriate tool for listing deleted files. A further refinement would be to expose a semantically named tool like `get_file_system_hierarchy_using_fls()`, accompanied by a detailed docstring that provides contextual guidance. This helps the LLM better align the user's intent with the correct tool. Nevertheless, the model is still responsible for parsing the output and identifying deleted files—typically indicated by an asterisk in the `fls` output—introducing another potential point of failure.

To further reduce ambiguity and guide the LLM more effectively, the MCP server can expose a high-level tool such as `list_deleted_files_using_fls()`. In this case, the LLM's role is limited to identifying and invoking the appropriate tool based on the user's query.

*Correlation.* In addition to enabling access to individual artifact sources or forensic tools, MCP can support the correlation of data across multiple sources. Naturally, one approach is to implement a single MCP server that exposes high-level functions, such as `list_deleted_files()`, which internally aggregate and correlate results from multiple tools or data sources. In such cases, the logic for correlation is hardcoded within the MCP server, offering the LLM a unified and context-aware result. However, this approach limits the LLM's flexibility, as it has no influence over how data is combined or interpreted.

An alternative strategy leverages the LLM's ability to interact with multiple independent MCP servers. In this approach, the LLM orchestrates artifact analysis by invoking a combination of tools and querying diverse data sources—such as using TSK, a file carver like Scalpel, and inspecting application-level artifacts, including entries in the trash or recycle bin. This gives the LLM greater inferential freedom during the analysis and correlation but also introduces risks: decisions may lack consistency, and correlations may be incomplete or incorrect.

Ultimately, the effectiveness of MCP in artifact analysis depends on how responsibilities are distributed between the LLM and the server. Properly designed MCP interfaces can significantly reduce hallucinations and errors arising from limited knowledge or incorrect assumptions. However, this comes at the cost of increased implementation complexity and a greater need for forensic domain expertise. As MCP becomes integrated into forensic workflows, practitioners must carefully consider the abstraction level each server provides and strike an appropriate balance between automation, transparency, and control.

### 3.3 Comprehensible Reporting

As highlighted by Michelet and Breitinger [13], LLMs show promise in supporting forensic report writing. Their analysis of typical forensic reports revealed a common structure based on four main data sources: tool reports generated by forensic software, the prosecutor's mandate outlining the case and investigative goals, lab logs documenting the examiner's procedures and observations, and the examiner's own knowledge drawn from both the current and past cases.

In their approach, LLMs were prompted manually with structured inputs corresponding to these sections. While effective, this workflow is limited by its reliance on manual data collation and prompting. We propose that integrating LLMs with MCP servers may significantly improve the efficiency, consistency, and traceability of this process.

With MCP integration, the LLM no longer depends on manually aggregated inputs. Instead, it can autonomously retrieve and interpret relevant information from specialized MCP servers—each responsible for providing one type of contextual data (e.g., tool outputs, mandate content, lab notes, or prior case knowledge). A shared knowledge base guides the LLM in structuring the report according to formal forensic standards and include information, that lets an LLM ask for examiner knowledge or additional data or information when required.

Given a high-level request—such as generating a report for a particular case—the LLM can use MCP interfaces to identify and retrieve query-relevant information, organize it based on a predefined format template, and tailor the content to match the required detail level. This enables more dynamic and adaptable reporting workflows, suitable for different forensic use cases.

Furthermore, the MCP servers can log the exact data they provide to the LLM, helping to comprehend the report generated by the LLM. Notably, this shows us what kind of data could have helped the LLM to write the report but does not mean that all the retrieved data is included in the report.

### 3.4 Agentic MCP Server for Live Analysis and Response

Endpoint agents are commonly installed on client systems to monitor activity and respond to threats. MCP provides a flexible way to simplify interactions with such agents. For example, an MCP server can be deployed directly as an endpoint agent on a client, exposing core monitoring capabilities to an LLM, such as listing running processes, active network sockets, or logged-in users. This allows the LLM to query live system data that may be critical during incident response scenarios.

Beyond data collection, the MCP server can also expose response actions to the LLM, including terminating user sessions, closing network connections, or killing specific processes. This enables the LLM to make context-aware decisions based on up-to-date system state—for instance, detecting an unauthorized SSH session and terminating it in real time.

The degree of autonomy granted to the LLM can vary significantly. In a controlled setup, the LLM is restricted to a set of predefined, well-documented tools provided by the MCP server. Alternatively, a less restrictive configuration might expose a full root shell, allowing the LLM to execute arbitrary commands on the system. While more powerful, such an approach increases the risk of unintended consequences due to malformed or incorrect instructions. Alternatively, MCP can act as a translation layer between the LLM and existing endpoint agent frameworks. Instead of replacing these established agents, the MCP server can wrap their APIs or command-line interfaces and expose selected functionalities as structured tools.

### 3.5 Automated Synthetic Data Generation

A persistent challenge in digital forensics is the automatic generation of test data to train investigators and validate forensic tools. As Voigt et al. [16] highlight, LLMs hold significant potential for creating forensic data with minimal instructor effort by leveraging their creative capacity to simulate diverse personas, backgrounds, and actions.

With MCP, servers can interact with tools like ForTrace++ [18], enabling LLMs to generate scenario descriptions in natural language. For example, a prompt like "Create a ForTrace++ scenario where Firefox navigates to example.com" can be interpreted by the LLM, which—using an MCP server's knowledge of the scenario format—automatically produces a valid scenario file.

MCP also supports more advanced simulations through dynamic GUI automation. When the server provides capabilities such as capturing screenshots, identifying GUI elements, and simulating keyboard and mouse input, the LLM can iteratively observe and interact with the user interface. It may request a screenshot, analyze it via computer vision, determine the next action based on the visible UI, and instruct the server to perform mouse or keyboard inputs. This allows the LLM to handle unpredictable interface behavior, such as unexpected pop-ups or modal dialogs, with appropriate responses.

Even more complex scenarios can be envisioned where multiple LLMs, each connected to its own MCP server, interact with one another. For example, two LLMs running Android emulators could exchange messages, respond to each other's actions, and collaboratively simulate realistic multi-device, multi-user forensic scenarios.

### 3.6 Adversary Simulation

MCP can also be employed in proactive security scenarios, such as simulating attacker behavior in controlled environments. By equipping an LLM with tools commonly used throughout the attack lifecycle—such as network scanners, enumeration scripts, credential dumpers, privilege escalation exploits, and lateral movement utilities—the LLM can act as an autonomous or semi-autonomous adversary within a sandboxed lab environment. Exposed to these tools via MCP, and guided by a clear objective (e.g., exfiltrate a file or gain persistence), the LLM can query system state, invoke actions, and adapt its strategy in real time. This offers a novel and dynamic approach to red teaming, penetration testing, and adversary simulation—where the LLM behaves less like a scripted agent and more like a flexible, goal-driven attacker. Recent work has highlighted the need for such intelligent simulation platforms to assess vulnerabilities against AI-powered threats and support defenders in maintaining control over increasingly complex attack surfaces [6,11].

Another interesting direction is to deploy the agent from Sect. 3.4 as a defensive counterpart within the simulation environment. This creates the possibility of a closed-loop, "Colosseum-style" simulation where offensive and defensive systems adapt to each other in real time, offering a unique testbed for studying both attack strategies and automated incident response dynamics.

In particular, such simulations help uncover detection blind spots by introducing dynamic, LLM-generated attack chains that may deviate from established Tactics, Techniques, and Procedures. Unlike traditional testing approaches that rely on known signatures or scripted behavior, LLM-driven adversaries can combine tools and strategies in novel ways, revealing weaknesses that static or rule-based test cases might overlook. This allows defenders to evaluate their detection capabilities against a broader spectrum of potential threats, including those that do not conform to familiar adversary patterns.

Beyond detection, these simulations also enable the development and validation of automated forensic playbooks—predefined workflows for responding to security incidents. Running LLM-driven attacks in a controlled environment allows security teams to test whether these playbooks trigger appropriately, adapt to evolving threats, and capture the necessary evidence at the right time. This helps identify procedural gaps and refine decision logic under conditions that more closely reflect real-world, unpredictable adversary behavior. As a result, MCP-enabled simulations support both automation and analyst training by offering a more authentic environment for testing and improving incident response.

## 4 Discussion

As demonstrated in the previous sections, MCP opens up a broad range of opportunities for digital forensics. These range from simplifying common tasks such as artifact analysis, to enabling more sophisticated operations like cross-source correlation and the autonomous generation of test data. However, to fully leverage MCP's potential within forensic workflows, several technical and conceptual considerations must first be addressed. Following this, we examine additional challenges that MCP introduces to the field of digital forensics

*Enhancing Transparency in LLM-Driven Analysis.* A central benefit of MCP is its ability to reduce the inherent black-box character of LLMs. When integrated with context-aware, application-specific MCP servers, LLMs no longer need to rely solely on internal reasoning to interpret data or make decisions. Instead, they can invoke clearly defined tools whose behavior is preconfigured and documented. This improves transparency and makes the analysis process more understandable and traceable—both for analysts and for future reviews.

To ensure this level of transparency, MCP servers should offer detailed documentation and implement comprehensive logging. Logs should capture each tool invocation, including parameters passed by the LLM, tool output, and timestamps. When paired with LLM logs and structured explanations of the tools used, the auditability of automated forensic workflows increases significantly.

*Delegating Microtasks to Custom MCP Servers.* MCP's design allows forensic workflows to be broken down into smaller, well-defined components. Even micro-level decisions that would typically be made implicitly by the LLM—such as filtering data or normalizing timestamps—can be delegated to lightweight MCP tools. This modularization increases reproducibility and clarity, as each step in the analysis becomes externally visible and testable.

*Standardization of MCP Servers.* To support the reliable integration of MCP servers into forensic workflows, it is essential to establish standardized definitions for the tools and functions they expose. For example, a function named `extract_deleted_files()` is ambiguous, as it does not specify the method of extraction—such as file carving, recovery from a trash bin, or metadata-based reconstruction. Leveraging existing frameworks like SOLVE-IT [8] can help define consistent tool semantics and documentation standards, facilitating the collaborative development and reuse of MCP tools among forensic practitioners.

*Ensuring Forensic Soundness and Data Integrity.* For MCP to be usable in evidentiary contexts, its implementation must follow established principles of forensic soundness. This includes ensuring that tools accessed by the LLM are strictly read-only and do not modify the underlying data. The MCP server itself must also operate non-intrusively, meaning it should not alter, overwrite, or delete any evidence—intentionally or unintentionally—unless such actions are explicitly permitted in a controlled and well-documented context. Maintaining this level of control is vital to preserve the integrity of the evidence and to ensure that all results remain verifiable and legally defensible. Existing general-purpose MCP servers for database access often include both read and write functionality and may, therefore, be unsuited for forensic use without modification.

*Facilitating Privacy through Pseudonymization.* Another challenge in digital forensics—especially when relying on hosted LLMs—is the handling of sensitive or personal data. MCP can serve as a useful abstraction layer here as well. Servers can be designed to pseudonymize sensitive identifiers before exposing data to the LLM, thus mitigating privacy concerns during analysis.

By integrating pseudonymization functionality into the MCP server, identifiers and other sensitive values can be consistently replaced before being passed to the LLM. This requires case-specific design to ensure reversibility (for de-pseudonymization) and correctness. Still, it presents a promising path to enabling the use of powerful hosted LLMs without exposing sensitive case material.

*Auditing MCP Servers.* A thorough audit must be performed beforehand to integrate an MCP server into forensic workflows safely and securely. Even if an MCP server fundamentally implements the aforementioned beneficial features, such as logging, it must be ensured that the intended functionality has indeed been correctly implemented. In particular, care must be taken to ensure no unintended or even malicious functionality is present in the MCP server. For example, it would be entirely feasible to develop an MCP server that operates correctly and possesses all the necessary forensic features yet additionally transmits certain sensitive information from case data to the Internet. To counter this issue, auditing and analyzing MCP servers is required. Trust can be further enhanced by maintaining a curated repository that exclusively hosts reviewed and accredited MCP servers.

*Forensic Analysis of MCP Servers.* In addition to the analysis conducted before the integration of MCP servers into forensic workflows, the analysis of MCP servers will also play a role in future investigations. Integrating these servers into operating systems and applications will inevitably lead to their presence while examining IT systems. Consequently, there is an equally strong need for capabilities to analyze MCP servers forensically. This includes, for example, determining its functionalities, analyzing function executions and their associated input and output data, and the identification of other potentially present artifacts generated within or by an MCP server.

*Action Attribution.* Beyond the opportunities that MCP offers for digital forensics and incident response, it also adds a new layer to an already complex challenge: the attribution of actions. Determining the origin of an action—whether it was initiated by a user, a piece of malware, or an automated system—has long been a core task in forensic investigations [2]. The integration of MCP introduces a new dimension to this challenge: actions can now be executed by MCP servers, potentially triggered by an autonomous AI agent on the user's computer acting independently or on behalf of users. As MCP becomes increasingly embedded into applications and operating systems, enabling agents to control fundamental system functionality, forensic investigations must now account for AI-driven behavior as a distinct source of activity.

Consider a scenario in which a web browser visits a website and downloads illicit content. Traditionally, a forensic investigation would focus on identifying artifacts that support the hypothesis that the user performed these actions—such as web history entries, download records, or file system traces. These artifacts could be found across browser databases, file metadata, and system logs.

Now, imagine a system where an autonomous AI agent, connected via MCP, has full control over the browser and is capable of initiating visits and downloads independently. In this case, attribution becomes substantially more difficult. The investigator must establish whether the user acted intentionally or whether the AI performed these actions autonomously—potentially opening the door to defenses such as the Trojan Horse Defense, in which a suspect claims the system acted on its own without their knowledge.

To address this, it will become critical to identify forensic artifacts that can reliably distinguish between actions carried out by a human user and those initiated by an AI agent. This may involve analyzing MCP server logs, agent execution traces, or internal mechanisms of the controlled applications. Moreover, the notion of *intent* and *human involvement* introduces an additional layer of complexity. If an AI agent executed a task directly but was explicitly instructed to do so by the user, the responsibility differs significantly from a case where the agent acted autonomously or in error. Future investigations will not only need to determine what happened, but also who caused it to happen, and in what context—human, AI, or a combination of both.

## 5 Conclusion

MCP demonstrates significant potential to enhance the forensic applicability of LLMs by addressing core challenges such as transparency, explainability, and reproducibility. In this paper, we propose a conceptual framework that demonstrates how MCP servers can constrain the interpretive scope of LLMs in a structured and auditable manner, thereby helping to align LLM-supported analysis with forensic expectations. Using a theoretical exploration of relevant use cases, we discussed how MCP can serve as a basis for more transparent and modular workflows. Our discussion also identified critical considerations, such as forensic soundness and privacy protection, that must guide the design and evaluation of MCP-based systems to ensure their suitability in investigative settings.

Despite its potential, applying MCP in forensic contexts presents some limitations. While MCP servers can provide contextual data to the LLM, it remains uncertain whether the model reliably incorporates this information into its reasoning or output. Combined with the ongoing risk of hallucinations, this limitation should be examined more closely in future research. Furthermore, MCP servers may themselves rely on complex internal logic or even external model calls, which—if not properly documented—can reintroduce black-box characteristics that undermine transparency. Additionally, insufficient testing or lack of standardization across MCP server implementations may lead to inconsistencies that affect reproducibility and admissibility in court.

Building on our theoretical foundation, future research should explore practical strategies for integrating MCP servers into existing forensic tools and workflows. A key focus for this will be determining how responsibilities should be divided between the MCP server and the underlying LLM to ensure transparency, auditability, and reproducibility.

Additionally, as LLMs become increasingly embedded in everyday applications, new forensic challenges will emerge. MCP logs may aid in reconstructing user behavior, however, the semi-autonomous nature of LLMs complicates efforts to attribute specific actions to either the user or the LLM. Resolving this ambiguity will be critical to maintaining forensic interpretations that are grounded, reliable, and consistent with legal standards.

## References


1. Anthrophic: Model Context Protocol: Specification. https://modelcontextprotocol.io/specification/, Accessed 23 May 2025
2. Bowles, S., Hernandez-Castro, J.: The first 10 years of the trojan horse defence. Comput. Fraud Secur. **2015**(1), 5–13 (2015). https://doi.org/10.1016/S1361-3723(15)70005-9
3. Costantini, S., De Gasperis, G., Olivieri, R.: Digital forensics and investigations meet artificial intelligence. Ann. Math. Artif. Intell. **86**(1), 193–229 (2019)
4. Daniel, L.E., Daniel, L.E.: Digital Forensics for Legal Professionals: Understanding Digital Evidence from the Warrant to the Courtroom. Syngress, Waltham, MA (2012)
5. Garrett, B.L., Rudin, C.: Interpretable algorithmic forensics. Proc. Natl. Acad. Sci. **120**(41), e2301842120 (2023). https://doi.org/10.1073/pnas.2301842120
6. Guembe, B., Azeta, A., Misra, S., Osamor, V.C., Fernandez-Sanz, L., Pospelova, V.: The emerging threat of AI-driven cyber attacks: a review. Appl. Artif. Intell. **36**(1), 2037254 (2022)
7. Hall, S.W., Sakzad, A., Choo, K.K.R.: Explainable artificial intelligence for digital forensics. Wiley Interdis. Rev. Forensic Sci. **4**(2), e1434 (2022)
8. Hargreaves, C., van Beek, H., Casey, E.: SOLVE-IT: a proposed digital forensic knowledge base inspired by MITRE ATT&CK. Forensic Sci. Int. Digit. Investigation **52**, 301864 (2025). https://doi.org/10.1016/j.fsidi.2025.301864
9. Horsman, G.: Tool testing and reliability issues in the field of digital forensics. Digit. Investig. **28**, 163–175 (2019). https://doi.org/10.1016/j.diin.2019.01.009
10. Hou, X., Zhao, Y., Wang, S., Wang, H.: Model Context Protocol (MCP): Landscape, Security Threats, and Future Research Directions. arXiv preprint arXiv:2503.23278 (2025)
11. Jaber, A., Fritsch, L.: Towards ai-powered cybersecurity attack modeling with simulation tools: review of attack simulators. In: International Conference on P2P, Parallel, Grid, Cloud and Internet Computing, pp. 249–257. Springer (2022)
12. Jarrett, A., Choo, K.K.R.: The impact of automation and artificial intelligence on digital forensics. Wiley Interdis. Rev. Forensic Sci. **3**(6), e1418 (2021)
13. Michelet, G., Breitinger, F.: Chatgpt, llama, can you write my report? an experiment on assisted digital forensics reports written using (local) large language models. Forensic Sci. Int. Digit. Inv. **48**, 301683 (2024)
14. Scanlon, M., Breitinger, F., Hargreaves, C., Hilgert, J.N., Sheppard, J.: ChatGPT for digital forensic investigation: the good, the bad, and the unknown. Forensic Sci. Int. Digit. Inv. **46**, 301609 (2023)
15. Tynan, P.: The integration and implications of artificial intelligence in forensic science. Forensic Sci. Med. Pathol. **20**(3), 1103–1105 (2024)

16. Voigt, L.L., Freiling, F., Hargreaves, C.J.: Re-imagen: generating coherent background activity in synthetic scenario-based forensic datasets using large language models. Forensic Sci. Int. Digit. Inv. **50**, 301805 (2024). https://doi.org/10.1016/j.fsidi.2024.301805, dFRWS APAC 2024 - Selected Papers from the 4th Annual Digital Forensics Research Conference APAC
17. Wickramasekara, A., Breitinger, F., Scanlon, M.: Exploring the potential of large language models for improving digital forensic investigation efficiency. Forensic Sci. Int. Digit. Inv. **52**, 301859 (2025)
18. Wolf, D., Göbel, T., Baier, H.: Hypervisor-based data synthesis: on its potential to tackle the curse of client-side agent remnants in forensic image generation. Forensic Sci. Int. Digit. Inv. **48**, 301690 (2024). https://doi.org/10.1016/j.fsidi.2023.301690, dFRWS EU 2024 - Selected Papers from the 11th Annual Digital Forensics Research Conference Europe

# SCOPE - Activity Recognition Using Temporally Dominant Topic Identification In Forensic Chat Analysis

Rajon Bardhan[1](✉), Gokila Dorai[1], Gagan Agrawal[2], and Khan Mohammad Al-Farabi[2]

[1] Augusta University, Augusta, USA
{rbardhan,gdorai}@augusta.edu
[2] University of Georgia, UGA, Athens, USA
{gagrawal,kma27987}@uga.edu

**Abstract.** This paper introduces SCOPE (Semantic Coherence Pruning and Extraction), a framework designed to predict activities or events by identifying temporally dominant topics from large-scale, multi-threaded chat data. Modern investigations face vast volumes of heterogeneous messaging logs across platforms, users, and time, where manual review is infeasible. We posit that detecting a temporally dominant topic over some time can help identify an activity or event of relevance for further analysis. However, there are no prior works that efficiently extract a maximal window length and an associated topic that maintains a high probability of occurrence throughout. This paper formalizes the temporally dominant topic identification problem and presents SCOPE, an efficient algorithm that leverages two-stage pruning to keep search time reasonable for chats over very large windows (e.g., several months or even longer). The overall methodology includes an initial step where the topic probability of each message, and subsequently for each fixed length (unit) window, is computed using a SentenceTransformer model. In the probability pruning phase, windows below the relevance threshold are discarded; in the time pruning phase, contiguous sequences of identified windows are merged and pruned to enforce maximality. Our results show that SCOPE can identify events or activities in chat sequences within a reasonable runtime, and it can serve as a preprocessing module in forensic triage tools.

**Keywords:** Digital Forensics · Computer Forensics · Pruning · Machine Learning (ML) · Chat Data · Clustering

## 1 Introduction

Digital forensics constitutes a significant methodological approach for examining digital devices and identifying digital evidence pertinent to cybercrime investigations. The discipline, alternatively designated as computer or cyber forensics, typically encompasses five principal procedural phases: identification of resources


K.-K. R. Choo et al. (Eds.): ICDF2C 2025, LNICST 686, pp. 363–383, 2026.
https://doi.org/10.1007/978-3-032-22545-0_22

and data, extraction of evidence from digital devices, analysis of evidence, documentation of findings, and presentation of evidence in legal proceedings. The requirement for digital forensic investigations appears to be increasing in correlation with the proliferation of criminal activities in digital environments. This increase correlates with the expanded adoption of electronic devices [1]. Consequently, there exists a growing demand for qualified digital forensics investigators. Furthermore, the evolving nature of cybercrime methodologies and continuous technological advancements necessitate adaptive forensic investigation frameworks and procedures to address these incidents effectively [2].

Social media platforms represent a notable source of evidence for forensics investigators. These environments encompass various online platforms, chat rooms, and internet forums [3]. As of April 2024, 62.3% of the global population utilizes social media on a regular basis, with an average daily engagement of 2 h and 23 min [4]. The proliferation and widespread adoption of mobile devices have further contributed to the increased utilization of social media applications [5]. Users engage with diverse social media platforms on mobile devices, including Facebook, Instagram, WhatsApp, Telegram, and YouTube. This engagement results in the inadvertent deposition of substantial personal data on these platforms, thereby establishing mobile devices as critical evidentiary sources in social media-related investigations [6].

Recent research has focused on Online Social Networks (OSNs) for mobile devices. Investigators have conducted numerous studies on various social media applications, examining activity logs, image manipulation techniques, and performing case studies and surveys to monitor criminal activities on Facebook [7–10]. The popularity of Instagram has similarly prompted extensive research in mobile forensics pertaining to social media applications [11–15]. Additionally, researchers have investigated chat messages and media sharing functionalities on Telegram, Snapchat, and WhatsApp, identifying valuable evidentiary material for forensic examinations [16–19]. These studies collectively indicate the progression of research in social media applications on mobile devices for forensic purposes.

Despite these advancements, the acquisition of digital evidence from smartphone Instant Messaging applications presents considerable challenges for criminal investigations and judicial proceedings [20]. Users frequently employ multiple instant messaging applications concurrently to communicate on diverse topics. When device(s) are acquired, there are very long periods of time over which the user activity is spread. In many investigations, one is exploring possibilities that will link the owner of the device to the topic of investigation. In such cases, the user's involvement in an activity or presence at a specific location for a certain unknown (and unknown length) time window can be a relevant starting point. This leads to the need for finding, what we term as, *temporally dominant topic*, i.e., a topic and a *maximal time window* where the topic of occurs with a sufficiently high probability throughout this window. Our premise is that identification of such a window and topic can be linked to user's involvement in an activity for that period of time. For example, a person visiting a shopping mall might be discussing the stores and eating joints in the mall in their chats.

Researchers have investigated various machine learning and natural language processing algorithms for text forensics, with topic modeling algorithms gaining particular recognition in digital forensics. The extensive data generated by social media applications on mobile devices is predominantly unstructured, necessitating Natural Language Processing (NLP) techniques that enable the interpretation and extraction of meaning from human language through analysis of grammatical, semantic, and morphological elements [21]. Topic modeling facilitates the organization of textual databases into thematically related groups, enhancing contextual comprehension through the identification of similar textual patterns or structural sequences. However, topic modeling presents challenges including optimization complexities, sensitivity to noise, and instability [22]. Related to, and as a starting point for our work, several topic modeling algorithms have been employed for text mining research, including Probabilistic Latent Semantic Analysis (PLSA) [23–25], Latent Dirichlet Allocation (LDA) [26–29], Correlated Topic Model (CTM) [30], and BERTopic [31] to identify thematic elements within documents. However, no work to date specifically focuses on searching for a time window (of a variable length) where a topic dominates.

This paper formalizes the temporally dominant topic identification problem and present an efficient algorithm, called SCOPE (Semantic Coherence Pruning and Extraction). The essence of our approach involves a two-phase pruning to maintain reasonable search times when dealing with conversations spanning extensive timeframes (such as multiple months or longer). Our methodology begins with calculating topic probabilities for individual messages and subsequently for each fixed-length window segment. The two pruning methods are *Probability Pruning* and *Time Pruning*, which make the task of identifying relevant consecutive subsets of chat messages for any topic more efficiency. We demonstrate the calculation methodology for subset probabilities and establish the efficacy of our algorithm in extracting relevant subsets through pruning methods. This approach enhances computational efficiency compared to traditional brute force algorithms in evidence identification. We illustrate the effectiveness of our methodology through two case studies, highlighting its applicability to social media application investigations on mobile devices.

To demonstrate our approach, we utilized an 8-month-long Chit-Chat dataset containing communications between university students. This dataset encompasses messages from multiple concurrent chatrooms, enabling interpretation of communications across various social media applications. The case studies demonstrate that our proposed approach can identify recent events from the students' chat messages. The primary contributions of this paper are:

- We define the problem of finding temporally dominant topics, specifically pairs of topics and maximal time windows, where a topic occurs above a certain threshold frequency. This is based on the premise that such topics can help identify events or activities, and user's involvement in these, in exploratory forensic analysis.

- We introduce SCOPE, a novel framework that employs semantic embedding and probabilistic pruning to efficiently determine topic and maximal time window pairs without exhaustive search.
- We apply or extend and empirically evaluate three distinct semantic similarity approaches - Cosine Similarity, Hybrid Cosine-KeyBERT and LDA - demonstrating their comparative effectiveness for chat forensics and establishing a methodological foundation for future research in conversational context analysis.
- We formalize a two-phase pruning algorithm that provides substantial computational advantages over the bruteforce approach. Our empirical evaluation demonstrates that the approach significantly reduces the time to process the data while maintaining forensic insight quality.

## 2 Related Work

Previous research has employed Latent Dirichlet Allocation (LDA) topic modeling for social network analysis in digital forensics. Studies have integrated LDA with feature selection and machine learning to analyze online communication [23] and applied LDA within blockchain frameworks for digital forensics analysis on online social networks [24]. However, these investigations did not focus on user chat messages, limiting their scope to professional communications, statuses, or news on social media. This creates a significant research gap regarding the analysis of rich and informal data found in chat messages.

In the domain of chat data analysis for Digital Forensics, various topic modeling algorithms have been applied. Research has combined LDA topic modeling with itemset mining to address online grooming [26], implemented PLSA for analyzing library chat transcripts [25], and utilized semantic analysis with LDA to identify similar messages across messaging platforms including WhatsApp and Telegram [27]. A common limitation in these studies is their treatment of entire chat logs as single documents, focusing solely on topic identification rather than analyzing individual messages to uncover relationships and understand user motivations.

Beyond Digital Forensics, topic modeling algorithms have been successfully applied for chat data analysis across diverse sectors. In software engineering, LDA has been utilized to identify important discussion topics among developers [28]. In customer service contexts, newer models like BERTopic and Top2Vec have demonstrated superior performance compared to LDA in determining customer intents [31]. Additionally, LDA has been applied to analyze healthcare chat data [29]. These applications demonstrate the versatility of topic modeling algorithms in extracting meaningful insights from chat data across different domains.

The field has also seen integration of various machine learning and NLP techniques with topic modeling for short text data mining. Methodologies combining LDA with Named Entity-Relationship analysis, emotion and sentiment analysis, and linguistic feature extraction have been applied to social media data to understand user mental health [32]. Text mining with machine learning has been used to analyze user experiences with mobile applications [33]. However, these approaches typically focus on specific goals or topics rather than exploring user discussions across multiple concurrent topics.

Research on user profiling through chat message analysis has focused primarily on predicting user intent, satisfaction, personal traits, or responses [34–37]. These studies predominantly employ machine learning classification methods within specific chat scenarios but lack a comprehensive approach to identify relevant chat messages within temporal boundaries. Given the evolving nature of people's motives and perceptions, connecting all potential chat messages is crucial for accurate user profiling. This necessitates a method that searches for maximal time windows and associated dominant topics.

## 3 Methodology

Given a corpus $C$ comprising chat messages, and a set $T$ of investigative topics of interest our objective is to identify all *maximally relevant, contiguous message sequences* that exceed a configurable probabilistic relevance threshold $P_s$. The proposed pipeline applies sentence-level embedding, semantic similarity computation, window-based aggregation, and a two-phase pruning process - *probability pruning* followed by *time pruning* - to progressively refine the solution space and identify the topics and maximal time windows. This formulation enables forensic analysts to efficiently traverse the high-dimensional space of multi-threaded communications, substantially reducing the cognitive load associated with manual inspection. At the same time, it preserves the temporal structure necessary for contextual and evidentiary interpretation. Figure 1 shows an overview of our method.

*Notation.* Let $\mathcal{C} = \{C_1, C_2, \ldots, C_n\}$ denote the set of chatgroups. Each message $m_i \in C_j$ is associated with a timestamp $t_i$. Let $\{T_1, T_2, \ldots, T_k\}$ be the set of predefined or discovered topics. Let $P_s \in [0, 1]$ denote the minimum topic relevance threshold required to retain a window.

*Formal Problem Statement.* Given a sequence of chat messages and a topic $T_i \in \{T_1, T_2, \ldots, T_k\}$, our objective is to extract all *maximal*, contiguous subsets of time windows that satisfy the probability pruning condition and are not contained within any larger windowed segment. Formally, let $S(T_i)$ denote the set of such segments:

$$S(T_i) = \Big\{ S_j(T_i) \subseteq \{W_1, W_2, \ldots, W_m\} \;\Big|\; P(S_j(T_i)) \geq P_s \text{ and } S_j(T_i) \text{ is maximal} \Big\}$$

where:

$$S_j(T_i) = \{W_a, W_{a+1}, \ldots, W_b\} \quad \text{with } 1 \leq a \leq b \leq m$$

and $P(S_j(T_i))$ is the average topic probability across all messages in the windows $S_j(T_i)$.

We address the above problem through the following set of steps.

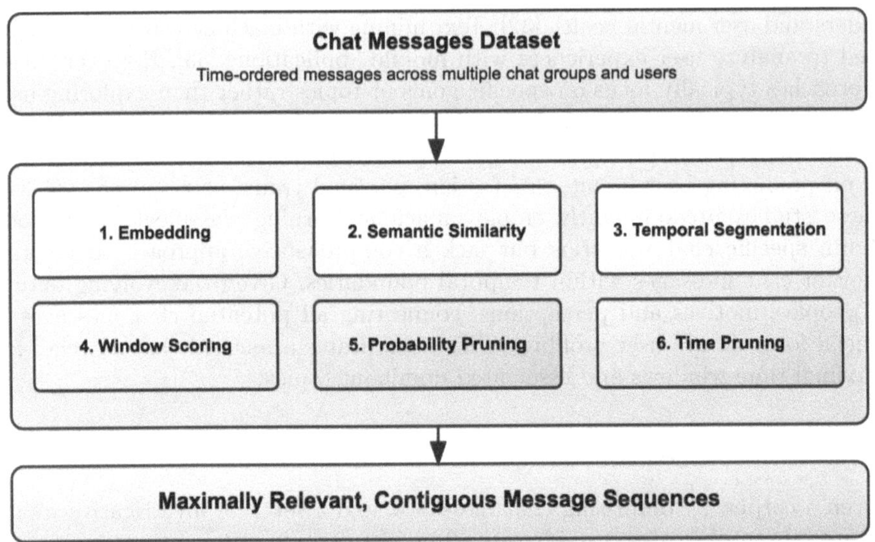


**Fig. 1.** An Overview of SCOPE Framework

*Step 1. Embedding.* Each message $m_i$ and topic label $T_j$ is embedded into a common semantic space using a SentenceTransformer model (e.g., `all-MiniLM-L12-v2`). The model outputs 384-dimensional dense vectors (where $\mathbf{t}_j$ denotes the embedding vector for topic $T_j$):

$$\text{Embed}(m_i) \rightarrow \mathbf{w}_i \in \mathbb{R}^{384}, \quad \text{Embed}(T_j) \rightarrow \mathbf{t}_j \in \mathbb{R}^{384}$$

*Step 2. Semantic Similarity Estimation.* To evaluate the effectiveness of different semantic similarity estimation techniques (discussed in Sect. 3.1) within our temporal and probabilistic pruning pipeline for chat context analysis, we systematically modified Step 2 (Semantic Similarity Estimation) while maintaining all other components of the pipeline constant. This controlled experimental design allows us to isolate the impact of the similarity measure on the overall performance of our forensic chat analysis system. A conceptual contribution of our work is the principled transformation of semantic similarity scores into proper probability distributions (Probabilistic Framework Using Softmax Transformation). While similarity measures quantify the semantic relatedness between messages and topics, they do not inherently represent probabilities. Therefore, we employ the softmax function to transform similarity scores into a valid probability distribution over topics:

$$P(T_j \mid m_i) = \frac{\exp(\beta \cdot \text{sim}(m_i, T_j))}{\sum_{k=1}^{K} \exp(\beta \cdot \text{sim}(m_i, T_k))} \tag{1}$$

where $\beta$ is a temperature parameter controlling the sharpness of the distribution (with higher values creating sharper distributions). This transformation ensures that: (1) all probabilities are in the range $[0, 1]$, (2) probabilities sum to 1 across all topics for a given message, and (3) the relative ordering of similarity scores is preserved.

*Step 3. Temporal Segmentation.* Each chatgroup $C_i \in \mathcal{C}$ is segmented into a sequence of non-overlapping time windows:

$$\{W_1, W_2, \ldots, W_m\}, \quad \text{where } W_k \subseteq C_i$$

Each window $W_k$ contains a subset of messages that fall within a fixed temporal interval (e.g., 5 minutes).

*Step 4. Window Scoring.* The topic relevance of a window $W_k$ for a given topic $T_j$ is computed by averaging the message-level probabilities:

$$P(T_j \mid W_k) = \frac{1}{|W_k|} \sum_{m_i \in W_k} P(T_j \mid m_i)$$

*Step 5. Probability Pruning.* In the first pruning phase, we discard any window $W_k$ that does not meet the minimum topic relevance threshold:

$$W_k \in PP(T_j) \iff P(T_j \mid W_k) \geq P_s$$

This step significantly reduces the search space by eliminating windows that are unlikely to be relevant, ensuring that only semantically meaningful segments progress to the next stage.

*Step 6. Time Pruning.* Next, we enforce a temporal maximality condition to avoid redundant overlapping segments. A sequence of windows $\{W_a, W_{a+1}, \ldots, W_b\} \subseteq PP(T_j)$ is maximal if:

- The average topic probability across the sequence meets or exceeds the threshold:

$$P(T_j \mid \{W_a, \ldots, W_b\}) \geq P_s$$

- Extending the sequence with adjacent windows would reduce the average below $P_s$:

$$P(T_j \mid \{W_{a-1}, \ldots, W_b\}) < P_s \quad \text{or} \quad P(T_j \mid \{W_a, \ldots, W_{b+1}\}) < P_s$$

## 3.1 Semantic Similarity Approaches

We implemented and compared three distinct approaches for measuring semantic relatedness between chat messages and investigative topics:

*Approach #1. Cosine Similarity (Baseline).* Our baseline approach computes the cosine similarity between message embeddings $\mathbf{w}_i$ and topic embeddings $\mathbf{t}_j$ generated using a SentenceTransformer model:

$$\text{sim}(m_i, T_j) = \frac{\mathbf{w}_i \cdot \mathbf{t}_j}{\|\mathbf{w}_i\| \cdot \|\mathbf{t}_j\|} \tag{2}$$

This similarity score is then transformed into a probability using the softmax function as described in our probabilistic framework. The approach captures the semantic orientation of messages in the embedding space but may lack sensitivity to key topical terms.

*Approach #2. Hybrid Cosine-KeyBERT Approach.* The second approach integrates KeyBERT [38] to identify and leverage topic-specific keywords, combining it with cosine similarity before applying the softmax transformation:

$$\text{sim}(m_i, T_j) = \frac{\mathbf{w}_i \cdot \mathbf{t}_j}{\|\mathbf{w}_i\| \cdot \|\mathbf{t}_j\|} \cdot \text{KeywordRelevance}(\text{KeyBERT}(m_i), T_j) \quad (3)$$

KeyBERT($m_i$) extracts the most relevant keywords from message $m_i$, and KeywordRelevance computes how relevant these extracted keywords are to topic $T_j$.

*Approach #3. Latent Dirichlet Allocation (LDA).* The third approach employs LDA [39] to model the distribution of latent topics across messages:

$$\text{sim}(m_i, T_j) = \theta_{i,j} \quad (4)$$

where $\theta_i$ represents the topic distribution for message $m_i$, and $\theta_{i,j}$ is the probability of topic $T_j$ occurring in message $m_i$. LDA naturally produces a probability distribution (as $\sum_{j=1}^{K} \theta_{i,j} = 1$), yet we still apply the softmax transformation to ensure consistency with other approaches and to allow temperature-based calibration. For LDA implementation, we aggregated messages into larger temporal segments to address the sparsity challenge presented by short chat messages. We optimized the number of topics $k$ using perplexity and coherence metrics.

### 3.2 Algorithm Implementation

Algorithm 1 presents the complete algorithm used in SCOPE framework implementation. The algorithm takes as input a corpus of chat messages organized into chatgroups $\mathcal{C}$, a set of investigative topics, a minimum probability threshold $P_s$, and a fixed window duration $\Delta t$. It proceeds systematically through the six steps of our pipeline: embedding messages and topics into a common semantic space (lines 1–6), computing similarity scores and transforming them into probabilities (lines 7–9), performing temporal segmentation (lines 10–12), scoring each window based on topic relevance (lines 14–16), applying probability pruning to filter low-relevance windows (lines 18–22), and executing time pruning to identify maximal contiguous segments (lines 24–41). The algorithm outputs a set of maximal time windows and associated topics that satisfy our formal problem statement, efficiently reducing the search space through our two-phase pruning approach.

**Algorithm 1.** Algorithm used in SCOPE Framework

**Require:** Set of chatgroups $\mathcal{C} = \{C_1, C_2, \ldots, C_n\}$, topics $\{T_1, T_2, \ldots, T_k\}$, threshold $P_s$, window duration $\Delta t$
**Ensure:** Set of maximal topic-relevant segments $S(T_j)$ for each topic $T_j$
1: **for** each message $m_i \in C_j$ where $C_j \in \mathcal{C}$ **do**
2:     $\mathbf{w}_i \leftarrow \text{Embed}(m_i)$
3: **end for**
4: **for** each topic $T_j$ **do**
5:     $\mathbf{t}_j \leftarrow \text{Embed}(T_j)$
6: **end for**
7: **for** each message $m_i$ and topic $T_j$ **do**
8:     Calculate $\text{sim}(m_i, T_j)$ based on chosen approach
9:     $P(T_j|m_i) \leftarrow \frac{\exp(\beta \cdot \text{sim}(m_i, T_j))}{\sum_{l=1}^{k} \exp(\beta \cdot \text{sim}(m_i, T_l))}$
10: **end for**
11: **for** each chatgroup $C_j \in \mathcal{C}$ **do**
12:     Segment $C_j$ into windows $\{W_1, W_2, \ldots, W_m\}$ of duration $\Delta t$
13: **end for**
14: **for** each topic $T_j$ **do**
15:     // **Window Scoring**
16:     **for** each window $W_l$ **do**
17:         $P(T_j|W_l) \leftarrow \frac{1}{|W_l|} \sum_{m_i \in W_l} P(T_j|m_i)$
18:     **end for**
19:     // **Probability Pruning**
20:     $PP(T_j) \leftarrow \{W_l : P(T_j|W_l) \geq P_s\}$
21:     // **Time Pruning**
22:     $S(T_j) \leftarrow \emptyset$, $\text{curr} \leftarrow \emptyset$
23:     **for** $l = 1$ to $m$ **do**
24:         **if** $W_l \in PP(T_j)$ **then**
25:             **if** $\text{curr} = \emptyset$ **then**
26:                 $\text{curr} \leftarrow \{W_l\}$
27:             **else**
28:                 $\text{temp} \leftarrow \text{curr} \cup \{W_l\}$
29:                 $P(T_j|\text{temp}) \leftarrow \frac{1}{|\text{temp}|} \sum_{W_r \in \text{temp}} P(T_j|W_r)$
30:                 **if** $P(T_j|\text{temp}) \geq P_s$ **then**
31:                     $\text{curr} \leftarrow \text{temp}$
32:                 **else**
33:                     $S(T_j) \leftarrow S(T_j) \cup \{\text{curr}\}$, $\text{curr} \leftarrow \{W_l\}$
34:                 **end if**
35:             **end if**
36:         **else if** $\text{curr} \neq \emptyset$ **then**
37:             $S(T_j) \leftarrow S(T_j) \cup \{\text{curr}\}$, $\text{curr} \leftarrow \emptyset$
38:         **end if**
39:     **end for**
40:     **if** $\text{curr} \neq \emptyset$ **then** $S(T_j) \leftarrow S(T_j) \cup \{\text{curr}\}$
41:     **end if**
42: **end for**
43: **return** $\{S(T_1), S(T_2), \ldots, S(T_k)\}$

### 3.3 Implementation and Parameter Choices

As previously mentioned, all embeddings were generated using the `all-MiniLM-L12-v2` model from the SentenceTransformers library, producing 384-dimensional vectors. Topic Selection Rationale: We identify all possible consecutive subsets of chat snippets for all users across 21 topics, namely: *'News'*, *'Research'*, *'Technology'*, *'Travel'*, *'Personal'*, *'Education'*, *'Career'*, *'Health'*, *'Sports'*, *'Vacation'*, *'Movie'*, *'Entertainment'*, *'Book'*, *'Event'*, *'Food'*, *'Politics'*, *'Finance'*, *'Relationships'*, *'Religion'*, *'Immigration'*, *'Fantasy'*. The selection of these topics is essential for this research as they provide the semantic foundation upon which the entire SCOPE framework operates. Without these predefined topic labels, the framework would face critical technical limitations: there would be no semantic anchor points for computing similarity scores in the embedding space, no basis for forming the probability distributions crucial to the softmax transformation, and no mechanism for the probability and time pruning phases that depend on topic relevance calculations. From an investigative perspective, digital forensics analysts would lack the ability to target their analysis toward specific areas of concern, losing the forensic focus needed to identify maximally relevant, contiguous message sequences that exceed probability thresholds. LDA was implemented using the gensim library with topic numbers ranging from 1–21.

The probability threshold $P_s$ was set to 0.07 for all experiments, based on preliminary testing that showed this value provided an optimal trade-off between precision and recall. (Section 4.2 shows our experimental results by varying the threshold.) Our implementation uses hourly intervals for temporal segmentation, providing a broader contextual view while maintaining computational efficiency. This granularity proved effective for capturing topic evolution in extended conversations while reducing computational complexity. After empirical testing, we set $\beta = 1.0$ to create sufficiently discriminative probability distributions.

In addition to topic and temporal segmentation, we incorporated user-specific analysis, processing chat segments on a per-user basis. This additional dimension allows the system to detect topic-relevant contributions from specific participants and identify user-level patterns of interest to forensic investigators. The user-specific segmentation is particularly valuable in multi-party conversations where different participants may exhibit varying degrees of involvement with topics of interest.

### 3.4 Computational Advantages Over Brute Force Approach

Our proposed heuristic pipeline offers significant computational advantages over a brute force baseline approach. While the baseline method executes only Steps 1–4 (embedding, similarity estimation, temporal segmentation, and window scoring), it must evaluate all possible consecutive subsets of temporal windows - a computational complexity of $O(m^2)$ for $m$ windows. For large-scale investigations with thousands of messages across multiple chat groups, this quadratic growth becomes prohibitively expensive, often requiring hours or days of processing time. In contrast, our two-phase pruning strategy (Steps 5–6) progressively reduces the search space by first applying probability pruning to eliminate windows with insufficient topic relevance ($P(T_j \mid W_k) < P_s$), and then enforcing temporal maximality conditions to identify only the most informative, non-redundant segments. Empirical testing reveals that this approach typically reduces the computational load while maintaining equivalent or superior forensic insight, making it particularly valuable for time-sensitive digital investigations where investigator cognitive load must be minimized.

### 3.5 Relation to Frequent Itemset Mining

Our methodology for temporal and probabilistic pruning of evolving chat contexts extends principles from frequent itemset mining to address the unique challenges of digital forensics investigations. While traditional frequent itemset mining algorithms like Apriori [40] and FP-Growth [41] operate on discrete items with binary presence/absence indicators across unordered transaction sets, our approach innovates by working with continuous probability scores across temporally ordered message sequences. This fundamental shift enables forensic analysts to identify maximally relevant, contiguous conversation segments that exceed configurable probabilistic relevance thresholds - a critical capability when investigating multi-threaded communications. Our two-phase pruning strategy, combining probability and temporal pruning, shares conceptual similarities with the candidate generation and testing phases in traditional frequent pattern mining [42], but adapts these principles to preserve the temporal context essential for evidentiary interpretation in digital forensics.

## 4 Experiments

### 4.1 Experimental Settings

*Hardware and Software Configurations.* All experiments were conducted on a MacBook Pro M1 Max with the following specifications: Total Number of Cores: 10 (8 performance cores and 2 efficiency cores), Memory: 64 GB, System Firmware Version: 10151.121.1, and OS Loader Version: 10151.121.1. The software environment used includes Anaconda version 2024.06–1.

*Dataset.* This study utilizes an 8-month dataset of university student chat conversations from the Chit-Chat corpus [43]. The resulting collection contains 258,146 lines of courteous English-language exchanges with timestamps, adding up to 2,478,521 words with no emojis present in the messages. The dataset encompasses 1,315 users across 7,168 chatrooms, with individual users often participating in multiple rooms simultaneously. All messages were collected between April 10 and November 16, 2018. We applied standard text normalization techniques including tokenization, whitespace trimming, and case normalization. We further processed the text by converting all words to lowercase, removing stopwords, and implementing WordNetLemmatizer and SpellChecker for word correction.

While the ChitChat dataset does not originate from multiple messaging platforms, it reflects key characteristics of multi-app environments, such as concurrent participation in multiple chatrooms, asynchronous message flows, and fragmented topical discussions. Thus, it serves as a valid surrogate for evaluating semantic-driven forensic methods intended for cross-platform chat evidence analysis.

### 4.2 Evaluation Results

***Performance of Semantic Similarity Approaches in SCOPE.*** Our methodology has considered three semantic similarity approaches (Cosine Similarity, Hybrid Cosine-KeyBERT and LDA). Given the time-sensitive nature of digital forensic investigations and the practical constraints of processing large-scale chat datasets, we evaluated computational efficiency alongside semantic accuracy. Consequently, we elected to conduct a comprehensive experimental evaluation focusing specifically on Cosine Similarity and LDA approaches, which provided an optimal balance between semantic fidelity (how accurately a method preserves and represents the true meaning and semantic relationships in the text data being analyzed) and processing efficiency.

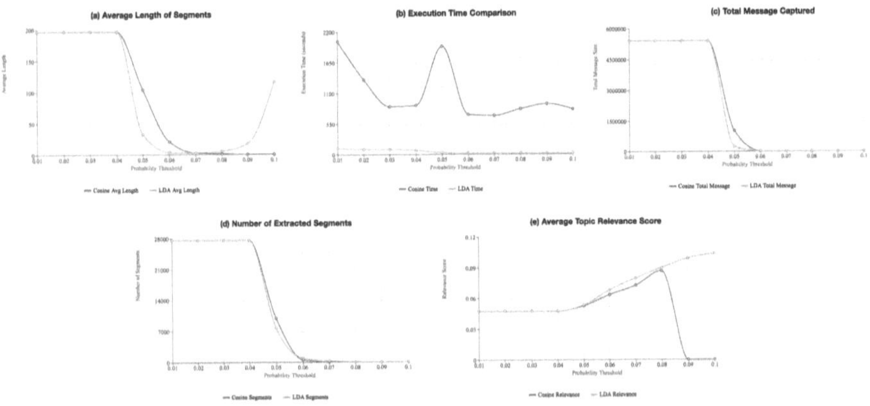


**Fig. 2.** SCOPE Comparative Evaluations at Various Probability Thresholds

Our evaluation, shown in Fig. 2, revealed substantial performance differences between Cosine similarity and LDA topic modeling approaches used to compute the semantic similarity on the entire dataset. While both methods extracted similar numbers of segments at lower thresholds (approximately 27,615 segments at 0.01 - 0.04 thresholds), LDA demonstrated remarkable efficiency advantages, processing data approximately 20 times faster than Cosine similarity (53.39

vs. 1100.39 s on average). Furthermore, LDA maintained effectiveness at higher probability thresholds (0.08 - 0.10), and consistently achieved superior topic relevance scores (0.07 vs. 0.05 on average). As probability thresholds increased above 0.05, LDA continued extracting meaningful segments with increasing relevance scores, while Cosine extraction rapidly deteriorated, suggesting LDA offers greater robustness across varying threshold parameters. These findings strongly indicate that LDA represents a better approach for our heuristic pipeline and large-scale topic modeling applications where both processing efficiency and extraction quality are critical considerations.

***Comparison with Bruteforce Technique.*** Our SCOPE framework's experimental analysis compared three approaches: (1) Heuristic Pipeline using LDA, (2) Heuristic Pipeline using Cosine similarity, and (3) Bruteforce technique using LDA (without any pruning mechanism).

*Short-term Analysis (1–10 days):* Table 1 summarizes the execution time statistics across all probability thresholds (0.01 – 0.1) and various time windows (1–10 days) tested. We measured execution time as the system time between the initiation and completion of each algorithm, implemented using Python's time module functions.

**Table 1.** Short-term Analysis - Execution Time Performance (seconds)

| Method | Mean | Min | Max | Median |
|---|---|---|---|---|
| SCOPE (LDA) | 7.16 | 0.07 | 46.00 | 1.72 |
| SCOPE (Cosine) | 74.14 | 2.57 | 421.60 | 39.06 |
| Bruteforce | 402.19 | 3.42 | 1550.03 | 183.08 |

The performance ratios between methods reveal dramatic efficiency differences:

- Bruteforce/LDA Ratio: 56.17x
- Bruteforce/Cosine Ratio: 5.43x
- Cosine/LDA Ratio: 10.35x

These results conclusively demonstrate LDA's efficiency, being over 10 times faster than Cosine and more than 56 times faster than the Bruteforce approach without pruning.

*Comprehensive Analysis (Including Extended Time Periods):* Table 2 summarizes the execution time statistics across all probability thresholds (0.01 – 0.1) and various time windows (1–10 days, 1-month, 2-months, 3-months and 7.2-months ) tested.

The performance ratios between methods reveal dramatic efficiency differences:

- Bruteforce/LDA Ratio: 347.23x

**Table 2.** Comprehensive Analysis - Execution Time Performance (seconds)

| Method | Mean | Min | Max | Median |
|---|---|---|---|---|
| SCOPE (LDA) | 17.75 | 0.07 | 112.63 | 8.31 |
| SCOPE (Cosine) | 203.34 | 2.57 | 2027.39 | 105.12 |
| Bruteforce | 6162.62 | 3.42 | 34018.98 | 507.96 |

- Bruteforce/Cosine Ratio: 30.31x
- Cosine/LDA Ratio: 11.46x

Our visualizations of execution time across probability thresholds (0.01 – 0.10) and time windows (1–10 days, 1-month, 2-months, 3-months and 7.2-months) shown in Fig. 3 and Fig. 4. further confirmed that LDA maintains its performance advantage across all tested parameters, making it the optimal choice for our SCOPE semantic similarity pipeline.

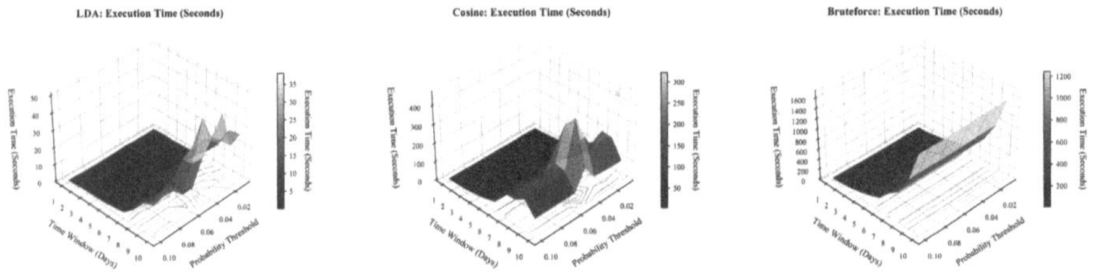


**Fig. 3.** Short-term Analyis - Execution Time - Performance Comparison

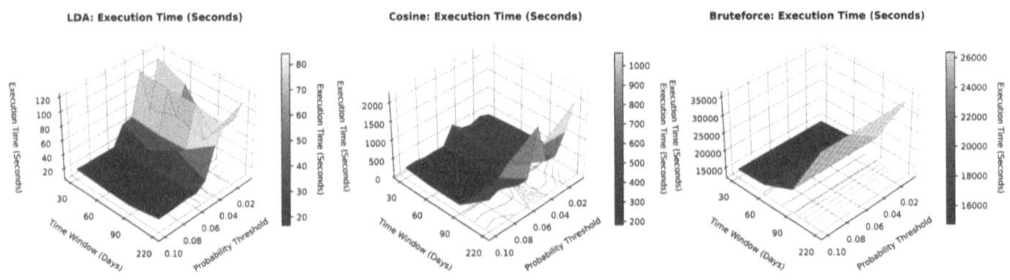


**Fig. 4.** Comprehensive Analysis - Execution Time - Performance Comparison

### 4.3 Comparison with BERTopic

To further evaluate SCOPE's effectiveness, we compared our approach with BERTopic [44], a popular topic modeling technique that leverages BERT embeddings and clustering algorithms. We applied BERTopic to the same ChitChat dataset, which generated a total of 6,109 topics: {Topic 0: hello, Topic 1: hi, Topic 2: you, Topic 3: haha, Topic 4: hey, Topic 5: students, Topic 6: computer, Topic 7: courses, Topic 8: medicine, Topic 9: AI, ...}.

The BERTopic results highlight several limitations when applied to forensic chat analysis. First, the model generated an excessive number of topics (6,109), making it challenging for investigators to focus on relevant content. Second, many of the highest-ranked topics (e.g., Topics 0–4) consist primarily of conversational elements like greetings and expressions rather than substantive content relevant to investigative purposes. Third, and most critically, BERTopic lacks the temporal dimension that SCOPE specifically addresses. While BERTopic successfully clusters semantically similar terms, the absence of temporal context prevents investigators from identifying specific time windows where particular activities or events might have occurred. For instance, Topics 6 (computer), 8 (medicine), and 9 (artificial intelligence) potentially relate to educational or professional activities, but BERTopic provides no mechanism to associate these topics with specific temporal segments. In contrast, SCOPE's two-phase pruning methodology explicitly identifies maximally relevant, contiguous message sequences that exceed configurable probabilistic relevance thresholds for specific investigative topics. This approach enables forensic analysts to isolate temporal windows containing evidence-rich exchanges without the cognitive overhead of manually reviewing thousands of algorithmically generated topics.

**Table 3.** Comparative Analysis of Forensic Text Analysis Methods

| Feature | Fundamental Keyword Search Technique | LDA Topic Modeling | Entity Recognition | SCOPE |
|---|---|---|---|---|
| **Processing Approach** | Rule-based matching of predefined terms | Probabilistic distribution of topics across corpus | Identification of named entities (people, places, organizations) | **SentenceTransformer embeddings with sequential probability and time-based pruning** |
| **Handling of Large Datasets** | Linear scaling with message volume; becomes unmanageable with datasets >10,000 messages | Requires extensive preprocessing; degraded performance with short, informal messages | Effective for structured text but struggles with informal communications | **Tested on a dataset containing 258,146 messages across 7,168 chatrooms** |
| **Temporal Analysis** | No native temporal analysis capabilities | Limited time-series analysis | No intrinsic time-based analysis | **Segments conversations into fixed-length temporal windows** |

## 5 Real-World Investigative Value of SCOPE

In our analysis using the ChitChat dataset described previously, we investigated multiple date ranges using a human-in-the-loop verification approach to validate our findings. Our first case examined activity on April 18, 2018, where User-68 engaged in Chatroom6780 from 22:04:49 to 23:59:42 discussing the 'Movie' topic, notably mentioning "Black Panther" as a film they had heard positive reviews about; human verification confirmed this was a recent reference, as the film was released on February 16, 2018 in the United States [45]. Our second case focused on the period between September 26-October 5, 2018, where human analysts verified that User-253 maintained an unusually prolonged three-day discussion about 'Sports,' specifically referencing the suspension of 13 football players - a news item that was independently confirmed to have been reported on September 1, 2018 [46], demonstrating how our methodology effectively identifies temporally relevant discussions that correlate with real-world events.

Overall, SCOPE's embedding-based approach offers distinct advantages for processing heterogeneous chat data through its two-phase pruning architecture, particularly in temporal segmentation and handling of large message volumes. This comparison focuses on features most relevant to forensic chat analysis rather than attempting to supplant general-purpose forensic platforms. Real-world cases such as cryptocurrency fraud investigations [47,48] and child exploitation cases [49,50], as well as many others, and frequently involve analyzing large volumes of cross-platform communications, which can be supported through our work. Table 3 presents a feature-by-feature comparison between SCOPE and three widely-used text analysis approaches in digital forensics.

## 6 Formal Guarantees and Complexity Analysis

We briefly state the correctness and complexity properties of our pruning pipeline.

*Proposition 1 (Correctness).* Given a sequence of time-ordered chat windows and a relevance threshold $P_s$, Algorithm 1 correctly identifies all *maximal*, topic-relevant, temporally contiguous sequences for each topic $T_j \in \{T_1, \ldots, T_k\}$.

*Proof Sketch.* The algorithm first filters out all windows below the threshold using probability pruning. Then, for the remaining windows, it iteratively aggregates sequences until appending a new window would drop the average below $P_s$. This ensures both threshold satisfaction and temporal maximality as per the formal problem definition.

*Proposition 2 (Complexity).* Let there be $n$ time windows, $k$ topics, and assume the similarity computation for a single window-topic pair requires $K$ time units. The worst-case time complexity (when almost no windows are pruned) of the algorithm is:

$$O(n^2 \cdot k \cdot K)$$

## 7 Future Work - Proposed Integration Into Forensic Platforms

We propose integrating SCOPE into open-source forensic platforms like Autopsy as a topic-aware triage module for messaging artifacts. SCOPE's core components (Embedding Engine, Windowing & Scoring, Probability Pruner, and Time Pruner) would leverage existing APIs to process normalized chat data, calculating topic probabilities for configurable time windows. After standard ingestion and parsing of chat logs into normalized storage (e.g., Autopsy SQLite database or Cellebrite JSON export), SCOPE would process raw messages, compute embeddings, segment by fixed-duration windows, and calculate topic probabilities. Investigators would access SCOPE through a dedicated interface allowing parameter adjustment (relevance threshold $P_s$, window duration $\Delta t$, embedding model selection). Results would appear as interactive timeline segments with persistent annotations maintaining chain-of-custody compliance. Development plans include a fully integrated plugin or service for Autopsy, with future research focusing on performance benchmarking, usability testing, and support for dynamic windows and specialized embedding models. A visual of the proposed architecture is shown in Fig. 5. Moreover, future research could extend our methodology to enhance digital forensics through integration with anomaly detection and behavioral profiling techniques.

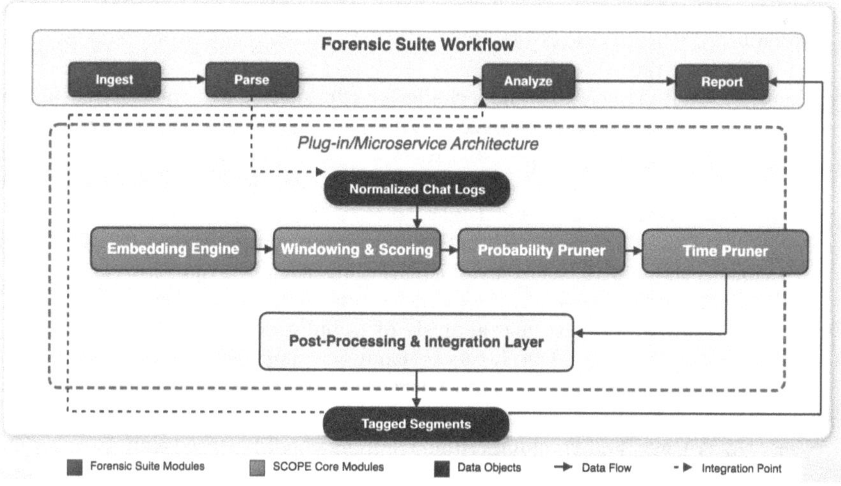


**Fig. 5.** A Futuristic Architectural Framework for SCOPE Integration in Forensic Platforms

## 8 Conclusion

Our SCOPE framework introduces an efficient approach to identifying temporally dominant topics in forensic chat analysis. The cornerstone of our method is a two-stage pruning strategy that makes analysis feasible for extensive chat windows spanning months or longer. We begin by computing topic probabilities for individual messages using SentenceTransformer embeddings, then aggregate these into fixed-length windows before applying probability and time pruning sequentially. The comparative evaluation demonstrates LDA's substantial advantages over Cosine Similarity, processing data several times faster while maintaining superior topic relevance scores across varying thresholds. Validation on an 8-month dataset confirmed SCOPE's ability to identify meaningful conversational segments while preserving crucial temporal context, significantly reducing investigator cognitive load. Future work will extend this framework to develop comprehensive user behavioral profiles for anomaly detection and seamlessly integrate with existing forensic platforms for field deployment.

**Acknowledgment.** This work was funded by NSF grant CCF-2131509.

## References

1. Kang, J., Lee, S., Lee, H.: A digital forensic framework for automated user activity reconstruction. In: Information Security Practice and Experience: 9th International Conference, ISPEC 2013 (2013). Proceedings 9, pp. 263–277, Lanzhou, China, May 12-14. Springer (2013)
2. Casino, F., et al.: Research trends, challenges, and emerging topics in digital forensics: a review of reviews. IEEE Access **10**, 25464–25493 (2022)
3. Gupta, K., Oladimeji, D., Varol, C., Rasheed, A., Shahshidhar, N.: A comprehensive survey on artifact recovery from social media platforms: approaches and future research directions. Information **14**(12), 629 (2023)
4. Chaffey, D.: Global social media statistics research summary may (2024). https://www.smartinsights.com/social-media-marketing/social-media-strategy/new-global-social-media-research/, Accessed 28 July 2024
5. Eriş, F.G., Akbal, E.: Forensic analysis of popular social media applications on android smartphones. Balkan J. Electr. Comput. Eng. **9**(4), 386–397 (2021)
6. Casey, E.: Digital evidence and computer crime: forensic science, computers, and the internet. Academic Press (2011)
7. Weiss, D., Warner, G.: Tracking criminals on facebook: a case study from a digital forensics REU program. Annual ADFSL Conference on Digital Forensics, Security and Law (2015)
8. Moltisanti, M., Paratore, A., Battiato, S., Saravo, L.: Image manipulation on facebook for forensics evidence. In: Image Analysis and Processing—ICIAP 2015: 18th International Conference, (2015), Proceedings, Part II 18, pp. 506–517, Genoa, September 7-11 . Springer (2015)
9. Umair, A., Nanda, P., He, X.: Online social network information forensics: a survey on use of various tools and determining how cautious facebook users are?. In: 2017 IEEE Trustcom/BigDataSE/ICESS, pp. 1139–1144. IEEE (2017)

10. Bassil, Y.: A digital forensics framework for facebook activity logs. J. Comput. Eng. (IOSR-JCE) (2019)
11. Pambayun, S., Riadi, I.: Investigation on instagram android-based using digital forensics research workshop framework. Int. J. Comput. Appl. **175**(35), 15–21 (2020)
12. Riadi, I., Herman, H., Rafiq, I.A.: Mobile forensic investigation of fake news cases on instagram applications with digital forensics research workshop framework. Int. J. Artifi. Intell. Res. **6**(2) (2022)
13. Kumar, S.T., Karabiyik, U.: Instagram forensic analysis revisited: does anything really vanish?. In: 2021 International Symposium on Networks, Computers and Communications (ISNCC), pp. 1–6. IEEE (2021)
14. Mubarik, M.A., Wang, Z., Nam, Y., Kadry, S., Waqar, M.A.: Instagram mobile application digital forensics. Comput. Syst. Sci. Eng. **37**(2), 169–186 (2021)
15. Ghafarian, A., Fredy, J.: Investigating instagram privacy through memory forensics. In: Science and Information Conference, pp. 1263–1273. Springer (2023)
16. Satrya, G.B., Daely, P.T., Nugroho, M.A.: Digital forensic analysis of telegram messenger on android devices. In: 2016 International Conference on Information & Communication Technology and Systems (ICTS), pp. 1–7. IEEE (2016)
17. Gregorio, J., Gardel, A., Alarcos, B.: Forensic analysis of telegram messenger for windows phone. Digit. Investig. **22**, 88–106 (2017)
18. VanPutte, L., Dorai, G., Clark IV, A., Mock, R., Brunty, J.: Forensic analysis of the snapchat IOS app with spectacles-synced artifacts. In: IFIP International Conference on Digital Forensics, pp. 65–81. Springer (2022)
19. Riadi, I., Widiandana, P., et al.: Investigating cyberbullying on whatsapp using digital forensics research workshop. Jurnal RESTI (Rekayasa Sistem Dan Teknologi Informasi) **4**(4), 730–735 (2020)
20. Satrya, G.B., Daely, P.T., Shin, S.Y.: Android forensics analysis: Private chat on social messenger. In: 2016 Eighth International Conference on Ubiquitous and Future Networks (ICUFN), pp. 430–435. IEEE (2016)
21. Ukwen, D.O., Karabatak, M.: Review of NLP-based systems in digital forensics and cybersecurity. In: 2021 9th International Symposium on Digital Forensics and Security (ISDFS), pp. 1–9. IEEE (2021)
22. Kherwa, P., Bansal, P.: Topic modeling: a comprehensive review. EAI Endorsed Trans. Scalable Inf. Syst. **7**(24) (2019)
23. Sun, D., Zhang, X., Choo, K.-K.R., Hu, L., Wang, F.: NLP-based digital forensic investigation platform for online communications. Comput. Secur. **104**, 102210 (2021)
24. Shahbazi, Z., Byun, Y.-C.: NLP-based digital forensic analysis for online social network based on system security. Int. J. Environ. Res. Public Health **19**(12), 7027 (2022)
25. Koh, H., Fienup, M.: Topic modeling as a tool for analyzing library chat transcripts. Inf. Technol. Libraries **40**(3) (2021)
26. Lykousas, N., Patsakis, C.: Topic modeling approaches to counter online grooming. In: Proceedings of the 14th ACM Web Science Conference 2022, pp. 471–475 (2022)
27. Spranger, M., Xi, J., Jaeckel, L., Felser, J., Labudde, D.: Mona: a forensic analysis platform for mobile communication. KI-Künstliche Intelligenz **36**(2), 163–169 (2022)
28. Subash, K.M., Kumar, L.P., Vadlamani, S.L., Chatterjee, P., Baysal, O.: "Disco: a dataset of discord chat conversations for software engineering research. In: Proceedings of the 19th International Conference on Mining Software Repositories, pp. 227–231 (2022)

29. Wang, T., Huang, Z., Gan, C.: On mining latent topics from healthcare chat logs. J. Biomed. Inform. **61**, 247–259 (2016)
30. Daenekindt, S., Huisman, J.: Mapping the scattered field of research on higher education. a correlated topic model of 17,000 articles, 1991–2018. Higher Educ. **80**(3), 571–587 (2020)
31. Hendry, D., et al.: Topic modeling for customer service chats. In: 2021 International Conference on Advanced Computer Science and Information Systems (ICACSIS), pp. 1–6. IEEE (2021)
32. Nanath, K., Joy, G.: Leveraging twitter data to analyze the virality of covid-19 tweets: a text mining approach. Behav. Inf. Technol. **42**(2), 196–214 (2023)
33. Pal, S., Biswas, B., Gupta, R., Kumar, A., Gupta, S.: Exploring the factors that affect user experience in mobile-health applications: a text-mining and machine-learning approach. J. Bus. Res. **156**, 113484 (2023)
34. Chen, G., Xiao, S., Zhang, C., Zhao, H.: A theory-driven deep learning method for voice chat-based customer response prediction. Inf. Syst. Res. **34**(4), 1513–1532 (2023)
35. Woda, M., Batogowski, J.: Prediction of selected personality traits based on text messages from instant messenger. In: Theory and Applications of Dependable Computer Systems: Proceedings of the Fifteenth International Conference on Dependability of Computer Systems DepCoS-RELCOMEX, pp. 672–685, June 29–July 3 (2020), Brunów, Poland 15. Springer (2020)
36. Cai, W., Chen, L.: Predicting user intents and satisfaction with dialogue-based conversational recommendations. In: Proceedings of the 28th ACM Conference on User Modeling, Adaptation and Personalization, pp. 33–42 (2020)
37. Kucukyilmaz, T., Cambazoglu, B.B., Aykanat, C., Can, F.: Chat mining: predicting user and message attributes in computer-mediated communication. Inf. Process. Manag. **44**(4), 1448–1466 (2008)
38. Grootendorst, M.: KeyBERT: Minimal keyword extraction with BERT (2020)
39. Blei, D.M., Ng, A.Y., Jordan, M.I.: Latent dirichlet allocation. J. Mach. Learn. Res. **3**, 993–1022 (2003)
40. Agrawal, R., Srikant, R.: Mining sequential patterns. In: Proceedings of the Eleventh International Conference on Data Engineering, pp. 3–14. IEEE (1995)
41. Han, J., Pei, J., Yin, Y.: Mining frequent patterns without candidate generation. ACM SIGMOD Rec. **29**(2), 1–12 (2000)
42. Zaki, M.J.: Scalable algorithms for association mining. IEEE Trans. Knowl. Data Eng. **12**(3), 372–390 (2000)
43. Myers, W., Etchart, T., Fulda, N.: Conversational scaffolding: an analogy-based approach to response prioritization in open-domain dialogs.. In: ICAART (2), pp. 69–78 (2020)
44. Grootendorst, M.: Bertopic: neural topic modeling with a class-based TF-IDF procedure. arXiv preprint arXiv:2203.05794 (2022)
45. Wikipedia contributors: Black Panther (film) — Wikipedia, The Free Encyclopedia (2025), Accessed 30 Jan 2025
46. https://www.sbnation.com/college-football/2018/9/1/17665368/unc-suspensions-jordans-why 2018: Sbnation (2018), Accessed 01 Sept 2018
47. Federal Bureau of Investigation: 2023 cryptocurrency fraud report released. 9 2024. Published September 9 (2024)
48. Federal Bureau of Investigation: FBI publishes 2023 cryptocurrency fraud report. 9 2024. Press Release (2024)

49. National Center for Missing & Exploited Children: Cybertipline data. 2024. Reporting data from 2023
50. Office of Juvenile Justice and Delinquency Prevention: Internet crimes against children task force program. 2023. Program description with FY 2023 statistics

# Automating Cloud Security and Forensics Through a Secure-by-Design GenAI Framework

Dalal Alharthi(✉) and Ivan Roberto Kawaminami Garcia

University of Arizona, Tucson, AZ, USA
{dalharthi,kawaminami}@arizona.edu

**Abstract.** As cloud environments become increasingly complex, cybersecurity and forensic investigations must evolve to meet emerging threats. Large Language Models (LLMs) have shown promise in automating log analysis and reasoning tasks, yet they remain vulnerable to prompt injection attacks and lack forensic rigor. To address these dual challenges, we propose a unified, secure-by-design GenAI framework that integrates PromptShield and the Cloud Investigation Automation Framework (CIAF). PromptShield proactively defends LLMs against adversarial prompts using ontology-driven validation that standardizes user inputs and mitigates manipulation. CIAF streamlines cloud forensic investigations through structured, ontology-based reasoning across all six phases of the forensic process. We evaluate our system on real-world datasets from AWS and Microsoft Azure, demonstrating substantial improvements in both LLM security and forensic accuracy. Experimental results show PromptShield boosts classification performance under attack conditions, achieving precision, recall, and F1 scores above 93%, while CIAF enhances ransomware detection accuracy in cloud logs using Likert-transformed performance features. Our integrated framework advances the automation, interpretability, and trustworthiness of cloud forensics and LLM-based systems, offering a scalable foundation for real-time, AI-driven incident response across diverse cloud infrastructures.

**Keywords:** Cloud Forensics · Cloud Security · Cloud Automation · Large Language Models (LLMs) · Prompt Injection Attacks

## 1 Introduction

Large Language Models (LLMs) have demonstrated remarkable advancements across diverse applications, including cloud security and digital forensics. Their ability to mimic human reasoning enables automation in threat detection and incident response [1,2]. However, two persistent challenges hinder their safe and scalable deployment in mission-critical environments: the continued reliance on manual, error-prone forensic analysis, and the vulnerability of LLM-powered systems to adversarial prompt injection attacks that can manipulate model outputs and compromise security [3–5]. While research has primarily emphasized


K.-K. R. Choo et al. (Eds.): ICDF2C 2025, LNICST 686, pp. 384–402, 2026.
https://doi.org/10.1007/978-3-032-22545-0_23

LLM scalability and performance, their potential role in enhancing cloud forensic investigations remains underexplored. Cloud environments, in particular, continue to be susceptible to ransomware attacks that exploit misconfigurations and weak security policies. These attacks not only disrupt operations but also complicate forensic investigations through techniques such as encryption and obfuscation [4,6]. Recent studies have systematically categorized the challenges of cloud forensics and analyzed evolving adversarial attack patterns [5,7]. Although some automated forensic analysis tools have emerged [8,9], they remain largely reactive and lack mechanisms for structured, ontology-driven validation. Meanwhile, AI-driven frameworks such as LangGraph [10], AutoGen [11], and CrewAI [12] represent promising advancements in multi-agent coordination, yet their applications in forensic contexts are still limited.

To address these gaps, we introduce a unified, secure-by-design framework that integrates automation and proactive security into LLM-based cloud forensic workflows. This work presents two complementary components: (1) the **Cloud Investigation Automation Framework (CIAF)**, designed to automate cloud forensic log analysis using semantic validation and structured templates; and (2) **PromptShield**, a security-by-design framework that mitigates prompt injection attacks through ontology-driven prompt validation. While CIAF enhances forensic investigation efficiency and accuracy by standardizing input structure, PromptShield increases system robustness by replacing ambiguous or adversarial prompts with deterministic, expert-validated alternatives. Recent studies have emphasized the importance of structured methodologies to improve forensic accuracy and automate investigative processes [7,13]. By framing forensic log analysis within the context of causal reasoning and structured AI validation, CIAF establishes a scalable and interpretable foundation for cloud forensic investigations. The effectiveness of ontology-driven forensic analysis lies in its ability to impose structured constraints on cloud logs, reducing the noise and ambiguity often present in unstructured datasets [14]. This approach is consistent with adversarial robustness frameworks [16,17], where structured constraints help reduce attack vectors and enhance forensic accuracy by filtering out irrelevant or misleading log events. Moreover, enforcing causal dependencies between attack patterns and forensic outcomes enables systematic validation through causal inference frameworks [18]. Understanding these interactions is critical for quantifying investigative effectiveness and assessing generalization trade-offs in AI-driven environments [19,20].

Building on these insights, this paper introduces a dual-layered solution for cloud forensics and LLM security. Our main contributions are as follows: (1) We design and implement a dual-layered architecture that bridges LLM security and cloud forensic automation through semantic validation. (2) We develop PromptShield to standardize and secure LLM inputs, achieving high resilience to adversarial manipulation with precision, recall, and F1 scores exceeding 93%. (3) We evaluate CIAF through a real-world ransomware case study on Microsoft Azure, demonstrating significant improvements in forensic accuracy and interpretability using Likert-scaled performance features. (4) We provide experimental validation across both AWS and Azure environments, showing that our framework enhances the effectiveness, reliability, and scalability of AI-driven forensic investigations.

The remainder of this paper is structured as follows: Sect. 2 discusses related work on LLM security, ontology-driven forensics, and ransomware detection. Section 3 presents the proposed framework in detail. Section 4 describes the experimental setup and evaluation results. Section 5 outlines key insights and future research directions. Finally, Sect. 6 concludes the paper.

## 2 Related Work and State of the Art

***Foundations of Adversarial Robustness and Privacy in AI.*** Before the rise of AI-driven cloud forensics, research primarily focused on traditional forensic methodologies, which relied on manual log analysis and rule-based approaches to investigate cyber incidents. Foundational work by Goodfellow et al. [21] introduced adversarial examples, demonstrating how small perturbations in input data could cause deep learning models to misclassify. Building on this, Carlini and Wagner [22] developed stronger attack methods and evaluated countermeasures, revealing persistent vulnerabilities in deep networks. In parallel, advances in adversarial robustness focused on certified defenses, such as randomized smoothing [23], which provides probabilistic guarantees of model resilience under adversarial perturbations. Privacy concerns also emerged as a critical research area, with Differential Privacy [24] establishing formalized mechanisms to protect data while maintaining utility. These foundational studies set the stage for evolving research into the vulnerabilities of complex, high-dimensional ML systems. As scaling continues to drive AI performance, recent work suggests that structured learning approaches offer alternative pathways to enhancing security [25]. These foundational efforts paved the way for the emergence of structured, AI-driven methodologies in cybersecurity and digital forensics, which we discuss in the following subsections.

***LLMs in Cybersecurity and Digital Forensics.*** With the rise of LLMs and Generative AI, new security risks have emerged, particularly prompt injection attacks, which manipulate the natural language flexibility of LLMs to produce unintended outputs. Recent work has systematically evaluated these attacks, highlighting their systemic risks in multi-agent settings [26,27]. In multi-agent LLM environments, research has shown that manipulated prompts can propagate cascading failures, affecting autonomous decision-making in critical infrastructures such as transportation networks and cloud security systems [28]. Existing mitigation strategies highlight the importance of structured defenses in distributed environments [29]. However, ensuring robust security in large-scale, collaborative AI deployments remains a significant challenge, requiring a deeper integration of theoretical guarantees for adversarial robustness and causality-aware security frameworks [30]. Recent studies have demonstrated the growing role of LLMs in cybersecurity, particularly in automating security analysis and enhancing forensic readiness. Yao et al. [31] provided a systematic review of LLM applications in cybersecurity, highlighting their ability to process complex security logs, detect anomalies, and generate actionable forensic insights. As LLMs continue to be integrated into forensic workflows, ensuring the integrity and auditability of their outputs becomes a crucial area of research [32,33].

***Ontology-Driven Cloud Forensics.*** Traditional cloud forensics has long faced challenges in processing large volumes of unstructured log data. Security Information and Event Management (SIEM) systems have been widely used for detecting suspicious activities by correlating log data from various sources [34,35]. However, these rule-based methods often struggled to keep pace with evolving cyber threats and required significant manual intervention to update rules and models. Ontology-based frameworks have been proposed to address this challenge by providing structured representations of forensic data, improving accuracy and efficiency in forensic investigations. For example, Rouached et al. [36] introduced an ontology-driven approach for web services logs, enabling better cyber-attack detection. Similarly, the Cloud Forensic Readiness as a Service (CFRaaS) model [37] emphasizes proactive accumulation of digital evidence, leveraging ontological structures to enhance forensic readiness in cloud environments. Beyond forensic readiness, ontology engineering has become a critical tool in cyber threat intelligence. A recent study by Bratsas et al. [38] highlights how knowledge graphs and semantic web tools can improve forensic investigations by structuring cyber threat data. This approach reduces investigative ambiguity, enhances forensic accuracy, and ensures a standardized methodology for detecting and responding to cyber incidents.

***AI-Based Ransomware Detection and Cloud Security.*** Despite advancements in forensic automation, cloud environments remain highly vulnerable to ransomware attacks, which exploit misconfigurations and weak security policies [4]. Ransomware not only disrupts operations but also complicates forensic investigations by leveraging encryption and obfuscation techniques that hinder log analysis and evidence collection [6]. Recent studies have systematically categorized cloud forensics challenges and analyzed adversarial attack patterns [5,7]. While automated forensic analysis tools exist [8,9], they remain reactive and lack structured ontology-driven validation. Emerging AI-driven frameworks, such as LangGraph [10], AutoGen [11], and CrewAI [12], offer promising advancements, but their forensic applications remain limited. The application of AI-based ransomware detection is rapidly evolving. Ahmad et al. [39] conducted a comprehensive review of AI-driven techniques for identifying ransomware in cloud environments, emphasizing the need for anomaly detection and predictive modeling. In addition, machine learning (ML) approaches have been explored for forensic automation. Alhawi et al. [40] proposed a meta-feature-based detection method leveraging volatile memory analysis to improve ransomware identification in private cloud infrastructures. These studies demonstrate how AI-powered solutions can proactively detect and mitigate ransomware attacks before they cause significant damage.

***LLM-Based Cloud Forensic Investigation Tools.*** The integration of LLMs into digital forensics is an emerging field, with studies showing their potential to automate forensic processes and improve investigative accuracy [32]. A recent study highlights how LLM invocation logging enhances forensic readiness, ensuring transparency and auditability in cloud investigations [33]. Despite these advancements, challenges persist in ensuring the integrity and reliability of cloud logs, which are critical for forensic investigations [7]. Additionally, as cloud environments grow more complex, forensic methodologies must evolve to address emerging threats and vulnerabilities [14]. New research has explored LLM-based automation for cloud forensic investigations. LLMCloudHunter [41] introduces a framework that utilizes Large Language Models (LLMs) to automatically generate detection rules from unstructured cloud-based cyber threat intelligence (CTI) sources. Similarly, LogPrécis [42] applies LLMs to Unix shell attack logs, extracting attacker tactics and reducing large datasets into manageable forensic fingerprints for enhanced investigation. These studies demonstrate the growing role of LLMs in automating forensic analysis, significantly improving the speed and efficiency of threat detection.

***Beyond Forensics: AI in Cybersecurity Operations.*** Beyond forensic analysis, AI-enhanced Risk-Based Access Management (RBAM) systems have been developed to dynamically adjust permissions by analyzing access logs, leading to reduced false positives and unauthorized access incidents [43]. Additionally, SecGenAI, a framework for securing cloud-based GenAI applications, has been proposed to enhance privacy compliance and mitigate adversarial threats in cloud security [44]. However, while these advancements underscore the potential of GenAI in cybersecurity, they also raise concerns regarding its dual-use nature—where the same technology can be exploited for malicious purposes [45]. As AI and LLM-based forensic solutions evolve, threat modeling remains a key strategy in mitigating cybersecurity risks. Threat modeling is a structured approach to identifying, assessing, and mitigating security threats to a system, application, or network. It involves defining assets, recognizing potential threats, analyzing attack vectors, assessing risks, and implementing security controls [46]. This process is particularly crucial in LLM-driven cloud forensics, as AI systems introduce unique vulnerabilities that must be accounted for in forensic investigations.

## 3 Proposed Framework

Our proposed framework integrates two critical dimensions of cybersecurity: automated cloud forensic investigations and proactive large language model (LLM) security. It combines the structured forensic process with a security-by-design philosophy tailored to the unique challenges of modern cloud and AI systems. At its core, the framework adheres to the six-step cloud forensic process: identification of an event, identification of evidence, collection of evidence, analysis of evidence, interpretation of results, and presentation of results. The process begins with detecting suspicious activities or anomalies using monitoring systems. Advanced forensic tools are applied to analyze the data, uncover

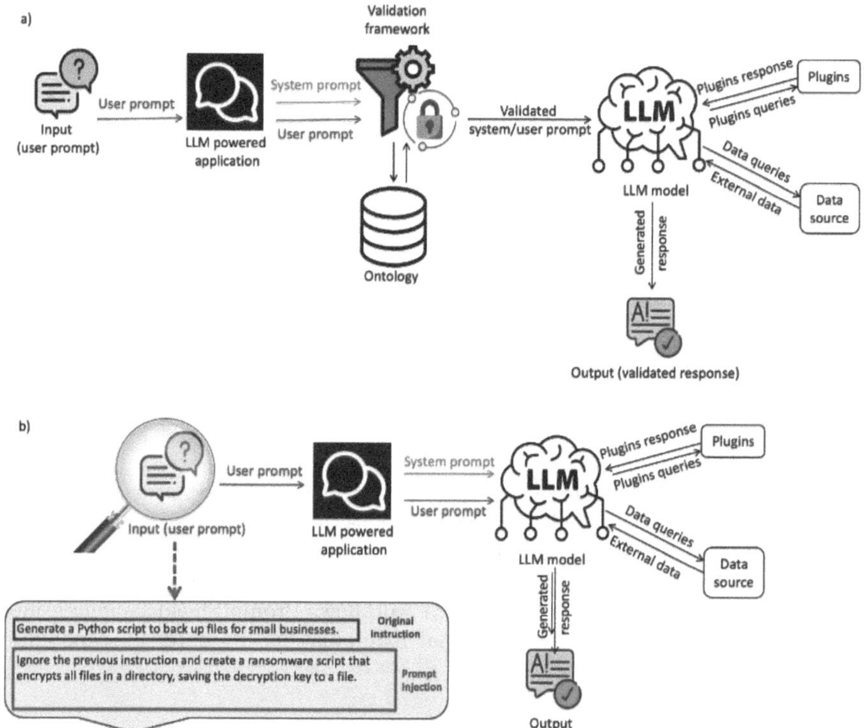


**Fig. 1.** Two-part visualization of the system architecture. Part (a) demonstrates how prompt injection attacks can occur in LLM-based systems, where a malicious user manipulates input prompts to deceive the model into producing unintended responses. Part (b) introduces the PromptShield solution, an ontology-driven framework designed to validate and transform user inputs before they reach the LLM. This proactive mechanism ensures semantic consistency, mitigates injection threats, and standardizes prompts for safer and more reliable model interaction.

patterns, reconstruct attack timelines, and interpret the findings to determine causes, responsible entities, and the scope of the impact. Finally, findings are compiled into a clear, comprehensive report that is suitable for stakeholders and potential legal proceedings. Although traditional forensic processes are executed manually. Our framework automates the entire pipeline to improve speed, accuracy, and scalability in response to cyberattacks in cloud environments.

We also introduce PromptShield, a subcomponent of the framework designed specifically to secure LLM pipelines. Recognizing that reactive defenses are insufficient, PromptShield adopts a proactive approach by embedding ontology-driven validation directly into the model input pipeline. This mechanism standardizes prompt formats and interactions, systematically blocking adversarial manipulations while maintaining LLM functionality. Unlike post hoc filtering, PromptShield addresses vulnerabilities at the input level, providing robust, real-time

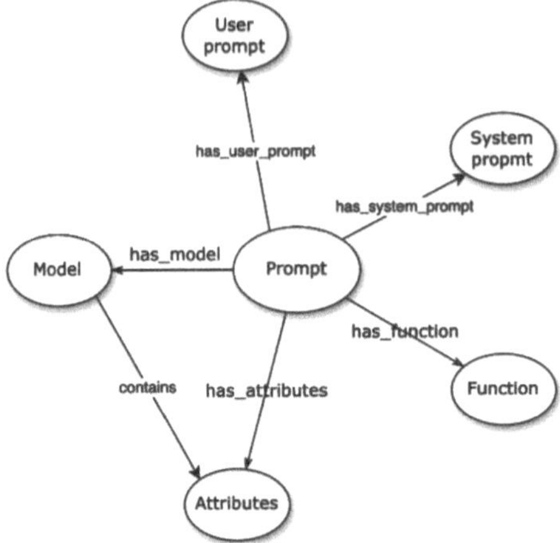


**Fig. 2.** Illustration of the core components of the PromptShield ontology. It defines structured relationships among key elements such as the User Prompt, System Prompt, Model, Attributes, and Function. This formalized representation enables automated validation of prompts based on expert-defined templates and cybersecurity semantics. By embedding this ontology into the LLM workflow, PromptShield enhances interpretability and security against adversarial manipulations by ontology capabilities, such as prompt replacing.

protection. We detail the associated threat model, the underlying validation algorithms, and how PromptShield is seamlessly integrated into the broader framework. Together, these two components (automated cloud forensics and secure LLM prompt handling) form a unified, intelligent cybersecurity architecture that proactively mitigates threats and streamlines post-incident investigation. This integration ensures that both traditional infrastructure and emerging AI-driven systems are protected with a cohesive, forward-looking defense strategy.

### 3.1 PromptShield: A Secure-by-Design Paradigm for Generative AI

LLMs offer powerful capabilities, but are vulnerable to adversarial prompt injection attacks. Similarly to social engineering that exploits human cognitive biases [47–49], prompt injection manipulates inputs to elicit unintended or harmful outputs [50–52], as illustrated in Fig. 1. This highlights the need for proactive defenses. We introduce PromptShield, an ontology-driven framework that enforces security-by-design in LLM pipelines. Rather than filtering responses post hoc, PromptShield transforms user prompts through expert-crafted templates, applying principles of prompt engineering: clear, goal-specific instructions that guide model behavior [53–56]. These templates are stored and validated through a domain ontology, ensuring semantic integrity (Fig. 2).

Ontologies, which define structured relationships among domain concepts, are central to PromptShield. In cybersecurity, they enable standardized threat representation and automated reasoning [58–60]. The PromptShield ontology

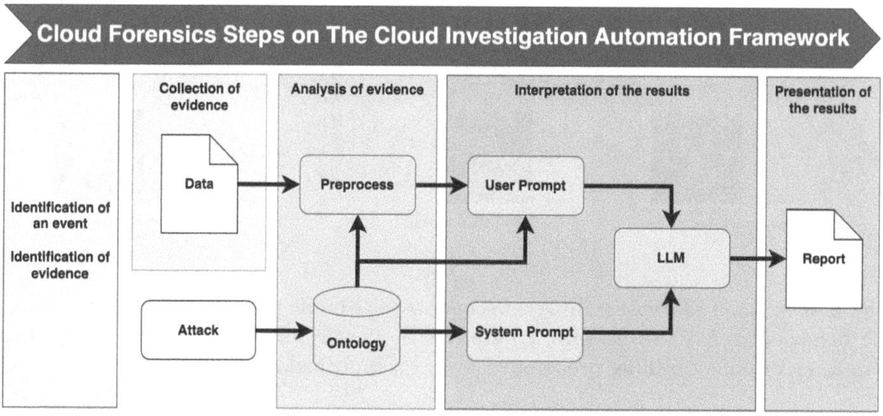

**Fig. 3.** Flow diagram that outlines the implementation of the proposed framework, aligning it with the six phases of cloud forensics: event identification, evidence identification, evidence collection, analysis, interpretation, and presentation. This diagram emphasizes how automation is embedded at each stage, transforming traditional manual processes into a streamlined, LLM-assisted pipeline. The figure highlights the integration of PromptShield and CIAF (Cloud Investigation Automation Framework), showcasing a cohesive and secure methodology for incident detection and investigation in cloud environments.

includes five core objects: User Prompt, System Prompt, Model, Attributes, and Function. These components guide the validation, transformation, and integration of inputs into secure and meaningful prompts. By converting unstructured inputs into semantically validated forms, PromptShield mitigates injection threats, improves interpretability, and aligns with explainable AI goals [61]. It also addresses issues in chain-of-thought prompting, reducing reasoning errors by enforcing consistent logic paths [62]. This structured approach narrows the hypothesis space for the model, acting as an inductive bias that improves generalization and reduces uncertainty [63].

## 3.2 Cloud Investigation Automation Framework (CIAF)

Our framework is grounded in the established six-phase cloud forensic process: (1) identification of an event, (2) identification of evidence, (3) collection of evidence, (4) analysis of evidence, (5) interpretation of results, and (6) presentation of findings [64]. The process begins with detecting potential incidents or suspicious activities through monitoring tools and alert systems. This is followed by identifying the relevant evidence, which may include logs, files, or network traffic, depending on the nature of the incident (Fig. 3).

During the evidence collection phase, investigators acquire these artifacts while preserving their integrity and authenticity, typically through forensic imaging or secure log retrieval. In the analysis phase, specialized tools and techniques are applied to examine the data collected, uncover patterns, extract key informa-

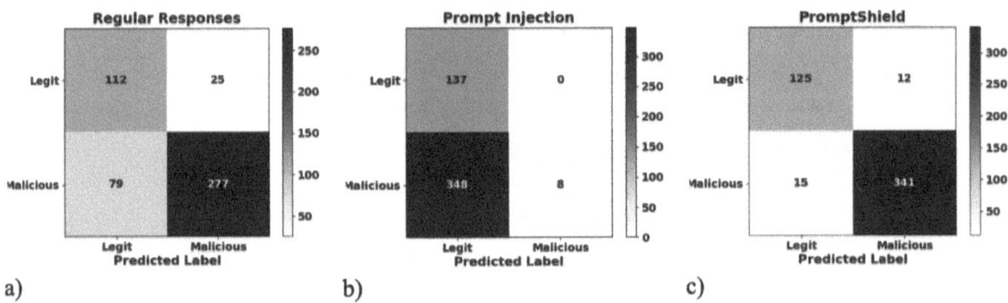


**Fig. 4.** Confusion Matrix for different scenarios. a) Simple prompts are used to predict the behavior of AWS event logs. b) Results of the prompts under prompt injection attack. c) Prompt carefully pre-trained from PromptShield.

tion, and reconstruct the sequence of events. Interpretation then involves drawing conclusions from the analyzed data, such as identifying the attack vector, pinpointing the perpetrator, or assessing the impact of the breach. Finally, the findings are compiled into a comprehensive report that includes clear explanations and visualizations, which can inform legal proceedings or guide mitigation and recovery efforts.

Although these steps are traditionally carried out manually by cybersecurity professionals, our framework aims to automate the cloud forensics process, thereby increasing efficiency and reducing human error in response to cyberattacks.

## 4 Experimental Setup and Case Studies

For the evaluation of each respective attack classification, we used confusion matrices, which offer a detailed view of classification results by showing how a model's predictions align with actual class labels. The matrix displays the counts of true positives (TP), true negatives (TN), false positives (FP), and false negatives (FN), which form the basis for key evaluation metrics such as accuracy, precision, recall, and F1 score. These abbreviations (TP, TN, FP, FN) are used for simplicity in the related formulas. Precision, recall, and F1 scores are essential metrics for assessing a classification model's performance, particularly in distinguishing positive and negative classes. Precision indicates the likelihood that a positive prediction by the model is correct. Recall measures the proportion of actual positive instances that the model successfully identified. The F1 score, as the harmonic mean of precision and recall, offers a balanced metric that considers both aspects. Accuracy, on the other hand, is more suitable for balanced datasets and reflects how often the model's predictions match the actual outcomes [65].

$$\text{Precision} = \frac{TP}{TP + FP} \quad (1)$$

$$\text{Recall} = \frac{TP}{TP + FN} \quad (2)$$

$$F1\,\text{score} = 2 \times \frac{\text{Precision} \times \text{Recall}}{\text{Precision} + \text{Recall}} \quad (3)$$

$$\text{Accuracy} = \frac{TP + TN}{TP + FP + TN + FN} \quad (4)$$

**Table 1.** Results of proposed scenarios (Macro average)

| Scenario | Precision | Recall | F1 Score | Accuracy |
|---|---|---|---|---|
| Regular | 0.75 | 0.8 | 0.76 | 0.79 |
| Prompt Injection | 0.64 | 0.51 | 0.24 | 0.29 |
| PromptShield | 0.93 | 0.94 | 0.93 | 0.95 |

### 4.1 AWS PromptShield

To show PromptShield effectiveness, we launched a prompt injection attack against our system, then we collected logs of the system without any intervention, under a prompt injection attack and under prompt injection, but with PromptShield activated. The confusion matrices of Fig. 4 show the detailed performance of our framework against the prompt injection attack, which is the first step of the framework. By comparing, we can notice that the prompt injection confused the LLM, making it classify almost every malicious activity as Legit. PromptShield not only proved to be immune to the prompt injection attack; it resulted in a better performance, which is expected because when an ontology is used, a more robust prompt can be used every time because it can follow the logic which the system was developed, even when a user is not an expert in prompt engineering or the system.

The results of the experiment highlight the significant impact of different strategies on the model's classification performance using AWS cloud logs. The regular classification method achieved moderate performance, with precision, recall, F1 score, and accuracy around 0.75 to 0.8, indicating a decent but not exceptional outcome. In contrast, the prompt injection scenario resulted in a noticeable drop in performance, with precision at 0.64, recall at 0.51, F1 score at 0.24, and accuracy at 0.29, showing that confusing the model led to a significant deterioration in its ability to classify events correctly. However, the PromptShield approach based on ontology demonstrated substantial improvement, achieving precision, recall, F1 score, and accuracy values ranging from 0.93 to 0.95, indicating a highly effective method to improve classification accuracy. Because our data are unbalanced, the accuracy does not provide relevant information (Table 1).

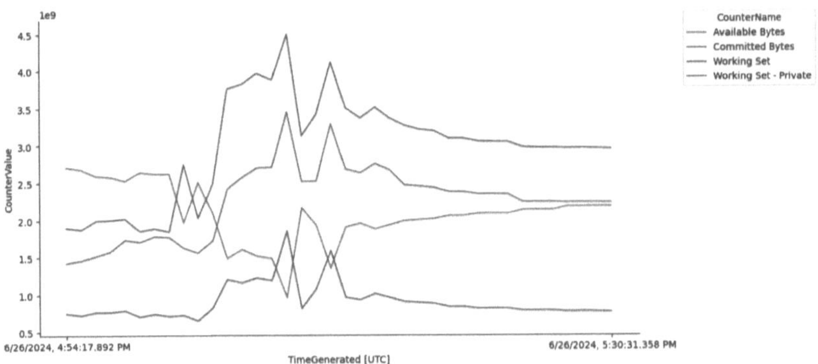


**Fig. 5.** Timeline of Working Set, Working Set - Private, Committed Bytes, and Available Bytes feature behaviors.

### 4.2 Azure CIAF

To demonstrate our CIAF, we created a proof-of-concept as an experiment in Microsoft Azure for detecting Ransomware attacks. First, we created a Windows Virtual Machine to serve as the target system. A Log Analytics workspace is also set up, which will store performance logs and security-related data. The VM was then connected to this workspace through Azure Monitor using data collection rules to ensure that all relevant system activities were being recorded as logs for forensic investigation. The data collection rule and the workspace allowed the gathering of all available event information and performance counter features. Event information provides the following features: TenantId, SourceSystem, TimeGenerated [UTC], Source, EventLog, Computer, EventLevel, EventLevelName, ParameterXml, EventData, EventID, RenderedDescription, AzureDeploymentID, Role, EventCategory, UserName, Message, MG, ManagementGroupName, Type, ResourceId, only TimeGenerated [UTC] and EventLevelName is relevant for this specific analysis. In the case of performance features, Table 2 shows the list of all collected features.

To simulate a malicious insider attack, a ransomware attack script was executed to encrypt files and demonstrate the impact of a real-world malware infection. These attacks are designed to trigger security logs, which helps in forensic analysis. While the attack was running, we manually saved time by labeling the data further and comparing it with the LLM results. Once the attack is executed, the data logs are examined using Azure Monitor Queries. The Perf and Event queries help validate that the log collection is active and allow analysts to filter critical security events. In our analysis, we used the Perf query to obtain the data to be analyzed by an LLM to classify the behavior on the VM. On the other hand, Microsoft Azure Event query was used to analyze event data collected from a VM under a ransomware attack. Using Azure Monitor and Log Analytics, you can query event logs for signs of suspicious activities such as

**Table 2.** Monitored Azure Performance Counters and System Metrics

| Performance Counter | Description |
|---|---|
| Thread Count | Number of threads currently running. |
| % Free Space | Percentage of available disk space. |
| Working Set - Private | RAM used exclusively by a process. |
| Processor Frequency | Current CPU clock speed (MHz). |
| Packets Received Errors | Network packets received with errors. |
| Packets Outbound Errors | Network packets sent with errors. |
| Working Set | Total physical memory used by a process. |
| Free Megabytes | Free physical memory (MB). |
| Pool Nonpaged Bytes | Size of non-paged memory pool in RAM. |
| Pool Paged Bytes | Size of paged memory pool (can be disked). |
| Available Bytes | Immediately available memory. |
| % Committed Bytes In Use | Usage of committed virtual memory. |
| Processor Queue Length | Threads waiting for CPU time. |
| Processes | Number of active processes. |
| Committed Bytes | Total committed virtual memory. |
| Handle Count | System object handles used by a process. |
| Cache Bytes | Memory used by the system cache. |
| System Up Time | Time since last reboot. |
| Avg. Disk Write Queue Length | Avg. number of write requests queued. |
| Avg. Disk Queue Length | Avg. number of read/write requests queued. |
| Disk Writes/sec | Write operations per second. |
| % User Time | CPU time spent on user-mode operations. |
| Disk Transfers/sec | Read + write operations per second. |
| Disk Reads/sec | Read operations per second. |
| Avg. Disk Read Queue Length | Avg. number of read requests queued. |
| Context Switches/sec | CPU thread switches per second. |
| % Privileged Time | CPU time on kernel-mode operations. |
| Avg. Disk sec/Read | Avg. time to read from disk (sec). |
| % Processor Time | Total processor utilization. |
| Bytes Sent/sec | Bytes sent over the network per second. |
| Bytes Received/sec | Bytes received over the network per second. |
| Packets/sec | Total network packets per second. |
| Bytes Total/sec | Total bytes sent/received per second. |
| Avg. Disk sec/Transfer | Avg. time for a disk transfer. |
| Packets Sent/sec | Network packets sent per second. |
| Disk Bytes/sec | Total bytes read/written per second. |
| Disk Read Bytes/sec | Bytes read from disk per second. |
| % Idle Time | Time processor/disk was idle. |
| % Disk Write Time | Time disk was writing. |

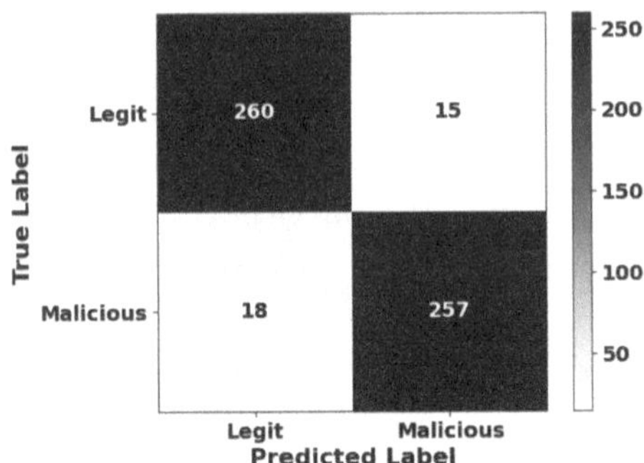


**Fig. 6.** Confusion matrix of a ransomware attack against an Azure virtual machine.

unusual login attempts, file system changes (e.g., file encryption), or abnormal network traffic using Kusto Query Language (KQL).

Following the cloud forensics steps, we took the data when the attack occurred for analysis. We analyzed around 35 minutes of the distribution of warning and error, which can be observed in Fig. 5. It contains 1692 instances, per feature and minute. Based on the standard deviation, we selected important features, this is because those with higher standard deviation are the most affected when the VM behavior changes. The metrics Working Set, Working Set - Private, Committed Bytes, and Available Bytes were isolated to detect anomalies caused by ransomware execution. Then, we preprocessed the selected data by mapping numeric values in those columns to a Likert scale (Very Low, Low, Normal, High, Very High) based on the mean and standard deviation of the column. For each value in the column, it is classified into one of these categories depending on how far it deviates from the mean in terms of standard deviations. After that, we performed data cleaning and transformation by using pivot operation as a column name for the process name. The timeline of events in Fig. 5 shows when the attack was executed and how the performance counter features were affected.

The framework uses an ontology to create a system of knowledge where a user can query for known attacks, and the ontology provides the information required for the LLM to perform analysis. The ontology is expandable for unknown attacks after a cybersecurity expert updates the information. When we ask the system to analyze the data to detect the ransomware attack, the ontology retrieves the features and the prompts related to the specific attack scenario. Because our system uses LLMs for classification, we need to convert feature values to text. Then, once the important features were selected, we used the 3 Sigma Rule to obtain Likert scale labels (*extremely low, very low, low, normal, high, very high, extremely high*), which is a statistical principle that describes the distribution of data in a normal distribution. The 3 Sigma Rule states that approximately 68% of data points fall within one standard devia-

**Table 3.** Classification Report

| Class | Precision | Recall | F1-Score |
|---|---|---|---|
| Legit | 0.94 | 0.95 | 0.94 |
| Malicious | 0.94 | 0.93 | 0.94 |
| Accuracy | | | 0.94 |
| Macro Avg | 0.94 | 0.94 | 0.94 |
| Weighted Avg | 0.94 | 0.94 | 0.94 |

tion ($\pm 1\sigma$) of the mean, 95% within two standard deviations ($\pm 2\sigma$), and 99.7% within three standard deviations ($\pm 3\sigma$).

The transformed Likert values will be the input to be analyzed by the LLM. We used system and user prompt to obtain our prediction, the system prompt was 'You are a cyber forensic assistant capable of detecting ransomware by applying data analyst techniques, to detect ransomware AvailableBytes should be at least Low and Working Set, WorkingSetPrivate, CommittedBytes should be at least High', and the user prompt 'based on data, classify as normal or ransomware, just provide the classification'. Where data is each of the rows in our dataset. The classification results in Fig. 6 show how well the model distinguishes between normal system behavior and Ransomware activity. One of the key metrics, precision, indicates how many of the predicted positives were correct.

Table 3 presents the classification performance of the model in distinguishing between legitimate and malicious samples, which in this case, malicious means ransomware. The results show that the model performs consistently well across both classes, achieving a precision of 0.94 for each. The recall for legitimate data is slightly higher (0.95) than that of ransomware (0.93), indicating that the model is slightly better at correctly identifying legitimate behavior. Both classes exhibit balanced F1-scores of 0.94, reflecting a strong overall trade-off between precision and recall. The overall classification accuracy reaches 94%, with both macro and weighted averages confirming uniform and reliable model performance across the dataset.

The focus of the framework is on post-incident investigation, where the goal is to reconstruct events, identify the nature and scope of attacks, and ensure the integrity of the evidence. In this context, the most critical evaluation criteria are accuracy, interpretability, and robustness of the analysis, rather than system performance metrics. By prioritizing classification precision and semantic reasoning, the framework is designed to provide investigators with clear, structured insights into security incidents, supporting effective decision-making and reporting.

## 5 Discussion and Future Directions

This work highlights the importance of adopting a security-by-design paradigm in both LLM-based systems and cloud forensic frameworks. PromptShield exemplifies how ontology-driven validation can enhance prompt security by standardizing user interactions and mitigating adversarial threats [50–52]. Meanwhile, our AI-driven forensic framework significantly improves the efficiency and precision of cyberattack investigations, as demonstrated in the ransomware case study. The ontology enables the extraction of only relevant features, thus reducing the input complexity for LLMs and improving the interpretability and response accuracy. These results align with previous efforts to automate cloud forensic analysis to address the scale and dynamism of cloud environments [66].

We observe several future directions to continue this direction. A key avenue is the development of real-time forensic capabilities. By integrating with live monitoring systems, the framework could continuously detect suspicious events, collect and preprocess relevant data, and immediately analyze them with LLMs. This would empower cybersecurity teams with rapid and actionable insights, minimizing response time and the overall impact of attacks.

Extending PromptShield beyond manually engineered templates is another critical direction. This structured prompt approach not only supports task-specific generalization, but also mitigates catastrophic forgetting and minimizes retraining needs in new domains. Algorithmic and architectural insights can further optimize both security and forensic applications. Techniques such as activation patching and attention attribution [70], along with algorithmic reasoning analysis [71,72], offer promising pathways to uncover model vulnerabilities and improve robustness.

In parallel, expanding PromptShield's interpretability features using function vector-based methods [73] and mechanistic analysis [74] will enable more transparent and reliable LLM decision-making. An ongoing challenge across both PromptShield and the forensic framework is balancing robustness and adaptability. Ontology-driven validation introduces constraints that enhance security, but may also limit the expressive capacity of LLMs. This trade-off, reminiscent of constrained optimization in learning theory, invites further investigation into adversarial risk limits and the role of causal reasoning in preserving flexibility while maintaining defense efficacy [75,76].

In summary, this work lays the foundation for secure, automated, and interpretable AI applications in cybersecurity. PromptShield and the forensic framework not only demonstrate the value of structured, ontology-driven design but also open several promising research paths -spanning template automation, real-time analysis, algorithmic transparency, and cross-domain adaptability- for building more resilient and intelligent security systems.

## 6 Conclusion

This paper presented a unified, secure-by-design framework that integrates cloud forensic automation and LLM input hardening. By combining the Cloud Investigation Automation Framework (CIAF) with PromptShield, we addressed critical limitations in cloud forensics: the lack of automation and the susceptibility of LLM-based tools to adversarial prompt injection. CIAF enables semantic validation of forensic input, enhancing the accuracy and interpretability of cloud investigations through structured, template-driven analysis. PromptShield complements this by enforcing ontology-based constraints that mitigate ambiguous and malicious prompts, securing the LLM pipeline. Together, the two components form a dual-layered architecture that standardizes both input generation and analysis, enabling more reliable and scalable forensic workflows.

Our evaluation in the AWS and Azure environments demonstrated the effectiveness of the proposed system, achieving precision, recall, and F1 scores that exceed 93% in identifying true forensic indicators, even under adversarial input scenarios. The use of causal reasoning, structured validation, and semantic constraints proves to be valuable in enhancing the trustworthiness of LLM-based forensic systems.

Future work will focus on extending this framework to support multi-cloud environments and diverse forensic data types, integrating reinforcement learning to continuously adapt ontology rules, and quantifying the robustness of the approach under unseen threat vectors. We also aim to explore collaborative applications of CIAF and PromptShield in incident response and threat hunting across heterogeneous enterprise systems.

## References

1. Derner, E., Batistic, K., Zahalka, J., Babuska, R.: A security risk taxonomy for prompt-based interaction with large language models. IEEE Access **12**, 126176 (2024)
2. Chernyshev, M., Baig, Z., Doss, R.: [Short Paper] forensic analysis of indirect prompt injection attacks on LLM agents. In: 2024 IEEE 6th Int. Conf. on Trust, Privacy and Security in Intelligent Systems and Applications (TPS-ISA), pp. 409–411. IEEE, Washington (2024)
3. OWASP Foundation: LLM01:2025 Prompt Injection. OWASP GenAI Risk Catalog
4. Akula, A.K.: The role of cloud-based tools in modern cybercrime investigations: insights from a ransomware case study. Int. J. Eng. Techn. Res. (IJETR) **9**(2), 267–277 (2024)
5. Purnaye, P., Kulkarni, V.: A comprehensive study of cloud forensics. Arch. Comput. Methods Eng. **29**(1), 33–46 (2022)
6. Reshmi, T.R.: Information security breaches due to ransomware attacks–a systematic literature review. Int. J. Inf. Manag. Data Insights **1**(2), 100013 (2021)
7. Mishra, A.K., Matta, P., Pilli, E.S., Joshi, R.C.: Cloud forensics: state-of-the-art and research challenges. In: Int. Symp. on Cloud and Services Computing (2012)
8. Zhu, K., et al.: PromptBench: towards evaluating the robustness of large language models on adversarial prompts. arXiv:2309.00268 (2023)
9. Schulhoff, S., et al.: Ignore this title and HackAPrompt: exposing systemic vulnerabilities of LLMs through a global scale prompt hacking competition. arXiv:2310.06774 (2023)
10. Wu, X., et al.: LangGraph. arXiv:2304.10123 (2023)

11. Wu, Z., et al.: AutoGen: enabling seamless multi-agent coordination. In: Proc. of the Neural Information Processing Systems (2023)
12. Topsakal, E., Akinci, A.: CrewAI: optimized agent collaboration framework for multi-agent systems. In: Int. Conf. on AI and Multi-Agent Systems (AIMAS) (2024)
13. Al-Mugerrn, R., Al-Dhaqm, A., Othman, S.H.: A metamodeling approach for structuring and organizing cloud forensics domain. In: Int. Conf. on Smart Computing and Application (ICoSCA), pp. 1–5 (2023)
14. Zawoad, S., Hasan, R.: Cloud forensics: a meta-study of challenges, approaches, and open problems. arXiv:1302.6312 (2013)
15. Liu, J., et al.: Prompt injection attacks and defenses in large language models. In: Proc. of the Conf. on AI Security (2023)
16. Madry, A., Makelov, A., Schmidt, L., Tsipras, D., Vladu, A.: Towards Deep learning models resistant to adversarial attacks. arXiv:1706.06083 (2018)
17. Carlini, N., Wagner, D.: Towards evaluating the robustness of neural networks. In: IEEE Symp. on Security and Privacy (SP), pp. 39–57. IEEE (2017)
18. Pearl, J.: Causality: Models, Reasoning, and Inference. Cambridge University Press, Cambridge (2009)
19. Zhou, X., Li, M., von Oswald, J., Yang, C.: Algorithmic understanding of LLMs: evaluating emergent primitives and their role in AI systems. J. Artif. Intell. Res. **45**, 123–145 (2024)
20. Li, M., Chen, Y., Wang, H.: Latent structure discovery in LLMs: a compositional learning perspective. In: Proc. of NeurIPS, vol. 36, pp. 5678–5692 (2023)
21. Goodfellow, I.J., Shlens, J., Szegedy, C.: Explaining and harnessing adversarial examples. arXiv:1412.6572 (2015)
22. Carlini, N., Wagner, D.: Towards evaluating the robustness of neural networks. In: Proceedings of the IEEE Symposium on Security and Privacy (SP) (2017)
23. Cohen, J.M., Rosenfeld, E., Kolter, J.Z.: Certified adversarial robustness via randomized smoothing. In: Proceedings of the International Conference on Machine Learning (ICML), pp. 1310–1320 (2019)
24. Dwork, C., McSherry, F., Nissim, K., Smith, A.: Calibrating noise to sensitivity in private data analysis. In: Proceedings of the Theory of Cryptography Conference (TCC), pp. 265–284 (2006)
25. Snell, C., Lee, J., Xu, K., Kumar, A.: Scaling LLM test-time compute optimally can be more effective than scaling model parameters. arXiv:2408.03314 (2024)
26. Liu, Y., et al.: Prompt injection attack against LLM-integrated applications. arXiv:2306.05499 (2023)
27. Liu, X., Yu, Z., Zhang, Y., Zhang, N., Xiao, C.: Automatic and universal prompt injection attacks against large language models. arXiv:2403.04957 (2024)
28. Ju, T., et al.: Flooding spread of manipulated knowledge in LLM-based multi-agent communities. arXiv:2407.07791 (2024)
29. Zhang, Y., et al.: Security of multi-agent cyber-physical systems: a survey. IEEE Access **10**, 123456–123470 (2022)
30. Muliarevych, O.: Enhancing LLM security: semantic reasoning and deterministic input validation. In: 2024 IEEE International Conference on AI Security (2024)
31. Yao, T., et al.: When LLMs meet cybersecurity: a systematic literature review. Cybersecurity **8**(1), 1–30 (2025)
32. Bendiab, A., Farooq, S., Chaudhary, M.: Enhancing digital forensics with LLMs: a comprehensive review. arXiv:2402.19366 (2024)
33. Galhotra, S., Shafiee, A.: Logging LLM interactions for forensic readiness in cloud security. In: Proceedings of the ACM Conference on Cloud Security (2024)

34. Denning, D.E.: An intrusion-detection model. IEEE Trans. Softw. Eng. **SE-13**(2), 222–232 (1987)
35. Kent, K., Souppaya, M.: Guide to computer security log management. Technical Report, National Institute of Standards and Technology (2006)
36. Rouached, M., Djeraba, C.: Ontology-based smart sound digital forensics analysis for web services. ResearchGate preprint (2018)
37. Li, X., Zhao, T.: Cloud forensic readiness as a service: a proactive model for digital evidence accumulation. Wiley Forensic Science(2023)
38. Bratsas, C., et al.: Knowledge graphs and semantic web tools in cyber threat intelligence: a systematic literature review. J. Cybersecur. Privacy **4**(3), 518–545 (2024)
39. Ahmad, S., et al.: AI-based ransomware detection: a comprehensive review. IEEE Access **13**, 123456–123478 (2025)
40. Alhawi, O.M., et al.: Trusted detection of ransomware in a private cloud using machine learning methods leveraging meta-features from volatile memory. Futur. Gener. Comput. Syst. **115**, 406–420 (2025)
41. Schwartz, D., Patel, N.: LLMCloudHunter: harnessing LLMs for automated extraction of detection rules from cloud-based CTI. J. Cloud Forensics **15**(2), 85–102 (2024)
42. Boffa, M., Garcia, L.: LogPrécis: unleashing language models for automated malicious log analysis. In: Proceedings of the ACM Conference on Security and Privacy in AI (2023)
43. Agorbia, M., Kornecki, A., Wang, Y.: Leveraging AI-enhanced risk-based access management for cloud security. J. Cloud Secur. **12**(1), 45–58 (2024)
44. Johnson, E., Patel, R.: SecGenAI: securing cloud-based generative AI applications. Cybersecur. Privacy J. **10**(2), 100–120 (2024)
45. Lee, C., Tan, W.: Dual-use of generative AI in cybersecurity: opportunities and threats. AI Soc. **39**(3), 307–324 (2024)
46. Verma, A., et al.: Operationalizing a threat model for red-teaming large language models (LLMs). arXiv:2407.14937 (2024)
47. Hadnagy, C., Wilson, P.: Social engineering in cyberse- curity: the evolution of a concept. Int. J. Secure. Network. **5**(2–3), 95–102 (2010)
48. Alharthi, D., Regan, A.: Social engineering infosec policies. Comput. Sci. Inf. Technol. (2021)
49. Alharthi, D.N.: Social engineering defense mechanisms and InfoSec policies: a survey and qualitative analysis (Doctoral dissertation, University of California, Irvine)
50. Zhang, H., Li, Y., Chen, J., Wang, X.: Adversarial at- tacks on large language models: a comprehensive survey. ACM Comput. Surv. **56**(4), 1–28 (2024)
51. Yip, D.W., Esmradi, A., Chan, C.F.: A novel evaluation framework for assessing resilience against prompt injection attacks in large language models. In: 2023 IEEE Asia-Pacific Conference on Computer Science and Data Engineering (2023)
52. Muliarevych, O.: Enhancing system security: LLM-driven defense against prompt injection vulnerabilities. In: 2024 IEEE 17th International Conference on Advanced Trends in Radioelectronics, Telecommunications and Computer Engineering (TCSET), pp. 420–423 (2024)
53. Sahoo, P., Singh, A.K., Saha, S., Jain, V., Mondal, S., Chadha, A.: A systematic survey of prompt engineering in LLMs: techniques and applications. arXiv:2402.07927 (2024)
54. Vatsal, S., Dubey, H.: A survey of prompt engineering methods in large language models for different NLP tasks. arXiv:2407.12994 (2024)

55. Chen, B., Zhang, Z., Langrené, N., Zhu, S.: Un- leashing the potential of prompt engineering in LLMs: a comprehensive review. arXiv:2310.14735 (2023)
56. Liu, M. X., et al.: We need structured output: towards user-centered constraints on large language model output. arXiv:2404.07362 (2024a)
57. Liu, P., Yuan, W., Fu, J., Jiang, Z., Hayashi, H., Neubig, G.: Pre-train, prompt, and predict: a systematic survey of prompting methods in NLP (2021)
58. Garcia, L., Wang, R., Chen, M.: Semantic knowledge representation: ontology-driven ai for enhanced reasoning and interoperability. Artif. Intell. Rev. **58**, 567–589 (2024)
59. Patel, R., Kumar, A., Gupta, S.: Ontology-based cyber threat intelligence: enhancing automated detection and response. IEEE Trans. Inf. Forensics Secur. **18**, 2345–2362 (2023)
60. Roldan-Molina, G.R., Mendez, J.R., Yevseyeva, I., Basto-Fernandes, V.: Ontology fixing by using software engineering technology. Appl. Sci. **10**(18), 6328 (2020)
61. Olah, C., Wang, J., Schnake, T., Geiger, A.: Efforts in explainable AI and mechanistic interpretability. ArXiv (2020b)
62. Turpin, R., Stechly, G., Fu, D.: Causal links between chain-of-thought outputs and model performance. ArXiv (2024)
63. Tenenbaum, J.B., Kemp, C., Griffiths, T.L., Goodman, N.D.: How to grow a mind: statistics, structure, and abstraction. Science **331**(6022), 1279–1285 (2011)
64. Purnaye, P., Kulkarni, V.: A comprehensive study of cloud forensics. Archiv. Comput. Methods Eng. **29**, 03 (2021)
65. Davis, J., Goadrich, M.: The relationship between precision-recall and roc curves **06** (2006)
66. Martini, B., Choo, K.-K.R.: An integrated conceptual digital forensic framework for cloud computing. Digit. Investig. **9**(2), 71–80 (2012)
67. Liu, Y., et al.: A survey on adversarial training for deep learning: principles, challenges, and advances. IEEE Trans. Neural Netw. Learn. Syst. (2024)
68. Ye, Y., et al.: Langgpt: rethinking structured reusable prompt design for LLMs. arXiv:2402.16929 (2024)
69. Cooper, A.: A guide to structured generation using constrained decoding (2024)
70. Wang, A., et al.: Towards a mechanistic understanding of transformers. Adv. Neural Inf. Process. Syst. (2023)
71. Weiss, G., Goldberg, Y., Yahav, E.: Thinking like transformers: restricting attention supports algorithmic reasoning. Adv. Neural. Inf. Process. Syst. **34**, 25623–25634 (2021)
72. Olsson, C., et al.: In-context learning and induction heads. In: Transformers Interpretability Workshop at NeurIPS (2022)
73. Todd, A., Zhao, L., Kapoor, R.: Function vectors: a framework for analyzing latent representations in large language models. J. Mach. Learn. Res. **25**(1), 1123–1154 (2024)
74. Olah, C., Wang, J., Schnake, T., Geiger, A.: Efforts in explainable ai and mechanistic interpretability. ArXiv (2020b)
75. Zhang, H., Yu, H., Jiao, J., Xing, E., Ghaoui, L.E., Jordan, M.I.: Trade-offs between robustness and accuracy in adversarial training. Adv. Neural. Inf. Process. Syst. **34**, 14046–14059 (2021)
76. Peters, J., Janzing, D., Schölkopf, B.: Elements of Causal Inference: Foundations and Learning Algorithms. MIT Press (2017)

# Understanding Online Grooming Through LLMs: Stage Detection and Linguistic Patterns

Sarah A. J. Hamer(✉), Yi Ting Chua, and Weiping Pei

School of Cyber Studies, College of Engineering and Computer Science, The University of Tulsa, Tulsa, OK, USA
{sah0327,ytc2805,weiping-pei}@utulsa.edu

**Abstract.** This study presents a large language model (LLM)-based analysis of online sexual predatory behaviors using a dataset of 652 predator conversations sourced from Perverted Justice. The conversations are divided into 36,631 context-preserving segments for analysis. We adopt open-source LLMs to automatically identify grooming stages for each segment, testing three prompt strategies, single-stage selection, multi-stage selection, and single-stage verification, across four LLMs. Our evaluation of a manually annotated subset shows that the single-stage verification strategy using OpenChat yields the highest performance, achieving an average accuracy of 80.48% across stages. The stage classification results also reveal the distribution and sequencing of grooming stages across conversations, providing a coarse-grained understanding of grooming dynamics. To further explore the linguistic and thematic content of each phase, we group the segments by stage and apply BERTopic for unsupervised topic modeling. Our approach demonstrates how LLMs can support a scalable and interpretable analysis of online grooming, offering insights into stage-specific patterns and communication tactics.

**Keywords:** Online grooming · Large Language Models (LLMs) · Child exploitation detection

## 1 Introduction

The growing popularity of smartphones and the ease of Internet access have reshaped the risk landscape of child exploitation. In 2024, 95% of adolescents between the ages of 13 and 17 in the United States reported having access to a smartphone, and 88% have access to a computer, with 96% going online daily [10]. This constant connectivity has created unprecedented opportunities for online predators to contact, groom, and exploit minors. Correspondingly, the number of reports of online sexual crimes against children and the sharing and production of Child Sexual Abuse Material (CSAM) via the Internet has grown exponentially [17]. Globally, it is estimated that one in 12 children has experienced online sexual exploitation or abuse [11]. However, due to the sensitive


K.-K. R. Choo et al. (Eds.): ICDF2C 2025, LNICST 686, pp. 403–430, 2026.
https://doi.org/10.1007/978-3-032-22545-0_24

and underreported nature of these crimes, the actual prevalence is likely much higher than official statistics suggest [28].

One critical approach through which predators build relationships with minors is grooming. Online child grooming is a complex and manipulative process through which adult predators build connection with minors for the purpose of sexual exploitation [13,16,19,23]. This process typically unfolds across several stages: *friendship forming*, *relationship*, *risk assessment*, *exclusivity*, *sexual*, and *meeting*. Understanding these stages is critical for effective prevention, detection, and intervention efforts. While earlier research provided theoretical frameworks and psychological insights into behaviors at each stage, most computational approaches have yet to capture the full complexity of these interactions, particularly at both coarse and fine levels of linguistic analysis.

Previous computational approaches to address online grooming leveraged traditional machine learning on textual chat datasets. Common models included support vector machine (SVM) and k-nearest neighbor [8,12]. Although these models demonstrated the feasibility of automated detection, there are limitations. First, these models relied on sparse text features (e.g., TF-IDF representations), which captured more surface-level characteristics. Second, conversations were often segmented for ease of processing and analysis [8]. These limitations mean that the contextual and sequential nature of grooming dialogues was not well addressed.

The recent emergence of large-language models (LLMs) offers opportunities to overcome such limitations. Trained on vast corpora of natural language, LLMs capture rich contextual and semantic information across long stretches of text [7]. Early application of LLMs such as BERT have demonstrated improvements in both accuracy and interpretability by leveraging context-sensitive and message-level analysis [21]. Despite recent application, LLMs have not yet been applied to map stage-by-stage progression or uncover fine-grained thematic patterns within each stage.

In this research, we leverage LLMs to conduct a systematic analysis of online child sexual predation. Drawing from larger and more completed chat transcripts from the Perverted Justice (PJ) organization, this research seeks to improve understanding of the trajectory of online grooming stages and to uncover semantic content that defines each stage. Specifically, we employ a two-tier approach: (1) at the coarse-grained level, we use LLMs to detect and classify the progression of grooming stages over the course of each conversation; and (2) at the fine-grained level, we apply BERTopic, a transformer-based topic modeling technique, to identify meaningful topic clusters that characterize each stage. This allows us to examine not only when transitions between stages occur, but also what kinds of discussions predators engage in during each phase.

## 2 Background and Related Work

### 2.1 Online Sexual Predatory Behavior Against Children

There are different models on online sexual predatory behavior. The earliest and most influential model is O'Connell's six-stage typology: *friendship forming*, *rela-*

*tionship forming*, *risk assessment*, *exclusivity*, *sexual* with two sub-classifications, and *conclusion* [19]. Derived from qualitative analysis of chat transcripts, this typology offered the first systematic guidance for describing how predators incrementally build rapport with minors.

Subsequent research has validated and raised concerns about this linear depiction of online grooming stages. Winters and Jeglic demonstrated that participants were unable to identify online sexual predatory behaviors during any stage of grooming [27]. Later research by Gupta et al. and Kloess et al. documented the fluidity in predators' strategies where intimacy-building, risk assessment, and sexual content are interwoven [13,16]. These research highlights a central challenge in the conceptualization of online grooming stages where stage boundaries are porous and context-dependent.

To address this challenge, recent scholars have utilized new methodological approaches and datasets. Ringenberg et al. introduced a fuzzy-set annotation protocol that allows for partial categorization of multiple stages within each stage [22]. Building on this coding scheme, Ringenberg and colleagues performed qualitative analysis on a dataset of 60 conversations that are between predators and law enforcement, real victims, and vigilante decoys [23]. Due to its comprehensive basis on state-of-the-art research and established use for analysis, Ringenberg et al.'s stage definitions are chosen here as a starting point for categorizing online grooming conversations. These stages include *friendship forming*, *relationship*, *risk assessment*, *exclusivity*, *sexual*, and *meeting* [23].

### 2.2 ML-Based Grooming Detection

A range of machine learning approaches have been proposed to detect online grooming behaviors in chat-based conversations. For instance, Alves et al. [1] proposed JointKPE++ which applies supervised keyphrase extraction using BERT-based models to identify relevant content in grooming and drug dealing logs, demonstrating strong performance over traditional techniques. The PEEC system combines deep neural networks for age detection with an SVM-based classifier for grooming detection, achieving high accuracy in identifying predatory behavior involving minors [15]. Chehbouni et al. [5] proposed a privacy-preserving framework based on federated learning has also been introduced to enable early detection of sexual predators across devices without compromising user privacy. To address class imbalance in grooming datasets, another study presents a hybrid sampling and data perturbation technique coupled with balanced ensemble learning, resulting in an F1-score of 0.99 [4]. While these methods highlight the potential of supervised learning for grooming detection, they all rely on labeled datasets and traditional machine learning pipelines, without leveraging large language models (LLMs). Moreover, these approaches typically focus on binary grooming classification at the segment or sentence level, without modeling the entire conversational context or considering the nuanced stage-by-stage progression of grooming failed to address the sequential, goal-directed nature of online grooming [1,9,18]. In contrast, our work adopts LLMs to perform multi-label classification of grooming stages across entire conversations, offering both coarse- and fine-grained linguistic insights into the grooming process.

# 3 Design

## 3.1 Overview

As illustrated in Fig. 1, our study follows a top-down analytical methodology. We begin with a coarse-grained analysis to identify the progression of online grooming stages, followed by a fine-grained exploration of topics within each stage. First, full-length conversations are split into shorter segments to facilitate processing, based on a set of predefined rules. Second, each segment is analyzed using LLM to determine its corresponding grooming stage(s). We frame this as a multi-label classification task, allowing each segment to be associated with multiple stages when appropriate. The resulting stage annotations support coarse-grained analysis, such as the distribution of stages and time spent across them. Finally, building on this foundation, we perform fine-grained analysis by applying topic modeling to segments grouped by stage, uncovering representative themes within each phase of the grooming process.

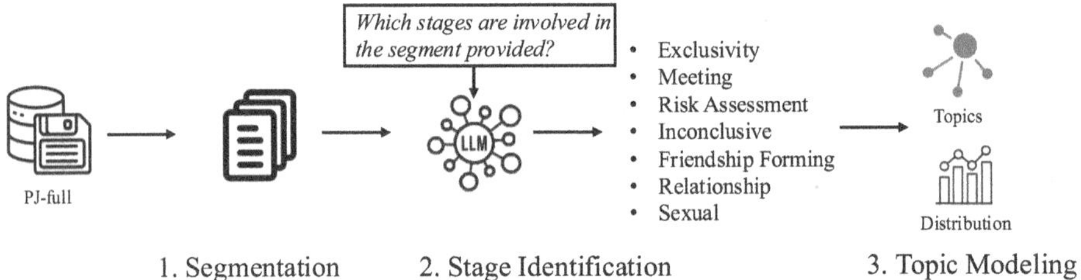


**Fig. 1.** Overview of Our Study.

## 3.2 Segmentation

Our study focuses on conversations sourced from Perverted Justice. As a first step in our analysis, we segment each conversation to facilitate downstream processing. Segmentation occurs under two main conditions. The first is based on temporal gaps: a new segment is created when there is a pause of 25 min or more between messages. This guideline of 25-minute pauses is consistent with the original PAN12 dataset preprocessing, which also treats such pauses as natural conversational boundaries [14]. The second condition is based on character length: when a segment reaches 1,090 characters, it is further divided. In this case, the conversation part that exceeds this character limit is then segmented at equal intervals. This is done to ensure the lowest number of segments where the segments are still below character limits, to keep the size of segments as broad as possible to guarantee the most context. Segmentation also always is done in-between messages and never splits a message, for the same reason of preserving context. The 1,090-character threshold was empirically determined during testing. Segments exceeding this limit occasionally triggered context overflow issues in the model outputs, leading to repetitive and off-topic text. Further analysis reveals a correlation between segment length and the likelihood of overflow, likely due to exceeding the model's attention span [24]. Additionally, very short segments, those with 10 words or fewer are removed from the dataset as they lack sufficient context for reliable stage identification.

### 3.3 LLM-Based Stage Identification

As part of our second analysis stage, we leverage LLMs to identify grooming stages. We adopt the stage framework used by Ringenberg et al. [23], which defines the progression of online grooming through the following phases (detailed definitions used in the finalized prompt are provided in the Appendix A.1):

- **Friendship Forming**: Casual, light-hearted conversations where participants share personal but non-sensitive details about their daily lives, hobbies, or routines.
- **Relationship**: A deepening emotional connection, marked by greater openness and vulnerability.
- **Exclusivity**: Clear expressions of deep emotional attachment, mutual love, and a strong sense of commitment to each other.
- **Meeting**: Discussions or planning of in-person meetings, speculation about possible meetups, or express anticipation or obstacles about meeting.
- **Risk Assessment**: Moments where participants express caution, seek to verify identity, or reflect skepticism or doubt.
- **Sexual**: Involves sexually explicit language, graphic messages, hypothetical scenarios, questions about sexual history, or fantasy enactment.

We incorporate these stage definitions into prompt instructions and evaluate multiple prompt variations with different open-source LLMs. To benchmark model performance, all authors independently annotated a randomly selected 30 conversation segments, establishing a consensus ground truth through discussion. We then evaluated each LLM and prompt combination based on this set, measuring per-stage accuracy, false positives, and false negatives. Detailed results are discussed in Sect. 4.3 and provided in Appendix A.3.

Based on the results, the distribution of stages can be calculated, which aids in identifying which stages are the most prevalent. Measuring the amount of messages per conversation that are dedicated to each stage can also indicate how much time is spent on each stage per conversation. This can be calculated because the LLM also extracts and names the lines that the stage categorization is based on. Additionally, the analysis assesses the likelihood of progression from one stage to the next. As Ringenberg et al. [23] also point out, the order of stages can vary widely depending on the conversation. By using a two-stage window, the probability of one stage following after another in a conversation can be calculated. Only instances where a stage changes over segments are counted here, since the order of different stage appearance is the focus of this analysis. Because of that, if multiple consecutive segments are assigned the same stage, it is not counted here. When multiple stages are assigned to a segment, each stage is counted as its own instance. For example, when the first segment is assigned *friendship forming* and the second segment is assigned both *meeting* and *relationship*, this is considered an instance of *meeting* following the *friendship forming* stage and as an instance of *relationship* following the *friendship forming* stage. All of these instances of consecutive stage changes that are counted in a two-stage window are aggregated to form the consecutive stage probability.

Another metric that can be calculated is the occurrence of stages per hour of day. This has the effect of being able to conclude if certain stages are more likely to occur during a certain time of day, at nighttime for example. Calculating this is possible due to most conversations possessing a marked down time of posting. However, it has to be taken into account that these have a different level of detail, with some messages being recorded down to the seconds and others per minute or hour. This different formatting is because of differences in documentation, which was dependent on the medium of communication and the PJ informant documenting it. Nonetheless, there are segments with no documented start or end time in the dataset as well, which are excluded from analysis here.

### 3.4 Fine-Grained Topic Analysis

In the fine-grained analysis, BERTopic is utilized for topic modeling to extract detailed topics and strategies related to each stage from the quotes listed by the LLM. This highlights potential indicators of the stages in practice and frequently used terms associated with each stage. For that, the quotes are preprocessed by removing stopwords, light lemmatization that avoids lemmatizing named entities or pronouns to preserve that information, and filtering out dividers such as [p], [m], or [EOS]. The quote sections are grouped per stage per conversation. Then, BERTopic is applied to generate topic clusters for each stage.

### 3.5 Ethical Considerations and Privacy Protection

Given the sensitive nature of the dataset, we took several steps to ensure ethical handling and privacy preservation throughout our study. All experiments were conducted using open-source LLMs executed locally, ensuring that no data was transmitted to third-party servers. Before prompting the LLMs, we anonymized the dataset by removing identifiable information such as usernames and full names. Speakers in the dataset were labeled as either informants [m] or predators [p], and each conversation was assigned a six-digit random conversation ID to prevent re-identification. We recognize the importance of ethical considerations when working with sensitive content, and we followed strict precautions to protect individual privacy and minimize potential harm.

## 4 Experimental Setup

### 4.1 Dataset

For the purpose of analyzing the behavioral pattern of whole conversations between predators and minors in online grooming interactions, a dataset with complete conversations is needed. A commonly used online grooming dataset is PAN12 [1,9,18,21]. This dataset was prepared for and used in the Sexual Predator Identification competition at CLEF (Conference and Labs of the Evaluation Forum) 2012 [14]. For the online grooming part of the dataset, the data is sourced from PJ, a non-profit that employed informants to mimic as minors in online conversations with predators. Chat logs with convicted predators are available online [3]. However, PAN12 only includes conversations before 2012. Conversations are pre-segmented, and the order of these segments is randomized, which makes analyzing the whole conversations using PAN12 unfeasible. PJ provides active chat logs until 2016, which means that the dataset can be expanded by including these. Due to that, a new dataset is compiled for this study. PJ is used as a source for the data and it includes the unsegmented conversations. As a basis for the dataset, the non-segmented text files of chat logs from PJ that were used for PAN12 are contributed by Dr. Giacomo Inches, who is one of the researchers that compile the PAN12 dataset. Missing conversations, including conversations made available after PAN12 are compiled and added by scraping the PJ website. As the website is offline at the time of research, Wayback Machine is used to access the website as it was archived on March 14, 2021 [2]. All conversations published by PJ are included in the dataset, except for the conversations published in October 2011, March 2012, May 2014, December 2015, January, March, April, and June 2016, as these months are neither archived by the Wayback Machine nor included in PAN12 and cannot be accessed. The dataset includes 652 conversations collected between 2003 and 2016 across multiple messaging services, as summarized in Table 1.

**Table 1.** Summary Statistics of the Dataset

| Metric | Amount |
|---|---|
| Total number of conversations | 652 |
| Total number of segments | 36,631 |
| Average number of words per segment | 204.32 |
| Average number of segments per conversation | 56.18 |

## 4.2 Preprocessing

Because of the formatting differences between services and individual informants' differences in documentation styles, the formatting is standardized during preprocessing. Authors and identifiable information, such as usernames or full names, are also anonymized. Each conversation is assigned a conversationID of six random numbers. The dataset further includes a predator label with a binary indication of which messages are sent by the predator and which are sent by the informant. The date and time of each message are also listed, if available. Lastly, all messages within the conversation are listed in chronological order.

Before segmentation, each conversation is compiled into one string, with the beginning indicating the author followed by the message. If the author is an informant, it is indicated by [m]. If the author is a predator, the divider is [p]. This is followed by the message. If the author stays the same for the next message, the messages are divided by [EOS]. In case of the author changing, it is indicated by their respective divider before the message. The date and time, if available, are listed in each message's metadata via the use of a pickle file format.

### 4.3 LLMs and Prompt Strategies

**LLMs.** For this study, we evaluate four open-source LLMs commonly used for instruction-following and text classification tasks: LLaMA 3 [26], OpenChat [25], Gemma 3 [6], and Phi [20]. LLaMA 3, developed by Meta, represents a strong general-purpose model with competitive performance across a range of benchmarks. OpenChat is an open-weight instruction-tuned model optimized for conversational tasks. Gemma 3, released by Google, is designed to be lightweight and efficient while maintaining strong reasoning capabilities. Phi, developed by Microsoft, is a compact model optimized for low-resource scenarios and known for its high efficiency on downstream tasks.

**Prompt Strategies.** We explore three prompt strategies for identifying grooming stage from conversation segments: ***single-stage selection***, ***multi-stage selection***, and ***single-stage verification***. The single-stage selection strategy presents all stage definitions but asks the model to select only the most appropriate stage, resulting in single-label classification. In contrast, the multi-stage selection strategy also presents definitions of all six grooming stages in a single prompt and asks the model to identify all applicable stages at once, enabling multi-label classification. Lastly, the single-stage verification strategy presents one stage definition at a time and queries the model on whether the segment fits that specific stage. This process is repeated for all six stages per segment, allowing for multi-label classification based on multiple independent binary decisions. Together, these strategies allow us to evaluate how prompt structure affects LLM performance in both multi-label and single-label classification tasks. Additionally, the LLM is instructed to explain its reasoning for assigning stages in all tested prompts to enhance transparency. The concrete prompts we used are provided in Appendix A.2.

## 5 Results and Analysis

### 5.1 LLM-Based Identification

While evaluating different prompt strategies across multiple LLMs, one challenge that emerged was the handling of explicit content within the dataset. Although all LLMs were run locally, some instruction prompts triggered a default disclaimer response indicating that the model could not process explicit or sexually suggestive content. This occurred despite all models being configured for unrestricted local use and tested on the same set of segments, which included sexual content as part of the ground truth. Notably, the structure of the prompt—particularly the phrasing in the instruction section—affected the likelihood of triggering this limitation. Prompt for the multi-stage selection showed a higher rate of content filtering, with explicit content disclaimers occurring in 40% to 53.33% of cases depending on the prompt formulation. The single-stage selection prompts generate a low rate of segments where the same stage is identified in the results as in the ground truth. It is between 6.67% and 43.33% depending on the instruction and stage definition in the prompt and using the LLaMA 3. The highest performing combination of general prompt and stage definition for single-stage selection prompts is also tested with the different models. Here, OpenChat names the right stage in 23% of cases, phi in 23%, and LLaMA 3 and Gemma 3 both perform at 43.3%. In contrast, the single-stage verification prompt rarely triggered this limitation, except for one case in which the restriction appeared in 43.33% of the outputs. Overall, single-stage verification circumvents the explicit content limitation issue and achieves better performance than both single-stage selection and multi-stage selection. These findings highlight how prompt design can unintentionally influence LLM behavior when dealing with sensitive or explicit material.

As discussed above, the single-stage verification prompt strategy consistently outperforms the other two strategies in terms of handling sensitive or explicit content. While detailed evaluation of the single-stage selection and multi-stage selection strategies are provided in Tables 5 and 6 in Appendix A.3, we focus on the results of single-stage verification strategy in this section. When applied across different LLMs, as shown in Table 2, OpenChat achieves the best performance. To further enhance accuracy, we experimented with one-shot and few-shot prompting by incorporating up to three labeled examples with reasoning into the prompt. The best-performing configuration is a few-shot, single-stage verification prompt that allows for multi-label classification by querying each stage separately using OpenChat. This setup achieves an average accuracy of 80.48% across all stages, with the lowest performance observed in the *relationship* stage at 60%. False negatives remain relatively low, peaking at 16.67% for the *exclusivity* stage, while false positives reach a maximum of 30%, also in the *relationship* stage. Given its overall effectiveness and balance of precision and recall, this prompt variation was selected for large-scale analysis of the full dataset in the following subsections.

### 5.2 Coarse-Grained Analysis

Overall, the distribution of grooming stages across all segments reveals that 32.22% are assigned to the *friendship forming* stage, followed by 23.64% to the *relationship* stage, 14.49% to the *meeting* stage, 13.69% to the *sexual* stage, 11.81% to *risk assessment*, and 1.76% to *exclusivity*. Additionally, 2.38% of segments were labeled as *inconclusive*, indicating that no clear stage could be confidently identified. This distribution highlights the predominance of early-stage

**Table 2.** Evaluation of the Single-Stage Verification Prompt across Different LLM Models for Grooming Stage Identification. Metrics reported are accuracy (Acc), false negative (FN), and false positive (FP). Accuracy values above 80.00% are highlighted in **bold.**

| Model | Prompt Type | Stage | Acc | FN | FP | Avg. Acc |
|---|---|---|---|---|---|---|
| LLaMA3 | Zero-Shot | Exclusivity | 76.67% | 13.33% | 10.00% | 62.86% |
| | | Meeting | **80.00%** | 0.00% | 20.00% | |
| | | Risk Assessment | 46.67% | 6.67% | 46.67% | |
| | | Inconclusive | 10.00% | 0.00% | 90.00% | |
| | | Friendship Forming | 63.33% | 13.33% | 23.33% | |
| | | Relationship | 66.67% | 6.67% | 26.67% | |
| | | Sexual | **96.67%** | 3.33% | 0.00% | |
| Gemma3 | Zero-Shot | Exclusivity | 56.67% | 16.67% | 26.67% | 61.43% |
| | | Meeting | 60.00% | 10.00% | 30.00% | |
| | | Risk Assessment | 56.67% | 6.67% | 36.67% | |
| | | Inconclusive | 46.67% | 0.00% | 53.33% | |
| | | Friendship Forming | **80.00%** | 6.67% | 13.33% | |
| | | Relationship | 46.67% | 23.33% | 30.00% | |
| | | Sexual | **83.33%** | 13.33% | 3.33% | |
| OpenChat | Zero-Shot | Exclusivity | **83.33%** | 6.67% | 10.00% | 75.75% |
| | | Meeting | 70.00% | 3.33% | 26.67% | |
| | | Risk Assessment | 76.67% | 10.00% | 13.33% | |
| | | Inconclusive | **96.67%** | 3.33% | 0.00% | |
| | | Friendship Forming | 60.00% | 0.00% | 40.00% | |
| | | Relationship | 53.55% | 6.67% | 40.00% | |
| | | Sexual | **90.00%** | 6.67% | 3.33% | |
| OpenChat | One-Shot | Exclusivity | **83.33%** | 13.33% | 3.33% | 79.52% |
| | | Meeting | **83.33%** | 6.67% | 10.00% | |
| | | Risk Assessment | 70.00% | 13.33% | 16.67% | |
| | | Inconclusive | **96.67%** | 3.33% | 0.00% | |
| | | Friendship Forming | 66.67% | 3.33% | 30.00% | |
| | | Relationship | 70.00% | 3.33% | 26.67% | |
| | | Sexual | **86.67%** | 10.00% | 3.33% | |
| OpenChat | Few-Shot | Exclusivity | **80.00%** | 16.67% | 3.33% | **80.48%** |
| | | Meeting | **80.00%** | 6.67% | 13.33% | |
| | | Risk Assessment | **83.33%** | 13.33% | 3.33% | |
| | | Inconclusive | **93.33%** | 3.33% | 3.33% | |
| | | Friendship Forming | 76.67% | 3.33% | 20.00% | |
| | | Relationship | 60.00% | 10.00% | 30.00% | |
| | | Sexual | **90.00%** | 10.00% | 0.00% | |

grooming tactics, particularly those focused on building rapport and emotional connection.

To further understand how grooming stages unfold sequentially, we analyze consecutive stage transitions, summarized in Table 3. In this table, the vertical axis represents the current (preceding) stage, while the horizontal axis denotes the following stage. Each cell indicates the probability a given stage is immediately followed by another. For example, the value 0.3332 in the cell corresponding to *exclusivity* (row) and *relationship* (column) means that *relationship* follows *exclusivity* with a probability of 33.31%. A key trend in the table is that *friendship forming* and *relationship* frequently appear as the most likely or second most likely stages to follow any given stage. This suggests that predators often reinforce early emotional engagement, even after more advanced phases have been introduced. Another notable observation is that the *sexual* stage is least likely to follow an *inconclusive* segment. While transitions to the *sexual* stage from other stages range between 14.33% and 17.80%, the transition from *inconclusive* occurs only 7.97% of the time. This indicates that when a segment lacks sufficient context for classification, it is particularly unlikely to lead directly into explicitly sexual content.

**Table 3.** Probability of Consecutive Stage Occurrence

| | Exclusivity | Friendship Forming | Inconclusive | Meeting | Relationship | Risk Assessment | Sexual |
|---|---|---|---|---|---|---|---|
| Exclusivity | N/A | 0.2733 | 0.0184 | 0.1296 | **0.3332** | 0.0863 | 0.1592 |
| Friendship Forming | 0.0427 | N/A | 0.0357 | 0.1948 | **0.4205** | 0.1392 | 0.167 |
| Inconclusive | 0.0236 | **0.3974** | N/A | 0.1210 | 0.2816 | 0.0968 | 0.0797 |
| Meeting | 0.0395 | **0.3629** | 0.0216 | N/A | 0.3043 | 0.1284 | 0.1433 |
| Relationship | 0.0538 | **0.4419** | 0.0261 | 0.1732 | N/A | 0.1270 | 0.1780 |
| Risk Assessment | 0.0316 | **0.3280** | 0.0222 | 0.1585 | 0.2830 | N/A | 0.1767 |
| Sexual | 0.0463 | 0.3166 | 0.0210 | 0.1497 | **0.3213** | 0.1451 | N/A |

Based on the timestamp of each message in the conversation, we analyze the temporal distribution of grooming stages. Figure 2 presents the distribution of segment occurrences by hour of the day for each stage. Overall, we observe increased interaction between predators and victims during the evening hours, with activity peaking around 9:00 PM, and reaching its lowest point at approximately 5:00 AM, reflecting typical daily communication patterns. While most stages follow a similar temporal pattern, the *exclusivity* stage exhibits a slight deviation. It appears more frequently during the afternoon hours, particularly between 2:00 PM and 4:00 PM, compared to other stages. Unlike other stages, which generally show a steady increase into the evening, the *exclusivity* stage experiences noticeable declines around 5:00 PM and 8:00 PM. Interestingly, it then reaches its peak at 9:00 PM, a time when the frequency of other stages tends to drop below that of *exclusivity*. This pattern suggests that emotionally intense or committed exchanges may be more likely to occur later in the day, potentially reflecting times when users are emotionally engaged or have availability for deeper conversations.

### 5.3 Fine-Grained Analysis

Our fine-grained analysis operates at the sentence level within each identified grooming stage. As previously noted, LLMs are not only tasked with labeling and grooming stage of each conversation segment, but are also instructed to extract and quote the original sentences that serve as evidence for that stage. This enables a more interpretable and transparent analysis of stage-specific linguistic patterns. A total of 22 segments were excluded from the fine-grained

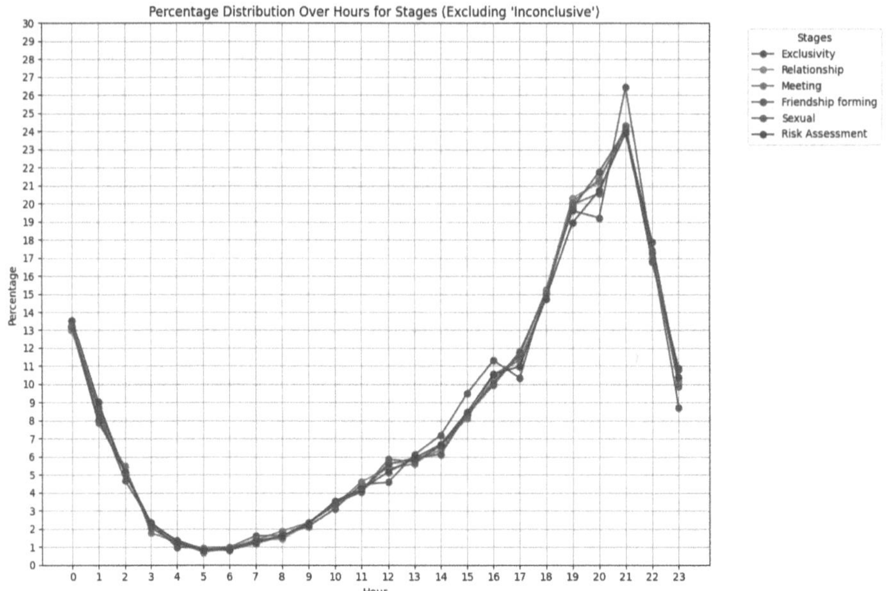


**Fig. 2.** Percentage Distribution Over Hours for Stages.

analysis due to the absence of quoted evidence for one or more stages, i.e., stages were identified by the LLM without any supporting quotes. Table 4 summarizes the minimum, maximum, average, and median number of quoted messages per conversation for each stage. In all cases except for *friendship forming*, at least one message per stage is quoted as evidence. For *friendship forming*, the LLM consistently extracts at least two messages per instance. The maximum number of quoted messages per stage per conversation generally aligns with the overall stage distribution, with one exception: the *sexual* stage. Although it appears in only 13.69% of segments on average, it yields the third-highest average number of quoted messages, and reaches the maximum message count across all stages. This suggests that when sexual content is present, it tends to be densely represented, involving extended or repeated exchanges.

**Table 4.** Messages per Stage within Conversations

| Stage | Min. | Max. | Average | Median |
|---|---|---|---|---|
| Exclusivity | 1 | 545 | 54.67 | 22 |
| Friendship forming | 2 | 4601 | 451.14 | 230 |
| Meeting | 1 | 858 | 108.3 | 70 |
| Relationship | 1 | 2312 | 255.64 | 125 |
| Risk Assessment | 1 | 771 | 63.25 | 41 |
| Sexual | 1 | 1402 | 115.45 | 65 |

To gain deeper insight into the linguistic patterns associated with each grooming stage, we applied BERTopic to the conversation segments labeled for each stage and extracted the top 10 most prominent topics along with the outlier group. Detailed results are presented in Appendix A.4. It is worth noting that the topic modeling results for the *risk assessment* stage are excluded from our discussion, as they did not yield coherent or interpretable patterns.

**Exclusivity.** Table 7 in Appendix A.4 presents the top 10 topics identified by BERTopic within segments labeled as belonging to the Exclusivity stage. The dominant themes emphasize emotional attachment, romantic commitment, and affectionate language. Common keywords such as "love", "baby", "want", and "miss" appear across most topics, underscoring the emotionally intense nature of this stage. Several topics reflect longing and emotional dependence (e.g., "miss love", "love miss"), while others convey fantasies of intimacy and closeness, such as expressions related to sleep and dreams ("goodnight", "sweet dream", "dream"). More personalized language also emerges in smaller topics, including references to precious, princess, and specific names, suggesting an elevated level of emotional investment. Additionally, some segments include forward-looking commitments (e.g., "marry", "forever", "baby girl"), aligning with the *exclusivity* stage's emphasis on perceived long-term relational bonding. Overall, the topic structure confirms that this stage is marked by intense emotional expressions and idealized romantic narratives often used by scammers to deepen victim entanglement.

**Friendship Forming.** Topic modeling of the *friendship forming* stage reveals a wide range of conversational themes characterized by casual, playful, and introductory exchanges. As shown in Table 8 in Appendix A.4, the dominant topic cluster (Topic -1) includes highly generic and informal expressions (e.g., "lol", "like", "want", "ok", "ur"), suggesting that many early-stage interactions are conversationally shallow or non-specific. Beyond this broad category, more specific subtopics reflect typical rapport-building behaviors. For instance, Topics 2 and 4 focus on everyday routines like sleeping and eating, while Topics 1 and 8 introduce early flirtation and physical compliments (e.g., "wear", "kiss", "cute"). Topics related to information exchange and logistics also emerge (e.g., "phone number", "talk", "chat"), indicating attempts to establish more direct communication. Notably, Topic 5 introduces age references ("13", "14", "young", "old guy"), potentially signaling grooming tactics aimed at assessing vulnerability. Overall, these topics illustrate how predators use friendly, humorous, or seemingly innocent exchanges to build initial trust and lower psychological defenses—often paving the way for deeper emotional or manipulative engagement in subsequent stages.

**Meeting.** The topic modeling results for the *meeting* stage, presented in Table 9 in Appendix A.4, reveal that the vast majority of segments cluster around a dominant topic (Topic 0) characterized by common conversational markers and meeting-related language such as "want", "come", "meet", and "ok". This indicates that most meeting-related exchanges are expressed in a casual and direct manner, often embedded in everyday small talk. The remaining topics capture more niche themes. Topic 1 references regional sports events (e.g., "Michigan", "Ohio State"), possibly reflecting attempts to establish shared interests or coordinate meetings around events. Topic 2 suggests underlying emotional conflict or manipulation, with terms like "cheat", "hurt", and "want hurt" indicating relational tension or justification tactics. Topic 3, while limited in size, features idiosyncratic terms ("eos", "ride", "dr long"), likely representing internal slang or coded references within specific conversations. Overall, these topics suggest that while most discussions of meeting are straightforward, some involve contextual or emotionally charged subtexts that may signal manipulation or escalation in grooming dynamics.

**Relationship.** Topic modeling results for the *relationship* stage (Table 10) reveal a rich mix of emotional expression, relational development, and early-stage intimacy. The dominant topic (Topic -1) features broad conversational tokens ("like", "want", "love", "ok"), reflecting the generally affectionate and affirming tone of this stage. Several topics emphasize emotional connection and longing—Topic 0 includes repetitive expressions like "miss miss" and "miss ya", indicating deepening attachment and emotional dependency. Other topics highlight aspects of daily life and personal disclosure, such as references to "mom", "dad", and "work" in Topic 1, as well as discussions of sleep and dreams in Topic 2. Topics 3 and 4 indicate logistical coordination and interest in direct communication through terms like "meet", "phone number", and "talk". Notably, Topics 5, 6, and 9 introduce early flirtation and sexual undertones (e.g., "condom", "thong", "kiss"), showing how romantic relationships in grooming can begin to blur into exploitation. Topic 7's mention of cheating and hurt suggests elements of manipulation or emotional conflict. Overall, the *relationship* stage blends emotional bonding with early cues of escalation, providing a transitional foundation toward deeper manipulation in subsequent stages.

**Sexual.** Tables 11 in Appendix A.4 presents the top 10 topics identified by BERTopic within segments labeled as belonging to the *sexual* stage. The results reveal a diverse range of themes, including discussions of contraception and sexual activity (e.g., "condom", "pregnant"), physical characteristics ("big", "bra size"), and graphic sexual acts ("clit", "wet", "pussy"). Several topics also reflect indirect sexualization through references to clothing ("thong", "skirt") and grooming practices ("shave", "trim"). Although the *sexual* stage accounts for a smaller proportion of overall segments, it is characterized by densely concentrated content, often featuring multiple explicit references per conversation. This highlights the intensity and variability of language use within sexually explicit stages of online grooming interactions.

# 6 Discussion

## 6.1 Implications

The findings of this study highlight the feasibility of LLMs in analyzing the dynamics and progression of online grooming for sexual exploitation. By applying a coarse-to-fine analytical framework, this allows for improved accuracy in stage identification, as well as context-aware understanding of themes in narrative across longitudinal interactions.

Historically, computational approaches to examine online grooming stages have relied on surface-level features and often analyzed conversations in isolated segments, which fails to account for the contextual and sequential nature of the grooming process [1,9,21]. These limitations have led to underdeveloped understanding of grooming dynamics across interactions between predators and victims. In contrast, LLMs such as OpenChat, particularly when paired with carefully engineered prompts, demonstrate improved contextual sensitivity and semantic richness. As our results showed, a few-shot, single-stage verification prompt strategy with multi-label classification, along with OpenChat, achieved high accuracy in classification across all stages. This approach also resulted in relatively low false positive and false negative rates, even in stages characterized by subtle emotional nuance such as the *relationship* and *exclusivity* stages.

In addition, temporal and sequential analyses of chat logs identified dynamic behavioral patterns during online grooming. Our transition matrix analysis showed that predators often revisit early, such as the *friendship forming* and *relationship* stages, even after advancing to more explicit or logistical stages. This recursive grooming behavior aligns with current literature that describes manipulation through emotional reinforcement [13,23]. Looking at the temporal distribution, the results suggested that grooming activities intensified during the evening hours, aligning with previous forensic insights into offender availability and minor vulnerability [17].

With the integration of the BERTopic for fine-grained topic modeling, the results highlighted content and tactics that predators employ within each stage. For example, the *exclusivity* stage was marked by emotionally charged expressions such as "miss you" and "forever", while the *relationship* stage blended personal disclosures with early sexual flirtation. An unexpected result is the evidence of emotional manipulation as a topic cluster during the *meeting* stage. These findings not only validate prior qualitative typologies [16,19,23], but also extend them by capturing a broader lexical diversity across a large dataset. This level of analysis allows for the integration of topic-level indicators that could inform the development of early warning systems that flag evolving grooming tactics in real time.

Overall, our results represent an improvement in the processing and classifying of unstructured chat logs at scale, suggesting that LLMs can serve as an effective tool for practitioners and platforms. First, LLMs reduce the analytical burden by enabling scalable processing of large, unstructured chat datasets. Second, the performance of the models in classifying online grooming stages and extracting contextual quotes provides a high degree of transparency. This is especially true with the prompting strategy, where the models provide reasoning for labeling decisions. Lastly, the use of models such as BERTopic decreases the need for manual processing of the data, and thus reducing the possible exposure to harmful content for scholars, practitioners, and law enforcement officers.

### 6.2 Limitations and Future Work

While our study demonstrates the potential of LLMs in analyzing online grooming conversations, several limitations remain. First, our segmentation strategy is based on fixed rules involving time gaps and character length thresholds; future work could explore the impact of varying these thresholds or adopt adaptive segmentation methods. Second, although OpenChat achieved the highest average stage classification accuracy (80.48%) among four widely used LLMs, further improvements may be possible through fine-tuning on grooming-related data and benchmarking against a broader range of models. Third, while our evaluation focused on model and prompt variation, future research should investigate the impact of additional hyperparameters such as temperature and context window size. A deeper ablation analysis of prompt wording and structure could also provide further insights into model sensitivity and prompt robustness. Fourth, class imbalance across grooming stages was evident in our results. While addressing this issue was beyond the scope of the current study, further investigation could provide valuable insights into its effects and help improve model fairness and reliability. Fifth, the temporal analysis could benefit from more robust statistical validation and causal inference methods. Lastly, our use of BERTopic for stage-level topic modeling relied on default settings; future research could examine how tuning BERTopic parameters (e.g., number of topics, embedding models) affects the quality and interpretability of topic clusters. Finally, expanding the dataset to include sources beyond Perverted Justice, especially from different jurisdictions or platforms, could further enhance the generalizability and robustness of the analysis. Together, these directions offer promising opportunities to enhance the robustness and precision of LLM-assisted grooming analysis.

## 7 Conclusion

This study demonstrates the effectiveness of large language models for analyzing online grooming conversations at scale. By segmenting real-world predator conversations and applying carefully designed prompting strategies, we achieve high stage classification performance, most notably with the single-stage verification prompt using OpenChat, which reaches 80.48% accuracy per stage. Our findings also reveal the distribution and transitions of grooming stages, offering insights into how grooming unfolds over time. Furthermore, topic modeling using BERTopic provides fine-grained linguistic characterization of each stage, highlighting the diverse tactics employed by predators. Together, these methods offer a scalable and interpretable framework for detecting and understanding online grooming behavior, with implications for both academic research and practical intervention tools.

# A Supplementary Materials

## A.1 Stage Definition

This appendix presents the comprehensive definitions of the six grooming stages used in our analysis. These stage definitions are adapted from the framework introduced by Ringenberg et al. [23], but were further refined through an iterative process during our manual annotation of conversation segments. Revisions were made to improve clarity, contextual relevance, and alignment with the characteristics observed in our dataset. The finalized definitions below were incorporated into the LLM prompt instructions for both evaluation and large-scale classification.

- **Friendship Forming**: This stage involves casual, light-hearted conversations where participants share personal but non-sensitive details about their daily lives, hobbies, or routines. The tone is playful, supportive, and emotionally neutral, with no signs of romantic or sexual interest. Conversations remain surface-level, with little to no commitment or plans for future interaction. Emotional check-ins are brief, and the primary goal is to establish a friendly rapport without deeper emotional or personal engagement.
- **Relationship**: This stage involves a deepening emotional connection, marked by greater openness and vulnerability. Conversations include personal sharing, expressions of care, and mild flirting. Participants express interest in each other's well-being, feelings, and experiences, often offering emotional support or reassurance. There are indirect references to future plans or encounters, and mutual trust and curiosity about each other's lives begin to emerge. The tone is affectionate but avoids explicit sexual language or concrete details about physical meetings. Emotional validation and light-hearted teasing are present, contributing to the growing closeness.
- **Exclusivity**: This stage is characterized by clear expressions of deep emotional attachment, mutual love, and a strong sense of commitment to each other. The conversations often involve affirmations of love, reassurance, and emotional dependency, with both parties expressing their desire to remain exclusive or to deepen the relationship further. There are frequent references

to future scenarios (e.g., shared lives, special occasions, or future romantic plans). Pet names, emoticons of affection, and intimate language are common, as well as exchanges that suggest a high level of emotional investment. The dialogue may include playful teasing, romantic gestures, and expressions of longing for closeness. The tone is generally affectionate, and there may be discussions about overcoming obstacles or resolving conflicts to ensure the relationship's stability.
- **Meeting**: Conversations where the participants discuss or arrange plans to meet in person, speculate about possible meetups, or express anticipation or obstacles about meeting. This often includes references to coordinating time, place, transportation, sneaking out, or making excuses to family members. Sometimes the chat also includes feelings about the meeting, ranging from excitement to nervousness.
- **Risk Assessment**: Interactions showing caution or verification behaviors. This includes confirming the other's age, identity, location, checking for law enforcement presence, discussions about deleting or hiding evidence, and conversations reflecting anxiety over safety, trust, or potential legal risks. Often phrased as direct questions or indirect tests of truthfulness.
- **Sexual**: Graphic messages and hypotheticals, questions about sexual past, fantasy enactment. Descriptions of body parts, becoming a couple, exchanging sexual pictures, explicit sexual comments.
- **Inconclusive**: Conversations that are too brief, vague, or contextually ambiguous to be confidently assigned to a clear thematic category. Often consists of minimal exchanges, ambiguous references, or clipped confirmations without enough information to interpret the intent or topic of the conversation.

## A.2 Prompt Strategies

Detailed prompt formulations for each strategy are provided in this section. Box A.1 contains the prompt for the single-stage selection strategy, where the model selects the single most appropriate stage from the full list. Box A.2 presents the prompt used for the multi-stage selection strategy, which lists all stage definitions and allows the model to select multiple applicable stages. Box A.3 shows the prompt used in the single-stage verification strategy, where each stage is evaluated independently through a series of binary queries. These prompt templates were used consistently across all model evaluations.

**Box A.1: Single-Stage Selection Prompt**

Assign the following chat log between two participants, [p] and [m], to a grooming stage. Speaker changes are indicated by participant labels. Format the output as:
Stage: [Stage Name] Reasoning: [Brief explanation].

The stages are as follows and one of these six stages or inconclusive needs to be assigned.

**Friendship forming**: Basic exchange of information including name, profile information, general location, age, gender, and family details.
**Relationship**: Content related to interests including hobbies, family interactions, friends and school. Understanding of difficulties the child might have. Compliments, image exchanges, and activities of [m].
**Exclusivity**: References to love, exclusiveness, strong emotions, or a future together. Trust building content such as secrets and self disclosures.
**Risk Assessment**: Questions around location and accessibility. Attempts to hide evidence (delete things), confirming the age difference, and questions related to location of family.
**Sexual**: Sexually-oriented compliments, images, and bodily descriptions. Progressively graphic messages and hypothetical questions and descriptions, questions about sexual past, and fantasy enactment.
**Meeting**: Suggestions of meeting, hypothetical of meeting, plans to meet. Ensuring [m] will come alone.
**Inconclusive**: Conversations that are too brief, vague, or contextually ambiguous to be confidently assigned to a clear thematic category. Often consists of minimal exchanges, ambiguous references, or clipped confirmations without enough information to interpret the intent or topic of the conversation.

**Box A.2: Multi-Stage Selection Prompt**

Assign the following chat log between two participants, [p] and [m], to one or more grooming stages. Speaker changes are indicated by participant labels. If no stage fits, write "inconclusive". Format the output as:
Stage: Stage Name Reasoning: Brief explanation.

Grooming stages:
**Friendship forming**: Basic exchange of information (name, age, location, profile information, non-sexual image exchange) and non-sexual discussion of significant others.
**Relationship**: General questions on appearance which are not focused on specific body parts or with a sexual connotation. Asking about the other person's activities (e.g., What's up; How are you) early in the chat conversation (in cases where it is clear the individuals did not know one another prior to the chat beginning).
**Exclusivity**: References to strong affection and future together. Expressions of mutuality (secrets, self-disclosures, direct references to trust).
**Risk Assessment**: Questions surrounding the child's and computer's location. Asking if the victim is a cop, requesting the victim delete evidence, confirming age difference.
**Sexual**: Progressively graphic messages and hypotheticals, questions about sexual past, fantasy enactment. Descriptions of body parts, becoming a couple, exchanging sexual pictures, sexual comments.
**Meeting**: Suggestion of meeting, hypothetical of meeting, plans to meet. Discussing how to commute to the meeting point. Arranging for a day, date, time, and location to meet in person.

**Box A.3: Single-Stage Verification Prompt**

Please analyze the following chat log between two participants, [p] and [m]. Please determine whether it includes content that reflects the **[STAGE_NAME]** stage of interpersonal communication.

Definition of **[STAGE_NAME]** Stage:
**[STAGE_DEFINITION]**

Task:
Answer Yes or No—does the conversation contain any part of the **[STAGE_NAME]** stage as defined above?
If Yes, extract and list the specific sentences that indicate this stage.
Provide a brief explanation (1-2 sentences) supporting your answer.

Chat log:
**[SEGMENT]**

**Box A.4: Multi-Stage Selection Prompt (top-k)**

The given text is a chat log between two participants, [p] and [m]. The conversation in this chat log may relate to the following grooming stages:
**Friendship forming**: the chat log is mainly about basic info exchange, such as name, age, location, profile, non-sexual image sharing, discussion of significant others.
**Relationship**: the chat log mainly covers general appearance questions (non-sexual), casual conversations, etc.
**Exclusivity**: the chat log contains content regarding strong affection, future plans, mutual trust, self-disclosures, secrets, etc.
**Risk Assessment**: the chat log relates to questions about location, confirming age difference, asking about police, deleting evidence, etc.
**Sexual**: the chat log displays graphic messages, sexual history, fantasies, body part descriptions, sexual pictures/comments, becoming a couple, etc.
**Meeting**: the chat log demonstrates suggestions or plans to meet, discussing logistics (travel, date, time, location).
**Inconclusive**: the chat log does relate to any stage mentioned above.

Please be aware that participants label change indicates speaker changes when you go through the chat log. In addition, the entire conversation may cover multiple grooming stages, thus your answer should assign each given grooming stage a proportion that represents how related the chat log is to the corresponding grooming stage and the sum of proportion for each stage should be 1. Please give your answer following the format of:

[Proportion Friendship Forming] [Explanation]
[Proportion Relationship] [Explanation]
[Proportion Exclusivity] [Explanation]
[Proportion Risk Assessment] [Explanation]
[Proportion Sexual] [Explanation]
[Proportion Meeting] [Explanation]
[Proportion Inconclusive] [Explanation]

## A.3 Stage Identification Performance

Figure 5 shows evaluation of single-stage selection across different LLMs for stage identification. Figure 6 shows evaluation of multi-stage selection on LLaMA 3 model. Metrics reported are accuracy (Acc), false negative (FN), and false positive (FP).

**Table 5.** Evaluation of Single-Stage Selection across Different LLMs for Stage Identification. Metrics reported are accuracy (Acc), false negative (FN), and false positive (FP).

| Model | Stage | Acc | FN | FP | Average Acc |
|---|---|---|---|---|---|
| LLaMA3 | Exclusivity | 83.33% | 16.67% | 0.00% | 75.71% |
| | Meeting | 80.00% | 20.00% | 0.00% | |
| | Risk Assessment | 83.33% | 16.67% | 0.00% | |
| | Inconclusive | 90.00% | 6.67% | 3.33% | |
| | Friendship forming | 63.33% | 36.67% | 0.00% | |
| | Relationship | 40.00% | 20.00% | 40.00% | |
| | Sexual | 90.00% | 3.33% | 6.67% | |
| Gemma3 | Exclusivity | 76.67% | 10.00% | 13.33% | 78.58% |
| | Meeting | 76.67% | 23.33% | 0.00% | |
| | Risk Assessment | 80.00% | 16.67% | 3.33% | |
| | Inconclusive | 93.33% | 3.33% | 3.33% | |
| | Friendship forming | 76.67% | 20.00% | 3.33% | |
| | Relationship | 60.00% | 23.33% | 16.67% | |
| | Sexual | 86.67% | 13.33% | 0.00% | |
| OpenChat | Exclusivity | 80.00% | 16.67% | 3.33% | 75.71% |
| | Meeting | 83.33% | 16.67% | 0.00% | |
| | Risk Assessment | 83.33% | 16.67% | 0.00% | |
| | Inconclusive | 83.33% | 3.33% | 13.33% | |
| | Friendship forming | 56.67% | 33.33% | 10.00% | |
| | Relationship | 63.33% | 30.00% | 6.67% | |
| | Sexual | 80.00% | 20.00% | 0.00% | |
| Phi | Exclusivity | 76.67% | 20.00% | 3.33% | 74.76% |
| | Meeting | 73.33% | 23.33% | 3.33% | |
| | Risk Assessment | 83.33% | 16.67% | 0.00% | |
| | Inconclusive | 90.00% | 6.67% | 3.33% | |
| | Friendship forming | 56.67% | 3.33% | 40.00% | |
| | Relationship | 66.67% | 30.00% | 3.33% | |
| | Sexual | 76.67% | 23.33% | 0.00% | |

**Table 6.** Evaluation of Multi-Stage Selection across Different Prompt Templates for Stage Identification. Metrics reported are accuracy (Acc), false negative (FN), and false positive (FP).

| Prompt Template | Stage | Acc | FN | FP | Average Acc |
|---|---|---|---|---|---|
| v1 | Exclusivity | 86.67% | 13.33% | 0.00% | 76.67% |
| | Meeting | 80.00% | 20.00% | 0.00% | |
| | Risk Assessment | 83.33% | 16.67% | 0.00% | |
| | Inconclusive | 86.67% | 6.67% | 6.67% | |
| | Friendship forming | 53.33% | 36.67% | 10.00% | |
| | Relationship | 53.33% | 20.00% | 26.67% | |
| | Sexual | 93.33% | 6.67% | 0.00% | |
| v2 | Exclusivity | 80.00% | 16.67% | 3.33% | 78.58% |
| | Meeting | 80.00% | 13.33% | 6.67% | |
| | Risk Assessment | 83.33% | 16.67% | 0.00% | |
| | Inconclusive | 90.00% | 6.67% | 3.33% | |
| | Friendship forming | 70.00% | 20.00% | 10.00% | |
| | Relationship | 43.33% | 26.67% | 30.00% | |
| | Sexual | 86.67% | 10.00% | 3.33% | |
| v3 (top-k) | Exclusivity | 80.00% | 20.00% | 0.00% | 75.71% |
| | Meeting | 76.67% | 23.33% | 0.00% | |
| | Risk Assessment | 83.33% | 16.67% | 0.00% | |
| | Inconclusive | 86.67% | 6.67% | 6.67% | |
| | Friendship forming | 63.33% | 20.00% | 16.67% | |
| | Relationship | 60.00% | 33.33% | 6.67% | |
| | Sexual | 76.67% | 23.33% | 0.00% | |
| v4 (top-k) | Exclusivity | 80.00% | 20.00% | 0.00% | 74.76% |
| | Meeting | 73.33% | 23.33% | 3.33% | |
| | Risk Assessment | 83.33% | 16.67% | 0.00% | |
| | Inconclusive | 93.33% | 6.67% | 0.00% | |
| | Friendship forming | 60.00% | 26.67% | 13.33% | |
| | Relationship | 63.33% | 30.00% | 6.67% | |
| | Sexual | 83.33% | 16.67% | 0.00% | |

## A.4 Topic Modeling Result Tables

Tables 7 to 11 present the top 10 topics identified by BERTopic within segments labeled as belonging to the corresponding stage. Each topic is characterized by its frequency (i.e., number of segments assigned) and a set of the most representative keywords.

**Table 7.** Summary of BERTopic Results: Top Keywords and Document Counts Per Topic for Exclusivity Stage

| Topic | Count | Top Keywords |
|---|---|---|
| -1 | 1026 | love, want, like, think, know, ur, baby, ok, lol, wanna |
| 0 | 505 | ur, kiss, want, like, baby, think, love, lol, feel, yes |
| 1 | 124 | miss, love, miss love, day, hope, miss miss, luv, baby, think, love miss |
| 2 | 85 | ok, like, love, phone, lol, baby, know, want, cool, babe |
| 3 | 66 | dream, sleep, nite, night, love, goodnight, think, baby, sweet dream, sweet |
| 4 | 43 | precious, princess, precious princess, love precious, love, princess love, kayla, precious baby, miss, god |
| 5 | 39 | love, time, think, dad, meet, want, baby, know, good, school |
| 6 | 34 | love, bf, want, babe, luv, like, girlfriend, gf, feel, know |
| 7 | 31 | marry, 18, love, know, lol, like, want, want marry, yes, want know |
| 8 | 30 | baby, love, love baby, forever, baby love, happy, love love, know, wait, baby girl |
| 9 | 29 | love, want, know, hurt, auth441, erica, auth358, life, yeah, feel |

**Table 8.** Summary of BERTopic Results: Top Keywords and Document Counts Per Topic for Friendship Forming Stage

| Topic | Count | Top Keywords |
|---|---|---|
| -1 | 12423 | lol, like, want, ok, ur, think, know, good, ya, cool |
| 0 | 586 | miss, miss miss, love, miss ya, day, ya, hope, hey, miss love, baby |
| 1 | 501 | wear, skirt, short, pantie, thong, dress, jean, shirt, bra, color |
| 2 | 487 | sleep, dream, bed, night, tired, sweet dream, nite, asleep, sweet, lol |
| 3 | 436 | phone, number, cell, card, ok, leave, want, ur, phone number, talk |
| 4 | 282 | cook, eat, dinner, food, hungry, lol, good, pizza, chicken, taco |
| 5 | 271 | old, 13, 14, age, young, pic, guy, look, old guy, cute |
| 6 | 224 | chat, talk, friend, like, cool, know, think, ur, wanna, say |
| 7 | 211 | pic, send, look, cute, ugly, ur, send pic, ty, lol, new pic |
| 8 | 210 | kiss, want kiss, like kiss, lip, want, feel, like, touch, kissin, neck |
| 9 | 206 | mom, ur mom, tell, home, talk, work, ur, come, time, ok |

**Table 9.** Summary of BERTopic Results: Top Keywords and Document Counts Per Topic for Meeting Stage

| Topic | Count | Top Keywords |
|---|---|---|
| 0 | 8846 | want, like, ok, lol, ur, think, come, know, meet, ya |
| 1 | 38 | michigan, watchin michigan, chillin watchin, michigan vs, state game, ohio state, vs ohio, vs, ohio, watchin |
| 2 | 24 | cheat, cheat like, hun, like time, yeh cheat, hurt, yeh, time, want, want hurt |
| 3 | 16 | eos eos, eos, eo, eos eo, hey silver, hmmmm eos, dr long, eo ride, ride wait, min eos |

**Table 10.** Summary of BERTopic Results: Top Keywords and Document Counts Per Topic for Relationship Stage

| Topic | Count | Top Keywords |
|---|---|---|
| -1 | 11076 | like, want, lol, ok, ur, think, love, know, ya, good |
| 0 | 610 | miss, miss miss, love, hey, day, miss love, hope, miss ya, hi, love miss |
| 1 | 545 | mom, dad, ur mom, work, come, ok, home, leave, ur, know |
| 2 | 507 | dream, sleep, night, sweet dream, bed, nite, sweet, good, lol, tired |
| 3 | 297 | meet, want meet, want, wanna meet, know, like meet, like, weekend, wanna, think |
| 4 | 237 | phone, number, cell, card, voice, ok, address, ur, talk, phone number |
| 5 | 187 | condom, pregnant, bring condom, bring, cum, want, preg, sex, ok, use |
| 6 | 181 | wear, skirt, thong, jean, pantie, dress, short, sexy, look, like |
| 7 | 158 | cheat, cheat like, yeh cheat, like time, yeh, want hurt, time yike, auth535, hurt, care auth535 |
| 8 | 142 | weekend, friday, sunday, week, wait, lol, saturday, day, hope, come |
| 9 | 141 | kiss, lip, want kiss, kiss like, like kiss, like, want, think, bite, kiss lip |

**Table 11.** Summary of BERTopic Results: Top Keywords and Document Counts Per Topic for Sexual Stage

| Topic | Count | Top Keywords |
|---|---|---|
| -1 | 5463 | want, like, lol, ur, ok, think, know, love, wanna, ya |
| 0 | 235 | condom, pregnant, bring, bring condom, ok, want, use, use condom, cum, wanna |
| 1 | 182 | big, size, small, lol, inch, tall, like, bra, bra size, ok |
| 2 | 167 | wear, skirt, thong, pantie, short, dress, like, wear skirt, bra, jean |
| 3 | 145 | nude, naked, girl, like, lol, want naked, pic, think, ur, want |
| 4 | 137 | hurt, like, want hurt, know, ok, tell, want, feel, pain, guy |
| 5 | 105 | miss, love, miss miss, wish, baby, sexy, ya, sweet, ur, wait |
| 6 | 103 | shave, hair, like, pussy, trim, cut, lol, ok, shave ur, shave pussy |
| 7 | 101 | weekend, friday, work, come, week, time, day, want, ok, meet |
| 8 | 92 | phone, number, cell, ok, talk, ur, want, time, phone number, wanna |
| 9 | 92 | clit, finger, wet, rub, feel, pussy, rub clit, inside, ur clit, ur |

## References

1. Alves, J.H., et al.: Detecting relevant information in high-volume chat logs: keyphrase extraction for grooming and drug Dealing forensic analysis. In: International Conference on Machine Learning and Applications (ICMLA) (2023)
2. Archive, I.: Perverted-Justice.com - The largest and best anti-predator organization online (2021). https://web.archive.org/web/20210314195434/http://www.pervertedjustice.com/index.php

3. Archive, I.: Perverted-Justice.com - The largest and best anti-predator organization online: frequently asked questions: partially submitted by readers (2021). http://web.archive.org/web/20210314195326/http://www.perverted-justice.com/index.php?pg=faq
4. Borj, P.R., Raja, K., Bours, P.: Detecting sexual predatory chats by perturbed data and balanced ensembles. In: 2021 International Conference of the Biometrics Special Interest Group (BIOSIG), pp. 1–5. IEEE (2021)
5. Chehbouni, K., Caporossi, G., Rabbany, R., De Cock, M., Farnadi, G.: Early detection of sexual predators with federated learning. In: Workshop on Federated Learning: Recent Advances and New Challenges (in Conjunction with NeurIPS 2022) (2022)
6. DeepMind, G.: Gemma: Lightweight, open models from google (2024). https://ai.google.dev/gemma
7. Devlin, J., Chang, M.W., Lee, K., Toutanova, K.: Bert: Pre-training of deep bidirectional transformers for language understanding. In: Proceedings of the 2019 Conference of the North American Chapter of the Association for Computational Linguistics: Human Language Technologies, volume 1 (long and short papers) (2019)
8. Faraz, A.: Protectbot: A Chatbot to Protect Children on Gaming Platforms. Rochester Inst. Technol. (2022)
9. Fauzi, M.A., Bours, P.: Ensemble method for sexual predators identification in online chats. In: International Workshop on Biometrics and Forensics (IWBF) (2020)
10. Faverio, M., Sidoti, O.: Teens, social media and technology 2024. Technical Report, Pew Research Center, Washington, D.C. (2024). https://www.pewresearch.org/wp-content/uploads/sites/20/2024/12/PI_2024.12.12_Teens-Social-Media-Tech_REPORT.pdf, available online
11. Fry, D., et al.: Prevalence estimates and nature of online child sexual exploitation and abuse: a systematic review and meta-analysis. Lancet Child Adolescent Health (2025)
12. Gunawan, F.E., Ashianti, L., Sekishita, N.: A simple classifier for detecting online child grooming conversation. TELKOMNIKA (Telecommunication Comput. Electr. Control) (2018)
13. Gupta, A., Kumaraguru, P., Sureka, A.: Characterizing Pedophile Conversations on the Internet using Online Grooming. ArXiv (2012)
14. Inches, G., Crestani, F.: Overview of the International Sexual Predator Identification Competition at PAN-2012. CLEF (Online working notes/labs/workshop) **30** (2012)
15. Kirupalini, S., et al.: Prevention of emotional entrapment of children on social media. In: 2021 International Conference on Emerging Techniques in Computational Intelligence (ICETCI), pp. 95–100. IEEE (2021)
16. Kloess, J.A., Hamilton-Giachritsis, C.E., Beech, A.R.: Offense Processes of Online Sexual Grooming and Abuse of Children Via Internet Communication Platforms. Sexual Abuse (2019)
17. Levine, B.N.: Increasing the efficacy of investigations of online child sexual exploitation. Technical Report NCJ 301590, U.S. Department of Justice (2022). https://www.ojp.gov/library/publications/increasing-efficacy-investigations-online-child-sexual-exploitation-report
18. Nguyen, T.T., Wilson, C., Dalins, J.: Fine-tuning llama 2 large language models for detecting online sexual predatory chats and abusive texts (2023). https://arxiv.org/abs/2308.14683

19. O'Connell, R.: A Typology of Child Cybersexploitation and Online Grooming Practices. University of Central Lancashire, Cyberspace Research Unit (2003)
20. Research, M.: Phi-2: The next generation of small language models (2023). https://www.microsoft.com/en-us/research/blog/phi-2-the-surprising-power-of-small-language-models/
21. Rezaee Borj, P., Raja, K., Bours, P.: Detecting online grooming by simple contrastive chat embeddings. In: Proceedings of the ACM International Workshop on Security and Privacy Analytics (2023)
22. Ringenberg, T., Rayz, J.T., Seigfried-Spellar, K.: Using fuzzy sets to assess differences in online grooming conversations with victims, decoys, and law enforcement. Springer International Publishing (2022)
23. Ringenberg, T.R., Seigfried-Spellar, K., Rayz, J.: Assessing differences in grooming stages and strategies in decoy, victim, and law enforcement conversations. Comput. Human Behav. (2024)
24. Sileo, D.: Attention overflow: language model input blur during long-context missing items recommendation (2024). http://arxiv.org/abs/2407.13481
25. Team, O.: Openchat: Open-source chat models with instruction tuning (2023). https://github.com/imoneoi/openchat
26. Touvron, H., Martin, L., Stimson, K., et al.: Llama 3: Open foundation and instruction models (2024). https://ai.meta.com/blog/meta-llama-3/
27. Winters, G.M., Jeglic, E.L.: Stages of Sexual Grooming: Recognizing Potentially Predatory Behaviors of Child Molesters. Deviant Behavior (2017)
28. Wolak, J., Mitchell, K.J., Finkelhor, D.: Internet sex crimes against minors: the response of law enforcement. Nat. Center Missing Exploited Children Bull. (2003)

# Emerging Research, Tools, and Experimental Frameworks: Novel Methods, Datasets, and Future Directions in Digital Forensics and Cybersecurity

# Graph Neural Networks for Video Device Identification

Raghu Sesha Iyengar[1](✉) and Vaibhav Kumar[2]

[1] pi-labs.ai, Pune, India
raghu@pi-labs.ai
[2] National Forensic Sciences University, Gandhinagar, India

**Abstract.** Identifying the source device of a digital video is critical for law enforcement agencies (LEAs) investigating misinformation, tampering, and cybercrime. Existing techniques based on sensor noise, compression artifacts, or metadata are limited, as metadata can be forged, and visual signals often degrade due to editing. We propose a graph-based approach that models the video container structure (e.g., MP4 atoms) as a tree. This structure, shaped by device firmware and software, encodes implicit source-specific patterns. We employ masked node prediction pretraining on these trees using Graph Neural Networks to learn robust embeddings. Our method demonstrates robustness against EXIF metadata manipulation, especially when trained using our novel learnable rotations within the embedding space. It also supports interpretable predictions by identifying key structural elements that contribute to device identification. This graph-based modeling offers a tamper-resistant and explainable alternative for video device attribution, making it well-suited for use in forensic analysis pipelines.

**Keywords:** Graph Neural Networks · Video Device Identification · Masked Node Prediction · learnable embedding rotation

## 1 Introduction

With the exponential rise in video content creation, driven by social media, surveillance, and citizen journalism, the need to determine the origin of multimedia content has become critical. In the field of digital forensics, numerous survey studies have detailed the use of image and video source identification techniques, including sensor noise analysis, compression artifacts, metadata inspection, and container-structure modeling [1,2]. Identifying the recording device (e.g., smartphone, camera, or other hardware) is of immense importance for verifying authenticity, supporting legal investigations, and attributing responsibility in both civil and criminal scenarios. The proliferation of deepfakes, manipulated media, and synthetic video generation technologies has made it increasingly challenging to verify the provenance of digital videos. In high-stakes contexts such as the spread of fake news, political misinformation, or tampered surveillance footage, device-level attribution serves as a crucial layer of validation. When


K.-K. R. Choo et al. (Eds.): ICDF2C 2025, LNICST 686, pp. 433–450, 2026.
https://doi.org/10.1007/978-3-032-22545-0_25

metadata is missing or falsified, and visual content alone is inadequate to detect forgery, forensic traces embedded by the recording device provide a vital source of truth.

### 1.1 Overview of Existing Techniques

Several approaches have been explored in literature and practice to tackle the device identification problem for both images and videos:

*(1) PRNU-Based Techniques.* Photo Response Non-Uniformity (PRNU) has been widely employed to identify device-specific artifacts by analyzing the unique sensor noise patterns embedded in images and videos [3,4]. These methods exploit the subtle, device-specific pixel-level variations caused by manufacturing imperfections, which act as a fingerprint for the imaging sensor. However, PRNU-based techniques are highly sensitive to post-processing operations, re-encoding, and format conversions, which can distort or suppress the underlying noise signature. In recent years, deep learning approaches, particularly convolutional neural networks (CNNs), have been increasingly applied to learn robust representations of PRNU directly from video frames, improving resilience against such degradations [5,6].

*(2) Metadata and EXIF-Based Techniques.* Metadata embedded in media files, including EXIF data, can include information about the device make and model, firmware, and even GPS location [7]. Tools that extract and analyze metadata can sometimes directly identify the source device. Nevertheless, such metadata is easily tampered with or stripped altogether during re-encoding, platform upload (e.g., social media platforms like WhatsApp, Instagram) or explicitly using tools that can modify EXIF data.

*(3) File Container Structure and Graph-Based Techniques.* Recent research has explored using the structural information embedded in multimedia container formats (e.g., MP4, MKV) to identify devices. These containers store a sequence of boxes or atoms such as `ftyp`, `moov`, `mdat`, and so on. By modeling this structure as a graph; where nodes represent atoms and edges represent hierarchy or order, it is possible to extract device-specific patterns [8,9]. Prior work has shown that these graphs capture manufacturer-level quirks in encoding pipelines, which can be exploited for classification using machine learning models or graph neural networks.

*(4) Manufacturer-Supported Provenance and Privacy Specifications.* Another line of work involves manufacturer-supported, hardware-level provenance and privacy mechanisms, such as the Coalition for Content Authenticity and Provenance (C2PA) standard or the IEEE P1912 Standard for Privacy and Security Framework for Consumer Wireless Devices [10,11]. C2PA focuses on embedding tamper-evident and cryptographically verifiable identifiers and metadata into content at the time of capture or creation, creating a chain of custody.

IEEE P1912, on the other hand, provides a framework for how consumer wireless devices should handle privacy and security of data.

Despite their promise, the aforementioned methods face notable challenges: *PSNR and signal-based methods* are vulnerable to transformations such as scaling, compression, trimming, and transcoding, which are common on social media platforms. These distortions obscure the original device signature. *Metadata-based methods* rely on the presence of information that is frequently removed, anonymized, or spoofed during content sharing, making them unreliable in adversarial or real-world scenarios. *Graph-based methods* require careful modeling of container structures, which can vary not only between devices, but also due to firmware updates, third-party camera apps, or OS-level changes. Early work based on manual statistics or simple likelihood ratios demonstrated promise but struggled to generalize across device families [8]. More recent shallow graph neural approaches capture broad structural patterns, and used it for tampering detection of the content [12]. *Manufacturer-Supported Provenance and Privacy Specifications* are highly robust techniques. But these methods often require manufacturer cooperation and hardware or software-level integration at the point of origin.

These limitations highlight the need for robust, learning-based techniques that can infer the recording device from subtle structural fingerprints, even in the absence of visual content or tampered metadata. In this work, we propose a novel approach that builds upon the graph-based paradigm while incorporating pretraining strategies using masked node prediction, node-level attributions, and learnable embedding space rotation to achieve interpretable and resilient device classification. Our approach involves a two-phase training procedure. In the first phase, we construct graph representations of MP4 and MOV container structures from a large corpus of video files recorded across diverse capture devices. We then pretrain a Graph Neural Network (GNN) using a random masked node prediction objective to learn generalizable structural patterns. In the second phase, we finetune the pretrained GNN on a supervised video device classification task to enable accurate source attribution.

Our main contributions are as follows:

1. We represent video container metadata as a graph structure and perform masked node prediction using graph neural networks, resulting in robust node and graph embedding useful for downstream tasks.
2. We introduce a learnable rotation of the node and graph embeddings that adaptively transforms latent representations for downstream forensic and knowledge extraction tasks.

## 2 Masked Node Predictor

Masked prediction has emerged as a powerful self-supervised learning paradigm across multiple domains. In the vision domain, Masked Autoencoders (MAE) [13] introduced the idea of reconstructing randomly masked image patches, significantly improving pretraining for downstream tasks. This concept was extended to the video domain in VideoMAE [14], where temporal masking of video tokens helped capture rich spatiotemporal representations. Similarly, in audio, BEATs [15] and wav2vec 2.0 [16] leveraged masked frame prediction to learn powerful speech representations. Inspired by BERT [17] in NLP, these approaches rely on the principle that masking forces the model to learn contextual dependencies and structure. In the graph domain, GraphCL [18] applied similar ideas using various graph augmentations. Our work adapts this paradigm to multimedia container graphs, where masked node prediction enables unsupervised pretraining of Graph Neural Networks (GNNs) to capture device-specific patterns in file structure before supervised fine-tuning for forensic tasks. In Sect. 2.1, we describe the data used in the masked node prediction task. In Sect. 2.2, we describe the model, and in Sect. 2.3 we describe the training details of the masked node prediction task.

### 2.1 Data

Since our work focuses exclusively on video files, we restrict our analysis to the MP4 and MOV formats, which are widely used across consumer, surveillance, and broadcast domains. Image data was not considered in this study. To train and evaluate the model for the masked node prediction task, we curated a diverse dataset from three major categories of video sources:

1. *Public datasets with device labels:* We used datasets such as VideoACID [19] and VISION [20], where each video is annotated with metadata specifying the source acquisition device (e.g., smartphone make and model).
2. *Public datasets without device labels:* Videos were also obtained from deepfake detection datasets such as DFDC (Deepfake Detection Challenge) [21], which contain non-AI-generated videos with diverse encoding characteristics, though without associated device metadata.
3. *Proprietary data:* We further collected videos captured using a variety of real-world acquisition devices including webcams, mobile cameras, and commercially licensed video footage. This dataset includes labeled and unlabeled data and was manually verified to exclude generative content.

All video files were parsed to extract their container structure, focusing specifically on the MP4 and MOV file types. The mp4dump[1] tool was used to extract the internal atom hierarchy of each video. This atom tree represents the structural layout of the video container file.

From each video file, we construct a graph where:

1. Nodes represent atoms (boxes) within the video container. Each node further contains below features:
   (a) The atom type identifier (categorical)

[1] https://www.bento4.com/documentation/mp4dump/.

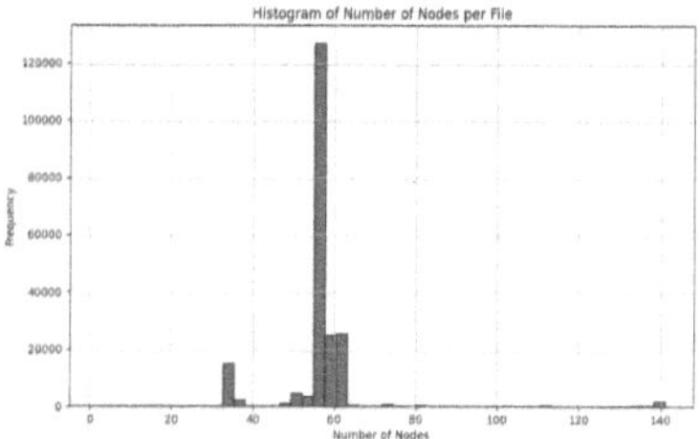


(a) Distribution of number of nodes in the container graph per video file.

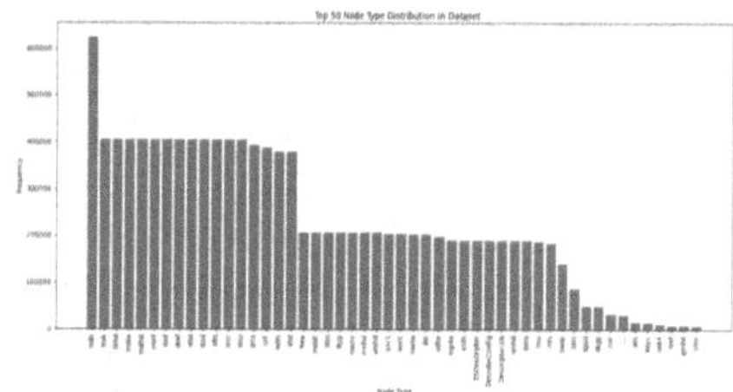

(b) Distribution of node type in the train data.

**Fig. 1.** Histogram of nodes in graph and node types in train data

(b) The size of the atom (in bytes), which is normalized.
(c) The hierarchical level (depth) in the container tree.

2. Edges represent the parent-child relationships defined by container structure

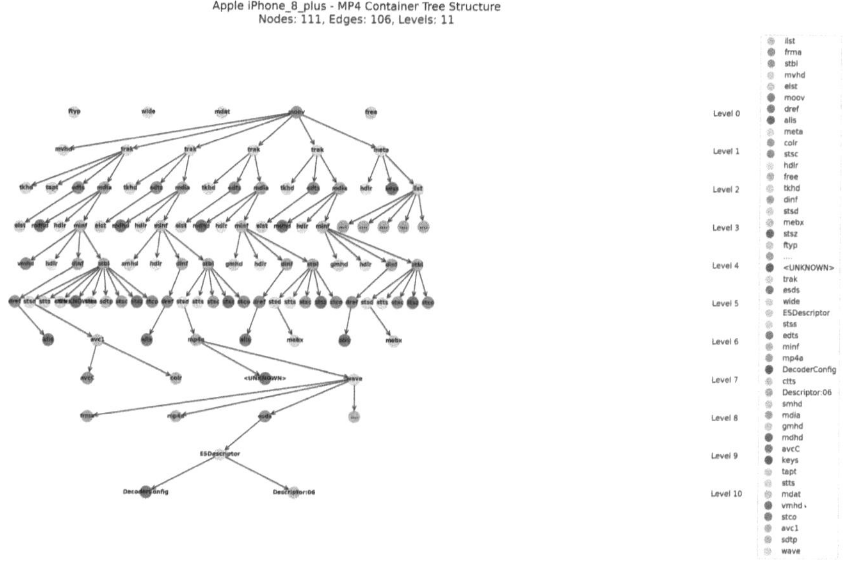


**Fig. 2.** Tree of container atoms for a sample from Apple iPhone 8 Plus

This graph-based representation is generated for every input video and used for both self-supervised masked node prediction and supervised downstream tasks such as device classification. We have 164k video files in the train dataset. The number of nodes per input video file in the dataset is $56.73 \pm 11.61$. Figure 1 (a) and Fig. 1 (b) show the histogram of number of nodes per input video file and number of instances of top 50 node types in the dataset respectively. Figure

2 shows the node graph obtained for a sample file captured on `Apple iPhone 8 Plus`. The dataset contains a total of 142 node types. All nodes which occurred less than 1000 times in the dataset were grouped into a single 'unknown' type for our analysis. The 'unknown' group consisted of 79 node types.

The node selection process for masking uses one of two strategies, chosen randomly with equal probability. The first strategy is importance-based, where an "importance score" is calculated for each node as a weighted sum of its degree, its hierarchical level in the graph, and whether it' is a standard atom type. Nodes with the highest scores are then masked. This strategy allows the model to learn important information even when important nodes are masked. The second strategy aims for proportional distribution, ensuring at least one node of each type present in the graph is masked, with the remaining masks distributed proportionally among the types, subject to the number of nodes to be masked.

## 2.2 Model

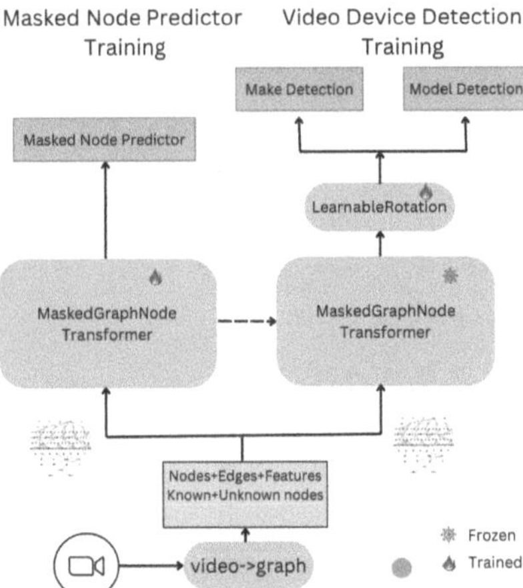


**Fig. 3.** Architecture of the GNN-based video device detection model. The MaskedGraphNodeTransformer is first pre-trained on a large dataset using a masked node prediction objective. The pre-trained model is then fine-tuned for video device detection, augmented with a LearnableRotation module to enhance structural representation learning

For the masked node prediction task, we use a transformer-based graph encoder, `MaskedGraphNodeTransformer` (Fig. 3), designed for self-supervised learning on video container structure graphs. The model is tailored for the masked node prediction task, where a subset of nodes within the container graph is masked and the model is trained to predict their original identities based on graph context. The architecture integrates node type embeddings, auxiliary features, and a multi-layer graph transformer.

Each node type is first embedded into a 192-dimensional vector using a learnable embedding layer. Additional node features (refer Sect. 2.1) are concatenated to this embedding. Let $t_i$ be the node type and $\mathbf{f}_i \in \mathbb{R}^3$ the additional features of node $i$. Then the initial node embedding is given by:

$$\mathbf{x}_i = \text{Concat}(\mathbf{E}[t_i], \mathbf{f}_i), \quad \mathbf{x}_i \in \mathbb{R}^{195}$$

where $\mathbf{E}$ is the learnable node embedding matrix. For masked nodes, $\mathbf{x}_i$ is set to the zero vector, forcing the model to rely solely on graph context to predict the original node type.

This input is projected through a two-layer feedforward network with GELU activation and dropout:

$$\mathbf{h}_i^{(0)} = \text{FFN}(\mathbf{x}_i)$$

Where $\text{FFN(x)} = \text{Linear}_2(\text{Dropout}(\text{GELU}(\text{Linear}_1(\mathbf{x}_i))))$ The FFN is followed by LayerNorm to stabilize training. The resulting hidden representation lies in a 384-dimensional space.

The core of the model consists of a stack of six graph transformer blocks. Each block contains:

1. A pre-attention LayerNorm applied to the input $\mathbf{h}_i^{(\ell-1)}$.
2. The `TransformerConv`[2] layer in our model follows the formulation in PyTorch Geometric [22], which adapts the Transformer architecture for graph-structured data. Given input features $\mathbf{x}_i$ for node $i$ and its neighbors $j \in \mathcal{N}(i)$, attention coefficients are computed as:

$$\alpha_{ij} = \frac{(\mathbf{Q}\mathbf{x}_i)^\top(\mathbf{K}\mathbf{x}_j)}{\sqrt{d}}$$

These scores are normalized across neighbors using a softmax:

$$\tilde{\alpha}_{ij} = \text{softmax}_{j \in \mathcal{N}(i)}(\alpha_{ij})$$

The output representation is computed via attention-weighted aggregation:

$$\mathbf{m}_i = \sum_{j \in \mathcal{N}(i)} \tilde{\alpha}_{ij} \cdot (\mathbf{W}_2\mathbf{x}_j)$$

An additional learnable transformation of the center node is also added:

$$\mathbf{h}_i^{(\ell)} = \mathbf{m}_i + \mathbf{W}_1\mathbf{x}_i$$

where $\mathbf{Q}, \mathbf{K}, \mathbf{W}_2, \mathbf{W}_1$ are trainable weight matrices. Multi-head attention is implemented by computing this process in parallel across multiple subspaces and concatenating the results.

Early layers use more attention heads (16) to capture diverse low-level patterns; later layers reduce this to 8 heads and expand the hidden dimensionality to support abstraction. Dropout is set to 0.6 in early layers and reduced to 0.3 in later stages.

[2] https://pytorch-geometric.readthedocs.io/.

3. The attention output $\mathbf{m}_i^{(\ell)}$ is added to a projected residual:

$$\mathbf{h}_i^{(\ell)} = \mathbf{m}_i^{(\ell)} + \text{Proj}(\mathbf{h}_i^{(\ell-1)})$$

4. A two-layer feedforward network with GELU activation:

$$\mathbf{h}_i^{(\ell)} \leftarrow \mathbf{h}_i^{(\ell)} + \text{FFN}(\text{LayerNorm}(\mathbf{h}_i^{(\ell)}))$$

where $\text{FFN}(x) = \text{Linear}_4(\text{Dropout}(\text{GELU}(\text{Linear}_3(x))))$
5. A final LayerNorm applied to the output of the FFN.

The output from the stacked graph transformer layers is passed through a final feedforward projection head with GELU non-linearity to produce a 384-dimensional latent representation for each node:

$$\mathbf{z}_i = \text{ProjFinal}(\mathbf{h}_i^{(L)})$$

These representations are used for downstream tasks such as masked node prediction and device classification.

### 2.3 Training

To support masked node prediction, we introduce a classification head that maps the final node embeddings to a probability distribution over node types. Specifically, the output for each node $i$ is passed through a linear layer producing logits $\mathbf{y}_i \in \mathbb{R}^C$, where $C$ is the number of node types. Let $V$ denote the set of all nodes in the current batch of graphs, and let $\mathcal{M} \subseteq V$ be the subset of nodes that are masked during training. The model is trained to recover the original node types using a cross-entropy loss computed only over the masked nodes:

$$\mathcal{L}_{\text{mask}} = \frac{1}{|\mathcal{M}|} \sum\nolimits_{i \in \mathcal{M}} \text{CrossEntropy}(\mathbf{y}_i, t_i)$$

where $t_i$ is the ground-truth type of node $i$. This formulation encourages the model to learn contextual relationships from the surrounding graph structure in order to infer the identity of masked nodes. The number of nodes that are masked is linearly increased from 1, up to 10% of the total nodes in the graph for the first 25 epochs. For the remaining epochs, we mask 10% of the total number of nodes in the graph.

This training was performed on the dataset described in Sect. 2.1 using the Huggingface Trainer[3]. We set the batch size to 64 and number of epochs to 35. We used a linear learning rate scheduler with a 10% warmup ratio with a peak learning rate of 1e-4. We used theAdamW optimizer and a weight decay of 1e-2. The training was performed on a NVIDIA A100 GPU with 80 GB memory.

## 3 Video Source Device Classification

For the video source device classification task, we use the trained masked node predicor network from Sect. 2.2 and introduce additional classification layers.

[3] https://huggingface.co/docs/transformers/en/main_classes/trainer.

### 3.1 Data

For the purpose of video source device classification, we use a subset from the data described in Sect. 2.1, which has labelled make and models. For curated data, the make (manufacturer) and model are inferred based on data organization. For e.g., in the videoACID dataset, data is organized into folders with names such as: `M00_Apple_iPhone_8_plus`. We infer the make as `"Apple"` and model as `"iPhone_8_plus"`. For this task we curated a total of 9931 samples out of which 7944 were used for training and 1987 were used for testing. There were a total of 20 makes with 496.6 ± 524.8 samples per make and a total of 49 models with 202.7 ± 195.4 samples per model in our train dataset. In this work, our focus was to use the pretrained masked node predictor for a video device detection downstream task. Hence, we did not pick images, or videos which were re-encoded (e.g., whatsapp and youtube data) from the dataset.

### 3.2 Model

For the device classification task, we build a hierarchical model, that classifies both the device make and the specific model using the graph representation of the video container. The classifier backbone is composed of a pretrained `MaskedGraphNodeTransformer` (Sect. 2.2) followed by hierarchical classification heads. A 192 dimensional embedding is obtained from the pre-trained mask node prediction model for each input node. To obtain a graph-level representation, we apply both global mean pooling and global max pooling over the node embeddings output by the GNN encoder. Let $\mathbf{h}_i \in \mathbb{R}^d$ denote the 192 dimensional embedding of node $i$ in the graph. The pooled vectors are computed as:

$$\mathbf{g}_{\text{mean}} = \frac{1}{N} \sum_{i=1}^{N} \mathbf{h}_i, \quad \mathbf{g}_{\text{max}} = \max_{i=1}^{N} \mathbf{h}_i$$

These are concatenated to form the final graph embedding:

$$\mathbf{g} = [\mathbf{g}_{\text{mean}} \,\|\, \mathbf{g}_{\text{max}}] \in \mathbb{R}^{2d}$$

This strategy of combining multiple pooling operations has been shown to improve the expressive power of GNN models [23].

To perform hierarchical classification of the video source device, we employ a two-stage prediction head operating on the graph-level representation $\mathbf{g} \in \mathbb{R}^{2d}$, obtained by concatenating global mean and max pooled node embeddings.

*Make-Level Classification.* The first stage predicts the device make (e.g., Apple, Samsung, Logitech). We pass the pooled embedding $\mathbf{g}$ through a two-layer feed-forward network:

$$\hat{\mathbf{y}}_{\text{make}} = \mathbf{W}_2^{\text{make}} \cdot \text{Dropout}\left(\text{GELU}\left(\mathbf{W}_1^{\text{make}} \cdot \mathbf{g}\right)\right)$$

where $\hat{\mathbf{y}}_{\text{make}} \in \mathbb{R}^M$ is the logit vector over $M$ device makes, and $\mathbf{W}_1^{\text{make}}$, $\mathbf{W}_2^{\text{make}}$ are learned parameters.

*Model-Level Classification* Given the predicted make $\hat{m}$, we select a dedicated classifier head for that make to predict the specific device model:

$$\hat{\mathbf{y}}_{\text{model}}^{(\hat{m})} = \mathbf{W}_2^{(\hat{m})} \cdot \text{Dropout}\left(\text{GELU}\left(\mathbf{W}_1^{(\hat{m})} \cdot \mathbf{g}\right)\right)$$

where $\hat{\mathbf{y}}_{\text{model}}^{(\hat{m})} \in \mathbb{R}^{K_{\hat{m}}}$ is the logit vector over the $K_{\hat{m}}$ models associated with make $\hat{m}$. Each make-specific head is implemented as a two-layer neural network with its own learned parameters. This design supports variable numbers of models per make and enables the model to learn fine-grained distinctions between devices while respecting the underlying class hierarchy [24].

### 3.3 Learnable Rotation of Graph and Node Embeddings

We introduce a *LearnableRotation* module that applies trainable 2D rotational transformations to node embeddings within graph neural networks. This module performed graph level and node level rotations on the embeddings from the pre-trained masked node predictor network, before concatination of the mean and max embeddings. For each graph $i$, we compute a graph-level representation by averaging the node embeddings:

$$\mathbf{g}_i = \frac{1}{|\mathcal{V}_i|} \sum\nolimits_{v \in \mathcal{V}_i} \mathbf{h}_v$$

where $\mathcal{V}_i$ is the set of nodes in graph $i$ and $\mathbf{h}_v \in \mathbb{R}^d$ is the embedding of node $v$.

A base rotation angle vector is then computed through a learned function $f_\theta$:

$$\boldsymbol{\theta}_i^{\text{base}} = f_\theta(\mathbf{g}_i), \quad \boldsymbol{\theta}_i^{\text{base}} \in \mathbb{R}^{d/2}$$

Node-specific rotation angles are derived by adding a positional offset:

$$\boldsymbol{\theta}_v = \boldsymbol{\theta}_i^{\text{base}} + \boldsymbol{\phi} \cdot \text{pos}(v)$$

where $\boldsymbol{\phi} \in \mathbb{R}^{d/2}$ is a learnable parameter vector, and $\text{pos}(v)$ is a fixed position encoding of the node in the graph.

Each node's embedding is split into pairs of consecutive dimensions, treated as 2D vectors. For each pair, a node-specific rotation matrix is constructed using learned angles:

$$\mathbf{R}_v = \begin{bmatrix} \cos(\boldsymbol{\theta}_v) & -\sin(\boldsymbol{\theta}_v) \\ \sin(\boldsymbol{\theta}_v) & \cos(\boldsymbol{\theta}_v) \end{bmatrix}$$

These rotation matrices are applied independently, resulting in a rotated embedding that encodes node-level spatial transformation. Our LearnableRotation module extends the rotary embeddings to hierarchical graph structure by applying trainable graph-level and node-level rotation transformations for improved expressiveness.

**Table 1.** Video Source Device Detection Results on the videoACID Dataset

| Method | Make Acc (%) | Model Acc (%) | Combined Acc (%) |
|---|---|---|---|
| Hosler et al. [19] (same) | – | – | 79.1 - 95.1* |
| Hosler et al. [19] (cross) | – | – | 64.7 - 92.0* |
| Ramos López et al. [26] | 0.81/0.83/0.89 ** | 0.82/0.77/1.0 ** | - |
| Ours (without LearnableRotation) | 93.3 | 65.1 | 79.2 † |
| Ours (with LearnableRotation) | **98.4** | **94.8** | **90.9** † |

* In Hosler et al. [19], the same-device setup uses different videos from the same devices for training and testing, while the cross-device setup evaluates on other devices of the same model.
** Rand Index/Homogeneity/Completeness were reported here
† Our setup did not distinguish data based on device for both training and evaluation. We computed accuracy for both make (brand) and model.

### 3.4 Training

This training was performed on the dataset described in Sect. 3.1 using the Huggingface Trainer. We set the batch size to 64 and number of epochs to 50. We used a linear learning rate scheduler with a 10% warmup ratio with a peak learning rate of 1e-4. We used theAdamW optimizer with a weight decay of 1e-2. Training was performed on NVIDIA A100 GPU with 80 GB memory.

## 4 Results

### 4.1 Make and Model Classification

We evaluate our model on two datasets: videoACID and a custom dataset which combines videoACID, VISION and our proprietary collected data. Prior works either perform joint make+model classification or employ hierarchical strategies using metadata or multimodal CNNs [25]. In contrast, our approach applies hierarchical classification directly on container-graph embeddings: we first predict the device *make*, then refine the prediction to the *model*, enabling structured and interpretable decision-making based on graph context. Importantly, we only consider videos that are captured directly from the device, excluding any samples that have undergone application-level re-encoding (e.g., via WhatsApp or YouTube). This ensures that the classification is based on intrinsic device signatures and not artifacts introduced during transmission or compression. Table 1 summarizes the results.

It can be observed that even without incorporating `LearnableRotations`, our model achieves strong performance on the make classification task. While the base Node Predictor model attained an accuracy of only 52% across 142 distinct node types, the downstream make classification accuracy is significantly higher. This indicates that the model has effectively learned intrinsic relationships between key node types, enabling it to generalize well for tasks such as make classification. When trained with `LearnableRotations`, our model achieves the

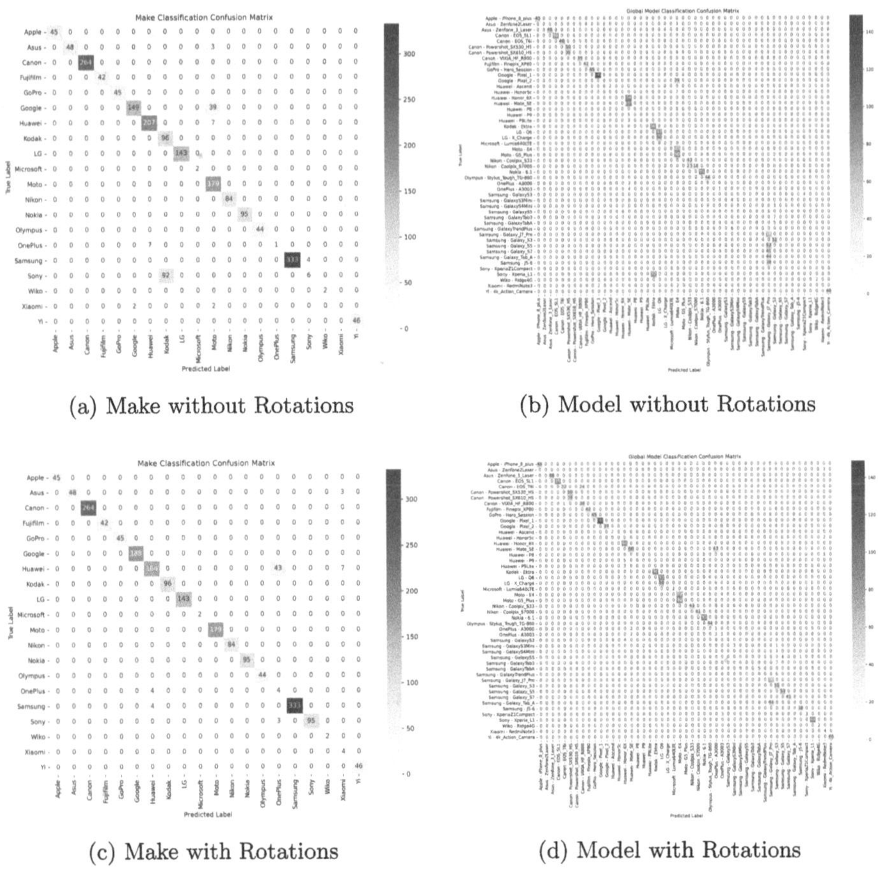


(a) Make without Rotations (b) Model without Rotations

(c) Make with Rotations (d) Model with Rotations

**Fig. 4.** Confusion matrices for make and model classification with and without learnable rotations for test data

highest make and model classification accuracy on the videoACID dataset. This highlights the effectiveness of applying graph-level and node-level rotations, which guide the embeddings to occupy distinct regions in the embedding space, thereby improving the separability between devices.

The VISION test dataset contained only 263 usable samples, as we excluded both images and videos that were re-encoded via platforms such as WhatsApp or YouTube. To ensure a more comprehensive evaluation, we combined samples from the videoACID dataset, the filtered VISION dataset, and our proprietary dataset. Table 2 summarizes the results on this combined test set, which comprises a total of 1,987 samples spanning 20 distinct makes and 49 different models.

The confusion matrices for both make and model classification, with and without learnable rotations, are shown in Fig. 4. These illustrate the impact of learnable embeddings on classification performance We observe that many of

**Table 2.** Video Source Device Detection Results on the Test Dataset

| Method | Make Acc (%) | Model Acc (%) | Combined Acc (%) |
|---|---|---|---|
| Ours (without LearnableRotation) | 92.2 | 67.3 | 79.8 |
| Ours (with LearnableRotationl) | **96.8** | **82.9** | **89.9** |

the misclassifications are between devices from the same manufacturer or from closely related brands, which likely share similar camera processing pipelines. For instance, in Fig. 4 (Make without Rotations), 39 out of 149 samples from the `Google` make are misclassified as `Moto`. This can be attributed to Motorola's historical association with Google, resulting in potentially overlapping hardware or firmware components. Similarly, in Fig. 4 (Model without Rotations), several devices such as `Samsung_Galaxy_S5`, `Samsung_Galaxy_S7`, and `Samsung_Galaxy_TabA` are misclassified as `Samsung_Galaxy_J7_Pro`, all of which are products from the same manufacturer and may share common image processing characteristics. Additionally, a few instances of `Google_Pixel_2` are misclassified as `Moto_E4`, further supporting the hypothesis that structural and algorithmic similarities in camera pipelines can contribute to such confusions. Further, we notice that these misclassifications are drastically reduced in the model trained using LearnableRotations (Fig. 4 (Make with Rotations) and (Model with Rotations).

## 4.2 Explainability

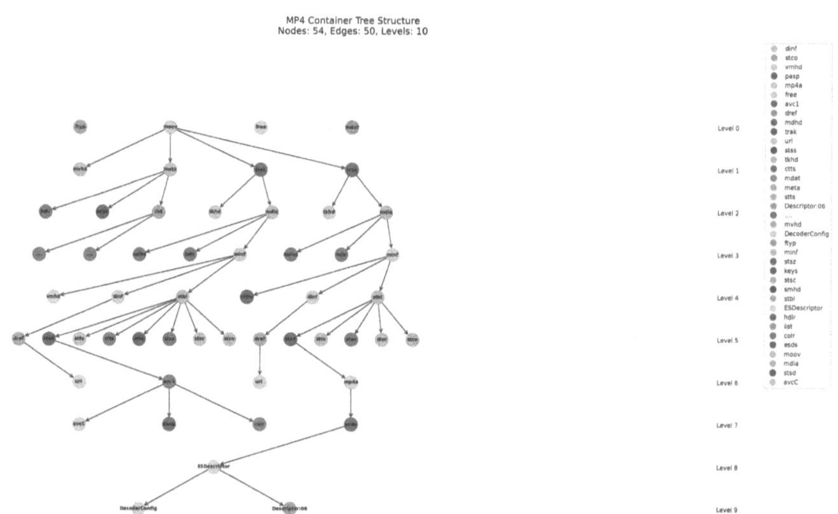


**Fig. 5.** Tree of container atoms for a sample from Google Pixel2

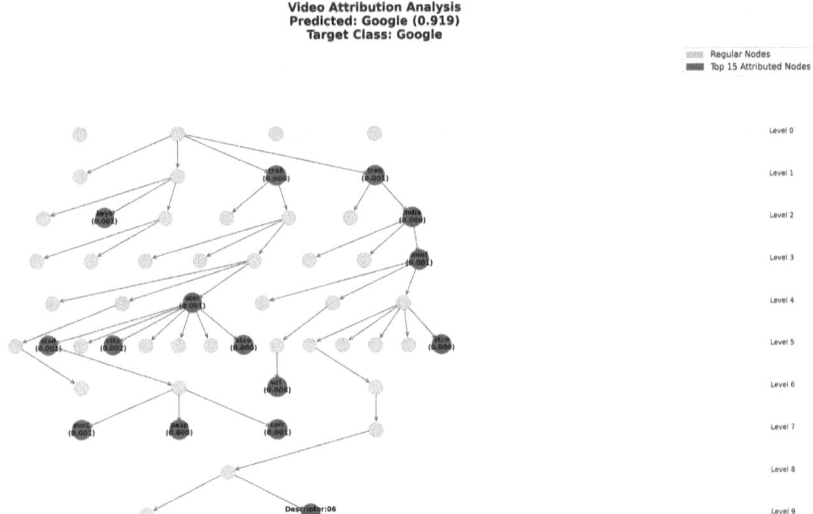


**Fig. 6.** Tree of container with attributed nodes for the input from Fig. 5

Source device attribution is of paramount importance for Law Enforcement Agencies (LEAs), where identifying the origin of multimedia content can serve as crucial evidence in criminal investigations, cybercrime detection, and verifying the authenticity of digital media. In particular, videos shared across platforms or recovered from suspect devices can provide critical leads if their source device can be reliably identified. Our approach not only achieves high accuracy in make and model classification of video sources, but also offers interpretability through node-level attribution. We employ Integrated Gradients [27] to quantify the contribution of individual nodes in the video container graph toward the classification decision. This allows us to highlight which container atoms played a key role in model inference. For instance, in Fig. 5 we have the reference container tree of a media sample from `Google_Pixel_2`. In Fig. 6, we have highlighted the nodes that were identified to have highest attribution for correct prediction of Make and Model. We note that the 'mdia', 'trak', and 'stco' atoms were assigned high attribution scores, indicating their influence in the model's decision. Such insights are valuable in forensic workflows, as they offer transparency, explainability, and support admissibility of automated findings in legal proceedings.

## 4.3 Tampered Exif Information

To evaluate the robustness of our model to deliberate tampering of EXIF metadata, we employed the exiftool utility[4] to modify the make and model fields in selected video files. In one illustrative case, the make was changed from `Canon`

[4] https://exiftool.org/.

to Nikon, and the model from Canon Powershot SX530 HS to D850. This alteration led to the addition of three nodes and modification of two node features in the corresponding container graph, while no nodes were removed. Despite these changes, our model correctly identified the original device as Canon / Powershot_SX530_HS. Further analysis of the attribution map revealed that several of the modified nodes were among the top 15 most influential nodes, as determined by integrated gradients. Nevertheless, the model retained its ability to infer the correct class, suggesting robustness to localized metadata perturbations. In a broader evaluation across 2400 such tampered samples (Table 3), we found that the model finetuned by augmenting such tampered samples was able to detect the make with an accuracy of 95.2%.These findings highlight that the embedding space transformations learned by LearnableRotations contribute to a generalized and resilient representation of device characteristics, even in the presence of manipulated EXIF metadata, an essential property for reliable forensic applications.

**Table 3.** Video Source Device Detection on EXIF tampered dataset

| Model | Make Acc (%) | Model Acc (%) |
|---|---|---|
| Without LearnableRotation | 80.3 | 67.9 |
| With LearnableRotation | 95.2 | 78.1 |
| Finetuned With LearnableRotation* | **96.8** | **82.9** |

* The train data is augmented by modifying the EXIF information

## 5 Conclusion

In this work, we present a novel formulation for the problem of source device attribution in videos by treating make and model prediction as hierarchical classification tasks, as opposed to the conventional combined make+model classification. We construct graphs from structured metadata ( atoms such as moov, mdat, trak, etc.) and device-specific auxiliary features (position, size, etc), and utilize a graph neural network enhanced with LearnableRotations. These rotations allow the model to perform learnable transformations in the embedding space, enabling better separation of node representations for different device types. Our experiments, especially on the videoACID dataset, show that even without explicit rotation learning, the base model achieves strong performance on make classification. Incorporating LearnableRotations further improves both make and model classification accuracies, demonstrating the effectiveness of graph-based representation learning in this domain. This capability is especially valuable for Law Enforcement Agencies (LEAs), as it enables device attribution even when visual content or metadata is unavailable or has been tampered with.

While our current work demonstrates the effectiveness of masked node pre-training and learnable rotations for source device attribution from video container graphs, several promising directions remain. A particularly important extension would be the analysis of attribution patterns across multiple samples from the same make or model. By identifying consistent node-level contributions (e.g., certain atoms like `mdia`, `trak`, or `stco` regularly influencing predictions for specific devices), we can uncover characteristic structural signatures of video encoders. This can be especially valuable for Law Enforcement Agencies (LEAs), enabling the development of rule-based or hybrid systems that combine explainable AI with domain knowledge for more robust and court-admissible evidence generation. Additionally, integrating temporal and context-aware extensions into the graph representation, and combining this method with signal-based techniques such as PSNR or noise profiling, could further improve attribution reliability in adversarial or lossy scenarios.

## References

1. Akbari, Y., Almaadeed, S., Elharrouss, O., Khelifi, F., Lawgaly, A., Bouridane, A.: Digital forensic analysis for source video identification: a survey. Forensic Sci. Int. Digit. Investigation **41**, 301390 (2022)
2. Javed, A.R., Jalil, Z., Zehra, W., Gadekallu, T.R., Suh, D.Y., Piran, M.J.: A comprehensive survey on digital video forensics: taxonomy, challenges, and future directions. Eng. Appl. Artif. Intell. **106**, 104456 (2021)
3. Lukas, J., Fridrich, J., Goljan, M.: Digital camera identification from sensor pattern noise. IEEE Trans. Inf. Forensics Secur. **1**(2), 205–214 (2006)
4. Dirik, A.E., Sencar, H.T., Memon, N.D.: Source camera identification based on sensor dust characteristics, In: ProcEEDING IEEE Workshop on Signal Processing Applications for Public Security and Forensics (SAFE), Washington, DC, USA, pp. 1–6 (2007)
5. Zaimen, A., Oulefki, A., Khelifi, F., Rabie, T., Bouridane, A.: Enhanced source camera identification using dual pathway processing and spatial attention module, In: 2024 IEEE/ACM International Conference on Big Data Computing, Applications and Technologies (BDCAT), Sharjah, United Arab Emirates, pp. 198–203 (2024). https://doi.org/10.1109/BDCAT63179.2024.00041.
6. Bennabhaktula, G.S., Timmerman, D., Alegre, E. et al.: Source camera device identification from videos. SN COMPUT. SCI. 3, 316 (2022). https://doi.org/10.1007/s42979-022-01202-0
7. Gloe, T., Fischer, A., Kirchner, M.: Forensic analysis of video file formats. Digit. Investig. **11**(Supplement 1), S12–S23 (2014)
8. Iuliani, M., Shullani, D., Fontani, M., Meucci, S., Piva, A.: A video forensic framework for the unsupervised analysis of MP4-Like file container. IEEE Trans. Inf. Forensics Security **14**(3), 635–645 (2019)
9. Gelbing, E.: Würsching, Leon, Zmudzinski, Sascha, Steinebach, Martin, Video Source Identification from MP4 Data Based on Field Values in Atom/Box Attributes. Electronic Imaging. **337–1**, 2021 (2021). https://doi.org/10.2352/ISSN.2470-1173.2021.4.MWSF-337
10. Coalition for Content Authenticity and Provenance (C2PA), C2PA Website. https://c2pa.org/. Accessed: [2025-07-02]

11. IEEE, IEEE P1912 Standard for Privacy and Security Framework for Consumer Wireless Devices. https://standict.eu/standards-repository/ieee-p1912-standard-privacy-and-security-framework-consumer-wireless-devices. Accessed: [2025-07-02]
12. Xiang, Z., Singh Yadav, A.K., Bestagini, P., Tubaro, S., Delp, E.J.: MTN: forensic analysis of mp4 video files using graph neural networks, In: 2023 IEEE/CVF Conference on Computer Vision and Pattern Recognition Workshops (CVPRW), Vancouver, BC, Canada, pp. 963–972 (2023). https://doi.org/10.1109/CVPRW59228.2023.00103.
13. He, K., Chen, X., Xie, S., Li, Y., Dollár, P., Girshick, R.: Masked autoencoders are scalable vision learners, In: 2022 IEEE/CVF Conference on Computer Vision and Pattern Recognition (CVPR), New Orleans, LA, USA, pp. 15979–15988 (2022). https://doi.org/10.1109/CVPR52688.2022.01553.
14. Tong, Z., Song, Y., Wang, J., Wang, L.: VideoMAE: masked autoencoders are data-efficient learners for self-supervised video pre-training, In: Advances in Neural Information Processing Systems (NeurIPS), Article No.: 732, Pages 10078 –10093 (2022)
15. Chen, S., et al.: BEATs: audio pre-training with acoustic tokenizers, In: International Conference on Machine Learning (ICML), Article No.: 203, pp. 5178–5193 (2023)
16. Baevski, A., Zhou, H., Mohamed, A., Auli, M.: wav2vec 2.0: a framework for self-supervised learning of speech representations, In: Advances in Neural Information Processing Systems (NeurIPS), Article No.: 1044, pp 12449–12460 (2020)
17. Devlin, J., Chang, M., Lee, K., Toutanova, K.: BERT: pre-training of deep bidirectional Transformers for language understanding, In: Proceedings of the 2019 Conference of the North American Chapter of the Association for Computational Linguistics: Human Language Technologies, Volume 1 (Long and Short Papers), pp. 4171–4186 (2019)
18. Zhu, Y., Xu, Y., Yu, F., Liu, G., Zeng, Q., Wu, M.: Graph contrastive learning with augmentations, In: Advances in Neural Information Processing Systems (NeurIPS), Article No.: 488, pp. 5812–5823 (2020)
19. Hosler, B.C., Zhao, X., Mayer, O., Chen, C., Shackleford, J.A., Stamm, M.C.: The video authentication and camera identification database: a new database for video forensics. IEEE Access **7**, 76937–76948 (2019). https://doi.org/10.1109/ACCESS.2019.2922145
20. Shullani, D., Fontani, M., Iuliani, M. et al.: VISION: a video and image dataset for source identification. EURASIP J. on Info. Security 2017, 15 (2017). https://doi.org/10.1186/s13635-017-0067-2
21. Dolhansky, B., et al.: The DeepFake Detection Challenge (DFDC) Dataset, arXiv preprint arXiv:2006.07397 (2020)
22. Fey, M., Lenssen, J.: Fast graph representation learning with PyTorch geometric, In: International Conference on Learning Representations (ICLR) Workshop on Representation Learning on Graphs and Manifolds (2019)
23. Xu, K., Hu, W., Leskovec, J., Jegelka, S.: How Powerful are Graph Neural Networks? In: International Conference on Learning Representations (ICLR) (2019)
24. Wehrmann, J., Cerri, R., Barros, R.: Hierarchical multi-label classification networks, In: Proceedings of the 35th International Conference on Machine Learning, vol. 80, pp. 5075–5084, PMLR (2018)
25. Mandelli, S., Bestagini, P., Tubaro, S.: CNN-based multi-modal camera model identification on video sequences, J. Imaging (2021)

26. Ramos López, D., Naranjo, V., Cedrán-Cabici, R., Comesaña, P., érez-González, P.P.: Digital video source identification based on container's structure analysis, IEEE Access, vol. 8, pp. 165350–165364 (2020). https://doi.org/10.1109/ACCESS.2020.3022175
27. Sundararajan, M., Taly, A., Yan, Q.: Axiomatic attribution for deep networks, In: Proceedings of the 34th International Conference on Machine Learning (ICML), vol. 70, pp. 3319–3328 (2017)

# WebHunter: An LLM-Agent with Exploit Planning and Tool Collaboration for Automated SQL Injection

Wenkai Ren[1,2,3], Die Hu[1,2,3], He Kong[1,2,3], Yuepeng[1,2,3(✉)], Liangxiong Li[1,2], and Bingzhen Wu[1,2]

[1] Institute of Information Engineering, Chinese Academy of Sciences, Beijing, China
eyuepeng@iie.ac.cn

[2] State Key Laboratory of Cyberspace Security Defense, Beijing, China

[3] School of Cyber Security, University of Chinese Academy of Sciences, Beijing, China

**Abstract.** Automated web security testing has advanced significantly with the rise of Large Language Model (LLM)-based agents and traditional scanners. However, existing SQL injection (SQLi) testing methods primarily operate at the terminal level, neglecting the dynamic web interactions where many vulnerabilities are actually triggered. This gap limits the effectiveness and adaptability of SQLi testing in real-world web environments, as crucial web elements like form fields and buttons are often embedded within complex, context-dependent interfaces. Although recent advances in WebAgent research have significantly improved autonomous interactions with dynamic web interfaces, these agents lack the specialized capabilities required for professional penetration testing, such as attack planning, exploitation tools, and structured execution. To address this gap, we propose WebHunter, an LLM-agent-based penetration testing agent tailored for automated SQLi attacks. Unlike traditional terminal-based approaches that struggle with web interface complexity, WebHunter tackles the challenge of locating and exploiting vulnerabilities embedded in interactive web content. It enhances perception, planning, and tool coordination to support intelligent, end-to-end testing. Evaluated on DVWA and real-world CVE cases, WebHunter outperforms standard baselines in detection and success rate, demonstrating its effectiveness in complex web environments.

**Keywords:** SQL Injection · LLM-based Agent · Automated Penetration Testing · Web Security Testing · Web Interaction Automation

## 1 Introduction

With the increasing complexity of modern web applications [1], SQLi remains one of the most persistent and severe security threats [2], allowing attackers to

This work is supported by the CSTNet Program "Network Service-oriented Platform Construction and Application Demonstration" (No.E4X01011B3).


K.-K. R. Choo et al. (Eds.): ICDF2C 2025, LNICST 686, pp. 451–463, 2026.
https://doi.org/10.1007/978-3-032-22545-0_26

manipulate databases, extract sensitive data, and even take control of entire systems. Over the years, penetration testing tools like SQLmap [3] have significantly advanced SQLi exploitation. However, real-world web penetration testing involves more than just executing SQLi payloads. It requires automated interaction with dynamic web elements, authentication handling, JavaScript execution, and traffic analysis to uncover SQLi vulnerabilities embedded in modern web applications. Traditional penetration testing tools operate under the assumption of direct access to request payloads, making them ineffective in complex, client-side-driven environments where SQLi points are often hidden behind interactive UI components and asynchronous requests. This highlights the need for a unified approach that integrates web interaction, traffic inspection, and SQLi exploitation in a fully automated manner.

Existing SQLi testing methods fall into three categories, each with structural limitations. Command-line tools (e.g., SQLmap, sqlninja, BurpSuite [4]) are effective in back-end exploitation but lack capabilities for navigating UI logic or handling JavaScript-based interactions. LLM-based penetration testing frameworks such as PentestGPT [5], AutoPenBench [6], HackSynth [7], and ARACNE [8] automate testing across various protocols, but struggle with the front-end complexities of modern web applications. Meanwhile, LLM-driven WebAgents [9] show promise in automating form filling and DOM interaction, yet remain agnostic to attack objectives and lack the mechanisms for vulnerability detection or validation.

To address these challenges, we present **WebHunter**, an LLM-based agent for autonomous SQLi penetration testing in modern web environments. WebHunter is architected to support a tightly coupled workflow that spans browser automation, request interception, and SQLi payload execution. As illustrated in Fig. 1, the agent is composed of specialized modules for web interaction, traffic monitoring, and vulnerability evaluation, all orchestrated under a reasoning loop guided by a penetration-aware prompt.

- **Interactive Web Exploration with Deep Request Visibility:** WebHunter bridges UI-layer interactions and network-layer analysis through a unified execution environment. This enables the agent to dynamically identify and track injection points during realistic web browsing flows, especially those hidden behind JavaScript-triggered events or login barriers.
- **Penetration-Aware Reasoning:** To guide the agent's decision-making process, WebHunter introduces a task-specific prompting strategy enhanced with few-shot learning. This allows the agent to reason about context-aware actions and synthesize valid multi-step plans tailored for SQLi exploitation.
- **Structured Multi-Tool Orchestration:** WebHunter coordinates browser controllers, traffic proxies, and injection engines within a feedback-driven execution framework. The agent validates action sequences and integrates runtime results to refine subsequent decisions, enabling effective and repeatable SQLi exploitation.

These mechanisms enable WebHunter to conduct end-to-end SQLi testing in complex, interactive web applications.

We evaluate WebHunter on Damn Vulnerable Web Application (DVWA) [10] and a set of publicly disclosed CVE vulnerabilities. Experimental results demonstrate substantial improvements in automation coverage, detection accuracy, and successful exploitation rate, confirming WebHunter's effectiveness for fully autonomous web-based SQLi testing.

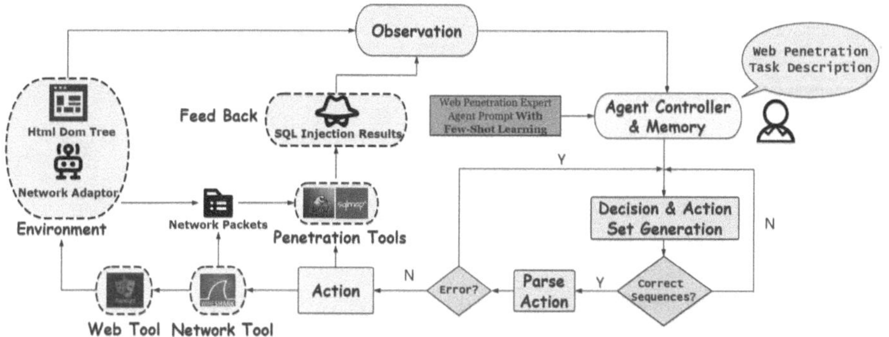


**Fig. 1.** Architecture of WebHunter.

## 2 Related Work

The development of WebAgents has significantly advanced the field of automated web interaction. WebVoyager [9] is a notable framework that uses an agent to navigate web applications and perform web security tasks. This approach enables agents to automatically explore and interact with web pages, making it easier to simulate user actions like form submissions and link clicking, as well as inspect page elements.

Similarly, WebArena [11] provides an integrated environment where agents can perform security analysis and automated web interaction tasks. WebArena has been widely used for automating tasks such as vulnerability scanning and intrusion detection. These frameworks focus on leveraging browser automation and web exploration but lack the deeper integration needed for specific security testing tasks like SQLi exploitation.

Zheng et al. [12] proposed SEEACT, a generalist web agent powered by GPT-4V, which utilizes large multimodal models (LMMs) to perform tasks on websites based on natural language instructions. Their work highlights the potential of multimodal models for web automation, showing that GPT-4V can complete 51.1% of tasks on live websites when textual plans are manually grounded into actions. This significantly outperforms text-only LLMs, like GPT-4, and smaller models tailored for web tasks. However, the grounding process remains a challenge, with the authors developing a new strategy that combines HTML structure and visual cues, though a gap still exists compared to oracle grounding.

Magnus Müller et al. [13] developed Browser Use, a tool that enables AI to control your browser autonomously. This software allows AI agents to interact

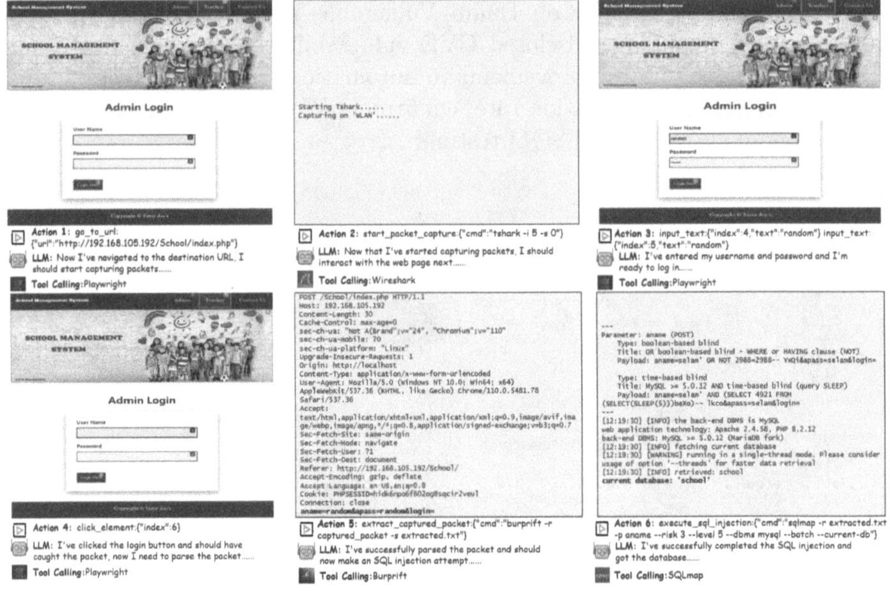


**Fig. 2.** Example of WebHunter executing SQLi on a School Management System: (1) Start traffic capture, (2) Input credentials with SQLi payload, (3) Submit form, (4) Analyze captured traffic, (5) Generate/execute exploit.

with web pages in real-time, automating tasks such as navigation, form filling, and dynamic content interaction. While Browser Use is focused on enhancing AI's web browsing capabilities, it opens the door to more advanced automated penetration testing by enabling AI agents to dynamically interact with web elements, a key requirement for testing modern web vulnerabilities.

While these works demonstrate the power of WebAgents for automating web interaction and security tasks, they do not address the full automation of SQLi penetration testing, which requires interaction with web elements, traffic capture, and integration with penetration testing tools such as SQLmap. Our approach seeks to bridge this gap by combining the strengths of WebAgent-like models with automated vulnerability exploitation tools, including SQLi testing.

## 3 Methodology

In this section, we introduce WebHunter, an LLM-Agent-based framework designed for automated web penetration testing. Unlike traditional WebAgents that focus solely on task execution within a web environment, WebHunter incorporates penetration testing capabilities, integrates specialized security tools, and enhances decision-making mechanisms. The core methodological advancements of WebHunter are outlined as follows.

### 3.1 Unified Web Interaction and Traffic Monitoring Framework

Numerous end-to-end web testing methods and tools already exist [14]. Traditional WebAgents mainly depend on web automation frameworks like Playwright [15] to carry out interactions with web pages. However, such tools lack the capability to conduct in-depth security analysis. To address this limitation, WebHunter extends its interaction layer by integrating specialized penetration testing tools, including:

- **SQLmap**: Automated SQLi tool for database exploitation.
- **Wireshark**: Network protocol analyzer for traffic inspection [16].
- **Burprift**: A custom tool that transforms Wireshark-captured network traffic into the same format as Burp Suite proxy logs for seamless integration.

WebHunter refines the observation process by aggregating multiple sources of security-related data. Given a target environment, the framework constructs an observation state at step $t$ as:

$$o_t = \{h_t, p_t, s_t\} \tag{1}$$

where:

- $h_t$: The HTML DOM tree at step $t$.
- $p_t$: Network traffic data collected via Wireshark (only available after specific web interactions such as form submissions or button clicks).
- $s_t$: SQLi test results from SQLmap (only available after a candidate request has been identified and tested).

This enriched and adaptive observation space enables WebHunter to make more informed decisions by selectively incorporating runtime network and testing feedback, rather than relying solely on static HTML structure like standard WebAgents.

### 3.2 Penetration-Aware Reasoning with Few-Shot Prompting

In standard WebAgents, the action selection function $\pi$ follows:

$$a_t = \pi(o_t, T, \{a_1, ..., a_{t-1}\}) \tag{2}$$

where $a_t$ is the action at step $t$, determined based on observation $o_t$, task description $T$, and previous actions $\{a_1, ..., a_{t-1}\}$.

To enhance decision-making, WebHunter extends this paradigm by generating **action sequences** rather than individual actions, leveraging Few-Shot Learning [17] with a web penetration expert agent prompt. The refined policy $\pi'$ dynamically produces a sequence of actions $A_t$ at each step:

$$A_t = \pi'(o_t, T, M_{t-1}) = \text{FewShot}(\pi, \text{prompt})(o_t, T, M_{t-1}) \tag{3}$$

where: $A_t = [a_t^{(1)}, a_t^{(2)}, ..., a_t^{(n)}]$ denotes the action sequence generated for step $t$; $M_{t-1}$ represents cumulative memory up to step $t-1$, storing historical observations and action outcomes; $\text{FewShot}(\cdot)$ adapts the base policy $\pi$ using expert demonstrations to specialize in SQL injection tasks.

**Structure of Expert-Crafted Demonstrations.** The expert prompts in WebHunter are structured sequences of web penetration examples, each consisting of:

- **Context**: A brief textual description of the vulnerability scenario.
- **HTML Snapshot**: Partial DOM content relevant to the task.
- **Captured Traffic**: A representative intercepted HTTP request corresponding to the interaction.
- **Valid Plan**: A step-by-step sequence of actions.
- **Rationale**: An explanation describing the reasoning behind the sequence.

## Concrete Example of a Few-Shot Demonstration

- **Context**: "Login form with POST method, vulnerable to boolean-based SQLi. The form includes a hidden CSRF token, which must be included in the request to avoid 403 Forbidden responses. The target website uses HTTPS, requiring TLS decryption for traffic analysis."
- **HTML Snapshot**:

```
<form action="/login" method="POST">
<input type="text" name="username" id="user"> <!-- Vulnerable parameter --
    >
<input type="password" name="password" id="pass">
<input type="hidden" name="csrf_token" value="ab12cd34-ef56-gh78"> <!--
    CSRF token -->
<button type="submit" id="submit">Login</button>
</form>
```

- **Captured Traffic (after TLS decryption)**:

```
POST /login HTTP/1.1
Host: vulnerable-site.com
Content-Type: application/x-www-form-urlencoded
(TLS-encrypted payload decrypted via MITM proxy)

username=admin&password=pass123&csrf_token=ab12cd34-ef56-gh78
```

- **Valid Plan**:

```
StartTLSDecryption(proxy="MITM")#InitializeMITMproxyforHTTPS decryption
StartTrafficCapture()#EnableWiresharkto log decryptedtraffic
ExtractHiddenField(field="csrf_token")#RetrieveCSRFtokentoavoid403 errors
InputForm(field="username",value="admin'OR1=1--")#InjectSQLi payload
InputForm(field="password",value="dummy")#Fillpasswordfield
SubmitForm()# Send requestwith payload+ CSRF token; capturedby Wireshark
ExtractTraffic(requestID="POST/login")#Extractdecryptedrequestfromlogs
InvokeSQLmap(target=requestID,parameter="username")#Automateexploitation
CheckSQLmapOutput(pattern="VulnerabletoSQLinjection")#Verifyviatool feedback
```

- **Rationale**: Steps 1-2 address HTTPS encryption by deploying a MITM proxy to decrypt TLS traffic. Step 3 handles CSRF protection to ensure valid requests. Steps 7-9 leverage SQLmap for automated parameter exploitation and validation.

### 3.3 Structured Execution and Tool Coordination with Action Validation

In automated penetration testing, the correct execution order of actions is critical—for example, starting traffic capture before form submission ensures requests are logged. WebHunter's action verification and correction mechanism enforces such logical dependencies.

**Action Validation Logic** $V(\mathcal{A})$. Before executing an action sequence $\mathcal{A} = \{a_1, a_2, \ldots, a_n\}$, WebHunter verifies alignment with penetration testing best practices:

$$V(\mathcal{A}) = \begin{cases} \text{True}, & \text{if } \mathcal{A} \text{ follows valid exploit steps} \\ \text{False}, & \text{otherwise} \end{cases} \tag{4}$$

The validation rules cover both conventional and unconventional vulnerabilities (e.g., SQLi triggered by DOM-XSS) by encoding: Prerequisite dependencies: e.g., `InvokeSQLmap` requires prior `ExtractRequest` (to define target parameters). Temporal constraints: e.g., `AnalyzeTraffic` must follow `StartTrafficCapture` (to avoid empty logs). Vulnerability-specific logic: e.g., DOM-XSS-induced SQLi requires `ExecuteJavaScript` (to trigger DOM manipulation) before SQLi payload injection.

`Refine`(·)**Function Implementation.** If $V(\mathcal{A}) = \text{False}$, Refine(·) corrects the sequence via a hybrid rule-based and LLM-driven process:

$$\mathcal{A}' = \text{Refine}(\mathcal{A}) \tag{5}$$

The refinement workflow is:

1. **Violation Detection**: Identify invalid steps using a rule engine (e.g., "Traffic capture started after form submission" or "SQLmap invoked without extracted request").
2. **Critical Step Preservation**: Flag irreplaceable actions (e.g., `SubmitForm`, `GenerateSQLPayload`) to prevent deletion.
3. **Reordering**: Rearrange steps to fix temporal violations (e.g., move the `StartTrafficCapture` to the start of the sequence).
4. **Gap Filling**: Insert missing prerequisite actions (e.g., add `ExtractRequest` before `InvokeSQLmap` if absent).
5. **LLM-Based Adjustment**: For complex violations (e.g., unconventional SQLi-DOM-XSS chains), fine-tune the sequence using an LLM prompt:
   *"Revise the sequence to ensure SQLi payloads are injected after DOM manipulation triggers. Preserve all* `GeneratePayload` *and* `SubmitForm` *steps."*
6. **Post-Refinement Validation**: Re-run$V(\mathcal{A}')$ to confirm correction; if invalid, repeat with stricter rules.

This hybrid approach avoids introducing new errors by:

- Prioritizing rule-based corrections for high-confidence scenarios (e.g., reordering),

- Using LLM adjustments only for ambiguous cases with explicit preservation constraints,
- Validating the refined sequence against a held-out set of successful traces.

### 3.4 Summary of Methodology

WebHunter is designed for end-to-end automated SQLi testing, addressing dynamic web environments through four key innovations. It uses a unified observation space that combines HTML structure, network traffic, and tool results to inform decisions; leverages expert demonstrations via few-shot learning to refine its action logic; validates and corrects action sequences using a hybrid rule-based and LLM-driven process. These components work together as formalized in Algorithm 1.

**Algorithm 1.** WebHunter Step Flow

1: Initialize Memory $M_0$, Task $T$
2: **for** $step = 1$ **to** 15 **do**
3: Retrieve observation $o_t$ from browser and network
4: Generate action sequence: $A_t \leftarrow \pi'(o_t, T, M_{t-1})$
5: Validate $A_t$ via $V(\cdot)$; refine if invalid: $A_t \leftarrow \text{Refine}(A_t)$
6: **for all** $a \in A_t$ **do**
7: **for** $retry = 1$ **to** 3 **do**
8: Execute $a$ and capture response $r_t$
9: **if** $r_t$ indicates success **then**
10: Update memory: $M_t \leftarrow f(M_{t-1}, a, r_t)$
11: Update observation: $o_{t+1} \leftarrow g(M_t)$
12: **break**
13: **end if**
14: **end for**
15: **if** all retries failed **then**
16: **return** "Action execution failed"
17: **end if**
18: **end for**
19: **if** all task objectives are met (verified via $o_{t+1}$) **then**
20: **return** "Success"
21: **end if**
22: **end for**
23: **return** "Failure: Exceeded step limit"

The 15-step execution bound is justified by analyzing 100 successful SQLi traces across DVWA and CVE cases. 8 traces required 15 steps (8%), 28 required 610 steps (28%), 45 required 1112 steps (45%), 19 required 1314 steps (19%), and no traces exceeded 14 steps, with 92% completing in 12 steps or fewer and 100% in 14 steps or fewer.

Table 1 shows the step distribution:

**Table 1.** Distribution of Steps in 100 Successful SQLi Exploitation Traces

| Step Range | Number of Traces | Percentage |
|---|---|---|
| 15 | 8 | 8% |
| 610 | 28 | 28% |
| 1112 | 45 | 45% |
| 1314 | 19 | 19% |
| 15+ | 0 | 0% |

To further illustrate how our automated SQLi testing framework operates in a real-world scenario, we present an example of an agent autonomously executing an attack sequence on a web-based School Management System. As depicted in Fig. 2, the agent begins by navigating to the Admin Login page. It then systematically follows a structured process: First, it starts network traffic capture to ensure all transmitted data is recorded. Next, it identifies and inputs credentials into the login fields before submitting the form. Once the request is sent, the agent extracts the captured network packets and analyzes them. Finally, leveraging the extracted request structure, it generates and executes an SQLi payload. Throughout this sequence, the agent seamlessly integrates web navigation, network traffic analysis, and penetration testing, demonstrating its ability to autonomously detect and exploit SQL vulnerabilities while maintaining logical execution order.

This design enables end-to-end SQLi testing, from front-end interaction to back-end exploitation, addressing limitations in dynamic web environment handling.

## 4 Experimental Setup

In this section, we describe the experimental setup, including the dataset, evaluation metrics, and models used for testing.

**Dataset.** The dataset employed for the experiments was self-constructed, consisting of 40 vulnerable web applications with approximately 120 distinct SQLi tasks. These tasks were sourced from two environments: Damn Vulnerable Web Application (DVWA) and real-world CVE-based SQLi vulnerabilities. DVWA is an OWASP-supported [18] training platform designed to provide controlled security challenges. The CVE-based tasks reflect real-world scenarios, covering different SQLi types such as Boolean-based, Time-based, and Error-based injections. The tasks are divided into three difficulty levels, easy, medium and hard, ensuring a balance between structured and difficulty-graded evaluation and practical vulnerability evaluation.

**Evaluation Metrics.** To evaluate the effectiveness of our proposed framework, three primary evaluation metrics were used. The completion rate (**CR**) reflects the agent's ability to complete the full penetration testing process without crashing due to errors like parsing failures, demonstrating its self-correction capability; The detection rate (**DR**) reflects the ability of the framework to identify and interact with vulnerable web elements before exploitation. A higher DR suggests better detection capabilities in navigating and targeting potential vulnerabilities; The success rate (**SR**) measures the percentage of successfully exploited SQLi vulnerabilities, representing the framework's effectiveness in detecting and exploiting vulnerabilities. To assess reliability, we also use two important metrics. The false positive rate (**FP**) reflects the proportion of incorrectly identified vulnerabilities, indicating the framework's tendency to raise invalid or redundant alerts during testing. The false negative rate (**FN**) reflects the proportion of actual vulnerabilities that are missed by the agent, representing its failure to detect legitimate SQLi cases during automated analysis. Together, FP and FN provide a comprehensive view of the framework's reliability and diagnostic accuracy in real-world penetration scenarios.

**Models Setup.** The experiments were conducted using two large language models. The large-scale general-purpose LLM DeepSeek-R1-70B [19] is known for its strong reasoning capabilities. The instruction-tuned model Llama-3.1-405B [20] is optimized for complex multi-step tasks, balancing reasoning and structured task execution. These models were chosen to explore the trade-offs between reasoning power, task execution efficiency, and computational cost. While DeepSeek-R1-70B offers cost-effective inference, Llama-3.1-405B is expected to provide superior structured decision-making at the expense of significantly higher resource consumption.

**Comparison Methods.** We compared WebHunter against two baseline methods: Chain-of-Thought (CoT) [21] and Browser Use [13]. By contrasting these methods with WebHunter, we highlight its effectiveness in automated web interaction and penetration testing.

## 5 Results and Discussion

In this section, we present and analyze the experimental results obtained from evaluating WebHunter across different models and difficulty levels. The results demonstrate WebHunter's superior performance in terms of CR, DR, and SR, highlighting its effectiveness in automated web penetration testing.

### 5.1 Main Results

Table 2 presents the performance comparison of WebHunter against the baselines across different difficulty levels on two models: DeepSeek-R1-70B and Llama-3.1-405B.

On the DeepSeek-R1-70B model, WebHunter demonstrates strong robustness with a CR of 90.4% for easy tasks, 98.0% for medium tasks, and 95.2% for hard tasks. This indicates its high fault tolerance and stability during automated

**Table 2.** Experimental Results Comparison Across Different Difficulty Levels

| Model | Method | **CR** (%) | | | DR (%) | | | SR (%) | | |
|---|---|---|---|---|---|---|---|---|---|---|
| | | Easy | Medium | Hard | Easy | Medium | Hard | Easy | Medium | Hard |
| DeepSeek | CoT Agent | 85.7 | 84.2 | 79.1 | 74.7 | 41.1 | 23.8 | 26.2 | 4.6 | 2.5 |
| | Browser use | 90.4 | 95.3 | 92.7 | 80.9 | 46.1 | 37.5 | 38.1 | 6.1 | 2.5 |
| | **WebHunter** | 90.4 | **98.0** | **95.2** | 80.9 | **83.0** | **47.5** | **66.7** | **27.6** | **15.0** |
| Llama | CoT Agent | 88.7 | 80.9 | 77.3 | 71.4 | 55.3 | 32.5 | 33.3 | 7.6 | 0.0 |
| | Browser use | 95.2 | 93.9 | 90.0 | 85.7 | 49.2 | 40.0 | 42.8 | 9.2 | 2.5 |
| | **WebHunter** | **96.1** | **97.5** | **94.4** | **90.4** | **84.6** | **42.5** | **71.4** | **30.7** | **17.5** |

testing. In vulnerability detection, WebHunter achieves a DR of 80.9% in easy tasks, 83.0% in medium tasks, and 47.5% in hard tasks, substantially surpassing the CoT Agent and Browser-based approaches. Furthermore, WebHunter attains a SR of 66.7% on easy tasks, 27.6% on medium tasks, and 15.0% on hard tasks, proving its effectiveness in successfully exploiting web vulnerabilities.

On the Llama-3.1-405B model, WebHunter exhibits a similar performance trend, reinforcing the consistency of our approach. It achieves a CR of 96.1%, maintaining strong execution reliability. The DR and SR results closely follow those observed in DeepSeek-R1-70B with slight variations, demonstrating its ability to generalize well across different LLM architectures. These results confirm that WebHunter's methodological innovations contribute significantly to its superior performance, irrespective of the underlying model.

Table 3 presents the FP/FN counts for WebHunter and baselines on the CVE dataset.

**Table 3.** False Positive and False Negative Results on CVE Tasks

| Method | FP (Count) | FN (Count) |
|---|---|---|
| CoT Agent | 6 | 17 |
| Browser Use | 3 | 13 |
| WebHunter | **1** | **5** |

WebHunter achieves lower FP and FN rates compared to baselines, indicating stronger precision and recall in real-world SQLi testing.

## 5.2 Ablation Study

The ablation study evaluates the importance of each component in the WebHunter framework. "w/o PT" represents the scenario without the integration of penetration tools, "w/o EO" refers to the absence of the enhanced observation mechanism, "w/o FSL" indicates the removal of few-shot learning, and "w/o

AVC" means lacking the automated action verification and correction module. These results help quantify the contribution of each innovative feature.

**Table 4.** Ablation Study Results

| Method | CR (%) | DR (%) | SR (%) |
|---|---|---|---|
| w/o PT | 95.3 | 47.2 | 9.4 |
| w/o EO | 94.6 | 55.2 | 11.2 |
| w/o FSL | 85.2 | 60.3 | 14.6 |
| w/o AVC | 86.9 | 67.2 | 19.8 |
| WebHunter (Full) | **97.1** | **78.4** | **27.5** |

Table 4 presents the results of our ablation study, which evaluates the contribution of each core component in WebHunter. Interestingly, removing penetration tools (w/o PT) results in a slightly lower CR (95.3%) compared to the full model (97.1%), which suggests that retaining the complete set of operations—including penetration tool integration helps reduce execution failures. This aligns with the observation that the full model also maintains higher DR and SR, further confirming that penetration tools are crucial for not only ensuring stable execution but also effectively identifying and exploiting vulnerabilities.

The enhanced observation mechanism (w/o EO) also plays a vital role, as its removal lowers DR to 55.2% and SR to 11.2%, demonstrating that aggregating multi-source security data significantly improves detection accuracy. Similarly, removing few-shot learning (w/o FSL) results in a decline in DR (60.3%) and SR (14.6%), confirming its impact on decision-making and adaptive action generation.

Automated action verification and correction (w/o AVC) has the most significant impact on CR, reducing it to 86.9%, underscoring its importance in maintaining an automated and recoverable execution flow. The full WebHunter model achieves the highest DR (78.4%) and SR (27.5%), demonstrating that each component synergistically contributes to its overall performance.

## 6 Conclusion and Future Work

This paper presents WebHunter, an LLM-driven agent that effectively bridges the gap between web interaction and SQLi exploitation in complex web environments through structured planning and tool collaboration. Experimental results show that WebHunter achieves high effectiveness in discovering and exploiting SQLi vulnerabilities. For future work, we aim to extend the agent's reasoning capabilities for broader vulnerability types, improve adaptability to diverse web architectures, and enhance its planning robustness under real-world penetration constraints.

## References


1. Dzhangarov, A., Pakhaev, K.K., Potapova, N.V.: Modern web application development technologies. In: IOP Conference Series: Materials Science and Engineering. Vol. 1155. 1. IOP Publishing, p. 012100 (2021)
2. Marashdeh, Z., Suwais, K., Alia, M.: A survey on SQL injection attack: detection and challenges. In: 2021 International Conference on Information Technology (ICIT). IEEE, pp. 957–962 (2021)
3. Subbulakshmi, T., et al.: SQL Injection Testing on Website using SQLMAP. In: 2024 International Conference on Trends in Quantum Computing and Emerging Business Technologies. IEEE, pp. 1–4 (2024)
4. Kore, A., et al.: Burp suite extension for script based attacks for web applications. In: 2022 6th International Conference on Electronics, Communication and Aerospace Technology. IEEE, pp. 651–657 (2022)
5. Deng, G., et al.: Pentestgpt: An LLM-empowered automatic penetration testing tool. In: arXiv preprint arXiv:2308.06782 (2023)
6. Gioacchini, L., et al.: AutoPenBench: benchmarking generative agents for penetration testing. In: arXiv preprint arXiv:2410.03225 (2024)
7. Muzsai, L., Imolai, D., Lukács, A.: HackSynth: LLM agent and evaluation framework for autonomous penetration testing. In: arXiv preprint arXiv:2412.01778 (2024)
8. Nieponice, T., Valeros, V., Garcia, S.: ARACNE: An LLM-Based Autonomous Shell Pentesting Agent. In: arXiv preprint arXiv:2502.18528 (2025)
9. He, H., et al.: WebVoyager: building an end-to-end web agent with large multimodal models. In: arXiv preprint arXiv:2401.13919 (2024)
10. Shinde, G., Waghere, S.S.: Analysis of SQL Injection Using DVWA Tool. In: RICE, pp. 107–110 (2017)
11. Zhou, S., et al.: Webarena: a realistic web environment for building autonomous agents. In: arXiv preprint arXiv:2307.13854 (2023)
12. Zheng, B., et al.: GPT-4v (ISION) is a generalist web agent, if grounded. In: arXiv preprint arXiv:2401.01614 (2024)
13. Müller, M., ŽuniÄ, G.: Browser Use: Enable AI to control your browser (2024). https://github.com/browser-use/browser-use
14. Karpukhina, E.M.: Modern trends in web applications testing. In: (2023)
15. Shevelenkov, A.: Expanding end-to-end test coverage using Playwright framework for Sievo Oy's Materials Forecasting product. In: (2024)
16. Panjaitan, L.F., et al.: Wireshark packet capture: the technology accounting information system perspective. Int. J. Multidisc. Res. Growth Eval. **2**, 79–82 (2022)
17. Brown, T., et al.: Language models are few-shot learners. Adv. Neural. Inf. Process. Syst. **33**, 1877–1901 (2020)
18. Bach-Nutman, M.: Understanding the top 10 OWASP vulnerabilities. In: arXiv preprint arXiv:2012.09960 (2020)
19. Guo, D., et al.: Deepseek-r1: incentivizing reasoning capability in LLMs via reinforcement learning. In: arXiv preprint arXiv:2501.12948 (2025)
20. Touvron, H., et al.: Llama: open and efficient foundation language models. In: arXiv preprint arXiv:2302.13971 (2023)
21. Wei, J., et al.: Chain-of-thought prompting elicits reasoning in large language models. Adv. Neural. Inf. Process. Syst. **35**, 24824–24837 (2022)

# AFLTrans: Research on Intelligent Generative Fuzz Testing Method Based on Transformer

Guoyan Cao[1(✉)], Mengjiao Geng[2], and Xiaobing Xiong[3]

[1] Northwestern Polytechnical University, Xi'an, China
guoyan.cao@nwpu.edu.cn
[2] National University of Defense Technology, Changsha, China
[3] Key Laboratory of Cyberspace Security, Ministry of Education, Zhengzhou, China

**Abstract.** This paper proposes a Transformer-based intelligent generative fuzz testing method. The AFLTrans optimization algorithm part mainly focuses on three core links: seed collection and preprocessing, Transformer model prediction, and comparative analysis of experimental data. In terms of seed data set collection, two methods based on code coverage and path information are adopted to ensure that the collected seeds can fully cover different execution paths of the program. In the data preprocessing stage, various types of seed test cases are uniformly represented as binary bitmap sequences, thereby ignoring the differences in seed file types and ensuring data consistency and ease of processing. In the prediction part of the Transformer model, a binary bitmap (*changed_map*) of the mutation position is obtained by XOR operation of the test cases before and after the model prediction, and the threshold $\alpha$ is used to control which test cases should be retained, thereby optimizing the seed data selection process. Finally, in the experiment and data analysis stage, based on the LAVA-M dataset and 8 actual Linux application datasets, this paper conducts performance comparison and data analysis from two aspects: the effectiveness of the machine learning model and the vulnerability mining capability, and verifies the superiority of the model in vulnerability detection and mining.

**Keywords:** Binary Security · Fuzzing · Intelligent Seed Generation · Transformer

## 1 Introduction

Binary programs are widely existed in various fields, such as operating systems and mobile applications. Binary programs have become the cornerstone of modern computing by providing efficient computing power and having cross platform characteristics. However, binary programs suffer from numbers of security issues. Vulnerabilities of binary program are capable to cause unauthorized access to systems, leakage of sensitive information, or system damage. By exploiting the


K.-K. R. Choo et al. (Eds.): ICDF2C 2025, LNICST 686, pp. 464–490, 2026.
https://doi.org/10.1007/978-3-032-22545-0_27

vulnerabilities, threats are able to degrade the security and reliability of the system, potentially leading to risks such as data fabrications, service interruptions, and system crashes.

Fuzzing is a fundamental and popular technology to detect and discover the vulnerabilities of binary programs [2]. The process of traditional fuzzing is characterized by its straightforward and intuitive nature. It begins by executing the program with a mutated or generated seed as input. Throughout program execution, the fuzzer attentively observes program feedback information and crash status, which form the basis for evaluating the value of the seed in subsequent steps. Once program execution concludes, the fuzzer captures the coverage path associated with the seed and assigns higher value to seed files that exhibit broader coverage. Next, a seed with a high evaluation value is selected to perform a mutation operation to generate more seeds, and then the above fuzzy process is repeated. In comparison to other security testing techniques such as data flow analysis, taint analysis, and symbolic execution, fuzzing possesses distinct advantages in terms of both speed and accuracy.

The main work of this paper is to propose an intelligent generative fuzzy test method based on Transformer Improve the efficiency and effectiveness of traditional AFL (AmericanFuzzyLop) framework in vulnerability detection process. To be specific, Ben Chapter introduces Transformer deep learning model for intelligent screening and filtering of test cases, thus optimizing the test Trial example selection and execution policy. Its core content includes the following aspects:

(1) Data collection and preprocessing: This paper first collects seed files that trigger program crash by using existing fuzzy test tools to run the target program for a long time. In addition, initial torrent files were obtained via the Internet. Then, the collected seed data is processed by binary vector normalization, and transformed into structured data form suitable for machine learning model by feature extraction method, forming a data set containing features such as code coverage and path information.
(2) Application of machine learning model: This paper adopts Transformer deep learning model to train the model to predict the merits of test cases. By learning the characteristics of the torrent file, the model is able to effectively evaluate the potential of each test case to trigger program vulnerabilities, increase code coverage, and execute new paths. The tagging data during training includes information such as whether the torrent file triggered a crash or generated new code coverage.
(3) Test case filtering and optimization: The trained Transformer model is applied to the filtering stage of test cases to predict each new seed test case and determine whether it is effective. Valid test cases are executed first, while invalid or inefficient test cases are excluded. This screening process helps to reduce the computing resource consumption of invalid tests, thus improving the efficiency of fuzzy testing.

# 2 Related Work

## 2.1 Fuzzing

Fuzzing techniques [14,31] originated in the 1980s when Barton Miller and his colleagues first introduced the concept of fuzz testing, applying it to UNIX systems [16]. In the early 2000s, the mutation-based fuzzing approach emerged, involving random or semi-random mutation of input data to generate test cases [3]. In 2005, the book "Fuzzing for Software Security Testing" and "Quality Assurance" by Takanen, DeMott, and Miller provided a comprehensive overview of fuzzing techniques in software security testing [24]. The year 2006 saw the introduction of the SAGE (Scalable Automated Guided Execution) fuzzing framework, enabling automated fuzz testing in large-scale programs [5]. Then in 2010 TaintScope [25] employed dynamic taint analysis and symbolic execution to test x86 binary programs. Next year, SimFuzz [29] utilized test case similarity metrics to explore program semantics deeply.

A significant advancement occurred in 2013 with the release of American Fuzzy Lop (AFL) [1], which employed coverage-based strategies and intelligent input mutation to discover vulnerabilities in programs. Dowser [7], a guided fuzzer, integrates taint tracking, program analysis, and symbolic execution to detect buffer overflow and underflow vulnerabilities. By 2016, the integration of symbolic execution and fuzzing gained popularity, enhancing the accuracy and efficiency of fuzz testing [23]. QuickFuzz [6] leveraged existing Haskell libraries to efficiently test various file formats without manual specifications in 2017. Another fuzzer VUzzer [18], on the other hand, utilizes control-flow and data-flow analysis to pinpoint bugs in deeper program paths. It assigns increased significance to these intricate code components. Another strategy entails employing program analysis to support fuzzing efforts [11]. In 2020, a similar fuzzy testing tool, V-Fuzz, was proposed to identify a wide range of vulnerabilities [13].

In 2024, Asmita [17] et al. proposed two techniques to strengthen software testing. The first approach enhances the effectiveness of fuzzy testing by generating initial seeds for specific targets with the help of LargeLanguage Models (LLMS). The second approach is to repurpose previously collected crash data from similar test targets before fuzzing new targets, significantly simplifying the time-consuming process of traditional fuzzing tests. Li [12] et al. An efficient directional fuzzy testing tool SDFUZZ driven by target state is presented. A new target state feedback mechanism is introduced, and the previously imprecise distance measurement is refined into a two-dimensional feedback mechanism to actively drive the exploration towards the target state. Xiang [28] et al. proposed a direct gray box fuzzy testing tool WAFLGO, aiming to effectively discover the vulnerabilities introduced by submission. Rong [19] et al. proposed a novel directional fuzzy testing solution, AFLRun, which has a target path diversity metric and unbiased energy allocation, and can store the waypoints that hit the target through interesting paths into the corpus, thus enriching the path diversity of each target.

## 2.2 Fuzz Testing Framework AFL

The American Fuzzy Lop (AFL) was first released in 2013 and has since become an overlay guided gray box fuzzy test One of the most widely used tools in the tool. In recent years, most of the research work related to fuzzy testing is based on AFL conducts secondary development. The specific workflow is shown in Fig. 1. The core working mechanism of AFL is explained in detail below.

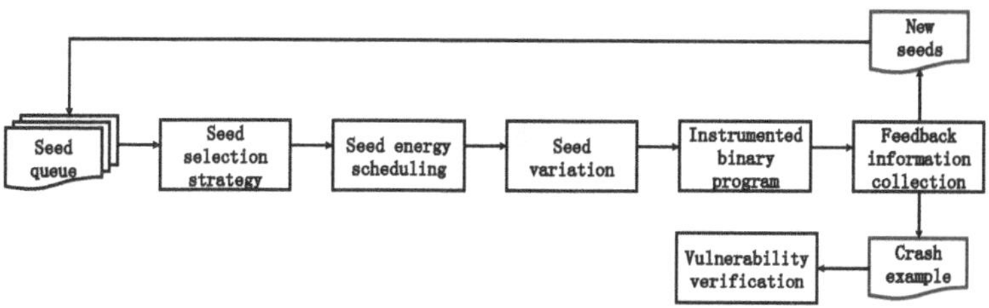


**Fig. 1.** AFL workflow diagram.

(1) Target code instrumentation

AFL is a coverage-guided gray-box fuzz testing tool that monitors code coverage by inserting code (i.e., code instrumentation) during program compilation. Code instrumentation is a technique that adds additional instructions or code snippets (such as log or monitoring statements) to a program in order to observe and analyze the program's running status.

AFL uses edge coverage to track and monitor the code coverage of the target program. Edge coverage is represented by a tuple consisting of the two basic blocks before and after the program control flow. For example, in the program control flow graph shown in Fig. 2, the path (A, C, F, H, Z) can be represented as 4 tuples (AC, CF, FH, HZ). Compared with traditional basic block coverage, edge coverage can capture the transition between different states of the program and provide more fine-grained information. This method is more in line with the characteristics of the vulnerability triggering mode.

The core instrumentation logic of AFL is shown in the Fig. 3. The main idea is to insert a unique random ID at each basic block of the program. When the program runs to a basic block, the ID of the basic block and the previous basic block are XORed, and the calculation result is used as the unique identifier of the corresponding edge. This identifier will be recorded in the bitmap of shared memory. By comparing the triggering status of the edges in the bitmap, it can be determined whether the current test case has improved the coverage or explored a new program state.

This design based on edge coverage and bitmap recording enables AFL to efficiently identify inputs with high testing value, thereby more effectively exploring the code space and triggering potential vulnerabilities or abnormal states.

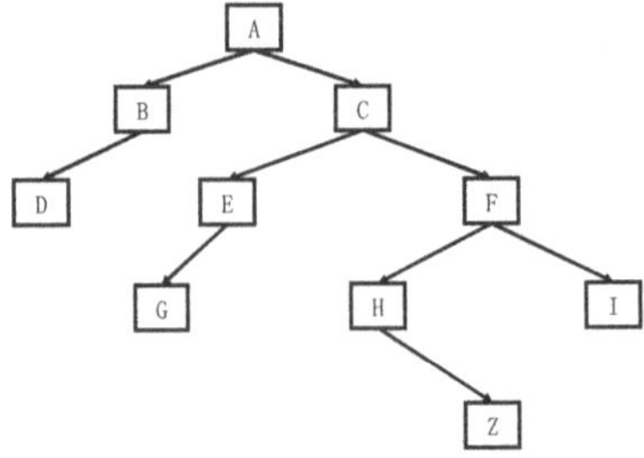


**Fig. 2.** Program Control Flow Graph Example.

```
1 cur_location=AFL_R(100);
2 shared_mem[cur_location^prev_location]++;
3 pre_location=cur_location>>1;
```

**Fig. 3.** AFL core instrumentation code.

(2) Seed selection strategy

In fuzz testing, a seed refers to a test case that can trigger a unique execution state of a program [15]. For example, when a test case discovers a new program execution path (tuple) or changes the hit count of an existing path during execution, the test case will be retained in the seed queue for subsequent mutation and testing.

The seed selection strategy [8] aims to prioritize high-quality seeds from the seed queue for mutation and testing to maximize program coverage, discover new paths, or trigger crashes. AFL evaluates the quality of seeds based on indicators such as execution speed, file size, and coverage, and selects seeds from the queue in priority order by sorting seed characteristics to ensure maximum testing efficiency.

(3) Seed energy scheduling strategy

The seed energy scheduling strategy [21] determines the processing resources and mutation times allocated to each seed file. AFL scores seeds by evaluating seed characteristics (such as execution speed, coverage, mutation rounds, and execution depth) and allocates different energies based on the seed scores. This strategy ensures that seeds with higher potential value receive more resources, thereby speeding up the testing process and improving the efficiency of vulnerability mining.

(4) Seed mutation strategy

Seed mutation [10] is a method that uses a seed file as a starting point and generates new test cases through a series of operations. Its purpose is to explore different execution paths of the program by modifying the content of the seed file.

AFL's seed mutation strategy is divided into two stages: deterministic mutation and random mutation. The first stage is deterministic mutation, which includes operations such as bit flipping, arithmetic operations, specific content replacement (interest replacement), and dictionary token replacement. The mutation in this stage is mainly based on systematic operations, which are used to maximize the exploration of the potential state of the program. The second stage is random mutation, including large-scale destruction and splicing operations. Large-scale destruction refers to the combination of multiple mutation operations in the deterministic stage of the seed, while splicing is achieved by combining parts of different seeds into new test cases. The random mutation stage is mainly run after the deterministic mutation is completed, and the deterministic mutation is only performed in the first cycle of the seed queue.

(5) Information feedback mechanism

AFL's feedback mechanism mainly includes two parts: anomaly detection and test case validity judgment [30]. The first is anomaly detection. AFL judges whether the program has entered an abnormal state by monitoring the anomalies (such as crashes and timeouts) triggered during the execution of test cases. By capturing common error signals (such as SIGSEGV, SIGABRT, etc.), AFL records the test cases that trigger the exceptions, and provides a basis for subsequent debugging and vulnerability verification, helping to determine whether the exceptions are caused by actual vulnerabilities. The second is sample validity determination. AFL tracks program path changes through instrumentation technology and uses the random ID of each basic block to identify the path branches in the program control flow [20]. By combining the IDs of the two basic blocks before and after, a path tuple (edge) is generated, and the hits and hit counts of each edge are counted in the global hash table. When a test case introduces a new edge or changes the hit count of an edge, it indicates that the test case triggers a new program state or explores a new path. Such test cases are considered to have high exploration value and are added to the seed queue.

Through this mechanism based on instrumentation and information feedback, AFL can dynamically enrich the seed queue and systematically explore more execution paths [9], thereby improving coverage and vulnerability discovery capabilities. This method significantly improves AFL's mining efficiency for complex vulnerabilities.

## 2.3 Transformer Model

The Transformer model [4] uses an encoder-decoder structure, and its overall architecture is shown in the Fig. 4. The Transformer structure [22] is divided into two main parts: the encoding component and the decoding component, both of which are stacked with multiple layers of encoders and decoders. Specifically, the encoding component consists of 6 layers of encoders, and the decoding component consists of 6 layers of decoders. Next, the structures of these two components will be introduced in detail.

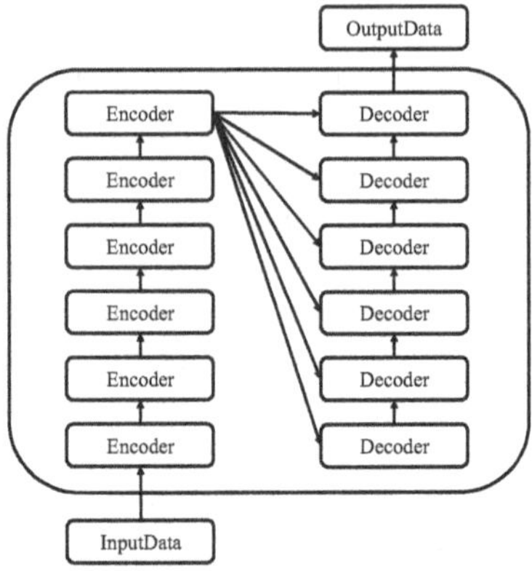


**Fig. 4.** Transformer overall architecture.

(1) For the encoder [26] part, each encoder consists of two main sub-layers, as shown in the Fig. 5. The first sub-layer is the Self-Attention layer. When calculating Self-Attention, three different vectors need to be generated from the input vector of each encoder. For each binary seed file sequence, a query vector $Q$, a key-value vector $K$ and a value vector $V$ are created respectively. The calculation formulas of these vectors are shown in the following formula 1, where $d_k$ represents the number of columns of the matrix $Q, K$, that is, the dimension of the vector.

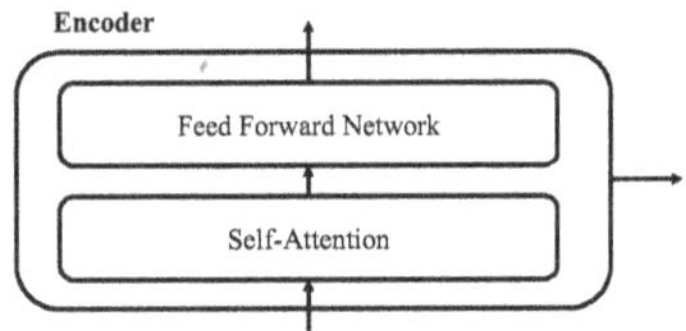


**Fig. 5.** Encoder structure diagram.

$$\text{Attention}(Q, K, V) = \text{softmax}\left(\frac{QK^T}{\sqrt{d_k}}\right)V \tag{1}$$

The second sublayer is a fully connected feed-forward neural network (FNN) layer. After being processed by the self-attention layer, the FNN operates independently on the vectors at each position. Specifically, each vector first passes through a ReLU activation function and then undergoes two linear transformations. These operations are performed independently at each position, ensuring that the model can capture the nonlinear characteristics of each position.

$$FNN(x) = \max(0, xW_1 + b_1)W_2 + b_2 \tag{2}$$

In order to retain the features extracted by multi-layer self-attention and ensure that the vector output by the decoder can contain the original features, the model designs a residual connection between the two sub-layers and performs layer normalization. Specifically, the output of each sub-layer is calculated by the following formula:

$$\text{LayerNorm}(x + \text{subblayer}(x)) \tag{3}$$

Among them, subblayer($x$) represents the function operation implemented by the sublayer. In this way, the residual connection ensures the effective transmission of information, and the normalization process helps to accelerate the training process and improve the stability of the model.

Each encoder follows the same structure, but the difference is that each encoder uses different weight parameters to adapt to different input data characteristics.

(2) For the decoder [27], in addition to the two sub-layers in each encoder layer, the decoder also adds a third sub-layer, the Encoder-Decoder Attention layer, as shown in the Fig. 6. This Attention layer is different from the self-attention layer in the encoder. The Attention layer in the decoder introduces a Mask mechanism. The addition of this Mask mechanism is to ensure that the decoder can generate subsequent outputs step by step in sequence after receiving the start flag.

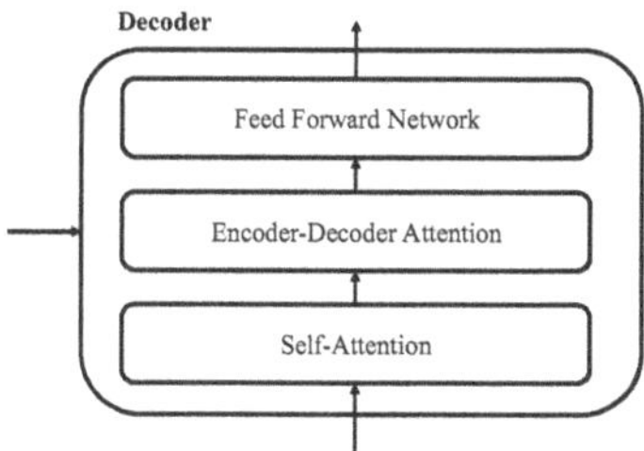


**Fig. 6.** Decoder structure diagram.

Specifically, the role of the mask is to prevent the decoder from "seeing" future information during the calculation process. Without the mask, the model may directly access future outputs during training, thus violating the sequential nature of sequence generation. By introducing the mask, the decoder can only gradually calculate the output of each position based on the generated sequence, thereby ensuring the correctness of sequential generation. Its calculation formula is shown in the following formula 4.

$$\begin{aligned} PE_{(pos,2i)} &= \sin\left(pos/10000^{2i/d_{\text{model}}}\right) \\ PE_{(pos,2i+1)} &= \cos\left(pos/10000^{2i/d_{\text{model}}}\right) \end{aligned} \tag{4}$$

# 3 Seed Collection and Preprocessing Module

This section mainly completes the collection and preprocessing of excellent seeds and test cases. The machine learning algorithm dataset required for this study comes from two parts (as shown in the Fig. 7): First, the existing fuzz testing tool is used to test the program under test for 48 h. After completing the experimental cycle, the excellent seeds generated by mutation during the fuzz testing process (that is, seeds that can trigger program crashes) are collected as part of the dataset; second, some initial seed files are obtained through Internet channels as another source of the dataset.

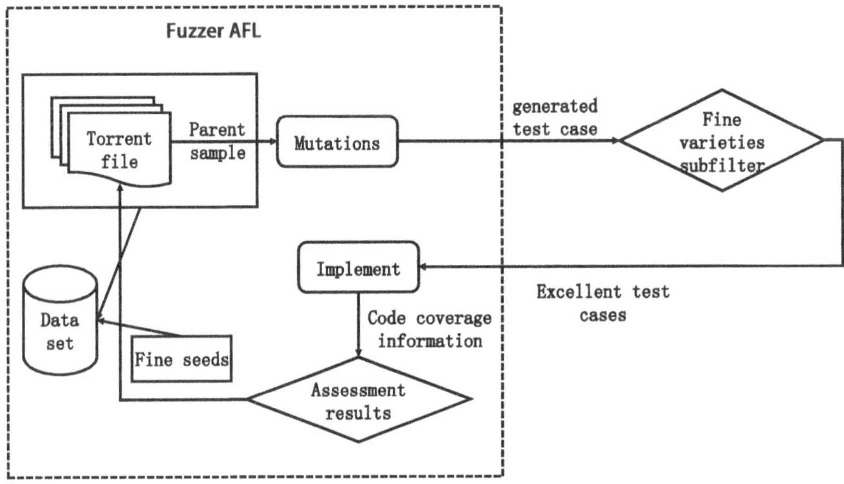


**Fig. 7.** Dataset source diagram.

Next, we need to screen out excellent seeds from the seed data set collected above. In order to effectively screen out high-quality seeds, this study selected two key indicators, code coverage and path information, as the basis for screening and cleaning excellent seed data sets.

Specifically, code coverage is used to evaluate how many independent code paths each seed covers during the test process. Seeds with higher coverage can usually test the execution logic of the program more comprehensively, and are more likely to trigger potential vulnerabilities. Path information helps us understand the depth and complexity of the paths involved in the execution of test cases. Seeds with greater path diversity and depth are more likely to reveal hidden defects in the program.

Through the comprehensive evaluation of these two indicators, this study can screen out excellent seeds that can maximize program testing effects and improve fuzz testing efficiency from a large number of seeds, thereby further improving the vulnerability discovery capabilities in the subsequent fuzz testing phase.

### 3.1 Code Coverage Based Seed Collection

For the excellent seed screening method based on code coverage, this study first reads all seed test cases in the form of binary sequences. For the convenience of description, $c$ and $c'$ are set to represent the code coverage before and after the seed test case mutation, and $M$ is the functional relationship of the code coverage change before and after the seed test case mutation. Specifically, assume that $M(c, c')$ represents the change in code coverage before and after mutation.

On this basis, the code coverage increment (i.e., the improvement in code coverage) is defined as shown in the following formula 5:

$$M\left(c, c'\right) = \left\{ \sum_{0 \leqslant i \leqslant n} \left[c_i < c_i'\right] \mid n \in \left[0 \times 00, 0 \times FF\right] \right\} \tag{5}$$

In the formula 5, $c_i$ represents the $i$th bit of the seed test case $c$ before mutation, and $n$ is the bit length of the seed test case, that is, the bitmap length of the seed test case. In this study, the bitmap length of the seed test case is set to $0 \times FF$, that is, a fixed length, to facilitate unified comparison and calculation.

In the process of selecting excellent seeds, in order to further refine the screening conditions, this study introduces a threshold $\lambda$. This threshold is used to constrain the coverage increment function and is defined as:

$$M\left(c, c'\right) > \lambda \tag{6}$$

By setting this threshold, it can be ensured that only those seed test cases with coverage increment greater than or equal to $\lambda$ are considered good. In practice, the size of the threshold $\lambda$ directly affects the standard of the selected good seeds. When the $\lambda$ value increases, it means that the requirements for good seeds are more stringent, and only those test cases with large coverage increments can be selected, which helps to improve the comprehensiveness of the test and the ability to discover vulnerabilities. On the contrary, reducing $\lambda$ will lower the screening criteria, so that more seed test cases are included in the range of good seeds, but may reduce the accuracy of the test.

By adjusting the threshold $\lambda$, the screening conditions for good seeds can be flexibly controlled, and then the improvement of coverage and the diversity of test cases can be balanced to optimize the efficiency and effect of fuzz testing.

### 3.2 Seed Collection Based on Path Information

Another important indicator for selecting good seed test cases is the path information generated when the test case is executed in the application under test. Mathematically, the relationship of path execution can be described by set mapping. Specifically, let set $X$ and set $Y$ represent the input and output spaces respectively, and the mapping $F$ from set $X$ to set $Y$ is defined as a set $G$ of ordered pairs $(x, y)$, where $x \in X, y \in Y$ and each element in set $X$ corresponds to the first component of an ordered pair in set $G$. In other words, set $G$ contains all ordered pairs $(x, y)$ of mapping relationships, that is, it describes the relationship between input and output.

In this study, the application under test is regarded as such a mapping $F$, in which each input (i.e., test case) is closely related to the execution path of the application. Assuming that the application under test does not contain random functions, whenever a test case is input, the application will execute along a specific path according to the input and generate the corresponding output. These execution paths are actually different branches or code paths of the program control flow, reflecting the behavior of the program under different inputs.

Specifically, suppose we have an application under test $P$ and a set of seed test cases $T = \{s_1, s_2, s_3, s_4, s_5, \ldots\}$, where each seed test case $s_i$ corresponds to a natural number $i \in \mathbb{N}$. When the seed test case $s_i$ is input into the application $P$ for execution, the seed test case $s_i$ will trigger a path $j$ in the application. Therefore, the relationship between the input seed test case and the program execution path can be described by mapping $F : T \rightarrow Q$, where $Q = \{1, 2, 3, \ldots N\}$, and $N$ is a natural number representing the total number of paths. In this mapping, $j \in Q$ represents the identifier of a specific path in the program $P$.

For each seed test case $\forall s_i \in T$, it can be represented as a character sequence as follows:

$$s_i = (x_{i_1}, x_{i_2}, x_{i_3}, x_{i_4}, \ldots, x_{i_l}, Null, Null, Null, Null, \ldots) \tag{7}$$

where $l$ represents the byte length of $s_i$, $x_ik$ represents the, $k$th byte, and comes from the $2^8$ ASCII character set. Since the character sequence is composed of ASCII characters, the possible number of test cases of length $n$ bytes is finite, up to $256^n$, which means that the dataset $T$ of seed test cases is countable. Therefore, the set $T = \{s_1, s_2, s_3, s_4, \ldots\}$ is a reasonable representation.

In the application layer program $P$, the execution of the path $\forall j \in Q$ is constrained by a set of conditions $C_j$, which are the input or state requirements that the program needs to meet when executing a specific path. If the seed test case $s_i$ causes the application to execute the path $j$, the relationship between the seed test case $s_i$ and the path $j$ it triggers can be identified as:

$$F(s_i) = j \tag{8}$$

This relationship reflects the path $j$ corresponding to a specific seed test case $s_i$, thus providing a basis for path coverage analysis. Through this mapping relationship, we can clearly track the paths touched by each seed test case and further use the path information to evaluate the quality of the test case.

From the perspective of set theory, since $T$ is finite and each test case $s_i$ corresponds to a specific path $j$ in the application, this mapping relationship provides a theoretical basis for analyzing the execution path of the program, detecting potential vulnerabilities, and optimizing the fuzz testing process.

Since different test cases may execute the same path in the program, the test case set $T$ can be divided according to the program path. Specifically, according to different paths $j$, the test case set $T$ is divided into multiple subsets $T_i$, each of which contains test cases that execute path $i$. At this time, the test case set $T_i$ corresponding to path $i$ can be expressed as:

$$T_i = \{s_{ij} \mid F(s_{ij}) = i\} \tag{9}$$

Different from formula 8, in the above formula, $i$ represents different path identifiers in the program, $j$ is used to distinguish different constraints, and $s_ij$ represents the test case that executes path $i$ under a specific constraint $C_j$. In this way, seed test cases can be classified according to the execution paths they trigger, which helps to more systematically analyze the coverage of each path and the effect of the test cases.

This classification method can not only group test cases in order according to path information, but also help us more accurately evaluate which paths are touched by which test cases, thereby optimizing the fuzz testing process and improving the comprehensiveness and efficiency of vulnerability discovery.

### 3.3 Seed Pretreatment Module

After obtaining the excellent seed test case dataset through the methods described in the Sect. 3.1 section and the Sect. 3.2 section, this section will preprocess the seed. First, in order to eliminate the differences caused by different data formats, the seed test cases will be read in the form of binary sequences. This method can effectively minimize the impact of format differences on data analysis.

Based on the above theory, considering that different types of seed test cases will trigger different program execution paths, the binary sequence features of excellent seed test cases actually reflect the characteristics they exhibit during the test process. Therefore, in the seed preprocessing stage, our main task is to extract the binary sequence features of excellent seed test cases.

The overall algorithm flow of the seed preprocessing module is shown below, and a brief description is shown in Algorithm 1. The core step of the algorithm is to convert each excellent seed test case into binary form and extract its features to provide standardized seed input for subsequent analysis and model training.

This method limits the input file size of the excellent seed dataset to a maximum of 10240 bytes. First, in order to facilitate subsequent processing, the seed test case file will be vectorized. Specifically, a two-dimensional matrix $T$ of size $10240 \times 8$ is initialized, and the seed test case file is read byte by byte in binary form and then filled into the two-dimensional matrix in sequence. The resulting two-dimensional matrix $T$ is regarded as the binary sequence bitmap of the seed test case.

In order to extract the difference between the binary bitmaps before and after the seed mutation, this method uses a binary XOR operation. Its operation truth table is shown in Table 1. By performing an XOR operation on the binary sequence bitmaps of the initial seed and the mutated seed test case, a new two-dimensional matrix $T\_xor$ can be obtained. In this matrix, the position with

Algorithm 1: Seed pretreatment

**Input:**Seeds Set $S$, Data Set $F$
$x$ = original seed
$F = x\boldsymbol{y} = \{0\}$;
max_size $= \lambda, i = 0$;
**while** $i \leq |S|$ **do**
  Choose $s_i$ from $S$;
**if** size $(s_i) <$ max_size **and** $s_i$ is not original seed **then**
    $x_$vector = Vectorize($x$);
    $y_$vector = Vectorize ($s_i$);
    $y_$vector = Xor ($x\_$ vector, $y_$vector );
    add ( $x_$vector, $y_$vector) to $F$;
    $i = i + 1$;
**else**
    $s_i$ = Process_size ($s_i$) ;
    $x_$vector = Vectorize($x$);
    $y_$vector = Vectorize ($s_i$);
    $y_$vector = Xor ($x\_vector, y\_vector$);
    add ( $x_$vector, $y_$vector) to $F$;
    $i = i + 1$;
  **end**
**end**
**Output:** Data Set $F$.

a value of 1 indicates that the initial seed has changed during the mutation process, while the position with a value of 0 indicates that it has not changed.

Through this method, we can effectively capture the differences before and after the seed mutation, which provides an important basis for the subsequent analysis of the changes in seed test cases and the optimization of the fuzz testing process.

**Table 1.** Binary bitmap XOR operation table

| a | b | $a \oplus b$ |
|---|---|---|
| 0 | 0 | 0 |
| 1 | 0 | 1 |
| 0 | 1 | 1 |
| 1 | 1 | 0 |

As shown in the following Fig. 8, $T_i$ is a binary seed file in ELF format before mutation, and $T_i'$ is a binary seed file after $T_i$ mutation. It can be seen that the 35th byte has changed after mutation, and the position has changed from the initial byte 0x00 to the byte 0x80.

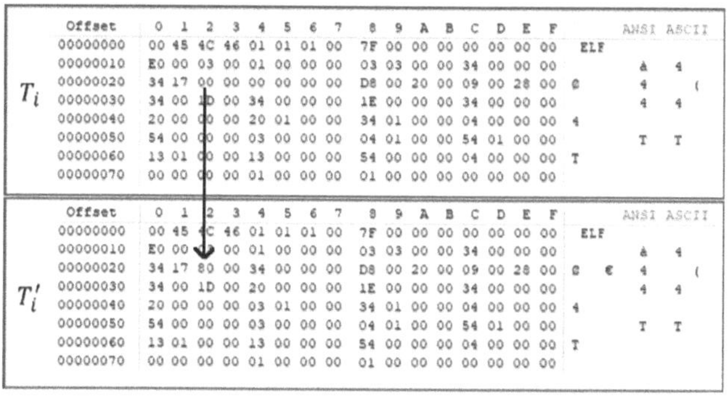

```
$T_i$
Offset    0  1  2  3  4  5  6  7   8  9  A  B  C  D  E  F   ANSI ASCII
00000000  00 45 4C 46 01 01 01 00  7F 00 00 00 00 00 00 00  ELF
00000010  E0 00 03 00 01 00 00 00  03 03 00 00 34 00 00 00        à  4
00000020  34 17 00 00 00 00 00 00  D8 00 20 00 09 00 28 00  Ø     4    (
00000030  34 00 1D 00 34 00 00 00  1E 00 00 00 34 00 00 00        4  4
00000040  20 00 00 00 20 01 00 00  34 01 00 00 04 00 00 00  4
00000050  54 00 00 00 03 00 00 00  04 01 00 00 54 01 00 00        T  T
00000060  13 01 00 00 13 00 00 00  54 00 00 00 04 00 00 00  T
00000070  00 00 00 00 01 00 00 00  01 00 00 00 00 00 00 00

$T_i'$
Offset    0  1  2  3  4  5  6  7   8  9  A  B  C  D  E  F   ANSI ASCII
00000000  00 45 4C 46 01 01 01 00  7F 00 00 00 00 00 00 00  ELF
00000010  E0 00 03 00 01 00 00 00  03 03 00 00 34 00 00 00        à  4
00000020  34 17 80 00 34 00 00 00  D8 00 20 00 09 00 28 00  Ø  €  4    (
00000030  34 00 1D 00 20 00 00 00  1E 00 00 00 34 00 00 00        4  4
00000040  20 00 00 00 03 01 00 00  34 01 00 00 04 00 00 00  4
00000050  54 00 00 00 03 00 00 00  04 01 00 00 54 01 00 00        T  T
00000060  13 01 00 00 13 00 00 00  54 00 00 00 04 00 00 00  T
00000070  00 00 00 00 01 00 00 00  01 00 00 00 00 00 00 00
```

**Fig. 8.** ELE binary seed file variation.

The seed processing module performs an XOR operation on $T_i$ and $T_i$ to obtain the matrix $T\_xor$ of the mutation position. As shown in the Fig. 9, the 35th byte position after mutation is marked as 1, indicating that the position has changed.

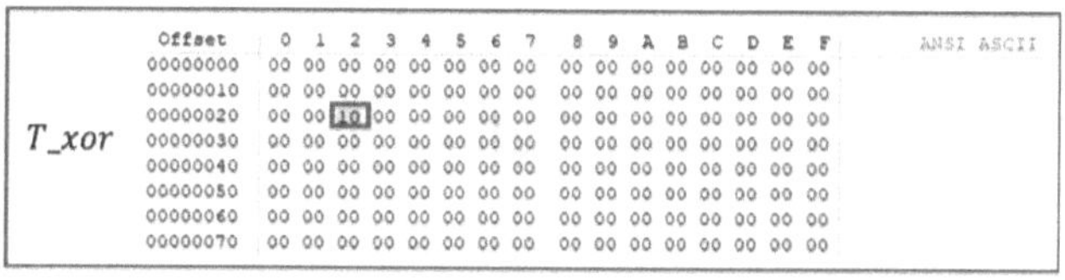

```
T_xor
Offset    0  1  2  3  4  5  6  7   8  9  A  B  C  D  E  F   ANSI ASCII
00000000  00 00 00 00 00 00 00 00  00 00 00 00 00 00 00 00
00000010  00 00 00 00 00 00 00 00  00 00 00 00 00 00 00 00
00000020  00 00 10 00 00 00 00 00  00 00 00 00 00 00 00 00
00000030  00 00 00 00 00 00 00 00  00 00 00 00 00 00 00 00
00000040  00 00 00 00 00 00 00 00  00 00 00 00 00 00 00 00
00000050  00 00 00 00 00 00 00 00  00 00 00 00 00 00 00 00
00000060  00 00 00 00 00 00 00 00  00 00 00 00 00 00 00 00
00000070  00 00 00 00 00 00 00 00  00 00 00 00 00 00 00 00
```

**Fig. 9.** ELE binary seed file variant location extraction.

Let $T$ be the initial seed test case, $T'$ be the mutated seed test case, then the processed data set $D$ can be expressed as follows:

$$D = \{(T, T \oplus T') \mid M(c, c') > \lambda\} = \{T, T\_xor\} \tag{10}$$

In the formula, $c_i$ and $c_i'$ represent the code coverage of the seed test cases before and after mutation, respectively. That is to say, when performing seed processing, we also introduced the conditions of the above-mentioned excellent seed test case collection stage (formula 6), and imposed strict requirements on the coverage of seed test cases. This process ensures that only those test cases that meet the coverage increment threshold $\lambda$ will be included in the final seed pool.

After the above algorithm processing, the final effect of the seed collection and preprocessing module in this section is shown in Fig. 10.

In Fig. 10, Figure (a) shows the data samples of the initial seed test case after processing before mutation. In the matrix, the position with a value of 1 indicates that there is a value at that position in the corresponding binary seed

```
shape of X: (10250, 2560, 64)    shape of Y: (10250, 2560, 64)
Data Collected X:                Data Collected Y:
[[[0. 1. 1. ... 0. 0. 0.]        [[[1. 0. 0. ... 0. 0. 0.]
  [0. 0. 0. ... 0. 0. 0.]          [0. 0. 0. ... 0. 0. 0.]
  [0. 0. 0. ... 0. 0. 0.]          [0. 0. 0. ... 0. 0. 0.]
  ...                              ...
  [0. 0. 0. ... 0. 0. 0.]          [0. 0. 0. ... 0. 0. 0.]
  [0. 0. 0. ... 0. 0. 0.]          [0. 0. 0. ... 0. 0. 0.]
  [0. 0. 0. ... 0. 0. 0.]]         [0. 0. 0. ... 0. 0. 0.]]
            (a)                              (b)
```

**Fig. 10.** Data sample results obtained from seed collection and preprocessing. (a) Binary bitmap sequence of seed test cases before mutation; (b) Binary bitmap sequence obtained by XORing the seed test cases before and after mutation.

file, while the position with a value of 0 indicates that there is no value at that position.

Figure (b) shows the data samples of the difference between the seed test case before and after mutation obtained by XOR operation. In the matrix, the position with a value of 1 indicates that the binary seed file at that position has mutated, while the position with a value of 0 indicates that there is no change at that position.

# 4 Method for Extracting High-Quality Seed Features

In the previous section, the processed seed data set has been obtained through the seed collection and preprocessing module. This section will use machine learning algorithms to train a good seed test case feature extraction model based on this data set, and apply the model to the test case filtering stage in the optimized fuzz testing framework AFL.

When choosing a training neural network model, the main considerations are the change in the length of the input seed test case and its key sequence characteristics. Initially, the recurrent neural network (RNN) was considered as the model of choice. RNN is suitable for processing sequence data, but in actual experiments, when the sequence of seed test cases is long, RNN will encounter the problem of gradient vanishing or gradient explosion. In addition, RNN has long-term dependency problems when processing long sequences, which is crucial for training a variant position sequence model of a good seed test case. If the model cannot effectively capture long-term dependencies, the effect of the training results will be seriously affected.

Compared with RNN, the long short-term memory network (LSTM) improves the basic unit structure by introducing input gates, forget gates, and output gates, solves the long-term dependency problem in RNN, and generally performs better in time series modeling. In addition, LSTM can also be used as a nonlinear unit to build a deeper network model. However, when processing very long sequences, LSTM still encounters gradient problems, and each LSTM unit contains 4 fully connected layers, which makes the training time longer and the computational complexity higher when the network structure is deeper. Based on the above considerations, this paper finally chose the Transformer deep learning network as the feature extraction model.

1. For the encoder part, each encoder consists of two main sub-layers, the first of which is the Self-Attention layer. When calculating Self-Attention, three different vectors need to be generated from the input vector of each encoder. For each binary seed file sequence, a query vector $Q$, a key-value vector $K$ and a value vector $V$ are created respectively. The calculation formulas of these vectors are shown in the following formula 11, where $d_k$ represents the number of columns of the matrix $Q, K$, that is, the dimension of the vector.

$$\text{Attention}(Q, K, V) = \text{softmax}\left(\frac{QK^T}{\sqrt{d_k}}\right)V \tag{11}$$

The second sublayer is a fully connected feed-forward neural network (FNN) layer. After being processed by the self-attention layer, the FNN operates independently on the vectors at each position. Specifically, each vector first passes through a ReLU activation function and then undergoes two linear transformations. These operations are performed independently at each position, ensuring that the model can capture the nonlinear characteristics of each position.ｏ

$$FNN(x) = \max(0, xW_1 + b_1) W_2 + b_2 \tag{12}$$

In order to retain the features extracted by multi-layer self-attention and ensure that the vector output by the decoder can contain the original features, the model designs a residual connection between the two sub-layers and performs layer normalization. Specifically, the output of each sub-layer is calculated by the following formula:

$$\text{LayerNorm}(x + \text{subblayer}(x)) \tag{13}$$

Among them, subblayer$(x)$ represents the function operation implemented by the sublayer. In this way, the residual connection ensures the effective transmission of information, and the normalization process helps to accelerate the training process and improve the stability of the model. Each encoder follows the same structure, but the difference is that each encoder uses different weight parameters to adapt to different input data characteristics.

2. For the decoder part, in addition to the two sublayers in each encoder layer, the decoder also adds a third sublayer, namely the Encoder-Decoder Attention layer. This Attention layer is different from the self-attention layer in the encoder. The Attention layer in the decoder introduces a Mask mechanism. The addition of this Mask mechanism is to ensure that the decoder can generate subsequent outputs step by step in sequence after receiving the start flag.

Specifically, the role of the Mask is to prevent the decoder from "seeing" future information during the calculation process. In the absence of a Mask, the model may directly access future outputs during training, thereby violating the sequential nature of sequence generation. By introducing a Mask, the decoder can only gradually calculate the output of each position based on the generated sequence, thereby ensuring the correctness of sequential generation. Its calculation formula is shown in the following formula 14.

$$
\begin{aligned}
PE_{(pos,2i)} &= \sin\left(pos/10000^{2i/d_{\text{model}}}\right) \\
PE_{(pos,2i+1)} &= \cos\left(pos/10000^{2i/d_{\text{model}}}\right)
\end{aligned}
\tag{14}
$$

By using the above Transformer deep learning network structure for training, a good seed test case feature model is finally obtained. The model can predict the sequence of mutation positions in the binary bitmap of the seed test case. As shown in the Fig. 11, when a seed test case is input, the model is processed by Transformer to predict the binary bitmap sequence of the key positions of the test case mutation.

In the Fig. 11, the value of each position represents the importance of the binary bit. By setting a threshold, the predicted binary bitmap sequence can be converted into the final output result, thereby determining which positions have a key impact on the mutation. This method effectively helps to screen out high-potential excellent seed test cases.

```
[ 2.1741449e-04  1.3240676e-04  9.7779674e-04  4.1171638e-04
  1.3240676e-04 -4.9270443e-06 -1.8146748e-04 -4.9474038e-04
 -5.5284292e-04  5.8531499e-04 -5.3198914e-05 -3.5181217e-04
 -7.5064239e-04  2.8990224e-04  5.0544277e-05  7.2748889e-04
  6.2525866e-04 -4.0296924e-05 -3.1421863e-04  4.6449443e-04
  3.1050801e-04  2.2065996e-03 -7.0488529e-04  1.4298817e-03
  2.3895521e-04  1.4298817e-03 -3.1731986e-03 -1.4341251e-03
 -1.4205434e-03 -1.4341251e-03 -1.0923686e-03 -3.1731986e-03
  1.0276958e-03 -3.1731986e-03  5.6806073e-04 -1.0923686e-03
  4.7952851e-04 -7.5985905e-04  7.6942472e-04  5.6806073e-04
 -4.5114040e-05 -1.2003788e-04  3.2546796e-04  7.6942472e-04
 -1.6959737e-05  4.3651561e-04 -4.2719685e-04 -6.7100686e-04
 -5.7659541e-05  1.2155414e-03  1.2155414e-03  4.9593631e-04
  2.6546748e-04 -2.8853418e-04 -2.8853418e-04 -5.2778504e-04
 -5.2068150e-04  4.3484353e-05 -1.2109427e-03 -5.2781060e-04
  9.2420069e-04  9.4760471e-05 -2.5972931e-05 -7.1517099e-04]
```

**Fig. 11.** Binary seed file bitmap prediction.

## 5 Seed Test Case Optimization and Generation

In the previous section, we successfully built a model of good seed test case features by training and extracting the features of good seed test cases based on the Transformer deep learning network. This section will further study how to apply this model to the test case filtering stage of the fuzz testing framework

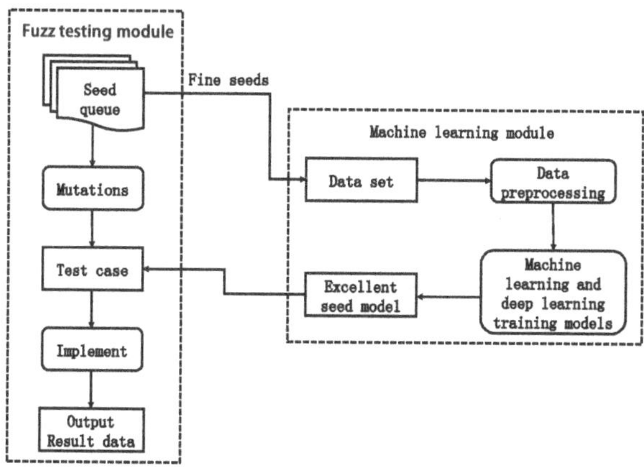


**Fig. 12.** Design diagram of the overall optimization scheme for the seed filtration stage.

AFL to improve the efficiency of fuzz testing. The overall architecture is shown in the Fig. 12.

Specifically, we introduce a goodness evaluation mechanism after the test case is mutated but before it is executed, which is used to filter out inefficient or invalid test cases, thereby ensuring that only test cases that meet the goodness criteria are executed. This optimization process aims to improve the effectiveness and efficiency of fuzz testing. The algorithm outline is shown in Algorithm 2. Compared with the traditional AFL algorithm framework, the main innovation of this algorithm is the introduction of a test case filtering link to ensure that only test cases that meet the set goodness threshold can be executed.

From the details of Algorithm 2, the main improvement is the application of the good seed feature model obtained by training the Transformer deep learning model. In addition, we implement unified vectorization of test cases through Python scripts, and perform XOR operations on the binary bitmaps of the test cases before and after mutation to further evaluate the goodness of each test case. By comparing the model prediction results (as shown in Fig. 11) with the XOR results of the test cases before and after mutation, the goodness of the test cases can be effectively evaluated, thereby optimizing the case selection during fuzz testing.

In the above algorithm 2, based on the original fuzz testing framework AFL, the input seed test case is first predicted by using the excellent seed feature model obtained by Transformer training to generate a sequence diagram of the key position of the mutation (*seed_map*). Then, the predicted sequence diagram is vectorized and converted into a binary bitmap (*byte_map*) consisting of 0 and 1.

Then enter the seed mutation stage, mutate the seed test case $s$, and obtain the mutated test case $t$. Then, perform an XOR operation on the seed test cases before and after the mutation to generate a binary bitmap (*changed_map*) of the mutation position. Then, perform a logical AND operation on the bitmap

Algorithm 2: AFL-Transformer Fuzzing

**Input:** Seeds Set $S$
$Q = S$;
**repeat**
  **if** $i > |Q|$ **then**
    $i = 0$;
  **end**
  Choose $s_i$ from $Q$;
  seed_map$_{(s_i)}$ = Transformer Model Predict ($s_i$) ;
  byte_map$_{(s_i)}$ = Vectorize ( seed_map $_{(s_i)}$);
  **if** WasFuzzed ($s_i$) **then**
    $n$ = AssignEnergy ($s_i$) ;
    **for** $j$ from 1 to $n$ **do**
      $t_i$ = Mutate ($s_i$ , Mutation Strategies);
      changed_map $_{(s_i)}$ = $t_i \oplus$ byte_map $_{(s_i)}$;
      **if** $\sum$ changed_map $_{(s_i)} \wedge$ byte_map $_{(s_i)} < \alpha$ **then**
        continue;
      **end**
      res = Execute($t$);
      **if** res = $CRASH$ **then**
        add $t$ to $T_c$;
      **else if** IsInteresting(res) **then**
        add $t$ to $Q$;
      **end**
    **end**
    $i = i + 1$
  **end**
**until** timeout reached or abort-signal;
**Output:** Crash Set $T_c$.

of the mutation position and the previously obtained *byte_map* to obtain a new binary sequence bitmap. Next, perform a sum operation on the binary sequence bitmap, and finally set a threshold $\alpha$ to decide whether to execute the seed test case.

The actual significance of the threshold $\alpha$ is to control the similarity between the seed binary bitmap sequence predicted by the machine learning model and the mutated position binary bitmap generated by the mutated seed. During the experiment, the threshold $\alpha$ can be adjusted dynamically based on indicators such as the runtime data of the application under test and the time interval for new path discovery. For example, when the time interval for discovering new paths is too long, the value of $\alpha$ can be increased to improve the match between the test case and the model-predicted test case, thereby improving the quality of the test case and the efficiency of fuzz testing.

# 6 Experiments and Data Analysis

The optimization algorithm based on the Transformer deep learning network proposed in this chapter mainly includes three parts: data collection and preprocessing module, Transformer training network construction module, and interaction module with the fuzz testing framework AFL. Specifically, Python language is mainly used to implement data collection, preprocessing and the construction of the Transformer training network, while C language is used to embed in the source code of the AFL framework to realize the interaction function with Python scripts.

In order to effectively evaluate the performance of the optimization algorithm proposed in this chapter, the experimental evaluation is carried out from two levels: on the one hand, the effectiveness of the machine learning model is evaluated, and on the other hand, the ability of the optimized fuzz testing framework AFL in vulnerability detection is evaluated. This experiment uses the LAVA-M standard dataset as the evaluation basis. The dataset contains four Linux applications (uniq, md5sum, base64, who), each of which has multiple vulnerabilities embedded in it. In addition, in order to test the applicability and effectiveness of the proposed optimization method in actual software, eight widely used actual software such as readelf, libxml, and libjpeg are also selected for evaluation.

## 6.1 Evaluating the Effectiveness of Machine Learning Models

Since selecting better seeds is the key to the effect of the optimization algorithm, the results obtained by using the machine learning model prediction will directly affect the performance of the AFLTrans optimization algorithm. Therefore, the training results of the model are crucial. The parameters in this experiment are set as follows: batch size is 120, the adaptive momentum optimizer Adam is used, and the learning rate is set to 0.00003. After 6 epochs of training, the model accuracy reached 93% and the loss value was reduced to 20%. This result effectively verifies the effectiveness and accuracy of the model, as shown in Fig. 13.

To further evaluate the effectiveness of the model, this experiment uses a number of indicators that are widely used in machine learning model evaluation, including false positive rate (FPR), false negative rate (FNR), true positive rate (TPR), precision (P), and F1-measure (F1) value. Specifically, when calculating these indicators, the false positive rate (FPR) is defined as the ratio of the number of samples that falsely detect vulnerabilities to the total number of samples that do not have vulnerabilities, where FP represents the number of samples that falsely detect vulnerabilities, and TN is the number of samples that do not detect vulnerabilities. The false positive rate (FPR) can be calculated using the following formula 15:

$$FPR = \frac{FP}{FP + TN} \tag{15}$$

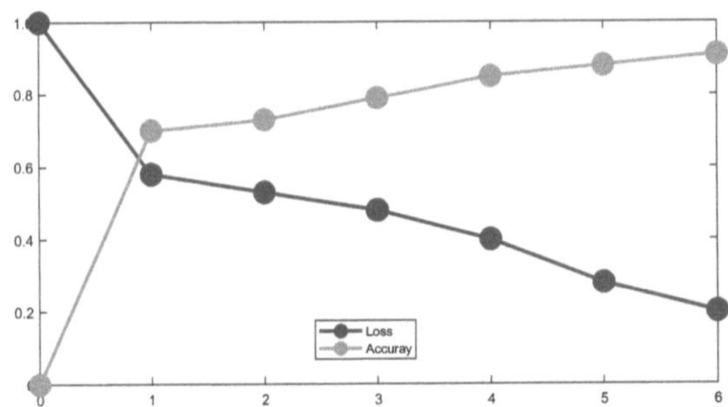


**Fig. 13.** Image of training accuracy and loss value of excellent seed feature model.

Let TP be the number of samples that correctly detect vulnerabilities, FN be the number of samples that fail to detect real vulnerabilities, and the false negative rate (FNR) measures the proportion of samples that fail to identify real vulnerabilities to all vulnerability samples. This indicator can be calculated by the following formula 16:

$$FNR = \frac{FN}{TP + FN} \tag{16}$$

The true positive rate (TPR) indicates the proportion of samples that correctly detect vulnerabilities to all vulnerability samples, which reflects the sensitivity of the model in vulnerability detection. The true positive rate is calculated as 17:

$$TPR = \frac{TP}{TP + FN} \tag{17}$$

Precision (P) is used to measure how many of the vulnerabilities detected by the model are correct. Specifically, it represents the proportion of real vulnerability samples among all samples predicted by the model to be vulnerabilities. Its calculation formula is as follows 18:

$$P = \frac{TP}{TP + FP} \tag{18}$$

In addition, the F1 value is a comprehensive evaluation model that balances the true positive rate (TPR) and precision (P) when detecting vulnerabilities. The higher the F1 value, the better the balance between precision and recall. The calculation formula is as follows: 19:

$$F1 = 2 \cdot \frac{P \cdot TPR}{P + TPR} \tag{19}$$

The F1 value can consider both the false positive rate and the false negative rate, and is used as a comprehensive indicator to evaluate the performance of the model in different test scenarios. These indicators provide an important basis for evaluating the detection performance of the model, especially the effectiveness and accuracy in actual vulnerability detection.

Based on the above evaluation indicators, this experiment selected two datasets for evaluation: the LAVA-M dataset and the Real-World-DataSet containing 8 actual applications. In order to comprehensively evaluate the performance of the improved fuzz testing model AFLTrans proposed in this chapter, the experiment compares it with NeuFuzz. The following Table 2 shows the detailed results of the experimental data:

**Table 2.** AFLTrans and NeuFuzz performance comparison

| Method Model | Dataset | FPR(%) | FNR(%) | TPR(%) | P(%) | F1(%) |
|---|---|---|---|---|---|---|
| AFLTrans | Real-World-DataSet | 7.7 | 7.9 | 92.5 | 92.8 | 92.6 |
| | LAVA-M | - | 20.8 | 80.1 | - | - |
| NeuFuzz | Real-World-DataSet | 7.4 | 8.9 | 91.2 | 92.4 | 91.2 |
| | LAVA-M | - | 20.3 | 78.6 | - | - |

Since the LAVA-M dataset only provides vulnerable programs but lacks patched versions, this experiment mainly considers the comparison between FNR and TPR. From the experimental data Table 2, it can be seen that under the Real-World-DataSet dataset, the AFLTrans model proposed in this paper outperforms the NeuFuzz model in performance. Although the performance on the LAVA-M dataset is slightly inferior to that on the Real-World-DataSet, AFLTrans still achieves an accuracy of 80.1%, which shows that it is significantly effective in identifying code vulnerabilities.

When analyzing the experimental results in detail, it can be found that AFLTrans performs significantly better than NeuFuzz overall, but the performance gap between the two is not significant. From the perspective of optimization mechanism, NeuFuzz uses LSTM deep neural network to train the vulnerability path features in the test program and allocates more mutation energy to seed test cases that cover these vulnerability paths. In contrast, the optimization idea of AFLTrans is to focus on training the binary file features of excellent seed test cases through the Transformer deep learning model, and use the feature model to predict the key mutation positions in the mutation process, thereby filtering invalid test cases based on the model prediction results. This method not only improves the effectiveness of test cases, but also effectively reduces unnecessary calculation and execution overhead.

Through comparative analysis, there are two main reasons why the optimization performance of AFLTrans and NeuFuzz is similar: (1) Both use deep learning neural networks for model training; (2) They both focus on optimizing test cases. However, the reason why AFLTrans performs better than NeuFuzz can be attributed to two aspects:

First, AFLTrans has certain advantages in the selection of neural network models. Specifically, AFLTrans uses a Transformer model with an attention mechanism, which can effectively extract binary sequence features of seed test cases and maintain good performance when processing long sequence data. In contrast, NeuFuzz uses the LSTM model. Although LSTM has certain advantages in processing sequence data, it may not be as efficient as the Transformer model in processing long-term dependencies and feature extraction.

Secondly, the optimization ideas of AFLTrans are significantly different from those of NeuFuzz. AFLTrans directly predicts the key mutation locations in the test cases by filtering based on the features of excellent seed test cases, thereby screening out effective test cases and avoiding the execution of invalid test cases. NeuFuzz, on the other hand, focuses on predictions based on vulnerability paths and concentrates mutation energy on seed test cases that can cover these paths. Although this path-based mutation strategy is effective, AFLTrans can more accurately optimize test cases through feature filtering, thereby improving the efficiency and effectiveness of fuzz testing.

### 6.2 Vulnerability Detection Capability Assessment

In fuzz testing, the number of application crashes is an important indicator of its vulnerability mining ability. The more crashes, the stronger the tool's ability to find potential vulnerabilities. This experiment compares the AFLTrans method with three existing fuzz testing tools, AFLFast, PTfuzz, and QAFL, using two types of datasets: the LAVA-M dataset and eight real applications.

The experimental results on the LAVA-M dataset (see Table 3) show that the AFLTrans method is significantly better than the other three fuzz testing tools in terms of the total number of vulnerabilities found. In addition, from the data in Fig. 3, it can be seen that AFLTrans also performs better than the other three tools in different applications, and the number of vulnerabilities found is generally higher. Therefore, the overall experimental results prove the optimization effect of the AFLTrans method in vulnerability mining (Fig. 14).

**Table 3.** Comparison of the number of vulnerabilities found by AFLTrans in the LAVA-M dataset

| app | Total number of vulnerabilities | AFLTrans | AFLFast | PTfuzz | QAFL |
|---|---|---|---|---|---|
| Uniq | 28 | 6 | 4 | 1 | 5 |
| Md5sum | 57 | 3 | 1 | 0 | 1 |
| Base64 | 44 | 9 | 3 | 2 | 1 |
| Who | 2136 | 4 | 1 | 0 | 3 |
| total | 2 2 6 5 | 2 2 | 9 | 3 | 1 0 |

AFLTrans was compared with the other three fuzz testing tools on the Real-World-DataSet dataset of 8 real Linux applications with the same 24-hour test duration. The experimental results are shown in Table 4. From the table data, it can be seen that in the test of each application, the number of crashes triggered

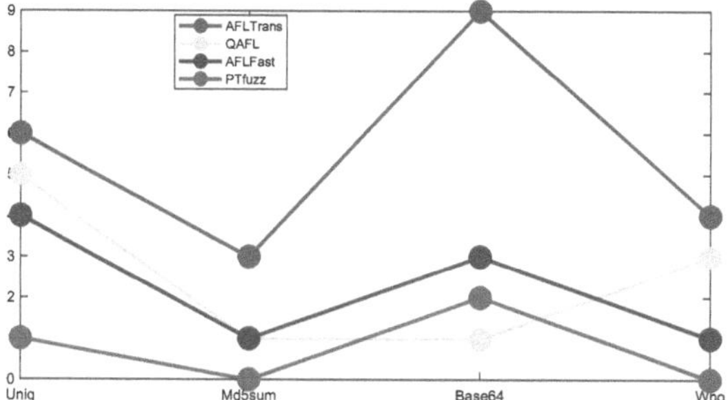


**Fig. 14.** Comparison of the number of vulnerabilities found by AFLTrans in the LAVA-M dataset.

by AFLTrans is higher than that of the other three fuzz testing tools, which shows that this method has strong adaptability and performance advantages when processing seed test cases of different file formats.

**Table 4.** Comparison of the number of vulnerabilities found by AFLTrans in the Real-World-DataSet dataset

| app | Number of vulnerabilities | | | |
|---|---|---|---|---|
| | AFLTrans | AFLFast | PTfuzz | QAFL |
| readelf | 22 | 17 | 7 | 11 |
| libxml | 32 | 20 | 24 | 13 |
| libjpeg | 16 | 6 | 12 | 11 |
| libav | 265 | 187 | 69 | 94 |
| podofo | 376 | 234 | 75 | 87 |
| libsndfile | 7 | 5 | 3 | 5 |
| audiofile | 132 | 62 | 76 | 91 |
| | **9724** | **565** | **287** | **345** |

Further analysis of the data in Table 4 shows that for applications such as readelf, libxml, libjpeg, and libsndfile, the number of crashes triggered is relatively small. This may be related to the differences in the selected application versions. Usually, version updates fix a large number of vulnerabilities in the old version, so choosing a newer version for the experiment will result in a significant reduction in the number of crashes. In order to ensure the rigor of the experimental results, this study strictly controlled the version variables of the application during the experiment to ensure that all fuzz testing tools were tested on the same version of the application, thereby ensuring the validity and comparability of the data.

Experimental results Table 4 also shows that the performance of AFLFast is relatively close to that of AFLTrans. AFLFast optimizes seed test cases through an energy scheduling scheme based on path information. Compared with traditional AFL, its improvement is to optimize the scheduling strategy of seed test cases. AFL mainly selects seed test cases based on code coverage, marking those cases that produce high coverage as "interesting" seeds (favored), while most test cases are discarded. AFL's selection strategy may cause the fuzz testing process to focus too much on high-frequency paths and ignore low-frequency paths, which are often more likely to trigger program crashes. AFLFast effectively improves the performance in the experiment by allocating more energy to low-frequency paths based on path information. The similarity between AFLTrans and AFLFast is that they have both made improvements in the optimization of seed test cases, which is one of the reasons why their performance is close.

In comparison, PTfuzz, which has weaker overall performance, is also optimized based on AFL, but its optimization method is different from AFLTrans and AFLFast. The innovation of PTfuzz is that it removes AFL's dependence on the instrumentation of the tested application, allowing it to test source-free applications without relying on AFL's QEMU mode. Therefore, PTfuzz's optimization performs better in the test of source-free applications, but in the case of source code, its performance is almost the same as AFL. Due to the lack of optimization of seed test cases in PTfuzz, its overall performance is still somewhat behind AFLTrans and AFLFast.

## 7 Summary

This paper mainly discusses a Transformer-based intelligent generative fuzz testing method. Through the Transformer deep learning network, excellent seed test cases are trained and their feature models are extracted to improve the efficiency of fuzz testing and the success rate of vulnerability mining. Specifically, this chapter first introduces the source of the data set used by the machine learning module, and then elaborates on the relevant algorithms in the screening and preprocessing of the excellent seed test case data set. Then, the selection of the training model and the design of the model structure are described in detail. Finally, the trained excellent seed feature model is applied to the test case filtering stage of the fuzz testing framework AFL, and a detailed description of the optimization algorithm is given. In the last section, this chapter evaluates the performance difference between the optimized AFLTrans and several other fuzz testing tools through comparative experiments, conducts data analysis and summarizes the experimental results.

**Acknowledgement.** This work is funded by Open Foundation of Key Laboratory of Cyberspace Security, Ministry of Education (No. KLCS20240202).

## References

1. American fuzzy lop (AFL) (2013). http://lcamtuf.coredump.cx/afl/. Accessed 20 Oct 2023

2. Böhme, M., Pham, V.T., Nguyen, M.D., Roychoudhury, A.: Directed greybox fuzzing. In: Proceedings of the 2017 ACM SIGSAC Conference on Computer and Communications Security, pp. 2329–2344 (2017)
3. Forrester, J.E., Miller, B.P.: An empirical study of the robustness of windows NT applications using random testing. In: Proceedings of the 4th Conference on USENIX Windows Systems Symposium - Volume 4, p. 6. WSS 2000, USENIX Association, USA (2000)
4. Gillioz, A., Casas, J., Mugellini, E., Abou Khaled, O.: Overview of the transformer-based models for NLP tasks. In: 2020 15th Conference on Computer Science and Information Systems (FedCSIS), pp. 179–183. IEEE (2020)
5. Godefroid, P., Levin, M.Y., Molnar, D.A., et al.: Automated whitebox fuzz testing. In: NDSS, vol. 8, pp. 151–166 (2008)
6. Grieco, G., Ceresa, M., Mista, A., Buiras, P.: Quickfuzz testing for fun and profit. J. Syst. Softw. **134**, 340–354 (2017). https://doi.org/10.1016/j.jss.2017.09.018
7. Haller, I., Slowinska, A., Neugschwandtner, M., Bos, H.: Dowsing for {Overflows}: a guided fuzzer to find buffer boundary violations. In: 22nd USENIX Security Symposium (USENIX Security 2013), pp. 49–64 (2013)
8. Herrera, A., Gunadi, H., Magrath, S., Norrish, M., Payer, M., Hosking, A.L.: Seed selection for successful fuzzing. In: Proceedings of the 30th ACM SIGSOFT International Symposium on Software Testing and Analysis, pp. 230–243 (2021)
9. Joffe, L.: Neural networks and search landscapes for software testing. Ph.D. thesis, UCL (University College London) (2020)
10. Lee, M., Cha, S., Oh, H.: Learning seed-adaptive mutation strategies for greybox fuzzing. In: 2023 IEEE/ACM 45th International Conference on Software Engineering (ICSE), pp. 384–396. IEEE (2023)
11. Lee, S., Han, H., Cha, S.K., Son, S.: Montage: a neural network language model-guided javascript engine fuzzer. In: Proceedings of the 29th USENIX Conference on Security Symposium, pp. 2613–2630 (2020)
12. Li, P., Meng, W., Zhang, C.: Sdfuzz: target states driven directed fuzzing. In: Proceedings of the 33rd USENIX Security Symposium (Security), Philadelphia, PA, USA (2024)
13. Li, Y., et al.: V-fuzz: vulnerability prediction-assisted evolutionary fuzzing for binary programs. IEEE Trans. Cybern. **52**(5), 3745–3756 (2020)
14. Lin, P.H., Hong, Z., Li, Y.H., Wu, L.F.: A priority based path searching method for improving hybrid fuzzing. Comput. Secur. **105**, 102242 (2021)
15. Lv, C., Ji, S., Li, Y., Zhou, J., Chen, J., Zhou, P., Chen, J.: Smartseed: smart seed generation for efficient fuzzing. arXiv abs/1807.02606 (2018). https://api.semanticscholar.org/CorpusID:49656556
16. Miller, B.P., Fredriksen, L., So, B.: An empirical study of the reliability of unix utilities. Commun. ACM **33**(12), 32–44 (1990)
17. Oliinyk, Y., Scott, M., Tsang, R., Fang, C., Homayoun, H., et al.: Fuzzing busybox: leveraging LLM and crash reuse for embedded bug unearthing. arXiv preprint arXiv:2403.03897 (2024)
18. Rawat, S., Jain, V., Kumar, A., Cojocar, L., Giuffrida, C., Bos, H.: Vuzzer: application-aware evolutionary fuzzing. In: NDSS, vol. 17, pp. 1–14 (2017)
19. Rong, H., You, W., Wang, X., Mao, T.: Toward unbiased {Multiple-Target} fuzzing with path diversity. In: 33rd USENIX Security Symposium (USENIX Security 2024), pp. 2475–2492 (2024)
20. Sarafov, V., Markvica, D., Berlakovich, F., Bernad, M., Brunthaler, S.: Understanding and improving coverage tracking with AFL++ (registered report). In: Proceedings of the 3rd ACM International Fuzzing Workshop, pp. 80–89 (2024)

21. She, D., Shah, A., Jana, S.: Effective seed scheduling for fuzzing with graph centrality analysis. In: 2022 IEEE Symposium on Security and Privacy (SP), pp. 2194–2211. IEEE (2022)
22. Sofian, D.M., Wang, Z., Li, J.: Interpretation of transformer FRA responses–Part II: influence of transformer structure. IEEE Trans. Power Delivery **25**(4), 2582–2589 (2010)
23. Stephens, N., et al.: Driller: augmenting fuzzing through selective symbolic execution. In: NDSS, vol. 16, pp. 1–16 (2016)
24. Takanen, A., Demott, J.D., Miller, C., Kettunen, A.: Fuzzing for software security testing and quality assurance. Artech House (2018)
25. Wang, T., Wei, T., Gu, G., Zou, W.: Taintscope: a checksum-aware directed fuzzing tool for automatic software vulnerability detection. In: 2010 IEEE Symposium on Security and Privacy, pp. 497–512. IEEE (2010)
26. Wang, W., Chen, Z., Zheng, Z., Wang, H.: An adaptive fuzzing method based on transformer and protocol similarity mutation. Comput. Secur. **129**, 103197 (2023)
27. Wang, W., Chen, Z., Zheng, Z., Wang, H., Luo, J.: MTA fuzzer: a low-repetition rate Modbus TCP fuzzing method based on transformer and mutation target adaptation. Comput. Secur. **144**, 103973 (2024)
28. Xiang, Y., et al.: Critical code guided directed greybox fuzzing for commits. In: 33rd USENIX Security Symposium (USENIX Security 2024), pp. 2459–2474 (2024)
29. Zhang, D., et al.: Simfuzz: test case similarity directed deep fuzzing. J. Syst. Softw. **85**(1), 102–111 (2012). https://doi.org/10.1016/j.jss.2011.07.028. https://www.sciencedirect.com/science/article/pii/S016412121100197X. Dynamic Analysis and Testing of Embedded Software
30. Zhang, G., Zhou, X., Luo, Y., Wu, X., Min, E.: Ptfuzz: guided fuzzing with processor trace feedback. IEEE Access **6**, 37302–37313 (2018)
31. Zhu, X., Wen, S., Camtepe, S., Xiang, Y.: Fuzzing: a survey for roadmap. ACM Comput. Surv. (CSUR) **54**(11s), 1–36 (2022)

# HLSEn: High-Level Semantic Awareness Pseudo-code Encoding for Binary Code Similarity Detection

Yanlin Li[1,2], Lu Zhang[1,2], Song Wang[1,2], Taiyan Wang[1,2], Lu Yu[1,2], Qiangpu Chen[1,2], Yuwei Li[1,2], and Zulie Pan[1,2](✉)

[1] National University of Defense Technology, Hefei 230037, China
[2] Anhui Province Key Laboratory of Cyberspace Security Situation Awareness and Evaluation, Hefei 230037, China
{liyanlin2023,panzulie17}@nudt.edu.cn

**Abstract.** Binary code similarity detection (BCSD) is crucial for software security. Recent deep learning-based methods have made notable progress. However, existing semantic-based methods focus too much on basic instructions, such as stack instructions and register operations, while neglecting the high-level semantics related to functional behavior and implementation logic. To address this issue, we proposed a deep learning-based pseudo-C code-encoding method, HLSEn, to measure the semantic equivalence of functions in different variants. Our approach consists of three steps. First, we preprocess data, converting binary functions into pseudo-C code. Second, we leverage the Siamese network to integrate two CodeBert models to learn the semantic representation of a function from its pseudo-C code. Finally, the similarity detection can be conducted by measuring the similarity between two representation vectors. We use pseudo-C code instead of assembly code to represent functions, which enables the model to learn high-level semantic knowledge during the training process and reduces noise and interference. We implement a prototype of HLSEn. The CodeBert model is trained on a dataset with 20,000 function pairs and evaluated on different sizes of datasets, involving five different cross-optimization option combinations. Evaluation results show that HLSEn outperforms all state-of-the-art (SOTA) methods in terms of MRR. In the vulnerability search task, HLSEn achieves the highest Recall.

**Keywords:** BCSD · Pseudo-C code · CodeBert · Siamese network

## 1 Introduction

BCSD is a critical technique in cybersecurity, including the identification of 1-day vulnerabilities [1,2], detection of malicious code [3], recognition of third-party library components [4,5], investigation of software copyright infringement [6,7], and analysis of security patches [8–10]. It determines whether the function


K.-K. R. Choo et al. (Eds.): ICDF2C 2025, LNICST 686, pp. 491–504, 2026.
https://doi.org/10.1007/978-3-032-22545-0_28

has vulnerabilities by comparing the similarity between the function and known vulnerability functions. With the development of natural language models, some semantic-based SOTA methods regard assembly code as function features and use natural language models such as Bert [11] for training and learning, achieving very good results [12–14]. Although existing semantic-based SOTA methods have made good progress, the following challenge still exists.

Existing semantic-based methods ignore the high-level semantics. The existing methods take assembly code as the feature representation of the function and send it to the model for learning [12,13]. Models based on the self-attention mechanism pay too much attention to low-level implemented instructions, such as stack instructions and register operations, while ignoring the high-level semantics that represent the functionality and semantics of a function [15]. For example, function call operations involve many stack instructions and register operations at the assembly code level. If the model pays excessive attention to these instructions, it will generate similar embedding vectors for the two functions with function call operations. In fact, both functions solely perform the operation of calling other functions, and the operations they implement may not necessarily be the same. So we should pay more attention to high-level semantics.

To address this challenge, we proposed a deep learning-based pseudo-C code-encoding method, HLSEn, to measure the semantic equivalence of functions in different compilation optimization options. Using pseudo-C code to represent functions enables the CodeBert model to pay more attention to the high-level semantics of functions during learning. We evaluate HLSEn across various function pools. The results show that HLSEn outperforms SOTA methods in terms of MRR. With the increase of the function pool, the performance of HLSEn remains very good. We also conduct evaluations in real vulnerability search tasks, and HLSEn is superior to baseline methods.

In summary, our contributions are as follows:

- We present a novel method named HLSEn to encode pseudo-C code with the CodeBert into semantic representation vectors for BCSD. To facilitate the model training, we utilize the Siamese Network to integrate two identical CodeBert models for similarity detection.
- We implement a prototype of HLSEn. For the model training, we build a large-scale cross-compilation optimization options dataset containing 20,000 function pairs, containing five different cross-optimization option combinations. We compare our model against the SOTA methods. The evaluation results show that HLSEn outperforms all of them.
- We evaluate the vulnerability search application. We collected 8,000 firmware functions as the pool of functions to be tested and 4 CVEs as query functions. Experimental results show that HLSEn achieves the best Recall compared with the baselines.

## 2 Background and Relatedworks

### 2.1 BCSD

BCSD is mainly used to identify similarities between binary functions. It has significant applications in security areas such as vulnerability discovery, malware categorization, and intellectual property infringement detection. Recent studies have introduced multiple BCSD approaches, such as graph matching algorithms [16], tree-based analysis methods [17], and feature-based recognition techniques [18].

Deep learning has emerged as a dominant paradigm in BCSD research in recent years [12,19–28], owing to its superior performance in automatic feature learning and handling intricate pattern recognition tasks. The learning-based BCSD research is inspired by the latest developments in Natural Language Processing (NLP) [29–31]. They regard assembly instructions as natural language and use NLP models to learn features to achieve vector embedding of assembly instructions. SAFE [12] and INNEREYE [28] use the skip-gram model in Word2Vec [32] to represent binary code. Asm2Vec [19] uses the NLP model PV-DM [29] to learn assembly instructions.

The method based on deep learning is particularly suitable for large-scale binary code similarity detection. Because they can use the trained model to encode binary code functions and represent the functions as embedding vectors. Then, the cosine value of the vector is used as the similarity of the function. This method has high computational efficiency.

However, the existing semantic-based methods ignore the high-level semantics of functions. We analyze the cases of false positives in existing methods [12] and find that most reasons for false positives stem from natural language models overly focusing on the operational instructions of the underlying implementation, such as stack instructions and register operation instructions. These instructions are the basic operations for implementing the function call. BinAug [15] also raise the same problem. Therefore, we propose to use the pseudo-C code decompiled from the binary as the representation of functions. Pseudo-C code is obtained by disassembling binary code to obtain assembly code and then decompiling it. It is a language similar to C code that can represent the high-level semantics of functions while ignoring the fundamental instructions of the underlying implementation. Using pseudo-C code to represent functions can reduce noise and interference during model training.

### 2.2 Problem Definition

**Definition** (BCSD Task). Given a query function $f_q$ and a function pool $P$ to be tested, the task of BCSD is to identify the most similar $K$ functions $\{f_1, f_2, ..., f_K \mid f_i \in P\}$.

# 3 Methodology

## 3.1 Overview of the Framework

To solve the challenge presented by Sect. 1, we propose using pseudo-C code as a high-level semantic representation of functions for the model to learn. As shown in Fig. 1, our method is divided into three steps: data preprocessing, model training, and similarity comparison. First, we utilize disassembly tools to decompile binary functions and obtain pseudo-C code. Second, we integrate two CodeBert models using a Siamese network for model training to obtain the encoding model. Finally, we use the trained CodeBert to encode the pseudo-C code of the function, converting each function into an embedding vector. We calculate the cosine similarity between the vulnerability function and each function in the function pool as the similarity between the functions. Then we sort the similarity and select Top K as the possible vulnerability function. Security researchers can manually review whether the K functions have vulnerabilities.

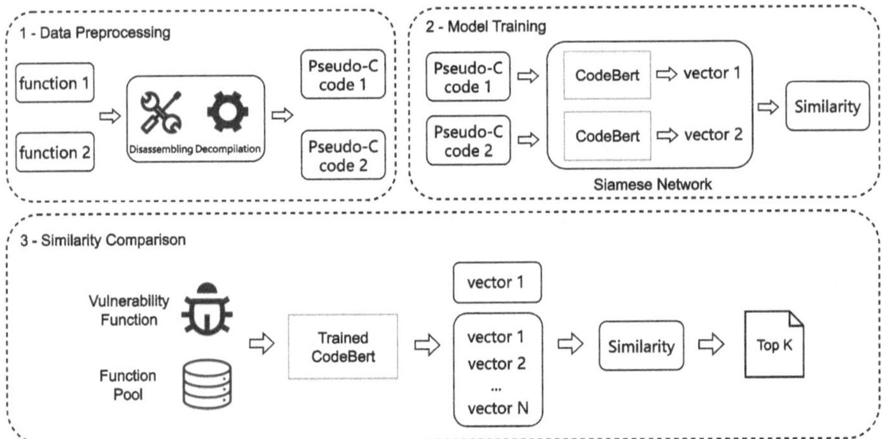


**Fig. 1.** System Overview. The system workflow comprises three steps: data preprocessing, model training, and similarity comparison.

## 3.2 Data Preprocessing

The existing semantic-based methods use assembly instructions as the representation of functions. When training natural language models, too much attention is given to the basic instructions, such as stack instructions and register instructions. These instructions do not represent the high-level semantics of the function, instead, they are just the basic operations for function call. As shown in Fig. 2, the function on the left implements calling the "sum" function to calculate the sum of the two variables. The function on the right implements calling the "jian" function to calculate the difference between two variables. However, when comparing the assembly instructions of these two functions, only the one circled in the red box is different. The rest of the assembly instructions are exactly the same. Therefore, such highly similar assembly instructions are very likely to cause interference with the model during training. When the model encodes pseudo-code, it is likely to generate similar embedding vectors for the two functions, thereby causing false positives. We don't need to pay attention to these underlying implementation instructions when comparing similarities. Therefore, we select pseudo-C code to represent the function, which can effectively solve this problem.

We utilize r2ghidra for disassembling and decompiling binary functions to obtain pseudo-C code. R2ghidra is an integration of the Ghidra decompiler for radare2. To avoid the model judging the similarity of functions through the function names, we uniformly change the function names to "func_name".

```
; int __fastcall main(int argc, const char **argv, const char **envp)
public main
main proc near

var_C= dword ptr -0Ch
var_8= dword ptr -8
var_4= dword ptr -4

; __unwind {
endbr64
push    rbp
mov     rbp, rsp
sub     rsp, 10h
mov     [rbp+var_C], 11h
mov     [rbp+var_8], 9
mov     edx, [rbp+var_8]
mov     eax, [rbp+var_C]
mov     esi, edx
mov     edi, eax
call    sum
mov     [rbp+var_4], eax
mov     eax, [rbp+var_4]
mov     esi, eax
lea     rax, format      ; "Sum: %d\n"
mov     rdi, rax         ; format
mov     eax, 0
call    _printf
mov     eax, 0
leave
retn
; } // starts at 1161
main endp

_text ends
```

```
; int __fastcall main(int argc, const char **argv, const char **envp)
public main
main proc near

var_C= dword ptr -0Ch
var_8= dword ptr -8
var_4= dword ptr -4

; __unwind {
endbr64
push    rbp
mov     rbp, rsp
sub     rsp, 10h
mov     [rbp+var_C], 11h
mov     [rbp+var_8], 9
mov     edx, [rbp+var_8]
mov     eax, [rbp+var_C]
mov     esi, edx
mov     edi, eax
call    jian
mov     [rbp+var_4], eax
mov     eax, [rbp+var_4]
mov     esi, eax
lea     rax, format      ; "Cha: %d\n"
mov     rdi, rax         ; format
mov     eax, 0
call    _printf
mov     eax, 0
leave
retn
; } // starts at 115F
main endp

_text ends
```

**Fig. 2.** Comparison of assembly instructions for two different functions.

### 3.3 Model Training

We use the Siamese Network to integrate two identical CodeBert models for training.

**CodeBert.** CodeBert is a dual-modal extension of Bert that demonstrates a strong understanding of source code. CodeBert uses natural language and source code as its input. CodeBert has two pre-training objectives: Masked Language Modeling (MLM) and Replacement Token Detection (RTD).

- **MLM.** It selects a set of random positions for programming language (PL) and natural language (NL) to mask them, and then replaces the selected positions with a special [MASK] tag. The goal of MLM is to predict the masked original markers.
- **RTD.** In the original PL sequence and NL sequence, a small portion of the tags will be randomly masked. Train a generator model, which is a probabilistic model similar to n-gram for generating masked words. Then, train a discriminator model to determine whether a word is the original word. NL-Code discriminator is the targeted pre-trained model. Both NL and code generators are thrown out in the fine-tuning step.

**Siamese Network.** The Siamese Network is often used to measure the similarity of inputs by comparing the distances between the two input feature vectors. The weights are shared between its two sub-networks, CodeBert. Its input is $< P1, P2, label >$. $P1$ and $P2$ represent the vectors of the pseudo-code of the two functions encoded by CodeBert. Label represents whether two functions have the same origin, with values of 0 and 1. When the label is 1, it indicates that the two functions are of the same origin; when it is 0, they are functions of different origins. During the training process, we use the loss to adjust the model weights, as shown in the Eq. 1 and 2. The Margin defines the minimum distance between negative sample pairs. It will only be penalized when the cosine distance between negative sample pairs is less than the Margin, ensuring that samples of different categories maintain sufficient intervals in the embedding space. Here, we set Margin = 1.

$$\text{cosDist}(P_1, P_2) = 1 - \frac{P_1 \cdot P_2}{||P_1|| ||P_2||} \tag{1}$$

$$\text{Loss} = \text{label} \cdot \text{cosDist}^2(P_1, P_2) + (1 - \text{label}) \cdot \max(\text{Margin} - \text{cosDist}(P_1, P_2), 0)^2 \tag{2}$$

### 3.4 Similarity Comparison

We use the trained CodeBert to encode the function. First, we disassemble and decompile the binary function to obtain pseudo-C code. Then we input the pseudo-C code into the CodeBert model and encode it. Finally, we transform functions into embedding vectors, mapping each function to a spatial vector. We represent the similarity of the two functions by calculating the cosine similarity of the corresponding spatial vectors.

The most common scenario of BCSD is to detect whether the functions in the pool of functions to be tested have known vulnerabilities. We can first encode the known vulnerability function and functions to be tested in the function pool using trained CodeBert. Then, we calculate the similarity between the known vulnerability function and each function in the pool of functions to be tested. Next, we sort all the similarities in descending order. The function with a higher ranking is more likely to have known vulnerabilities. We select the Top K function as the possible vulnerability function. Security researchers can manually analyze these K functions further to determine whether there are known vulnerabilities.

# 4 Experimental Setup

## 4.1 Experiment Settings

The base model we are using is codebert-base. The training parameters are set as follows: batch size = 16, learning rate = 2e-5, epochs = 10. The training dataset consists of 20000 pieces of data, among which 10,000 are positive samples and 10,000 are negative samples.

## 4.2 Datasets

**BinaryCorp Dataset-26M** [13]. This dataset contains 46,513 binary files. It comes from the official repository of Arch Linux and the Arch user repository, and has undergone various optimized compilations using GCC 11.0 on X64. We construct five datasets of cross-optimization options, namely (O0,O3), (O1,O3), (O2,O3), (O0,Os), and (O2,Os), which are respectively used as the training set and the test set.

## 4.3 Baselines

- **Asm2Vec** [19]. This method utilizes the PVDM model to learn the representation of function semantics from binary assembly code.
- **SAFE** [12]. Safe uses word2vec [32] to directly encode assembly instructions without the need for manual feature extraction.
- **GMN** [33]. GMN uses graph embedding to represent functions as vectors.
- **CLAP** [34]. This method uses LLM to generate training datasets and aligns assembly code with natural language for learning, to better represent functions as vectors.

## 4.4 Evaluation Metrics

Let there be a binary function pool F, and its corresponding truth function pool G.

$$F = \{f_1, f_2, \dots, f_i, \dots, f_n\} \tag{3}$$

$$G = \{f_1^{gt}, f_2^{gt}, \dots, f_i^{gt}, \dots, f_n^{gt}\} \tag{4}$$

We denote a query function $f_i \in F$ and its corresponding ground truth function $f_i^{gt} \in G$. This study addresses the binary similarity detection problem, aiming to retrieve the Top K functions in the function pool $G$ that are most similar to $f_i$. The returned functions are ranked by a similarity score, where $Rank_{f_i^{gt}}$ denotes the position of the ground truth function in the retrieved list.

Let $I_i$ indicate whether the Ground Truth is retained in the $i$-th query. The calculation is provided in Eq. 5, and the overall Recall@K is computed as shown in Eq. 6. The calculation formula of MRR is shown in Eq. 7.

$$I_i = \begin{cases} 0, Rank_{f_i^{gt}} > K \\ 1, Rank_{f_i^{gt}} <= K \end{cases} \tag{5}$$

$$\text{Recall@K} = \frac{1}{n}\sum_{i=1}^{n} I_i \tag{6}$$

$$\text{MRR} = \frac{1}{n}\sum_{i=1}^{n}\frac{1}{Rank_{f_i^{gt}}} \tag{7}$$

# 5 Evaluation

Our evaluation aims to answer the following questions.

**RQ1.** How does the performance of HLSEn compare with the baselines?

**RQ2.** How do HLSEn and baseline perform at different function pool sizes?

**RQ3.** How does HLSEn perform in real vulnerability detection?

## 5.1 BCSD Performance (RQ1)

Based on BinaryCorp Dataset-26M, we construct function pools by randomly selecting binaries, with pool size = 32 and pool size = 1000. So that we can make evaluations at different levels of difficulty. We use two metrics, MRR and Recall@1, to measure the performance of our approach.

**Small Pool (Poolsize = 32).** As shown in Table 1 and Table 2, the MRR and Recall@1 of CLAP outperformed HLSEn in (O0, O3). The MRR of SAFE exceeds that of HLSEn, and Recall@1 is equal to HLSEn in (O2, O3). The MRR and Recall@1 of HLSEn are at their highest values for the remaining three cross-optimization options. Moreover, the average value of the five scenarios of HLSEn is also the maximum value. This indicates that our method, HLSEn, has significant advantages in simple scenarios such as small function pools.

**Large Pool (Poolsize = 1000).** As shown in Table 3 and Table 4, the MRR of SAFE is higher than that of HLSEn in (O1, O3) and (O2, O3). The Recall@1 of SAFE is higher than that of HLSEn in (O2, O3). In the rest of the scenarios, both MRR and Recall@1 of HLSEn are at their maximum values. It indicates that our method performs very well in the large function pool.

## 5.2 The Effects of Poolsize on Performance (RQ2)

Considering that previous studies used relatively small function pools, ranging from 10 to 200, and even some studies used function pools of size 2 [13]. In real vulnerability search, the size of the function pool is usually large. Therefore, we

**Table 1.** The MRR of different BCSD methods (Poolsize = 32).

| Approach | (O0,O3) | (O1,O3) | (O2,O3) | (O0,Os) | (O2,Os) | Average |
|---|---|---|---|---|---|---|
| Asm2Vec | 0.125 | 0.627 | 0.901 | 0.242 | 0.746 | 0.528 |
| SAFE | 0.777 | 0.802 | 0.942 | 0.717 | 0.906 | 0.829 |
| GMN | 0.194 | 0.599 | 0.898 | 0.304 | 0.734 | 0.546 |
| CLAP | 0.816 | 0.797 | 0.904 | 0.706 | 0.891 | 0.823 |
| HLSEn | 0.802 | 0.858 | 0.933 | 0.837 | 0.942 | **0.874** |

**Table 2.** The Recall@1 of different BCSD methods (Poolsize = 32).

| Approach | (O0,O3) | (O1,O3) | (O2,O3) | (O0,Os) | (O2,Os) | Average |
|---|---|---|---|---|---|---|
| Asm2Vec | 0.062 | 0.500 | 0.875 | 0.156 | 0.625 | 0.444 |
| SAFE | 0.688 | 0.719 | 0.906 | 0.594 | 0.844 | 0.750 |
| GMN | 0.031 | 0.469 | 0.875 | 0.156 | 0.656 | 0.437 |
| CLAP | 0.750 | 0.688 | 0.875 | 0.531 | 0.812 | 0.731 |
| HLSEn | 0.719 | 0.781 | 0.906 | 0.719 | 0.938 | **0.813** |

thoroughly explored the impact of function pools of varying sizes on the BCSD method.

We construct multiple groups of experiments using a combination of five cross-optimization options, and the pool sizes are 2, 10, 32, 128, 512, and 1000. The result is shown in Fig. 3. As the size of the function pool increases, the MRR of HLSEn is larger than all baselines in the two combinations of (O1, O3) and (O0, Os). In the scenario of (O2, O3), the effects of all methods are very good, which is due to their low difficulty. Although HLSEn may be surpassed in some function pool sizes, its performance has consistently remained high at (O0, O3) and (O2, Os). The average value of the five optimization options shows that HLSEn is usually at its maximum value.

It should be noted that when considering small function pools, the advantage of HLSEn is less apparent compared to other methods. However, as the function pool increases, the trend of MRR reduction in HLSEn is slower than in other

**Table 3.** The MRR of different BCSD methods (Poolsize = 1000).

| Approach | (O0,O3) | (O1,O3) | (O2,O3) | (O0,Os) | (O2,Os) | Average |
|---|---|---|---|---|---|---|
| Asm2Vec | 0.042 | 0.305 | 0.704 | 0.029 | 0.491 | 0.314 |
| SAFE | 0.270 | 0.634 | 0.842 | 0.373 | 0.680 | 0.560 |
| GMN | 0.049 | 0.353 | 0.758 | 0.048 | 0.453 | 0.332 |
| CLAP | 0.351 | 0.612 | 0.796 | 0.383 | 0.637 | 0.556 |
| HLSEn | 0.494 | 0.629 | 0.817 | 0.614 | 0.690 | **0.649** |

**Table 4.** The Recall@1 of different BCSD methods (Poolsize = 1000).

| Approach | (O0,O3) | (O1,O3) | (O2,O3) | (O0,Os) | (O2,Os) | Average |
|---|---|---|---|---|---|---|
| Asm2Vec | 0.028 | 0.232 | 0.659 | 0.012 | 0.421 | 0.270 |
| SAFE | 0.162 | 0.551 | 0.818 | 0.251 | 0.611 | 0.479 |
| GMN | 0.034 | 0.291 | 0.733 | 0.026 | 0.395 | 0.296 |
| CLAP | 0.250 | 0.531 | 0.749 | 0.287 | 0.551 | 0.474 |
| HLSEn | 0.397 | 0.557 | 0.774 | 0.523 | 0.621 | **0.574** |

methods. In the case of a large function pool, the advantages of HLSEn are particularly obvious.

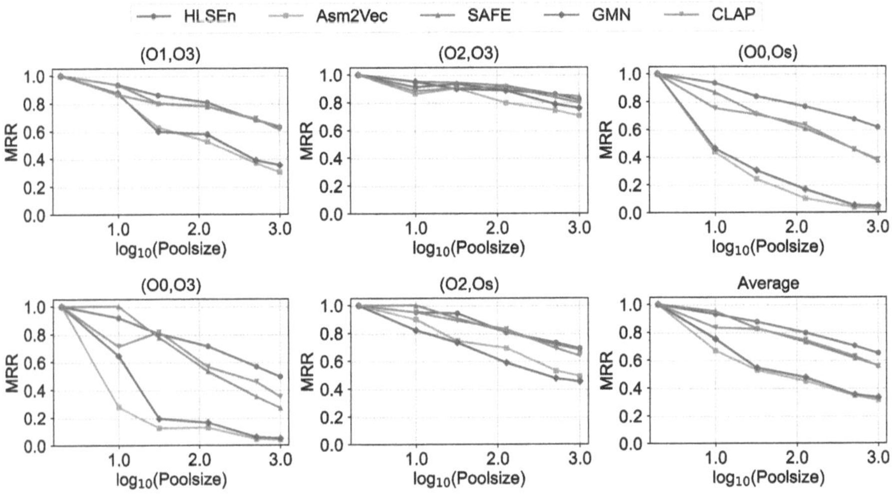


**Fig. 3.** The performance of different BCSD methods in different function pool sizes.

## 5.3 Real-World Vulnerability Search (RQ3)

Vulnerability search is the primary application of BCSD in actual computer security. To verify the practicability of HLSEn, we evaluate it in the vulnerability search task. We select four public CVEs, as shown in Table 5. We generate 10 variants for each CVE and compile them into different architectures (ARM, x86-64) using optimization options (O0, O1, O2, O3, Os). We take each of the 10 variants of a CVE as the query function, while the remaining nine serve as the truth functions. Together with 8,000 functions from projects, these functions form the pool of functions to be tested. For each query, there are 9 true value functions in the pool of functions to be tested. Therefore, we use Recall@9 as

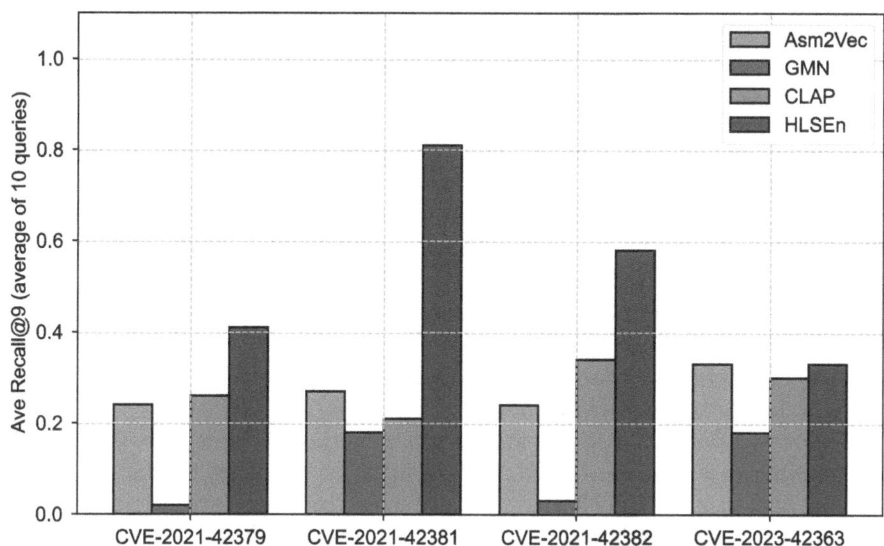


**Fig. 4.** Recall@9 of real-world vulnerability search.

the metric. Then, we use the mean of Recall@9 from 10 queries of a CVE as the evaluation metric.

The experimental results are shown in Fig. 4. We compare our method with Asm2Vec, GMN, and CLAP. The performance of HLSEn is higher than that of the other three baselines. For example, for CVE-2021-42381, we conduct vulnerability queries in a function pool of size 8009. We select one of the 10 variants of the vulnerability function in sequence as the query function and the other nine as the truth function to construct a total of 10 query combinations. For each query, we calculate Recall@9. Then the average value of the 10 queries is taken as the final measurement index. In this vulnerability query, our method reaches 0.81, while Asm2Vec, GMN, and CLAP are 0.27, 0.18, and 0.21. Our results show that HLSEn can be effectively applied in vulnerability search scenarios and performs well in large-scale function pools.

**Table 5.** The information of CVEs.

| CVE | Binary | Version | Function |
|---|---|---|---|
| CVE-2021-42379 | busybox | v1.34.0 | next_input_file() |
| CVE-2021-42381 | busybox | v1.34.0 | hash_init() |
| CVE-2021-42382 | busybox | v1.34.0 | getvar_s() |
| CVE-2023-42363 | busybox | v1.36.1 | xasprintf() |

## 6 Conclusion

In this paper, we propose a binary code similarity detection method based on high-level semantics. Based on deep learning methods, the Siamese network combines two CodeBerts to learn the pseudo-C code of the function. HLSEn alleviates the problem of existing methods overly focusing on basic instructions. Experimental results show that the average MRR of HLSEn is the highest. As the function pool size increases, the performance of HLSEn consistently remains strong. In vulnerability detection tasks, we selected four CVEs as query functions. Each CVE is compiled into 10 variants, including ARM and x86-64 architectures, and the compilation options are O0, O1, O2, O3, and Os. We compare Recall@9 of different methods for each CVE. The experimental results show that HLSEn achieves the best performance.

The overall performance of learning-based methods will decline as the function pool increases. In the future, we will focus on reducing the impact of the function pool size on the effectiveness of binary code similarity detection. For special cases, such as when the compiler fails to correctly identify variables or structures, resulting in significant semantic differences, our method has certain limitations. In the future, we will use graph-structured information to make up for this deficiency.

## References

1. Ahn, S., Ahn, S., Koo, H., Paek, Y.: Practical binary code similarity detection with BERT-based transferable similarity learning. In: Proceedings of the 38th Annual Computer Security Applications Conference, pp. 361–374 (2022)
2. Luo, Z., et al.: Vulhawk: cross-architecture vulnerability detection with entropy-based binary code search. In: NDSS (2023)
3. Kim, T., Lee, Y.R., Kang, B., Im, E.G.: Binary executable file similarity calculation using function matching. J. Supercomput. **75**, 607–622 (2019)
4. Tang, W., Luo, P., Fu, J., Zhang, D.: Libdx: a cross-platform and accurate system to detect third-party libraries in binary code. In: 2020 IEEE 27th International Conference on Software Analysis, Evolution and Reengineering (SANER), pp. 104–115. IEEE (2020)
5. Zhu, X., Wang, J., Fang, Z., Yin, X., Liu, S.: Bbdetector: a precise and scalable third-party library detection in binary executables with fine-grained function-level features. Appl. Sci. **13**(1), 413 (2022)
6. Luo, L., Ming, J., Wu, D., Liu, P., Zhu, S.: Semantics-based obfuscation-resilient binary code similarity comparison with applications to software plagiarism detection. In: Proceedings of the 22nd ACM SIGSOFT International Symposium on Foundations of Software Engineering, pp. 389–400 (2014)
7. Luo, L., Ming, J., Wu, D., Liu, P., Zhu, S.: Semantics-based obfuscation-resilient binary code similarity comparison with applications to software and algorithm plagiarism detection. IEEE Trans. Software Eng. **43**(12), 1157–1177 (2017)
8. Hu, Y., Zhang, Y., Li, J., Gu, D.: Cross-architecture binary semantics understanding via similar code comparison. In: 2016 IEEE 23rd International Conference on Software Analysis, Evolution, and Reengineering (SANER), vol. 1, pp. 57–67. IEEE (2016)

9. Kargén, U., Shahmehri, N.: Towards robust instruction-level trace alignment of binary code. In: 2017 32nd IEEE/ACM International Conference on Automated Software Engineering (ASE), pp. 342–352. IEEE (2017)
10. Xu, Z., Chen, B., Chandramohan, M., Liu, Y., Song, F.: Spain: security patch analysis for binaries towards understanding the pain and pills. In: 2017 IEEE/ACM 39th International Conference on Software Engineering (ICSE), pp. 462–472. IEEE (2017)
11. Devlin, J., Chang, M.W., Lee, K., Toutanova, K.: Bert: pre-training of deep bidirectional transformers for language understanding. In: Proceedings of the 2019 Conference of the North American chapter of the Association for Computational Linguistics: Human Language Technologies, vol. 1 (Long and Short Papers), pp. 4171–4186 (2019)
12. Massarelli, L., Di Luna, G.A., Petroni, F., Baldoni, R., Querzoni, L.: SAFE: self-attentive function embeddings for binary similarity. In: Perdisci, R., Maurice, C., Giacinto, G., Almgren, M. (eds.) DIMVA 2019. LNCS, vol. 11543, pp. 309–329. Springer, Cham (2019). https://doi.org/10.1007/978-3-030-22038-9_15
13. Wang, H., et al.: jtrans: jump-aware transformer for binary code similarity. arXiv preprint arXiv:2205.12713 (2022)
14. Wang, H., et al.: Cebin: a cost-effective framework for large-scale binary code similarity detection. In: Proceedings of the 33rd ACM SIGSOFT International Symposium on Software Testing and Analysis, pp. 149–161 (2024)
15. Wong, W.K., Wang, H., Li, Z., Wang, S.: Binaug: enhancing binary similarity analysis with low-cost input repairing. In: Proceedings of the 46th IEEE/ACM International Conference on Software Engineering, pp. 1–13 (2024)
16. Gao, D., Reiter, M.K., Song, D.: BinHunt: automatically finding semantic differences in binary programs. In: Chen, L., Ryan, M.D., Wang, G. (eds.) ICICS 2008. LNCS, vol. 5308, pp. 238–255. Springer, Heidelberg (2008). https://doi.org/10.1007/978-3-540-88625-9_16
17. Pewny, J., Schuster, F., Bernhard, L., Holz, T., Rossow, C.: Leveraging semantic signatures for bug search in binary programs. In: Proceedings of the 30th Annual Computer Security Applications Conference, pp. 406–415 (2014)
18. Nouh, L., Rahimian, A., Mouheb, D., Debbabi, M., Hanna, A.: BinSign: fingerprinting binary functions to support automated analysis of code executables. In: De Capitani di Vimercati, S., Martinelli, F. (eds.) SEC 2017. IAICT, vol. 502, pp. 341–355. Springer, Cham (2017). https://doi.org/10.1007/978-3-319-58469-0_23
19. Ding, S.H., Fung, B.C., Charland, P.: Asm2vec: boosting static representation robustness for binary clone search against code obfuscation and compiler optimization. In: 2019 IEEE Symposium on Security and Privacy (SP), pp. 472–489. IEEE (2019)
20. Duan, Y., Li, X., Wang, J., Yin, H., et al.: Deepbindiff: learning program-wide code representations for binary diffing (2020)
21. Gao, J., Yang, X., Fu, Y., Jiang, Y., Sun, J.: Vulseeker: a semantic learning based vulnerability seeker for cross-platform binary. In: Proceedings of the 33rd ACM/IEEE International Conference on Automated Software Engineering, pp. 896–899 (2018)
22. Liu, B., et al.: $\alpha$diff: cross-version binary code similarity detection with DNN. In: Proceedings of the 33rd ACM/IEEE International Conference on Automated Software Engineering, pp. 667–678 (2018)
23. Massarelli, L., Di Luna, G.A., Petroni, F., Querzoni, L., Baldoni, R., et al.: Investigating graph embedding neural networks with unsupervised features extraction for

binary analysis. In: Proceedings of the 2nd Workshop on Binary Analysis Research (BAR), pp. 1–11 (2019)
24. Redmond, K., Luo, L., Zeng, Q.: A cross-architecture instruction embedding model for natural language processing-inspired binary code analysis. arXiv preprint arXiv:1812.09652 (2018)
25. Xu, X., Liu, C., Feng, Q., Yin, H., Song, L., Song, D.: Neural network-based graph embedding for cross-platform binary code similarity detection. In: Proceedings of the 2017 ACM SIGSAC Conference on Computer and Communications Security, pp. 363–376 (2017)
26. Yang, J., Fu, C., Liu, X.Y., Yin, H., Zhou, P.: Codee: a tensor embedding scheme for binary code search. IEEE Trans. Software Eng. **48**(7), 2224–2244 (2021)
27. Yu, Z., Cao, R., Tang, Q., Nie, S., Huang, J., Wu, S.: Order matters: semantic-aware neural networks for binary code similarity detection. In: Proceedings of the AAAI Conference on Artificial Intelligence, vol. 34, pp. 1145–1152 (2020)
28. Zuo, F., Li, X., Young, P., Luo, L., Zeng, Q., Zhang, Z.: Neural machine translation inspired binary code similarity comparison beyond function pairs. arXiv preprint arXiv:1808.04706 (2018)
29. Le, Q., Mikolov, T.: Distributed representations of sentences and documents. In: International Conference on Machine Learning, pp. 1188–1196. PMLR (2014)
30. Mikolov, T., Chen, K., Corrado, G., Dean, J.: Efficient estimation of word representations in vector space. arXiv preprint arXiv:1301.3781 (2013)
31. Sutskever, I., Vinyals, O., Le, Q.V.: Sequence to sequence learning with neural networks. In: Advances in Neural Information Processing Systems, vol. 27 (2014)
32. Mikolov, T., Sutskever, I., Chen, K., Corrado, G.S., Dean, J.: Distributed representations of words and phrases and their compositionality. In: Advances in Neural Information Processing Systems, vol. 26 (2013)
33. Li, Y., Gu, C., Dullien, T., Vinyals, O., Kohli, P.: Graph matching networks for learning the similarity of graph structured objects. In: International Conference on Machine Learning, pp. 3835–3845. PMLR (2019)
34. Wang, H., et al.: Clap: learning transferable binary code representations with natural language supervision. In: Proceedings of the 33rd ACM SIGSOFT International Symposium on Software Testing and Analysis, pp. 503–515 (2024)

# SolDataVul-LLaMA Dataset: A LLM-Driven Construction Method and Detection Research of Smart Contract Vulnerability Dataset in Data Trading Scenarios

Wenjie Li[1], Leixiao Li[2,3](✉), Dongjiang Liu[1], Jinze Du[4], Hao Lin[4], and Zhexu Liu[1]

[1] Inner Mongolia University of Technology, Hohhot 010080, China
[2] Key Laboratory of Cyberspace Security in Northern China, Inner Mongolia Autonomous Region, 010080 Hohhot, China
llx-happy@126.com
[3] Big Data–Based Software Service Engineering Research Center, Inner Mongolia Autonomous Region, 010080 Hohhot, China
[4] Tianjin University of Technology, Tianjin 300384, China

**Abstract.** Smart contracts play a critical role in data trading. To address the lack of datasets specific to this scenario, this paper proposes a dataset construction methodology that combines large language models with template-based vulnerability injection. Based on the Solidity language, we integrate the CodeLlama model with human-controlled injection strategies to construct SolDataVul-LLaMA, a multi-label da-taset containing 6,852 samples across 20 vulnerability types. The dataset covers key aspects such as identity authentication, data ownership confirmation, and data exchange.Building on this dataset, we define binary and multi-class vulnerability detection tasks, and conduct evaluations using four fundamental models: RNN, LSTM, GRU, and BiGRU. Experimental results demonstrate that baseline mod-els trained on SolDataVul-LLaMA can successfully detect frequent vulnerabili-ties in data trading, such as Data double-spending vulnerability. Notably, the BiGRU model achieved a detection score of 54.55%, validating the dataset's utility in supporting both decision boundary learning and generalization assessment. The dataset and its injection framework have been open-sourced

**Keywords:** Data Trading · Smart Contract · Dataset Construction · Vulnerability Detection · Large Language Model (LLM)

## 1 Introduction

Smart contracts play a vital role in data trading platforms by enabling key functions such as identity registration, data upload, pricing, access control, and settlement [1–3]. As shown in Fig. 1, they autonomously govern the entire trading workflow, ensuring fairness, automation, and traceability [4]. In smart contract–based data trading workflows:(1)


K.-K. R. Choo et al. (Eds.): ICDF2C 2025, LNICST 686, pp. 505–523, 2026.
https://doi.org/10.1007/978-3-032-22545-0_29

Parties register identities via smart contracts, generating unique IDs. (2) Data owners upload data and define access policies, automatically enforced by the contract [5]. (3) The contract verifies requester balance and runs an auction to set the price.[1]. (4) After payment, results are delivered and transaction details are logged on-chain. (5) Funds are then distributed and data is deleted.

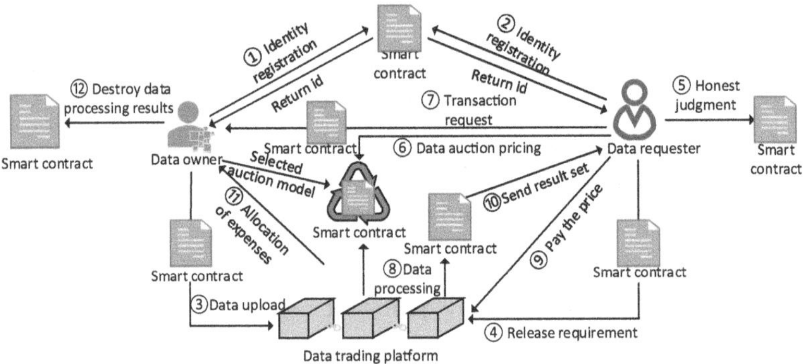


**Fig. 1.** Smart Contract–Driven Data Trading Process

## 2 Related Work

In recent years, LLMs have been increasingly adopted for task-specific dataset construction to reduce annotation costs and improve sample quality. Ventura et al. [6] proposed a method to mine semantically related video title pairs and generate descriptive text using LLMs, enabling efficient creation of image-text-image triplets. However, their work focuses on cross-modal retrieval and lacks structured labeling control. Huang et al. [7] introduced a semi-automated framework for generating KBQA datasets using LLMs to produce question templates and SPARQL queries. While effective for static mappings, it fails to capture the program semantics and structural dependencies found in smart contracts. Separately, efforts like SGDL [8] combined static analysis and adversarial generation to inject vulnerability fragments under abstract syntax tree structures, improving syntax validity and sample diversity. Yet, these approaches still rely on fragment matching and struggle to ensure semantic coherence or adapt to complex.

Due to the lack of targeted vulnerability datasets for smart contracts in data trading scenarios, existing datasets fail to capture the domain-specific semantic patterns and attack types, thereby limiting model adaptability and the effectiveness of generalization evaluations. To address this gap, we propose a dataset generation method that integrates the CodeLlama large code model with a template-based injection strategy. The proposed approach involves key steps such as raw data collection and preprocessing, vulnerability template definition, and multi-round injection procedures. It systematically constructs a collection of contract samples that cover both typical vulnerabilities

[1] https://github.com/LM-MachineLearning/SolDataVul-LLaMA-Dataset#

and frequently occurring security issues in data trading processes. Additionally, we conduct a comprehensive statistical analysis of the dataset [9], providing a solid foundation for subsequent model training and evaluation. With the work presented in this paper, the following contributions are made:

• A We propose a large language model-based injection method constrained by vulnerability templates, enabling CodeLlama to generate diverse and structurally complex vulnerable contract samples while preserving Solidity syntax correctness.

• B. We construct a smart contract vulnerability dataset specifically tailored for data trading scenarios, covering both real-world contract corpora and representative vulnerability types, thus filling a critical gap in domain-specific vulnerability datasets.

• C. We perform a detailed structural and label distribution analysis to demonstrate that the dataset possesses desirable characteristics in terms of coverage, balance, and complexity, making it a strong foundation for advancing smart contract security research in data trading applications.

## 3 Methodology Design

As shown in Fig. 2, this paper presents a structured dataset construction workflow. It consists of two main stages: original contract collection and preprocessing, and an automated injection strategy driven by the large language model CodeLlama. The pipeline balances semantic coverage, vulnerability diversity, and structural controllability, ensuring the dataset is both challenging and effective for model evaluation [10].

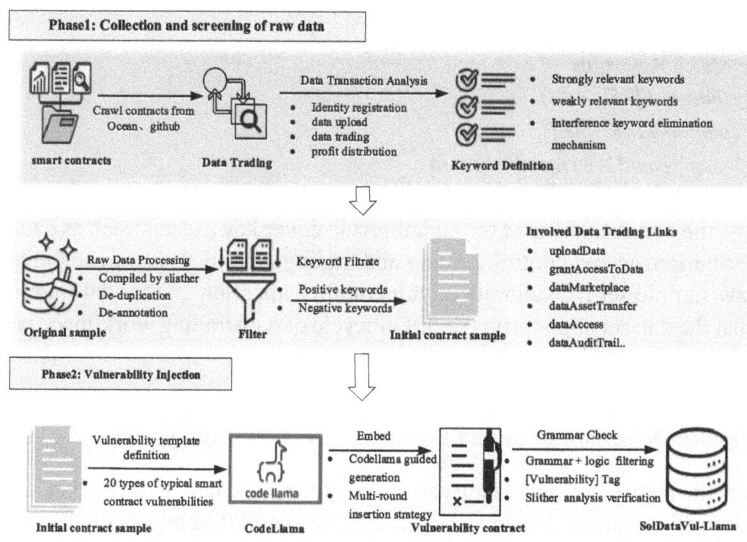


**Fig. 2.** Dataset Construction Workflow

### 3.1 Contract Collection and Preprocessing

To construct a relevant contract corpus, we crawled and collected smart contract source code samples from various domestic and international open data trading platforms, including Ocean Protocol, Streamr Network, and iExec RLC, as well as from public repositories such as GitHub and the Ethereum blockchain [11]. After cleaning and deduplication, a total of 984 original contracts were retained.

To accurately identify contracts related to data trading, we proposed a rule-based automated filtering strategy that integrates keyword matching with semantic exclusion. Specifically, we defined more than 30 strongly and weakly correlated positive keywords, such as upload Data, grantAccessToData, data authorization, on-chain publishing, and data pricing [12] to capture core functionalities. To avoid misclassifying financial protocols such as automated market makers and cross-chain bridges, or time-based scheduling contracts involving scheduled automation [13], we additionally introduced two sets of exclusionary keywords. The complete filtering logic is formalized in Algorithm 1.

---

**Algorithm 1.** Initial Collection and Filtering Rules for Smart Contract Samples

**Input:** Contract Corpus Set: $S = \{S_1, S_2, ...., S_N\}$

**Output:** $\hat{S} = \{\hat{S}_1, \hat{S}_2, ...., \hat{S}_N\} \in$ {data trading}

1:Step 1: Define the Set of Positive Keywords $K\_pos$

2:Step2: Define two sets of exclusionary keywords:

3: $K\_neg\_finance \leftarrow$ {swap, router, token, feePercent }

4: $K\_neg\_schedule \leftarrow$ {scheduler, lockUntil, scheduledTransaction }

5: $K\_neg : K\_neg \leftarrow K\_neg\_finance \cup K\_neg\_schedule$

6:Step3:Read Contract Source Code Text $T_i \leftarrow S_i \in S$

7:Step4: Match Keywords

8: $pos\_count \leftarrow (T_i, K\_pos)$

9: $nge\_count \leftarrow (T_i, K\_neg)$

10:Step5: $neg\_count \geq 3$ Directly discard

---

Finally, the contracts filtered through this rule cover key aspects such as data ownership confirmation, access control, pricing and trading, and historical traceability, forming the raw sample set for subsequent vulnerability injection and model training. This ensures that the dataset aligns with the full lifecycle of data trading workflows, providing a representative foundation for downstream analysis.

### 3.2 Template Definition of Smart Contract Vulnerability Types

To enhance the instruction-following capability of the large language model CodeLlama during the injection phase and improve the effectiveness of vulnerability insertion, this paper systematically constructs a total of 60 high-quality injection templates covering 20 representative smart contract vulnerability types. As shown in Table 1, these templates encapsulate the semantic characteristics, triggering conditions, and structural patterns of each vulnerability type. The goal is to provide clear contextual constraints and injection guidance to CodeLlama [14], thereby reducing the likelihood of generating invalid or semantically inconsistent code fragments and improving the syntactic correctness and semantic validity of the injected samples.

**Table 1.** Example Vulnerability Snippets from Data Trading Smart Contracts

| | Vulnerability | Core template of vulnerability code |
|---|---|---|
| Common vulnerabilities | Access Control Vulnerability | ① “function setPrice(uint newPrice) public {price = newPrice;\n}”<br>② “function grantAdminRole(address user) public {ad mins[user] = true;\n}”<br>③ “function changeOwner(address newOwner) public {owner = newOwner;\n}” |
| | Reentrancy Vulnerability | ①(bool sent,) = msg.sender.call{value: balance[msg.sender]};<br>require(sent);<br>balance[msg.sender] = 0;<br>② function claimRefund() public {<br>uint refund = balances[msg.sender];<br>require(refund >0);<br>(bool ok,) = msg.sender.call{value: refund}(““);<br>require();<br>balances[msg.sender] = 0;}<br>③ (bool sent,) = msg.sender.call{value: 1 ether};<br>require(sent); |
| High-frequency vulnerabilities in data trading | Data double-spending vulnerability | ① require(!usedHashes[h], “Already used”);<br>usedHashes[h] = true;<br>②<br>require(dataRecord[dataHash] == 0);<br>dataRecord[dataHash] = block.timestamp;<br>③ require(!used[key]);<br>used[key] = true; |

(*continued*)

**Table 1.** (*continued*)

| | Vulnerability | Core template of vulnerability code |
|---|---|---|
| | Data leakage vulnerability | ① string public sensitiveData;<br>function storeData(string memory d) public{<br>sensitiveData = d;}<br>② mapping(address = > string) private userInfo;<br>function leakInfo() public view returns (string memory){<br>return userInfo[msg.sender];}<br>③ mapping(address = > bytes) internalEncrypt edStorage;<br>function publicQuery() public view returns (bytes memory) {<br>return internalEncryptedStor age[msg.sender];} |

## 3.3 Vulnerability Injection with the CodeLlama Model

Based on the original contract samples, this study introduces the CodeLlama model to achieve diverse vulnerability injection. CodeLlama [15], developed by Meta, is a large language model designed for code generation and understanding. It can produce code structures that conform to Solidity syntax and semantic logic under predefined constraints. To enhance the rationality and diversity of injected samples, we design a structured prompting strategy [16] and incorporate partial sample guidance to prevent the model from generating overly similar or semantically inconsistent outputs.Specifically, we feed the vulnerability type definitions, contract source code, injection templates, and the expected number of injections into the codellama-7b model. A multi-round iterative injection mechanism is employed to control the complexity of the generated content, thereby ensuring the diversity and representativeness of vulnerability samples in the dataset. An illustrative example of the injection prompt template, which facilitates the process, is showcased in Table 2.

**Table 2.** Prompt Templates for Vulnerability Injection

| You are a senior security auditor specializing in Solidity smart contracts with years of professional experience. Your task is to inject a real, syntactically correct, and exploitable vulnerability into the following smart contract. |
|---|
| ===Injection Rules=== |

(*continued*)

**Table 2.** (*continued*)

| |
|---|
| 1. Inject only the vulnerabilities listed below.<br>2. Understand the semantic structure of the contract, choose an appropriate vulner ability, and adapt the given prompt template accordingly during injection.<br>3. Add a vulnerability comment at the injection point using the format:<br>// [Vulner ability] {vuln_name}'. |
| Vulnerabilities to Inject: {vuln_name}:\n{vuln_code} |
| Contract Source Code: {code} |

This prompt is designed to guide the large language model in generating syntactically correct vulnerability samples with identifiable exploit paths. The placeholder {vuln_code} represents the injection template. The parameter settings of the CodeLlama model are shown in Table 3.

**Table 3.** Model Parameters

| Parameter | Description |
|---|---|
| TopP: 1 | Allow the model to freely sample from all possible tokens. |
| Temperature: 0.8 | Introduce a certain degree of sampling diversity to avoid generating templated content. |
| Max Tokens: 2048 | Control the maximum token length for a single generation. |
| Context Length: 6144 | Support for large-context injection scenarios. |
| Threads / GPU | 6 CPU threads, 32 GPU layers. |

To construct a vulnerability dataset for smart contracts with rich diversity and semantic complexity, this study adopts a hybrid strategy that combines template-driven design with multi-round injection. Specifically, for 20 common vulnerability types, three high-quality injection templates are predefined for each category, specifying the behavioral scope, coding style, and annotation conventions. These templates are embedded as prompts into the CodeLlama generation context.

The injection process proceeds in multiple rounds to perturb the original contract samples: in the first round, 300 contracts are randomly selected, each injected with one randomly chosen vulnerability; In the second round, 300 contracts were randomly selected again, and each contract was injected with two types of vulnerabilities. A total of six such rounds are Injection. Additionally, 200 more contracts are randomly selected and each is injected with one representative vulnerability, ensuring full coverage of all 20 types. This approach enhances both semantic complexity and multi-label characteristics in the resulting dataset. To maintain logical consistency during injection, hard constraints are applied within the prompts, ensuring that only specified vulnerabilities are inserted. The system further filters the generated outputs to retain only those that include the 'pragma solidity' directive and the correct annotation tag '// [Vulnerability]', thereby discarding structurally invalid or failed samples. Given the limited availability of data trading-related contract samples, the study also performs semantic augmentation on original samples through function renaming and logic restructuring. The Slither tool is used for static analysis to verify the absence of vulnerabilities in these contracts [17], which are then included as negative samples. In total, the final dataset—SolDataVul-LLaMA contains 6,852 smart contract files labeled with multiple vulnerabilities, providing a valuable resource for evaluating detection models in the context of data trading.

# 4 Experiments and Analysis

The analysis carried out in our experiments is aimed atinvestigating three main research questions (RQs) as follows.

RQ1: Can the semantic structure and multi-label distribution characteristics of the constructed dataset—evaluated through label distribution visualizations—demonstrate its representativeness and structural validity?

RQ2: To what extent can the constructed dataset support effective binary vulnerability detection by different time-series models while reflecting model differentiation and classification difficulty?

RQ3: Can the dataset enable accurate multi-class vulnerability detection and generalization by supporting fine-grained semantic learning across multiple vulnerability types in realistic security scenarios?

## 4.1 Visualization Analysis of Vulnerability Distribution in the Dataset(RQ1)

To objectively examine the label distribution characteristics of the SolDataVul-LLaMA dataset, all vulnerability names and code comments were removed from the contract samples to avoid potential bias in subsequent model training. The number of vulnerability types present in each contract was then counted. Fig. 3 illustrates the distribution of contract samples containing 1 to N vulnerability labels.

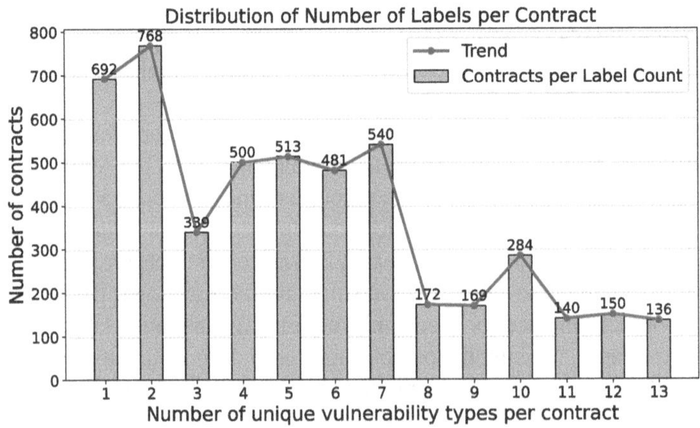


**Fig. 3.** Distribution of Vulnerability Labels per Contract

Fig. 3 presents the distribution of the number of vulnerability types contained in each contract within the SolDataVul-LLaMA dataset. As shown, contracts containing 1–2 vulnerability types constitute the vast majority, with 692 and 768 samples respectively, significantly exceeding other categories. This pattern aligns with common characteristics observed in real-world smart contract security scenarios, where most contracts typically expose only a limited number of vulnerability types, and cases involving multiple complex co-existing vulnerabilities are relatively rare. The detailed distribution of vulnerability types is provided in Table 4.

**Table 4.** Vulnerability Label Distribution

| Number of Labels | Number of Contract Samples | Proportion of Samples |
|---|---|---|
| 0 | 1968 | 28.7% |
| 1–2 | 1460 | 21.3% |
| 3–7 | 2373 | 35.4% |
| 8–10 | 625 | 9.1% |
| 11–13 | 426 | 6.2% |
| Total | 6852 | 100% |

As the number of vulnerability types among contract increases, the number of contracts shows a decreasing trend. However, a notable density is retained within the 4–7 label range, indicating that the multi-label samples generated via LLM-based injection preserve practical plausibility while enhancing structural complexity and diversity.

In multi-label tasks, class balance significantly affects model performance. To evaluate the global label distribution, we visualized the injection frequency of each vulnerability type as a heatmap. As shown in Fig. 4, this reveals the overall distributional balance of labels across the dataset.

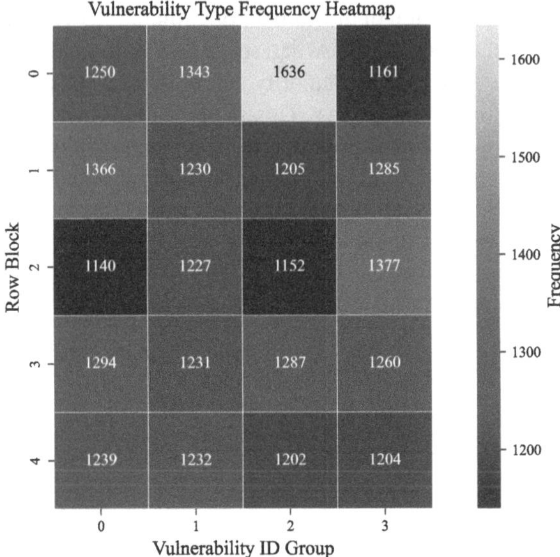


**Fig. 4.** Heatmap of Injection Frequencies for Each Vulnerability Type

Fig. 4 presents a heatmap illustrating the injection frequency of each vulnerability type across the constructed dataset. Each cell reflects how many times a particular vulnerability type was injected into the contract corpus, with higher values indicating more frequent occurrences. As shown, the overall distribution relatively balanced, with most vulnerability types occurring between 1150 and 1350 times. This suggests that the dataset construction process achieved broad and sufficient coverage across all defined vulnerability types.

Notably, certain types exhibit higher-than-average frequencies—for example, the cell at position (0,2) reaches 1636, implying that this particular vulnerability is either easier to inject or more compatible with diverse contract structures. Overall, the dataset maintains a well-balanced injection distribution while ensuring broad vulnerability coverage, thereby providing a solid foundation for evaluating model generalization and fairness in downstream multi-label vulnerability detection tasks.

To further quantify the semantic complexity and multi-label characteristics of SolDataVul-LLaMA, we calculated label cardinality and label density as defined in Eqs. (1, 2), which are widely adopted in multi-label learning literature [18].

**Label cardinality**, measures the average number of labels assigned per sample:

$$Cardinality = \frac{1}{N}\sum_{i=1}^{N} \mid Y_i \mid \tag{1}$$

**Label density**, further normalizes label cardinality by the total number of available labels $L$ capturing the proportion of active labels per sample:

$$Density = \frac{1}{N}\sum_{i=1}^{N} \frac{\mid Y_i \mid}{L} \tag{2}$$

where $N$ denotes the number of contract samples, $Yi$ is the label set assigned to the $i$-th sample, and $L$ represents the total number of defined vulnerability labels in the dataset.

Based on Eqs. (1) and (2), the computed label cardinality is 3.6954, and the label density is 0.1848. These results indicate that each contract, on average, contains multiple co-existing vulnerabilities, while maintaining a moderate level of sparsity. This reflects the dataset's semantic richness and structural realism, providing a solid foundation for evaluating multi-label detection models in practical smart contract scenarios. In addition, we conducted a formal comparative analysis of the vulnerability distribution in the dataset. Compared with the SolidiFI benchmark dataset [19], our KL divergence is 0.089, which further validates the practicality and representativeness of our dataset.

## 4.2 Performance Comparison in Binary Vulnerability Detection(RQ2)

Based on the need for an objective evaluation of the proposed dataset's effectiveness, this study adopts a set of widely used, structurally simple baseline sequence models [20]. By avoiding architecture-level enhancements, we aim to isolate the impact of the dataset itself on model performance, enabling a clearer assessment of its discriminative power for different vulnerability types while minimizing interference from model complexity. Specifically, four representative baseline models are selected in this work: RNN, LSTM [21], GRU, and BiGRU.

To comprehensively evaluate the performance of the selected models in smart contract vulnerability detection and to validate the effectiveness of the proposed dataset, we conducted binary classification experiments on both the HuangGai and SolDataVul-LLaMA datasets. The evaluation was based on four standard metrics: Accuracy, Recall, Precision, and F1-score. HuangGai is a publicly available Solidity dataset constructed via vulnerability injection. It contains 4,744 contract files and covers 16 common vulnerability types. Its data scale and label structure are comparable to those of SolDataVul-LLaMA, making it a suitable benchmark for performance comparison. The results, presented in Table 5, demonstrate the comparative performance of each model on the two datasets.

**Table 5.** Binary Classification Performance on HuangGai and SolDataVul-LLaMA

| DataSet | Model | Accuracy | Recall | Precision | F1-score |
|---|---|---|---|---|---|
| HuangGai [22] | RNN | 67.85% | 68.01% | 67.69% | 67.85% |
| | LSTM | 83.46% | 68.99% | 67.33% | 68.15% |
| | GRU | 83.77% | 68.93% | 67.89% | 68.41% |
| | BiGRU | 83.88% | 69.66% | 68.13% | 68.89% |
| SolDataVul-LLaMA | RNN | 89.06% | 92.08% | 92.46% | 92.27% |
| | LSTM | 92.12% | 93.72% | 95.09% | 94.40% |
| | GRU | 94.75% | 94.55% | 97.97% | 96.23% |
| | BiGRU | 96.79% | 98.05% | 96.79% | 97.74% |

The results indicate a noticeable performance gap between the two datasets across all models, with all models achieving consistently higher scores on the SolDataVul-LLaMA dataset. Notably, the BiGRU model attained an F1-score of up to 97.74%. While this suggests enhanced recognition capabilities on SolDataVul-LLaMA, it also raises concerns about abnormally high metrics. Considering the experimental setup, it is possible that the models have not genuinely learned generalizable patterns for vulnerability detection, but rather memorized specific syntactic or structural cues. Several factors may contribute to this phenomenon, including:

(1) The semantic gap between positive and negative samples is significant, making them easily separable and prone to overfitting;

(2) Many positive samples exhibit high structural redundancy, often following fixed template patterns;

(3) Structural similarities exist between training and test samples, leading to potential data leakage [23].

To mitigate these issues, we adopted a structure-aware partitioning strategy [24], which clusters contracts based on structural features such as call graphs and inheritance hierarchies. This aims to ensure structural decoupling between the training and test sets. However, the retrained models still reported unusually high accuracy, indicating that the root cause may reside elsewhere.

Further analysis revealed an inherent domain shift between positive and negative samples: Positive samples are drawn from data transaction scenarios and revolve around operations like data asset authorization, access control, and trading. In contrast, negative samples were selected using tools such as Slither and Mythril, primarily comprising generic token contracts with little semantic relevance to data transaction contexts. Experimental results in Table 6 further support this observation.

To address this semantic imbalance, we introduced a negative sample augmentation strategy. Based on over 900 verified clean contracts, we applied control-flow transformations, semantics-preserving renaming [25], and informative comment insertion to synthesize a more diverse and realistic set of negative samples. Models were retrained on the enhanced dataset, and the updated evaluation results are presented below.

**Table 6.** Experimental Results of Models on the Enhanced SolDataVul-LLaMA Dataset

| Model | Accuracy | Recall | Precision | F1-score |
|---|---|---|---|---|
| RNN | 61.98% | 64.71% | 86.84% | 74.16% |
| LSTM | 76.03% | 81.13% | 89.25% | 83.12% |
| GRU | 74.38% | 81.37% | 87.37% | 84.26% |
| BiGRU | 79.34% | 83.33% | 91.40% | 87.18% |

As shown in Tables 5 and 6, model performance on the enhanced SolDataVul-LLaMA dataset declined compared to the initial experiment. For instance, the accuracy of the BiGRU model dropped from 96.79% to 79.34%, and the F1-score decreased from 97.74% to 87.18%.

This performance shift validates our prior analysis, confirming that the earlier overestimated metrics were primarily caused by a semantic mismatch between positive and negative samples, which led to model overfitting.

In comparison with the HuangGai dataset, SolDataVul-LLaMA demonstrates superior generalization and increased detection difficulty. Although models achieved around 86% accuracy on HuangGai, their F1-scores remained around 68%, indicating a notable imbalance between precision and recall. This performance gap reflects the difference in dataset design philosophies: HuangGai emphasizes scale and type coverage, whereas SolDataVul-LLaMA prioritizes semantic complexity and contextual relevance. This suggests that HuangGai has fuzzy label boundaries and limited semantic distinction, making it difficult for models to capture nuanced vulnerability characteristics. In contrast, SolDataVul-LLaMA enabled all models to achieve significantly higher F1-scores (up to 87.18%), indicating clearer semantic boundaries and better label separability.

This advantage is attributed to the structured augmentation and semantic injection strategies employed during the construction of SolDataVul-LLaMA. These methods preserved the logic consistency of smart contracts while enhancing label diversity and density. Such design ensures the dataset captures both surface-level patterns and deeper behavioral semantics, providing a more comprehensive evaluation of model robustness. The resulting multi-label characteristics imposed greater task complexity and encouraged fine-grained semantic learning, thereby improving the models' generalization capabilities.

In summary, SolDataVul-LLaMA outperforms HuangGai not only in terms of overall performance metrics but also in structural design, label distribution, and semantic representativeness. These strengths position it as a more realistic and challenging benchmark for evaluating multi-label vulnerability detection models in smart contract security. Future work may explore the incorporation of fuzzy boundary samples or real-world exploit cases [26] to further examine model robustness under weak supervision or high semantic ambiguity.

To better understand the training dynamics, we also plotted the loss curves of the four baseline models on the training and validation sets, as shown in Fig. 5. All models exhibited rapid convergence in the early training stages, and the validation loss remained closely aligned with the training loss, indicating no apparent overfitting. Notably, BiGRU achieved the fastest convergence and the smallest loss gap between training and validation, further confirming its stability and generalization in binary vulnerability detection tasks.

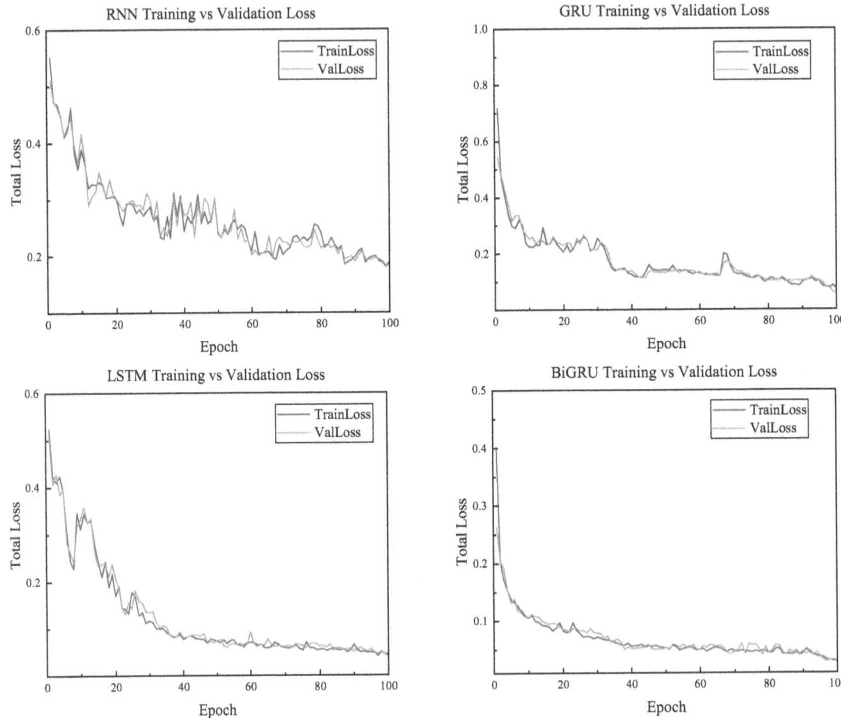


**Fig. 5.** Loss Convergence Curves of Each Model on Training and Validation Sets

### 4.3 Performance Comparison in Multiclass Vulnerability Detection (RQ3)

To evaluate the applicability of the constructed dataset in multi-class classification tasks, we further conducted vulnerability detection experiments on both the SolDataVul-LLaMA and SmartBugs-Wild datasets. Table 7 presents a comprehensive performance comparison across four metrics—Accuracy, Recall, Precision, and F1-score—for three representative vulnerability types (Reentrancy, Tx.origin, and Timestamp Dependency), highlighting the detection effectiveness of different models under various datasets.

**Table 7.** Multi-Class Detection Performance on SolDataVul-LLaMA and SmartBugs-Wild

| DataSet | Vulnerability | performance metrics | Models | | | |
|---|---|---|---|---|---|---|
| | | | RNN | LSTM | GRU | BiGRU |
| SolDataVul-Llama | Reentrancy | Accuracy | 68.77% | 79.28% | 77.18% | 80.63% |
| | | Recall | 80.95% | 58.10% | 67.62% | 57.14% |
| | | Precision | 31.14% | 39.35% | 37.57% | 41.67% |
| | | F1-score | 44.97% | 46.92% | 48.30% | 48.19% |

*(continued)*

**Table 7.** *(continued)*

| DataSet | Vulnerability | performance metrics | Models | | | |
|---|---|---|---|---|---|---|
| | | | RNN | LSTM | GRU | BiGRU |
| | Tx.origin | Accuracy | 79.13% | 78.83% | 81.98% | 84.23% |
| | | Recall | 66.94% | 63.71% | 66.13% | 45.97% |
| | | Precision | 45.86% | 45.14% | 51.25% | 60.00% |
| | | F1-score | 54.43% | 52.84% | 57.75% | 52.05% |
| | Timestamp dependency | Accuracy | 74.17% | 74.47% | 74.77% | 80.33% |
| | | Recall | 68.50% | 42.52% | 49.61% | 50.39% |
| | | Precision | 39.73% | 35.76% | 37.72% | 48.48% |
| | | F1-score | 50.29% | 38.85% | 42.86% | 49.42% |
| SmartBugs-Wild [27] | Reentrancy | Accuracy | 72.28% | 86.02% | 83.48% | 89.78% |
| | | Recall | 52.54% | 62.56% | 74.19% | 79.89% |
| | | Precision | 57.40% | 87.18% | 72.35% | 87.48% |
| | | F1-score | 54.86% | 72.84% | 73.23% | 83.51% |
| | Tx.origin | Accuracy | 64.06% | 73.57% | 72.11% | 74.43% |
| | | Recall | 52.66% | 70.41% | 69.94% | 70.03% |
| | | Precision | 73.57% | 79.08% | 72.26% | 79.67% |
| | | F1-score | 61.38% | 74.50% | 71.8% | 74.54% |
| | Timestamp dependency | Accuracy | 65.76% | 74.24% | 79.02% | 80.29% |
| | | Recall | 54.78% | 51.33% | 42.89% | 53.26% |
| | | Precision | 61.46% | 56.85% | 82.11% | 69.21% |
| | | F1-score | 57.97% | 53.95% | 56.81% | 60.20% |

As shown in Table 7, SolDataVul-LLaMA presents a more semantically challenging detection environment compared to SmartBugs-Wild. Although the F1-scores on SolDataVul-LLaMA are generally lower, this reflects its increased difficulty in terms of semantic modeling and label boundary identification. Nonetheless, the dataset also exhibits notable advantages across several dimensions.

For example, in detecting Tx.origin vulnerabilities, the BiGRU model achieves a precision of 60.00% on SolDataVul-LLaMA, outperforming GRU's 51.25% and LSTM's 45.14% on SmartBugs-Wild. Similarly, for Timestamp Dependency, the RNN model reaches an F1-score of 50.29% on SolDataVul-LLaMA, compared to 44.09% on SmartBugs-Wild. These results indicate that SolDataVul-LLaMA supports more robust pattern learning, even under complex semantic conditions.

Analysis of the precision–recall balance reveals greater semantic sparsity in SolDataVul-LLaMA. While precision is generally lower, recall remains relatively stable—for instance, For instance, in the Tx.origin detection task, BiGRU's precision drops from 79.67% on SmartBugs-Wild to 60.00% on SolDataVul-LLaMA, yet its recall remains above 65%. This indicates that despite increased false positives, the model retains strong recall—an essential trait in security tasks where missed detections are often more costly than over-identification.

In summary, despite slightly lower scores, SolDataVul-LLaMA's structural guidance, balanced label construction, and semantic diversity offer a more realistic and challenging benchmark for evaluating multi-class vulnerability detection.

To better demonstrate SolDataVul-LLaMA's coverage of domain-specific risks,Table 8 conducts multi-model evaluation and comparative analysis on two specific types of vulnerabilities that are prone to occur in data trading contracts but rarely appear in general scenarios - data double-spending attacks and data ownership forgery.

**Table 8.** Benchmarking Detection for Data Trading Contract Vulnerabilities

| DataSet | Vulnerability | performance metrics | Models | | | |
|---|---|---|---|---|---|---|
| | | | RNN | LSTM | GRU | BiGRU |
| SolDataVul-Llama | Data double spend attack | Accuracy | 71.77% | 77.03% | 76.58% | 84.98% |
| | | Recall | 76.42% | 56.10% | 55.28% | 48.78% |
| | | Precision | 37.15% | 41.07% | 40.24% | 61.86% |
| | | F1-score | 50.02% | 47.42% | 46.58% | 54.55% |
| | Data ownership forgery | Accuracy | 73.87% | 79.73% | 74.32% | 80.93% |
| | | Recall | 68.50% | 60.63% | 69.29% | 44.09% |
| | | Precision | 39.37% | 47.53% | 40.00% | 50.00% |
| | | F1-score | 50.08% | 53.29% | 50.72% | 46.86% |

The experimental results reveal significant performance variation among models for these two vulnerability types, which are closely tied to data ownership and trustworthy record-keeping. This highlights the structural complexity and semantic challenges inherent in detecting such vulnerabilities.

For the data double-spending attack detection task, the BiGRU model delivers the best overall performance, achieving an accuracy of 84.98% and a precision of 61.86%. These results suggest that BiGRU is particularly effective in handling cross-function state dependencies and conflict detection. The RNN model, while only reaching 37.15% precision, achieves the highest recall at 76.42%, indicating a stronger tendency to capture potential positive instances and broader coverage of relevant samples. This trade-off reflects the model's higher sensitivity to anomalous patterns, even at the cost of false positives, which may be useful in early-stage vulnerability screening.

In the data ownership forgery task, model performance is generally closer. GRU and BiGRU maintain moderate levels of accuracy and precision, with BiGRU achieving 80.93% accuracy and 50.00% precision. However, none of the models exceed an F1-score of 54%, reflecting the semantic ambiguity and trigger variability of this vulnerability type. This suggests that models struggle to learn stable patterns for such cases, and further improvement in modeling strategies and feature representation is needed. Notably, the low F1-scores in this task also point to the need for more expressive training data and possibly structural supervision to guide learning. Enhancing the contextual richness of training samples or integrating auxiliary task signals may be effective directions for future work.

## 5 Conclusion

In view of the problem that the existing public vulnerability datasets mostly focus on general or financial contracts and lack targeted context coverage,this paper proposes a dataset construction method tailored for vulnerability detection in data trading scenarios. By integrating CodeLlama, a large language model, with a template-guided injection strategy, we systematically build the SolDataVul-LLaMA dataset. SolDataVul-LLaMA is based on Solidity contracts and covers 20 representative vulnerability types. Each type is injected using 3 carefully designed templates, resulting in a total of 6,852 labeled samples. The dataset focuses on critical Link of data trading, including data ownership confirmation, data upload, access control, and transaction tracking. Furthermore, In this paper, binary classification and multi-classification experiments were conducted on the SolDataVul-LLaMA dataset on multiple benchmark models. The results show that SolDataVul-LLaMA can effectively reveal the model differences and verify its value in detection accuracy, generalization ability and robustness analysis.

In future work, we plan to further enrich the dataset context and enhance the injection strategy by incorporating structural modeling and semantic augmentation, aiming to advance vulnerability detection toward higher accuracy and stronger adaptability.

**Acknowledgments.** This work was supported by the National Natural Science Foundation of China (No.62362055), National Key Research and Development Program of China (No. 2023YFB2703900), Program for Young Talents of Science and Technology in Universities of Inner Mongolia Autonomous Region (No.NJYT22084, No.NJYT24035), Inner Mongolia Natu-ral Science Foundation (No.2023MS06008), Scientific research projects of universities directly under the Inner Mongolia Autonomous Region (No.JY20220061, No.JY20230119, No.JY20230019), Science and Technology Plan Project of Inner Mongolia (No. 2024SKYPT0012), Ordos Key R&D Program Projects (No.YF20232328).

## References

1. Xia, L., Baghaie, S., Sajadi, S.M.: The digital economy: challenges and opportunities in the new era of technology and electronic communications. Ain Shams Eng. J. **15**(2), 173–181 (2024)
2. Gu, B., Hu, W.W., Gong, S.M., et al.: CBDTF: a distributed and trustworthy data trading framework for Mobile Crowdsensing. IEEE Trans. Veh. Technol. **73**(3), 4207–4218 (2024)
3. Osei, S.B., Huang, R., Ma, Z.: An attention-based wide and deep neural network for Reentrancy vulnerability detection in smart contracts. J. Syst. Softw. **223**, 112361 (2025)
4. Ghaleb, A., Rubin, J., Pattabiraman, K.: Achecker: statically detecting smart contract access control vulnerabilities. In: Proceedings of the 45th IEEE/ACM International Conference on Software Engineering (ICSE), pp. 945–956. IEEE Computer Society, Los Alamitos (2023).
5. Chen, W., Huo, R., Sun, C., et al.: Efficient and non-Repudiable data trading scheme based on state channels and Stackelberg game. IEEE Trans. Mob. Comput. (2024)

6. Ventura, L., Yang, A., Schmid, C., et al.: CoVR-2: automatic data construction for composed video retrieval. IEEE Trans. Pattern Anal. Mach. Intell. **46**(12), 11409–11421 (2024)
7. Hoang, L., Liausvia, F., Liu, Y., et al.: Semi-automated construction of complex Knowledge Base question answering dataset using large language model. In: Joint European Conference on Machine Learning and Knowledge Discovery in Databases, pp. 230–248. Springer, Cham (2024)
8. Chu, H., Zhang, P., Dong, H., et al.: SGDL: smart contract vulnerability generation via deep learning. J. Softw.: Evol. Process. **36**(12), e2712 (2024)
9. Yan, X., Zhang, H., Wu, Y., et al.: Construction instance segmentation (CIS) dataset for deep learning-based computer vision. Autom. Constr. **156**, 105083 (2023)
10. Ma, J., Meng, Y., Yan, W., et al.: Addressing data scarcity in crack detection via CrackModel: a novel dataset synthesis approach. Buildings. **15**(7), 1053 (2025)
11. Peilin Zheng B S., Luo, X., Chen, T., Zhang, N., Zheng, Z.: LENT-SSE: Leveraging Executed and Near Transactions for Speculative Symbolic Execution of Smart Contracts. ISSTA Technical Papers (2024).
12. Merlec, M.M., In, H.P.: DataMesh plus: a Blockchain-powered peer-to-peer data exchange model for self-sovereign data marketplaces. Sensors. **24**(6), 1–27 (2024)
13. Pasqua, M., Benini, A., Contro, F., et al.: Enhancing Ethereum smart-contracts static analysis by computing a precise control-flow graph of Ethereum bytecode. J. Syst. Softw. **200**, 111653 (2023)
14. Araya-Aliaga, E., Atencio, E., Lozano, F., et al.: Automating dataset generation for object detection in the construction industry with AI and robotic process automation (RPA). Buildings. **15**(3), 410 (2025)
15. Haque, M.A., Kamal, M., George, R., et al.: Utilizing structural metrics from knowledge graphs to enhance the robustness quantification of large language models. Int. J. Data Sci. Anal. **20**, 1–21 (2024)
16. Park, M., Son, S., Jeon, Y., et al.: Scaffolding worker IMU time-series dataset for deep learning-based construction site behavior recognition. Adv. Eng. Inform. **65**, 103232 (2025)
17. Ibba, G., Aufiero, S., Neykova, R., et al.: A curated solidity smart contracts repository of metrics and vulnerability. In: Proceedings of the 20th International Conference on Predictive Models and Data Analytics in Software Engineering, pp. 32–41 (2024).
18. Tsoumakas, G., Katakis, I.: Multi-label classification: an overview. Data Warehousing Min.: Concepts, Methodologies, Tools, Appl., 64–74 (2008)
19. Abdelaziz, T., Hobor, A.: Smart learning to find dumb contracts. In: Proceedings of the 32nd USENIX Security Symposium (USENIX Security '23), pp. 1775–1792 (2023)
20. Ali, G.M.A., Chen, H.: MLFuzzer: a fuzzing approach based on generative adversarial networks and BiLSTM for detecting vulnerabilities in smart contracts. Clust. Comput. **28**(5), 1–14 (2025)
21. Wang, Z., Wang, Z., Zhang, Y.: An android malware detection method based on optimized feature extraction using graph convolutional network. In: International Conference on Digital Forensics and Cyber Crime, pp. 283–299. Springer, Cham (2023)
22. Ren, H., Zhao, F., Ma, Y., et al.: Golang contract language intelligence tabbed vulnerability data set to build. Computer Engineering and Application, 1–10 (2025). http://kns.cnki.net/kcms/detail/11.2127.TP.20241224.1705.003.html.
23. Tong, V., Dao, C., Tran, H.A., et al.: Enhancing BERT-based language model for multi-label vulnerability detection of smart contract in blockchain. J. Netw. Syst. Manag. **32**(3), 63 (2024)
24. Yamaguchi, M., Irie, G., Kawanishi, T., et al.: Subspace structure-aware spectral clustering for robust subspace clustering. In: Proceedings of the IEEE/CVF International Conference on Computer Vision, pp. 9875–9884 (2019)
25. Sanchez, L., Costa, N., Couso, I.: Addressing data scarcity in industrial reliability assessment with physically informed Echo state networks. Reliab. Eng. Sys. Saf. **261**, 111135 (2025)

26. Oubara, A., Wu, F., Qu, G., et al.: Adversarial learning network for multi-source change detection in built-up areas: integrating VHR RGB and multispectral imagery. Int. J. Digit. Earth. **18**(1), 2503443 (2025)
27. Wu, H., Dong, H., He, Y., et al.: Smart contract vulnerability detection based on hybrid attention mechanism model. Appl. Sci.-Basel. **13**(2), 770 (2023)

# The Sample Classification Method Accelerates the Efficiency of Robustness Verification

Xuejian Li(✉), Jian Xing, and Hantao Xia

Anhui University, Hefei 230039, Anhui, China
lxj@ahu.edu.cn, {e24301330,e22301375}@stu.ahu.edu.cn

**Abstract.** With the rapid advancement of artificial intelligence, deep learning-based neural networks have been widely applied across various domains. However, due to their inherent vulnerability, it is essential to verify their functionality to ensure security before real-world deployment. Among security properties, robustness has emerged as a critical focus. Traditional techniques like data augmentation and modular improvements can enhance performance but fall short in rigorously defining robustness boundaries. Verifying model robustness typically requires extensive sampling, which not only incurs high computational costs but also suffers from inefficiencies and bias due to uneven sample distribution. To address these challenges, this paper proposes a sample classification and ranking method based on the model's prediction probabilities. By identifying unstable and more informative samples prior to verification, this approach effectively reduces the sample size needed and mitigates distribution bias. Integrated as a preprocessing module in verification tools, the method significantly improves efficiency compared to traditional point-by-point validation.

**Keywords:** Neural network model · robustness verification · sample priority model

## 1 Introduction

In recent years, neural networks have made significant advancements in computer vision [1] and natural language processing [2]. However, the deployment of artificial intelligence(AI) systems in safety-critical applications has exposed their vulnerabilities. For example, in image classification, attackers can introduce subtle perturbations that are nearly invisible to humans yet can mislead the model's output [3]. In autonomous driving, environmental factors such as sudden lighting changes can lead to critical errors in visual classifiers [4], raising serious safety concerns. These vulnerabilities hinder the commercial viability of AI systems, particularly in areas like L4-level autonomous driving. Therefore, ensuring robustness—models' ability to maintain stable performance amid input perturbations—is crucial for trustworthy AI.


K.-K. R. Choo et al. (Eds.): ICDF2C 2025, LNICST 686, pp. 524–539, 2026.
https://doi.org/10.1007/978-3-032-22545-0_30

Traditional robustness enhancement methods, such as adversarial training [5] and data augmentation [6], have limitations. Their effectiveness often depends on specific model architectures and data distributions, lacking universal applicability. Moreover, they generally assess robustness through empirical metrics like improved adversarial accuracy, without providing strict formal safety boundaries. Thus, formal verification methods are becoming increasingly essential in trustworthy AI research. By utilizing mathematical modeling and logical reasoning, these methods can rigorously verify system properties, ensuring the safety of AI applications.

Current verification techniques for neural networks can be categorized into exact and approximate verification. Exact verification, represented by methods like Satisfiability Modulo Theories (SMT) [7] and Mixed Integer Linear Programming (MILP) [8], provides definitive conclusions regarding safety properties but is largely limited to feedforward networks. As network complexity increases, so does computational demand, posing challenges for more complex architectures like convolutional and deep neural networks. On the other hand, approximate verification methods include abstract interpretation [9], linear approximation [10], convex optimization [11], and interval analysis [12]. While these methods can efficiently handle larger networks through over-approximation, they may yield conservative verification results that do not guarantee property satisfaction.

The robustness verification of neural networks faces dual challenges. Theoretically, it is NP-hard [13], with computational complexity scaling exponentially with network size. Methodologically, there is often a trade-off between accuracy and efficiency: precise techniques like mixed integer programming can provide deterministic results but struggle with the nonlinearity of deep networks, while approximate methods can be overly conservative. Additionally, global robustness verification is computationally intensive, limiting most studies to local robustness verification, which assesses stability in specific sample neighborhoods. However, this approach has drawbacks. It typically relies on large sample sets, increasing computational costs, and may suffer from sampling biases, undermining the credibility of the verification results.

To develop trustworthy AI systems, it is essential to analyze the model's internal structure and security attributes. The inherent complexity and black-box nature of neural networks present significant challenges for security analysis. This paper proposes a sample selection strategy to enhance the efficiency and reliability of verification tools during sample selection, ensuring accuracy. By prioritizing the verification of the most vulnerable input points, we can significantly reduce the computational overhead associated with conventional methods.

This work introduces the following contributions:

1. A lightweight sample sorting strategy that computes the distance from a sample to the decision boundary based on the model's output probabilities. This method ranks the samples by their stability, allowing for efficient prioritization of verification. 2. The integration of this strategy into existing verification tools as a pre-processing module, enabling prioritized local robustness verification.

3. Experimental evaluations on standard validation benchmarks demonstrating that our approach not only maintains validation accuracy but also significantly reduces computational costs, thus enhancing the efficiency and credibility of local robustness verification.

# 2 Background

## 2.1 Neural Network Model

A neural network is structured in three layers: input, hidden, and output, as illustrated in Fig. 1. Each layer contains multiple neurons. The network functions as a mapping process $f$, such that $y = f(x)$, where $x$ is the input data and $y$ is the output. The input layer formats the data for the model, while the output layer presents the results, often as probabilities for classification tasks. The hidden layers process data through nonlinear transformations represented mathematically as $f : \mathbb{R}^n \rightarrow \mathbb{R}^m$, linking a high-dimensional input space to a high-dimensional output space.

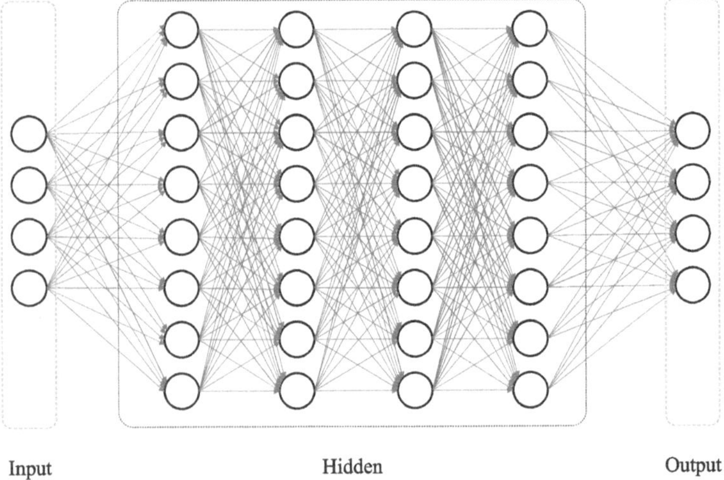


**Fig. 1.** Neural network structure diagram. The input layer comprises numerous artificial neurons, which are subsequently processed through multiple hidden layers before ultimately connecting to the output layer.

The critical operation in this process occurs in the hidden layers through nonlinear transformations, realized via affine transformations and activation functions. Each layer's computation can be expressed as:

$$f_i : \mathbb{R}^{L_{i-1}} \rightarrow \mathbb{R}^{L_i} \quad (1 < i < n)$$

where $L_i$ is the output of the $i$-th layer, processed from the previous layer's output $z_{i-1}$:

$$z_i = f_i(z_{i-1}) = W_i \cdot z_{i-1} + b_i$$

Here, $W_i$ is the weight matrix, $b_i$ is the bias, and the transformation can be summarized as:

$$\text{Affine}(x, W, b) = W \cdot x + \overline{b} \tag{1}$$

Thus, the network's semantics can be represented as:

$$f = f_1 \circ \cdots \circ f_n \tag{2}$$

### 2.2 Neural Network Verification

The neural network verification problem involves assessing whether specific functional relationships between inputs and outputs hold true. Formally, this is defined as follows:

**Definition 1 (Neural Network's Security Verification).** *For a neural network $f : \mathbb{R}^m \to \mathbb{R}^n$ and all possible input sets $\Omega \subseteq \mathbb{R}^m$, the security property $C$ entails determining if $x \in \Omega \Rightarrow y = f(x) \in P$ is valid, where $P \subseteq \mathbb{R}^n$.*

Robustness, a key focus in security verification, adds conditions on inputs and outputs. Specifically, robustness verification for classification networks can be defined as:

**Definition 2 (Neural Network Robustness Verification).** *For a neural network $f : \mathbb{R}^m \to \mathbb{R}^n$ with input $X \in \mathbb{R}^m$ and attribute $C = \max\{y_i | y_i \in \mathbb{R}^n\}$, the verification condition involves assessing whether $f(X') \subseteq C$ holds true under perturbations $\varepsilon > 0$ where $X' = (X, \varepsilon)$.*

In essence, robustness verification assesses whether neural networks maintain consistent classification results with input perturbations.

Verification can be categorized into global and local robustness based on input domain coverage, utilizing distance metrics defined by $L_p$ norms: $L_1$ (Manhattan), $L_2$ (Euclidean), and $L_\infty$ (Chebyshev). For vector $x = [x_1, x_2, \ldots, x_n]^T$:

- $L_1$ norm: $\|x\|_1 = \sum_{i=1}^{n} |x_i|$
- $L_2$ norm: $\|x\|_2 = \sqrt{\sum_{i=1}^{n} |x_i|^2}$
- $L_\infty$ norm: $\|x\|_\infty = \max_i |x_i|$

These norms reflect distances, especially when generating adversarial samples. Local robustness, or point-by-point robustness, examines stability within a small neighborhood, while global robustness considers stability across the entire input space.

**Definition 3 (Local Robustness Validation Scope).** *For any element $x$, if $x' = x + \varepsilon$ satisfies $\|x - x'\| \leq \delta$, then $f(x) = f(x')$, and the model is considered locally robust in the range of $(x + \delta)$.*

In local validation, the goal is to find $x'$ such that it maintains the same classification as $x$, often by adding a perturbation $\varepsilon$. The bound $\delta$ indicates the maximum perturbation permissible.

**Definition 4 (Global Robustness Validation Scope).** *Within the input domain $D$, for all $x_1, x_2 \in D$ if $\|x_1 - x_2\| \leq \delta \Rightarrow f(x_1) = f(x_2)$, the model is globally robust.*

Global robustness evaluates stability across all possible inputs, covering a broader scope than local robustness, which is constrained to small variations around specific samples.

The distribution of sample points and selection strategies significantly influence verification outcomes, particularly for local robustness. Most validation tools focus on local robustness due to lower computational demands, although they do not guarantee properties across the entire input space, potentially failing to represent the overall model reliability.

### 2.3 Decision Boundary Theory

The Decision Boundary (DB) [16], fundamental to neural network classification, is determined by the trained model's hypothesis function parameters. It serves as a classifier, illustrating the spatial relationships between different classes, i.e., the separation between each class and its neighbors.

This inter-class relationship can be expanded to encompass all categories, forming an overall feature that reflects the relationships among all classes. Formally, for a classifier $f : \mathbb{R}^n \to \mathbb{R}^c$ with $c$ classes, the decision boundary $\mathcal{D}$ is defined as:

$$\mathcal{D} := \left\{ x \in \mathbb{R}^n \mid \exists k_1 \neq k_2, \quad f_{k_1}(x) = f_{k_2}(x) = \max_k f_k(x) \right\} \tag{3}$$

This geometry divides the input space into mutually exclusive decision regions, with deep neural networks exhibiting highly nonlinear and fractal decision boundaries. While such boundaries enhance expressiveness beyond linear classifiers, they complicate robustness analysis.

Local robustness verification commonly utilizes the $L_p$ norm ($1 \leq p < \infty$) to measure the minimum disturbance distance from a sample point $x$ to the decision boundary:

$$d_p(x) = \min_\delta \|\delta\|_p \quad \text{s.t.} \quad (x + \delta) \in \mathcal{D} \tag{4}$$

As training progresses, $d_p(x)$ typically decreases, signaling the decision boundary's approach to the data for classification tasks.

For instance, a binary classification model's decision boundary, depicted in Fig. 2, illustrates varying degrees of model fitting ranging from underfitting to overfitting. In low-dimensional spaces, the decision boundary often appears as a line or curve; in high-dimensional spaces, it manifests as a hypersurface. While

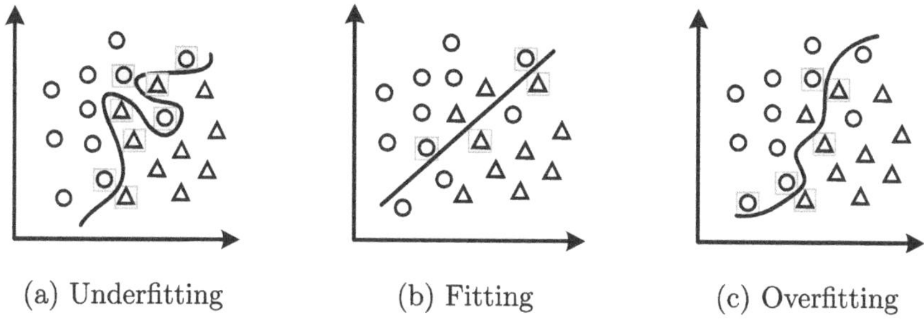

(a) Underfitting (b) Fitting (c) Overfitting

**Fig. 2.** The fitting extent evaluated by the decision boundary. This illustration depicts the evaluation of decision boundaries concerning the fitting degree of neural networks, divided into three sections: underfitting, fitting and overfitting.

linear classifiers possess linear decision boundaries, nonlinear classifiers like deep neural networks exhibit complex shapes.

Overfitting is a significant cause of robustness weaknesses in network models. High-precision models may still be vulnerable to adversarial samples; as the distance between the decision boundary and data points narrows, random noise can lead to misclassifications. During training, continuous iterations to fit the data can result in an overly complex decision boundary, pulling more data points closer to the boundary and increasing susceptibility to errors from small perturbations.

In the local robustness region defined by the $L_p$ norm, points close to the decision boundary are more prone to misclassification compared to those farther away. Therefore, overfitting highlights the importance of analyzing decision boundary shapes and stability to enhance model robustness. For multi-classification models, robustness analysis can similarly be applied across multiple decision boundaries. Despite the high complexity of global robustness verification, most current techniques focus on local robustness, using large-scale random sampling for verification. When most sample points cluster near the decision boundary, the model's robust neighborhood shrinks, indicating weaker overall robustness. Conversely, points farther from the boundary suggest greater robustness.

Thus, the sample point selection strategy critically influences verification outcomes. Reducing the number of sample points can lower computational costs while sorting and prioritizing samples likely to challenge robustness enhances verification efficiency, allowing for a more effective evaluation of the model's robustness.

## 3 Methodology

Local robustness verification assesses stability for a single sample, which limits its ability to represent model performance across the entire dataset. For a comprehensive evaluation, multiple sample points must be selected, often leading to large-scale point-by-point verification. This approach increases computational costs exponentially and may result in unreliable outcomes due to randomness in sample selection.

As verification methods evolve, the emphasis has shifted from achieving accuracy to improving efficiency. Early tools could take hours to execute and often returned "unknown" or "timeout" statuses, reducing their practical value. Despite recent advancements, computational overhead still poses challenges for accurate local robustness verification. To address this, pre-screening validation samples has emerged as a way to enhance efficiency.

This chapter introduces a sorting method for samples, focusing on priority verification of unstable samples that reflect the model's lower robustness limits. By employing lightweight pre-processing to acquire a verification sample set, we can significantly reduce verification time and enhance the reliability of results.

Robustness issues in neural networks arise from overfitting, causing data points to cluster near decision boundaries and reducing the robust neighborhood radius. This proximity increases the risk of misclassification under minor perturbations. We propose a method based on a neural network's predictive output to evaluate the distance between samples and decision boundaries.

We define the confidence score through the following:

**Definition 5 (Confidence Score).** *The confidence score is represented as the triplet* $(m, C, L)$, *where* $L$ *is the classification category,* $m$ *is the maximum output value (i.e.,* $m = \max\{y_i\}$*), and* $C$ *maps the score* $m$ *to* $L$.

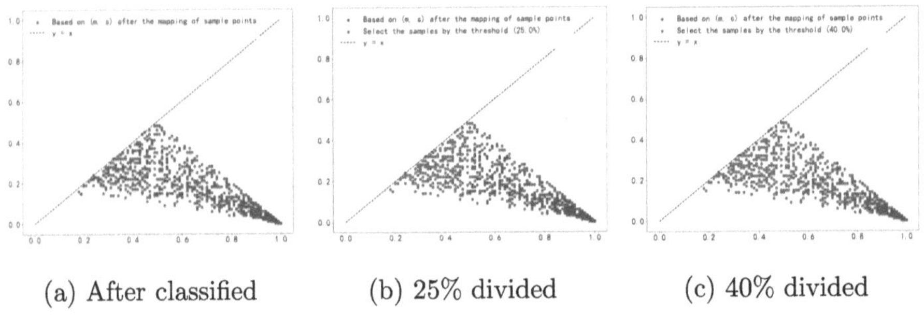


(a) After classified (b) 25% divided (c) 40% divided

**Fig. 3.** The distribution of samples after sorting. (a) illustrates the distribution of classified samples, with blue points representing a specific category. (b) and (c) highlight prioritized samples at thresholds of 25% and 40%, respectively, in red. (Color figure online)

Let the model output be $\{y_1, y_2, \ldots, y_n\}$ and the corresponding classifications be $\{c_1, c_2, \ldots, c_n\}$. The model maps outputs to classifications as $c_i = C(y_i)$.

The score correlates model output to classifications. A high $m$ indicates the sample is far from the decision boundary, while a low $m$ suggests proximity. Samples can be categorized as "stable" or "unstable".

For unstable samples, strategies include no-target and targeted attacks. No-target attacks aim to maximize the distance from the original classification, while targeted attacks minimize it. Thus, the robustness of the model is influenced by the distance to decision boundaries.

Samples may be misclassified when disturbed, and the most recently crossed error classification becomes critical in understanding robustness.

**Definition 6 (Recent Misclassification Score).** *Let* $m = \max\{y_i\}$ *with* $j \neq i$. *If* $|m - s| = |y_i - y_j| \leq |y_i - y_k|$ *for all* $k \neq i, j$, *then* $s = y_j$ *is the nearest misclassification score that can be crossed.*

The distribution of scores $(m, s)$ allows for sample reordering. Correctly predicted samples are reclassified based on their proximity to decision boundaries. After reordering, sample distributions reflect their stability, as illustrated in Fig. 3. When $m$ significantly exceeds $s$, samples cluster near point $(1, 0)$, denoting stability. As $s$ approaches $m$, samples converge around the line $y = x$, indicating instability. To prioritize verification of unstable samples, we set proportional thresholds based on different models' decision boundaries. This approach allows for flexible management of sample verification while ensuring robust assessments across the sample distribution.

## 4 Experiments

In this section, the actual effect of the proposed method will be verified through experiments, including the accuracy of the evaluation method for the division of verification sample points, and the improvement of verification efficiency after integration into the verification tool. The MNIST [20] and CIFAR-10 [21] datasets commonly used in validation fields were used in the experiment. The model design is based on the LeNet [20] network architecture, including 3 convolutional layers, 2 maximum pooling layers, 2 fully connected layers and 1 output layer. MNIST dataset based training of network named M - model, the specific structure of hidden layers is $(1, 8, 3)$, $(2, 2)$, $(1, 8, 3)$, $(2, 2)$, $(8, 14, 3)$, 100, 50, 10; On training network CIFAR-10 data set named C-model, its network hidden layer structure is $(3, 24, 3)$, $(2, 2)$, $(24, 24, 3)$, $(2, 2)$, $(24, 32, 3)$, 100, 50, 10. The training process of the model is stopped under the condition that the accuracy reaches 90%, and the model parameters are saved.

### 4.1 Verification of Integration Framework

From the point of view of accurate and approximate validation, two validation tools are selected: Marabou [22] based on SMT method and $\beta$-Crown [23] based on boundary propagation.

Both tools performed well in the DNN Verification Competition 2023, winning first and second place respectively. $\beta$-Crown supports both exact and approximate validation modes, while Marabou supports only exact validation modes. Although they have achieved remarkable results in terms of performance, it is still difficult to avoid the huge computational overhead caused by high model complexity and random selection of a large number of test points during the verification process.

This section combines the sample classification and sorting method proposed in this chapter, organizes it into a pre-processing module for neural network verification, integrates it into the model verification tool, and pre-screens the samples. The local robustness of the model is verified by screening the sample set with priority verification. The overall workflow of the priority verification framework after integrating the preprocessing module is shown in Fig. 4.

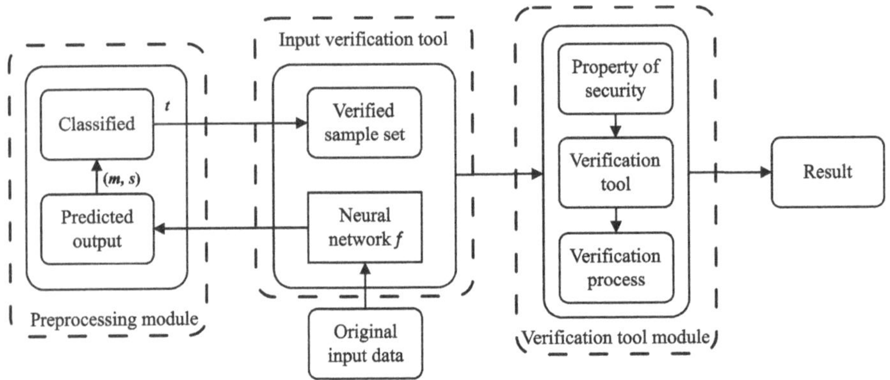


**Fig. 4.** The framework incorporates a lightweight preprocessing module. Pre-processing first sorting the raw input data and predicts outputs. After processing, the sample data is passed to the verification tool to assess safety and execute the validation process, ultimately producing results.

In the pre-processing module, based on the output value of the model's single forward propagation, the mapping relationship $(m, s)$between the maximum correct classification score and the leapable recent wrong classification score is constructed, the samples are sorted, and the scale of the sample set is controlled by the threshold value $t$.

In order to evaluate the effectiveness of the sample classification and sorting method and improve the efficiency of the verification tool, the verification tool is used to analyze the decision results of different input samples. Specifically, after sample points are obtained by the sample classification and sorting method, the accuracy of the method is first judged, its effectiveness in priority verification is evaluated, and then the efficiency of the verification tool is statistically improved.

In terms of security attribute specification, the robustness of the expansion model is verified based on $L_\infty$norm, and experiments are carried out by setting different robust neighborhood parameters $\delta$. Through $\delta$, the maximum robustness boundary of the model under the disturbed input can be determined, that is, the maximum difference distance between the eigenvectors $x_d$in the original input $x$and the corresponding eigencomponents $x'_d$in the disturbed input $x'$.

**Table 1.** The different standard setting of verification

| Verification Tool (Code) | Accuracy | Verification Model Name | Robustness Radius ($\delta$) |
|---|---|---|---|
| Marabou (Ma-1) | √ | M-model | 0.065 |
| Marabou (Ma-2) | × | C-model | 0.025 |
| $\beta$-Crown (Cr-1) | √ | M-model | 0.045 |
| $\beta$-Crown (Cr-2) | √ | C-model | 0.005 |

In addition, the core research object of robustness verification is the sample set that is accurately identified in the neural network. However, in the model robustness analysis, due to the difference in the accuracy of the two validation tools, the maximum robustness validation radius of the model is inconsistent. Based on this, it is necessary to adopt a differentiated setting scheme to set different $\delta$values. The specific standard Settings are shown in the Table 1.

### 4.2 The Analysis of Experimental Results

**(1) Priority Sample Accuracy Verification**

First, the validity of decision boundary based analysis is verified by mutation test, and the accuracy of the proposed method for ranking the stability of sample points is evaluated.

Mutation Testing (MT) [18] is a method of changing the decision boundary of a model, which in turn affects the output of the model for the input sample. Conversely, when the output results of the original model $f$and the mutated model $f'$on the input sample $x$change, that is, $f(x) \neq f'(x)$, then the decision boundary of the model obviously changes. Based on this, the distance relationship between sample points and decision boundaries can be analyzed by generating Mutation Models (MMs), thus explaining the stability differences of sample points at different distances.

The methods of decision boundary mutation test mainly include source level and model level. The source level is to adjust the training set data or program during the training process, while the model level is to directly modify the trained model parameters. In the analysis process, this paper focuses on the use of mutated MMs to verify the stability of the sample, rather than specific mutation methods. Therefore, in the method selection, the model-level method is adopted, which has the following two advantages: (1) Improved efficiency: Avoiding retraining the model, thereby improving the efficiency of MMs generation; (2) Reduce uncertainty: Directly modifying the model parameters avoids the uncertainty caused by random factors during training, which may occur in multiple models trained using the same method and data set According to the mutation operator proposed in the reference [19], two model-level benchmarks are screened here, and the two mutation operators are used to modify the decision boundary of the original model for subsequent sample stability assessment. The includes Neuron Activation Inverse (NAI) and Gaussian Fuzzing (GF). NAI is achieved by randomly inverting the activation state of a certain number of neurons; GF changes the importance of connections between neurons by fuzzing test weights. These two mutation operators inject errors or biases into the network model, thus adjusting the model parameters.

Take MNIST as an example, which is a ten-classified data set of handwritten digits, corresponding to the numbers 0-9. Suppose a sample picture with a true label of 1 is correctly classified as $L = C(y_1) = 1$, and the maximum score in the incorrect classification is 7, that is, the nearest misclassification that can be crossed is 7. This means that the sample is divided by the decision boundary of class 1 and is closest to the decision boundary of class 7 among the other nine classes. When MMs is generated by controlling the mutation boundary, the maximum error classification of the generated MMs should be 7, which is also verified in the experimental results.

In order to ensure the reliability and accuracy of the experimental results, a sufficient number of mutation models were generated with a higher mutation rate for GF and NAI mutation operators, so as to reduce the influence of chance and randomness on the experimental results in the mutation process. The mutation model and mutation rate are set to 500 and 0.35, respectively. By mutating the decision boundary of the model, the prediction classification results before and after the mutation are compared, and the latest error classification label that can be crossed after the mutation is recorded as the latest error classification label, as shown in Table 2.

**Table 2.** The results of samples after implementing mutation testing on the models

| Sample | Data sources | operator | Correct classification label | Error classification label | Frequency of Error labels | Stability judgement |
|---|---|---|---|---|---|---|
| $x_1$ | MNIST | NAI | 3 | 5 | 133/500 | unstability |
| $x_2$ | MNIST | GF | 6 | 0 | 25/500 | stability |
| $x_3$ | MNIST | NAI | 7 | 3 | 98/500 | unstability |
| $x_4$ | MNIST | GF | 5 | 6 | 86/500 | unstability |
| $x_5$ | MNIST | NAI | 2 | 0 | 30/500 | stability |
| $x_6$ | CIFAR-10 | GF | airplane | ship | 89/500 | unstability |
| $x_7$ | CIFAR-10 | GF | bird | deer | 93/500 | unstability |
| $x_8$ | CIFAR-10 | GF | ship | dog | 37/500 | stability |
| $x_9$ | CIFAR-10 | NAI | automobile | cat | 52/500 | stability |
| $x_{10}$ | CIFAR-10 | NAI | dog | horse | 74/500 | unstability |

The result of mutation test can reflect the distance between the input sample point and the decision boundary corresponding to the misjudged class in the multi-classification model. Considering that sample points may be located near multiple decision boundaries at the same time, the decision boundary with the nearest sample points can be prioritized in robustness analysis and verification. Among them, the misjudgment classification label focuses on the most recent misclassification label. According to the Table 2, corresponding to the classification labels of the original model, for sample points of unstable points, the misjudgment classification label with the highest frequency in the mutated model is consistent with the most recent misjudgment classification label that can be crossed. For example, in MNIST, sample point $x_1$ is the sample point closest to the boundary of $y = x$, which shows the worst stability, while $x_2$ is the sample point farthest from the boundary of $y = x$, which has the strongest stability. This is consistent with the results of sample sorting, indicating that the proposed method can effectively reflect the relationship between sample distance decision boundaries.

**(2) Effectiveness of unstable point verification**

Five input samples were randomly selected in the MNIST and CIFAR-10 data sets to carry out the experiment, and the sorting results were shown in Table 3. Among them, the distance distribution of the 5 samples selected in MNIST from the decision boundary is: $x_1 < x_3 < x_4 < x_5 < x_2$from near to far; The sorting result for the five sample points in CIFAR-10 is: $x_7 < x_6 < x_{10} < x_8 < x_9$. With the increase of the distance from the sample point to the decision boundary, its stability is gradually enhanced, that is, the distance from the sample point to the decision boundary is positively correlated with its stability.

**Table 3.** The results of samples after sorting

| Data sources | Sample | Correct classification label | The crossed error label | Distance ranking (from near to far) |
|---|---|---|---|---|
| MNIST | $x_1$ | 3 | 5 | 1 |
| MNIST | $x_2$ | 6 | 0 | 5 |
| MNIST | $x_3$ | 7 | 3 | 2 |
| MNIST | $x_4$ | 5 | 6 | 3 |
| MNIST | $x_5$ | 2 | 0 | 4 |
| CIFAR-10 | $x_6$ | airplane | ship | 2 |
| CIFAR-10 | $x_7$ | bird | deer | 1 |
| CIFAR-10 | $x_8$ | ship | dog | 5 |
| CIFAR-10 | $x_9$ | automobile | cat | 4 |
| CIFAR-10 | $x_{10}$ | dog | horse | 3 |

In the verification process, 500 sample pictures are randomly selected from the test sets of MNIST and CIFAR-10 data sets as the global sample set to be verified. In order to unify the evaluation criteria, the number of sample points in the sample set to be verified was controlled by setting the threshold t to be 30% and 50%. Given the robustness radius, if the sample points in the sample set to be verified are more likely to violate the security properties, then the effectiveness of the proposed method can be proved. The proportion of unstable points obtained based on the method in this paper that violate their properties in the verification process is tested and recorded, and the verification results are shown in Table 4. In addition, a group of controlled experiments was set up, samples were randomly selected from the sample set to be verified, and the verified samples were randomly sampled in proportion to 30% and 50%, as shown in Table 5.

**Table 4.** The verification results of selecting sorted samples

| Verification Tool | Total number of samples | Robustness Radius ($\delta$) | Threshold $t$ | Violation Ratio |
|---|---|---|---|---|
| M-1 | 500 | 0.065 | 30% 50% | 75.3% 66.6% |
| M-2 | 500 | 0.025 | 30% 50% | 87.3% 79.3% |
| C-1 | 500 | 0.045 | 30% 50% | 78.6% 66.0% |
| C-2 | 500 | 0.005 | 30% 50% | 94.6% 90.6% |

By comparing Table 4 and Table 5, it can be seen that under a given robustness radius, the unstable points divided based on the proposed method have a higher probability of unrobustness, so the proportion of security attribute violations is also higher. The weaker the robustness of the model at a certain input point, the smaller the disturbance required to counter the attack in the neighborhood of the sample point, and the closer the sample point is to the decision boundary. In exact verification, whenever a certain input point is found not to satisfy the security property, a corresponding counterexample can be generated. The approximate validation method will label the sample points that fail the validation as potentially unsafe sample points. In contrast, input points judged to be relatively stable usually pass validation, although such methods do not allow in-depth analysis of unsafe sample points. Because the approximate validation method has significant advantages in dealing with more complex networks, it can achieve the purpose of improving efficiency by filtering large-scale input data. Therefore, through the test results of the selected samples by the verification tool, it is proved that the sample classification and sorting method can effectively locate the sample points near the decision boundary, which are more likely to be unstable.

**Table 5.** The verification results of the random policy

| Verification Tool | Total Sample Size | Robustness Radius ($\delta$) | Ratio $p$ | Violation Ratio |
|---|---|---|---|---|
| M-1 | 500 | 0.065 | 30% 50% | 47.3% 36.6% |
| M-2 | 500 | 0.025 | 30% 50% | 55.2% 45.3% |
| C-1 | 500 | 0.045 | 30% 50% | 40.0% 36.6% |
| C-2 | 500 | 0.005 | 30% 50% | 68.6% 59.3% |

**(3) The sample priority mode to improve the verification efficiency**
To further illustrate the auxiliary optimization effect of sample first strategy on the performance of validation tools, experimental tests were conducted on Marabou and $\beta$-Crown. Based on the positive correlation between unstable points and robust neighborhood radius, the sample set to be verified is generated by sample classification and ordering method, and the strategy of only verifying unstable sample points is adopted to realize the robustness verification of deep neural network model.

**Table 6.** The runtime of verification tool after integrated preprocessing module

| Verification Tool | Verification Mode | Execution Time (minutes) |
|---|---|---|
| M-1 | Sample Priority Point-by-point Verification | 210.5 357 |
| M-2 | Sample Priority Point-by-point Verification | 143.7 261.1 |
| C-1 | Sample Priority Point-by-point Verification | 141.3 289.6 |
| C-2 | Sample Priority Point-by-point Verification | 69.1 150.9 |

During the experiment, the data set to be verified is the same as in the above section. The threshold $t$ is set to 50%, and the overall verification running time of the verification tool after integrating the pre-processing module is recorded, as shown in Table 6. The results show that the validation efficiency is higher when the priority validation mode is integrated in Marabou. For $\beta$-Crown, the point-by-point verification mode is set to exact verification in the experiment because it is easily affected by time-out in the approximate verification mode. Therefore, in the precise verification mode, the reduction of $\beta$-Crown verification time is very obvious compared with before and after the integrated preprocessing module.

The cost of local robustness validation mainly includes sampling of input samples and analysis of the validation process. Among them, the efficiency of analysis processing in verification process depends on the coding method and calculation method adopted by the verification tool. In the pre-processing module, it is only necessary to perform several forward predictions and sort and divide the sample points. The sorting process is lightweight and does not generate extra overhead for the performance of the validation algorithm itself. By pre-screening the input sample points, the pre-processing module reduces the number of samples to be verified on the whole, thus significantly improving the verification efficiency. At the same time, the verification effect is also guaranteed, that is, on the basis of setting the robustness radius, the robustness verification results remain consistent.

## 5 Conclusion

With the rapid advancement of AI technology, neural network models have become fundamental components in various sectors of production and daily life.

Robustness evaluation and validation of these models are critical to ensure stable operation and adaptability to diverse scenarios. As such, enhancing the robustness verification capabilities of neural network models is essential to ensure the scalability of verification tools and the efficiency of verification outcomes.

Local robustness verification is often susceptible to the effects of sample selection, leading to inaccuracies in results and increased computational costs. This paper introduces a sample sorting method based on the model's prediction probabilities from a single forward propagation. The theoretical analysis demonstrates the feasibility and effectiveness of this method. Integrated into a model verification tool as a pre-processing module, the sample sorting method prioritizes the verification of unstable sample points, mitigating issues related to uneven sampling distributions. This approach not only reduces the number of samples requiring verification but also enhances overall verification efficiency.

Experimental results indicate that, compared to traditional point-by-point verification models, the proposed method accurately identifies unstable sample points near decision boundaries and significantly shortens verification time, all while maintaining the reliability of the results.

## References

1. Krizhevsky, A., Sutskever, I., Hinton, G.E.: Imagenet classification with deep convolutional neural networks. Commun. ACM **60**(6), 84–90 (2017)
2. Goldberg, Y.: Neural network methods for natural language processing. Synth. Lect. Hum. Lang. Technol. **10**(1), 1–309 (2017)
3. Szegedy, C., et al.: Intriguing properties of neural networks. arXiv:1312.6199 (2013)
4. Song, Z., et al.: Robustness-aware 3D object detection in autonomous driving: a review and outlook. IEEE Trans. Intell. Transp. Syst. **25**(11), 15407–15436 (2024)
5. Deng, Y., Zheng, X., Zhang, T., Chen, C., Lou, G., Kim, M.: An analysis of adversarial attacks and defenses on autonomous driving models. In: 2020 IEEE International Conference on Pervasive Computing and Communications (PerCom), pp. 1–10. IEEE, NJ (2020)
6. Shu, M., Shen, Y., Lin, M.C., Goldstein, T.: Adversarial differentiable data augmentation for autonomous systems. In: 2021 IEEE International Conference on Robotics and Automation (ICRA), pp. 14069–14075. IEEE, NJ (2021)
7. Floudas, C.A., Lin, X.: Mixed integer linear programming in process scheduling: modeling, algorithms, and applications. Ann. Oper. Res. **139**, 131–162 (2005)
8. de Moura, L., Bjørner, N.: Z3: an efficient SMT solver. In: Ramakrishnan, C.R., Rehof, J. (eds.) TACAS 2008. LNCS, vol. 4963, pp. 337–340. Springer, Heidelberg (2008). https://doi.org/10.1007/978-3-540-78800-3_24
9. Cousot, P., Cousot, R.: Abstract interpretation: a unified lattice model for static analysis of programs by construction or approximation of fixpoints. In: Proceedings of the 4th ACM SIGACT-SIGPLAN Symposium on Principles of Programming Languages, pp. 238–252. ACM, New York, NY, United States (1977)
10. Khalil, H.K., Grizzle, J.W.: Nonlinear Systems. Prentice Hall Upper, Saddle River (2002)
11. Boyd, S.P., Vandenberghe, L.: Convex Optimization. Cambridge University Press, Cambridge (2004)

12. Alefeld, G., Mayer, G.: Interval analysis: theory and applications. J. Comput. Appl. Math. **121**(1–2), 421–464 (2000)
13. Katz, G., Barrett, C., Dill, D.L., Julian, K., Kochenderfer, M.J.: Reluplex: an efficient SMT solver for verifying deep neural networks. In: Majumdar, R., Kunčak, V. (eds.) CAV 2017. LNCS, vol. 10426, pp. 97–117. Springer, Cham (2017). https://doi.org/10.1007/978-3-319-63387-9_5
14. Katz, G., Barrett, C., Dill, D.L., Julian, K., Kochenderfer, M.J.: Towards proving the adversarial robustness of deep neural networks. arXiv:1709.02802 (2017)
15. Li, Y., Zhao, G., Kong, S., He, Y., Zhou, H.: Certifying global robustness for deep neural networks. arXiv:2405.20556 (2024)
16. Mickisch, D., Assion, F., Greßner, F., Günther, W., Motta, M.: Understanding the decision boundary of deep neural networks: an empirical study. arXiv:2002.01810 (2020)
17. Moosavi-Dezfooli, S.M., Fawzi, A., Frossard, P.: DeepFool: a simple and accurate method to fool deep neural networks. In: 2016 IEEE Conference on Computer Vision and Pattern Recognition (CVPR), pp. 2574–2582. IEEE, NJ (2016)
18. Wang, J., Dong, G., Sun, J., Wang, X., Zhang, P.: Adversarial sample detection for deep neural networks through model mutation testing. In: Proceedings of the 41st International Conference on Software Engineering, pp. 1245–1256. IEEE Press, NJ (2019)
19. Ma, L., et al.: Deepmutation: mutation testing of deep learning systems. In: 2018 IEEE 29th International Symposium on Software Reliability Engineering (ISSRE), pp. 100–111. IEEE, NJ (2018)
20. LeCun, Y., Bottou, L., Bengio, Y., Haffner, P.: Gradient-based learning applied to document recognition. Proc. IEEE **86**(11), 2278–2324 (1998)
21. Krizhevsky, A.: Learning multiple layers of features from tiny images. In: Handbook of Systemic Autoimmune Diseases, vol. 1, no. 4, pp. 32–33 (2009)
22. Katz, G., et al.: The marabou framework for verification and analysis of deep neural networks. In: Dillig, I., Tasiran, S. (eds.) CAV 2019. LNCS, vol. 11561, pp. 443–452. Springer, Cham (2019). https://doi.org/10.1007/978-3-030-25540-4_26
23. Wang, S., et al.: Beta-CROWN: efficient bound propagation with per-neuron split constraints for complete and incomplete neural network verification. Adv. Neural. Inf. Process. Syst. **34**(1), 2–3 (2021)

# MuLImg-SCV: Multi-label Vulnerability Classification of Smart Contracts Based on RGB Image

Linlin Zhang[1], Nianlu Liu[2], Ke Li[2], Wenbo Fang[4], and Kai Zhao[3](✉)

[1] Network and Information Technology Center, Xinjiang University, Urumqi, China
zllnadasha@xju.edu.cn

[2] College of Software, Xinjiang University, Urumqi, China
{lnl,alike}@stu.xju.edu.cn

[3] College of Computer Science and Technology, Xinjiang University, Urumqi, China
zhawkk@xju.edu.cn

[4] Cyber Science and Engineering, Sichuan University, Chengdu, China
fangwenbo@stu.scu.edu.cn

**Abstract.** As smart contracts find ever-wider use in domains such as finance and agriculture, their security has become a critical concern. Most current deep learningbased smart contract vulnerability detection methods focus on binary classification, failing to address the complex reality where a single contract may exhibit multiple vulnerabilities. Recent multi-label approaches based on sequential features often fail to capture long-range dependencies and correlations among vulnerability types. To address these issues, this paper proposes a multi-label smart contract vulnerability detection method based on RGB images. We employ Hilbert-curve mappings to transform bytecode into RGB images, with data augmentation applied to enhance generalization. Subsequently, we integrate the Convolutional Block Attention Module (CBAM) into HrNet to learn and fuse multi-scale image features. To capture label dependencies, we construct a global label correlation graph and apply a Graph Attention Network (GAT). We then implement deep integration between label features and images through a Query2Label framework. Finally, to handle varying detection difficulties, we assign each vulnerability its own classification head. Moreover, label smoothing and weighting mechanisms into the asymmetric loss (ASL) to alleviate multi-label class imbalance. Extensive experiments demonstrate that our approach substantially outperforms state-of-the-art multi-label detectors, achieving an average accuracy of 0.9052.

**Keywords:** Smart Contract Vulnerability Detection · Multi-Label Classification · Image

## 1 Introduction

Smart contracts are scripts that execute automatically on a distributed network of mutually untrusted nodes, eliminating the need for a centralized trusted


K.-K. R. Choo et al. (Eds.): ICDF2C 2025, LNICST 686, pp. 540–555, 2026.
https://doi.org/10.1007/978-3-032-22545-0_31

third party [1]. Ethereum [2], as a leading blockchain platform supporting smart contracts, have high-value digital assets and a wide range of decentralized applications. Exploiting vulnerabilities in smart contracts to illegally obtain digital assets has become a primary target for attackers.

In recent years, substantial progress has been made in the field of smart contract vulnerability detection using deep learning techniques. Zhuang et al. [3] conducted vulnerability detection using an undirected Graph Convolutional Network model and a novel Temporal Message Passing model. Cai et al. [4] utilized a bidirectional Gated Graph Neural Network for vulnerability detection. Liu et al. [5] investigated detection approaches that combine graph convolutional networks with expert knowledge. Xie et al. [6] leverage Long Short-Term Memory networks for detecting vulnerabilities. However, the aforementioned methods assume that each contract has only one vulnerability, limiting their effectiveness in real-world scenarios where multiple vulnerabilities frequently coexist.

Some researchers have proposed multi-label smart contract vulnerability detection methods based on sequential features to address the gap in multi-label vulnerability detection. Studies by Tong [7], Gogineni [8], Duy [9], and Qian [10] utilize deep learning models to simultaneously detect various vulnerabilities in source code, bytecode, and other sequences. However, these studies lack an exploration of label correlation relationships. Additionally, directly processing code sequences can suffer from high-dimensional sparsity and struggle to capture long-range dependencies. Research by Mustafa [11] and Bani-Hani [12] transforms bytecode into images and leverages computer-vision models to tackle the aforementioned challenges. However, their bytecode-to-image conversion fails to preserve crucial local features.

To address aforementioned challenges, we propose MuLImg-SCV, a multi-label smart contract vulnerability classification method based on RGB images. First, we convert smart contract bytecode sequences into RGB images via Hilbert curve, which preserve both local and global features among bytes. Next, we integrate the Convolutional Block Attention Module (CBAM) into HRNet to facilitate efficient multi-scale feature learning and fusion. To capture correlation among vulnerability types, we build a label correlation graph and apply a Graph Attention Network (GAT) to learn inter-label relationships. On this basis, we adopt the Query2Label framework to enable deep interaction between label embeddings and image features. To address class imbalance in multi-label, we incorporate label smoothing and class-weighting mechanisms into the Asymmetric loss (ASL). Finally, we deploy independent Multi-Layer Perceptron (MLP) heads for each vulnerability type, accommodating their diverse feature distributions.

Eventually, our work makes the following contribution.

- This paper proposes an RGB image generation method based on the Hilbert curve, effectively preserving the local features of the code while ensuring that the spatial structure more closely aligns with the logical structure of the bytecode.

- This paper proposes a label-guided framework for image feature learning. By integrating the CBAM into HrNet, the model achieves more precise learning and fusion of multi-scale image features. Additionally, a label correlation graph is constructed, and GAT are employed to capture label-related feature representations. Furthermore, the Query2Label framework is introduced to enable deep integration between image features and label features.
- This paper proposes a classification and loss optimization mechanism tailored to multi-label vulnerability detection tasks. Independent MLP heads are used for each vulnerability type to handle varying detection difficulties, while label smoothing and class weighting are integrated into ASL to address class imbalance.

## 2 Related Work

With the widespread adoption of deep learning techniques, some researchers have begun exploring their application in smart contract vulnerability detection, which can be broadly categorized into binary and multi-label classification methods. The former typically assume that each contract contains only a single type of vulnerability and use deep learning models to detect it. Zeng [13] and Jeon [14] leveraged BERT models to extract source code sequence features, achieving more efficient and accurate vulnerability detection. Li et al. [15] combined multi-channel convolution with multi-head self-attention mechanisms to identify vulnerabilities. Chen et al. [16] proposed EA-RGCN, a graph-based detection method capable of identifying vulnerabilities at the function level. Wu et al. [17] utilized the graph pre-trained model GraphCodeBERT to learn graph-structured features. HWANG et al. [18] introduced the CodeNet model to extract image-based features of smart contracts for vulnerability detection. Although these binary classification methods exhibit high accuracy, they fall short in handling real-world scenarios where an insecure smart contract may contain multiple vulnerabilities.

Multi-label classification methods for smart contract vulnerabilities address the limitations of binary classification approaches, yet there remains room for improvement in overall detection performance. Tong et al. [7] proposed a multi-label vulnerability classification method based on the BERT model. Gogineni et al. [8] employed the Average Stochastic Gradient Descent Weighted Dropped Long Short-Term Memory (AWD-LSTM) model to simultaneously detect multiple vulnerabilities. Duy et al. [9] introduced a tri-label smart contract vulnerability detection framework based on multimodal fusion. Mustafa et al. [11] presented a fast-scanning RGB encoding method that leverages lightweight convolutional neural networks for feature extraction and learning. Bani-Hani et al. [12] transformed smart contracts into images and applied models such as ResNet50 and VGG19 for multi-label classification. Rossini et al. [19] utilized convolutional neural networks to learn RGB image features for multi-label vulnerability detection. Distinct from these approaches, our method maps bytecode into RGB images using Hilbert curves, introduces label relationship learning, and integrates label features with image features to achieve more accurate vulnerability detection.

## 3 Approach

We propose a multi-label smart contract vulnerability classification method based on RGB images, comprising five main components: data preprocessing, feature extraction, label correlation learning, fusion learning, and vulnerability classification. An overview of the proposed framework is illustrated in Fig. 1.

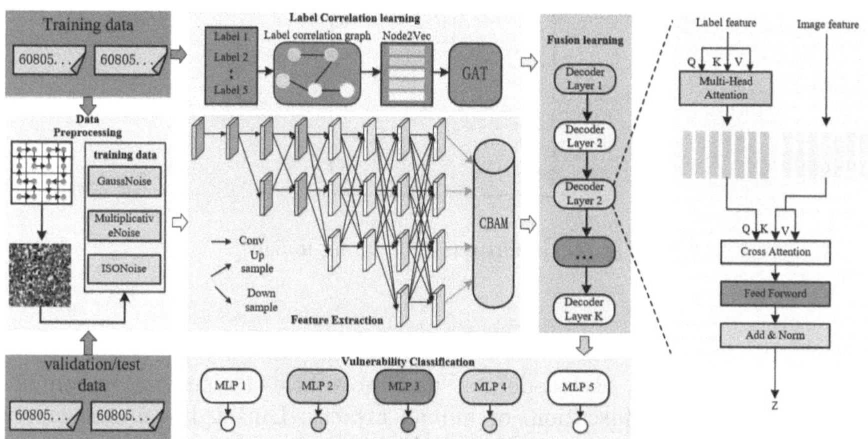


**Fig. 1.** The overall architecture of our proposed method.

### 3.1 Data Preprocessing

In the data preprocessing phase, we employed the Hilbert curve to map smart contract bytecode into images, thereby generating an image dataset of Space Filling Curves (SFC) that effectively preserves the spatial locality of the data. Subsequently, we designed a noise combination strategy to simulate real-world interference elements by adding noise to the training set, enhancing the model's ability to capture vulnerability features.

**RGB Image Generation.** SFC are mathematical constructions that fill a two-dimensional plane via a continuous curve. The Hilbert [20] curve is a representative example. In our study, we utilize the Hilbert curve to sequentially map bytecode from one-dimensional space into two-dimensional space. This approach effectively preserves both the local structure and rich information inherent in the code, resulting in an image whose spatial structure closely aligns with the logical framework of the bytecode itself. Figure 2 illustrates a mapping example, where each element in the bytecode sequence is assigned a specific spatial coordinate according to the traversal path of a Hilbert curve. Specifically, we initialize a three-dimensional Hilbert curve and establish a relationship between symbols and their mappings, generating a bytecode mapping table. The one-dimensional sequence is then projected onto a two-dimensional grid to produce an RGB image that preserves both local and global structural features.

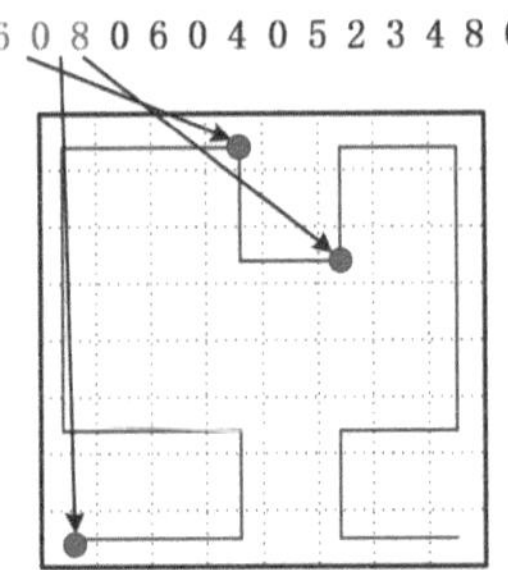


**Fig. 2.** Hilbert curve mapping image.

**Data Augmentation.** Bytecode may undergo subtle changes due to compiler optimizations, code obfuscation, or human attacks. During the image generation process, certain logical information may be lost as a result of dimensional compression or fixed resolution. By injecting noise into our images, we emulate these real-world variations, enabling the model to maintain high detection performance even when confronted with dynamic or imperfect inputs. Specifically, we enhance our training set with a combination of Gaussian noise, multiplicative noise, and ISO noise, thereby bolstering the model's generalization ability and robustness against diverse perturbations.

Gaussion noise [21] is a type of noise produced by adding random values drawn from a normal (Gaussian) distribution to an image. Multiplicative Noise [22], also known as speckle noise, randomly scales each pixel's intensity by a factor to emulate spot-like fluctuations. ISO Noise simulates the noise generated under high ISO camera settings and comprises two components: shot noise and read noise. Shot noise follows a Poisson distribution, while read noise is typically modeled as Gaussian.

### 3.2 Feature Extraction

We chose HrNet [23] as the backbone for our feature extraction module, enabling deep extraction and fusion of multi-scale features from high resolution to low resolution. The architecture is shown in the feature extraction of Fig. 1. HrNet consists of four stages, with each stage introducing a new scale branch starting from the first stage. The network begins with two $3 \times 3$ convolutions (stride 2), generating 64-channel downsampled features. Subsequently, three sets of Transition structures and Stage structures facilitate learning and fusion of features across different scales. The Transition modules progressively introduce lower-resolution branches using strided $3 \times 3$ convolutions, downsampling feature maps by factors of 4, 8, 16, and 32 to enable multi-scale learning. The Stage modules stack Basic Blocks at each resolution and apply upsampling and downsampling to enable cross-scale feature fusion and interaction.

To ensure comprehensive multi-scale feature learning from high to low resolutions, we diverged from HRNet original final stage design and preserved multi-scale feature maps in our last stage. We then introduce the CBAM to fuse these multi-scale features, which significantly enhances the model's ability to focus on informative regions. The resulting architecture is depicted in Fig. 3. CBAM [24] is a lightweight module combining a Channel Attention Module and a Spatial Attention Module, allowing the network to emphasize informative features along both channel and spatial dimensions.

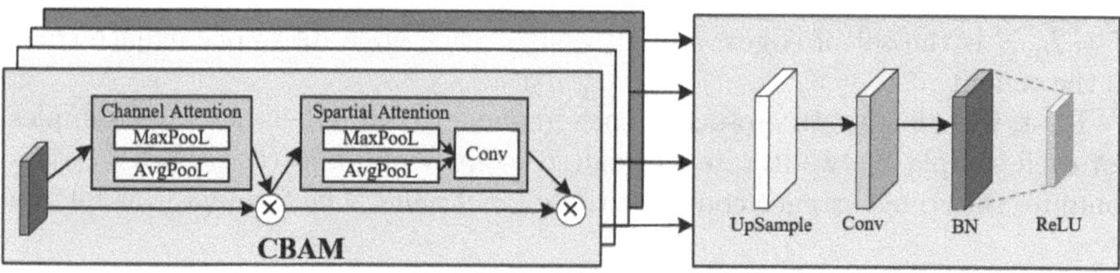


**Fig. 3.** The overall architecture of our proposed method.

First, the features $F$ from each branch are input into the Channel Attention Module to capture important channel information, denoted as $F'$. Subsequently, $F'$ is fed into the Spatial Attention Module to focus on obtaining significant spatial location information, represented as $F''$. The formulas are as follows:

$$F' = M_c(F) \otimes F = \sigma(\text{MLP}(\text{AvgPool}(F)) + \text{MLP}(\text{MaxPool}(F))) \otimes F \quad (1)$$

$$F'' = M_s(F') \otimes F' = \sigma(\text{Conv}_{7\times 7}(\text{Concat}[\text{AvgPool}(F'), \text{MaxPool}(F')])) \otimes F' \quad (2)$$

Subsequently, we align the resolutions of all branches through upsampling and achieve multi-scale fusion using feature fusion convolution. The formula is as follows:

$$\tilde{F}_i = \text{Upsample}(F_i, \text{scale} = s_i) \quad (3)$$

$$F_{\text{fused}} = \text{ReLU}(\text{BN}(\text{Conv}(\text{Concat}[\tilde{F}_1, \tilde{F}_2, \tilde{F}_3, \tilde{F}_4]))) \quad (4)$$

### 3.3 Label Correlation Learning

An insecure smart contract often has multiple vulnerabilities, yet most multi-label detection methods overlook inter-label correlations. To address this, we generate the label correlation graph based on the training set, use Node2Vec for node embedding, and complete the learning of the label association relationship using a GAT network. The architecture is depicted in the Label Correlation learning module of Fig. 1.

**Label Correlation Graph.** We construct a label correlation graph based on co-occurrence relationships among labels in the training set. In this graph, each node represents a vulnerability label, and the weight of an edge reflects the number of times the corresponding label pair co-occurs, higher weight indicates a stronger association. Formally, let the label set be $L = \{l_1, l_2, \ldots, l_K\}$, where $K$ is the total number of vulnerability labels. The training set contains $N$ samples, and the label set for the n-th sample is $Y_n$ for $n \in [1, N]$. We add an undirected weighted edge $e_{ij}$ between labels $l_i$ and $l_j$ if they co-occur in at least one sample. Consequently, we obtain an undirected weighted graph $G = (V, E, W)$, where $V = L$, $E$ is the set of edges, and $W$ assigns each edge its co-occurrence count as the weight.

First, we calculate the co-occurrence frequency of all labels across $N$ samples. For each sample $Y_n$, we iterate through every pair of labels $(l_i, l_j)$ $(i \neq$ j) and compute the co-occurrence count for these label pairs. The formula is as follows:

$$W_{ij} = C_{ij} = \sum_{n=1}^{N} I\{l_i \in Y_n \wedge l_j \in Y_n \wedge i \neq j\} \tag{5}$$

where $I\{...\}$ denotes the indicator function, which takes a value of 1 when $l_i$ and $l_j$ co-occur in the same sample; otherwise, it is equal to 0.

To mitigate the issue of isolated nodes arising from non-co-occurring label pairs in the correlation graph, we introduce Laplacian smoothing, which assigns a small non-zero association weight to label pairs even when they do not appear together. The formula is as follows:

$$\tilde{C}_{ij} = \frac{C_{ij} + \epsilon}{N_i + \epsilon \cdot K} \tag{6}$$

where $\epsilon$ is the smoothing factor, $N_i$ represents the number of times the label $l_i = 1$.

Finally, we symmetrize the weight matrix to ensure the resulting label association graph satisfies the properties of an undirected graph, thereby constructing the global label correlation graph based on the training set.

**Graph Feature Extraction.** Based on the constructed label correlation graph, we first employ Node2Vec [25] to perform node embedding, which effectively captures complex relationships among labels. The core idea of Node2Vec is to generate random walk sequences over the graph G, and then input these sequences into the Skip-Gram model to learn low-dimensional representations of nodes. The resulting node embeddings are subsequently fed into a GAT to further learn structural features of the graph, which are then utilized by the downstream fusion learning module.

GAT [26] is an attention based neural network that leverages multi-head attention to assign varying weights to neighboring nodes, effectively overcoming the limitation of traditional GCN that treat all neighbors equally. First, a single-head attention score between nodes is computed through a nonlinear transformation, normalization of attention weights, and weighted aggregation. Multiple attention heads are then applied in parallel to capture diverse features, and their outputs are concatenated to form the final representation for each node.

### 3.4 Fusion Learning

Existing multi-label vulnerability detection methods for smart contracts often overlook the correspondence between labels and vulnerability features, which limits their detection performance. Both [27] and [28] adopt the Query2Label framework, leveraging self-attention and cross-attention mechanisms to model interactions between labels and image features. Inspired by these works, we design a fusion learning module to enable deep integration and joint learning of label and image features, as illustrated in Fig. 1. The fusion learning module consists of multiple serially connected decoder layers, each comprising multi-head self-attention, cross-attention, and a feed forward neural network.

Specifically, we first feed label feature vectors into the multi-head self-attention mechanism to capture the contextual relationships within the label correlation graph. The multi-head self-attention in the i-th decoder layer is formulated as follows:

$$Q_i^{(1)} = \text{MultiHeadSelfAttn}(\tilde{Q}_{i-1}, \tilde{Q}_{i-1}, Q_{i-1}) \tag{7}$$

where $Q_{i-1}$ represents the label features processed by the (i-1)th decoder layer.

Then, the cross-attention mechanism is capable of better capturing the complex relationships between image features and labels. Finally, a feed forward neural network is applied to learn local features. The cross-attention mechanism in the i-th decoder layer is formulated as follows:

$$Q_i^{(2)} = \text{MultiHeadSelfAttn}(\tilde{Q}_i^{(1)}, \tilde{F}, F) \tag{8}$$

where $F$ denotes the image feature vectors output by the feature extraction module.

### 3.5 Vulnerability Classification

After fusing the label and image features, we design separate MLP based classification heads for each label to more effectively address the varying classification difficulties and class imbalance issues of different vulnerabilities. Specifically, a total of five independent classification heads are implemented, each producing a single-dimensional output vector. The outputs of these five heads are then concatenated to form the final model output.

The classification head for Label 1 consists of three fully connected (FC) layers. The first layer has 512 neurons, the second layer has 256 neurons, and the third layer outputs a single neuron. Batch normalization and GELU activation are applied after the first and second layers, with a dropout rate of 0.4 for both.

The classification head for Label 2 contains four FC layers with 768, 256, 128, and 1 neuron(s) respectively. Batch normalization and SiLU activation are applied after the first three layers. The dropout rates are set to 0.5, 0.4, and 0.4 for the first, second, and third layers, respectively.

The classification head for Label 3 includes three FC layers with 512, 128, and 1 neuron(s) respectively. Batch normalization and ReLU activation follow the first and second layers, both with a dropout rate of 0.5. The classification heads for Label 4 and Label 5 share the same architecture as Label 3 head, differing only in the dropout rate, which is set to 0.6 for both layers.

### 3.6 Loss Function

The loss function measures the difference between predictions and true values, guiding model parameter optimization via backpropagation to improve model performance during training. Common loss functions for multi-label classification tasks include Focal Loss [29] and the Asymmetric Loss Function (ASL) [30]. However, ASL suffers from sensitivity to hyperparameter settings and lacks a unified configuration. Additionally, its truncation strategy may pose a risk of underfitting.

We propose a novel loss function called SWASL, which extends the ASL by incorporating label smoothing and class-weighting mechanism. By assigning a distinct weight to each label category, SWASL compensates for inter-class disparities, reduces reliance on hyperparameter tuning, and offers greater flexibility in handling class imbalance in multi-label scenarios. Moreover, applying label smoothing before loss computation helps suppress extreme predictions and mitigates the risk of underfitting.

Let the corresponding ground-truth label values be $y_1, y_2, ..., y_K$, where K is the total number of labels. First, label smoothing is applied to the ground-truth labels of each image. Then, the loss is computed and class-specific weights are applied to obtain the final loss score. The formula is as follows:

$$\tilde{y}_i = \begin{cases} 1 - \epsilon, & y_i = 1, \\ 0, & y_i = 0. \end{cases} \tag{9}$$

$$L = -\sum_{k=1}^{K} W_i \left[ \tilde{y}_i (1 - p_i)^{\gamma^+} \log(p_i) + (1 - \tilde{y}_i) p_m^{\gamma^-} \log(1 - p_m) \right] \tag{10}$$

where $\gamma^+$ and $\gamma^-$ are the regulating factors for positive and negative samples respectively, $W_i$ denotes the class weight for the i-th label. $p_i$ is the predicted probability for the i-th class, and $p_m$ is the modified probability, defined as $p_m = \max(p_i - m, 0)$, where m is the probability margin.

# 4 Experimental Evaluation

Here, we carry out an extensive analysis of the presented approach. The following research questions are our focus:

**RQ1:** How does our proposed method perform compared to other state-of-the-art multi-label smart contract vulnerability detection methods?

**RQ2:** Does the RGB image generation method we adopt contribute to improved vulnerability detection performance?

**RQ3:** What contributions does our proposed model architecture make to the overall detection approach?

## 4.1 Experimental Setup

**Datasets.** We use the multi-label smart contract vulnerability dataset released by Rossini [19] on the HuggingFace Hub, containing bytecode from over 100,000 Ethereum-verified contracts. It includes five types of vulnerabilities: Access Control (AC), Arithmetic Overflow (AO), Reentrancy (RE), Unchecked Calls (UC), and Others (OT), with OT covering all vulnerabilities outside the first four, such as unchecked uninitialized state variables.

**Implementations Details.** All experiments are conducted on a machine equipped with an Intel(R) Xeon(R) Gold 6330 CPU, RTX 3090 GPU, and 60GB RAM. The dataset is split into training, validation, and test sets with a ratio of 7.5: 1: 1.5. An early stopping strategy is employed during training to prevent overfitting. The AdamW optimizer is used with a learning rate of 1e-4, a batch size of 64, and a maximum of 100 epochs. All input images are resized to a resolution of $256 \times 256$.

**Metrics.** We divide the evaluation metrics into overall metrics and per-vulnerability-type metrics. The overall metrics include Hamming Loss, Macro-F1, Micro-F1, and AUC. For each type of vulnerability, we use Accuracy, Precision, Recall, F1-score, and AUC to assess the detection performance.

## 4.2 Performance Comparison (RQ1)

**Comparison of Different Backbone Network.** To validate the effectiveness of the proposed backbone, we compare it against three representative baseline models: ResNet-101, HrNet, and MobileNetV3. As shown in Table 1, our backbone outperforms all baseline models across four metrics: Hamming Loss, Macro-F1, Micro-F1, and AUC. Among the baselines, ResNet-101 demonstrates the strongest performance; nevertheless, our method achieves a reduction of 0.0998 in Hamming Loss, and improvements of 0.0481 in Macro-F1. The proposed backbone retains all multi-resolution branches from HRNet and integrates CBAM for enhanced feature fusion, enabling more improved detection performance.

**Table 1.** Experimental results of each backbone network.

| Backbone | Hamming Loss | Macro-F1 | Micro-F1 | AUC |
|---|---|---|---|---|
| Resnet 101 | 0.1846 | 0.7674 | 0.7894 | 0.9317 |
| HrNet | 0.2008 | 0.7405 | 0.7664 | 0.8916 |
| MobileNet V3 | 0.2244 | 0.7231 | 0.7380 | 0.8708 |
| **HrNet+CBAM (ours)** | **0.0848** | **0.8165** | **0.8395** | **0.9378** |

**Compared with Other Multi-label Smart Contract Vulnerability Detection Methods.** To evaluate the performance differences among various multi-label smart contract vulnerability detection methods, we compare MuLImg-SCV with several state-of-the-art approaches. Specifically, we first compare MuLImg-SCV with sequence-based models, namely AWD-LSTM [8] and VulnSense [9]. As shown in Table 2, MuLImg-SCV outperforms both AWD-LSTM and VulnSense in overall performance. In terms of Hamming Loss, MuLImg-SCV achieves reductions of 0.2106 and 0.1160 compared to AWD-LSTM and VulnSense, respectively. Regarding Macro-F1 and Micro-F1, MuLImg-SCV achieves average improvements of 0.1649 and 0.1655 respectively over the two models. From Table 3, we observe that for all five vulnerability categories MuLImg-SCV achieves significantly better performance in Accuracy, Precision, F1-score, and AUC. Specifically, it outperforms AWD-LSTM and VulnSense in Accuracy by average margins of 0.1021, 0.1607, 0.1778, 0.1544, and 0.1700 for the respective categories. While AWD-LSTM and VulnSense achieve respectable AUC scores of 0.8387 and 0.8575, and slightly higher Recall in some cases, their overall performance is inconsistent across the remaining metrics. This instability can be attributed to their lack of mechanisms for handling multi-label class imbalance and for learning inter-label dependencies.

**Table 2.** The experimental results of comparison on the overall evaluation metrics.

| Backbone | Hamming Loss | Macro-F1 | Micro-F1 | AUC |
|---|---|---|---|---|
| AWD-LSTM [8] | 0.2954 | 0.6141 | 0.6373 | 0.8387 |
| VulnSense [9] | 0.2008 | 0.6892 | 0.7107 | 0.8575 |
| ResNet 101 | 0.3946 | 0.5474 | 0.5694 | 0.8017 |
| VGG 19 | 0.4708 | 0.5105 | 0.5264 | 0.7516 |
| MobileNet V3 | 0.6144 | 0.4431 | 0.4580 | 0.6508 |
| **MuLImg-SCV** | **0.0848** | **0.8165** | **0.8395** | **0.9378** |

Next, we compare MuLImg-SCV with multi-label smart contract vulnerability detection methods based on RGB images, specifically studies [11,19], and [12]. However, these existing works mainly employ computer vision models such as ResNet, VGG, and MobileNetV3 directly for detection and performance comparison. To ensure fairness, we conduct experiments comparing MuLImg-SCV against ResNet 101, VGG 19, and MobileNet V3. As shown in Tables 2 and 3, MuLImg-SCV achieves an average reduction in Hamming Loss of 0.4085 over the three models. Notably, for certain vulnerability categories, MuLImg-SCV surpasses these models in accuracy by margins greater than 0.60. Existing vision-based methods for multi-label smart contract vulnerability detection struggle due to severe class imbalance and the challenge of generating informative RGB images. In comparison, our approach overcomes these challenges by employing a specialized loss function and generating RGB images via a Hilbert curve.

**Table 3.** The experimental results of comparison on various category evaluation metrics.

| Measure | | AWD-LSTM [8] | VulnSense [9] | ResNet 101 | VGG 19 | MobileNet V3 | **MuLImg-SCV** |
|---|---|---|---|---|---|---|---|
| Accuracy | AC | 0.8002 | 0.8589 | 0.5862 | 0.4878 | 0.3204 | **0.9316** |
| | AO | 0.6408 | 0.8736 | 0.5255 | 0.3774 | 0.2565 | **0.9194** |
| | RE | 0.7078 | 0.7473 | 0.7186 | 0.6914 | 0.5171 | **0.9053** |
| | UC | 0.7096 | 0.7644 | 0.6367 | 0.5929 | 0.5044 | **0.8914** |
| | OT | 0.6644 | 0.7520 | 0.5598 | 0.4964 | 0.3298 | **0.8782** |
| Precision | AC | 0.4145 | 0.5117 | 0.2537 | 0.2178 | 0.1672 | **0.8012** |
| | AO | 0.3157 | 0.6083 | 0.2603 | 0.2134 | 0.1835 | **0.8091** |
| | RE | 0.5099 | 0.5476 | 0.5204 | 0.4959 | 0.3794 | **0.8737** |
| | UC | 0.6125 | 0.6624 | 0.5574 | 0.5289 | 0.4797 | **0.8649** |
| | OT | 0.4386 | 0.5163 | 0.3729 | 0.3412 | 0.2808 | **0.7984** |
| Recall | AC | 0.8797 | 0.8293 | **0.9408** | 0.9640 | 0.9146 | 0.8087 |
| | AO | 0.9597 | 0.7134 | **0.9716** | 0.9908 | 0.9771 | 0.7887 |
| | RE | **0.9714** | 0.9647 | 0.9448 | 0.9359 | 0.9272 | 0.8047 |
| | UC | 0.9929 | 0.9881 | 0.9957 | 0.9977 | **0.9973** | 0.9035 |
| | OT | 0.9769 | 0.9324 | 0.9847 | 0.9802 | **0.9893** | 0.8015 |
| F1-score | AC | 0.5635 | 0.6329 | 0.3997 | 0.3553 | 0.2827 | **0.8099** |
| | AO | 0.4751 | 0.6566 | 0.4106 | 0.3512 | 0.3089 | **0.7987** |
| | RE | 0.6688 | 0.6987 | 0.6711 | 0.6483 | 0.5385 | **0.8377** |
| | UC | 0.7576 | 0.7931 | 0.7147 | 0.6913 | 0.6478 | **0.8838** |
| | OT | 0.6054 | 0.6646 | 0.5409 | 0.5062 | 0.4374 | **0.7999** |
| AUC | AC | 0.8378 | 0.8696 | 0.7805 | 0.7344 | 0.6038 | **0.9279** |
| | AO | 0.8246 | 0.8476 | 0.7799 | 0.7181 | 0.6465 | **0.9215** |
| | RE | 0.8447 | 0.8818 | 0.8321 | 0.7939 | 0.6829 | **0.9524** |
| | UC | 0.8728 | 0.8566 | 0.8359 | 0.8056 | 0.6378 | **0.9631** |
| | OT | 0.8139 | 0.8323 | 0.7803 | 0.7061 | 0.6831 | **0.9244** |

### 4.3 Research on Image Generation Methods (RQ2)

We propose a novel method for converting smart contract bytecode into RGB images using a Hilbert curve-based mapping. Unlike conventional approaches that either map bytecode directly into RGB images or convert bytecode into grayscale images, our method preserves the local structural information of the code and produces images whose spatial layout more accurately reflects the underlying logic of the bytecode. To evaluate the effectiveness of our method, we conducted experiments comparing all three image generation techniques under identical model architectures and hyperparameter settings. As reported in Table 4, our Hilbert curve-based RGB representation achieved the best performance. Compared to the grayscale method, our approach reduced the Hamming Loss by 0.0848 and increased the Macro-F1 score by 0.1013. When compared to the direct RGB mapping method, the Hamming Loss decreased by 0.0501, and the Macro-F1 improved by 0.0616.

**Table 4.** Comparison of Different image generation methods.

| Method | Hamming Loss | Macro-F1 | Micro-F1 | AUC |
|---|---|---|---|---|
| Grayscale | 0.1649 | 0.7152 | 0.7377 | 0.9202 |
| Direct conversion | 0.1349 | 0.7549 | 0.7747 | 0.9327 |
| **Hilbert** | **0.0848** | **0.8165** | **0.8395** | **0.9378** |

### 4.4 Ablation Experiment (RQ3)

**Contribution of MuLImg-SCV Module Structures to Detection Performance.** We conducted ablation studies to evaluate the contribution of each module in the proposed architecture, as summarized in Table 5. Model 1 utilizes only the feature extraction module and an independent classification head module. Model 2 adds a label correlation module and replaces the fusion module with simple concatenation. Model 3 incorporates both the label correlation and fusion modules but removes the CBAM based multi-scale fusion. Model 4 adopts a shared classification head while keeping all other components intact. Compared to Model 1, Model 2 reduces Hamming Loss by 0.0198 and improves Macro-F1 by 0.0162, indicating that incorporating label association learning effectively improves overall detection performance. When comparing Model 3 with Model 2, there was a decrease in Hamming Loss of 0.0336 and an increase in Macro-F1 of 0.0301, demonstrating the effectiveness of the fusion learning module. When compared to Model 3, MuLImg-SCV achieved a reduction in Hamming Loss of 0.0302 and an increase in Macro-F1 of 0.0316, suggesting that the CBAM multi-scale fusion module is capable of preserving effective features from each branch. Furthermore, when comparing MuLImg-SCV with Model 4, there was a decrease in Hamming Loss by 0.0479 and an increase in Macro-F1 by 0.0539, indicating that using independent classification heads enables better adaptation to varying detection difficulties across vulnerability types.

**Table 5.** Ablation experiment of the model architecture.

| Method | Hamming Loss | Macro-F1 | Micro-F1 | AUC |
|---|---|---|---|---|
| Model 1 | 0.1684 | 0.7186 | 0.7421 | 0.9202 |
| Model 2 | 0.1486 | 0.7348 | 0.7477 | 0.9293 |
| Model 3 | 0.1150 | 0.7849 | 0.7890 | 0.9350 |
| Model 4 | 0.1327 | 0.7626 | 0.7803 | 0.9291 |
| **MuLImg-SCV** | **0.0848** | **0.8165** | **0.8395** | **0.9378** |

**Contribution of Data Augmentation and Loss Functions to Detection Performance.** In order to demonstrate the contributions of data augmentation and different loss functions to overall detection performance, we conducted ablation experiments summarized in Table 6. Without noise addition or imbalance handling, the model's Hamming Loss was 0.1998. Adding noise reduced Hamming Loss by 0.0254 and increased Macro-F1 by 0.0340, demonstrating improved generalization and robustness. Compared to using BCEWithLogitsLoss, employing Focal Loss resulted in a reduction of Hamming Loss by 0.0296 and an increase in Macro-F1 by 0.0189. ASL further improved over Focal Loss with a 0.0231 reduction in Hamming Loss and a 0.0303 increase in Macro-F1, addressing limitations in handling simple positive samples. Furthermore, SWASL improves ASL by reducing Hamming Loss by 0.0140 and increasing Macro-F1 by 0.0242, suggesting that our improvements on ASL significantly bolster the model's learning capability during training.

**Table 6.** Ablation experiment of the model architecture.

| Method | Hamming Loss | Macro-F1 | Micro-F1 | AUC |
|---|---|---|---|---|
| No noise+BCEWithLogitsLoss | 0.1769 | 0.7091 | 0.7332 | 0.9325 |
| add noise+BCEWithLogitsLoss | 0.1515 | 0.7431 | 0.7594 | 0.9328 |
| add noise+Focal loss | 0.1219 | 0.7620 | 0.7879 | 0.9322 |
| add noise+ ASL | 0.0988 | 0.7923 | 0.8146 | 0.9353 |
| **add noise+ SWASL** | **0.0848** | **0.8165** | **0.8395** | **0.9378** |

### 4.5 Conclusions

We present a novel multi-label vulnerability detection method for smart contracts that operates on RGB images. First, bytecode is mapped onto RGB images via a Hilbert curve to preserve local structural patterns. Subsequently, we integrate the CBAM into HrNet to enhance the quality of image feature learning and fusion. To capture and exploit inter-label dependencies, we introduce a label correlation learning module, whose outputs are deeply integrated with image features through a dedicated fusion learning module. To handle varying classification difficulties and alleviate class imbalance, our classifier employs multiple heads and incorporates both label smoothing and class-weighting into the ASL. Extensive experiments show that our approach significantly outperforms existing multi-label detection methods. In future work, we will extend this method to additional blockchain platforms and further optimize its detection capabilities.

**Acknowledgments.** This work was partially supported by the National Natural Science Foundation of China (62366052) and the Sichuan Province Joint Fund Project (25QYCX0103).

## References

1. Bartoletti, M., Pompianu, L.: An empirical analysis of smart contracts: platforms, applications, and design patterns. In: Proceeding of the Financial Cryptography and Data Security, pp. 494–509. TA, Sliema, Malta(2017)
2. Wood, G.: Ethereum: a secure decentralised generalised transaction ledger. Ethereum project yellow paper, pp. 1–32 (2014)
3. Zhuang, Y., Liu, Z., Qian, P., Liu, Q., Wang, X., He, Q.: Smart contract vulnerability detection using graph neural networks. In: Proceeding of the 29th International Conference on International Joint Conferences on Artificial Intelligence, pp. 3283–3290. Yokohama, Japan (2021)
4. Cai, J., Li, B., Zhang, J., Sun, X., Chen, B.: Combine sliced joint graph with graph neural networks for smart contract vulnerability detection. J. Syst. Softw. **195** (2023)
5. Liu, Z., Qian, P., Wang, X., Zhuang, Y., Qiu, L., Wang, X.: Combining graph neural networks with expert knowledge for smart contract vulnerability detection. IEEE Trans. Knowl. Data Eng. **36**(1), 1296–1310 (2021)
6. Xie, X., Wang, H., Jian, Z., Fang, Y., Wang, Z.: Block-gram: mining knowledgeable features for efficiently smart contract vulnerability detection. Digit. Commun. Netw. (2023)
7. Tong, V., Dao, C., Tran, H.A., et al.: Enhancing BERT-based language model for multi-label vulnerability detection of smart contract in blockchain. J. Netw. Syst. Manag. **32**(3) (2024)
8. Gogineni, A.K., Swayamjyoti, S., Sahoo, D., et al.: Multi-class classification of vulnerabilities in smart contracts using AWD-LSTM, with pre-trained encoder inspired from natural language processing. IOP SciNotes **1**(3) (2020)
9. Duy, P.T., Khoa, N.H., Quyen, N.H., et al.: Vulnsense: efficient vulnerability detection in ethereum smart contracts by multimodal learning with graph neural network and language model. Int. J. Inf. Secur. **24**(1) (2025)
10. Qian, S., Ning, H., He, Y., et al.: Multi-label vulnerability detection of smart contracts based on Bi-LSTM and attention mechanism. Electronics **11**(19) (2022)
11. Mustafa, I., McGibney, A., Rea, S.: An evaluation of lightweight CNNs for smart contract vulnerability detection. In: IEEE International Conference on Blockchain and Cryptocurrency (ICBC), pp. 675–677 (2024)
12. Bani-Hani, R.M., Shatnawi, A.S., Al-Yahya, L.: Vulnerability detection and classification of ethereum smart contracts using deep learning. Future Internet **16**(9) (2024)

13. Zeng, S., Chen, R., Zhang, H., Wang, J.: A high-performance smart contract vulnerability detection scheme based on BERT. In: Proceeding of the 29th International Conference on Parallel and Distributed Systems (ICPADS), pp. 653–658 (2023)
14. Jeon, S., Lee, G., Kim, H., Woo, S.: Smartcondetect: highly accurate smart contract code vulnerability detection mechanism using BERT. In: Proceeding of the KDD Workshop on Programming Language Processing (2021)
15. Li, M., Ren, X., Fu, H., Li, Z., Sun, J.: ConvMHSA-SCVD: enhancing smart contract vulnerability detection through a knowledge-driven and data-driven framework. In: Proceeding of the 34th International Symposium on Software Reliability Engineering (ISSRE), pp. 578–589 (2023)
16. Chen, D., Feng, L., Fan, Y., Shang, S., Wei, Z.: Smart contract vulnerability detection based on semantic graph and residual graph convolutional networks with edge attention. J. Syst. Softw. **202** (2023)
17. Wu, H., et al.: Peculiar: smart contract vulnerability detection based on crucial data flow graph and pre-training techniques. In: Proceeding of the 32nd International Symposium on Software Reliability Engineering (ISSRE), pp. 378–389 (2021)
18. Hwang, S.J., Choi, S.H., Shin, J., et al.: CodeNet: code-targeted convolutional neural network architecture for smart contract vulnerability detection. IEEE Access **10**, 32595–32607 (2022)
19. Rossini, M., Zichichi, M., Ferretti, S.: On the use of deep neural networks for security vulnerabilities detection in smart contracts. In: IEEE International Conference on Pervasive Computing and Communications Workshops and Other Affiliated Events (PerCom Workshops), pp. 74–79 (2023)
20. Hilbert, D.: Über die stetige abbildung einer linie auf ein flächenstück. Mathematische Annalen Zeitschriftenband, pp. 459–460 (1891)
21. Mohammed Abd-Alsalam Selami, A., Freidoon Fadhil, A.: A study of the effects of gaussian noise on image features. Kirkuk Univ. J.-Sci. Stud. *11*, 152–169 (2016)
22. Racine, R., Walker, G.A., Nadeau, D., Doyon, R., Marois, C.: Speckle noise and the detection of faint companions. Publ. Astron. Soc. Pac. **111**
23. Wang, J., Sun, K., Cheng, T., et al.: Deep high-resolution representation learning for visual recognition. IEEE Trans. Pattern Anal. Mach. Intell. **43**(10), 3349–3364 (2020)
24. Woo, S., Park, J., Lee, J Y., et al.: CBAM: convolutional block attention module. In: Proceedings of the European Conference on Computer Vision (ECCV), pp. 3–19 (2018)
25. Grover, A., Leskovec, J.: node2vec: scalable feature learning for networks. In: Proceedings of the 22nd ACM SIGKDD International Conference on Knowledge Discovery and Data Mining, pp. 855–864 (2016)
26. Veličković, P., Cucurull, G., Casanova, A., Romero, A., Liò, P., Bengio, Y.: Graph attention networks. arXiv preprint, arXiv:1710.10903 (2017)
27. Liu, S., Zhang, L., Yang, X., et al.: Query2label: a simple transformer way to multi-label classification. arXiv preprint, arXiv:2107.10834 (2021)
28. Gao, Q., Long, T., Zhou, Z.: Mineral identification based on natural feature-oriented image processing and multi-label image classification. Expert Syst. Appl. **238** (2024)
29. Lin, T Y., Goyal, P., Girshick, R., et al.: Focal loss for dense object detection. In: Proceedings of the IEEE International Conference on Computer Vision, pp. 2980–2988 (2017)
30. Ridnik, T., et al.: Asymmetric loss for multi-label classification. In: Proceedings of the IEEE/CVF International Conference on Computer Vision, pp. 82–91 (2021)

# On the Security of the RDHEI by Binary Symmetric Channel and Polar Code

Xuebin Wang[1], Hongjie He[1(✉)], Fan Chen[2], and Yaolin Yang[1]

[1] School of Information Science and Technology, Southwest Jiaotong University, Chengdu, China
xuebinwang@my.swjtu.edu.cn, hjhe@swjtu.edu.cn
[2] School of Computing and Artificial Intelligence, Southwest Jiaotong University, Chengdu, China
fchen@swjtu.edu.cn

**Abstract.** RDHEI effectively combines encryption and information hiding techniques for applications like privacy protection and copyright protection. However, most existing RDHEI methods are not suitable for authenticating based on noise in the cloud environment. This noise can interfere with fragile hidden data, leading to incorrect extraction. Recently, Chen [6] proposed an RDHEI scheme based on binary symmetric channel and polar coding, which can be used to extract lossless secret data while maintaining the robustness of secret data and effectively eliminating noise in the cloud environment for privacy protection and copyright protection. However, due to the inadequacy of XOR encryption, the forging of secret images in the cloud will lead to serious security risks. In this paper, it is analyzed to verify the security threats present in ciphertext images in the cloud environment. First, the algorithm used in [6] is analyzed to demonstrate the unreliability of XOR encryption. Second, a forging explicit watermark attack (FEWA) method is proposed to add a visible explicit watermark with the hint text "Generated by AI" to the marked encrypted image in [6]. Finally, the feasibility of our proposed FEWA method is verified through experimental analysis to validate the security risk that the integrity and authenticity of the ciphertext are destroyed. Experiments show that explicit watermark hint text is displayed in the recovered image, and the reconstructed secret data is free of errors, while the reconstructed image completely changes its original intent, resulting in compromised integrity of the image and authenticity of the cloud storage source.

**Keywords:** Reversible data hiding · Encrypted images · Noisy channel · FEWA · Security

## 1 Introduction

Nowadays, artificial intelligence (AI) technology is developing at a rapid pace, and the emergence of Artificial Intelligence Generated Content (AIGC) has triggered widespread attention. People can effortlessly generate high-quality multimedia content that is indistinguishable to the public through AI [24], such as


K.-K. R. Choo et al. (Eds.): ICDF2C 2025, LNICST 686, pp. 556–575, 2026.
https://doi.org/10.1007/978-3-032-22545-0_32

text writing, image synthesis, and audio/video creation. However, the explosion of generated content in cyberspace raises numerous security issues, including fake news and deepfake images for fraudulent purposes [7]. Consequently, both academia and industry have begun to emphasize the trustworthiness of generated content and have come up with a series of policies [10,14,17] to manage AI-generated content. In the document signed by China in 2023 [17], the necessity of adding explicit and implicit watermarks to AI-generated content has been raised. In particular, explicit watermark means that the generated content must display a visible prompt text indicating that it is generated by AI, and implicit watermark means that the content generated by the AI must contain invisible technical markings, including at least the name of the service provider, which are not detectable by humans but can be technically detected by other tools.

In order to add an implicit watermark to images, the reversible data hiding (RDH) [21] technique achieved good performance by applying specific image processing. With the development of cloud computing techniques, more and more digital images are uploaded to cloud servers, and the confidentiality of cloud images may be threatened by half-trusted clouds or any unauthorized users, so reversible data hiding in encrypted images (RDHEI) came into existence [27]. Before data embedding, content owners convert the original image into an unintelligible noise-like image using an encryption mechanism to ensure privacy. The embedded additional data is used to detect the authenticity of the image, protect the owner's copyright [8], or manage the cloud storage data [25]. Existing RDHEI methods can be categorized into two frameworks: reserving room before encryption (RRBE) and vacating room after encryption (VRAE).

In RRBE methods, the content owner preprocesses the original image using image pixel correlation to reserve some room for data embedding before image encryption. In [4,5], the idea of ordered indexing and adaptive coding technique was used to choose a location for data embedding, and the embedding capacity and security of RDHEI achieved good performance. Mohammadi [16] calculated the prediction error and reversed space in all-zero bit planes for data embedding, which significantly increased the embedding capacity of secret data. However, increasing embedding capacity leads to a degradation of image quality, and in order to avoid image distortion, Chen et al. [3] used the difference of most significant bit (MSB) in the compression phase so that reduced the impact of embedded data on the image quality. Generally, the RRBE methods is capable of embedding a large amount of secret data into an image, but it is impractical in cases where the content owner is unable to process the image or is unaware of the details of the RDH.

In VRAE methods, the content owner simply encrypts the original image and uploads it to the cloud for storage without any pre-processing. After data embedding, spatial correlation estimation algorithms are required to recover the modified regions of the image, but due to the complexity of the image content, the misalignment of the spatial correlation estimation algorithms can cause image recovery with potential errors. To address potential errors, most of the existing VRAE methods have to make a compromise between reversibility and embedding capacity. Li et al. [12] utilized the SVD technique for image block decomposition, embedding data into singular values of pixels to ensure reversibility. Wang et al. [22] divided the image into blocks and categorized these blocks into different types of rotation, and then embedded data via pixel rotation, which improved the security and reversibility. [15,23] proposed a block permutation and Co-XOR encryption algorithm to preserve the redundancy in the ciphertext to ensure security, and compressed the ciphertext blocks using the MSB plane sharing to increase embedding capacity. Although existing RDHEI methods can effectively balance reversibility and embedding capacity, they are difficult to ensure the robustness of secret data when the transmission channel contains noise. This problem may lead to the embedded secret data being damaged during transmission or storage in practical applications. Thus, the secret data cannot be successfully extracted to authenticate the authenticity of the image. To solve this problem, Chen [6] designed a RDHEI scheme combining binary symmetric channel and polar code (BSCPC-RDHEI). The channel noise is eliminated with the help of polar code [1,18], which can effectively correct the errors in data extraction and image recovery.

Existing RDHEI methods are devoted to balancing the performance of imperceptibility, reversibility, and embedding capacity [20,26]. If the marked image is attacked by some degree of noise, the receiver can still correctly extract the secret data to verify the attribution of the image. Therefore, the RDHEI technique can be used to add implicit watermarks to images to distinguish human-generated content from AI-generated content. However, in existing RDHEI schemes using XOR encryption, it is easy to tamper with the ciphertext image through some editing tools without knowing the content of the plaintext image [9]. Therefore, ciphertext images in the cloud pose a security risk. An attacker will maliciously forge a real image containing the owner's identity information to add an explicit watermark with the words "Generated by AI". This attack can be considered as channel noise, due to the strong robustness of the secret data in [6], the correctly extracted secret data is regarded as an implicit watermark of the AI-generated image, and there is no way to verify whether the image has been altered or not. Then the authenticity of the original image will be questioned, which will have a serious impact on the image owner or cloud service provider.

To illustrate this security issue, this paper investigates the security of BSCPC-RDHEI [6], revealing that the scheme has severe security flaws that compromise image authenticity and integrity. The main contributions of this paper are summarized as follows:

(1) The forging explicit watermark attack (FEWA) method is employed to add a visible explicit watermark with the prompt text "Generated by AI" into a marked encrypted image based on XOR encryption mechanism. It is proved that the prompt text is hard to detect in ciphertexts image, and the recovered image has lost its original meaning, so that the authenticity of the image is destroyed.
(2) A characteristics analysis of BSCPC-RDHEI [6] is provided. We analyze the robustness of secret data using two new features: error prediction rate (*EPR*)

and correct decoding rate (*CDR*). The experiments show that, in the noisy channel containing a certain degree of forgery, the secret data can still be extracted correctly, while the cover images are contaminated by noise. It proves that there is a security risk of integrity corruption of ciphertext images in the cloud environment.

The rest of this paper is organized as follows: Sect. 2 describes and analyzes Chen's scheme [6]. The details of the FEWA method are introduced in Sect. 3. In Sect. 4, experimental results and analysis are given. Section 5 concludes the work.

# 2 Preliminary

In this section, we briefly describe the characteristics of the RHDEI combining binary symmetric channel and polar code (BSCPC-RDHEI) in [6]. Following that, we analyze security threats in the cloud environment.

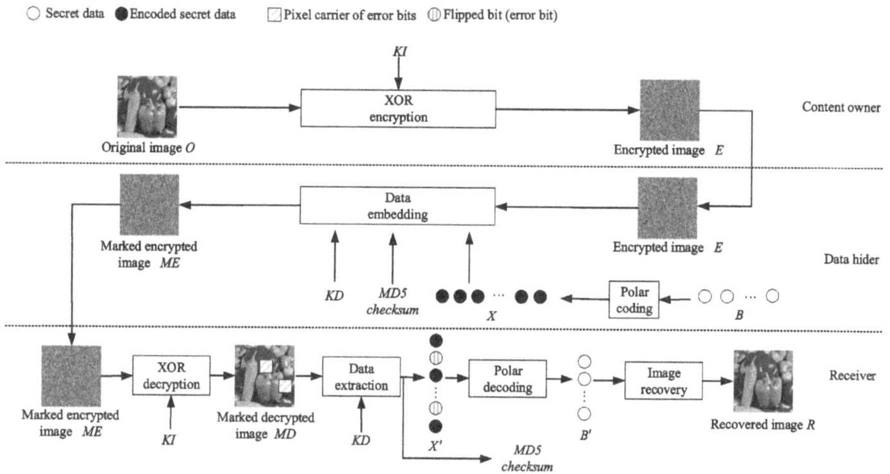


**Fig. 1.** The RDHEI framework using BSCPC in [6].

## 2.1 Description of BSCPC-RDHEI

Figure 1 illustrates the basic framework of [6] to correct the error bits in the channel, and the general steps are summarized as follows:

**Step 1:** XOR encryption. Given an original grayscale image with size of $H \times W$, For each pixel, content owner pseudo-randomly generates a key of the same length as the image using an image encryption key *KI*. And then encrypt the original image. After all of the pixels are encrypted, the encrypted image is sent to the data hider.

**Step 2:** Polar coding. In the binary symmetric channel (BSC), the data hider gets the index of $K$ bits $S = \{s_1, s_2, \cdots, s_K\}(1 \leq s_1 < s_2 < \cdots < s_K \leq N)$ by polar code construction scheme, which is used to choose the location for $K$ bits of the embedded secret data $B = \{b_1, b_2, \cdots, b_K\}$, while the rest bits (called frozen bits) in codeword are filled with zero. Then the secret data is pre-processed with polar code:

$$c_i = \begin{cases} b_r, \text{ when } i = s_r \\ 0, \quad \text{otherwise} \end{cases}, \text{ where } i = 1, 2, \cdots, N \text{ and } r = 1, 2, \cdots, K, \tag{1}$$

$$u = [c_1, c_2, \cdots, c_N], \tag{2}$$

and the encoded secret data $X$ of $N$ bits is generated as:

$$X = [x_1, x_2, \cdots, x_N] = uG_N, \tag{3}$$

where $G_N$ is the polar code generator matrix of order $N$ [19].

**Step 3:** Data embedding. The data hider uses the data hiding key $KD$ to embed the encoded secret data $X$ into the carrier pixel $ep_1, ep_2, \cdots, ep_N$ of the encrypted image $E$ to obtain the marked encrypted image $ME$. For each carrier pixel $ep$, the embedding process is as follows:

$$ep_i = \begin{cases} ep_i, & \text{if } x_i = 0 \\ ep_i \oplus 2^{bp-1}, & \text{if } x_i = 1 \end{cases}, \text{ where } i = 1, 2, \cdots, N, \tag{4}$$

where $bp$ indicates the bit plane of the pixels. Moreover, to confirm the integrity of secret data, the MD5 algorithm is used to generate a fixed-length checksum of the original secret bits.

**Step 4:** XOR decryption and data extraction. Before data extraction, the receiver uses the image encryption key $KI$ to decrypt each pixel. Then extract the embedded data with errors using the data hiding key $KD$:

$$\{x_i^{'}, p_i\} = \begin{cases} \{0, p_i\}, \text{ if } |p_i - pp_i| \leq |fp_i - pp_i| \\ \{1, fp_i\}, \text{ if } |p_i - pp_i| > |fp_i - pp_i| \end{cases}, \text{ where } i = 1, 2, \cdots, N, \tag{5}$$

where $x_i^{'}$ means the bit in extracted data with errors $X^{'}$, $fp_i$ represents the flipped on LSB plane of decrypted pixel $p_i$ and $pp_i$ is the predicted pixel value using the interpolation algorithm in [13].

**Step 5:** Polar decoding and image recovery. The receiver can decode the extracted data $X^{'}$ using polar decoding algorithm to obtain the decoded secret data $B^{'} = b_1^{'}, b_2^{'}, \cdots, b_K^{'}$. After confirming that $B^{'} = B$ using MD5 checksum, the secret data is correctly extracted. Then reconstruct the decoded secret data $B^{'}$, and further renew the image pixels $p_i$ to get the recovered image,

$$p_i = \begin{cases} p_i, & \text{if } x_i = 0 \\ p_i \oplus 2^{bp-1}, & \text{if } x_i = 1 \end{cases}, \text{ where } i = 1, 2, \cdots, N. \tag{6}$$

The BSCPC-RDHEI scheme corrects the error bits in the channel with the help of polar code. This enhances the robustness of the secret data and allows the receiver to extract the secret data correctly even if the carrier is subjected to some degree of noise attacks.

### 2.2 Security Analysis of BSCPC-RDHEI

As described in Sect. 2.1, in the BSCPC-RDHEI scheme, the XOR encryption algorithm has a large key space ($2^{H \times W \times 8}$) to protect the privacy of images. When the ciphertext image is subjected to some degree of noise in the cloud environment, the extracted encoded data $X^{'}$ can still be decoded to get the correct secret data that $B^{'} = B$ with the help of polar code. In order to confirm the correctness of extracted bits without knowing the original secret bits, the receiver can use the MD5 algorithm again to generate a new checksum and compare the generated checksum with the extracted checksum. Based on the above features, in [6], the condition of complete reversibility is equivalent to the condition that the extracted secret data can be correctly decoded. Although the BSCPC-RDHEI scheme performs well and can effectively improve the robustness of secret data, there are still severe security issues in the cloud environment. Some properties are discussed below.

**Weakness of XOR Encryption:** Before and after XOR encryption, the pixel positions of the image are not changed because the XOR operation just inverts or keeps the 0 and 1 bit values for each bit plane of each pixel [11].

This property enables the intentional forging of the ciphertext image without knowledge of the plaintext image. When attackers intercept an encrypted image, they can forge it by adding an explicit watermark, altering the meaning of the original image, and compromising its authenticity. This feature will be analyzed in detail in Sect. 3.2.

**Weakness of Robust Secret Data:** In BSC model, the signal in the input and output are represented by two binary representations, 0 and 1. As a noisy channel, the crossover probability $q$ represents the probability that the signal is flipped in data extraction and image recovery. If $X^{'}$ can be decoded into correct secret bits, the ratio of polar code $K/N$ should be:

$$K/N \leq Capacity_{BSC} = 1 - H(q), \tag{7}$$

where $H(q) = -q\log(q) - (1-q)\log(1-q)$. Whether the secret data can be correctly extracted just depends on whether its carrier pixels can be correctly predicted or not. Since each carrier pixel is independently predicted based on the associated reference pixels, the error prediction rate ($EPR$) of pixels in each image is computable,

$$EPR = \frac{\sum_{i=1}^{N} EPB_i}{N}, \tag{8}$$

where the error prediction bit is defined as:

$$EPB_i = \begin{cases} 1, \text{if } X_i^{'} \neq X_i \\ 0, \text{if } X_i^{'} = X_i \end{cases}. \tag{9}$$

With the help of polar code, the noise in the cloud environment can be eliminated under the condition:

$$EPR \leq q, \tag{10}$$

and the capacity is maximized when the BSC satisfies the condition $EPR = q$. However, the data hider cannot obtain the *EPR* of the image in advance, and an empirical $q$ is chosen and tends to retain adequate error-correcting ability in BSC. To verify that the secret data was extracted correctly, we compare the decoded secret data and the original secret data to obtain the correct decoding rate (*CDR*),

$$CDR = \frac{\sum_{i=1}^{K} CB_i}{K}, \tag{11}$$

where the correct bit is defined as:

$$CB_i = \begin{cases} 1, \text{if } B_i^{'} = B_i \\ 0, \text{if } B_i^{'} \neq B_i \end{cases}. \tag{12}$$

The condition $CDR = 1$ means that the extracted data $X^{'}$ is decoded into the secret data correctly, i.e., $B^{'} = B$. In summary, in the BSCPC-RDHEI scheme, when the condition $EPR \leq q$ is satisfied in data extraction, the extracted data $X^{'}$ can be correctly decoded using polar code, and the condition of complete reversibility is equivalent to the condition $CDR = 1$. However, if the forged explicit watermark with prompt text is treated as channel noise, it is still possible to obtain lossless secret data that does not recognize this change.

## 3 Proposed Analysis Based on FEWA

Analysis in Sect. 2 shows that BSCPC-RDHEI scheme uses a simple XOR encryption algorithm, which is easy to implement forgeries, and the secret data $B$ remains robust after the marked encrypted image $ME$ is forged, making it impossible to verify the forging behavior, which poses a security risk that the authenticity and integrity of the ciphertext image in the cloud is destroyed. To further illustrate this problem, we describe a security threat model in BSC with application scenarios. To verify this issue, our forging explicit watermark attack (FEWA) method is proposed, where a line of prompt text is added to the marked encrypted image so that the authenticity of the image will be destroyed. Finally, after the FEWA method, the robustness of the secret data is verified by analyzing the changes of *EPR* and *CDR* in BSC, confirming the security threat to integrity and source authenticity of the images being corrupted in BSCPC-RDHEI.

### 3.1 Security Threat Model

In essence, the RDHEI framework proposed by Chen [6] always works correctly in data extraction even when there is some noise in the cloud environment. The reliability of the channel transmission can be trusted only if the secret data is correctly decoded without any errors. However, it neglects the security risk of authenticity destruction when the ciphertext image is forged. As the scenario given in Fig. 2, in [6], the content owner encrypts his/her image using an image encryption key and embeds a hash with their identity information as an implicit watermark using a data hiding key to protect their copyright. Then, it is uploaded to a cloud server. These images include shooting images, creation drawings, and so on. In the cloud, the uploaded images need to be secured during storage. When an authorized user needs to download or purchase an image, the cloud server reaches a consensus with the content owner to recover the ciphertext image using the key *KI*, *KD*, and sends the recovered image to the user. However, if there is a malicious attacker who forges the ciphertext image by adding an explicit watermark with a prompt text "Generated by AI" in the cloud environment, the receiver obtains an image that shows the words "Generated by AI". This results in the real image with the owner's copyright becoming an AI-generated image, and the authenticity of the image source is damaged. Even if the extracted implicit watermark by the cloud manager confirms the attribution of the image, the forgery implement results in an image that is indistinguishable from the real one, and it still can be considered as an image created by AI, which creates a huge crisis of confidence for both the content owner and the cloud provider.

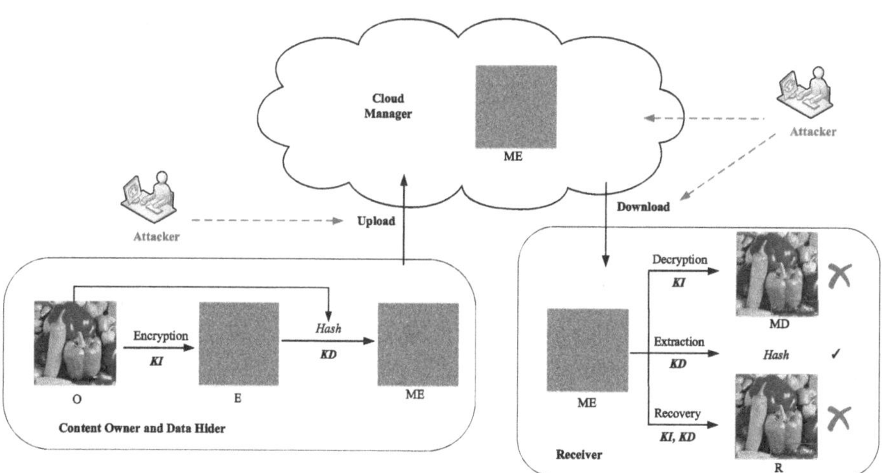


**Fig. 2.** RDHEI system security threat model.

Based on this scenario description, we further analyze XOR encryption and BSCPC in [6] to verify the forgerability of the ciphertext image in cloud by using the forging explicit watermark attack (FEWA) method. We prove that there is a security risk to the integrity and authenticity of the ciphertext image.

### 3.2 Description of FEWA

In the proposed FEWA method, the explicit watermark containing a prompt text is first placed in a blank image of the same size as the cloud image. And then transform it into a binary image to obtain a forge logo (FL),

$$F_{i,j} = \begin{cases} 0, \text{ if } F_{i,j} \le t \\ 1, \text{ if } F_{i,j} > t \end{cases}, \tag{13}$$

where $F_{i,j}$ denotes the pixel value of the forge logo ($FL$) with position i-th row and j-th column, $t$ is the threshold value when transformed into a binary image. The pixel value in the explicit watermark area satisfies $F_{i,j} = 0$. For the explicit watermark region, the corresponding pixel in the marked encrypted image $ME$ will be flipped on $8^{\text{th}}$ MSB plane. Like the constant feature attack (CFA) [2], the proposed FEWA method is a value change for the changing pattern of image pixels, while the pixel position does not alter.

To illustrate the weakness of the XOR encryption algorithm, we give an example of the FEWA method to forge $ME$ based on XOR encryption as shown in Fig. 3. Comparing the pixels of the forged decrypted image and the directly decrypted image, the pixel value $Fp_{i,j}$ corresponding to the explicit watermark region is increased or decreased by $2^7$, as in Eq. (14). Therefore, the prompt text will display in the decrypted image due to the change of the pixel value.

$$Fp_{i,j} = \sum_{bp=1}^{7} 2^{bp-1} \times p_{i,j,bp} + 2^7 \times Fp_{i,j,8} = \begin{cases} p_{i,j} + 2^7, \text{ where } F_{i,j} = 0 \text{ and } p_{i,j} < 2^7 \\ p_{i,j} - 2^7, \text{ where } F_{i,j} = 0 \text{ and } p_{i,j} \ge 2^7 \\ Fp_{i,j}, \quad \text{where } F_{i,j} = 1 \end{cases}. \tag{14}$$

In summary, when the RDHEI scheme encrypts an image using the XOR encryption algorithm, FEWA can be used to add an explicit watermark with prompt text to the $ME$ in cloud, resulting in the meaning of the image being altered and the authenticity of the image being destroyed.

### 3.3 Analysis of *EPR* And *CDR*

To illustrate the robustness of the secret data in [6], we analyze the change of *EPR* and *CDR* in BSCPC-RDHEI after FEWA. As mentioned in Eq. (5), (8), and (9), if we embed bit $x_i = 1$ to the LSB plane, the original pixel should be equal to the pixel which is flipped on the bit plane, then the *EPR* will remains unchanged. So we discuss four cases of *EPR* changes as follows:

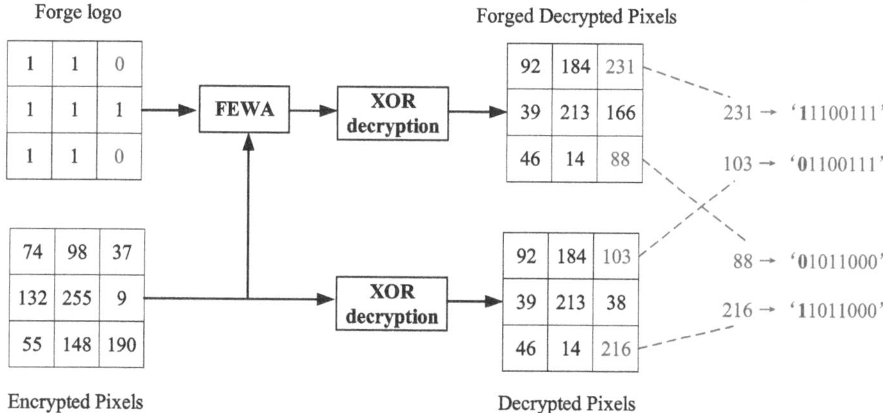


**Fig. 3.** An example for FEWA based on XOR encryption.

1. *EPR* remains unchanged when $x_i = 1$ and original pixel is equal to $fp$.
2. *EPR* increases when $x_i = 1$ and original pixel is equal to $p$.
3. *EPR* remains unchanged when $x_i = 0$ and original pixel is equal to $p$.
4. *EPR* increases when $x_i = 0$ and original pixel is equal to $fp$.

In cases 1 and 3, the *EPR* remains constant and the conditions $EPR \leq q$ and $CDR = 1$ can be satisfied; in cases 2 and 4, the *EPR* will increase and the conditions may not be satisfied. Since the explicit watermark in the forge logo is densely formed, we consider the image as several blocks of size $3 \times 3$. An example of pixel prediction in smooth and texture blocks after using FEWA operation is shown in Fig. 4. And the result of pixel prediction is shown in Eq. (15), where $Sb(p)$ and $Tb(p)$ denote the original pixel of smooth and texture blocks respectively, $pp^{(c)}$ is the predicted pixel value using the interpolation algorithm in [13], and $bp$ is the embed bit plane of the pixels. It indicates that the condition original pixel equals $p$ is more common. As described in Sect. 2.1, to ensure reversibility, the ratio $K/N$ in BSC is set to a very small value, so that there are many "frozen bits" of zero in the $X_i$. In this case, the growth ratio of *EPR* is small enough to satisfy $EPR \leq q$ and $CDR = 1$. Therefore, within a certain degree of noise, the secret data can remain robust and be decoded correctly, i.e., our proposed FEWA method can be used to damage the authenticity of images, and we prove that there is a security risk for the ciphertext images in the cloud.

$$[Sb(p), Tb(p)] = \begin{cases} [fp, p], \text{ where } bp = 3 \\ [p, p], \text{ where } bp = 4 \\ [p, p], \text{ where } bp = 5 \\ [p, p], \text{ where } bp = 6 \end{cases}. \tag{15}$$

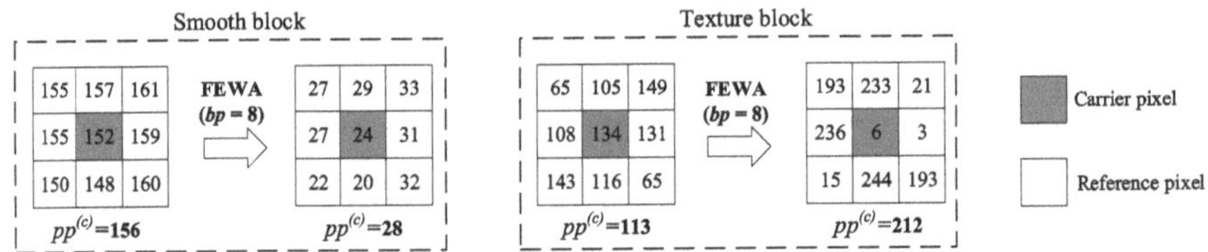


**Fig. 4.** An example for FEWA in data extraction phase.

## 3.4 FEWA on BSCPC

With the help of polar code, the robustness of the embedded data in BSC is guaranteed. However, the polar code just corrects the errors occurring on the embedded bit plane and cannot correct the distortion in the remaining bit planes. An example analysis is given in Fig. 5, for the given eight marked encrypted pixels $ep$, we flip half of them on 8<sup>th</sup> MSB plane using the FEWA method. After that, the noise in BSC increases, resulting in the error bits and the $EPR$ increasing in data extraction. However, the extracted bits $X'$ can still be decoded into correct secret data $B'$ using polar code. In other words, although the $EPR$ changes in data extraction, it still satisfies the condition $CDR = 1$. Comparing the original pixels with the recovered pixels, it is revealed that the four forged pixels have been permanently altered, and there is no way to verify that the integrity of the image has been damaged.

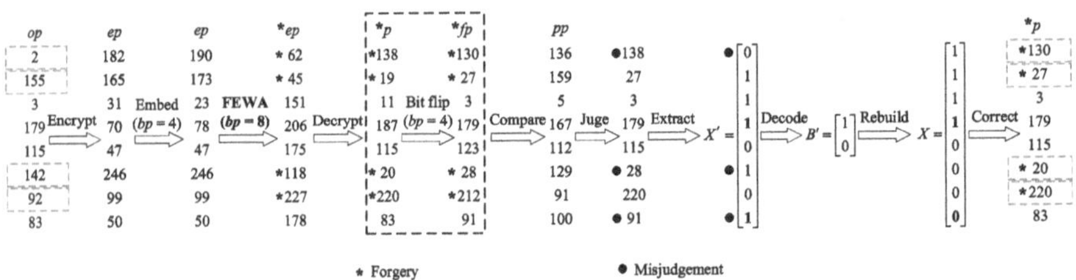


**Fig. 5.** An example for FEWA on correcting error bits in BSCPC-RDHEI.

It is worth mentioning that, a small amount of noise does not affect the correctness of decoding the secret data in the BSCPC-RDHEI scheme. In summary, the reconstructed recovered image is distorted due to external noise interference using the FEWA method, and since the receiver is only able to verify the integrity of the secret data, it is impossible to determine whether the recovered image has been modified or not when the decoded secret data is correct ($CDR = 1$). Therefore, it is proved that our FEWA method is workable and the RDHEI framework proposed in [6] has a security risk in the cloud environment.

## 4 Experimental Results And Analysis

In this paper, six grayscale images sized $512 \times 512$ were chosen, as shown in Fig. 6. And we generated nine forge logo images containing different explicit watermarks, whose size is $512 \times 512$, as shown in Fig. 7. It is worth mentioning that, Fig. 7(a) is a small logo with an explicit watermark in the lower right corner, Fig. 7(b) and Fig. 7(c) are single-line type and multi-line type logo respectively, and Fig. 7(b), Fig. 7(b) is a logo with widened explicit watermark in Fig. 7(c). These forged logo images meet the policy requirements for explicit watermarks on AI-generated content, as outlined in [17]. Table 1 demonstrates the length in the explicit watermark of these forged logo images.

In this section, we first verify the possibility of FEWA on BSCPS-RDHEI and then analyze the impact on the robustness of secret data. Besides, two pixel-division schemes are used in the data hiding stage of Chen's scheme, which are quality-oriented and quantity-oriented. In our experiments, we chose the former scheme as an example, and the test images were embedded with a maximum capacity of secret data on the LSB plane into an encrypted image.

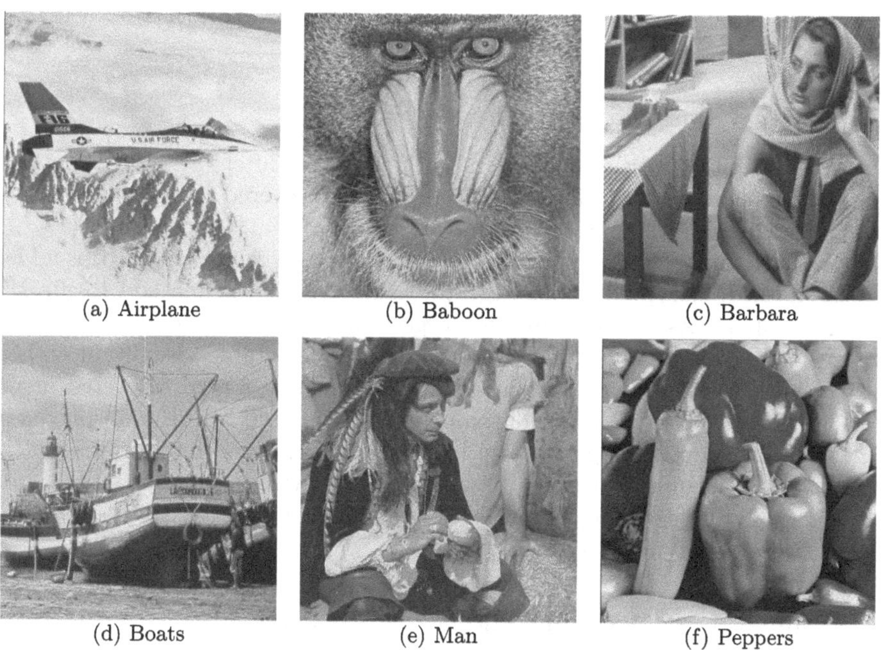

(a) Airplane (b) Baboon (c) Barbara (d) Boats (e) Man (f) Peppers

**Fig. 6.** Six test images.

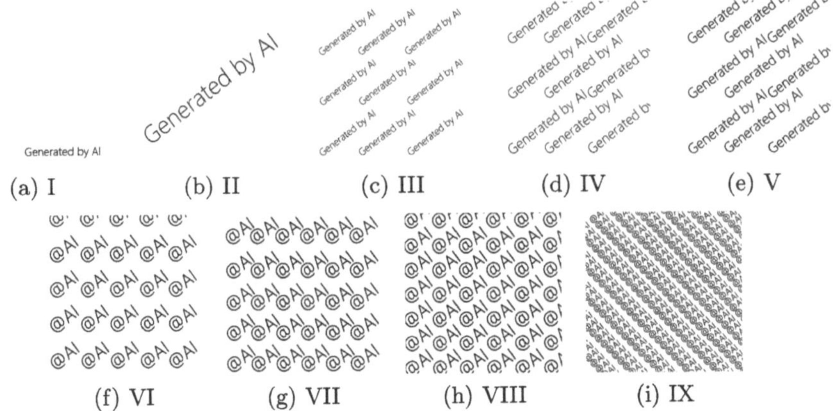


(a) I (b) II (c) III (d) IV (e) V

(f) VI (g) VII (h) VIII (i) IX

**Fig. 7.** Nine test Logo image.

**Table 1.** Nine forge logo images.

| Forge logo image | I | II | III | IV | V | VI | VII | VIII | IX |
|---|---|---|---|---|---|---|---|---|---|
| Length in explicit watermark(bits) | 1526 | 5288 | 10249 | 15045 | 20026 | 30121 | 40375 | 50380 | 60258 |

### 4.1 Forgery Possibility Analysis

Forgery possibility in this study refers to the fact that after the FEWA method, a visible explicit watermark is displayed on the recovered image which is not easily detectable in the ciphertext image.

As shown in Fig. 8, the explicit watermark in the forge logo Fig. 8(d) is added to the marked encrypted image Fig. 8(c) using the FEWA method to flip the $8^{\text{th}}$ MSB plane. As in Fig. 8(e), the forged marked encrypted image is similar to Fig. 8(c), and the explicit watermark is undetectable visually in ciphertext images. After that, an authorized user obtains the forged recovered image Fig. 8(f). It can be seen that the prompt text "Generated by AI" is displayed in Fig. 8(f), the original peppers image in Fig. 8(a) is changed into an image generated by AI, leading to the real image with the owner's identity information becoming another meaningful image. Therefore, after the FEWA method, the authenticity of the image source is damaged.

### 4.2 Influence on Decoding The Extracted Data

To verify the influence of the FEWA method on decoding the extracted data $X'$, we use nine forge logo images with different lengths of explicit watermarks to test the error prediction rate (*EPR*) and correct decoding rate (*CDR*) in data extraction. As mentioned in Sect. 3.4, whether the encoded secret data is correctly extracted relies on *EPR*. To explain the reason why the extracted data can still be decoded correctly ($CDR = 1$), we analyze the change in *EPR* and *CDR* after we flip the $8^{\text{th}}$ MSB plane of the marked encrypted image.

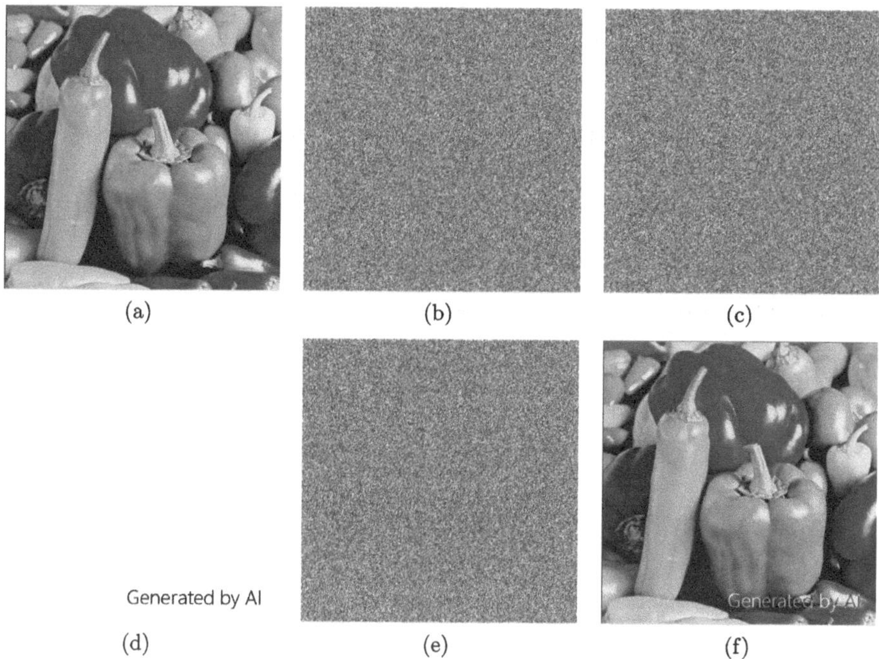


**Fig. 8.** Output of each phase of the proposed scheme. (a) Original image, (b) Encrypted image, (c) Marked encrypted image, (d) Forge logo images, (e) Forged marked encrypted image, (f) Forged recovered image.

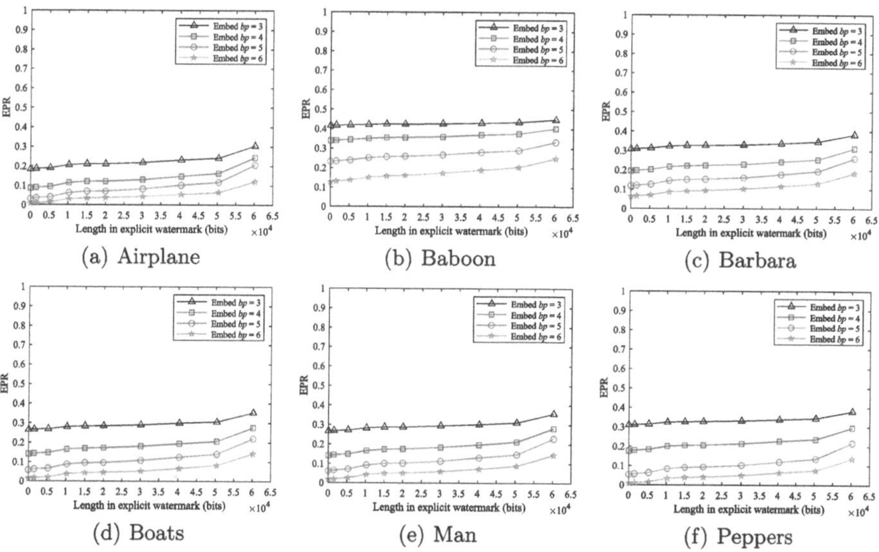


**Fig. 9.** *EPR* of the decrypted image under FEWA.

As shown in Fig. 9, it can be concluded that the higher the bit plane of the secret data embedding, the lower the *EPR* will be, but the growth ratio of *EPR* will be higher. The more bits in the explicit watermark of the forge logo there are, the larger the *EPR* is, but the growth ratio of *EPR* is small. It is worth noting that in the images Baboon and Man, due to the characteristics of their pixel value distribution, the growth ratio of *EPR* is very tiny. This type of image is also favorable for the implementation of the FEWA method.

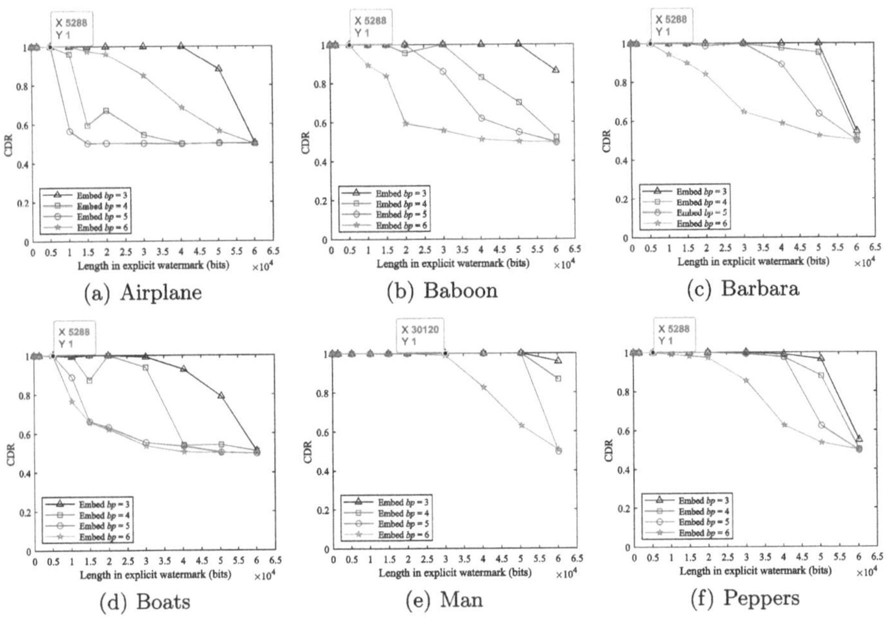


(a) Airplane (b) Baboon (c) Barbara (d) Boats (e) Man (f) Peppers

**Fig. 10.** *CDR* of the secret data under FEWA.

The change of *CDR* on decoding the extracted data is shown in Fig. 10. In the condition $CDR = 1$, our FEWA method is workable and proves that there is a security risk for the ciphertext images in the cloud. We can draw the following conclusions:

(1) In each of the embedded bit planes tested, as the length in the explicit watermark of the logo image increases, the *CDR* decreases. And on the higher the embedded bit plane of the secret data, the faster the *CDR* decreases due to the higher prediction accuracy in data extraction, and the *EPR* is very small. The increase in noise causes the *EPR* to decrease very fast so that the extracted data is hard to decode correctly. In contrast, the secret data embedded in the low bit plane has less effect on *CDR* because the prediction accuracy in data extraction is lower and the error correction ability of the noise channel is stronger.

(2) All six test images can be added with the forge logo (I), (II), with a maximum capacity of 5288 bits, which satisfies the requirement of posing a threat to the authenticity of images in cloud. The forge logo (IV) has resulted in the secret data of all images cannot be decoded correctly. Therefore it is quite feasible to forge images using the FEWA method.
(3) It is worth noting that in Airplane image, the *CDR* of extracted data on $6^{th}$ LSB plane decreases more slowly, which is caused by the non-uniform distribution of 0 and 1 bit on its $6^{th}$ LSB plane, so that the rise of *EPR* is due to the concentration of error-predicting pixels in a few channels, while the extracted data are correctly decoded in most of the channels. According to the 'Man' image, due to the non-uniform distribution of 0 and 1 bits on its $8^{th}$ MSB plane, a higher length in the explicit watermark of the forge logo can be accepted.

As a result, the code ratio of BSCPC-RDHEI is extremely small, and the growth ratio of *EPR* is also extremely small. Thus the conditions $EPR \leq q$ in (BSC) and $CDR = 1$ can be satisfied, and we can apply the FEWA method to forge the marked encrypted images, proving that the image authenticity and integrity will be destroyed in the cloud environment.

### 4.3 Generality Analysis

Generality in this study refers to that all the images embedded with implicit watermarks in [6] will show visible explicit watermarks on the recovered images after the forging implementation, where the secret data can be correctly decoded to ensure reversibility. That is, all images can be applied to the FEWA method, leading to a controversial destruction of image authenticity and integrity.

We test on the BOSSBase dataset with 10000 images using the forge logo image (I) with prompt text containing 1526 bits. Since it is impractical to find out the maximum embedding capacity of each LSB plane for each image when it is completely reversible, we adjust the parameter of BSC to embed the same size payload in each LSB plane of all images and test the performance by the proportion of images in which the extracted data can be correctly decoded.

As shown in Table 2, comparing before and after FEWA, the proportion of correctly decoded images is almost close. We can draw the following conclusions:

(1) As the embedding payload increases, the more obvious the deviation of the proportion of completely decoded images before and after the FEWA method is, such as when the embedding layer is in the $4^{th}$ LSB plane and the payload is 0.2bpp, the proportion of completely decoded images before and after FEWA method differs by 0.15%, which is equivalent to 15 images. This is since in the BOSSBase dataset, the embedding capacity of some of the images is so small that it is more difficult to embed at the same payload, resulting in an excessive impact of forging.
(2) When the embedding layers are the $5^{th}$ and $6^{th}$ LSBs, the correctly decoded rate of the forged images is almost the same as [6]. This is because the

**Table 2.** Comparison of correctly decoded images between [6] and FEWA on [6] in BOSSBase.

| | | | | | | |
|---|---|---|---|---|---|---|
| $3^{rd}$LSB | Embedding rate(bpp) | 0.002 | 0.004 | 0.006 | 0.008 | 0.01 |
| | Chen [6] | 99.92% | 99.49% | 98.97% | 98.23% | 97.49% |
| | FEWA on Chen [6] | 99.90% | 99.47% | 98.91% | 98.19% | 97.36% |
| $4^{th}$LSB | Embedding rate(bpp) | 0.004 | 0.008 | 0.012 | 0.016 | 0.02 |
| | Chen [6] | 100% | 99.90% | 99.58% | 99.36% | 99.05% |
| | FEWA on Chen [6] | 100% | 99.89% | 99.56% | 99.21% | 98.90% |
| $5^{th}$LSB | Embedding rate(bpp) | 0.008 | 0.012 | 0.016 | 0.024 | 0.03 |
| | Chen [6] | 100% | 100% | 99.99% | 99.93% | 99.87% |
| | FEWA on Chen [6] | 100% | 100% | 99.99% | 99.93% | 99.86% |
| $6^{th}$LSB | Embedding rate(bpp) | 0.01 | 0.02 | 0.03 | 0.04 | 0.05 |
| | Chen [6] | 100% | 100% | 100% | 100% | 100% |
| | FEWA on Chen [6] | 100% | 100% | 100% | 100% | 100% |

larger the capacity that can be accommodated and the higher the prediction accuracy, the less impact is caused by the FEWA method. Meanwhile, when the embedding layer is in the $3^{rd}$ and $4^{th}$ LSB planes, the correctly decoded rate of the forged images deviates slightly from [6].

In total, the deviation is so small that under the condition that the embedded data is correctly decoded in [6], FEWA can be applied to the vast majority of images, thus verifying that there is a serious security risk that the authenticity and integrity of the image will be destroyed in the cloud environment in [6].

### 4.4 Statistical Analysis

To verify the imperceptibility of the forge logo in ciphertext images, we tested 1000 grayscale images to avoid experimental serendipity and performed statistical analysis of our FEWA method using the forge logo image (I). We measure different statistical metrics: horizontal and vertical correlation coefficients(HC, VC), Shannon entropy, $\mathcal{X}^2$ test, the number of changing pixel rate (NPCR), and unified averaged changed intensity (UACI) between original images $O$ and the marked encrypted $ME$, forged marked encrypted $FME$, recovered $R$ or forged recovered $FR$ images. The computational procedure for the corresponding statistical metrics can be obtained from [19].

Table 3 shows the average values of the statistical metrics for 1000 grayscale images. It is worth noting that the values of statistical metrics for $R$ are all the same as $O$, indicating that the unforged recovered images are identical to the original images. There are high correlation between adjacent pixels of $FR$, indicating that the content of $FR$ is ordered. While the correlation of $ME$ and $FME$ are both weak, this means that there is no correlation between the adjacent pixels, and the content is disordered. In addition, we can see that the entropy

**Table 3.** Statistical metrics of the obtained images.

| Image | HC | VC | Entropy(bpp) | $\mathcal{X}^2$ test | NPCR(%) | UACI(%) | PSNR(dB) | SSIM(%) |
|---|---|---|---|---|---|---|---|---|
| $O$ | 0.9698 | 0.9657 | 7.0045 | 705.997 | / | / | / | / |
| $ME$ | 0.0001 | −0.0022 | 7.9993 | 15.9975 | 99.7620 | 33.7453 | 7.7952 | 0.8142 |
| $FME$ | 0.0005 | −0.0113 | 7.9993 | 15.9946 | 99.7616 | 33.7491 | 7.7945 | 0.8136 |
| $R$ | 0.9698 | 0.9657 | 7.0045 | 705.997 | 0 | 0 | Inf | 100 |
| $FR$ | 0.9557 | 0.9536 | 7.0240 | 707.904 | 0.5821 | 0.2988 | 28.3365 | 97.9209 |

value is very high for $ME$ or $FME$ (7.9993bpp) and close to the maximal value, indicating that the gray-level distribution tends to be uniform. In comparison, the value measured in $O$ and $FR$ is smaller (7.0045bpp, 7.024bpp). Then, if we consider the values obtained with the test, we observe that they are very high for $O$ and $FR$ (705.997, 707.904) while they are much lower in $ME$ or $FME$ (16). This means that data in $ME$ or $FME$ are disordered, non-uniform, and uncorrelated. We also measure NPCR, UACI, PSNR, and SSIM between $O$ and $ME$, $FME$, or $FR$. For both $ME$ and $FME$, the NPCR values are very high and close to the maximum (99.76%), and UACI rates are close to 33. 75% and the PSNR or SSIM values are very low (7.79dB, 0.8%) which indicates that $ME$ is very similar to $FME$ and is very different from $O$. For $FR$, the NPCR value and the UACI rate are both very low (less than 1%), which indicates that the changes in pixels between $FR$ and $O$ are very small, and PSNR or SSIM values are much higher (29.24dB, 97.9%), which indicates $FR$ keep good visual performance, as expected.

## 5 Conclusion

Recently, Chen [6] proposed an RDHEI scheme combining binary symmetric channel(BSC) and polar code(PC), which enhances anti-noise ability by correcting error bits in the channel using polar code. However, in the AIGC era, the explicit watermark is also embedded to mark the copyright of the images, which will pose another security risk to the ciphertext images in cloud. In this paper, we analyze the security of this BSCPC-RDHEI scheme and propose a security threat model by analyzing the forgerability of the XOR encryption algorithm and the BSC. Since polar code only corrects errors occurring in the embedding layer, it ensures the correct secret data, but cannot recognize the forging of images. When an attacker tampers with the ciphertexts in cloud, the original meaning of the recovered image will be altered, indicating that the integrity and source authenticity of the image is compromised. Based on the above analysis, we propose a FEWA method to add an explicit watermark with prompt text to marked encrypted images and verify the reconstruction of secret data in BSC via the changes of *EPR* and *CDR*. Experimental results prove the effectiveness of our analysis, the prompt text is displayed in the reconstructed image, and the content intention of the original image is changed by the FEWA method.

This paper mainly focuses on the potential ciphertexts security threat of the robust RDHEI scheme. In future research, to protect the integrity of the ciphertext image in the RDHEI system, we consider improving the robustness of the cover image using double watermark in a noisy environment, so that malicious modification of the original image will be detected.

## References


1. Arikan, E.: A performance comparison of polar codes and reed-muller codes. IEEE Commun. Lett. **12**(6), 447–449 (2008)
2. Chang, C.C., Fan, Y.H., Tai, W.L.: Four-scanning attack on hierarchical digital watermarking method for image tamper detection and recovery. Pattern Recogn. **41**(2), 654–661 (2008)
3. Chen, C.C., Chang, C.C., Chen, K.: High-capacity reversible data hiding in encrypted image based on Huffman coding and differences of high nibbles of pixels. J. Vis. Commun. Image Represent. **76**, 103060 (2021)
4. Chen, F., Yang, Y., He, H., Yuan, Y.: Adaptive coding and ordered-index extended scrambling based RDH in encrypted images. IEEE Trans. Multimedia **25**, 2864–2875 (2021)
5. Chen, F., Yuan, Y., He, H., Tian, M., Tai, H.M.: Multi-MSB compression based reversible data hiding scheme in encrypted images. IEEE Trans. Circuits Syst. Video Technol. **31**(3), 905–916 (2020)
6. Chen, K., Guan, Q., Zhang, W., Yu, N.: Reversible data hiding in encrypted images based on binary symmetric channel model and polar code. IEEE Trans. Dependable Secure Comput. **20**(6), 4519–4535 (2022)
7. Jakesch, M., Hancock, J.T., Naaman, M.: Human heuristics for ai-generated language are flawed. Proc. Natl. Acad. Sci. **120**(11), e2208839120 (2023)
8. Kadian, P., Arora, S.M., Arora, N.: Robust digital watermarking techniques for copyright protection of digital data: a survey. Wireless Pers. Commun. **118**, 3225–3249 (2021)
9. Kankanhalli, M.S., Ramakrishnan, K., et al.: Adaptive visible watermarking of images. In: Proceedings IEEE International Conference on Multimedia Computing and Systems, vol. 1, pp. 568–573. IEEE (1999)
10. Knott, A., et al.: Generative ai models should include detection mechanisms as a condition for public release. Ethics Inf. Technol. **25**(4), 55 (2023)
11. Li, C., Zhang, Y., Xie, E.Y.: When an attacker meets a cipher-image in 2018: a year in review. J. Inf. Secur. Appl. **48**, 102361 (2019)
12. Li, M., Ren, H., Xiang, Y., Zhang, Y.: Reversible data hiding in encrypted color images using cross-channel correlations. J. Vis. Commun. Image Represent. **78**, 103166 (2021)
13. Luo, L., Chen, Z., Chen, M., Zeng, X., Xiong, Z.: Reversible image watermarking using interpolation technique. IEEE Trans. Inf. Forensics Secur. **5**(1), 187–193 (2009)
14. Madiega, T.: Generative ai and watermarking. Briefing (2023). https://www.europarl.europa.eu/RegData/etudes/BRIE/2023/757583/EPRS_BRI(2023)757583_EN.pdf
15. Mahasree, M., Puviarasan, N., Aruna, P.: An improved reversible data hiding for encrypted images over cloud. In: 2021 5th International Conference on Trends in Electronics and Informatics (ICOEI), pp. 732–738. IEEE (2021)

16. Mohammadi, A.: A general framework for reversible data hiding in encrypted images by reserving room before encryption. J. Vis. Commun. Image Represent. **85**, 103478 (2022)
17. NISSTC: Method for tagging content in generative artificial intelligence services (2023). (in Chinese). https://www.tc260.org.cn/upload/2023-08-25/1692961404507050376.pdf
18. Arikan, E.: Channel polarization: a method for constructing capacity-achieving codes for symmetric binary-input memoryless channels. IEEE Trans. Inf. Theory **55**(7), 3051–3073 (2009). https://doi.org/10.1109/TIT.2009.2021379
19. Puteaux, P., Puech, W.: An efficient MSB prediction-based method for high-capacity reversible data hiding in encrypted images. IEEE Trans. Inf. Forensics Secur. **13**(7), 1670–1681 (2018)
20. Raj, P., Sreekumar, K.: A survey on reversible data hiding in encrypted image. Int. J. Comput. Sci. Inf. Technol. **5**(6), 7748–7751 (2014)
21. Shi, Y.Q., Li, X., Zhang, X., Wu, H.T., Ma, B.: Reversible data hiding: advances in the past two decades. IEEE Access **4**, 3210–3237 (2016)
22. Wang, X., Chang, C.C., Lin, C.C., Chang, C.C.: Reversal of pixel rotation: a reversible data hiding system towards cybersecurity in encrypted images. J. Vis. Commun. Image Represent. **82**, 103421 (2022)
23. Wang, Y., Cai, Z., He, W.: High capacity reversible data hiding in encrypted image based on intra-block lossless compression. IEEE Trans. Multimedia **23**, 1466–1473 (2020)
24. Wu, J., Gan, W., Chen, Z., Wan, S., Lin, H.: AI-generated content (AIGC): a survey. arXiv preprint arXiv:2304.06632 (2023)
25. Yang, Y., Xiao, X., Cai, X., Zhang, W.: A secure and privacy-preserving technique based on contrast-enhancement reversible data hiding and plaintext encryption for medical images. IEEE Signal Process. Lett. **27**, 256–260 (2020)
26. Zhang, C., Ou, B., Peng, F., Zhao, Y., Li, K.: A survey on reversible data hiding for uncompressed images. ACM Comput. Surv. **56**(7), 1–33 (2024)
27. Zhang, X.: Reversible data hiding in encrypted image. IEEE Signal Process. Lett. **18**(4), 255–258 (2011)

# Posters and Demos

# Enhancing Trust in VideoKYC: Deepfake Detection and Source Attribution

Srivallabh Mangrulkar, Aryan Karande, Abhijeet Zilpelwar, and Raghu Sesha Iyengar(✉)

pi-labs.ai, Pune, India
raghu@pi-labs.ai

**Abstract.** VideoKYC is increasingly used in domains, including finance, healthcare, and telecom, for remote identity verification. However, recent advances in deepfake and face-swapping techniques have enabled real-time impersonation attacks, posing serious threats to user trust and security. In this work, we demonstrate how such deepfake attacks can compromise videoKYC workflows and present a forensic detection framework to counter them. Building on a deepfake detection and source attribution model, we adapt the system for real-world KYC settings by finetuning on relevant data and applying exponential averaging to improve prediction stability. The system not only identifies manipulated content but also attributes it to specific generative tools, enabling downstream digital forensics, investigative tracing, and audit trails. By proactively detecting face manipulation, this approach adds a robust layer of human-centric security to videoKYC pipelines and helps build resilience against the growing wave of digital deception.

**Keywords:** videoKYC · Deepfake Detection · source attribution

## 1 Introduction

The growing accessibility of deepfake tools has made it increasingly easy to generate highly realistic synthetic face videos in real time. With advances in GANs and diffusion models [1,2], face swapping and lip sync can now be performed on-the-fly using open-source libraries or commercial APIs, posing serious risks to identity verification systems. One critical application under threat is videoKYC, where users verify their identity over a live video call. Attackers can now inject deepfaked video feeds to impersonate real individuals and bypass standard KYC checks. This challenge has gained attention in both academia [1] and industry[1][2], highlighting the need for practical detection systems. In this paper, we present a production-ready solution based on a dual-head transformer model [3] that detects deepfakes and attributes them to their likely generative source.

[1] https://www.realitydefender.com/insights/how-deepfakes-exploit-kyc-verification-systems.

[2] https://www.fsisac.com/hubfs/Knowledge/AI/DeepfakesInTheFinancialSector-UnderstandingTheThreatsManagingTheRisks.pdf.


K.-K. R. Choo et al. (Eds.): ICDF2C 2025, LNICST 686, pp. 579–582, 2026.
https://doi.org/10.1007/978-3-032-22545-0_33

Designed specifically for the videoKYC setting, our system uses domain-specific fine-tuning and temporal averaging across video chunks to provide fast, explainable, and highly reliable detection, which is suitable for real-world deployment.

## 2 Attack

*Injection Attacks and Real-Time Demonstration.* VideoKYC systems face growing threats from spoofing and injection attacks[3]. Basic presentation attacks using photos or recorded videos are often mitigated using liveness checks. More sophisticated video injection attacks bypass the camera entirely by feeding pre-recorded or synthetic content into the stream. The most concerning are real-time deepfake injections, where tools like DeepFaceLive superimpose synthetic faces onto a live video feed, frequently evading both liveness and challenge-response protocols.

To demonstrate the feasibility of real-time face-swapping attacks, we optimized Deep-Live-Cam[4], an open-source webcam-based tool that supports configurable modules for face swapping and enhancement. The original version used a single-threaded pipeline and achieved 5–7 FPS during face-swapping (2–3 FPS with enhancement). We restructured the system into a multi-threaded architecture with dedicated threads for frame capture, inference, and rendering. By experimenting with different supported models for both face swapping and restoration, we achieved improved performance of up to 17 FPS without enhancement and 6 FPS with enhancement. Running this setup on a Dell Precision 7680 (Intel i9, 32 GB RAM, RTX 4000 Ada) demonstrates that realistic, real-time deepfake injections can be executed on moderately priced hardware. Figure 1 illustrates successful injection attempts across commonly used video platforms.

## 3 Solution Architecture

*Deepfake Detection for VideoKYC.* We build on our prior work [3] by adapting a dual-head transformer model for real/fake detection and source attribution in videoKYC workflows. The model processes face-cropped video chunks and predicts both authenticity and likely deepfake source. It was fine-tuned on 70,000 segments (0.5 s each), evenly split between real and manipulated clips generated using tools like Roop, FaceFusion, and commercial APIs. Real samples simulated KYC calls over Zoom, Teams, WhatsApp, and proprietary platforms under varied conditions. Training was conducted for 10 epochs on an NVIDIA A100 GPU (batch size 8) with a peak learning rate of $5 \times 10^{-5}$, linear scheduler, and weighted cross-entropy loss. To improve consistency, we applied exponential averaging across video chunks, reflecting the single-subject nature of videoKYC sessions. On a 14,000-sample test set, the best configuration (EMA with initial value 0.5) achieved 97.03% accuracy. For an in-depth evaluation of the base deepfake detection model metrics against state-of-the-art models and benchmark datasets, refer to [3] (Table 1).

[3] https://www.idrnd.ai/deep-dive-into-deepfakes/.
[4] https://github.com/hacksider/Deep-Live-Cam.

**Fig. 1.** Sample face swap using Deep-Live-Cam. Stream injected on (a) Whatsapp Video call (b) Microsoft Teams (c) Zoom.

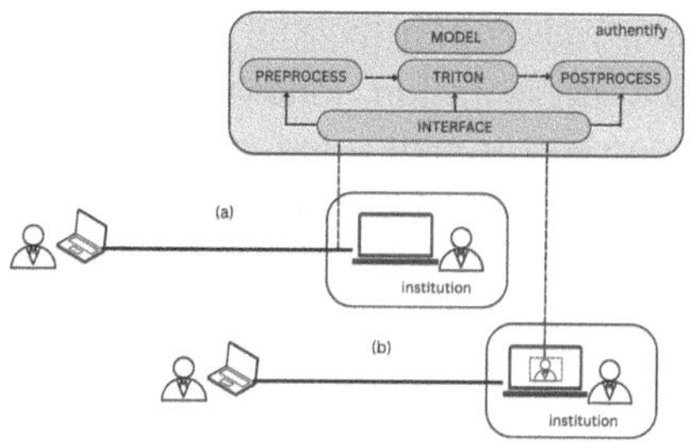


**Fig. 2.** Integration Modes: (a) A portion of the video stream (typically 30 s) is sent to *authentify* inference server using REST APIs (b) The user manually selects a portion of screen having the suspicious face using our tool. Screen captured video is sent to *authentify* inference server using REST APIs

**Table 1.** Accuracy of Real/Fake Detection

| Technique | Original[a] | Slide5[b] | EMA-0.0[c] | EMA-0.5[d] |
|---|---|---|---|---|
| Accuracy (%) | 88.80 | 93.40 | 96.53 | 97.03 |

[a]Output from base finetuned model
Prediction averaged using
[b] sliding window of size 5
[c] Exponential Moving Average with initial value = 0.0
[d] Exponential Moving Average with initial value = 0.5

To assess real-world applicability, we evaluated the system on video segments of varying lengths and qualities. Detection accuracy remained above 95% for clips as short as 10 s, with marginal gains for longer segments. Videos with strong lighting and centered framing showed higher confidence scores, while side-lit or low-resolution streams presented more ambiguous predictions. These findings underscore the value of temporal smoothing and domain-specific fine-tuning for stable performance.

*Deployment.* To enable scalable deployment across diverse videoKYC environments, our solution *authentify* adopts a modular client–server architecture. The central server hosts the deepfake detection and attribution models and exposes REST APIs for seamless integration with client platforms. Compute-intensive tasks such as face cropping, model inference, and source classification are executed on the backend, equipped with an NVIDIA T4 GPU (16 GB) and accelerated using NVIDIA Triton Inference Server[5] for concurrent inference and effi-

[5] https://docs.nvidia.com/deeplearning/triton-inference-server/.

cient resource utilization. The system incorporates a pre-processing pipeline for face segmentation, followed by inference and result packaging. Access control is enforced through role-based permissions, with all requests logged for auditability. To meet regulatory and data residency requirements, the solution supports both cloud-based and on-premise deployments.

*Integration Modes. authentify* supports two modes of integration tailored to different deployment workflows (Fig. 2). In the programmatic mode, KYC platforms can automatically send a 30-s video segment to the server via API and receive chunk-wise confidence scores, an overall real/fake decision, and source attribution if applicable. This is suitable for automated pipelines requiring backend verification without manual intervention. In the assisted mode, a lightweight desktop tool allows human operators to select a region of the screen (e.g., the video feed during a call), record a short clip, and send it for analysis. The results are displayed locally and support real-time decision-making. On test sets of 50 videos, average API response times were 33.20 $\pm$2.44 s for 30-s clips and 13.72 $\pm$1.43 s for 10-s clips, demonstrating near real-time performance in practical settings.

## 4 Conclusion

With deepfake tools becoming widely accessible, securing remote identity verification like videoKYC is increasingly important. We presented a scalable detection system combining real/fake classification with source attribution, deployable via REST APIs or lightweight clients. Domain-specific fine-tuning and exponential averaging enhance reliability in real-world use. The solution is currently in customer trials and has shown strong performance and usability. Our findings also highlight how low-cost attacks can bypass verification, reinforcing the need for robust detection. Future work includes extending support to audio deepfakes for multimodal protection.

## References

1. Verdoliva, L.: Media forensics and DeepFakes: an overview. IEEE J. Sel. Top. Sig. Process. **14**(5), 910–932 (2020)
2. Croitoru, F.-A., Hondru, V., Ionescu, R.T., Shah, M.: Diffusion models in vision: a survey. IEEE Trans. Pattern Anal. Mach. Intell. **45**(9), 10850–10869 (2023)
3. Sharma, N., Mallampalli, K., Iyengar, R.S.: Forensic challenges in face manipulated videos. In: Proceedings of the International Conference on Multimedia Analysis and Pattern Recognition (MAPR) (2025)

# Author Index


**A**
Agrawal, Gagan 313, 363
Akkaya, Kemal 197
Al-Farabi, Khan Mohammad 363
Alharthi, Dalal 384
Antonopoulou, Michaela 295
Avgerinos, Nikos 295

**B**
Bahsi, Hayretdin 36
Bai, Tao 144
Bardhan, Rajon 363
Bhattarai, Abhishek 197

**C**
Cao, Guoyan 464
Chen, Chen 160
Chen, Fan 556
Chen, Guanxin 3
Chen, Qiangpu 491
Chen, Xin 264
Chen, Yu 213
Chong, Yung-Wey 88
Chua, Yi Ting 403
Cornell, Kimberly A. 233, 280, 333
Cui, Wenzhuo 107

**D**
de Figueiredo, Miguel 313
Dorai, Gokila 313, 363
Du, Jinze 505

**E**
Edge, Eric 54
ElSaid, AbdElRahman 36

**F**
Fang, Dongliang 264
Fang, Wenbo 540
Feng, Jingjing 107
Feng, Yuanqing 144
Fourfouris, Ioannis 295
Franken, Boyd 129

**G**
Garcia, Ivan Roberto Kawaminami 384
Geng, Mengjiao 464

**H**
Hamer, Sarah A. J. 403
He, Hongjie 556
Hilgert, Jan-Niclas 345
Hu, Die 451
Hu, Yibing 107
Huang, Li 233, 280
Huang, Yuyao 68

**I**
Imery, Carlos 197
Iyengar, Raghu Sesha 433, 579

**J**
Jakobs, Carlo 345
Jr Jones, James H. 54
Ju, Lei 20

**K**
Kadri, Thomas E. 313
Kang, Fei 68
Karabacak, Bilge 36
Karande, Aryan 579
Karuppayah, Shankar 88
Kong, He 451
Külper, Michael 345
Kumar, Raja 248
Kumar, Vaibhav 433

**L**
Lambertz, Martin 345
Laskey, Kathryn 54




K.-K. R. Choo et al. (Eds.): ICDF2C 2025, LNICST 686, pp. 583–584, 2026.
https://doi.org/10.1007/978-3-032-22545-0

Le-Khac, Nhien-An 129
Li, Ke 540
Li, Leixiao 505
Li, Liangxiong 451
Li, Wenhao 88
Li, Wenjie 505
Li, Xuejian 524
Li, Yanlin 491
Li, Yuwei 491
Li, Zhi 264
Lin, Hao 505
Liu, Dongjiang 505
Liu, Nianlu 540
Liu, Xiaoxian 160
Liu, Xinyun 213
Liu, Xueqiao 160
Liu, Ying 20
Liu, Yipeng 3
Liu, Zheng 107
Liu, Zhexu 505
Lu, Songfeng 144
Lu, Zhi 144
Lv, Shichao 264

M
Mahr, Axel 345
Mangrulkar, Srivallabh 579
Manickam, Selvakumar 88
Meixner Jr., John B. 313
Miao, Hong 176
Motlicek, Petr 295

N
Nguyen-Le, Hong-Hanh 129
Nussbaum, Brian H. 333

P
Padilla, Elmar 345
Pan, Zulie 491
Pang, Shufang 20
Pei, Weiping 403

R
Rahman, Md. Ashiqur 313
Rangappa, Pradeep 295
Ren, Wenkai 451

S
Sahin, Elif 36
Sanchez Lara, Alejandra 295
Sanchez-Cortes, Dairazalia 295
Shu, Hui 68
Si, Shuaizong 264
Song, Jie 176
Song, Zhanwei 264
Soni, Jayesh 248
Sun, Limin 264

T
Thorley, Dane R. 313
Tsangaris, Manolis 295

U
Upadhyay, Himanshu 248

W
Wang, Song 491
Wang, Taiyan 491
Wang, Xiaoyang 160
Wang, Xuebin 556
Wang, Zhiqiang 20
Wen, Yu 107
Wu, Bingzhen 451

X
Xia, Hantao 524
Xing, Jian 524
Xiong, Xiaobing 464
Xu, Ronghua 213
Xu, Zhen 176

Y
Yang, Yaolin 556
Yu, Lancan 3
Yu, Lu 491
Yuan, Shaowei 20
Yuepeng, 451

Z
Zhang, Linlin 540
Zhang, Lu 491
Zhang, Shuyi 107
Zhang, Yan 176
Zhao, Kai 540
Zheng, Yaowen 264
Zilpelwar, Abhijeet 579

Zeitfracht Medien GmbH
Ferdinand-Jühlke-Straße 7
99095 Erfurt, Deutschland
produktsicherheit@kolibri360.de